# Parallel Architectures *and* Algorithms *for* Image Understanding

# Parallel Architectures *and* Algorithms *for* Image Understanding

V. K. Prasanna Kumar

Department of Electrical Engineering—Systems
University of Southern California
Los Angeles, California

ACADEMIC PRESS, INC.

*Harcourt Brace Jovanovich, Publishers*

Boston San Diego New York
London Sydney Tokyo Toronto

This book is printed on acid-free paper. ♾



ACADEMIC PRESS, INC.
1250 Sixth Avenue, San Diego, CA 92101



*United Kingdom Edition published by*
ACADEMIC PRESS LIMITED
24-28 Oval Road, London NW1 7DX

Library of Congress Catalog Card Data

Parallel architectures and algorithms for image understanding / [edited by] V.K. Prasanna Kumar.

p. cm.
Includes bibliographical references and index.
ISBN 0-12-564040-4 (alk. paper)
1. Image processing—Digital techniques. 2. Parallel processing (Electronic computers) 3. Computer architecture. I. Prasanna Kumar, V.K.
TA1632.P35 1991
621.39′9–dc20 90-41372
CIP



Printed in the United States of America
91 92 93 94 9 8 7 6 5 4 3 2 1 ▼

# Contents

## III. Implementations and Applications



## IV. Software Environments

## Contributors

Numbers in parentheses indicate pages on which authors' contributions begin.

Aggarwal, J. K. (121), *College of Engineering, The University of Texas at Austin, Austin, Texas 78712-1084*

Ahuja, Narendra (251), *Coordinated Science Laboratory, University of Illinois, 1101, W. Springfield Ave. Urbana, Illinois 61801*

Alnuweiri, Hussein M. (157), *Computer Engineering Department, King Fahd University of Petroleum and Minerals, Box No. 1729, Dhahran 31261, Saudi Arabia*

Burrill, James H. (525), *Department of Computer and Information Science, University of Massachusetts, Amherst, Massachusetts 01003*

Chakrabarti, Chaitali (3), *Department of Electrical Engineering, Systems Research Center, Institute for Advanced Computer Studies, University of Maryland, College Park, Maryland 20742*

Choudhary, Alok N. (251), *Department of Electrical and Computer Engineering, 111 Link Hall, Syracuse University, New York 13244-1240*

Cloud, Eugene L. (279), *Martin Marietta Electronic Systems, 6714 Bittersweet Lane, Orlando, Florida 32819*

Eshaghian, Mary Mehrnoosh (29), *Department of Electrical Engineering-Systems, SAL 317, University of Southern California, Los Angeles, California 90089-0781*

Fisher, Allan L. (307), *Department of Computer Science, Carnegie Mellon University, Pittsburgh, Pennsylvania 15213*

Hanson, Allen (399), *Department of Computer and Information Science, University of Massachusetts, Amherst, Massachusetts 01003*

Highnam, Peter T. (307), *Schlumberger Laboratory for Computer Science, PO Box 200015 Austin, Texas 78720-0015*

Hwang, Kai (59), *Department of Electrical Engineering-Systems, University of Southern California, Los Angeles, California 90089-0781*

JáJá, Joseph (3), *Department of Electrical Engineering, Systems Research Center, Institute for Advanced Computer Studies, University of Maryland, College Park, Maryland 20742*

Krikelis, Anargyros (339), *Aspex Microsystems Ltd., Brunel University, Uxbridge, Middlesex, United Kingdom UB8 3PH*

Lee, Sing H. (29), *Department of Electrical and Computer Engineering, Mail Code R-007, University of California at San Diego, La Jolla, California 92093*

Miller, Russ (185), *Department of Computer Science, State University of New York at Buffalo, Buffalo, New York 14260*

Nash, J. Greg (371), *Hughes Research Laboratories, 3011 Malibu Canyon Road, Mail Code RL-69, Malibu, California 90265*

Panda, Dhabaleswar Kumar (59), *Department of Electrical Engineering Systems, University of Southern California, Los Angeles, CA 90089-0781*

Parkinson, Dennis (209), *Active Memory Technology, 65, Suttons Park Ave., Reading, Berkshire, RG6-1AZ, United Kingdom*

Patel, Janak H. (251), *Coordinated Science Laboratory, University of Illinois, 1101, W. Springfield Ave. Urbana, Illinois 61801*

Prasanna Kumar, V. K. (157, 185), *Department of Electrical Engineering Systems, University of Southern California, Los Angeles, CA 90089-0781*

Przytula, K. Wojtek (95), *Hughes Research Laboratories, 3011 Malibu Canyon Road, Mail Code RL-69, Malibu, California 90265*

Ranka, Sanjay (227), *Department of Computer and Information Science, Syracuse University, Syracuse, New York 13244*

Reeves, Anthony P. (453), *School of Electrical Engineering, 410 Philips Hall, Cornell University, Ithaca, New York 14853-5401*

Reisis, Dionisios I. (185), *Department of Electrical Engineering, University of Southern California, Los Angeles, California 90089*

Riseman, Edward (399), *Department of Computer and Information Science, University of Massachusetts, Amherst, Massachusetts 01003*

Rosenfeld, Azriel (399), *Center for Automation Research, University of Maryland, College Park, Maryland 20742*

Sahni, Sartaj (227), *Department of Computer Science, University of Minnesota, 136 Lind Hall, 207 Church Street S. E., Minneapolis, Minnesota 55455*

Shaaban, Muhammad E. (29), *Department of Electrical Engineering-Systems, University of Southern California, Los Angeles, California 90089-0781*

Shu, David B. (371), *Hughes Research Laboratories, 3011 Malibu Canyon Road, Mail Code RL-69, Malibu, California 90265*

Stout, Quentin F. (185), *Department of Computer Science, University of Michigan, Ann Arbor, Michigan 48109*

Sunwoo, Myung H. (121), *College of Engineering, Computer and Vision Research Center, The University of Texas at Austin, Austin, Texas 78712-1084*

Tucker, Lewis (473), *Thinking Machines Corporation, 245 First Street, Cambridge, Massachusetts 02142*

Webb, Jon A. (499), *Department of Computer Science, Carnegie Mellon University, Pittsburgh, Pennsylvania 15213-3890*

Weems, Charles C. (399, 525), *Department of Computer and Information Science, University of Massachusetts, Amherst, Massachussets 01003*

# Preface

Computer scientists have been interested in problems in image-processing and image-understanding for many years. Numerous problems in low- and intermediate-level image-understanding offer parallelism in a natural fashion. Researchers in parallel processing have exploited this, leading to fast parallel solutions to these problems. However, at high-level image-understanding such parallelism is not apparent; parallelism cannot be easily employed to obtain desirable speed-ups. During the past decade, a number of new approaches to image-understanding tasks have been proposed. These are usually computationally demanding and often take several hours or even days on currently available serial machines. Indeed, novel architectural and algorithmic solutions are needed to employ these techniques in real world applications.

In the past few years several parallel machines have become available. Efforts are underway to use these machines for image-understanding tasks. In addition, researchers in image-understanding and parallel processing have been interested in understanding the computational requirements of solutions to these problems and identifying architectural and algorithmic approaches to these problems. This book presents contributions by leading researchers involved in designing and implementing parallel solutions to problems in image-understanding.

The book is organized into four parts: Architectures; Algorithms; Implementations; and Programming Environments.

In part one, a number of proposed architectures for image-understanding are described. Chaitali Chakrabarti and Joseph JáJá present VLSI architectures for template matching and block matching, which are widely used operations in image-processing. The authors provide optimal organizations for realizing these operations suitable for implementation in VLSI. Compared with known solutions, these organizations handle the I/O problem efficiently and have simple data and control flow, making these attractive for implementation.

Mary Eshaghian, Sing Lee, and Muhammad Shaaban consider optical interconnections for fine-grain image computations. They survey traditional approaches to using optical technology in image processing and propose a new model of computation suitable for image computations. In this model, computations are performed in traditional VLSI and communications are performed using free-space optics. This model provides a realization of the local memory PRAM. Simple, efficient parallel algorithms are shown for several intermediate-level vision tasks.

Kai Hwang and Dhabaleswar Panda propose RISC-based implementation of the Orthogonal Multiprocessor for image-processing, vision and neural network simulations. The architecture employs a novel orthogonal shared memory and is designed for integrated image-processing tasks. This chapter also describes design experiences and projected performance of the architecture.

The contribution by Wojtek Przytula describes a methodology for designing an application-specific architecture at Hughes Research Laboratories, suitable for a variety of tasks in signal and image-processing. In this methodology, a large class of problems is analyzed to arrive at data path, memory, and control requirements. Performance cost tradeoffs are then evaluated to lead to realizations in current technology.

M. H. Sunwoo and J. K. Aggarwal propose VisTA (Vision Tri-Architecture) for a general purpose computer vision system. To alleviate communication problems in using known architectures in a variety of tasks in image-understanding, an integrated system consisting of a sliding memory plane architecture for low-level operations, a medium grain flexibly coupled multiprocessor for intermediate-level operations, and a flexibly coupled hypercube multiprocessor for high-level vision is proposed.

In part two, parallel algorithms for image problems are studied on several organizations. The chapter by Hussein Alnuweiri and Viktor Prasanna Kumar describes solutions to several image problems when the number of available processors is limited. Organizations considered include the reduced-mesh-of-trees, mesh-connected modules, linear arrays, two-dimensional meshes, hypercube, and shuffle exchange networks. The RMOT organization introduced by the authors and others is shown to be well suited for a number of problems in intermediate-level analysis.

Russ Miller, Viktor Prasanna Kumar, Dionisis Reisis, and Quentin Stout show efficient parallel algorithms for many problems on the reconfigurable mesh architecture. The reconfigurable mesh captures the fundamental properties of CHiP, mesh computers augmented with broadcast buses, the bus automaton, the polymorphic torus network, and the coterie network in the content addressable array parallel processor of the image-understanding architecture. The chapter describes a number of fundamental data movement operations for image computations and derives asymptotically superior parallel algorithms for these problems. Dennis Parkinson considers the image-component labeling problem in detail and studies the performance of a number of parallel solutions on the AMT DAP 510 parallel machine. The results are very useful since the experiments are performed assuming a practical architecture consisting of a small number of processors to handle large images and since performance results are presented for various input cases.

Sanjay Ranka and Sartaj Sahni derive parallel algorithms for image transformations including shrinking, expanding, translation, rotation, and scaling on hypercube and mesh-connected computers. These algorithms can be applied to binary or grey scale images and are asymptotically optimal. A novelty of these algorithms is their simplicity, which makes them well suited for implementation on current mesh and hypercube machines.

In part three, implementation of several proposed parallel architectures for image-understanding are presented. Alok Choudhary, Janak Patel, and Narendra Ahuja present performance analysis of various image-understanding tasks on clusters of NETRA, a highly configurable architecture. Analytical performance results are derived which are also compared with implementation results. Preliminary results show suitability of NETRA for several image-understanding tasks including two-dimensional convolution, two-dimensional FFT, and median filtering.

The next chapter describes the implementation of the Geometric Arithmetic Parallel Processor (GAPP) at Martin Marietta Corporation. The GAPP has been designed to meet a number of constraints including real time processing requirements of images produced by infrared sensors, size, weight, reliability and power consumption arising in nighttime, air-to-ground attack mission capability. Eugene Cloud describes the design rationale to meet these requirements and the current status of the system implementation.

Allan Fisher and Peter Highnam describe the hardware and software components of the Scan Line Array Processor (SLAP) prototype system under development at CMU. In addition to architecture and implementation of SLAP, a directional compiling technique to optimize algorithms mapped onto SLAP is described. A number of applications drawn from image-understanding are shown to demonstrate performance improvements in using the proposed compilation technique.

Argy Krikelis describes the Associate String Processor for image-understanding. The ASP is designed to offer application flexibility, scalability, and computational efficiency. Comparative performance of the system on tasks from DARPA IU Benchmark is also shown.

David Shu and Greg Nash present a hierarchical architecture consisting of a SIMD content addressable array parallel processor, a set of digital signal processors, directed by a set of powerful general purpose processors at the highest level. The architecture is designed to support numeric as well as symbolic computations arising from the use of AI techniques in vision. Prototype hardware implementation and the programming environment are also described.

In the next chapter, Charles Weems, Edward Riseman, Allen Hanson, and Azriel Rosenfeld briefly describe the DARPA IU benchmark and the results of running the benchmark on SUN, Alliant, Sequent, and Warp computers, as well as simulation results of the UMass/Hughes Image-Understanding Architecture and Aspex Associate String Processor. In addition, partial benchmark results for the Connection Machine and Intel iPSC/2 are also presented.

The next section contains programming environments for designing and implementing solutions to image understanding tasks. Anthony Reeves describes the VISIX system, a unix-based software computer vision system. The Paragon programming environment for parallel program development is also described. A novel feature of the environment is its ability to handle data partitioning and functional decomposition. This is illustrated using several image-processing examples. Lewis Tucker describes "how to think parallel" using the data parallel programming notion on the Connection Machine. This is illustrated using a number of examples from image-understanding, including line of sight, line drawing, contour linking, pointer jumping, feature matching, and evidence accumulation problems.

Jon Webb describes two programming languages for application programming, Apply and Adapt, which are specialized for image-processing. Compilers have been developed to map the programs written in these languages onto parallel machines, including the iWarp machine at CMU. Ease of programming and efficiency of resulting Warp code are illustrated using a number of examples drawn from image-processing.

Finally, Charles Weems and James Burril present the programming environment of the Image-Understanding Architecture. They describe a simulator that runs on a SUN which can simulate the operations of each of the three levels of the IUA and also displays the state of the processors. This simulator, along with interaction with the system through the software console, can greatly simplify the development and debugging of application programs.

I would like to thank the authors for their (prompt) response and patience in bringing out this book. Special thanks to Ashfaq Khokhar for his assistance in formatting the manuscripts. Ju-wook Jang, David Okamura, and Anil Rao provided help with using LaTeX. I would also like to thank Sari Kalin and Alice Peters, for their helpful suggestions and patience in bringing this book to completion, and Pascha Gerlinger, for excellent production skill.

Viktor Prasanna Kumar

# Part I

# Parallel Architectures

# VLSI Architectures for Template Matching and Block Matching

**CHAITALI CHAKRABARTI and JOSEPH JÁJÁ**
*Department of Electrical Engineering*
*and Institute for Advanced Computer Studies*
*University of Maryland at College Park*
*College Park, Maryland*

## 1 Introduction

Image template matching and block matching are representative of many window-based tasks in image processing. Template matching is used in image location, scene matching, edge detection, filtering, and many other operations in image processing. Block matching is used to remove interframe redundancy in many video codecs such as video phone and teleconferencing. In view of all these applications, the problem of developing good architectures for computing template matching and block matching in real-time is very important.

Although the existing architectures for template matching and block matching consist of a systolic array of processors, most of them either ignore the I/O issues or employ schemes involving frequent off-chip memory accesses. In this chapter we present a brief overview of the existing architectures and then propose a systolic architecture consisting of a linear array of $P$ processors, which handles the I/O bandwidth problem efficiently. The proposed architecture achieves optimal speed-up with simple data and control flow. We use the minimum number of processors for real-time computation. The I/O problem is tackled by storing part of the input image in shift registers






ISBN 0-12-564040-4

in each processor and by circulating the shift registers so that the processor array can compute on the same input data multiple times. We choose the linear array so that all the processors can access data simultaneously from the I/O ports. Moreover, since the input is read in the line-scan mode, this configuration seems to be the natural choice.

The rest of the chapter is organized as follows. In section 2 we give the preliminaries for real-time template matching and full-search block matching. We briefly discuss the existing architectures in section 3. In section 4 we give an overview of the proposed architecture and algorithms and then give a detailed description in section 5.

# 2 Preliminaries

In this section we define template matching and block matching and give an estimate of the minimum number of processors that are required for real-time computation of these two operations.

## 2.1 Template Matching

Let the input image $I$ be an array of size $N_1 \times N_2$. If $W$ is a template of size $K \times K$, then the template matching of $W$ with $I$ is defined by

$$TM[i,j] = \sum_{m=0}^{K-1} \sum_{n=0}^{K-1} I[i+m, j+n] * W[m,n],$$

$0 \le i \le N_1 - K$, $0 \le j \le N_2 - K$. Figure 1 shows an $N_1 \times N_2$ input image, a $K \times K$ template, and a particular match configuration. We assume that the position of the template is defined by the coordinates of the input image covered by the upper-left corner of the template. Let SUB$(i,j)$ be the input block of size $K \times K$ whose upper-left corner is $(i,j)$ as shown in Fig. 1. The template is matched against every sub area SUB$(i,j)$ and for each such configuration TM$[i,j]$ is computed.

Template matching is an extremely time-consuming process since $K^2$ multiplication-accumulation (MAC) operations have to be computed for each of the $(N_1 - K + 1)(N_2 - K + 1)$ configurations in

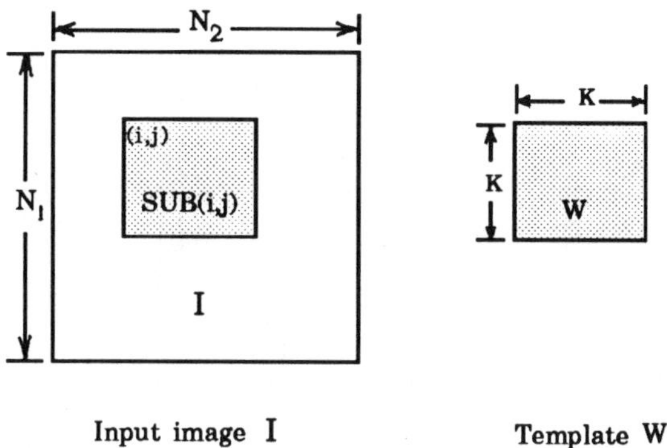


Figure 1: Input image $I$, template $W$, and a particular match configuration.

a frame. The total computation time for one frame is thus $T_v = (N_1 - K + 1)(N_2 - K + 1)K^2\alpha T_c$, where $T_c$ is the internal clock period, and $\alpha$ is a constant such that $\alpha T_c$ is the pipelined time required to compute one MAC. If $P$ is the minimum number of processors for real-time processing and if the speed-up is optimal, then the $P$-processor computation time $\frac{T_v}{P}$ is related to the frame frequency $f_F$ by $\frac{T_v}{P} \leq \frac{1}{f_F}$. Thus, the minimum value of $P$ is given by $P = \lceil (N_1 - K + 1)(N_2 - K + 1)K^2\alpha T_c f_F \rceil$. In 1.6 micron technology, if $T_c = 50$ ns and if the operations are bit parallel with eight bits per word, then the pipelined time required to compute one multiplication-accumulation is 400 ns. For the case when the size of the template is $8 \times 8$, the minimum number of processors required for Video Telephone Standard ($N_1 = 288, N_2 = 353, f_F = 10$ Hz) is 25 and for NTSC video signal ($N_1 = 512, N_2 = 480, f_F = 10$ Hz) is 61.

## 2.2 Block Matching

Full-search block matching determines a *displacement vector* for every *reference* block in the current frame, by comparing it with all *candidate* blocks in a search area surrounding the position of the reference block in the previous frame. Let the current frame $I_c$ of

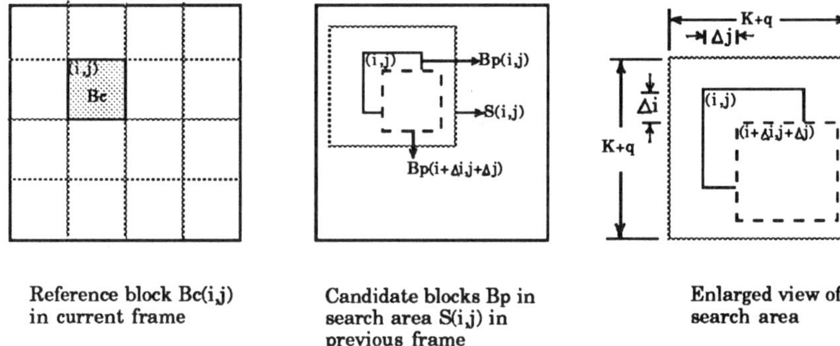


Figure 2: Reference block $B_c(i,j)$ and candidate blocks $B_p$ in search area $S(i,j)$.

size $N_1 \times N_2$ be divided into disjoint reference blocks of size $K \times K$. Let $B_c(i,j)$ be a reference block of $I_c$ whose top-leftmost coordinate is $(i,j)$ and let the corresponding search area $S(i,j)$ in the previous frame $I_p$ be of size $(K+q)\times(K+q)$. Let $B_p(i+\Delta i, j+\Delta j)$ be a candidate block in $S(i,j)$ whose top-leftmost coordinate is $(i+\Delta i, j+\Delta j)$, $-q/2 \leq \Delta i, \Delta j \leq q/2$. Figure 2 shows the relation between $B_c(i,j)$ and its candidate blocks in $S(i,j)$. Let $L_{i,j}(\Delta i, \Delta j)$ be the sum of absolute differences (SAD) between pixels $x_c$ of $B_c(i,j)$ and the corresponding pixels $x_p$ of $B_p(i+\Delta i, j+\Delta j)$; that is,

$$L_{i,j}(\Delta i, \Delta j) = \sum_{m=0}^{K-1} \sum_{n=0}^{K-1} |x_c(m,n) - x_p(m+\Delta i, n+\Delta j)|\,.$$

Let $(\Delta i, \Delta j)$ be the vector corresponding to $B_p(i+\Delta i, j+\Delta j)$ and let $(\Delta\hat{i}, \Delta\hat{j})_{i,j}$ be the displacement vector for $B_c(i,j)$. Then $(\Delta\hat{i}, \Delta\hat{j})_{i,j}$ is the vector corresponding to the candidate block of $B_c(i,j)$ with the minimum value of $L_{i,j}$; that is,

$$(\Delta\hat{i}, \Delta\hat{j})_{i,j} = \min_{\Delta i, \Delta j}{}^{-1} L_{i,j}(\Delta i, \Delta j).$$

Like template matching, block matching is also an extremely time-consuming process, since $(q+1)^2$ matches have to be computed for each of the $N_1N_2/K^2$ displacement vectors in a frame. This results in $N_1N_2(q+1)^2$ comparison–accumulation operations [1] per frame and a total computation time of $T_v = N_1N_2(q+1)^2\alpha T_c$, where $T_c$ is the internal clock period, and $\alpha$ is a constant such that $\alpha T_c$ is the pipelined time required to compute one comparison–accumulation operation. If $P$ is the minimum number of processors for real-time processing and if the speed-up is optimal, then $P = \lceil N_1N_2(q+1)^2\alpha T_c f_F\rceil$, where $f_F$ is the frame frequency. If $T_c = 50$ ns and if the operations are bit-parallel with eight bits per word, then the pipelined time required to compute one comparison–accumulation is 100 ns. For the case when $K = 8$ and $q = 8$, the number of processors required for Video Telephone Standard is seven and for NTSC video signal is 16.

## 3 Existing Architectures

Most of the existing architectures for template matching and block matching consist of a systolic array of processors and an external memory for storing the input images [2, 5, 6, 7, 9, 10, 12, 13]. These schemes differ in the number of processors, in the algorithms, and in the mappings of the algorithms into the architectures. In all these architectures the computations in the processor array are very efficient. However, the large number of off-chip memory accesses and complicated pointer circuitry make these designs unattractive. One way to overcome this limitation is to store part of the input image on-chip [3, 4, 8, 11].

Liao [11] proposed an architecture for template matching, which consists of a shift-buffer pipeline to store $K$ rows of the input image as shown in Fig. 3. The image data enter the buffer in line-scan format and are shifted in the pipeline. The multiplier array takes the data from the pipeline, computes in parallel, and sends the products to the adder tree. Unfortunately, this architecture produces $(K-1)$ invalid outputs for every $(N_2 - K + 1)$ valid outputs. Moreover, since the number of processors is fixed at $K^2$, this architecture is not versatile enough to compute template matching for any frame specification.

[1] A comparison–accumulation operation is $Z = Z + |A - B|$.

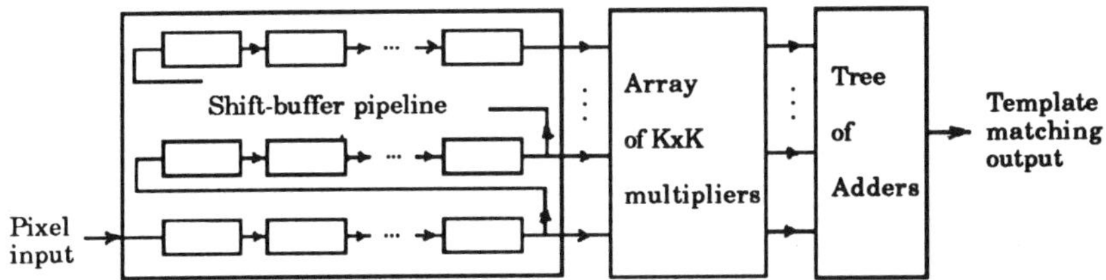


**Figure 3: Architecture proposed by Liao for template matching.**

To reduce off-chip memory accesses in block matching, Komarek *et al.* [8] suggested shift registers (for full search) and RAMs (for hierarchical search), whereas DeVos *et al.* [4] suggested on-chip line buffers, register chains, or memory blocks. In the scheme proposed by DeVos [4], the input is fed in block-scan mode. The processor array computes on one reference block at a time. For the case when the number of processors is $K$, the elements of the search area and the reference block are stored in the previous-block memory and current block memory as shown in Fig. 4. The processor array computes the sum of absolute differences of $(q+1)$ candidate blocks along a column of the search area. During this time, the next column of the search area is written into the previous-block memory and a column of the next reference block is written into the current-block memory. The processor array can then compute on the candidate blocks along the next column of the search area in the next iteration. The above process is repeated $(q+1)$ times.

# 4 Overview

In this section we give an overview of the proposed architecture and algorithms for template matching and block matching. We first briefly describe the architecture and then give the mappings of the algorithms for template matching and block matching into this architecture. Without loss of generality we assume that $N_1 = N_2 = N$.

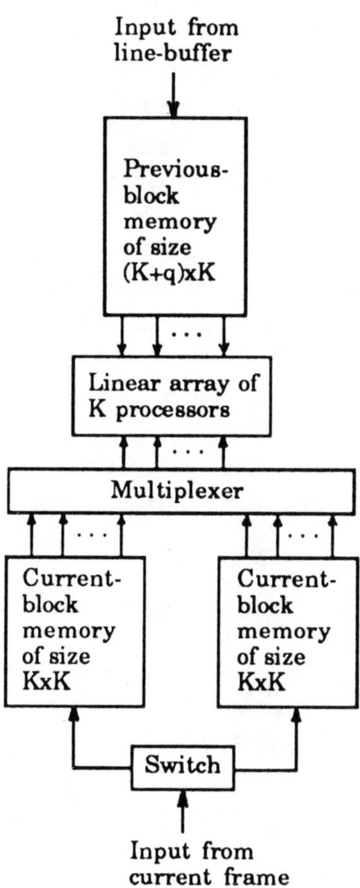


**Figure 4: Architecture proposed by DeVos et al. for block matching.**

## 4.1 Model

The proposed architecture consists of a linear array of $P$ processors. Each processor consists of a few storage registers and either a multiplier–accumulator [2] (for template matching) or a comparator–accumulator [3] (for block matching). A single number can be stored in each storage register. Attached to each processor are unidirectional shift registers as shown in Fig. 5. The input data are stored in shift registers, called the *data ring*, and the intermediate template-matching or block-matching outputs are stored in shift registers, called the *output ring*. By circulating the shift registers, the processors can compute on the same data multiple times. Each shift register consists of a linearly connected array of storage cells. When the shift register is clocked, the output of the $i$th storage cell is transferred to the $(i-1)$th storage cell in one clock cycle, where $1 \leq i < L$ and $L$ is the length of the shift register. When $i = 0$, the output of the shift register is transferred to a storage register. The input to the shift register is either the external image input or data from a storage register.

## 4.2 Algorithm and Mapping for Template Matching

Let $Y[i,j,m] = \sum_{n=0}^{K-1} I[i+m, j+n] * W[m,n]$; that is, $Y[i,j,m]$ is the row inner product (RIP) of the $m$th row of the template and the $m$th row of SUB$(i,j)$. Then $TM[i,j] = \sum_{m=0}^{K-1} Y[i,j,m]$; that is, $TM[i,j]$ is the sum of $K$ row inner products (corresponding to the $K$ rows of the template). The algorithm for template matching can be summarized as follows.

**Algorithm** *temp.match* :
1. **for** each row $i$ of input image **do**
2.     **for** each row $m$ of template **do**
3.         **for** each position $j$ of row $(i+m)$ of input image **do**
4.             Compute $Y[i,j,m]$ over row $(i+m)$ of input image
5.             Set $TM[i,j] = TM[i,j] + Y[i,j,m]$

[2] A multiplier–accumulator computes $Z = Z + A * B$.

[3] A comparator–accumulator computes $Z = Z + |A - B|$.

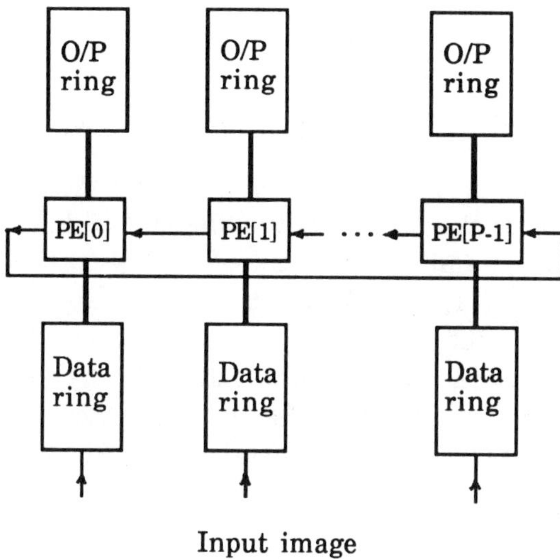


Figure 5: $P$-processor architecture.

The order of the for loops in algorithm *temp.match* is important. During the computation of template-matching outputs of row $i$, the $m$th row of the template is matched with row $(i+m)$th row of the input image for each $m$, $0 \leq m < K$.

The mapping of algorithm *temp.match* into the $P$-processor architecture is as follows: $P \geq K$ and $P$ divides $N$ evenly. The input image is read in line-scan mode and stored in cyclic mode in the shift registers of the $P$ processors. This means that $I[i,j]$ of the input image is read into the shift register of processor $p = j \bmod P$, $0 \leq i,j < N$. Thus, each row $i$ of the input image is divided into $N/P$ blocks and each block of $P$ consecutive elements is stored in the shift registers of $P$ processors. The $P$ processors compute template matching outputs for each row $i$ of the input image in the following way. The processors compute a set of $(N-K+1)$ RIPs between the $(i+m)$th row of the input image and the $m$th row of the template for each $m$, $0 \leq m < K$ (steps 2, 3, and 4 of *temp.match*). These RIPs are used to update the intermediate template-matching outputs stored in the shift registers. After $K$ updates, the shift register of processor $p = j \bmod P$ contains the template matching output $TM[i,j]$.

## 4.3 Algorithm and Mapping for Block Matching

Let $Y_{i,j}[\Delta i, \Delta j, m] = \sum_{n=0}^{K-1} |x_c(m,n) - x_p(m + \Delta i, n + \Delta j)|$; that is, $Y_{i,j}[\Delta i, \Delta j, m]$ is the row absolute difference (RAD) between the $m$th row of $B_c(i,j)$ and the $m$th row of $B_p(i + \Delta i, j + \Delta j)$. Then $L_{i,j}[\Delta i, \Delta j] = \sum_{m=0}^{K-1} Y_{i,j}[\Delta i, \Delta j, m]$; that is, $L_{i,j}[\Delta i, \Delta j]$ is the sum of $K$ row absolute differences (corresponding to the $K$ rows of the reference block). The displacement vector $(\Delta \hat{i}, \Delta \hat{j})_{i,j}$ is computed by first computing the vector corresponding to the best match over all $\Delta j$ and then over all $\Delta i$. The algorithm for block matching can be summarized as follows.

**Algorithm** *block.match* :

1. **for** $i = 0, K, 2K, \ldots$ of the current frame **do**
2.     **for** each row $(i + \Delta i)$ of the previous frame **do**
3.         **for** each row $m$ of the reference block **do**
4.             **for** $j = 0, K, 2K, \ldots$ of row $i$ of the current frame **do**
5.                 **for** each position $(j + \Delta j)$ of row $(i + \Delta i + m)$ of the previous frame **do**
6.                     Compute $Y_{i,j}[\Delta i, \Delta j, m]$
7.                     Set $L_{i,j}[\Delta i, \Delta j] = L_{i,j}[\Delta i, \Delta j] + Y_{i,j}[\Delta i, \Delta j, m]$
8.         Set $(\Delta \hat{i}, \Delta \hat{j})_{i,j} = \min^{-1}\{\min\{L_{i,j}(\Delta \hat{i}, \Delta \hat{j}), L_{i,j}(\Delta i, \Delta j)\}\}$

The mapping of algorithm *block.match* into the $P$-processor architecture is as follows. The input from the current frame and the previous frame external memory are read in line-scan mode and stored in cyclic mode in the shift registers of the $P$ processors. Thus, $I_c[i,j]$ of the current frame is read into a shift register of processor $p = j \bmod P$ and $I_p[i, \hat{j}]$ of the previous frame is read into a shift register of processor $p = \hat{j} \bmod P$, where $0 \leq i, j < N$ and $0 \leq \hat{j} < \hat{N}$, where $\hat{N} = N + q$. [4] The $P$ processors compute $N/K$ displacement vectors (corresponding to $N/K$ reference blocks of a row) for every

[4]The previous frame is appended with a ring of zeros of width $\frac{q}{2}$ so that the same procedure can be used to compute all the displacement vectors. This increases the size of the previous frame to $\hat{N} \times \hat{N}$, where $\hat{N} = N + q$.

$K$th row $i$ of the current frame in the following way. The processors compute a set of RADs between the $(i+m)$th row of the current frame and the $(i+m+\Delta i)$th row of the previous frame for each $m$, $0 \leq m < K$. The sum of these RADs gives a set of SADs, the intermediate values of which are stored in the shift registers of the processors. We refer to this set of SADs as $\text{SAD}(i, i+\Delta i)$. [5] The processors then compute the minimum value of SAD of the candidate blocks for each of the reference blocks and update the corresponding temporary displacement vectors. The above process is repeated for each $\Delta i$, $-\frac{q}{2} \leq \Delta i \leq \frac{q}{2}$.

# 5 Detailed Description

In this section we give the details of the processor architecture and algorithm for template matching and block matching. We first discuss the operations at the processor level and then elaborate on the I/O issues.

## 5.1 Template Matching

### Processor Architecture

Each processor consists of a multiplier–accumulator, a few storage registers, a data ring to store data from the input image, and an output ring to store the intermediate template-matching outputs. Figure 6 illustrates the design of a single processor.

The data ring is of size $KN/P$, since the pixels of the input image are read only once, and since the rows of the input image that are required for the computation of template-matching outputs of two consecutive rows overlap by $(K-1)$ rows. The elements in the data ring are partitioned into $K$ blocks such that $N/P$ elements of a row of the input image are in the same block of the data ring. Figure 7 shows the elements in the data rings prior to the computation of template-matching outputs of row 1 in an example where the image is of size

[5] $\text{SAD}(i, i+\Delta i)$ consists of $(q+1)N/K$ SADs between reference blocks whose top-leftmost coordinates are in row $i$ of the current frame and candidate blocks whose top-leftmost coordinates are in row $(i+\Delta i)$ of the previous frame.

$8 \times 8$, the template is of size $3 \times 3$ and the number of processors is four. The template values are broadcast to the processors via the $W$ line (see Fig. 6). The size of the output ring is $\lceil \frac{N-K+1}{P} \rceil = \frac{N}{P}$, since each processor computes at most $\lceil \frac{N-K+1}{P} \rceil$ intermediate template-matching outputs along a row. The intermediate template-matching outputs are stored in cyclic mode in the output ring and are updated $K$ times (once for each of the $K$ rows of the template).

### Processor Algorithm

We next discuss the operations of processor $p$ in the computation of template-matching outputs $TM[i, j]$, where $p = j \bmod P$ and $0 \leq i, j \leq N - K$. At the beginning of the computation of the template-matching outputs of row $i$, the data ring in each processor contains the elements corresponding to rows $i$ through $(i+K-1)$ of the input image in blocks 0 through $(K-1)$ (see Fig. 7). For each of the $K$ rows of the template $(0 \leq m < K)$, processor $p$ computes $Y[i, j, m]$s, where $j = \gamma P + p$ and $0 \leq \gamma < \lceil \frac{N-K+1}{P} \rceil$. Thus, processor $p$ computes $\lceil \frac{N-K+1}{P} \rceil$ RIPs of the $m$th row of the template and the $(i+m)$th row of the input image for each row of the template. The procedure to compute an RIP is as follows. The data ring loads two elements into registers $A$ and $C$ such that $A := data.ring[0]$ and $C := data.ring[1]$. Since the input is stored in the data ring in the cyclic mode, the $2P$ elements in the $A$ and $C$ registers of the $P$ processors are row-adjacent elements of the $(i+m)$th row of the input image. The output ring loads an intermediate template-matching output into register $Y$. The template values of the $m$th row are broadcast via the $W$ line. The product of the contents of register $A$ and $W$ gives one of the terms needed to compute a RIP. The contents of registers $A$ and $C$ are shifted[6] and a new term is computed. The above process is repeated for each of the $K$ values in a row of the template. The updated intermediate template-matching output is then loaded back into the output ring. The series of operations to compute a RIP corresponding to row $m$ of the template is summarized as follows.

---

[6]Register $A$ of processor $(P-1)$ is connected to register $C$ of processor 0, so that by shifting the contents of registers $A$ and $C$, register $A$ will always contain the correct value for the computation of an RIP.

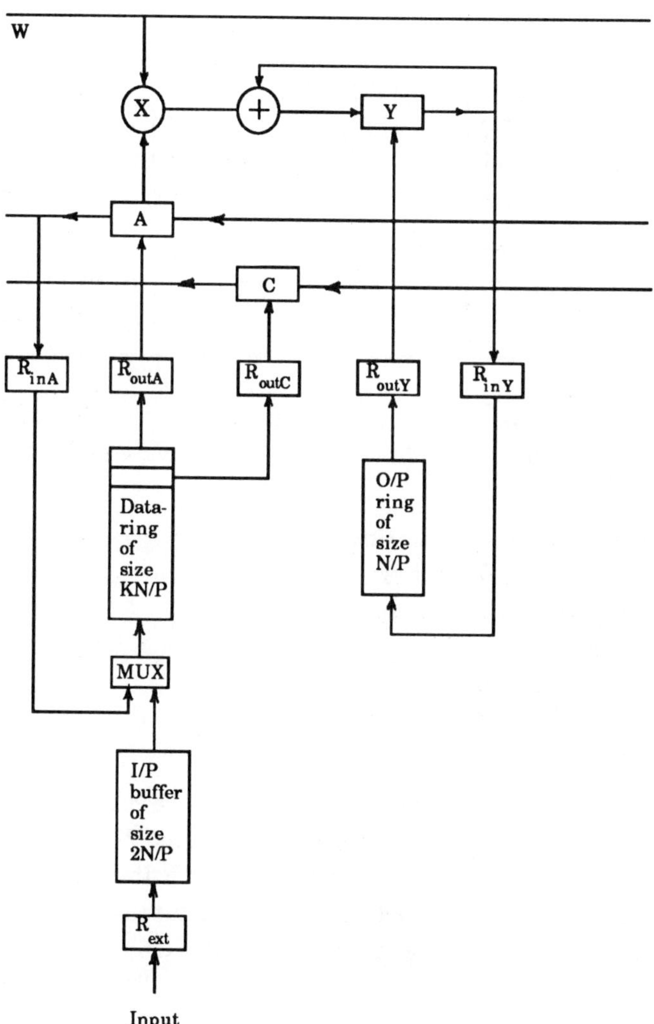


Figure 6: Design of a processor for template matching.

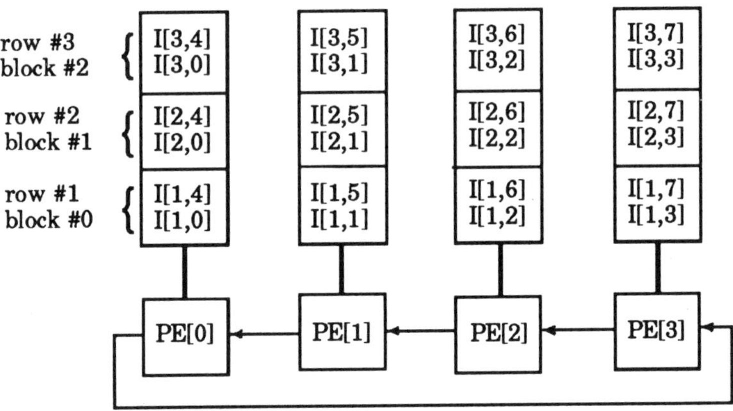


**Figure 7: Data ring configurations prior to computation of $TM[1,*]$ in an example with an $8 \times 8$ image, a $3 \times 3$ template and 4 processors.**

```
1.    load A, C from data ring
      load Y from output ring
2.    for q := 0 to K − 1 do
3.        broadcast W[m,q]
4.        Y := Y + A * W      (if flag = 0)
5.        Shift-left A and C by 1
6.    load Y into output ring
```

The data ring and the output ring are shifted and the above process is repeated $\lceil \frac{N-K+1}{P} \rceil = \frac{N}{P}$ times. Note that $flag$ is set to 1 in processors $(K-1)$ to $(P-1)$ in the $N/P$th iteration so that no invalid outputs are computed. The time taken to compute an RIP is $K\alpha T_c$. Thus, the data ring is clocked at $K\alpha T_c$.

## I/O Operations

We next discuss how the input image is loaded into the data ring. While the template-matching outputs of row $i$ are being computed, row $(i+K)$ is read from the input image into the input buffers (see Fig. 6) of the $P$ processors. Thus, each row is loaded into the input buffers in the time taken to compute all the template-matching outputs of a row. We propose two input-loading schemes, which differ in the way the data are loaded from the input buffer into the data ring. In the first scheme the data ring is circulated $(K+1)N/P$ times for the computation of the template-matching outputs of row $i$, $0 \leq i < N-K$. It is circulated $KN/P$ times so that all the elements of the data ring corresponding to rows $i$ through $(i+K-1)$ are incident on the processor array (and can be used for the computation of template-matching outputs of row $i$) and then for another $N/P$ times so that the elements corresponding to row $i$ are once again in block 0. In the next step the elements corresponding to the $(i+K)$th row are shifted in from the input buffer (while the elements corresponding to the $i$th row are shifted out). At the end of this step the data ring contains elements corresponding to rows $(i+1)$ through $(i+K)$, which are required for the computation of template-matching outputs of row $(i+1)$. The above scheme is illustrated in Fig. 8 in an example with an $8 \times 8$ image, a $3 \times 3$ template, and four processors. The input buffer is of size $N/P$. In this scheme the time taken to compute all the template-matching outputs of a row is $K(K+1)\alpha T_c N/P$. Note that this scheme does not achieve optimal speed-up. This is because the processor array is idle for $1/K$ of the time (it is idle for $K\alpha T_c N/P$ time for every $K^2 \alpha T_c N/P$ time that it is active).

The second scheme achieves optimal speed-up by pipelining the data in the following way. During the computation of the template matching outputs of row $i$–in particular, during the computation of $Y[i,*,0]$–the elements corresponding to row $(i+K)$ are loaded into the data ring from the input buffer, where $i = \beta K$ and $\beta$ is an integer in the range $0 \leq \beta \leq \lfloor \frac{N-K+1}{K} \rfloor$. In general, the elements corresponding to row $(i+K+j)$ are loaded into the data ring during the computation of $Y[i+j,*,j]$, $0 \leq j < K$. The input buffer is of size $2N/P$ since the elements of two rows, row $(i+2K-1)$ and row $(i+2K)$, are loaded into the data ring one after the other. [7]

In the second scheme the template values that are broadcast to

[7]Row $(i+2K-1)$ is loaded during the computation of $Y[i+K-1,*,K-1]$ (the last inner product in the computation of template-matching outputs of row $(i+K-1)$), and row $(i+2K)$ is loaded during the computation of $Y[i+K,*,0]$ (the first inner product in the computation of template-matching outputs of row $(i+K)$).

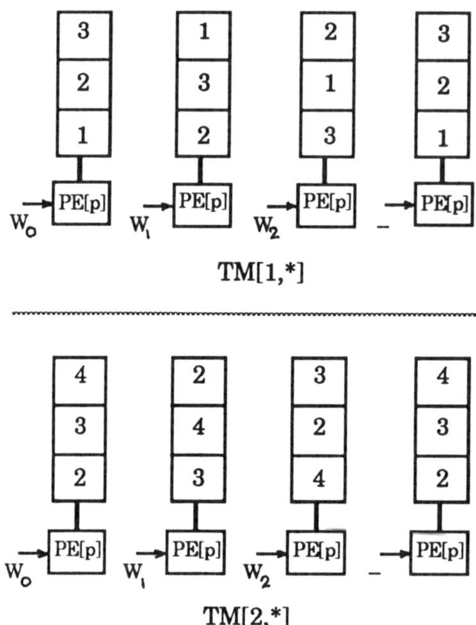


Figure 8: Rows of the input image in the data ring of processor $p$ during the computation of $TM[1,*]$, $TM[2,*]$ in scheme 1 in an example with an $8 \times 8$ image, a $3 \times 3$ template, and four processors.

the processor array are not the same for the computation of template-matching outputs of all rows. Let $W_j$ be the $j$th row of the template. The sequence of $W_j$s broadcast to the processor array for the computation of template-matching outputs of rows $i$ through $(i + K - 1)$, where $i = \beta K$ and $0 \leq \beta \leq \lfloor \frac{N-K+1}{K} \rfloor$, is as follows.

$$\underbrace{W_0, W_1, \ldots, W_{K-1}}_{TM[i,*]}, \underbrace{W_{K-1}, W_0, \ldots, W_{K-2}}_{TM[i+1,*]}, \ldots, \underbrace{W_1, W_2, \ldots, W_0}_{TM[i+K-1,*]},$$
$$\underbrace{W_0, W_1, \ldots, W_{K-1}}_{TM[i+K,*]}, \ldots$$

Note that there are $K$ different sets of $W_j$ sequences. The above scheme is illustrated in Fig. 9 for the example with an $8 \times 8$ image, a $3 \times 3$ template, and four processors. For details of the algorithm

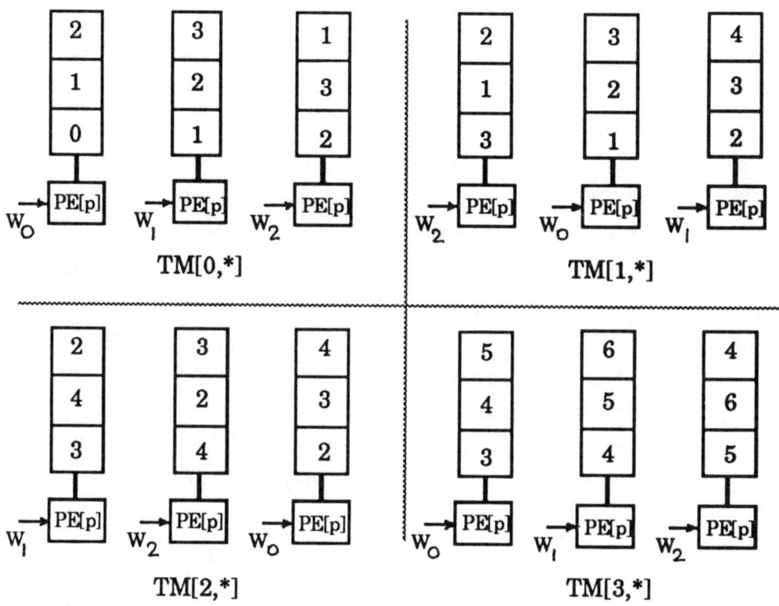


Figure 9: Rows of the input image in the data ring of processor $p$ during the computation of $TM[0,*]$, $TM[1,*]$, $TM[2,*]$, $TM[3,*]$ in scheme 2 in an example with an $8 \times 8$ image, a $3 \times 3$ template, and four processors.

refer to [1].

## 5.2 Block Matching

### Processor Architecture

In the architecture for block matching, there are two types of processors: type $A$ and type $B$. Although all the processors contain storage registers–a *previous-data ring* to store data from the previous frame and a *current-data ring* to store data from the current frame–only processors of type $A$ contain comparator–accumulators and output rings. Figure 10 illustrates the design of a single processor of type $A$. Let the processor array consist of $\delta$ groups with $K$ processors per group; that is, $P = \delta K$. In each group let there be $(q+1)$ processors of type $A$ and $(K - q - 1)$ processors of type $B$. We assume that $K > q$. We choose the number of processors of type $A$ to be $(q+1)$ so that the values of SAD of $(q+1)$ candidate blocks of a particular reference block are computed by the processors of the same group.

The previous-data ring is of size $K\lceil\hat{N}/P\rceil$, since $K$ rows of the previous frame are needed for the computation of a set of SADs along a row. (Recall that the previous frame is of size $\hat{N} \times \hat{N}$, where $\hat{N} = N + q$.) Although only $K$ rows of the current frame need to be stored, the current-data ring is of size $(K+1)\lceil\hat{N}/P\rceil$. This is because the current-data ring is clocked at the same rate as the previous-data ring and the previous-data ring is circulated $(K+1)\lceil\hat{N}/P\rceil$ times for the computation of the SADs along a row. The elements of the previous-data (respectively current-data) rings are partitioned into $K$ (respectively $(K+1)$) blocks such that $\lceil\hat{N}/P\rceil$ elements of a row of the previous (respectively current) frame are in the same block. Figure 11 shows the configurations of the previous-data ring and current-data ring prior to the computation of block-matching outputs of row 0 in an example with an $8 \times 8$ image, a $4 \times 4$ reference block, a $6 \times 6$ search area and four processors.

Note that the current-data ring has $N/P$ valid data (and one invalid datum) in each of its $K$ blocks and $\lceil\hat{N}/P\rceil$ invalid data in its $(K+1)$th block. The output ring is of size $\lceil\hat{N}/P\rceil$ (instead of $N/P$) [8] so that it can be clocked at the same rate as the data rings.

## Processor Algorithm

We next discuss the operations of a processor in the computation of a displacement vector. Recall that for each $\Delta i$ the processors first compute SAD$(i, i + \Delta i)$ which is a set of SADs between reference blocks whose top-leftmost coordinates are in row $i$ of the current frame and candidate blocks whose top-leftmost coordinates are in row $(i + \Delta i)$ of the previous frame.Then each group computes the minimum value of SAD and updates the temporary displacement vector. At the beginning of the computation of SAD$(i, i + \Delta i)$, the

[8]Since $\gamma(q+1)$ processors of type $A$ compute $(q+1)N/K$ SADs along a row, the minimum size of the output ring is $N/(K\gamma) = N/P$.

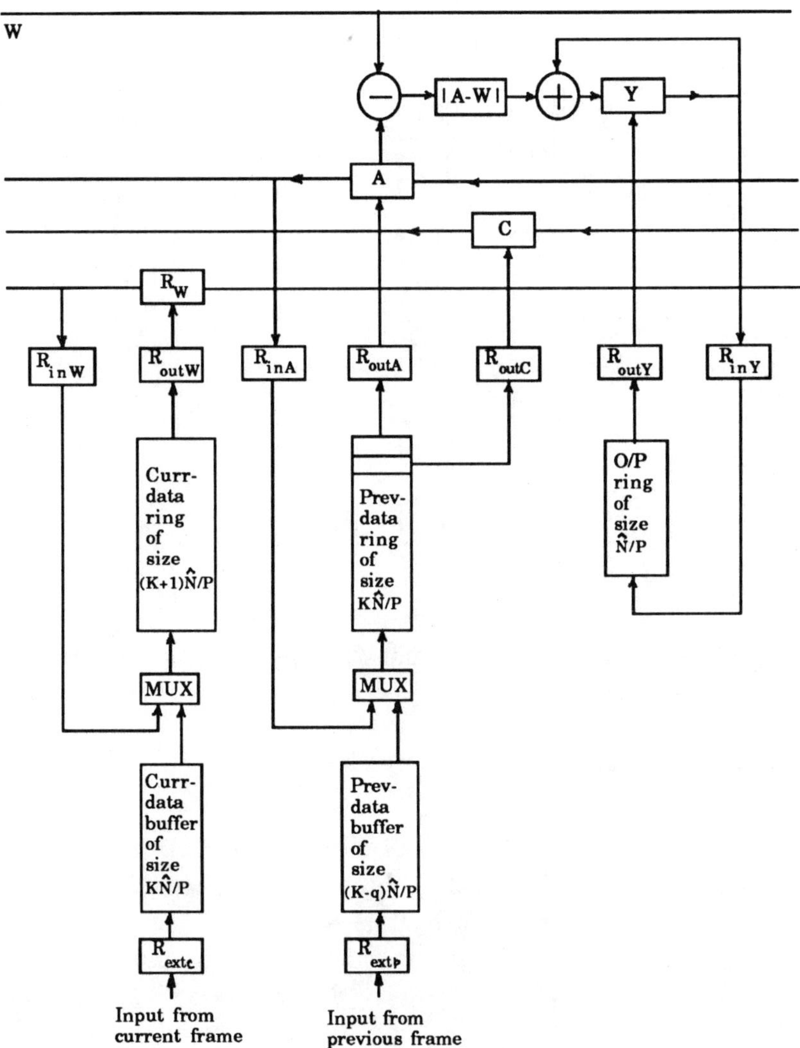


**Figure 10: Design of a processor of type *A* for block matching.**

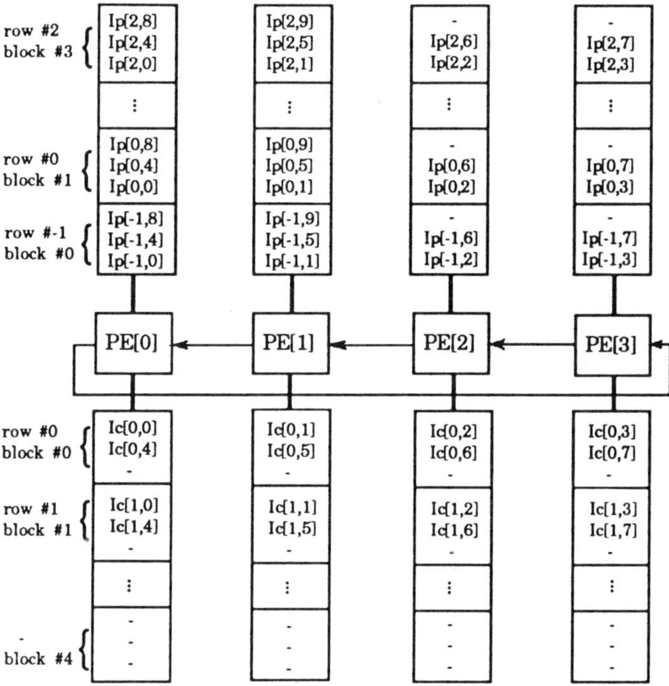


Figure 11: Previous-data ring and current-data ring configurations prior to the computation of displacement vectors of row 0 in an example with an $8 \times 8$ image, a $4 \times 4$ reference block, a $6 \times 6$ search area and 4 processors.

previous-data ring and the current-data ring of each processor contain elements of rows $(i + \Delta i)$ through $(i + \Delta i + K - 1)$ of the previous frame and rows $i$ through $(i + K - 1)$ of the current frame (see Fig. 12). For each of the $m$ rows of the current block, processor $p$ computes $Y_{i,j}[\Delta i, \Delta j, m]$, where $p = j \bmod P + \Delta j + \frac{q}{2}$, $0 \leq j < N$, and $j$ is a multiple of $K$. Thus, processor $p$ computes $N/P$ RADs for each $m$, $0 \leq m < K$. The procedure to compute a RAD is as follows. The previous-data ring loads two elements into registers $A$ and $C$ such that $A := prevdata.ring[0]$ and $C := prevdata.ring[1]$. The current-data ring loads an element into register $R_W$ such that $R_W := currdata.ring[0]$. The contents of $R_W$ of the leftmost processor in a group are broadcast via the $W$ line to all the processors of type $A$ of that group. The absolute difference of the contents of $A$ and $W$ gives one of the terms needed to compute a RAD. The contents of registers $A$, $C$, and $W$ are shifted and a new term is computed. The above process is repeated for each of the $K$ values in a row of the reference block. Note that by shifting the contents of $R_W$ $K$ times, the $K$ elements in a row of the reference block are incident to all the processors of type $A$ of that group. The series of operations to compute a RAD is summarized as follows.

1. load $A$ and $C$ from previous-data ring
   load $R_W$ from current-data ring
   load $Y$ from output ring
2. for $t := 0$ to $K - 1$ do
3. $\quad$ $Y := Y + |A - W|$ $\quad$ (*if flag* $= 0$)
4. $\quad$ shift-left $A$, $C$, $R_W$ by 1
5. load $Y$ into output ring

The previous-data ring, current-data ring and output ring are shifted and the above process is repeated $\lceil \hat{N}/P \rceil$ times. Note that *flag* is set to 1 when invalid data are loaded from the current-data ring. The time taken to compute a RAD is $K\alpha T_c$. Thus, the previous-data ring and the current-data ring are clocked at $K\alpha T_c$.

After the computation of SAD$(i, i+\Delta i)$, each group computes the minimum value of SAD and stores it in its *dvector* register, along with the corresponding temporary displacement vector. Computation of the minimum value of SAD is done in parallel with the computation of the first set of RADs of SAD$(i, i+\Delta i+1)$. The value of the dvector register is updated in successive iterations of $\Delta i$, so that at the end of $(q + 1)$ iterations of $\Delta i$, this register contains the minimum value of SAD and the corresponding displacement vector. Note that each group contains $N/P$ dvector registers, since each group computes the displacement vectors for $N/P$ reference blocks in a row. For details of the algorithm refer to [1].

## I/O Operations

The input from the current-frame and previous-frame external memory are loaded into the current-data ring and previous-data ring in

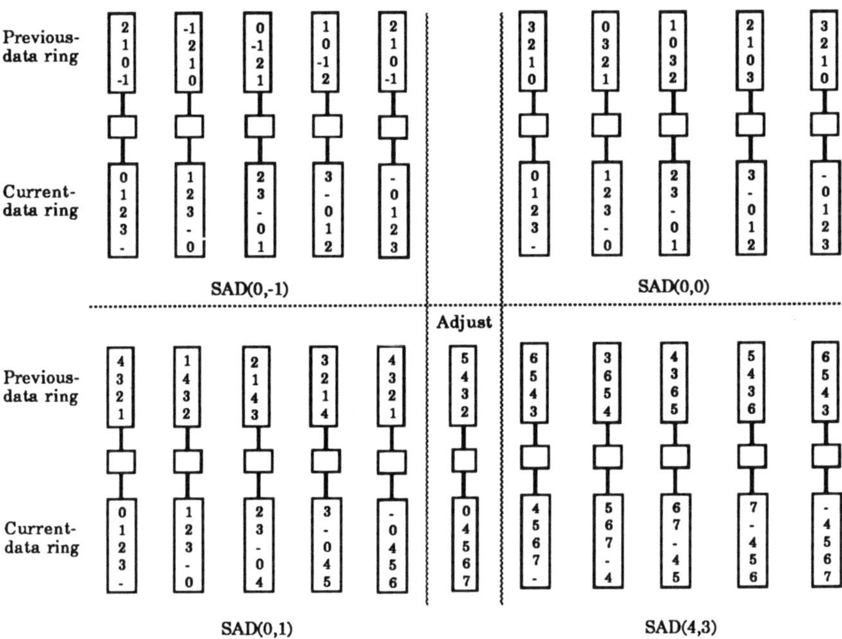


**Figure 12: Rows of the previous frame and current frame in the data rings of a processor during the computation of $SAD(i, i + \Delta i)$, $-\frac{q}{2} \leq \Delta i \leq \frac{q}{2}$, and $SAD(i + K, i + K - \frac{q}{2})$ for $i = 0$ in an example with an $8 \times 8$ image, a $4 \times 4$ reference block, a $6 \times 6$ search area and 4 processors**

the following way. During the computation of the displacement vectors of row $i$, $K$ rows of both the current frame as well as the previous frame are read in. The $K$ rows of the current frame are stored in shift registers of size $KN/P$, called the *current-data buffer* (see Fig. 11). Of the $K$ rows of the previous frame, $q$ rows are required for the computation of SAD$(i, i + \Delta\hat{i})$ where $-\frac{q}{2} + 1 \leq \Delta\hat{i} \leq \frac{q}{2}$, and $(K - q)$ rows are required so that the delay between the computation of SAD$(i + K, i + K - \frac{q}{2})$ and SAD$(i, i + \frac{q}{2})$ is minimum. These $(K - q)$ rows are stored in shift registers of size $(K - q)\lceil\hat{N}/P\rceil$, called the *previous-data buffer* (see Fig. 11).

Both the current-data ring and the previous-data ring are circulated $(K + 1)\lceil\hat{N}/P\rceil$ times for the computation of SAD$(i, i + \Delta i)$, for each $\Delta i$. $q$ rows of the previous frame are read into the previous-data ring in the following way. The previous-data ring is circulated $K\lceil\hat{N}/P\rceil$ times so that every element of rows $(i + \Delta i)$ through $(i + \Delta i + K - 1)$ of the previous frame is incident on the processor array, and then for another $\lceil\hat{N}/P\rceil$ times so that the elements of row $(i + \Delta i)$ of the previous frame are once again in block 0. In the next step the elements of the $(i + \Delta i + K)$th row are shifted in from the previous-data buffer while the elements of the $(i + \Delta i)$th row are shifted out. At the end of this step the previous-data ring contains elements of rows $(i+\Delta i+1)$ through $(i+\Delta i+K)$, which are required for the computation of SAD$(i, i + \Delta i + 1)$. The remaining $(K - q)$ rows (rows $(i + K + \frac{q}{2})$ through $(i + 2K - \frac{q}{2} - 2)$) are shifted into the previous-data ring after the computation of SAD$(i, i + \frac{q}{2})$. This period is known as *adjustment* time (the processor array is idle for this period of time). In the meantime the current-data ring shifts $(q + 1)$ rows (rows $(i + K)$ through $(i + K + q)$) during the computation of SAD$(i, i + \frac{q}{2})$ and the remaining $(K - q - 1)$ rows (rows $(i + K + q + 1)$ through $(i + 2K - 1)$) during the adjustment time. At the end of this step the previous-data ring contains the elements of rows $(i + K - \frac{q}{2})$ through $(i + 2K - \frac{q}{2} - 1)$ and the current-data ring contains elements of rows $(i + K)$ through $(i + 2K - 1)$, which are required for the computation of SAD$(i + K, i + K - \frac{q}{2})$. This process is illustrated in Fig. 12 for $i = 0$ in an example with an $8 \times 8$ image, a $4 \times 4$ reference block, a $6 \times 6$ search area and four processors.

The time required to compute $N/K$ displacement vectors of a row is $T_{row} = ((q+1)(K+1)+K-q-1)K\alpha T_c\lceil \hat{N}/P \rceil$, and the total computation time is $(q+2)K\alpha T_c N\lceil \hat{N}/P \rceil$.

### Acknowledgments

This research was supported in part by the Parallel Processing Group, Advanced Systems Division, National Institute of Standards and Technology, NSF Grant No. DCR-86-00378, and by the Systems Research Center Contract No. OIR-85-00108.

## Bibliography

[1] C. Chakrabarti, *VLSI architectures for real-time signal processing*, Ph.D dissertation, Department of Electrical Engineering, University of Maryland, College Park, Maryland, 1990.

[2] J. F. Coté, C. Collet, D. D. Haule and A. S. Malowany, *A high performance convolution processor*, Proc. SPIE vol. 1001 Visual Communications and Image Processing, 1988, pp. 469–475.

[3] N. Demassieux, F. Jutand, M. Bernard and C. Joanblanq, *A VLSI architecture for real-time image convolution with large symmetric kernels*, Proc. ICASSP, 1988, pp. 1961–1964.

[4] L. DeVos and M. Stegherr, *Parametrizable VLSI Architectures for the full-search block-matching algorithm*, IEEE Trans. on Circuits and Systems, vol. 36, no. 10, 1989, pp. 1309–1316.

[5] R. Dianysian, R. L. Baker and J. L. Salinas, *A VLSI architecture for template matching and motion estimation*, presented at ISCAS, 1988.

[6] E. R. Dougherty and C. R. Giardina, *Universal systolic architecture for morphological and convolutional image filters*, Proc.

SPIE vol. 1001 Visual Communications and Image Processing, 1988, pp. 739–746.

[7] O. Ersoy, *Semisystolic array implementation of circular, skew circular and linear convolutions*, IEEE Trans. on Computers, vol. C-34, no. 2, 1985, pp. 190–196.

[8] T. Komarek and P. Pirsch, *Array architectures for block matching algorithms*, IEEE Trans. on Circuits and Systems, vol. 36, no. 10, 1989, pp. 1301–1308.

[9] H. T. Kung and S. W. Song, *A systolic 2-D convolution chip*, Tech. Rep. CMU-CS-81-110, Carnegie Mellon University, Computer Science Department, March 1981.

[10] H. K. Kwan and T. S. Okulla-Oballa, *Two-dimensional systolic arrays for two-dimensional convolution*, Proc. SPIE vol. 1001 Visual Communications and Image Processing, 1988, pp. 724–731.

[11] Y. C. Liao, *VLSI architecture for generalized 2-D convolution*, Proc. SPIE vol. 1001 Visual Communications and Image Processing, 1988, pp. 450–455.

[12] P. A. Ruetz and R. W. Brodersen, *Architectures and design techniques for real-time image-processing IC's*, IEEE Journal of Solid State Circuits, vol. SC-22, no. 2, 1987, pp. 233–250.

[13] K. Yang, M. Sun and L. Wu, *VLSI implementation of motion compensation full-search block-matching algorithm*, Proc. SPIE vol. 1001 Visual Communications and Image Processing, 1988, pp. 892–899.

# Parallel Image Computing with Optical Technology

MARY M. ESHAGHIAN
*Grumman Data Systems*
*San Diego, California*

and

SING H. LEE
*Department of Electrical and Computer Engineering*
*University of California*
*San Diego, California*

and

MUHAMMAD E. SHAABAN
*Department of Electrical Engineering-Systems*
*University of Southern California*
*Los Angeles, California*

## 1 Introduction

Many massively parallel architectures have been studied over the past few decades for solutions to fine grain image computing tasks [19, 20, 21]. However, due to the communication-intensive nature of these tasks, their performance depends heavily on the underlying interconnection network. Optics offers an excellent medium for interprocessor communication by providing an extra dimension of connectivity. In this chapter we study parallel algorithms for intermediate-level vision processing of proposed optical models. In addition, we

Parallel Architectures and
Algorithms for
Image Understanding





ISBN 0-12-564040-4

will discuss the use of basic optical elements for preprocessing tasks, feature extraction, and pattern recognition. These techniques reflect the natural capabilities of optical technology in parallel and real-time processing of two-dimensional images.

Generating the Fourier transform and/or performing a correlation on a two-dimensional image input are classical examples where the parallel and real-time features of optical systems are exploited. The original works of Lendaris and Stanley [18] and VanderLugt [26] have established a solid basis for the discipline of coherent optical pattern recognition (OPR). A review paper by Casasent [5] gives a brief introduction to OPR techniques and architectures for feature extraction and correlation. In this chapter, we describe briefly integrated and optical implementations of a few preprocessing tasks, feature extraction, and statistical pattern recognition.

Taking advantage of the properties of free-space optics, we then propose a class of parallel architectures with reconfigurable interconnection networks. The operation and organization of these designs are based on a generic optical model of computation called OMC. Unlike other multiprocessor models using electrical interconnections, OMC allows unit delay interconnects among bounded degree processor nodes. Furthermore, its computational limits are similar to those of three-dimensional VLSI models. To demonstrate the accuracy and generality of OMC, we present a few physical implementations, using various forms of optical devices to program their interconnectivity in real time. Using these models, we present a set of pointer-based optimal $O(\log N)$ algorithms for problems such as connectivity, proximity.

The rest of the chapter is organized as follows. In section 2 we study a set of optical organizations for image preprocessing. In the following section, using free space interconnects, we propose models and algorithms for fine grain parallel processing of intermediate-level computer vision. Finally, in section 4, we discuss optical techniques for feature extraction and pattern recognition.

# 2 Optical Image Preprocessing

In the first part of this section we give a brief introduction to basic devices and concepts used in optical image processing. This introduction should aid in understanding the natural role optics can play in parallel image computing. In the second part of this section we concentrate on applications of optical techniques in image preprocessing tasks such as texture analysis, histograming, and edge detection. These operations are performed optically and in parallel over the entire image. This marks a great improvement in speed over conventional digital image preprocessing methods.

## 2.1 Basic Concepts

The processing power of optics stems from the wavelike properties of light and, to a much lesser extent, on its elementary composition of photons. Frequency, wavelength, amplitude, phase, and speed of propagation are some of the wavelike properties used to describe the characteristics of light. The speed of light depends on the index of refraction of the medium through which it is propagating. When light passes (at an angle) from one medium to another, its change of speed causes a change of direction; this is called refraction. Lenses, prisms, and other optical devices use this phenomenon to redirect beams of light.

When all the wave components of a light beam are in phase, it can be described as a harmonic wave such as $sin(x)$. This type of light is said to be coherent. Coherent light contains both phase and amplitude information, whereas incoherent light has no phase information. Optical image-processing systems that use coherent light offer immense processing power over classical digital image processing techniques. The simplest coherent optical processor in Fig. 2.1 consists of a thin convex lens of focal length $f$ illuminated by a beam of coherent light passing through a transparency with complex transmittance $g(x, y)$ positioned at a distance $f$ in front of the lens. The light distribution at a distance $f$ on the other side of the lens $G(u, v)$ turns out to be the Fourier transform of $g(x, y)$. This ability of a lens to produce an analog two-dimensional Fourier transform instantly (at the speed of light) is an important operation often used in various image-processing operations. Fourier transform is a good example of a class of image-processing tasks with efficient optical implementation. Such problems usually involve simultaneous global operations over all the points of the input image.

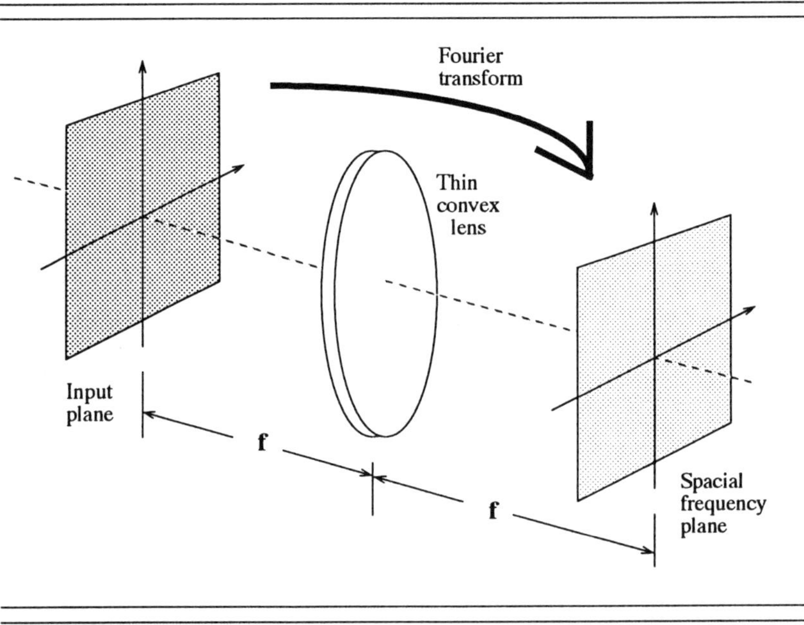


Figure 1: Simplified diagram of a coherent optical Fourier transform system.

Modern optical image processing systems combine the use of classical optical elements, such as lenses, with the use of modern optical devices. Spatial light modulators (SLM) are relatively new optical devices that play an important role in these systems. An SLM is a device that creates a form of modulation on the cross-section of a light beam. A transparency is a simple example of an SLM. These devices are usually used as spatial filters, or masks, in image-processing systems. Several types of SLMs have been developed in recent years, reflecting technological advances and the demands of modern optical processing systems [6]. Several applications in optical image processing will become evident throughout our discussion in the following sections.

Holography is another technological advancement that is considered an important part of modern optics. A hologram records both the amplitude and phase of an image, usually on photographic film, as a real positive valued image. This is achieved by having a light beam from the object interfere with a reference beam. A hologram with an arbitrary diffraction pattern also can be generated using computers [10]. Unlike a lens which has a global effect on the incident light beam, a hologram modulates the amplitude and phase of each part of the beam individually. This makes it possible to have optical elements with arbitrary deflection characteristics not achievable with conventional optics. This feature of holograms is used to implement many transformations that are needed as part of optical image processing. In addition, holograms find many applications in providing random optical interconnects, as discussed in section 3.

## 2.2 Optical Preprocessing

Traditional methods of image preprocessing utilize digital techniques and transformations [23]. However, these operations can be performed in analog fashion more efficiently using optical methods. In this section we study optical implementations of several tasks such as texture analysis, histograming, edge detection, dilation, and contraction.

### Texture Variance

One of the important tasks in image preprocessing is the texture enhancement of the input image. This operation is important to facilitate further processing such as image segmentation [27]. Texture variance is defined as

$$\sigma^2(x,y) = \overline{[g(x,y) - g_0]^2}$$

where $g(x,y)$ is the input transmittance, $g_0$ is its average value, and the bar denotes the total average. This variance can be computed optically by illuminating the input (using coherent light), forming its optical Fourier transform with a lens, blocking the dc portion of the transform, and performing the inverse transform on the result [15]. The desired variance image is formed on a ground glass diffuser, on which a TV camera is focused (Fig. 2.2).

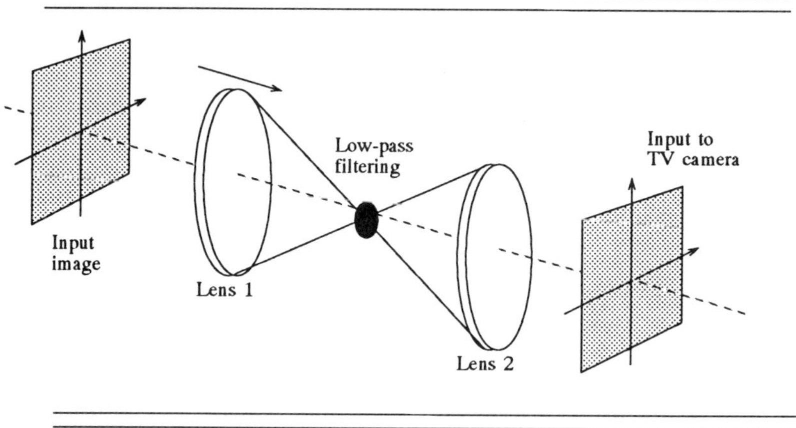


Figure 2: Optical system for extracting feature variance information.

## Gray-level Histogramming

Gray-level histograming of an image is a function that gives the frequency of occurrence of each gray level in the image. Histogram information is valuable for contrast and dynamic range adjustments. Using a microchannel, or a silicon/PLZT [16] SLM that can perform thresholding, one can obtain intensity level sliced images. Then the frequency of occurrence of each gray level in the image can be obtained using a condensed lens (Fig. 2.2).

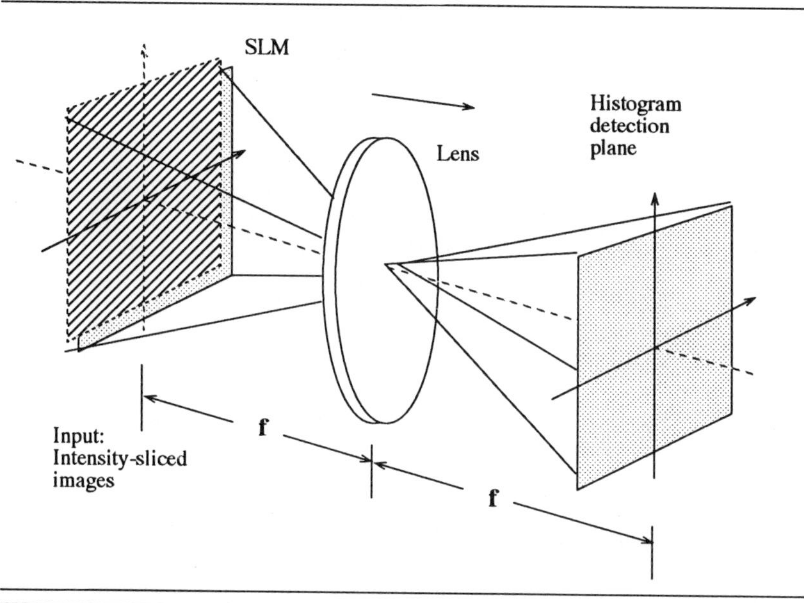


Figure 3: Optical system for extracting histogram information.

## Edge Extraction

An edge operator is a mathematical operator with a small spatial extent designed to extract edges and boundaries of objects in an image. Gradient, Laplacian, and Sobel operators are examples of edge operators frequently employed in computer vision [15]. These edge operators can be optically implemented using a multiple-exposed or computer-generated hologram filter of impulse response $h(x,y)$ in an optical correlator [14], where $h(x,y)$ is a sum of delta functions at different adjacent spatial locations (similar to Fig. 2.2 with low-pass filtering replaced with h(x,y) ). For example, performing the Sobel operation on an input $f(x,y)$ will yield the output $g(x,y)$ where $g$ and f are related by

$$g(x,y) \quad = \quad [((\langle\frac{\partial f}{\partial x}\rangle_y)^2 + ((\langle\frac{\partial f}{\partial y}\rangle_x)^2]^{\frac{1}{2}}$$

$$= f(x,y) * h(x,y)$$

where $\langle\ \rangle_x$ and $\langle\ \rangle_y$ denote averages over $x$ and $y$, respectively, $*$ represents correlation and

$$\begin{aligned} h(x,y) &= (1+j)\delta(x-d,y-d)+2\delta(x-d,y)+(1-j)\delta(x-d,y+d) \\ &\quad +2j\delta(x,y-d)-2j\delta(x,y+d)-(1-j)\delta(x+d,y-d) \\ &\quad -2\delta(x+d,y)-(1+j)\delta(x+d,y+d) \end{aligned}$$

where $d$ is the spacing between pixels.

### Dilation and Contraction

Dilation and contraction are operations useful for linking together segments of broken lines, as well as for filtering noise from an edge-extracted image [15]. Dilating an object S by a structured element B involves extending the border of S by adding B all around it (Fig. 2.2). The expansion or dilation operation can be performed as a combination of convolution and thresholding operations. Convolution is readily achieved using either an out-of-focus incoherent processing system or a low-pass filtered coherent processing system. While thresholding operations involve the use of a microchannel or a Si/PLZT SLM, contracting an object S by a structured element b involves shrinking the border of S by subtracting b from it (Fig. 2.2). The shrinking or contracting operation can be performed as a combination of complementation, expansion and operations (Fig. 2.2). Microchannel and Si/PLZT SLMs, which can be operated or designed to perform thresholding operations, also can be operated or designed to perform complementation. Linkage of broken segments is possible using a combination of expansion and shrinking operations, whereas noise filtering can be accomplished using only a combination of shrinking operations.

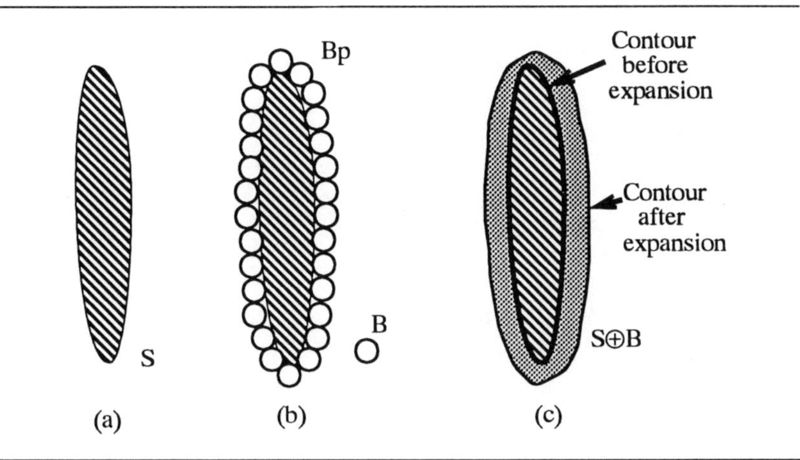


Figure 4: Expansion operation. (a) S input image. (b) Selecting the pixels p such that translated images $B_p$ of the structured shape B centered in pixel p intersect with S. (c) Expanded image of $S \oplus b$.

# 3 Intermediate-level Vision

In this section, we concentrate on the solutions to intermediate-level vision tasks using optical technology. These problems have been studied extensively over the past decade on various mesh-based VLSI organizations [19, 20, 21]. Due to the communication-intensive nature of these problems, significant time improvements can be obtained using more powerful and flexible interconnection networks. Optics provides an excellent medium for processor interconnectivity. In what follows, we introduce a set of parallel architectures with optical interconnects and then present efficient algorithms for connectivity, convexity, etc. A related computational model has been proposed by Huang, Jenkins, and Sawchuk. In [11], they have summarized digital optical cellular image processing, including binary image algebra and architectures.

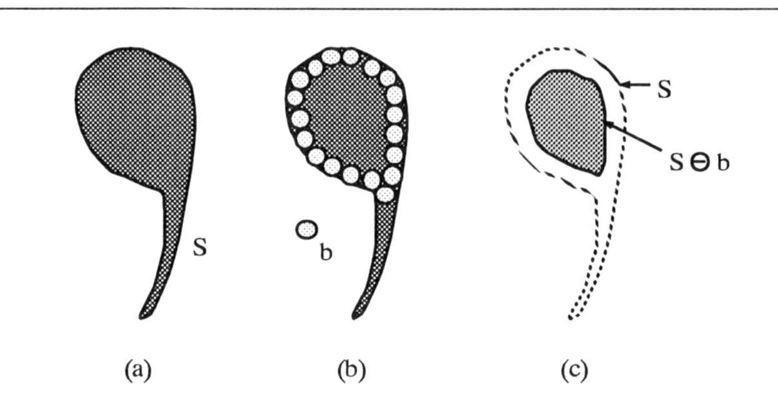


Figure 5: Shrinking operation. (a) S input image. (b) Selecting the pixels p such that the translated images $b_p$ of the structured shape b centered in pixel p intersect with S. (c)$S \ominus b$.

## 3.1 Optical Interconnection Networks

In the first part of this section we define an optical model of computation (OMC), which is an abstraction of currently implementable optical and electro-optical computers. Similar to the VLSI model of computation [25], this generic model can be used to understand the limits on computational efficiency in using optical technology. In the second part of this section, we present possible physical realizations of the optical interconnection network defined by OMC. Each of the proposed designs reflects the capabilities and limitations of the device technology used for the redirection of optical beams.

### An Optical Model

Based on the properties of free-space optics and VLSI technology, an optical model of computation is defined as follows:

**Definition 1** *An optical model of computation represents a network of N processors each associated with a memory module and a deflect-*

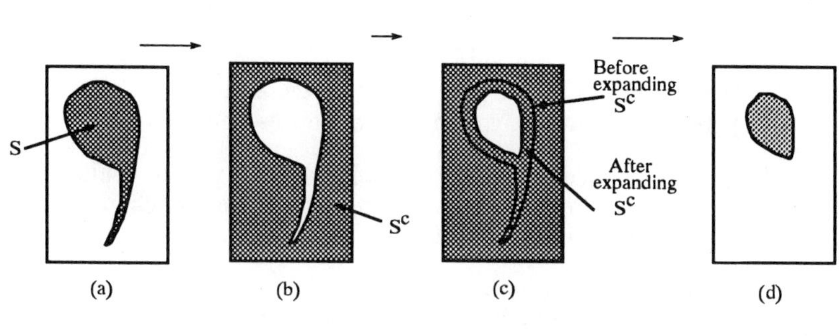


Figure 6: Performing shrinking by using expansion and complementation. (a) S input image. (b) Complementation of S:$S^c$. (c) Result of expansion of $S^c$ : $S^c \oplus b$. (d) Complementing the result of (c) :$(S^c \oplus b)^c = S \ominus b$ .

*ing unit capable of establishing direct optical connection to another processor. The interprocessor communication is performed satisfying the following rules similar to [1]:*

1. *At any time a processor can send at most one message. Its destination is another processor.*
2. *The message will succeed in reaching the processor if and only if it is the only message sent to that processor at that time step.*
3. *All messages succeed or fail (and thus are discarded) in unit time.*

To ensure that every processor knows when its message succeeds, we assume that the OMC is run in two phases. In the first, read/write messages are sent; in the second, values are returned to successful readers and acknowledgments are returned to successful writers. We assume that the operation mode is synchronous and that all processors are connected to a central control unit. The above definition is supplemented with a complete set of assumptions for accurate analysis in [7]. Some of these assumptions are listed below:

1. Processors are embedded in a Euclidean plane. This is referred to as the processing layer, and each of the processing/memory elements occupies one unit area.
2. Deflectors are embedded in a Euclidean plane. This is referred to as the deflecting layer, and each deflecting unit occupies at least one unit area.
3. The total volume is the sum of the space occupied by the processing layer, the deflecting layer, and the space for optical beams.
4. Intercommunication is done through free-space optical beams using deflectors capable of redirecting the incident beams in one unit of time.

To be able to compare our results with those using VLSI model of computation [25] without loss of generality, we assume that there are $N$ processors placed on an $N^{1/2} \times N^{1/2}$ grid called the processing layer. Similarly, there are $N$ deflecting modules on a layer above the processing layer, called the deflection layer. The interconnection beams are established in the free space between these two layers, as shown in Fig. 3.1. Hence, the amount of data that can be exchanged in a cycle between two sets of processors (two-way information transfer rate) is $N$. The time ($T$) required to solve a problem is the number of cycles required to exchange the minimum required information ($I$). This leads to

$$AT = \Omega(I)$$

where $A$ is the area occupied by the processing layer.

A related model is VLSIO [3], which is a three-dimensional generalization of the wire model of the two-dimensional VLSI with optical beams replacing the wires as communication channels. Compared with the three-dimensional VLSI model of computation [22], our model is more resource-efficient [7]. In the following sections, three different parallel architectures are presented as possible realizations of OMC.

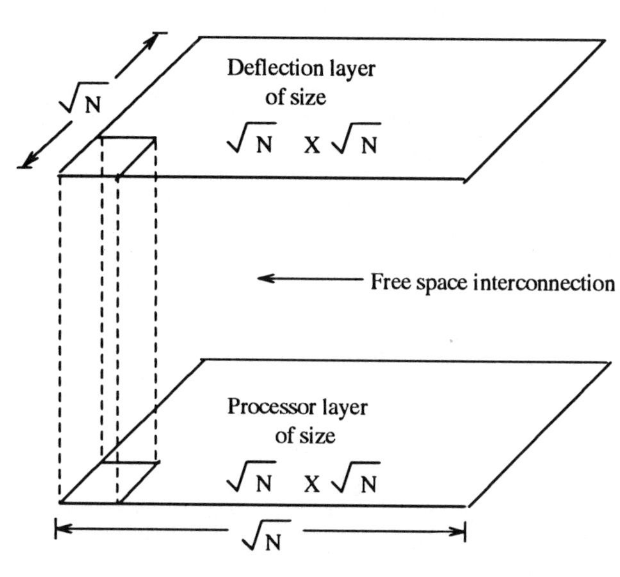


Figure 7: Optical model of computation.

## Parallel Organizations

In this section, we present a class of optical interconnection networks as a realization of the OMC presented in the previous section. Each of the proposed designs uses a different optical device technology for redirection of the optical beams to establish a new topology at any clock cycle, and each represents an upper bound on the volume requirement of OMC.

**Optical Mesh Using Mirrors:** In this design, there are $N$ processors on the processing layer of area $N$. Similarly, the deflecting layer has area $N$ and holds $N$ mirrors. These layers are aligned so that each of the mirrors is located directly above its associated processor (see Fig. 3.1). Each processor has two lasers. One of these is directed up toward the arithmetic unit of the mirror; the other is directed toward the mirror's surface. A connection phase would consist of two cycles. In the first cycle, each processor sends the address of its desired destination processor to the arithmetic unit of its associated mirror using its dedicated laser. The mirror's arithmetic unit computes a rotation degree such that both the origin and destination processors have an equal angle with the line perpendicular to the mirror's surface, which is in the plane formed by the mirror, the source processor, and the destination processor. Once the angle is computed, the mirror is rotated to point to the desired destination. In the second cycle, connection is established by the laser beam carrying the data from the source to the mirror and the data being reflected toward the destination. Since the connection is done through a mechanical movement of the mirror, using current technology, this leads to an order of millisecond reconfiguration time. Therefore, this architecture is suitable for applications where the interconnection topology does not have to be changed frequently. The space requirement of this architecture is $O(N)$ under the assumptions listed in [7].

**Reconfiguration Using Acousto-Optical Devices:** In this organization, $N$ processors are arranged to form a one-dimensional processing layer, and the corresponding acousto-optical devices are similarly located on a one-dimensional deflecting layer (see Fig. 3.1). The size of each of the acousto-optical devices is proportional to the size of the processing array, leading to an $O(N^2)$ area deflection layer. Similar to the design using the mirrors, every processor has two lasers, and each connection phase is made up of two cycles. In the first cycle, each processor sends the address of its desired destination processor to the arithmetic unit of its associated acousto-optical device using its dedicated laser. Each arithmetic unit computes the frequency of the wave to be applied to the crystal for redirecting the incoming optical beam to the destination processor. Using the other laser in the second cycle, each processor sends its data directly to the mirror located above it. This mirror is fixed such that its reflected beam passes through its corresponding acousto-optical device and then gets redirected toward the desired processor. One of the

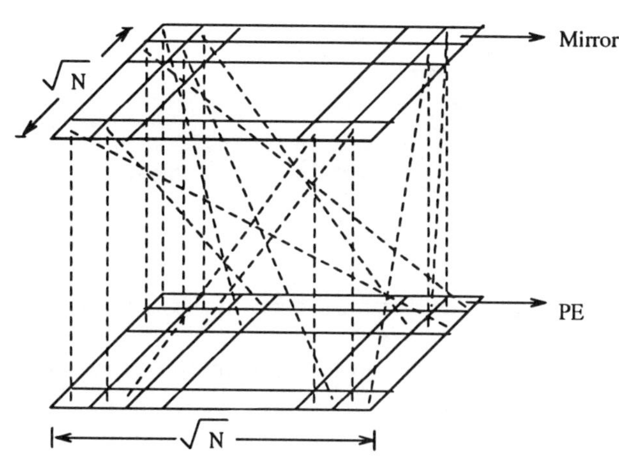


Figure 8: An optical mesh using mirrors.

advantages of this architecture over the previous design is that it has a reconfiguration time in the order of microseconds due to the speed of sound waves. The other advantage is its broadcasting capability, which is due to the possibility of generating multiple waves through a crystal at a given time.

**Electro-Optical Crossbar:** This design uses a hybrid reconfiguration technique for interconnecting processors. There are $N$ processors, each located in a distinct row and column of the $N \times N$ processing layer. For each processor, there is a hologram module having $N$ units, such that the $i^{th}$ unit has a grating plate with a frequency leading to a deflection angle corresponding to the processor located at the grid point $(i, i)$. In addition, each unit has a simple controller and a laser beam. To establish or reconfigure to a new connection pattern, each processor broadcasts the desired destination processor's address to the controller of each of $N$ units of its hologram module, using an electrical bus (see Fig. 3.1). The con-

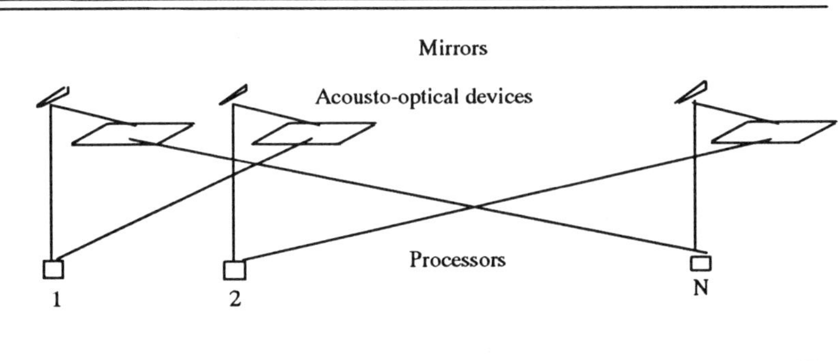


Figure 9: Reconfiguration using acousto-optical devices.

troller activates a laser (for conversion of the electrical input to optical signal) if its ID matches the broadcast address of the destination processor. The connection is made when the laser beams are passed through the predefined gratings. Therefore, since the grating angles are predefined, the reconfiguration time of this design is bounded by the laser switching time, which is in the order of nanoseconds using gallium arsenide (GaAs) technology [12].

## A Related Organization

In this section, we briefly describe the architecture and fundamental features of a programmable optoelectronic multiprocessor (POEM) [13] as shown in Fig. 3.1. The organization and operation of POEM is based on OMC concepts extended to wafer scale integration of optoelectronic processors and reconfigurable free-space optical interconnects. The POEM machine can be realized with an integrated optoelectronic technology, such as silicon/PLZT for the processor arrays and dichromated gelatin as the volume holographic storage medium for the interconnects. The POEM architecture can be enhanced to be reprogrammable or reconfigurable using a real-time volume holographic medium such as photorefractive crystals.

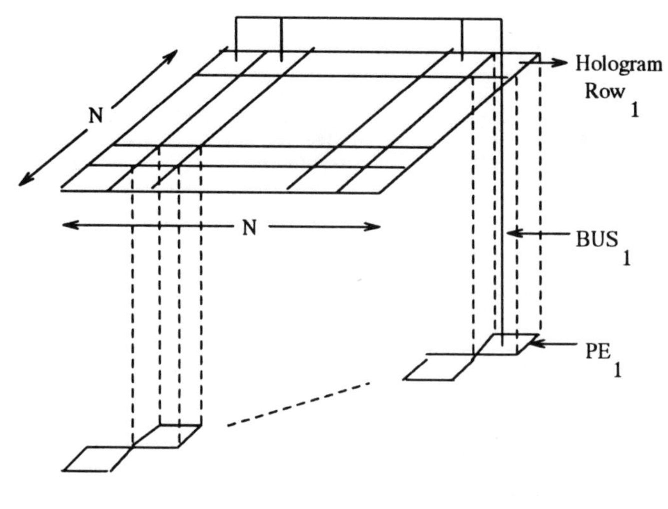


Figure 10: Reconfiguration using an electro-optical crossbar

**Implementation:** As an example, we describe a fine-grain POEM machine containing a very large number (100,000 or more) of simple one-bit silicon processors. An optoelectronic controller, connected to a sequential host computer, is used to broadcast optically the instruction stream and master clock through a computer-generated hologram to the processors. Interprocessor communication in POEM is implemented by activating different interconnection holograms in a volume holographic material of large storage capacity, such as dichromated gelatin. Each interconnection hologram is recorded with a different random phase code. These holograms can be activated independently at speeds compatible with the system clock rate by displaying the appropriate random phase code on a small spatial light modulator. Therefore, unlike conventional parallel systems, there are no limitations due to fixed connections among processors. Instead,

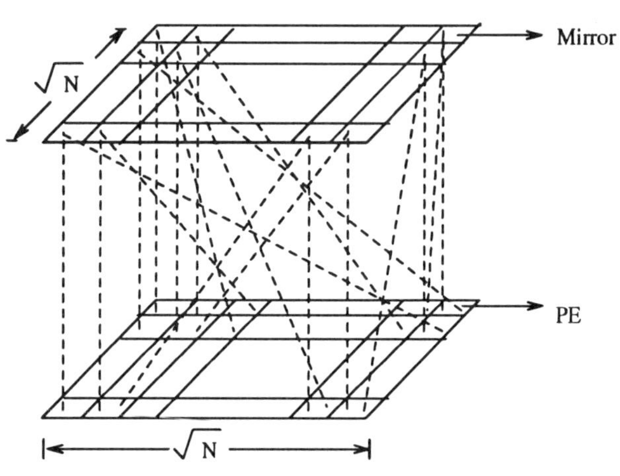


Figure 11: POEM architecture.

the programmable optical interconnects are determined by the opto-electronic controller to implement a topology that best matches the current algorithm. In addition, the interconnection storage capacity requirement on the holographic material can be reduced if real-time reprogrammable material requirements can be added. For example, one may envision using photorefractive crystals or other nonlinear optical materials to apply reprogrammable interconnects to the processors. In this case, the users will be capable of reconfiguring the POEM in a very short time to match their algorithmic requirements.

### 3.2 Parallel Algorithms

In this section, we present parallel algorithms for medium-level vision. As a general introduction to the design of algorithms on OMC, the following discussion is listed first.

## General Introduction

It is easy to see that an OMC with $N$ processors can simulate, in real time, an exclusive read exclusive write PRAM having $P$ processors and $M$ memory locations, where $N$ = maximum $\{P, M\}$. We start by formally defining an optical mesh and illustrating its operation in the simulation of EREW algorithms.

**Definition 2** *An optical mesh of size $N^2$ has a processor layer consisting of an $N \times N$ array of processors, which can intercommunicate in unit-time using their corresponding optical device residing on the deflection layer of the same size.*

A simple implementation of optical mesh is possible using mirrors (under the unit delay rotation assumption, which was discussed in the previous sections). The communication patterns needed for performing digital FFT of $N$ points can be easily realized using an optical mesh of size $N$ processors in $O(\log N)$ time. Note that as described in the first part of the paper, using optical lenses, FFT can be efficiently done in constant time. Similarly, image convolution can be easily carried out using an optical correlator system. However, in the following discussion, to familiarize the reader with OMC and its basic operations, we describe a digital image convolution technique.

Template matching is a basic operation in image processing and computer vision [23]. It is used as a simple method for filtering, edge detection, image registration, and object detection [24]. Template matching can be described as comparing a template (window) with all possible windows of the image. The result of each window operation is stored at the image position located at the window's top-left corner. Let $IMAGE\ (i,j)$ represent an $N^{1/2} \times N^{1/2}$ image where $0 \leq i,j \leq N^{1/2} - 1$. Let $W(s,t)$ represent the template where $0 \leq s,t \leq k-1$. Then the result $C(i,j)$ is as given below:

$$C(i,j) = \sum_{s=0}^{k-1} \sum_{t=0}^{k-1} IMAGE((i+s) mod N^{1/2}, (j+t) mod N^{1/2}) * W(s,t)$$

Note that the computation can be done in $O(N \times k^2)$ time using a uniprocessor.

Using $N/\log N$ processors, the above computation can be done in $O(k^2 \log N)$ time by partioning the processors into groups of size $(k/\log^{1/2} N) \times (k/\log^{1/2} N)$. Each of these groups checks the template of size $k \times k$ with the image of corresponding size. Since the number of processors is less than the image size, each processor is assigned to check a region of size $\log^{1/2} N \times \log^{1/2} N$. In $O(\log N)$ time, the results are obtained for this particular position of the template. This is repeated for all $k^2$ positions.

## Optimal Geometric Algorithms

In this section, we present $O(\log N)$ algorithms for problems such as finding connected components, and locating the nearest neighboring figure to each figure in an $N \times N$ image. The input to our algorithms is a *digitized* picture with $PE(i,j)$ storing the pixel $(i,j), 0 \leq i,j, \leq N-1$ in the plane.

We are concerned with black and white (binary) images, where the black pixels are 1-valued and white pixels are 0-valued. Connectivity among pixels can be defined in terms of their adjacency. Two black pixels $(i_1, j_1)$ and $(i_2, j_2)$ are *8-neighbors* if

$$\max\{\mid i_1 - i_2 \mid, \mid j_1 - j_2 \mid\} \leq 1$$

and *4-neighbors* if

$$\mid i_1 - i_2 \mid + \mid j_1 - j_2 \mid \leq 1$$

Two black pixels $(i_1, j_1)$ and $(i_k, j_k)$ are said to be connected by a *8-path(4-path)* if there exists a sequence of black pixels $(i_p, j_p)$, $2 \leq p \leq k$, such that each pair of pixels $(i_{p-1}, j_{p-1})$ and $(i_p, j_p)$ are 8-neighbors(4-neighbors). A maximal connected region of black pixels is called a *connected component*.

In a 0/1 picture, the connected 1's are said to form a figure. Thus, associated with each PE is a label, which is the unique $ID$ of the figure to which the PE belongs. The label associated with PE's $(i,j)$ and $(r,s)$ are the same if $(i,j)$ and $(r,s)$ are connected by a series of 1's. For more details see [19].

**Labeling Digitized Images:** An early step in intermediate-level image processing is identifying figures in the image. Figures correspond to connected 1's in the image. An $N \times N$ digitized picture may contain more than one connected region of black pixels. The problem is to identify to which figure (label) each 1 belongs.

**Lemma 1** *Given an $N \times N$ 0/1 image, all figures can be labeled in $O(\log N)$ time using an $(N \times N)$-optical mesh [7].*

The following code is the skeleton of the algorithm that each of the processors could run simultaneously to label the figures in an $N \times N$ image in $O(\log N)$ time.

```
procedure Label ; main program
     call Multiply ; multiplies picture fourfold
     call Border ; each border point points to its neighbor
     call Unify ; all borders are labeled uniquely
     call Propagate ; all outer borders propagate their
                          labels
end
```

In the following we use fewer processors to obtain an optimal solution.

**Theorem 1** *Given an $N \times N$ 0/1 image, all figures can be labeled in $O(\log N)$ time using an $(N/\log^{1/2} N \times N/\log^{1/2} N)$-optical mesh [7].*

**Distance Problems:** Another interesting problem is to identify and compute the distance from the nearest figure to each figure in a digitized image. In the following, we use the $l_1$ metric. However, it can be modified to operate for any $l_k$ metric.

**Theorem 2** *Given an $N \times N$ 0/1 image, the nearest figure to all figures can be computed in $O(\log N)$ time using an $(N/\log^{1/2} N \times N/\log^{1/2} N)$-optical mesh [7].*

## 4 Image Understanding

In this section we study solutions to high-level image processing tasks. Optics is a mature technology in image understanding and analysis. In fact, many of the earlier results in the area of pattern recognition are due to the use of optical methods. In this section we present a few architectures for feature extraction and pattern recognition. In the first part of the section, however, we look at a different approach for image enhancement using optical interconnects to implement an iterative technique.

## 4.1 Iterative Methods for Image Enhancement

Solutions to many problems in image understanding can be posed in terms of iterative improvement to an initial configuration. For example, discrete relaxation-based approaches to scene labeling can be viewed as an iterative improvement process. In such problems, the underlying graph is usually sparse. But this sparsity is not regular. Efficient parallel implementations of such relaxation methods are possible with OMC.

Consider the iterative method

$$x^{k+1} = Mx^k + g$$

where $M$ is sparse and nonsingular. Let $n_i$ be the number of nonzero elements in the $i$th row of $M$, and let $j_1, j_2, \ldots, j_{n_i}$ be the columns corresponding to these elements. Thus, the above equation can be rewritten as

$$x_i^{k+1} = \sum_{s=1}^{n_i} m_{ij_s} x_{j_s}^k + g_i.$$

Suppose there are $n$ processors and each of the processors stores exactly one nonzero element in matrix $M$. The structure of the coefficient matrix is used to define the holographic connections. The interconnection pattern remains the same throughout the computation. An optimal $O(\log m)$ time can be achieved by this design, where $m$ is the number of nonzero elements in the matrix [7]. This method is attractive when many computations are to be performed in which the structure of the coefficient matrix is fixed, such as the iterative methods [8].

## 4.2 Optical Feature Extraction Techniques

In this section, we propose optical implementations of four useful digital feature extraction techniques.

### Optical Hough Transform

The Hough transform (HT) is an efficient curve detector. It is useful when little is known about the location of a boundary but its shape can be described as a parametric curve (for example, a straight line or a circle). One possible implementation of the Hough transform maps a point in the $x - y$ plane into a straight line in the (m,c) transform plane using the formula $y' = mx' + c$ . A straight line in the $x - y$ plane is mapped into a point in the transform plane (see Fig. 4.2). All colinear edge elements are mapped into the same point in the transform plane. The total number of unit length colinear line segments forms a histogram at a point in the transform plane. A single long or many short colinear line segments can yield the same histogram value. Images that contain edge elements only, the so-called shape function, always can be decomposed as a set of approximate line segments. The HT maps these line segments into a smaller feature space to form the HT shape descriptors. Therefore, the HT is relatively unaffected by gaps in the curve and by noise[2].

To implement the HT optically, one method would be to computer generate a two-dimensional array of holograms; each hologram reconstructs the space-variant impulse response, which is a straight line of slope $(-x)$ and intercept y:

$$\hat{f}(m,c) = \int_{-\infty}^{+\infty} f(x,y)\delta(y - mx - c)dxdy$$

Where $\hat{f}(m,c)$ is the output and $f(x,y)$ is the input (Fig. 4.2).

### Optically Generated Moment Features

Geometrical moments of an image characterize its dark pixels distribution and are important in distortion-invariant pattern recognition. The geometrical moments of an input are defined by:

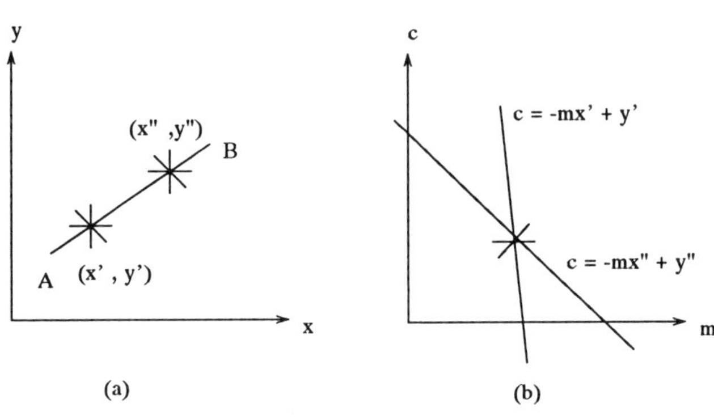


Figure 12: Principle of Hough transform. A line in (a) image space and (b) parameter space.

$$m_{pq} = \int_{-\infty}^{\infty} f(x,y)x^p y^q dx dy$$

They are easily calculated optically on the system of Fig. 4.2. In this system the input object $f(x,y)$ at $p_1$ is imaged at $p_2$ onto a mask, whose transmittance is the sum of the different $x^p y^q$, each on a different frequency carrier. The transmittance is given by:

$$g(x,y) = \sum_{p=-M}^{M} \sum_{q=-N}^{N} x^p y^q e^{[j2\pi(pu_0 x + qv_0 y)]}$$

Then $m_{pq}$ can be found on $P_3$ at the locations corresponding to the spatial frequency carriers. The $g(x,y)$ mask can be computer generated [4], and moments up to the third or fourth order should be obtained. From the optically computed $m_{pq}$, we can then digitally calculate normalized central moments $\eta_{pq}$, which is much less time-consuming than computing $m_{pq}$ digitally. From the first three orders

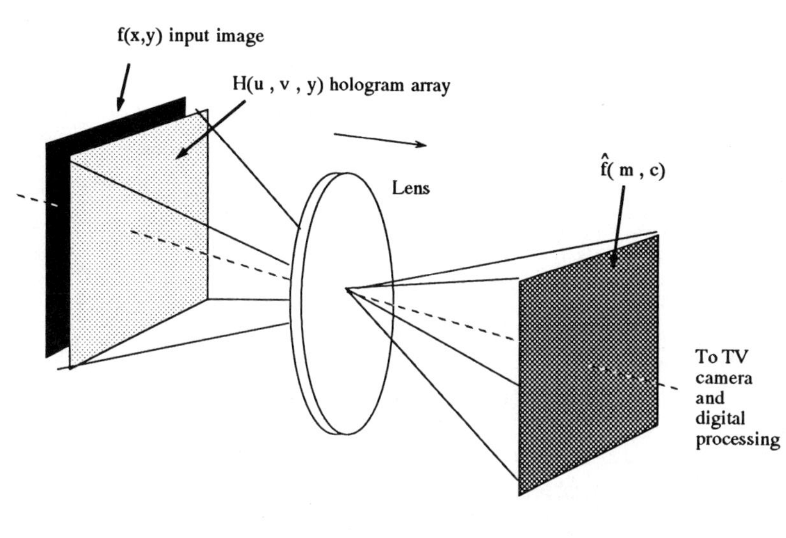


Figure 13: Optical setup to implement Hough transform.

of $\eta_{pq}$, another set of seven moments that is invariant to translation, rotation, and scale change can be digitally calculated.

## Optical Transform Followed by Digital Postprocessing

When the space-bandwidth product of an image is very large, Fourier Transform (FT) and cosine transform (CT) are good feature-extraction and data-reduction algorithms. The FT is obtained optically at the back focal plane of a lens using a coherent light source. The CT can be similarly obtained optically by replicating the input symmetrically. A detector with 32 wedges in one half and 32 rings in the other half of the detector plane is frequently inserted in the back focal plane of a lens to obtain the Fourier or cosine spectrum of the input [15]. The spectrum is shift-invariant because a shift in the input object contributes only a linear phase factor to the FT. The output from the wedge detectors is scale-invariant and the output from the ring detectors is rotationally invariant. After the data are reduced by optical FT or CT, digital algorithms can be applied readily for further feature extraction and decision making.

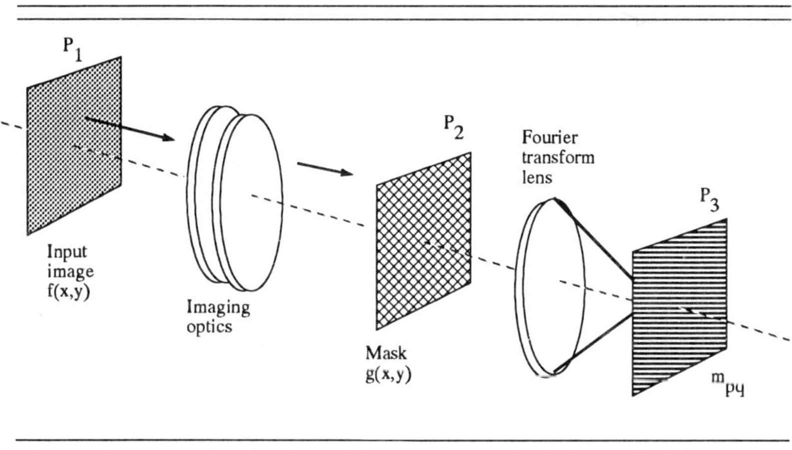


Figure 14: Optical system to compute in parallel the geometrical moment features of an input pattern.

## 4.3 Optical Statistical Pattern Recognition

Matched filters do not perform well when faced with the problem of recognizing objects belonging to a certain class (such as birds, fish) but differing in shape, size, or rotation. Statistical pattern recognition algorithms aim at classifying such objects by using a set of sample images from each class called a training set. The objects within each class display typical interclass statistical variances and similarities.

To perform optical statistical pattern recognition (OSPR), we begin with given image training sets. By applying digital statistical pattern-recognition algorithms adapted for large images (see [15, 17, 9] for detail on the image training sets), we can synthesize the synthetic discriminant functions (SDF) off-line. The SDFs are then encoded in a computer-generated hologram (CGH) that is to be inserted into the filter plane of an optical system for on-line processing of new images. Since the same CGH can be applied to any new images that have the same statistical properties as those of the training sets, OSPR can be performed in real time. We have optically implemented the Fukunaga-Koontz (F-K) transform for two-class image classification (for details refer to [15]).

To extend our results, we also have optically implemented the least-squares linear mapping techniques and Hotelling trace transform for multiple-class problems, in ways similar to that of the F-K transform. Equally reliable classification data were obtained [15].

# 5 Conclusion

In this chapter, we studied the impact of optical technology in image computing. Starting from low-level preprocessing tasks, we presented various optical systems and techniques. In solving intermediate-level vision tasks that tend to be more communication intensive in nature, we proposed a set of parallel architectures with free-space optical interconnects. The computational complexity and optimality of our designs were analyzed based on a proposed generic model of computation called OMC. We also discussed a few optical implementations for pattern recognition and feature extraction. Optical technology is the most mature in the area of high-level image understanding and then in low-level preprocessing tasks. Our results to medium-level tasks, such as connectivity, convexity, and proximity, are processor-time-product optimal but only utilize interconnectivity features of optical technology. In summary, optics as an alternative to electronics can be an efficient and attractive environment for solutions to parallel-image computing. However, we have yet to learn how to benefit from its parallel nature more effectively.

# Bibliography

[1] R. Anderson and G. L. Miller, *Optimal parallel algorithms for list ranking*, Technical report, Dept. of Computer Science, Uni-

versity of Southern California, 1987.

[2] D. H. Ballard and C. M. Brown, Computer Vision, Prentice-Hall.

[3] R. Barakat and J. Reif, *Lower bounds on the computational efficiency of optical computing systems*, Journal of Applied Optics, 26(6), 1987, pp. 1015–1018.

[4] D. Casasent, L. Cheatham, and D. Fetterly, *Optical system to compute intensity moments: design*, Appl. Opt., vol. 21, 1982, pp. 3292–3298.

[5] David Casasent, *Coherent optical pattern recognition: a review*, Optical Engineering, vol. 24, 1985, pp. 26–31.

[6] U. Efron, *Spacial light modulators for optical information processing*, Intl. Optical Computing Conf., Proc. SPIE, pp. 132–145,

[7] M. M. Eshaghian, Parallel Computing with Optical Interconnects, PhD thesis, Dept. of Computer Engineering, University of Southern California, 1988.

[8] D. J. Evans, ed., Sparsity and its Applications, Cambridge University Press, 1985.

[9] Z. H. Gu, J. R. Leger, and S. H. Lee, *Optical implementation of the least-squares linear-mapping technique for image classification*, J. Opt. Soc. Am., vol. 72, 1982, pp. 787–793.

[10] R. Hauck and O. Bryngdahl, *Computer holography: review and digressions*, Intl. Conf. Computer Generated Holography, Proc. SPIE, pp. 2–6.

[11] K. S. Huang, B. K. Jenkins, and A. A. Sawchuck, *Binary image algebra and optical cellular logic processor design*, Computer Vision, Graphics, and Image Processing.

[12] H. Ito, N. Komagata, H. Yamada, and Humio Inaba, *New structure of laser diode and light emitting diode based on coaxial transverse junction*, Technical report, Research Institute of Electrical Communication, Tohoku University, Sendai 980, Japan.

[13] F. Kiamilev, S. C. Esener, R. Paturi, Y. Feinman, P. Mercier, C. C. Guest, and Sing H. Lee, *Programmable optoelectronic multiprocessors and their comparison with symbolic substitution for digital optical computing*, Opt. Eng., vol. 28, 1989, pp. 396–409.

[14] S. H. Lee, *The synthesis of complex spatial filters for coherent optical data processing*, Patt. Recog., vol. 5, 1973, pp. 21–35.

[15] S. H. Lee, *Optical implementation of digital algorithms for pattern recognition*, Opt. Eng., vol. 25, 1986, pp. 69–75.

[16] S.H. Lee, S. C. Esener, M. A. Title, , and T. J. Drabik, *Two-dimensional silicon/plzt spatial light modulators: design considerations and technology*, Opt. Eng., vol. 25, 1986, pp. 250–260.

[17] J. R. Leger and S. H. Lee, Image classification by optical implementation of the Fukunaga-Koontz transfor, J. Opt. Soc. Am., vol. 72, 1982, pp. 556–564.

[18] G. G. Lendaris and G. L. Stanley, Proc. of the IEEE, vol. 58, 1979, pp. 198–216.

[19] R. Miller and Q. F. Stout, *Parallel geometric algorithms for digitized pictures on mesh connected computers*, IEEE transactions on Pattern Analysis and Machine Intelligence, March 1985, pp. 216–228.

[20] R. Miller and Q. F. Stout, *Efficient parallel convex hull algorithms,* IEEE transactions on Computers, December 1988, pp. 1605–1618.

[21] V. K. Prasanna-Kumar and M. Mary Eshaghian, *Parallel geometric algorithm for digitized pictures on mesh of trees*, Proc.

of IEEE International Conference on Parallel Processing, 1986, pp. 270–273.

[22] A. L. Rosenberg, *Three-dimensional integrated circuits*, H. T. Kung, R. Sproul, and G. Steel, ed., VLSI Systems and Computations, Computer Science Press, 1981, pp. 69–79.

[23] A. Rosenfeld and A. Kak, Digital Picture Processing, Academic Press, 2nd edition, 1982. (2 volumes).

[24] L. J. Siegel, H. J. Siegel, and A. E. Feather, *Parallel processing approaches to image correlation*, IEEE Trans. on Computers, C–31, March 1982.

[25] C. D. Thompson, A Complexity Theory for VLSI, PhD thesis, Dept. of Computer Science, Carnegie Mellon University, 1980.

[26] A. VanderLugt, IEEE Trans. Inf. Theory IT-10, vol. 139, 1964, pp. 139–145.

[27] A. G. Weber and A. A. Sawchuk, *Segmentation of textured images*, Tech. Digest on Machine Vision, OSA, 1985.

# The USC Orthogonal Multiprocessor for Image Understanding

**KAI HWANG and DHABALESWAR KUMAR PANDA**
*Department of Electrical Engineering - Systems*
*University of Southern California*
*Los Angeles, California*

## 1 Introduction

The advent of RISC processors on monolithic CMOS chips [20, 21], the increasing use of parallel processing software standards [8], and better programming paradigms have widened the development of high-performance supercomputing systems for image-understanding tasks [5, 22]. The last decade has seen several research and commercial systems geared toward image-processing applications [4]. But, no attempt has been made to blend the state-of-the art RISC processing technology with a flexible system architecture to develop a real-time imaging system, which can support integrated (low, medium, and high) levels of image-processing operations efficiently. In this chapter, we report the design experience and research results of such a system, to be constructed at the University of Southern California, known as *orthogonal multiprocessor* (OMP). This system uses 64-bit RISC microprocessors as the basic computational units together with an orthogonally structured two-dimensional memory organization, and a spanning bus network [9]. The 16-processor OMP prototype is targeted to achieve a peak performance of 400 RISC integer MIPS or a maximum of 640 Mflops. The objective of this project is to prove the suitability and scalability of the OMP architecture

Parallel Architectures and
Algorithms for
Image Understanding




ISBN 0-12-564040-4

for integrated image-processing tasks including computer vision and neural network simulation applications.

This OMP architecture was conceived at the University of Southern California [12, 14] in 1985. Presently, a 16-processor OMP prototype is under the final designing stage. This chapter is based upon our initial specification, simulation validation, and performance projection. Some of the design parameters are subject to further refinement in the remaining phases of the OMP project.

In this chapter, we emphasize hardware architectural features of the OMP prototype. These features are targeted towards high-performance image processing and matrix structured computation. The scope of the OMP system for vision and neural computing applications as reported in [7]. Parallel algorithm development on the OMP system is based on an extended C language known as *Trojan-C* [2]. This language facilitates efficient compilation (vectorization and parallelization) and resource allocation using the interleaved orthogonal memory structure. The architectural design choices were validated by a C-language-based OMP simulator [3, 15], developed using CSIM[1] package [19]. Simulated performance results were reported in [16]. These simulation results verify linear scalability in performance as machine size increases.

The rest of the chapter is organized as follows. The inherent characteristics of an integrated imaging system are described in Section 2. The orthogonal multiprocessor architecture and the prototype implementation is described in Section 3. Section 4 describes *vector register windows* ('VRWs') support in the OMP system to achieve efficient matrix computation. Section 5 presents simulated performance results of the OMP system. The architectural extension of OMP to three dimensions is illustrated in Section 6. Finally, we conclude with contributions of the OMP project to the parallel-processing and image-processing community.

This chapter is revised from six journal/conference papers [7, 9, 10, 11, 16, 18] that appeared from October 1988 to September 1990. The respective references can be referred to for detailed information.

---

[1]CSIM has been copyrighted by the Microelectronics and Computer Technology Corporation.

# 2 Integrated Image Understanding

Image-processing algorithms, from low-level to high-level, exhibit varying characteristics and demand different architectural features. An architecture, to be suitable for such integrated image-processing applications, should have a balance between these features without sacrificing the performance [6]. Our OMP prototype follows such a track and stands distinct with its architectural features. In this section, we highlight a spectrum of architectural characteristics for integrated image-processing and emphasize on their trade-offs associated with the OMP. A set of image-processing and pattern-recognition algorithms targeted for the OMP prototype is presented. These algorithms with their varying characteristics justify the integrated image-understanding capability of the OMP architecture.

## 2.1 Fine-Grain versus Coarse-Grain Parallelism

While the low-level image-processing tasks exhibit fine-grain parallelism at the pixel level, the high-level image-processing tasks are associated with coarse-grain parallelism at the object or the segment levels. The former tasks are traditionally known as SIMD algorithms; the latter ones fall into MIMD category. The OMP architecture provides a unified framework defined as *multiple program multiple data* (MPMD) to implement both SIMD and MIMD computational models efficiently. This also allows clustering of processors to exploit medium-grain parallelism. More details of this MPMD computational model are described in Section 3.1.

## 2.2 Local versus Global Communication

The efficiency of different image-processing algorithms relies on local communication, global communication, or both. Various existing architectures supporting image-processing are geared towards either efficient near-neighbor communication or efficient global point-to-point communication, but not both. The OMP architecture provides uniform overhead for all these communication schemes. Based on an *orthogonal vector communication paradigm* [17], the OMP prototype even supports one-to-many and many-to-many communication efficiently.

## 2.3 Scalar versus Vector Processing

Although imaging algorithms rely heavily on scalar processing, the algorithms based on neural network models and those associated with matrix-array structured data exhibit inherent vector-processing capability. The OMP prototype supports superscalar processing with RISC microprocessors as the basic computational elements. The prototype also exhibits efficient vector-processing capability with orthogonal memory organization (Section 3.2) and support by vector register windows (section 4).

## 2.4 Computation versus Data Manipulation

Data movement operations constitute a significant amount of the overall processing time of a parallel algorithm. The OMP prototype, with 64-bit *i*860 processors as the basic computational elements, delivers high throughput both for integer and floating-point operations. An *on-the-fly index manipulation* scheme (Section 4.3, [18]) performs data movement operations with least participation from the processor. This also allows overlapping of computation with data manipulation. This leads to high processing bandwidth available with the OMP system.

## 2.5 Memory Structure and Data Types

Various imaging algorithms demand a wide spectrum of data types and efficient underlying architectures to support these data types. Besides supporting the common data structures needed for a parallel environment, the OMP prototype provides efficient vector-matrix data types for structured image processing using a two-dimensional interleaved orthogonal memory organization. A *reconfigurable vector-register-windows organization* (section 4) provides such a modular and structured abstraction for matrix-structured image data.

## 2.6 Dynamic Reconfigurability

Several parallel-imaging algorithms have been developed in the past for a number of computational structures. Specific architectures have demonstrated efficiency in solving a class of problems, but not all. A system targeted for a broad range of imaging applications should support dynamic reconfiguration over a set of architectures with least overhead. The OMP prototype provides such dynamic reconfigurability [17] over a large class of interesting parallel architectures, such as the mesh, the hypercube, and the pyramid.

## 2.7 Cache Coherency and Synchronization Mechanisms

Although many parallel imaging algorithms demonstrate good theoretical speed-up for a given architecture, their implementation drastically suffers from practical difficulties like cache coherence and synchronization. The former provides overhead with large shared data, where as the later becomes severe in SIMD mode of operation with a large number of processors. The OMP prototype using a vector-register-windows mechanism supports effective caching with minimal overhead for maintaining cache coherency (Section 4.2). Similarly, the OMP prototype provides efficient synchronization schemes (Section 3.4) to support both SIMD and MIMD models of computation.

So, overall, the OMP prototype supports balanced architectural, hardware, and software characteristics to implement varying classes of imaging operations, computer vision, and neural network simulation applications. This theme is echoed throughout the following sections with substantiative explanations associated with the appropriate architectural features.

Table 1 presents a set of candidate image-processing and pattern-recognition algorithms. Depending on the initial data distribution, the total computational load, and the volume of interprocessor communications, the algorithms are classified into three major categories. A linear speed-up has been observed [11] for algorithms in all of these three classes.

| *Class* | *Algorithms* |
|---|---|
| Independent SISD | Image subsampling and expansion<br>Gray-level transformation<br>Temporal averaging<br>Temporal modeling and spectral estimation |
| Partially Synchronized MIMD | Convolution<br>Hough transform for line detection<br>Image compression using block truncation coding<br>Pattern clustering and recognition<br>Histogram equalization<br>Motion detection using optical flow<br>Image enhancement using median filter<br>Image and texture segmentation<br>Two-dimensional interpolation by spline functions<br>Simulated annealing |
| Fully Synchronized MIMD | Simulation of artificial neural networks:<br>image restoration<br>stereo matching<br>motion analysis<br>Pattern recognition using matrix operations<br>Multidimensional transforms (FFT, Hotelling, etc.)<br>Kalman and Wiener filtering<br>Scene labeling by discrete relaxation<br>Feature extraction using statistical methods<br>Shape from shading (Pentland method)<br>Symbolic search operations<br>Multidimensional spectral estimation |
| | |

Table 1: Candidate image-processing and pattern recognition algorithms for orthogonal multiprocessor.

# 3 Orthogonal Multiprocessor Architecture

A two-dimensional OMP consists of $n$ *processors*, $P_i, 0 \leq i \leq n-1$, and $n^2$ partially shared *memory modules*, $M_{i,j}, 0 \leq i,j \leq n-1$. The processors and the memory modules are interconnected by a mesh of *spanning buses*. In a two-dimensional OMP, the processor-memory bus spans into two orthogonal directions. Each memory module, $M_{i,j} (i \neq j)$, is shared by two processors, $P_i$ and $P_j$. But only one of the two processors can access the memory module at a given time. Each processor uses a dedicated pair of spanning buses and operates in either *row* mode or *column* mode access. The processor $P_k$, $0 \leq k \leq n-1$, can access the memory modules $M_{k,j} (M_{j,k})$, $0 \leq j \leq n-1$, in row (column) mode. It should be noted that the diagonal memory module, $M_{i,i}$, is only accessed by the processor $P_i$ as a private memory and participates in both row-mode and column-mode accesses. Such a two-dimensional structured memory organization is called *orthogonal access memory* (OAM). The two access modes are mutually exclusive; that is, at any given time, the OAM remains either in row or in column mode, but not in a mixed-access mode. Figure 1 illustrates an OMP consisting of 16 processors and 256 partially shared memory modules interconnected by a mesh of 16 spanning buses. The processors are also connected together through a common bus for *interprocessor communication* and *synchronization.*

## 3.1 Prototype Implementation

The prototype OMP offers a *multiple program multiple data* (MPMD) architecture using partially shared OAM structure. In the MPMD mode of operation, a large program is partitioned into many subprograms for parallel execution by multiple processors over different data sets. A special case of MPMD mode is *single program multiple data* (SPMD) mode, in which the partitioned subprograms executing on all processors are identical. The interprocessor communication and synchronization are handled at the subprogram level rather than at the instruction level as in the conventional SIMD or MIMD machines.

Figure 2 shows the board-level implementation of the OMP pro-

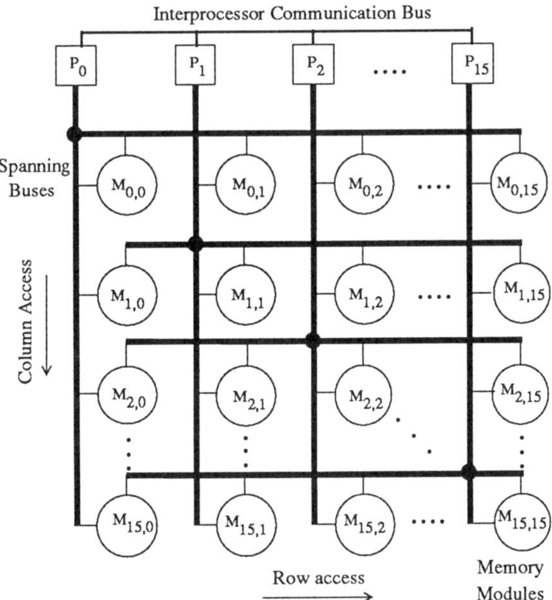


Figure 1: Logical architecture of the USC orthogonal multiprocessor.

totype. The processors, the orthogonal access memory, and the spanning buses constitute the back-end machine, which is attached to a front-end host through a VME [23] bus. The host handles all input-output functions with the external world, performs parallelization or vectorization of user programs, downloads compiled programs to the back-end, supervises data movement between the orthogonal memory and mass storage in the host, controls allocation of back-end resources, and monitors performance of the entire OMP system. We are customizing the Mach OS to handle these system-level functions.

Each of the 16 processor modules is packaged on a single *processor board* (PB). The 256 memory modules are partitioned into 4 × 4 subarrays and each subarray is housed in a single *memory board* (MB). The memory modules are interleaved (S-access interleaving) in both row and column directions. The S-access interleaving allows access of $n$ words from $n$ interleaved memory modules with a single address offset. The $n$ interleaved words are transferred between a processor and the OAM in a pipelined fashion. The row- and column-

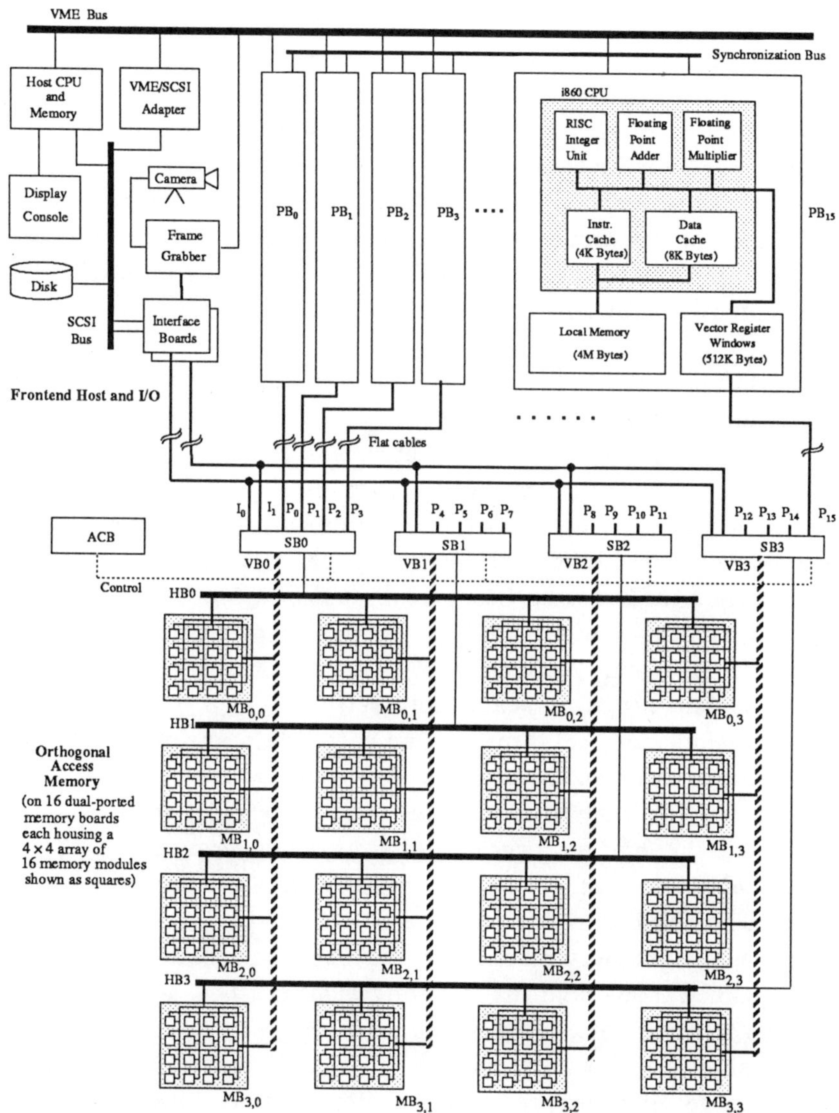


**Figure 2: Board-level implementation of the orthogonal multiprocessor with 16 i860 processors and 256 memory modules interconnected by eight spanning buses ($PB_i$: processor boards; $MB_{i,j}$: memory boards; SBi: switchboards; ACB: access control board; HBi: horizontal bus; VBi: vertical bus).**

mode OAM accesses from the processors are always performed in an interleaved manner. For example, a processor $P_k, 0 \leq k \leq 15$, fetches 16 memory words from 16 memory modules, $M_{j,k}, 0 \leq j \leq 15$, in a single column access. This interleaved access results in implicit *vector data access* from the OAM. A processor in an OMP system is allowed to access its own row (column) memory modules only. Hence, matrix-structured data with uniform allocation across the OAM results into row (column) vector data from a single processor's perspective. This two-dimensional interleaving scheme allows the access of $n^2$ memory words ($n$ vectors of $n$ words long each) for $n$ processors during a single OAM cycle. This provides high-bandwidth shared memory access for the overall system.

As shown in Fig. 2, eight spanning buses, HBi and VBi, $0 \leq i \leq 3$, are built on the memory backplane, forming a *spanning bus network*. Due to packaging constraints, the spanning buses from a group of four processors are multiplexed through a switchboard. The spanning bus network and the host subsystem are discussed in detail in Sections 3.3 and 3.5, respectively.

The local memory associated with each processor holds user program, system program, scalar data sets, and local variables. The orthogonal memory holds matrix and vector data sets, which are partially shared between the processors. Figure 3 shows the three levels of memory hierarchy from each processor's perspective. The internal instruction and data cache of the processor forms the first level. The local memory and the vector register windows form the second level. The third level consists of a single row and a single column of orthogonal memory modules. The respective access latencies in a nonpipelined mode hold the following relation : $t_1 \leq t_2 \leq t_3 \leq t_4$.

The internal data cache of the *i*860 processor serves as a buffer for nonshared scalar data from the local memory, while the VRWs form a large set of programmable vector registers for buffering and manipulating vector data sets from the orthogonal memory. The use of these register windows instead of an external cache avoids cache flushing, which is needed when the orthogonal memory access mode changes. The set of processors, operating in a producer-consumer relationship, synchronizes itself before mode switching. Special lan-

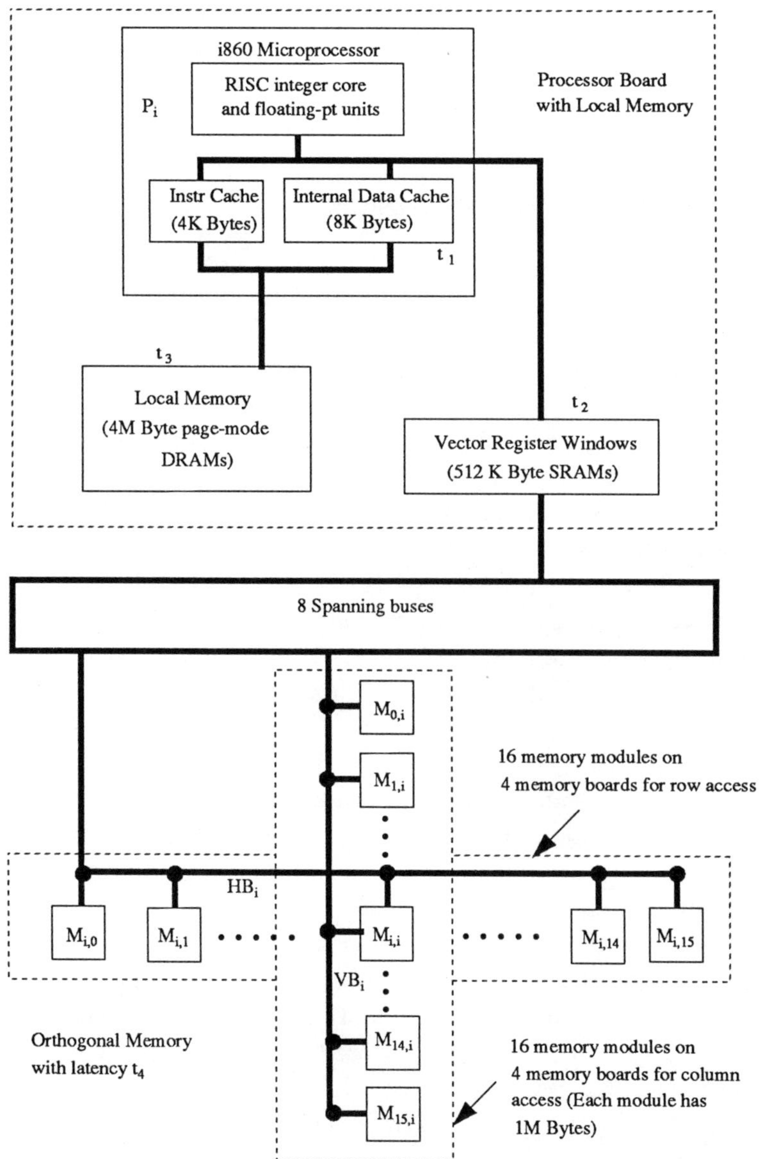


**Figure 3: Memory hierarchy and access latencies from the perspective of processor $P_i$, $0 \leq i \leq 15$, in the prototype orthogonal multiprocessor.**

guage primitives together with vectorizing and parallelizing compilers are under development to enable the programmer to use the vector register windows and the orthogonal memory more effectively. More features of vector register windows are discussed in Section 4.

## 3.2 Orthogonal Access Memory

The OAM consists of 16 memory boards plugged into a memory backplane. Each board houses 16 memory modules, forming a $4 \times 4$ subarray of the $16 \times 16$ array as shown in Fig. 2. Thus, every logical row (column) of memory modules is distributed across four memory boards. The memory backplane provides the horizontal bus (HB) and the Vertical Bus (VB) connectivity to facilitate interleaved memory access across four boards. Processors use the HB and the VB for row and column accesses respectively. Since row and column accesses are mutually exclusive, their address and control signals are multiplexed to a single bus on each memory board.

Each of the 16 modules on a memory board is organized as 256K $\times 36$ bit DRAM modules, for a word size of 32 bits and four bits for parity check. The capacity of each module is 1 MB resulting in a total OAM capacity of 256 MB. Each module is provided with and intermediate register for temporary storage of data for S-access interleaving. A memory controller on each board generates the appropriate control signals required for DRAM operation. The 32-bit memory word size can hold either a single-precision floating-point number or four eight-bit image pixels. A double-precision number is stored in two consecutive locations of a memory module.

Data are interleaved across the 16 memory modules in each of the two orthogonal directions. Thus the $i$th row of an $n \times n$ matrix has its $j$th element ($j = 0, 1, \ldots, n-1$) stored in module $M_{i \bmod 16,\, j \bmod 16}$. Similarly, the $k$th column has its $l$th element ($l = 0, 1, \ldots, n-1$) stored in $M_{l \bmod 16,\, k \bmod 16}$. Each processor accesses a vector of 16 data elements at a time. These elements are stored at the same offset location across the 16 modules. A reference to a row or column of $n$ elements in a user program is translated to $\lceil \frac{n}{16} \rceil$ accesses of 16-element vectors by the compiler. A *vector-load* is performed by simultaneously reading data from all 16 DRAM modules into the intermediate registers and then streaming the elements of the vector from these registers onto the bus, in a pipelined fashion. Similarly, a *vector-store* is performed by a pipelined write into the intermediate registers followed by a parallel write to the DRAM modules.

In our two-dimensional interleaving scheme, every processor $P_i$ 'sees' only discontiguous portions of the OAM as illustrated in Fig. 3. Moreover, the addressing scheme should be such that the OAM address spaces seen by all $P_i$s are identical. This means that each memory location in the shared module $M_{i,j} (i \neq j)$ should have two addresses: an address $A_r$, when accessed in the row-access mode by processor $P_i$, and an address $A_c$, when accessed in the column-access mode by processor $P_j$. Even though the physical addresses $A_r$ and $A_c$ are different, they have the same displacement within the module. The address format of an OAM location is shown in Fig. 4a.

The complete address of a memory word consists of four fields indicating the *module number*, the *displacement* of that word within the module, an *R/C bit* to indicate the row or column mode, and the *row (column) number*. The second and the third fields are supplied by the processor board. Module numbers are automatically generated by the memory controller. The row (column) number is generated by the switchboard to support circuit-switching of the processor buses into HB (VB) buses. Only the displacement address is used to fetch a word from a memory module. Figs. 4b and 4c show the two-dimensional interleaved addressing for an OAM array having four words in each memory module.

## 3.3 Spanning Bus Network

The spanning buses between processors and the OAM are built on a custom-designed memory backplane. To reduce the routing complexity of the buses on the backplane, the 16 pairs of logical buses (Fig. 1) are implemented with only four pairs of multiplexed physical buses as shown in Fig. 2. Four consecutive logical row (column) buses are multiplexed into one physical HB (VB) bus. As shown in Fig. 2, the bus-switching logic for the spanning buses is built into four Switch Boards (SBs) and one access control board (ACB) mounted on the backplane. Although the OAM allows only one access mode

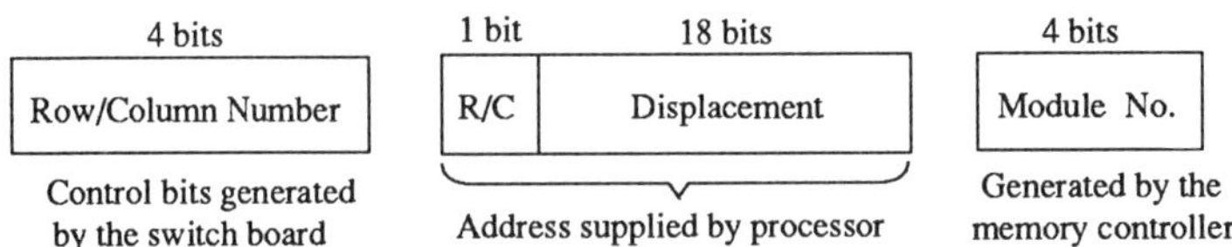


(a) Address format of a memory word for an orthogonal memory with 256 K words per module.

| 1 bit | 2 bits | 4 bits |
|---|---|---|
| R/C | Displacement | Module No. |

(b) 7-bit address used in part (c), where addresses for row-access are from 0 to 63 and for column-access from 64 to 127.

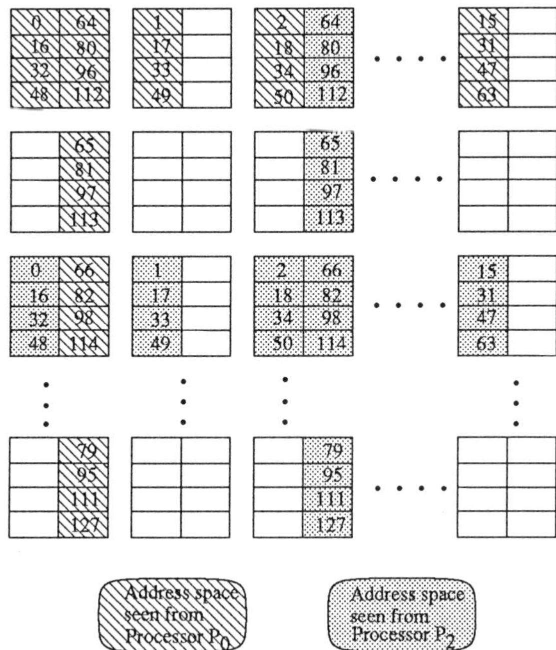


(c) Four words are illustrated in each memory module, where each memory words has two addresses, shown in two squares per row; the left one is for row-access and the right one for column-access.

**Figure 4: Two-dimensional, 16-way memory interleaving in an orthogonal memory organization for a 16-processor OMP system, where processor $P_i$ uses the $i$th row for row-access and the $i$th column for column access, for $i = 0, 1, \ldots, 15$.**

(either row or column) during a given OAM cycle, the processors are free to invoke OAM requests in different access modes. This type of orthogonal memory request characteristics is common in the MPMD operational mode of the system. Hence, the access control board arbitrates between access requests from all processors and determines the access mode of the OAM.

Each switch-board handles memory requests from four processor boards and two host interface boards. As a result, each pair of HB and VB is used in a six-way multiplexed circuit-switched fashion. The switchboards operate under the coordination of the access control board. If multiple memory-access requests occur at the same time, the requests from the I/O interface boards are given higher priority than those from the processors. A rotated daisy chain mechanism is adopted to resolve conflicting requests from four processors, ensuring fairness and no starvation. The arbitration is overlapped with the previous data transfer cycle to provide high OAM bandwidth.

## 3.4 Processor Subsystem

The processor subsystem consists of 16 processor boards plugged into a VME bus [23] backplane. Figure 5 shows the functional blocks on the processor board. The major component blocks on the board are processor module, local memory module, vector register windows memory, index memory, interrupt logic, VME bus interface, orthogonal memory interface, synchronization bus interface, and an RS-232 serial port interface. The processor module includes a 40 MHz i860 processor, its boot-eprom, and the associated decoding and cycle-control logic. The i860 processor was chosen because of its unique features, including a 64-bit external data bus, a 128-bit internal data bus, and high-speed floating-point units capable of executing two-floating point operations per clock cycle. The processor has the capability to perform vector operations with the aid of a vector library of subroutines. At its peak rate of operation, the i860 can execute two floating-point operations and one integer RISC operation concurrently in each cycle.

The 4 MB of local memory are organized in a 512K $\times$64 format

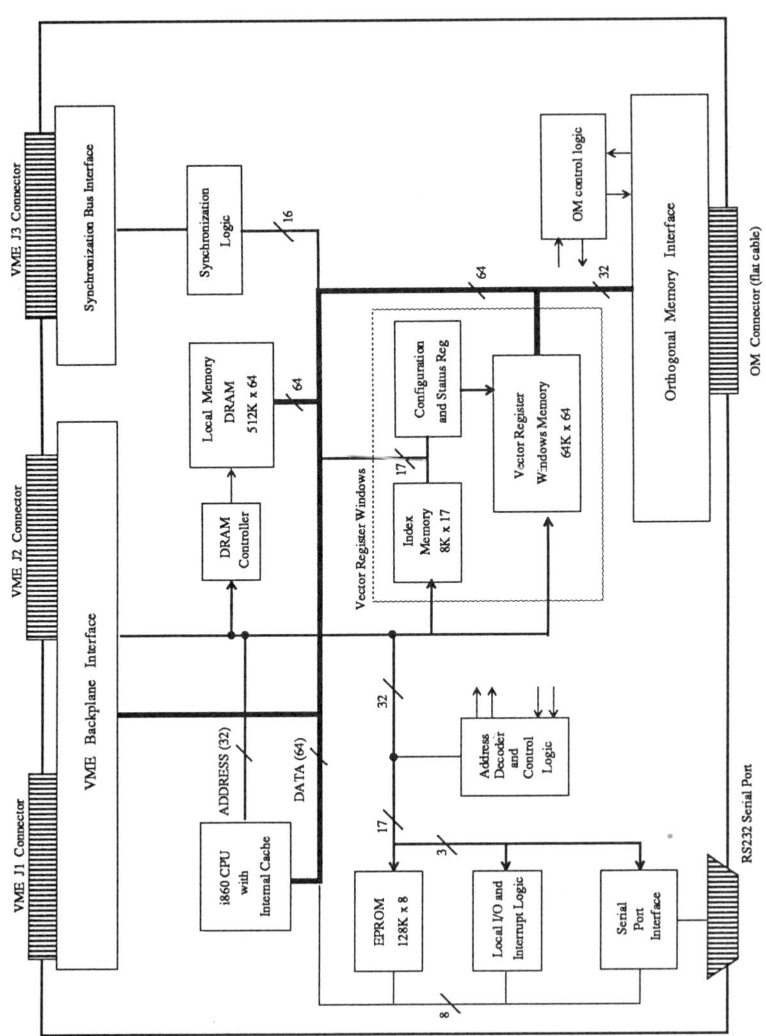


**Figure 5: Functional blocks on the processor board.**

using 70 nsec page-mode DRAMs. A miss in either the internal instruction cache or the data cache results in off-chip memory access. The decoding logic directs these off-chip requests to appropriate devices (local memory, VRWs, etc.). During a local memory data read operation, data caching to the internal data cache depends on the signal level at a cache enable (KEN/) input pin of the *i*860 processor [13]. The local memory is partitioned (user-programmable in steps of 16 KB) into two address spaces: cacheable and noncacheable. The shared data are mapped to the noncacheable space and the rest (program and data) to the cacheable space. The local memory supports fast page-mode access to match with the block-oriented transfers of the internal caches. The local memory subsystem supports zero wait state for a pipelined page-mode access and four wait states for a nonpipelined access. The local memory is dual-ported between processor's local bus and the VME bus. This dual-porting scheme provides a distributed shared memory address space between processors and host across the VME bus. The host communicates with processors using this shared address space. Any processor can communicate with other processors either through the VME interface or through the shared orthogonal memory. The partially shared orthogonal memory provides high-bandwidth parallel interprocessor communication as compared to the VME bus.

The VME interface has been expanded to support 64-bit data transfer/cycle across processors giving rise to a peak data transfer rate of 80 MB/s. The standard VME protocol has been enhanced to support *broadcast write*, where a single source can write common data to multiple destinations simultaneously. This feature is targeted for fast downloading of programs and common data from the host to all processors. Besides the normal VME interrupt structure, the processor board supports an *address-mapped interrupt* mechanism for fast interrupt handling across the processors [9]. This mechanism avoids the long interrupt latency encountered with standard VME interrupt protocol.

The VRWs act as buffers between a processor and the orthogonal vector memory. An *index memory* (IM) and the associated configuration registers are used to implement programmable and on-the-fly data manipulation during the data transfer between VRWs and the OAM. Both VRWs and IM are mapped to the local memory address space of the processor. The VRWs support zero wait state pipelined operation for vector accesses. The programmer's perspective of the VRWs together with their detailed implementation is described in Section 4.

The orthogonal memory data transfer is implemented as a DMA-like operation. The processor only initiates the operation by specifying a target orthogonal memory address, a target vector register address in the VRWs, and an associated index set. The orthogonal memory control logic takes care of rest of the data transfer, thus freeing the processor to perform other operations. The completion of the data transfer is intimated to the processor by an interrupt. This mechanism implements *posted-write* operations and facilitates the compiler to issue early OAM requests by code restructuring. This overlapped scheme of computation and data transfer is targeted to hide the long latency associated with orthogonal memory access to match with the RISC processing bandwidth.

Two different interprocessor synchronization mechanisms are implemented in the OMP. The distributed shared memory organization across the VME bus implements barrier synchronization with help of memory-mapped semaphores. This scheme provides flexibility to implement a large number of synchronization points in both SPMD and MPMD modes of operation. In addition to this, implementation of eight hardwired synchronization points, using a dedicated synchronization bus, enables fast synchronization in SPMD mode of operation. The synchronization bus is implemented using open-collector, wired-AND logic via the J3 connector of the VME backplane. This mechanism is targeted to achieve fast synchronization among processors with a minimal overhead of 100–200 ns.

The processor board is designed to run at 40 MHz, matching the 320 MB/s access rate for the internal instruction cache. The access rates of the internal data cache, the vector registers and the local memory are designed to be $B_1 = 640$ MB/s, $B_2 = 106.7$ MB/s, and $B_3 = 53.33$ MB/s, respectively. At 5325 ns per 16 32-bit data access, the orthogonal memory has a worst-case (assuming requests from all four processors are simultaneously active at a multiplexed switchboard during a given orthogonal memory cycle) bandwidth of $B_4 = 12.01$ MB/s per processor. The best case average latency from the OAM is 120 ns/word.

## 3.5 Host Interface and I/O Subsystem

The OMP back-end machine is controlled by a host computer, which is an integral part of the overall system as shown in Fig. 2. Presently, consideration is being given to either a SUN SPARC engine 300 or a Silicon Graphic IRIS workstation as the host. A customized Mach operating system will be ported to the host. The host is responsible for three major functions. The first is for general system control, system initialization, including program development, and preprocessing of user programs. The second responsibility is to provide data or program transfer to and from the OMP. The third function involves I/O operation with the external world.

To execute user programs on the back-end machine, the code generated by the host compiler is downloaded to processors. Similarly, uploading-downloading of data between processors and the host is supported. Transfer in either direction is performed through the VME bus. In real-time applications, the host issues operating system commands to move data between the peripheral devices and the orthogonal memory through a SCSI bus [1] directly without involving the back-end processors. In the synchronous mode, data are transferred in blocks with a maximum rate of 5 MB/s. For I/O-intensive applications, we have provision to add an additional SCSI adapter to the SCSI bus. It receives I/O commands through the VME bus either from the host or from processors and is able to initiate data transfers between peripheral devices on the SCSI bus. Other I/O devices connected to the host subsystem are a camera and a frame-grabber. Image is transferred at the rate of 10 MPixels/s from the frame-grabber.

# 4 Vector Register Windows

All arithmetic-logic operations on vector data mapped to the orthogonal memory are done from vector registers to vector registers in VRWs. An input vector operand must first be loaded from the orthogonal memory to a vector register before it can be used by a processor. Similarly, an output vector operand must be stored into a vector register first and written to the orthogonal memory later. The elements of VRWs are accessed by a processor in its local memory address space. The only OAM transfers possible are from OAM to vector registers (vector loads) and from vector registers to OAM (vector stores). A load (store) operation to (from) a designated vector register window from (to) the orthogonal memory is specified by the programmer and is implemented as a DMA-like operation.

## 4.1 Window Organization and Reconfigurability

The VRW's organization, associated with each processor in the OMP configuration, is shown in Fig. 6. The content of a memory location in an orthogonal memory module is defined to be an element. Each row or column access is done in an interleaved manner with a fixed address offset in each module resulting in a vector of 16 elements. A set of $v$ row or column vectors is grouped together to form a window of vectors. The VRWs consist of $w$ windows. We use 512 KB of static RAM memory with a capacity to represent 8K vectors. These vectors are dynamically reconfigured in variable-size windows as illustrated in Fig. 7.

For a target application using $n \times n$ matrices, any row or column of a matrix is folded onto several rows or columns in the orthogonal memory. A row or column of the application matrix becomes equivalent to $\lceil \frac{n}{16} \rceil$ vectors. Hence, $v = \lceil \frac{n}{16} \rceil$ provides a natural window size for the VRWs. The two least significant bits, $A_0$ and $A_1$, are used to select one of the four bytes within an element. The four bits $A_2 - A_5$ are used to select an element within a vector. The remaining 13 bits, $A_6 - A_{18}$, are dynamically partitioned between the vector field and the window field. Depending on the size of the application matrix, $\log_2 \lceil \frac{n}{16} \rceil$ bits are used for identifying a vector within a window. The

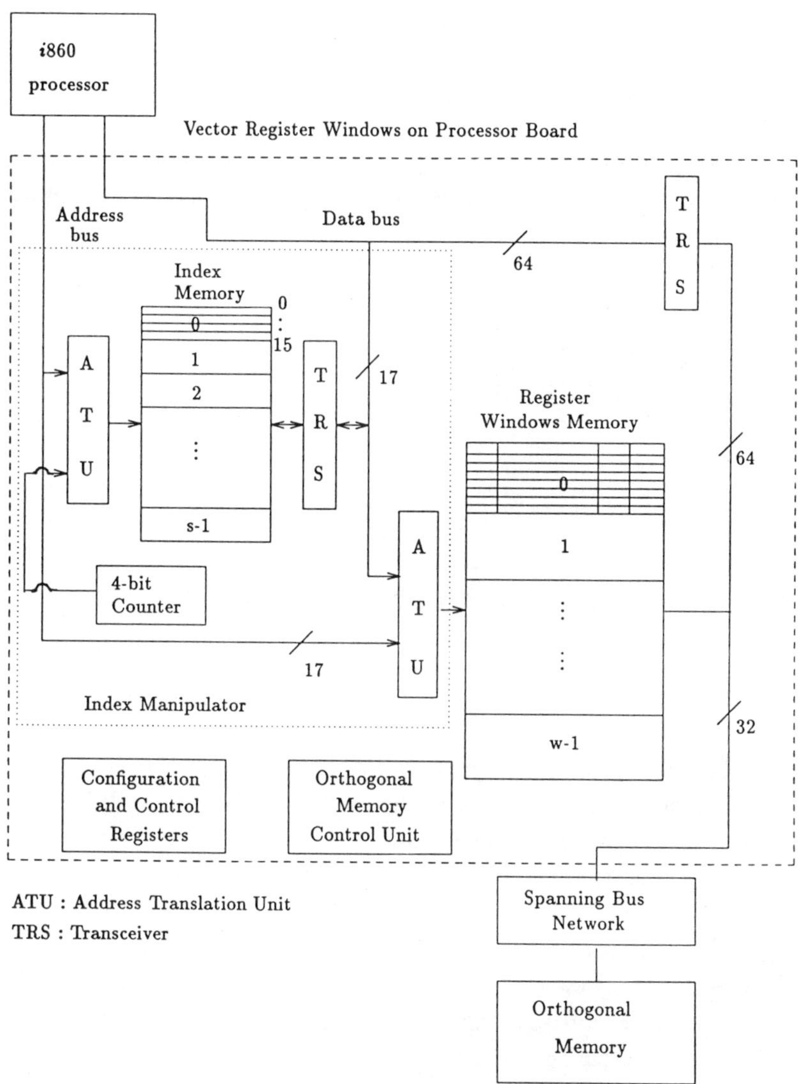


**Figure 6: Functional organization of the vector register windows with a built-in index manipulator.**

remaining $13 - \log_2\lceil \frac{n}{16} \rceil$ bits are used to identify a window.

Table 4.1 shows the number of available windows ($w$) in the OMP system together with the window size ($v$) for a wide range of application matrix sizes. The VRWs provide a sufficient number of windows for handling large matrices to encapsulate locality of data references. The dynamic reconfigurability of window size supports programming flexibility in applications involving multiple matrices with different dimensions.

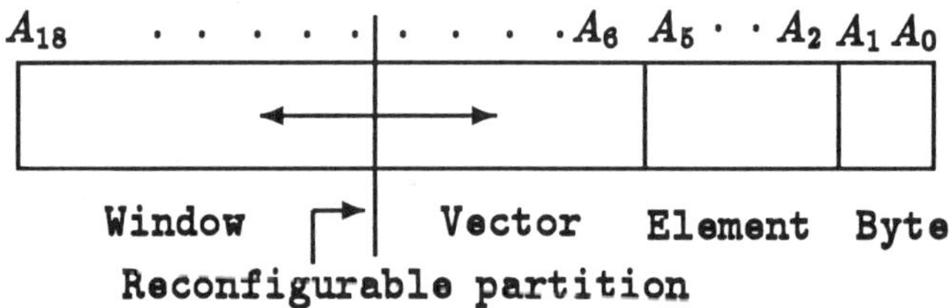


Figure 7: The address mapping scheme for a vector register window.

## 4.2 Data Coherency in VRWs

The VRWs are partitioned into two separate address spaces, from a processor's perspective, to treat the global read-write and the global read-only orthogonal memory data separately. These two address spaces separate the VRWs to noncacheable and cacheable spaces, respectively. The VRWs caching boundary allows a user to partition the VRWs into cacheable space in increments of 2 KB. The VRWs addresses falling below the caching boundary are cacheable. This programmable boundary can be dynamically moved upward during the execution of an application program.

If a vector operand corresponds to global read-only data type, it is loaded to a vector register in the cacheable space of the VRWs. Otherwise, it is loaded to the noncacheable space. So, when the processor accesses the elements of a global read-only vector from the VRWs, the elements are allowed (by activating the cache enable pin of the i860 processor by hardware decoding logic) to be cached to

| *Matrix Size* | *Window Size (v)* | *Number of Windows (w)* |
|---|---|---|
| 16 × 16 | 1 | 8192 |
| 32 × 32 | 2 | 4096 |
| 64 × 64 | 4 | 2048 |
| 128 × 128 | 8 | 1024 |
| 256 × 256 | 16 | 512 |
| 512 × 512 | 32 | 256 |
| 1024 × 1024 | 64 | 128 |
| 2048 × 2048 | 128 | 64 |
| 4096 × 4096 | 256 | 32 |
| 8192 × 8192 | 512 | 16 |

Table 2: Reconfigurability in vector register windows for variable matrix sizes. (window size = number of vector components in each window).

the internal data cache of the processor. The noncacheable data are directly accessed from the VRWs and hence bypass the internal cache. This scheme serves the following advantages:

1. If a read-only vector is used many times by an application, the computation becomes fast by keeping the data in the internal cache of the processor.

2. When the orthogonal memory is switched from row-access mode to column-access or vice versa, all global modified register windows in the non-cacheable address space of the VRWs are written back to the orthogonal memory. The cacheable register windows containing global read-only data are not written back to the orthogonal memory during mode changes.

3. For a small application, few selective windows need to be flushed. This provides a program-controlled, selective, and fast flushing scheme.

## 4.3 Index Manipulation and Window Reconfiguration

Each orthogonal memory access is associated with an index set for fast, on-the-fly index manipulation. An index set consists of 16 entries and specifies 16 destination (source) element locations in the VRWs for 16-way interleaved OAM data during a load (store) orthogonal memory operation. Figure 6 shows the VRW's implementation together with its built-in index manipulator. The index memory, mapped to the processor's local memory address space, is used to store a set of frequently used index sets. An index set, associated with an orthogonal memory transfer, is required to be resident in IM before the transfer takes place. The index sets can be stored in IM in the following ways: (a) downloading from the host to IM at the beginning of program execution; (b) the processor copying the index set entries from local memory to IM by load and store operations; or (c) the processor computing the entries based on some permutation and storing to IM. An *index-set base register* identifies the desired index set to be used during an orthogonal memory transfer. The index set base register is accessible by the processor as a memory-mapped I/O register.

The index memory is 17 bits wide to store index entries capable of indexing through 128 K elements in the VRWs. There is flexibility in using an index set together with either a *window base address register* or a *vector base address register* to achieve indexing restricted only to a window or to a vector, respectively. The window size can be dynamically reconfigured with the help of a *window size register*. The index set itself can be *directly* used to achieve indexing across all the elements of the VRWs. Hence, each entry in an index set may use 4-17 bits depending on the indexing scheme used [18]. This flexible usage of an index set allows it to be used multiple times with different windows or vectors by programming the respective base address registers. The window base address, vector base address, and window size registers are programmable and accessible by the processor as memory-mapped I/O registers. The IM, with an 8 K $\times 17$ organization, provides a storage of up to $s = 512$ index sets. The off-line computation and the storage of frequently used index sets reduce the overhead associated with on-the-fly data manipulation.

The indexing scheme is used only during the data transfer between the VRWs and the OAM. The accesses to the IM and the VRWs are pipelined, that is, the address generated by an index-set entry from IM during one minor cycle is used as the address to the VRWs in the next minor cycle. The design supports a fast minor cycle of 50 nsec duration.

The programmable and on-the-fly index-manipulation capability associated with the VRWs makes the OMP an attractive architecture for large-scale matrix data manipulation. Complex matrix manipulations like rotation, translation, shifting, and row-column exchanges can be efficiently done on the OMP with few orthogonal memory cycles. The detailed implementation of the VRWs and their use to achieve efficient matrix data manipulations are described in [18] with several illustrative examples.

The OAM data, once resident in the VRWs, is directly accessed by the processor in its local address space in a pipelined fashion. These data accesses bypass the IM and the associated data index manipulation logic. During this operation, the VRWs are physically addressed by the processor, based on the array addressing mechanism. To access an element in the VRWs, the window number, the vector number, and the element number are made *implicit* in the processor's address. For example, let us assume 16-way OAM interleaving and $v$ vectors/window. To access the $i$th element of $j$th vector in $k$th window, the effective address generated by the processor (with assistance from compiler) is

$$(k \times 16 \times v) + (j \times 16) + i + \text{base address of VRWs}.$$

By adding an offset argument to the effective address computation, several abstract data types are supported in the VRWs. This feature is used by the programmer to define overlapped-window access operation with VRWs [18]. A window provides a one-to-one mapping to a row (column) of the target application matrix. Several smaller windows can be grouped to form a larger window. This mechanism provides scope to define higher-level abstract data structures, like block-rows or block-columns. The flexibility also includes overlapped window access to define data structures on a set of contiguous elements of adjacent rows (columns) of an application matrix.

A window can be separated into multiple smaller windows to support subvector data structures. This modular and structured abstraction of the VRWs allows a programmer of the OMP system to operate on a large application matrix by defining the matrix as a small collection of vector windows rather than a large collection of orthogonal memory row (column) vectors.

# 5 Simulated Performance of OMP

The peak performance of the OMP prototype is targeted to be around 400 MIPS or 600 Mflops. An analysis of how this performance can be achieved was given in [9] based on the hardware latency parameters used in the prototype design. The OMP prototype design has been validated by running several scientific benchmark programs on an OMP simulator. The simulated performance of OMP was reported in [16].

Based on the simulation results, the OMP with 16 CPUs can perform 498 MOPS (million operations per second) for the multiplication of $128 \times 128$ matrices. The MOPS rating includes both RISC and floating-point operations, since they can be executed concurrently in each $i860$ processor. In the case of simulated run of a two-dimensional D FFT algorithm with 16 K data points, the speed was recorded as 450 MOPS. In both cases, speed-ups between 13 and 15 were achieved, as compared with sequential processing on a single $i860$ processor without using the orthogonal-access memory. These simulated performance results indicate that the OMP design can be 76% efficient, as compared with the absolute peak performance of 33 MIPS $\times 16 = 528$ MIPS, since each $i860$ processor can deliver a maximum of 33 MIPS.

A histogram modification algorithm has been parallelized for image enhancement using the OMP simulator. The following results were originally reported in [7]. Consider a digitized image frame with $M \times N$ pixels with $L$ gray levels. The pixels are represented as $P_{ij}$ for $0 \leq i \leq M-1$ and $0 \leq j \leq N-1$. Let $k$ be the index for gray level $0 \leq k \leq L-1$. Define a counting function $g_k(x) = 1$ if $x = k$, and 0 otherwise. The histogram of the given image frame is defined by the following pixel counts:

$$h(k) = \sum_{i=0}^{M-1}\sum_{j=0}^{N-1} g_k(P_{ij}) \text{ for } 0 \leq k \leq L-1.$$

The histogram equalization process involves the computation of the following partial sums:

$$S(k) = \sum_{t=0}^{k} h(t) \text{ for } 0 \leq k \leq L-1.$$

We use a transformation function

$$H(k) = \frac{S(k) - S(0)}{S(L-1) - S(0)} \cdot (L-1)$$

to normalize the histogram distribution. The new pixel counts are obtained by

$$P_{ij}^{new} = H(P_{ij}^{old}) \; for \; 0 \leq i \leq M-1, \; 0 \leq j \leq N-1.$$

The above computations can be executed in parallel on the OMP. Figure 8 shows the initial pixel distribution of an $8 \times 8$ image frame in the orthogonal-access memory of an OMP with four processors. Figure 8a shows the VRWs being used as buffers for accessing OAM data in column mode. As shown in Fig. 8b, row accesses are used in the completion of the histogram modification. Essentially, recursive doubling operations are performed in these alternate column and row operations to produce the new histogram count.

Figure 9a and 9b show the original image and the final image after running the above histogram equalization algorithm for an $M \times N = 120 \times 180$ image frame (the San Diego Mission Bay) on the 16-processor OMP simulator. Each pixel has $L = 256$ gray levels. Histograms corresponding to the respective images are shown. The simulated OMP execution time was recorded as 3.9 ms. The same program requires over 10 minutes to run on a uniprocessor SUN 3/60 workstation.

Compared with the use of a single *i*860-processor, the simulation result shows a sublinear speed-up as a function of the OMP machine

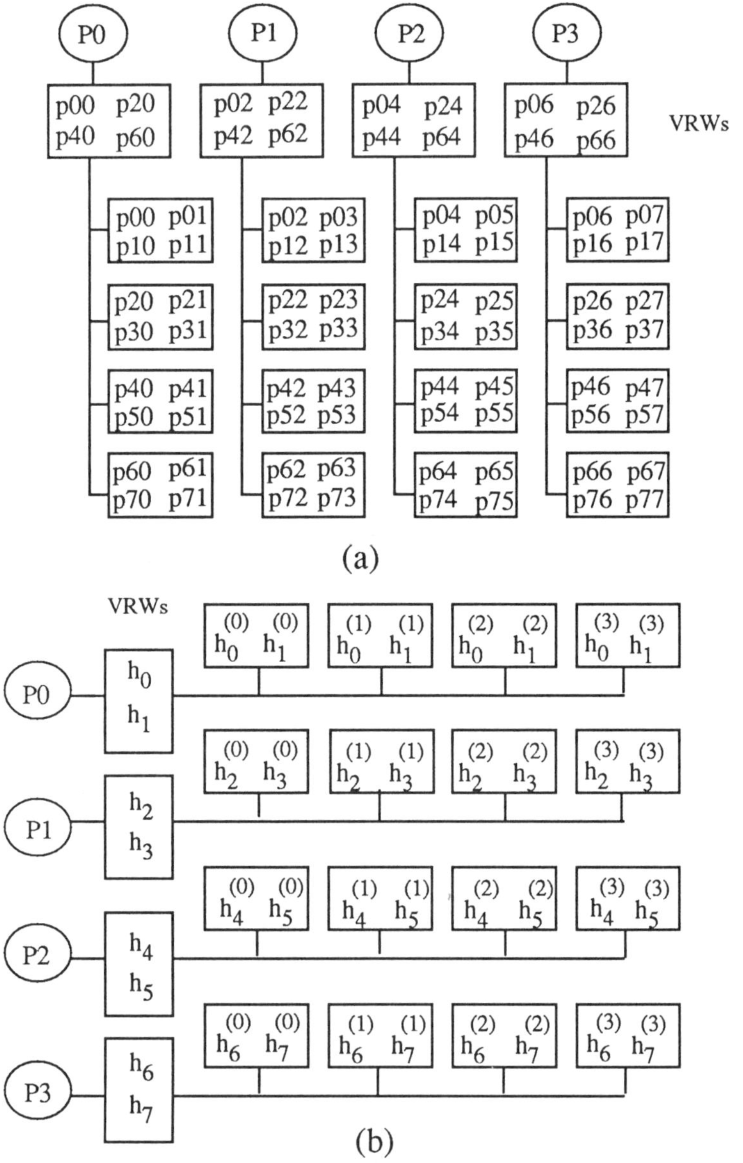


**Figure 8: Snapshots of data allocation in the orthogonal memory and in the vector register windows on a four processor OMP for computing histograms on an $8 \times 8$ image frame; (a) initial data distribution and (b) completion of histogram computation.**

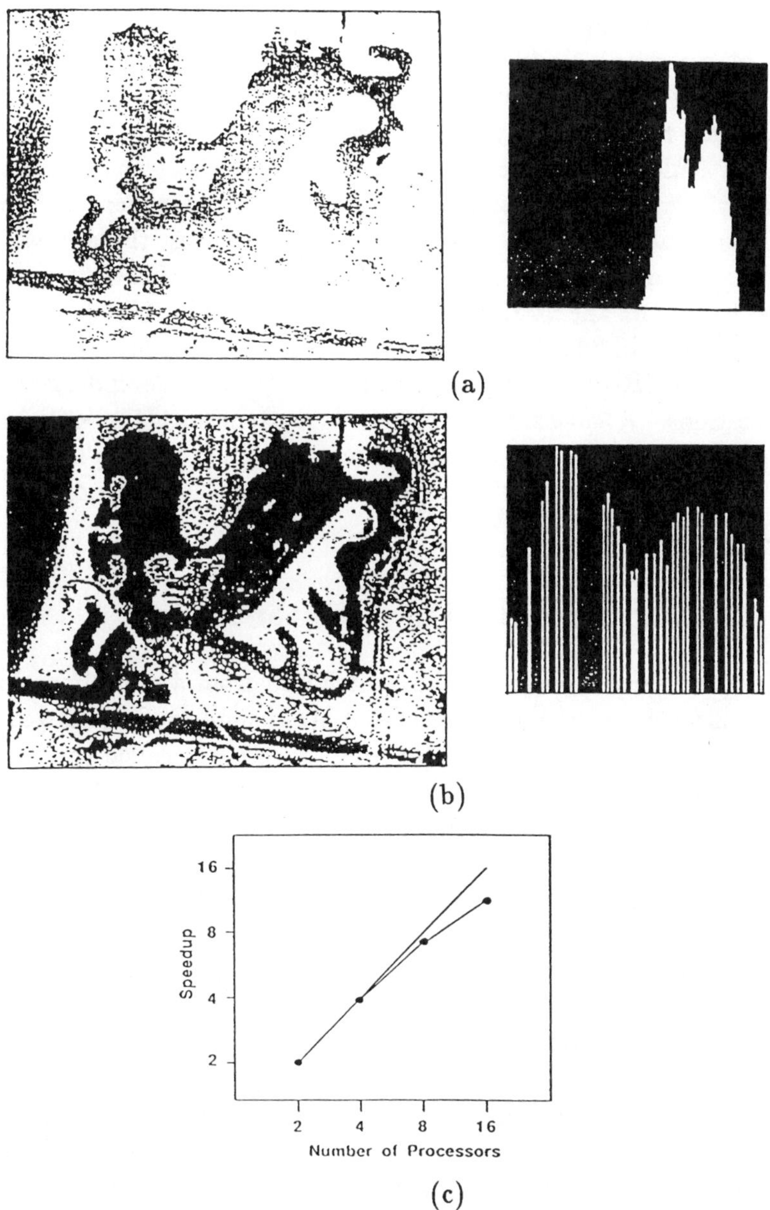


**Figure 9: The San Diego Mission Bay image (a) before and (b) after histogram equalization; (c) is the corresponding speed-up curve.**

size. As illustrated in Fig. 9c, the 16-processor OMP results in an 11.84 speed-up. Besides image enhancement, our research team is also using a neural network approach to achieve parallel processing on OMP for some early vision applications as reported in [7, 11]. In particular, we are interested in optical flow, static stereo, motion analysis, and image restoration by processing a sequence of time-varying image frames. Benchmark experiments in these areas are presently carried out using the OMP simulator and are planned for real testing on the OMP prototype once it is built.

The I/O bandwidth of the OMP prototype is estimated to be as high as 30 MB/s providing support for real-time image-understanding operations. A special-purpose I/O subsystem with frame-grabber, camera, and display unit is integrated into the system to match the OMP-processing bandwidth with the system I/O bandwidth as analyzed in [9].

# 6 OMP Architectural Extensions

The OMP architecture can be generalized from a two-dimensional structure to higher dimensions [10]. We denote the generalized orthogonal multiprocessor as OMP$(n, k)$, where $n$ is called the *dimension* and $k$ is the *multiplicity*. There are $p = k^{n-1}$ processors and $m = k^n$ memory modules in the system, where $p \gg n$ and $p \gg k$. The system uses $p$ memory buses, each spanning into $n$ dimensions. But, only one dimension is used in a given memory cycle. There are $k$ memory modules attached to each spanning bus. Each module is connected to $n$ out of $p$ buses through an $n$-way switch. It should be noted that the dimension $n$ corresponds to the number of accessible ports that each memory module has. This implies that each module is shared by $n$ out of $p = k^{n-1}$ processors.

For an example, the architecture of an OMP(3,4) is shown in Fig. 10, where the circles represent memory modules, the squares represent processor modules, and the circle-inside-square for a computer module. The 16 processors orthogonally access 64 memory modules via 16 buses, each spanning into three directions, called the $x$-access, $y$-access, and $z$-access, respectively. Various sizes of OMP

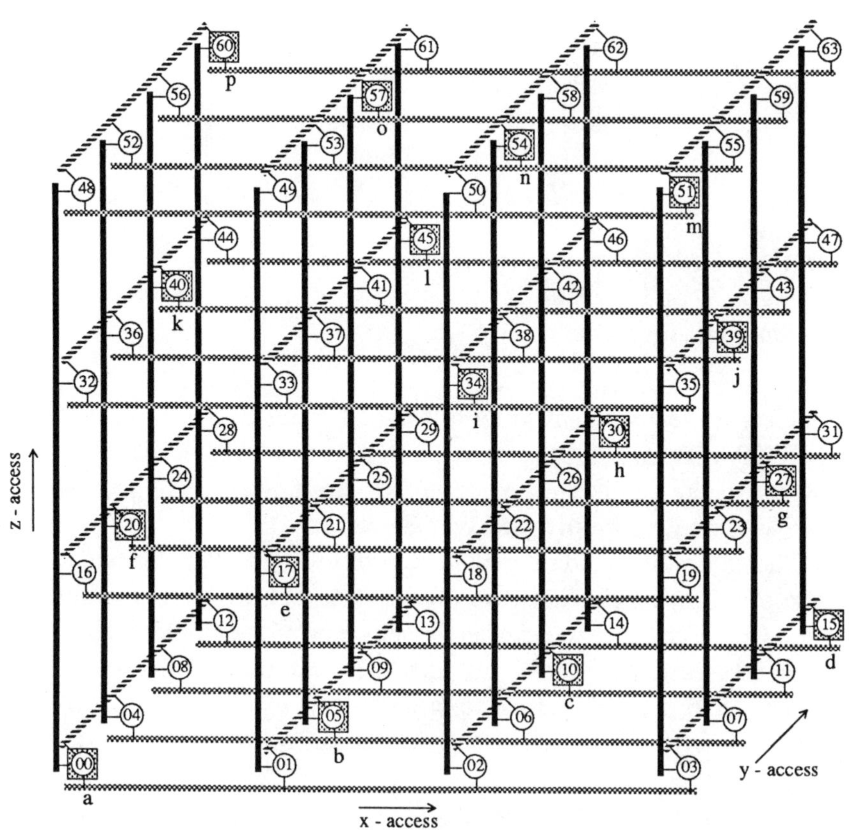


**Figure 10: The OMP(3,4) multiprocessor architecture with 16 processors (labeled as $a, b, \ldots, p$) accessing 64 memory modules (labeled as $00, 01, \ldots, 63$); each processor owns a private memory module, and the remaining 48 memory modules are shared by three processors.**

| OMP$(n,k)$ | $p = k^{n-1}$ | $m = k^n$ |
|---|---|---|
| OMP(2,8) | 8 | 64 |
| OMP(2,16) | 16 | 256 |
| OMP(3,8) | 64 | 512 |
| OMP(3,16) | 256 | 4,096 |
| OMP(4,8) | 512 | 4,096 |
| OMP(4,16) | 4,096 | 32,768 |
| OMP(5,16) | 65,536 | 524,288 |

Table 3: Orthogonal multiprocessor system sizes as a function of dimension $n$ and multiplicity $k$ ($p$ = no. of processors and $m$ = no. of memory modules).

architecture for different values of $n$ and $k$ are listed in Table 6. A 5D OMP with multiplicity $k = 16$ will have 65 K processors, comparable to the connection machine. In other words, the generalized OMP can easily support massive parallelism [10].

The three-dimensional orthogonal architecture is potentially useful in building special-purpose supercomputers for solving computational fluid dynamics and finite-element analysis problems, which use 3D matrix data structures. For example, one can duplicate approximately 16 times the hardware from an OMP(2,16), the prototype machine being built, to yield an OMP(3,16) system, which will have 256 processors and 4096 memory modules. This 3D OMP has the potential to achieve 12.8 Giga RISC instructions per second and 15.4 GFLOPS, assuming each processor delivers 50 MIPS and 60 Mflops as projected by Intel's future RISC technology. Our experience in building the current 2D OMP will pave the way to build the 3D OMP for extended supercomputing applications in the future.

# 7 Conclusions

We have reported the architectural design and the hardware features of the OMP system. The prototype OMP, based on RISC processors, demonstrates scalable performance for a range of image-processing algorithms and matrix-structured computation. The simulated performance of the OMP prototype with a 16-processor configuration is shown to be around 400 RISC integer MIPS or 600 Mflops. This processing capability is targeted toward large-scale real-time image-processing applications. The OMP prototype provides efficient implementation for applications demanding fine or coarse grain parallelism, local-global communication, and scalar-vector processing. The other features of OMP include easy system reconfigurability between SPMD and MPMD modes of operation, better match between processor-memory bandwidth, expandability to three-dimensional data structure for image and neural network applications, the use of orthogonal memory and spanning buses for orthogonal vector data communication, and the ability to embed almost all other parallel architectures onto it. The OMP prototype, with its balanced architectural features, stands distinct as a good research vehicle for new developments in image understanding.

### Acknowledgments

This research was supported by the United States National Science Foundation under grant no. 89-04172 at the University of Southern California.

We would like to thank the architecture group members of the Viscom Project. We appreciate the interactions with Michel Dubois, Chien-Ming Cheng, Navid Haddadi, Fon-Jein Hsieh, Mark Lytwyn, Weihua Mao, Sharad Mehrotra, Hemraj Nair, Santosh Rao, and Shisheng Shang during group meetings and technical discussions. We are also grateful to the technical assistance extended by Intel Corporation, AST Research, Microelectronics and Computer Technology, and Texas Instruments.

## Bibliography

[1] American National Standards Institute, ANSI X3.131, New York. *Small Computer System Interface (SCSI)*, 1986.

[2] V. Balan, Trojan-C language and its programming environment. Technical report, Laboratory of Parallel and Distributed Computing, Dept. of EE-Systems, Univ. of Southern California, Los Angeles, Calif., Mar. 1990.

[3] C. M. Cheng, Programmer's uide to the USC Orthogonal Multiprocessor simulator. Technical report, Dept. of EE-Systems, Univ. of Southern California, Los Angeles, Calif., Mar. 1990.

[4] P. M. Dew, R. A. Earnshaw, and T. R. Heywood, eds., Parallel Processing for Computer Vision and Display. Addision-Wesley, 1989.

[5] M. J. B. Duff, ed., Computing Structures for Image Processing. Academic Press, 1983.

[6] I. R. Greenshields, A Dynamically Reconfigurable Multimodal Architecture for Image Processing. Parallel Processing for Computer Vision and Display, pp. 153–165. Addison-Wesley, 1989.

[7] N. Haddadi, K. Hwang, and R. Chellappa, Viscom: An Orthogonal Multiprocessor for Early Vision and Neural Computing. In 10th International Conference on Pattern Recognition, Atlantic City, NJ, June 1990.

[8] K. Hwang and D. DeGroot, eds., Parallel Processing for Supercomputers and Artificial Intelligence. McGraw-Hill, New York, 1989.

[9] K. Hwang, M. Dubois, D. K. Panda, S. Rao, S. Shang, A. Uresin, W. Mao, H. Nair, M. Lytwyn, F. Hsieh, J. Liu, S. Mehrotra, and C. M. Cheng, OMP: A RISC-based Multiprocessor using Orthogonal-Access Memories and Multiple Spanning Buses. Proc. of ACM International Conference on Supercomputing, Amsterdam, June 1990.

[10] K. Hwang and D. Kim, Generalization of Orthogonal Multiprocessor for Massively Parallel Computations. In Proceedings of the Conference on Frontiers of Massively Parallel Computations, Fairfax, VA., Oct. 1988.

[11] K. Hwang, D. K. Panda, and N. Haddadi, The USC Orthogonal Multiprocessor for Image Processing with Neural Networks. 1990 SPIE/SPSE Symposium on Electronic Imaging, Santa Clara, Calif., Feb. 1990.

[12] K. Hwang, P.S. Tseng, and D. Kim, An Orthogonal Multiprocessor for Parallel Scientific Computations, IEEE Transactions on Computers, Vol. C–38(1), Jan. 1989, pp.47–61.

[13] Intel Corporation, i860 Programmer's Reference Manual, 1989.

[14] D. Kim, Orthogonal Architectures for Parallel Image Processing, Ph.D. thesis, Department of EE-Systems, University of Southern California, 1988.

[15] S. Mehrotra, Simulator Manual for the USC Orthogonal Multiprocessor, Technical report, Dept. of EE-Systems, Univ. of Southern California, Los Angeles, Calif., Feb. 1990.

[16] S. Mehrotra, C. M. Cheng, K. Hwang, M. Dubois, and D. K. Panda, Algorithm-Driven Simulation and Projected Performance of the USC Orthogonal Multiprocessor, Proc. of Intl. Conference on Parallel Processing, St. Charles, Ill., Aug 1990.

[17] D. K. Panda and K. Hwang, Embeddings of Parallel Architectures onto Orthogonal Multiprocessor, Technical report, Dept. of EE-Systems, Univ. of Southern California, Los Angeles, Calif., April 1990.

[18] D. K. Panda and K. Hwang, Reconfigurable Vector Register Windows for Fast Matrix Manipulation on the Orthogonal Multiprocessor, International Conference on Application Specific Array Processors, Princeton, N.J., Sept. 1990.

[19] H.D. Schwetman, CSIM: A C-Based, Process-Oriented Simulation Language, Proceedings of the 1986 Winter Simulation Conference, 1989, pp. 387–396.

[20] W. Stallings, Reduced Instruction Set Computer Architecture, Proceedings of the IEEE, Vol. 76(1), Jan. 1988, pp. 38–55.

[21] D. Tabak, High-Performance RISC Systems, J. of Microproc. and Microsys., Aug. 1989, pp. 355–372.

[22] L. Uhr, K. Preston Jr., S. Levialdi, and M. J. B. Duff, eds., Evaluation of Multicomputers for Image Processing, Academic Press, 1986.

[23] VME bus International Trade Association, The VME bus Specification Manual, 1990.

# Medium Grain Parallel Architecture for Image and Signal Processing

**K. WOJTEK PRZYTULA**
*Hughes Research Laboratories*
*Malibu, California*

## 1 Introduction

The chapter presents a discussion of a coprocessor for image and signal processing. The discussion centers around a particular methodology of design of application-specific architectures adopted by our group at Hughes. In a nutshell, there are two major steps in our design procedure. First, we define an abstract model of the architecture based on selected algorithms from the application domain. The model constitutes a high-level specification of the machine and includes a basic description of the data path, memory management, and control. Then, using the model as the starting point, we arrive at the complete architecture of the machine. The architecture specifies the design on a more detailed level and includes realizations of the building blocks of the model. The final realizations are obtained after a trade-off analysis of performance versus cost from the point of view of algorithms, hardware, and software (see Fig. 1).

The focus of this presentation is on discussion of various realization options, rather than on description of one specific final architecture. The algorithms are used to identify possible modifications of the basic model and realization options that provide optimal performance. Thus, the choice of algorithms has a critical impact on the design. The hardware point of view brings with it constraints

Parallel Architectures and
Algorithms for
Image Understanding




ISBN 0-12-564040-4

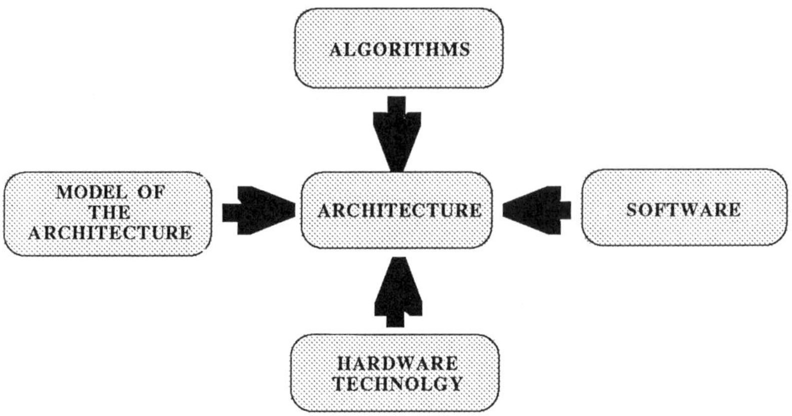


Figure 1: Approach to the design process of the application-specific computer.

imposed by specifications of the machine, such as cost, volume, and power, and by the state-of-the-art in technology, such as silicon chip feature sizes and areas, board densities and areas, numbers of pins in packages and connectors in boards, maximal clock rates. The software point of view onto the architecture design provides guidelines regarding efficiency, with which specific architectural options can be supported in a compiler and their impact on a complexity and therefore the cost of the software development.

In our methodology, identification of the architectural options is followed by the trade-off analysis, which leads to the definition of the final architecture. This analysis is not presented here, because it depends largely on specific assumptions regarding algorithms, hardware, and software and is, therefore, of little value in a general case. Instead, we provide a brief description of a coprocessor prototype for control of a robot arm, which was developed using the same design methodology and the same basic model of architecture.

The term *application-specific computers* is used in the literature to describe computers ranging from a single-chip processor for FFT computation to supercomputers for scientific computation. For the sake of this presentation we use the term to denote a programmable digital computer designed for an application such as sonar or radar signal processing or an entire application domain such as image or signal processing. This definition suggests an architecture tailored to the application but endowed with significant flexibility and generality. We use the term *coprocessors* to mean that the machine interacts with some front-end computer, which is responsible for the interface operations, some control functions, and some of the computations. We assume that an application-specific coprocessor should be characterized by a low cost, a small size, and a performance that is significantly better for the target application than that of general-purpose machines of similar cost.

The chapter consists of four sections. Section 2, following this introduction, is devoted to presentation of the basic model of the architecture. Section 3 contains the discussion of the realization options for the model. Section 4 describes the prototype of the coprocessor for robot arm control.

## 2 Abstract Model of the Architecture

This section presents the basic model of the architecture, which includes an outline of the data path, the memory management, and the control. The model constitutes a starting point for the search of the design space. The final architecture is obtained after analysis of various architectural options and modifications of the model from the point of view of software, hardware, and algorithms to be implemented on the machine (see Fig. 1). The level of detail in the definition of the model is much lower than in the final architecture. It is, however, sufficient to determine whether there is a good match between the model and the algorithms. The match is determined by mapping the algorithms onto the model and evaluating their performance. We have derived the model presented below in an iterative manner by mapping on it and its earlier versions various image- and signal-processing algorithms listed in Table 1. Some features of the model, such as number of processing units, number of registers of local memory, size of array memory, etc., are left unspecified as its parameters.

The section includes definitions of the model at the coprocessor and processing element level and description of the basic software for the machine.

## 2.1 Model of the Coprocessor

The machine described here is a coprocessor; therefore, it coexists in a computer system with a front-end machine, which is referred to as a host. The coprocessor is a programmable, medium-grain multiprocessor. It consists of three major building blocks: processor array, array memory, and the controller with program memory (Fig. 2). Programs stored in program memory are executed in the processor array on the data fetched from the array memory. The host loads the data and the programs into the coprocessor, initiates the execution of the programs, and unloads the results. It also initializes the coprocessor, checks its status, and supervises basic testing routines.

The processor array is a square array of processing elements interconnected to four nearest neighbors. The size of the array is one of the parameters of the model, and is intended to range from $8 \times 8$ (64 processing units) to no more than $64 \times 64$ (4096 processing units). The array is connected to the array memory on its north and south edge. The north edge is used for data read and the south edge for data write. The east and west edges are connected with each other by means of wraparound connections. Thus, the array and the array memory can be viewed as a toroidal structure. The processor array is characterized by small local memory in the processing units and high-bandwidth connections between the processors and between the array and the array memory. The array operates under the control of a single controller in SIMD (single instruction stream, multiple data stream) mode. Not all processors have to be active in any cycle; some of them can be disabled (masked out). The masking of processors can be deterministic or data-dependent.

The data memory is organized in columns matching the columns of the array. The memory has two ports. The top port is used for loading and unloading of data from the host as well as for input of data from the array. The bottom port is used exclusively for

**Signal-Processing Algorithms**

1. System of linear equations
2. Least squares –overdetermined, underdetermined, and generalized
3. Matrix operations (product, inverse, transposition)
4. Singular value decomposition (SVD)
5. 1-D FFT (radix 2 and 4)
6. Fast Hadamard transform
7. Fast HaarTtransform
8. FIR filtering with resampling

**Image Processing Algorithms**

1. 2-D Convolution
2. 2-D FFT (radix 2 and 4)
3. Connected component labeling
4. Feature vector computation
5. Template matching
6. Histogram

**Other Algorithms**

1. Regular permutations: bit reversed to sequential, transposition, etc.
2. General permutation without congestion
3. Sorting
4. Artificial neural networks models

**Sequences of Algorithms**

1. Synthetic aperture radar (spotlight and strip modes)
2. Airborne radar modes
3. Active sonar
4. Passive sonar
5. Adaptive antenna array processing

Table 1: Algorithms Used to design the model of the application-specific architecture for signal- and image-processing.

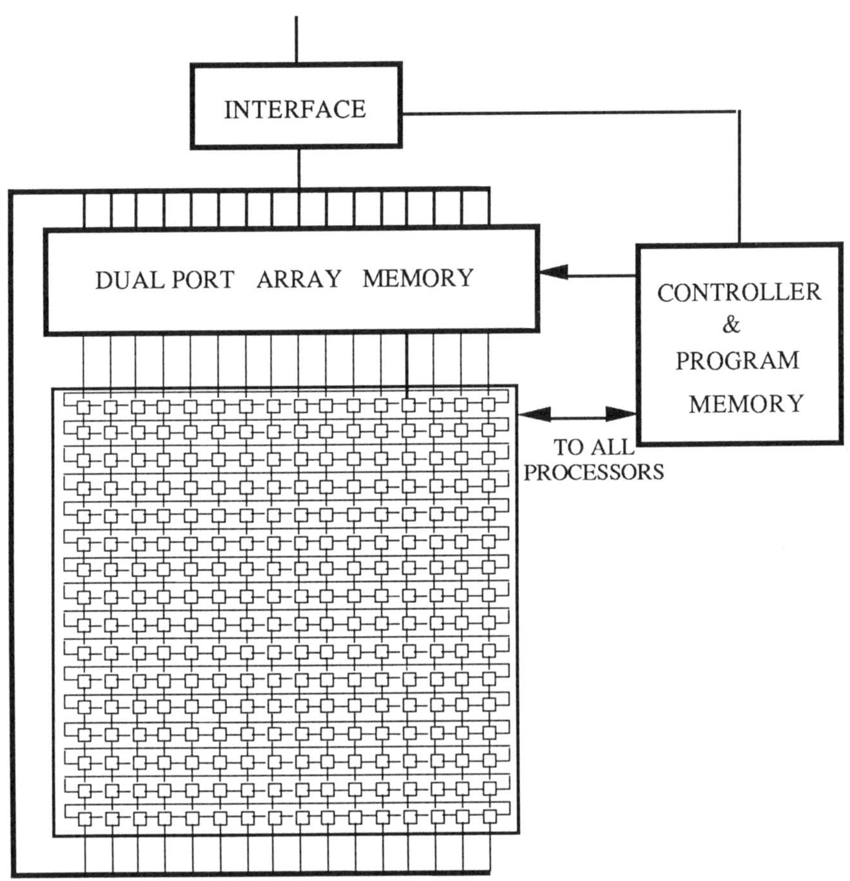


**Figure 2: Model of the coprocessor.**

data output into the processor array. During the program execution, the data flow from the memory through the bottom port into the processing array and the results are sent back into the data memory through its top port. The data are transferred between the array and the memory in rows; that is, a single address is used for each of the ports. The host is not limited to this form of access.

The controller sequences the lines of the program from the program memory, forms and distributes instructions to the processor array, and generates addresses and control signals for the data memory. The controller can also broadcast data from the program memory to the processor array. It receives a feedback of ORed flags and activity bits from all the processing elements of the array. The controller is also responsible for interaction with the host. It passes status information to the host and provides basic support for operations performed by the host on the coprocessor. These operations include loading and unloading of data and programs (this can be done concurrently with the execution of programs in the coprocessor), testing and diagnostics of the coprocessor, etc. The interaction with the outside world is relegated entirely to the host.

The coprocessor model is designed for two modes of operation: cellular and systolic. In the cellular mode there are three distinctive phases of the data processing: load, compute, and unload. First, the input data are loaded from the array memory into the local memory of processing elements of the array. Then the computation phase begins, and is followed by unloading of the results from the array into the array memory. A good example of a cellular algorithm for the architecture model is FFT [10]. In the systolic mode the distinctive phases are gone, and loading, computation, and unloading are pipelined and typically done at the level of an individual row or column of data. The modified Faddeev algorithm can be used as an example of a systolic algorithm suitable for the model [4].

## 2.2 Model of the Processing Element

The processing element consists of multiported local memory, several functional units (such as multiplier, adder, integer ALU ), I/O ports, and masking and instruction decoding unit (Fig. 3). The functional units are capable of concurrent computation. Also the I/O operations can be executed in parallel with local computations. This is accomplished by providing multiple fields in the processor instruction word (VLIW – very long instruction word) and multiple ports in the local memory. The number and the type of functional units as well as the number of ports and size of the memory are parameters of the model. Most of the control functions for the processing element are "factored out" to the main controller of the coprocessor. The remaining functions include generation of addresses for local memory (including indirect addressing), data dependent and deterministic masking of the processing element, and decoding of instructions to produce controls for the data path, that is, I/O ports, memory, functional units, and multiplexers associated with them.

## 2.3 Software

Design of an application-specific computer based on our methodology requires software tools to support development of both algorithms and the architecture. The algorithm development, also called algorithm mapping, involves derivation of a parallel version of a given algorithm, which can be efficiently executed on the architecture. It is often a difficult task, which could be simplified by software tools. The parallel versions of algorithms can be developed heuristically or systematically. In heuristic mapping, the parallel version is developed by trial and error, guided by familiarity with the algorithm and the architecture. The correctness of the parallel algorithms can be verified on the final architecture or on a software simulator of its model. An example of such a simulator is Parahacsis [11], which was developed for our model by modification of a tool from Stuttgart University [1]. The simulator takes in sample input data and a high-level language (Modula-2) specification of the parallel algorithm, and produces intermediate and final results, which are used for verification of correctness or debugging of the algorithm.

In the systematic approach, a parallel algorithm is developed by following a rigorous procedure involving typically an interactive session with a software tool. The tool requires a model of the architecture and implementation-independent formulation of the algorithm.

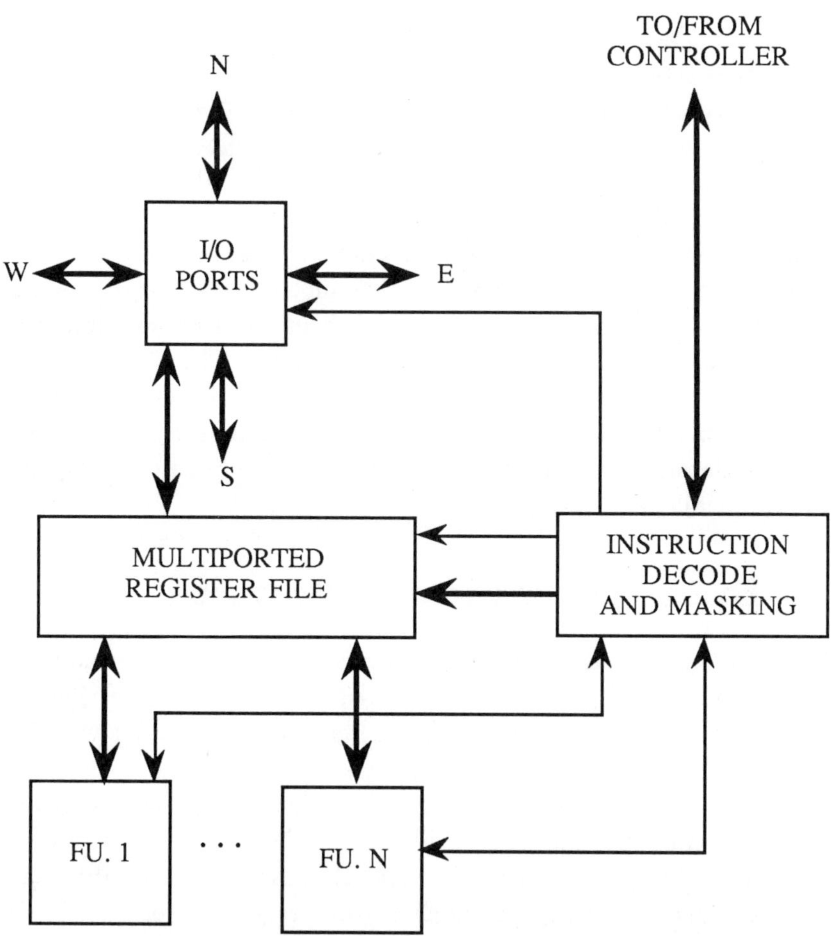


**Figure 3: Model of the processing element.**

The result is a provably correct parallel version of the algorithm suitable for the architecture and selected according to criteria of optimality defined by the user. The tools of this type proposed to date are restricted to a very limited class of algorithms and architectures. One example is a tool for mapping artificial neural networks onto mesh-connected processor arrays [6].

According to our methodology, the final architecture is obtained in a trade-off analysis step using the model defined in this section and architectural options presented in the next section. This step is best supported by an assembly-level retargetable simulator. The simulator captures the model and a particular realization version and produces performance estimates, for an algorithm coded in assembly language. The estimates include number of clock cycles, number of required local and array memory locations, etc. The simulator must be easy to modify so that multiple realization versions can be quickly encoded and compared. To make the performance estimates reliable, the simulator should provide automatic code compaction for optimal use of parallelism available in the machine.

## 3 Discussion of the Architecture

This section contains discussion of modifications of the model for image- and signal-processing, described in the previous section, and of details of the architectural definition, which are not part of the model. The model of the architecture augmented by various combinations of the modifications and architectural details leads to different versions of the final architecture. We will not design here any single final architecture, because this can be done only after a detailed trade-off analysis, which in turn requires precisely defined requirements for algorithms, hardware, and software. We will simply bring up a number of the modifications and architectural details in the context of algorithms, hardware, and software.

## 3.1 Algorithms

The model of the architecture described in the previous section was defined using algorithms from Table 1, which makes it capable of efficient execution of key image- and signal-processing algorithms. The discussion presented here revolves around the question of how to use the model and information contained in the algorithms to define the final architecture. It is natural that by selecting only a subset of the algorithms we would bias our realization and arrive at a more specialized architecture. There are, however, many other issues related to interpretation of the information provided by the algorithms that require attention.

The algorithms for a given application build a bridge between the sensor and the computational environment. For example, to form a high-resolution image from the radar sensor on a von Neumann electronic computer, there are synthetic aperture radar (SAR) algorithms of a particular type. The algorithms will be somewhat different if they are to be executed on a massively parallel computer. To define these algorithms one needs to know the architecture of the target computer, for instance, a specialized computer for SAR. On the other hand the algorithms must be known to define a specialized architecture that offers a good match between the application and the computer. One way to deal with this "chicken and egg" problem is to use the iterative approach proposed in this chapter, that is, to start with existing algorithms, develop a basic model of the architecture, derive parallel algorithms for the model, and then use the algorithms to refine the model and to design the final architecture.

In selecting appropriate representative algorithms in the design processes we need also to include algorithms, which are not used at present but promise to address future processing goals such as higher quality of processing, ability to deal with larger data sizes or rates, etc. For example, signal-processing algorithms based on singular value decomposition are rarely used in existing systems but they have great potential for high-resolution processing, provided that sufficient computational power is available in the future computer system.

In addition to identifying which algorithms are important, one needs to know their relative importance as well. This includes their frequency of use as well as their numerical complexity. For example, a small signal-processing problem, which among other computations includes FFT and matrix inversion, may be dominated in terms of computation time by the FFT. However, this domination may be turned in favor of matrix inversion as the problem size $N$ increases, because the computation time of the matrix inversion is proportional to $N^3$, whereas the computation time of the FFT is proportional to $N \log N$.

The algorithms should not be considered in isolation. An architecture optimal for individual algorithms may not be optimal for sequences of algorithms. In the mapping of individual algorithms we are free to assume the most favorable format for the input and output data. These formats may not agree with each other when the algorithms are put together into a sequence, thus requiring numerous data reorganization steps, which the architecture may not be able to support efficiently (for example, the need for reformating data on the output of FFT from bit reversed to sequential ordering).

The basic model of the processing element contains multiple functional units, of which number and choice are dictated by the algorithms. The signal-processing algorithms operate often on complex numbers and require a large number of multiply and add operations. It is therefore natural to provide at least these two units. The next most important arithmetic operation for signal-processing is division, which can be easily implemented together with square root operations. These two operations appear, for example, in solutions of linear systems and least-squares problems based on orthogonal transformations such as Givens rotations. Image-processing calls often for evaluation of conditional expressions and for indirect memory addressing. These operations require integer ALU. Some form of support is also needed for function generation such as exponent or sine and cosine, for example, a lookup table.

In our model of the architecture we assume that the local memory in the processing elements is small, and that most of the data are loaded into it when needed from the large array memory. The exact size of the local memory is one of the parameters in our model.

The systolic algorithms have typically very limited requirements for local storage, because they pipeline the computations with data flow from the array memory. These requirements may grow, however, if the level of pipelining is increased so that several rows of data are processed concurrently. Such pipelining is especially desirable when the processing elements have significant computational power, that is, very fast or very many functional units. Cellular algorithms require much more local memory and the size of the memory may have significant impact on their performance. This manifests itself as interruption in the computations for unloading of partial results and loading of more data (see, for example, FFT computation [10] or interpolation step in SAR [8]). Preferably, the size of the memory should be sufficient to meet requirements of the present computation and provide space for unloading of the previous results and loading of the new data. For example, in computation of multiple FFTs, we need local memory for twiddle factors and for two sets of data points, that is, one of the presently computed FFT and the other of the results of the previous FFT, which are being gradually unloaded and replaced during the computation by the inputs for the next FFT. The size of the local memory depends also on the application area. Typically, the image-processing algorithms have larger requirements for local memory than the signal-processing algorithms, because for many of them it is advantageous to save the entire image in the processor array as opposed to loading and unloading parts of them from the array memory.

The number of ports needed in the local memory is to a large degree a consequence of the number of functional units and I/O ports, which can access the memory in parallel. These in turn are determined, as we have seen, from the characteristics of the algorithms. The efficiency with which the ports are utilized depends on data dependencies in the algorithms and the degree of pipelining. Algorithms with more involved basic operations, which are pipelineable, such as complex Givens rotations in solution of linear systems or butterflies in multiple FFT computations, are more likely to use multiple ports efficiently than simple algorithms like matrix multiplication.

The processing elements in our model have connections with four nearest neighbors. They may be realized as concurrent connections that allow us to transfer data in north-south and east-west directions at the same time or as sequential connections, that is, in one direction at a time. The basic FFT implementation from [10] requires only sequential connections; however, if computation of FFT is to be overlapped with data loading and unloading, then concurrent communication in two directions must be possible. Systolic matrix multiplication algorithms also require concurrent connections, whereas for many permutations sequential connections are sufficient.

Realization of the processor array requires resolution of two questions: how large the array should be and how to implement its interconnections. The size of the array is probably the most important parameter of the architectural model and the hardest to resolve. The larger the array, the larger its computational throughput and its combined local memory, but larger also its dimensions and therefore more time is needed for loading and unloading data. The algorithms and data rates in real-time applications determine the required throughput and thus the minimal array size. The effective throughput is typically a nonlinear function of the array size and has to be determined separately for each algorithm. The simplest way to do it is to map the algorithm and estimate its performance for several a priori selected array sizes. A complicating factor here is the overheads due to partitioning of algorithms, which are needed when the data sets are larger than the processor array.

The choice of appropriate implementation of the array interconnections is dictated by the structure of algorithms rather than data sizes or data rates. Mesh connections are a very good match for most of the signal- and image-processing algorithms. Some algorithms such as permutations, neural networks [6], or window operations in image processing benefit from availability of wraparound connections. These connections decrease the diameter of the mesh network and as a result reduce by half the cost of some of the data transfers. The data reformating steps of some algorithms, for instance SAR [6], require more complicated wraparound connections, referred to as Illiac IV connections, in which the rightmost processor in a given row of array is connected to the leftmost processor of the next row. In image processing significant performance improvements can be obtained from augmentting the mesh by broadcasting connections along the columns, for instance in decision-tree-based image recognition. These connections would realize broadcasting from array memory as well as any of the processing elements in a given column to all the remaining processors in the column [8].

The architectural model specifies the transfer of data between the array memory and the processor array as unidirectional north-south flow. Some of the image-processing algorithms, such as graph connectivity algorithm, would benefit if a bidirectional flow, north-south and south-north, were available. Also the access to the memory only from the north and south boundaries of the array, is not sufficient for algorithms such as matrix multiplication or matrix transposition. They require access also from the east and west boundaries. In the case of matrix multiplication a concurrent flow in north-south and east-west directions is desirable; however, for matrix transposition sequential access (north-south followed by east-west) is sufficient.

Realization of the control of the coprocessor is the most challenging task because it depends not only on the algorithms but on the entire execution scenario prescribed for the application. The scenario specifies interaction with the outside world, including format and the rate of data, real-time or batch processing, communication protocol, etc. These issues are highly specific for a given system and will not be addressed here. More commonly encountered control issues have to do with execution of scalar computations, evaluation of conditional expressions, and address generation for the array memory. Some of the scalar operations occurring in the algorithms are best handled by the controller, especially if they can be executed concurrently with the parallel processing taking place in the array. To support scalar computations in the controller, there needs to be a connection for transfer of data between the array, array memory, and the controller. According to our model, the controller can broadcast data to the processor array; it also needs to be able to access the top port of the array memory in the same way as the host.

The controller provides support for deterministic masking, data dependent operation of the array, and conditional control flow. In deterministic masking it activates masking bits stored a priori in the processing elements. This function is critical in execution of permutation algorithms. The data-dependent operation makes it possible for processing elements to execute different branches of if-then-else instructions or terminate do-while loops depending on the result of locally evaluated conditions. This capability is of critical importance for many image processing algorithms, such as thresholding and histogramming, as well as some signal-processing algorithms such as nonlinear filtering. The conditional control flow is similar to that in the von Neumann computer and requires the controller to be capable of evaluating conditional expressions.

## 3.2 Hardware

The problem of implementing a given architecture in hardware reduces to assigning circuits to chips, chips to boards, connecting the boards with a backplane, and putting the entire system into a chassis, adhering in the process to hardware and technology specifications assumed a priori. The hardware specifications include computational throughput, maximal dissipated power, volume, cost, etc; the technology specifications include VLSI and packaging technology specifications. On the basis of the specifications, we select those architectural options, from the list suggested by the algorithms, that are implementable in terms of area and interconnections on chip and board, circuit complexity, system volume or power, etc. In this subsection we look at some of the architectural details from the hardware and technology point of view.

The present VLSI technology allows us to put a complex microprocessor on a single chip. The processing elements in our architecture are smaller than the microprocessor, because most of their control functions are moved to the external common controller; thus we can expect to put several of them on a single chip. The area of the processing element depends primarily on the number and area of functional units and local memory registers. The functional units can be implemented as fast and large pipelined circuits, of which only a couple could fit into the processing element, or as smaller and slower parallel-serial circuits with six or even more of them per processor (see description of the prototype in Section 4). The local memory contributes significantly to the area occupied by the processing element. Its size depends on the number of memory locations and the memory ports. For a fixed area the number of locations drops very fast with the growing number of ports, thus these two parameters have to be carefully weighted against each other. One way to alleviate the severity of the problem is to split the multiported local memory into several smaller memories with fewer ports. This results in saving area without reducing bandwidth, but complicates the compiler design (see the next subsection). A small area per chip has to be devoted to an instruction decoding logic, which is shared between the processing elements, and to the wiring of the control signals from the decoder to the processing elements. Each processing element has to include also a small masking circuit. The design of the decode and masking circuits is driven primarily by functionality and not the chip area considerations.

The processor array is implemented on several chips. Their number depends on the size of the array and number of processing elements per chip. The chips are integrated on a circuit board of a limited size. In many commercial and military systems these sizes are standarized. It is desirable to include the entire array and its memory on a single board (see the discussion of connector limitation that follows). Thus, the board-area limitation indirectly imposes a constraint onto the complexity of the processing element and directly imposes a constraint onto the size of array memory.

Some configurations of interconnections of the processor array may lead to large board area. For example, to implement both simple and Illiac IV wraparounds, which can be switched on demand, multiplexer chips have to be added on the boundaries of the array. These multiplexer circuits cannot be included on the processor chips because of extra connection pins required. The addition of the east-west access from the array to the memory is also costly. Here not only do the multiplexer chips have to be appended, but also the number of array memory chips may have to be increased to compensate for loss of memory locations due to the doubling of the number of memory ports.

Our architectural model is based on assumption of small local memory and very fast communication within the processor array and between the array and the memory. This fast communication translates into a large number of physical connections. Therefore, the limitation on number of connections on chip and on board rivals the area limitation in the impact on architectural realization. The mesh with wraparounds is characterized by a very large bisection width; thus, one needs to avoid partitioning the array and the memory into several boards, unless a very large number of connections is available (not the case in the present-day packaging technology). In case of an assignment of processing elements to a chip, it translates into only a few processors per chip. A small saving in the number of pins per chip can be obtained by reducing the number of physical connections per processing element from four to three [2]. This can be done so that logical connections to four nearest neighbors are still realizable, except for concurrent transfer in east-west and north-south directions. The saving for single processor per chip is 25%, for four processors 12.5% and for eight processors only 8.3%.

The connection limitation does not have to constrain the broadcasting along the columns proposed for some of the image-processing algorithms. This can be implemented using existing physical connections at some cost in the speed. The broadcast through the I/O ports encounters large capacitive load and takes several cycles.

The implementations, which fit well into the area and connection limitations, may still not be realizable because of the power or volume constraints. Some of the packaging systems such as standard electronic module-E (SEM-E) impose stringent power constraints, which may bottleneck hardware implementations. To overcome volume constraints it may be necessary to resort to advanced packaging techniques such as chip-on-board or three-dimensional electronics [3].

### 3.3 Software

A design of an application-specific coprocessor should guarantee not only good performance for the target applications and low-cost hardware implementation, but should be amenable also to efficient compilation of a high-level language code. It means that the architecture should avoid such features, which make efficient code generation by a compiler very difficult to accomplish. Split memory banks are good example of such a feature. Our modified model calls for multiported local and array memory, which can be easily implemented using multiple banks with fewer ports. This solution leads to smaller chip and board area, but complicates the compilation, because the compiler must allocate data to the appropriate bank in order to produce efficient code. The same applies to saving connections by reducing throughput in one of the directions of the data flow in the processor array, for instance east-west. Here, the compiler has to structure the flow so that the important data communication is done in the north south direction. There are many other examples of designs, especially in the data path of the processing units, which may lead to problems with efficient compilation. In some cases this efficiency can be accomplished at a cost of significantly complicating the compiler; in other cases, it may not be attainable at all.

# 4 System Prototype

This section contains a brief description of the implementation of our basic model, which is a coprocessor in a system of real-time control of redundant robot arm [9]. The host is a Sun 3 workstation and the coprocessor is connected to it via VME bus, on which it functions as a slave. The host views the coprocessor as a part of its memory space. The host-coprocessor system operates in two modes: halt mode and run mode. The halt mode is an idle mode of the coprocessor. It is used to load data and programs into the coprocessor's memories and to unload the results. This may take place before and after program execution or during temporary interruptions in the execution. In the run mode the coprocessor is under control of its own program.

The processor array is a $16 \times 16$ array of custom processors connected to its four nearest neighbors. The top and bottom rows of the array are connected to the data memory, and wraparound connections are provided between the boundary columns of the processors. The array is controlled by instructions of the coprocessor's program. The host does not have any direct control over the operation of the array. The array is divided into two parts. The boundary part consists of the processors in the leftmost column of the array. The remaining processors constitute the internal part. The two parts receive separate operation codes from two different fields of the program instruction. Thus, two sequences of instructions are executed concurrently by the array, one by the internal processors and the other one by the boundary processors. Depending on an application, these sequences may be identical or different. The processors in each part of the array process data in unison.

Not all of the processors have to be active in any given cycle. The processors are enabled by signals from the mask field of the machine instruction. There are two masking modes used: row-column masking and diagonal masking. In the first mode, the processors lying on the intersection of selected rows and columns of the processor array are activated, and in the second mode, selected diagonals are activated. Note that the variety of masking patterns that can be generated in this arrangement is limited. Nevertheless, computer simulations of a large number of robotics algorithms have shown it to be sufficient.

All the processors of the array are identical. They have four bidirectional I/O ports connecting them to the neighboring processors. The processors contain 24 registers of local memory and seven functional units: two adders, two multipliers, a sorter, a normalizer and a divider Fig. 4. The functional units are 32 bit, fixed-point parallel-serial devices. Two buses interconnect the registers and the functional units. Of the 24 random-access registers, eight can be accessed from both buses, eight from bus A, and eight from bus B. All the functional units are accessible from both buses, so that two operands can be loaded concurrently. The outputs of the functional units are accessible from one of the buses, and for some of the units 1's complements of the outputs are accessible from the other bus.

There is no control logic in the processing units. The functional units are hard-wired and their processing is initiated by a signal coming from the global controller. Several processing units can compute concurrently, although only one can receive its operands in a single cycle. This is possible because the computation in the multipliers

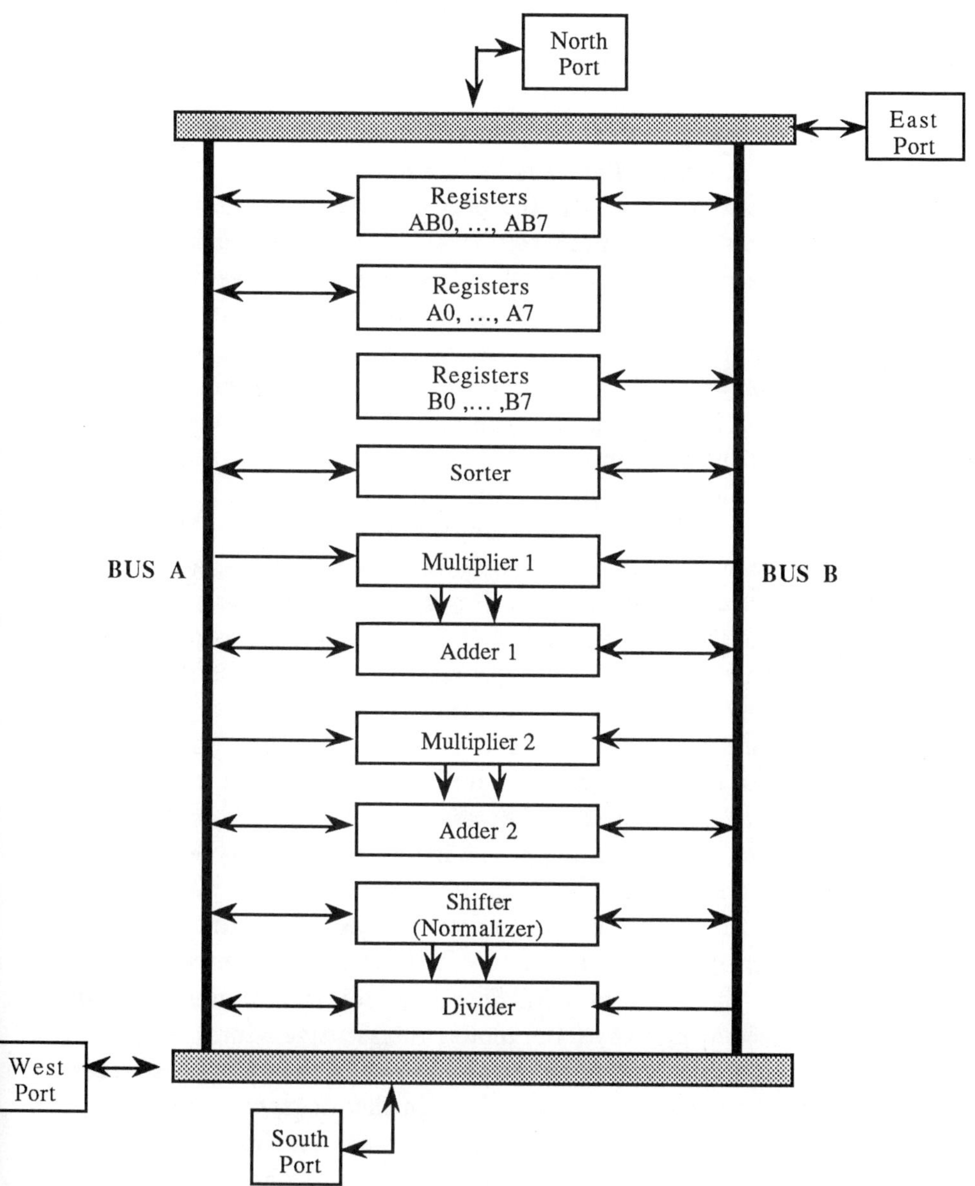


**Figure 4: Processing element.**

and the divider requires several cycles to complete, during which some other operations may also take place.

The data memory subsystem consists of a dual-ported data memory, two address counters (one for each port), and two address FIFOs (one for each port). The data memory is accessed by the host and by the processor array. The top port of the data memory is used by both the host and the processor array. The bottom port is accessed only by the processor array. The processor array uses the top port for output of data from the array into the memory and the bottom port for input from the memory into the array. The addresses for the top and bottom memory ports are located in two address counters. The counter for the top port contains the write addresses and the counter for the bottom port the read addresses. When a new data queue is to be read or written, the address of its head is loaded into the read or write counter from the read or write address FIFO. Consecutive items of the queue are accessed using addresses generated in the counters by incrementing or decrementing, depending on whether the queue is stored in ascending or descending memory locations.

The controller consists of a program memory, an instruction register, a program counter, a program FIFO, and a clock subsystem. The memory has separate input and output paths. The program memory and the program FIFO are loaded by the host in the HALT mode. In the RUN mode, the access to the memory is controlled by the program. In each cycle, a new instruction word is fetched from the memory and loaded into the instruction register. The memory address for the instruction comes from the program counter. To start the program execution, the host loads the starting address of the program from the program FIFO into the program counter, and puts the coprocessor into the RUN mode. Consecutive addresses are generated under the program control. Typically they will be obtained by incrementing the previous address in the program counter, unless a jump in the program flow is encountered. In this case, the new address is loaded into the program counter from the program FIFO. All the jumps are preprogrammed; that is, they do not depend on the input data.

The clock system of the coprocessor is independent of the host.

There are three types of clocks used in the coprocessor: system clock, multiplier clock, and divider clock. The system clock is in operation all the time in the power-on state of the coprocessor. It is used for all clocked operations of the coprocessor except for the operations of multiplication and division performed in the processors. The multiplier and divider clocks are controlled by the program and remain turned off most of the time. The multiplier clock is turned on by the multiplication instruction in the program. The clock produces 17 cycles of pulses and stops. This is the number of cycles necessary to perform the operation of multiplication. The divider clock is, similarly, turned on by the division instruction and executes 30 cycles of pulses, necessary for completion of division.

The coprocessor was implemented on five triple-hight VME boards (four for the processor array and one for the array memory) and three double-height VME boards (for the controller and the host interface), as in Fig. 5. The processing elements were implemented in $3\mu$ NMOS–one per chip.

### Acknowledgments

This research was supported in part by the National Science Foundation under grant MIP-8714680. The architecture, algorithms, and hardware prototype described in this document were developed by a team of researchers from Hughes Aircraft, University of Pennsylvania, and University of Southern California. I would like to acknowledge in particular the contributions of Lap Wai Chow, Miriam Hartholz, Tom Ireland, Prasanna Kumar, Charles Martin, George Miel, Greg Nash, James Radigan, David Schwartz, and Dale Sipma.

## Bibliography

[1] I. Barth, and T. Baunl, F. Sembach, Parallaxis User Manual, Computer Science Report, University of Stuttgart, March 1990.

[2] C. Fiduccia, *Pin-efficient interconnection networks*, private communication.

Figure 5: Prototype system for robotics.

[3] M. J. Little, R. D. Etchells, J. Grinberg, S. P. Laub, J. G. Nash, and M. W. Yung, *The 3-D computer*, presented at International Conference on Wafer Scale Integration, San Francisco, Jan. 1989, pp. 55-64.

[4] J. G. Nash and S. Hansen, *Modified Faddeeva algorithm for concurrent execution of linear algebraic operations*, IEEE Transactions on Computers, vol. 37, p. 129, 1988.

[5] V. K. Prasanna Kumar, *Mapping image processing algorithms and radar processing algorithms onto Hughes systolic/cellular processor*, Hughes Research Laboratories, 1990.

[6] V. K. Prasanna Kumar, and K. Wojtek Przytula, *Algorithmic Mapping of Neural Networks Models onto Parallel SIMD Machines*, Proceedings of International Conference on Application-Specific Array Processors, 1990, pp. 259-271.

[7] K. Wojtek Przytula, *Systolic/cellular system*, Hughes Research Laboratories, 1989.

[8] K. Wojtek Przytula, and J. G. Nash, *Parallel implementation of synthetic aperture radar algorithms*, Journal of VLSI Signal Processing, vol. 1, no. 1, 1989, pp. 45-56.

[9] K. Wojtek Przytula, and J. G. Nash, *A special purpose coprocessor for signal-processing*, Proceedings of the 21st Asilomar Conference on Signals, Systems and Computers, 1987, pp. 736-740.

[10] K. Wojtek Przytula, J. G. Nash, and S. Hansen, *Fast Fourier algorithm for two-dimensional array of processors*, Proceedings of SPIE 826, 1987, pp. 186-198.

[11] D. Schwartz, and J. Radigan Parahacsis, Hughes Research Laboratories, 1990.

# VisTA–An Image Understanding Architecture

M. H. SUNWOO
*Motorola Inc.*
*Digital Signal Processor Operations*
*Austin, Texas*

and

J. K. AGGARWAL
*Computer and Vision Research Center*
*College of Engineering*
*The University of Texas at Austin*
*Austin, Texas*

## 1 Introduction

Computation in a computer vision system may be divided into a three-level hierarchy [22,40]: low-, intermediate-, and high-level tasks. The architectures developed for one level, in general, are unsuitable for other levels of vision tasks. In addition, existing parallel architectures suffer from several disadvantages. Examples of such disadvantages include the communication overhead between processing elements (PEs), memory contentions in a shared memory, and inefficient data input and output (I/O) schemes.

To alleviate these disadvantages, to meet the heterogeneous computational characteristics in vision tasks, and finally, to improve performance, three new parallel architectures are proposed for the three levels of computer vision tasks: (1) VisTA/1: a new massively parallel *sliding memory plane array processor* (SliM), a fine-grained SIMD architecture, is proposed for low level vision to min-

Parallel Architectures and
Algorithms for
Image Understanding




ISBN 0-12-564040-4

imize the inter-processing element (inter-PE) communication overhead; (2) VisTA/2: a *flexibly (tightly/loosely) coupled multiprocessor* (FCM), a medium-grained MIMD architecture, is proposed for intermediate-level vision to alleviate the communication overhead in loosely coupled multiprocessors and memory contentions in tightly coupled multiprocessors; and (3) VisTA/3: a *flexibly coupled hypercube multiprocessor* (FCHM), a coarse-grained MIMD architecture, is proposed for high-level vision to reduce the disadvantages of existing hypercube multiprocessors. Finally, these three architectures are pipelined into VisTA(An Integrated Vision Tri-Architecture System) for a general-purpose computer vision system.

Computer vision tasks are divided into a three-level hierarchy. Low-level vision contains the operations applied to each pixel and to neighboring pixels, such as filtering, edge detection, convolution, etc. At this level, data locality is fully guaranteed and algorithms are usually simple. Intermediate-level vision consists of pixel grouping, region splitting, feature extraction, region labeling, segmentation, etc. At this level, data locality is usually guaranteed and algorithms are more complex. High-level vision tasks include image understanding, feature analysis, reasoning, symbolic processing, etc. At this final level, data locality is not guaranteed and algorithms are complex and nondeterministic.

A large number of parallel computer vision architectures have been proposed [24,46]. Most research in this field so far has been devoted to developing one architecture that covers all levels of vision tasks. However, such an approach has several drawbacks. SIMD mesh-connected architectures are suitable for low-level vision, but may be unsuitable for intermediate-level and high-level vision tasks [10]. Conversely, medium-grained or coarse-grained MIMD architectures are inappropriate for low-level vision. Tanimoto [40] properly points out the general problem of the missing architectural layer in computer vision, that is, the intermediate level. The gap between low and high levels must be filled by using an architecture for the intermediate level [40].

We briefly survey the existing parallel architectures for computer vision in each class, such as mesh-connected SIMD architectures, multiprocessors, and multilayer architectures, and discuss their features.

Most operations needed in low-level vision tasks are window-type operations that transform the value of each pixel into a new value, calculated from itself and the neighboring pixels. Such operations can be accomplished with a high degree of concurrency by using mesh-connected architectures well-suited to the structure of image data [15, 42]. Since Unger first proposed a computer based on a mesh topology for spatial problems [42], many mesh-connected architectures have been proposed [13, 15, 24]. Examples of such architectures include ILLIAC IV [2], MPP [3], the CLIP series [9, 14], DAP [27], GAPP [7], BAP [28], CM I with a hypercube topology [16], CAAPP [44], Polymorphic-Torus [23], Mesh with reconfigurable buses [26], etc.

However, these architectures have disadvantages. During processing, a great deal of local communication occurs between neighboring PEs. This inter-PE communication overhead is a considerable problem on existing mesh-connected array processors [11,15,19]. Moreover, when the size of a window operator is larger than $3 \times 3$, the overhead may seriously degrade the performance [15].

To reduce the inter-PE communication overhead, LIPP was proposed [11]. However, the scheme has several drawbacks. It requires complex gate logic circuits and complicated controls for multiplexing. Moreover, it needs a special purpose memory and processor [13]. Data from a memory module may be routed over several multiplexer levels inside one, two, or three different processors before reaching the final destination [11]. Thus, the propagation delay may be considerable. In addition, if the size of a window is larger than $3 \times 3$, or if other types of windows (circular, diamond, rectangular, etc.) used in low-level vision [21] are employed, the performance may degrade.

Among the aforementioned architectures, most of them do not include an I/O buffering capability. Thus, the I/O overhead may degrade the performance. In contrast, SliM provides an I/O buffering capability. Moreover, some architectures, such as CLIP4, CLIP5, CLIP6, CLIP7, BAP, and NTT, have six or eight communication links per PE instead of four. In contrast, on SliM, four communication links for each PE (north, east, west, and south) are sufficient instead of eight, thus simplifying the connectivity.

Many parallel architectures based on a multiprocessor configuration have been proposed for all levels of vision tasks. Examples of such architectures are ZMOB [18], PUMPS [4], PICAP II [6], VS [8], HBA [43], NETRA [5], etc. Besides these special-purpose multiprocessors, general-purpose multiprocessors (such as iPSC, Ncube, etc.) have also been used for computer vision [20,38]. However, these architectures may be unsuitable for low-level vision because of a relatively low degree of concurrency.

In general, there are two hardware mechanisms for data sharing among PEs in existing multiprocessors. The first is the shared-memory scheme in tightly coupled multiprocessors, and the second is the message-passing scheme in loosely coupled multiprocessors (multicomputers). PUMPS, PICAP II, etc., are examples of tightly coupled multiprocessors, and Cosmic Cube [30], iPSC, Ncube, etc. are examples of loosely coupled multiprocessors.

However, both types of multiprocessors have drawbacks. Loosely coupled multiprocessors have a communication overhead disadvantage due to message passing, whereas tightly coupled multiprocessors have a shared-memory contention problem. Another important drawback that is usually neglected is the data I/O overhead. Many papers have often assumed that the data to be processed are already in the processing structures. In other words, they ignore the time for the data I/O. However, it is not negligible, because in some cases, the I/O time may take longer than the computation time on existing multiprocessors.

There are several parallel architectures that consist of multiple layers in keeping with the three-level decomposition of computer vision tasks. Examples of such architectures are pyramidal architectures [39,41], such as PAPIA, GAM pyramid, a prototype pyramid machine, etc., which can be found in [22], and heterogeneous multilayer architectures, such as the UMass IUA [22,44].

In pyramidal architectures, in general, all PEs in all layers are identical, with each layer treated as an SIMD machine (that is, a homogeneous multilayer). These homogeneous multilayer architectures may not meet the heterogeneous computational characteristics of computer vision and are therefore inappropriate for general classes of vision applications [22,44]. Moreover, the large number of communication links between layers is also a disadvantage.

The UMass IUA [22,44] is a heterogeneous multilayer architecture. This architecture uses a content addressable array parallel processor (CAAPP) for low-level vision. However, associative processing may be inappropriate for low-level vision tasks because low-level vision processing is mainly numerical rather than symbolic. An intermediate communication associative processor (ICAP) and a symbolic processing array (SPA) are used for intermediate-level and high-level vision, respectively, in the UMass IUA. Tightly coupled shared memory modules and communication links are used between layers. However, memory contentions in shared memories may degrade the performance.

To alleviate the disadvantages of the existing parallel architectures, to meet the three levels of vision tasks, and to improve the performance, three architectures are proposed for the three levels of vision tasks. Then, these architectures can be pipelined into VisTA for a general-purpose computer vision system [35, 37]. VisTA was developed to exploit spatial parallelism and temporal parallelism within one architecture and through the whole pipelined architecture. VisTA does not require a large number of communication links between layers in multilayer architectures. In addition, VisTA eliminates memory contentions, since it does not have a shared memory between layers. The performance of each of the proposed architectures is evaluated through simulations and analytical models. Each architecture shows improvements in each class.

The remainder of this chapter is organized as follows. Section 2 introduces SliM and presents the overall scheme and details of one PE. The section then addresses the various communication schemes and the three autonomies. It also presents the performance evaluation for low-level vision tasks. Section 3 introduces FCM for intermediate-level computer vision and presents the details of the new architecture. For the performance evaluation, FCM is simulated on the Intel Personal SuperComputer/1 (iPSC/1). Section 4 introduces FCHM for high-level vision. FCHM is also simulated on iPSC/1. Section 5 addresses how to integrate the three architectures into a composite, general-purpose computer vision system and discusses the comparisons between VisTA and other integrated architectures. Finally, Section 6 summarizes the research effort and contains concluding remarks.

# 2 VisTA/1: A Sliding Memory Plane Array Processor for Low-Level Vision

This section presents a new mesh-connected array processor, called a sliding memory plane (SliM) array processor, for low-level computer vision tasks [33,34]. SliM alleviates several disadvantages of existing mesh-connected architectures, such as (1) the communication overhead between PEs; (2) the data I/O overhead; and (3) complicated interconnections. SliM is a fine-grained SIMD architecture operated in a unique scheme: bit-serial communication and bit-parallel computation.

In this architecture, the inter-PE communication can occur without interrupting PEs. In addition, two I/O planes provide a buffering capability. Thus, the communication, I/O, and computation occur simultaneously. The communication and I/O overheads can be overlapped with the computation and are greatly diminished. SliM provides various types of communication: local communication, nonlocal communication, and broadcast. Each PE can operate separately based on three autonomies: operation autonomy, addressing autonomy, and connection autonomy. SliM shows powerful applicability with these configurations. The performance of SliM shows improvements [33–36], illustrated with several examples of low-level computer vision tasks.

## 2.1 The Architecture of SliM

This section describes the architecture of SliM and compares its features with those of existing mesh-connected architectures. The section presents the overall scheme and structure of a PE, addresses the design choice between bit-serial and bit-parallel, and then discusses

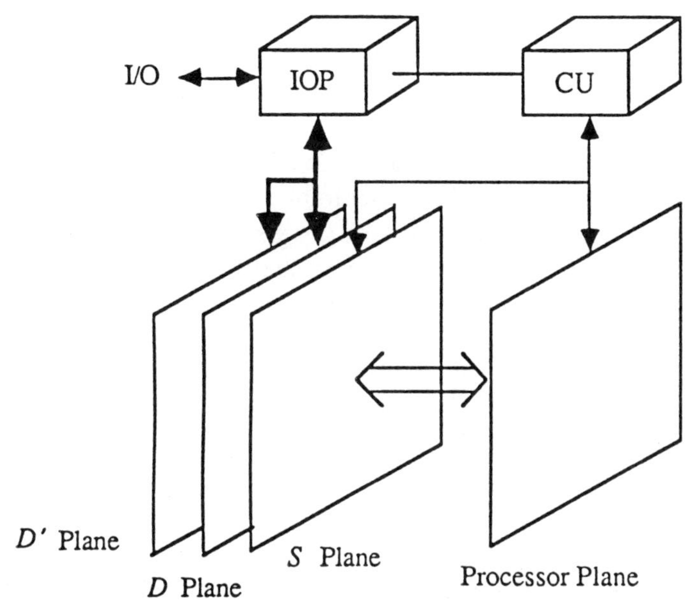


Figure 1: The sliding memory plane (SliM) array processor.

connectivity, communication, and autonomy issues.

## The Overall System

Figure 1 shows the logical diagram of SliM. The processor plane consists of $N \times N$ processors. Thus, the total number of PEs is $N^2$. The sliding memory plane $S$ consists of $N \times N$ shift registers connected by a wraparound mesh topology (torus). Thus, the $S$ plane, instead of the processor plane, forms a mesh topology. The I/O planes, $D$ and $D'$, consist of $N \times N$ shift registers connected to left and right neighbors.

$D$ and $D'$ are used exclusively for the data I/O, whereas $S$ is used for the inter-PE communication without interrupting PEs. The processors can process the data in $S$. The input and output processor (IOP) can load the input data in a row-parallel (or column-parallel) manner into $D$ or $D'$. Of course, if $D$ or $D'$ uses a sensory array, an image-parallel I/O can be achieved. After being loaded, the data in $D$ or $D'$ are shifted into $S$ in a one-unit cycle time (parallel shift).

The control unit (CU) shown in Fig. 1 consists of two subunits: the processor control subunit and the sliding memory plane control subunit. The processor control subunit broadcasts the instruction set to processors from the subunit's program memory, while the sliding memory plane control subunit mediates the data movement in the $S$ plane simultaneously. IOP controls the data I/O in the $D$ and $D'$ planes. Since each control unit can control separately, the computation, communication, and I/O occur simultaneously.

## A Processing Element

A PE, shown in Fig. 2, consists of an ALU, registers, multiplexers (MUXs), a demultiplexer (DMUX), and a $4 \times 2$ switching element (SW). The shift register $s$ is an element of the sliding memory plane $S$ shown in Fig. 1. Similarly, $d$ and $d'$ are elements of the I/O planes $D$ and $D'$. $s$ is connected to four neighboring registers via the switching element SW and a multiplexer. Thus, a PE is also connected to its four neighboring PEs via the register $s$. $d$ and $d'$ are connected only to their left and right neighboring registers.

While ALU processes the pixel in $s$ from $d$, a neighboring pixel can be shifted into $s$, and the I/O operation can occur through the $d'$ register. Again, while ALU processes the new pixel shifted into $s$, another neighboring pixel can be shifted into $s$, and the I/O operation can occur through $d'$. These operations can be executed by all PEs simultaneously. Each operation can be controlled separately by the processor control subunit, the sliding memory plane control subunit, or IOP. Thus, the inter-PE communication and I/O overheads can be overlapped with the computation, which significantly reduces the overheads.

All pixels are moved into the neighboring register cells simultaneously and in the same direction. Upon completing this sliding operation, the content in $s$ is transferred into a latch $l$ to avoid the data in $s$ conflicting with the newly incoming data from a neighbor.

The other major components of a PE consist of a shift register

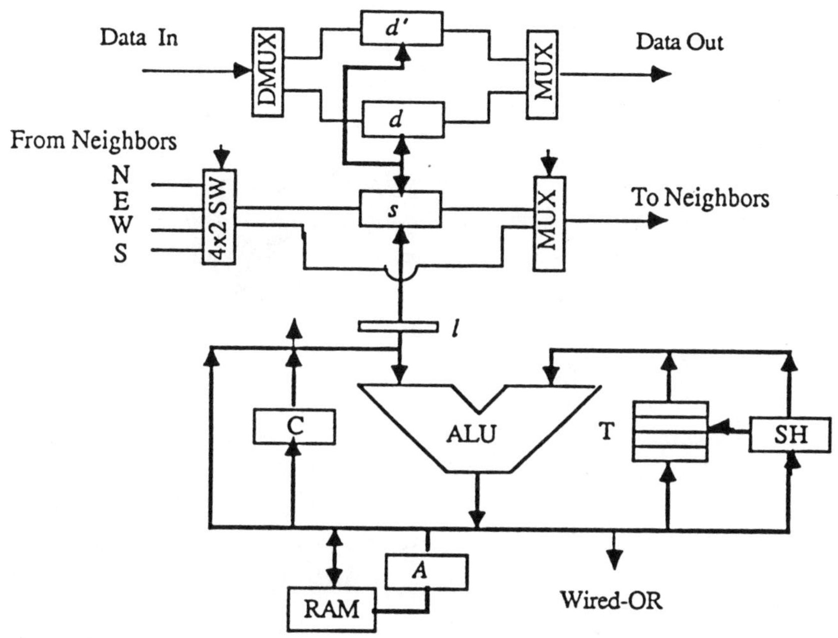


Figure 2: A processing element.

(SH), a condition register ($C$), an address register ($A$) for local addressing, four general registers ($T$'s), and a small amount of memory (RAM) that is located either inside or outside of a PE and is used for local data storage. ALU provides Boolean functions as well as arithmetic functions. SH performs arithmetic and logic shifts and is valuable for multiplication, division, and floating-point calculations. $C$ provides conditional operations and the control of SW and MUX for neighboring communication. $T$ is used for storing intermediate results. $s$ stores the data transferred from neighboring PEs.

For direct inter-PE communication, ALU stores the data to be transferred into $s$. During this communication, ALU can perform other operations. For fast shifting, sliding, and I/O operations, two different clock rates are used, one for normal operations and the other for shifting, sliding, and I/O operations. SliM has a bidirectional communication bus between the processor control subunit and the

PEs. Thus, every PE can communicate with the processor control subunit.

## Design Choice: Bit-Serial versus Bit-Parallel

Debate on bit-serial versus bit-parallel still continues [3, 14], each having advantages and disadvantages. Bit-serial gives cost-effectiveness and compactness, whereas bit-parallel gives high speed and easy programmability. The mesh-connected architectures proposed so far are based either on bit-serial communication and computation, such as MPP, CLIP, DAP, GAPP, CAAPP, etc., or on bit-parallel communication and computation, such as ILLIAC IV, CLIP6, CLIP7, etc.

Most operations in low-level computer vision are performed on gray-level rather than on binary data [14]. Hence, bit-parallel is better suited to low-level vision, and the speed of bit-parallel is faster than that of bit-serial [14]. Moreover, remarkable progress in VLSI technology makes it possible to develop much more compact systems [17].

SliM architecture can be implemented in either a bit-serial or bit-parallel manner. No matter which manner is used, the communication overhead overlaps with the computation. In practice, communication links between PEs occupy a large portion of the VLSI area and contribute to an increase in the number of pins in a VLSI chip. To reduce the VLSI area and the number of pins, we propose a unique scheme : bit-serial communication and bit-parallel computation-based on two different clock rates. The communication link between PEs in SliM is one-bit wide, so that more area of the VLSI can be saved and the number of pins can be reduced. Based on the current VLSI technology [17], it would be possible to build a number of the PEs of SliM on one VLSI chip.

In Fig. 2, the thick lines represent bit-parallel data paths while the thin lines represent bit-serial data paths. Each register cell contains one pixel. The 8-bit ALU operates in bit-parallel. Thus, SliM operates in bit-serial communication and bit-parallel computation.

## 2.2 Connectivities, Communication, and Autonomies

Figure 2 shows the two paths between SW and MUX for local communication. One path is via the *s* register; the other is direct. Using the two paths can result in three different connection modes : (1) *receiving mode* - the pixel received from a neighbor is stored in *s*; (2) *passing mode* - the pixel received from a neighbor is passed to another neighboring PE without storing; and (3) *receiving – passing mode* - the pixel received from a neighbor is stored in *s*, and this pixel or another pixel is passed to one of its neighbors.

Even though three connection modes are provided, only the receiving mode is necessary for the sliding operation. The other two connection modes are used for the different functions described below but not for the sliding operations. These connection modes are determined by the status of the condition register $C$ in each PE. The processor control subunit can globally change the status of $C$ in every PE and thus realize centralized control. Since each PE can control connectivity independently according to the status of $C$, distributed control is also achieved.

Three connection modes can realize the *virtual* communication links for two diagonal neighboring PEs. For example, the center PE sets the passing mode for its east neighbor, and its south PE sets the receiving mode for the center neighbor for the communication from east to south. Similarly, other virtual diagonal links can be realized. However, two neighboring PEs in the same row (or column) cannot send data to their diagonal PEs simultaneously because of communication link conflicts. These virtual links are especially advantageous for the computation along the border pixels of regions; such computation is commonly used for low-level vision tasks [45]. Even with four communication links, eight communication connectivities (four physical and four virtual connectivities) can be achieved by enhancing the internal structure.

Three different communication schemes are provided: local communication between nearest neighbors; non-local communication between non-nearest neighbors; and broadcast (row-broadcast, column-broadcast, and broadcast). See [34,36] for more details.

Maresca *et al.* [24] define three different autonomies of SIMD mesh-connected array processors: operation autonomy, addressing autonomy, and connection autonomy. With these autonomies, the SIMD architectures show great computational powers [14,24]. CLIP7A [14] introduces operation and addressing autonomies. Connection autonomy is presented in [23,26,44].

In contrast, SliM has three autonomies: (1) operation autonomy : the condition register $C$ provides operation autonomy. Each PE can execute different operations based on the status of $C$. Conditional operations can be efficiently accomplished by using the condition register; (2) addressing autonomy : The address register $A$ provides the local memory address. One bit in $C$ indicates whether the next address is in the register $A$ or in the broadcast instruction; and (3) connection autonomy : Each PE can control connection modes and communication schemes. SliM, with flexible connection modes and various communication schemes, achieves connection autonomy. More details can be found in [34,36].

## 2.3 Algorithm Complexities and Performance Evaluation on SliM

SliM is well-suited to low-level computer vision tasks where excessive data exchanges occur between neighbors, since it performs window-type operations with little or no communication overhead. This section discusses algorithm complexity, including the computation complexity and the communication complexity for low-level vision. The section then briefly presents the expected times of low-level vision tasks based on conservative assumptions on the PEs of SliM.

In many papers, algorithm complexity on mesh-connected architectures is based on the overall time complexity including the computation and communication complexities [12]. Fang et al. [12] describe the communication complexity of a generalized 2D convolution on array processors. The paper deals separately with the communication complexity and the computation complexity. A general 2D convolution algorithm on existing mesh-connected architectures requires an $O(W^2)$ communication time complexity [12], where $W$ is the size of a window operator. In contrast, the algorithm on SliM has a zero communication complexity because the inter-PE communication overhead can be entirely overlapped. Similarly, many parallel vision algorithms have either a zero or an $O(1)$ communication complexity on SliM.

The performance evaluation of SliM is based on the following conservative assumptions. First, the memory access time (1 byte) is 100 ns and is defined as a nominal instruction cycle time. Only one memory access without any operation can be executed in one cycle. Two operations at most can be merged into one instruction if no conflict exists, and can be executed within one cycle. Second, eight-bit passing to a neighboring PE is completed within one cycle time. Third, within one cycle the number of one-bit shifts is up to eight. Fourth, most of the operations are assumed to be executed within a cycle except for operations such as multiplication and division.

The method for the performance evaluation is as follows. The details of the relatively low-level algorithms (register transfer level) are made. Then, the instructions required for these algorithms are counted. The analytical model of SliM is described in [33,34,36]. Since sliding, (in other words, the inter-PE communication) can occur during the computation, the sliding operation and computing operation statements are put on the same line. In the following description of the algorithm, wherever more than one statement on the same line occurs, these statements can be considered to overlap.

### A Convolution Algorithm with a Zero Communication Complexity

Assume that window coefficients are in the broadcast instructions. Figure 3 shows the general algorithm, in which $s$ represents a shift register on the sliding memory plane $S$, and $T$ is a set of registers in a PE. As Fig. 3 shows, $W^2$ multiplications and $2(W^2 - 1)$ additions must be required, and the inter-PE communication entirely overlaps. Thus, the algorithm requires an $O(W^2)$ computation complexity; however, the algorithm requires a zero communication complexity.

If the window size is $3 \times 3$ and the number of bits per pixel is eight, the algorithm requires $9^*n_m + 16$ cycles, where $n_m$ is the number of

```
T ← l * w_00;    s ← a neighboring pixel;     /* Sliding */
for i ← 1 until W - 1 do
    for j ← 0 until W - 1 do
        T ← T + l * w_ij; s ← a neighboring pixel;    /* Sliding */
```

Figure 3: The parallel convolution algorithm on SliM.

cycles for two eight-bit integer multiplications. Since the register set $T$ is used instead of the memory, $n_m$ is assumed to be 8. Then, 88 cycles are required. The total estimated time is 8.8 $\mu$sec because the instruction cycle time is assumed to be 100 ns.

Some algorithms cannot be implemented without the communication overhead. The Sobel operator is one example. When the sliding operation passes the center, north, and south coefficients of the Sobel operator (that is, zero window coefficients), computation is not required. Thus, the communication overhead cannot entirely overlap. Hence, this algorithm has an $O(1)$ communication complexity.

The new parallel algorithms with a zero or an $O(1)$ communication complexity are developed in [34,36]. The performance evaluation of SliM for the DARPA image understanding benchmarks [45] shows improvements [34–36]. The performance of SliM is improved for several reasons. First, the inter-PE communication and the the data I/O overheads can overlap with the computation. Second, the bit-parallel processing is faster than the bit-serial processing. Third, instead of using memory, the $S$ plane, consisting of shift registers, is used for storing all pixels that can be transferred to neighbors and directly accessed by ALU. In addition, a set of registers ($T$) can be effectively used for storing intermediate results. Thus, the overhead for the memory access can be reduced.

# 3 VisTA/2: A Flexibly Coupled Multiprocessor for Intermediate-Level Vision

Existing multiprocessors have several disadvantages, such as the communication overhead in loosely coupled multiprocessors, memory contentions in tightly coupled multiprocessors, and the data I/O overhead in both types of multiprocessors. To alleviate these disadvantages and to improve performance, the flexibly (tightly/loosely) coupled multiprocessor (FCM) with a variable space memory scheme, which can merge a set of memory modules by a dynamically partitionable bus, is proposed for intermediate-level vision. Some features of FCM proposed in this chapter have several similarities to those of other architectures. [31,32,36] discuss the similarities and differences in detail. Two models of FCM are described next.

## 3.1 The FCM Model I

### The Architecture of FCM I

Figure 4 shows the flexibly (tightly/loosely) coupled multiprocessor Model I (FCM I). FCM I consists of $N$ PEs ($PE_i$), $N$ memory modules ($M_i$), a control unit (CU), and a high-speed input and output processor (IOP), where $0 \leq i \leq N-1$. $PE_i$ is connected to CU through the communication bus and to $M_i$ through the dynamically partitionable address and data (A/D) bus, using the partitionable arbiter described in [31,32,36]. $PE_i$ contains its own local memory for program and intermediate results. $M_i$ is used only for data.

A set of switches, $S_i$, which can connect and disconnect the A/D bus, is located between two memory modules, $M_i$ and $M_{i+1}$. All switches in $S_i$ are operated together (closed or opened together). CU can handle each switch set $S_i$ independently. IOP is directly connected to this memory and to CU.

Any two successive memory modules ($M_i$, $M_{i+1}$) can form one *contiguous addressable* memory module by closing $S_i$, in which case the two processing elements, $PE_i$ and $PE_{i+1}$ can access the module through the arbiter one at a time. Moreover, a set of consecutive memory modules can form one contiguous addressable memory module by closing all switch sets between these modules.

When all switch sets are closed, all memory modules become one contiguous addressable memory module, that is, one shared memory. Thus, any PE or IOP using the DMA scheme can access all memory modules. In this case, FCM I is referred to as a *fully tightly* coupled multiprocessor. With all switch sets closed, if more than one PE tries to access the memory simultaneously, memory contentions occur. To reduce memory contentions, CU opens switch sets. If all switch sets are opened, then any PE ($PE_i$) can access its corresponding module ($M_i$) without any memory contention. Accordingly, when all switch sets are open, the variable space memory scheme becomes $N$ memory modules, and no more shared memory exists. Therefore, each PE can access only its own memory module. Then, FCM I is referred to as a *fully loosely* coupled multiprocessor because no more shared memory exists.

When some switch sets are closed and the other sets are open, the network is split into a set of disjoint partitions. If all sets except $S_i$ are open, then $PE_i$ and $PE_{i+1}$ are referred to as *partially tightly* coupled, and the other PEs are referred to as *partially loosely* coupled. The variable space memory becomes $N-1$ disjoint memory modules, and the network forms $N-1$ partitions. To prevent memory contentions in tightly coupled partitions, a partitionable arbiter within the A/D bus is used between PEs and memory modules [31,32,36].

When all switch setsd except $S_i$ are closed, the variable space memory becomes two disjoint memory modules, and the network forms two partitions. Each partition, $PE_j$, $0 \leq j \leq i$, and $PE_k$, $i+1 \leq k \leq N-1$, is partially tightly coupled. The partitions are partially loosely coupled with respect to each other. Thus, FCM I is called a *flexibly (tightly/loosely)* coupled multiprocessor. The total number of different architectural configurations is $2^{N-1}$.

### Communication

There are three different types of communication: CU-to-PE communication (bidirectional); PE-to-PE communication; and broadcast from CU or from any PE. CU-to-PE communication can be

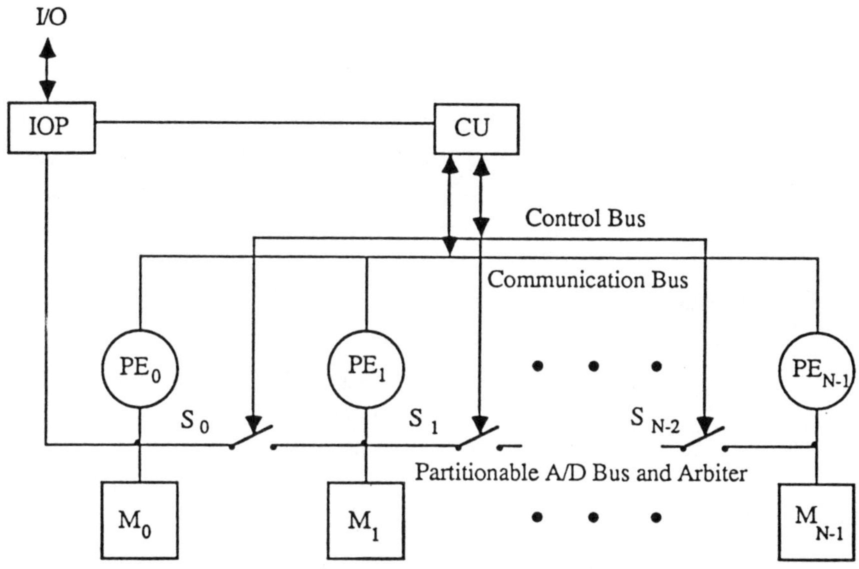


**Figure 4: The flexibly coupled multiprocessor model I (FCM I).**

**achieved via the communication bus. PE-to-PE communication can be achieved via the communication bus or the variable space memory. Broadcast from CU or from any PE can be realized by the communication bus in one cycle. For data sharing, the variable space memory can be used in tightly coupled partitions, and the communication bus can be used in loosely coupled partitions. Even in tightly coupled partitions, the communication bus can be used for message passing where messages are short. Thus, FCM supports both message passing and shared memory.**

**The variable space memory is advantageous for the exchange of large amounts of data whereas the communication bus is advantageous for the exchange of small amounts of data. To combine two**

sets of data in $M_i$ and $M_{i+1}$, only the switching time to close the switch set $S_i$ is needed instead of message passing.

## 3.2 The FCM Model II

FCM I does not have a buffering capability. Thus, the data I/O time still exists. To reduce the overhead, we propose another model (FCM II) described in [31,32,36]. FCM II has a buffering capability. Hence, even the data I/O time can overlap with the computation, and these times may disappear if the computation time is larger than the data I/O time. The architectural aspects of FCM II, except for its buffering capability, are the same as those of FCM I. See [31,32,36] for more details of FCM II. FCM II is useful for more general algorithms, such as pipelined algorithms, pipelined pseudoparallel algorithms [1], and tree-structured algorithms discussed in the next section.

## 3.3 Mapping Algorithms onto FCM

This section discusses examples of mapping strategies for FCM. Aggarwal and Jain [1] propose pipelined pseudoparallelism, where a serial algorithm is decomposed into a set of noninteractive, independent subtasks so that spatial parallelism can be used in each subtask level. However, in the pipelined pseudoparallel architecture, the communication overhead between stages is required. Spatial parallelism and temporal parallelism may be achieved by using multiprocessing (or array processing) and pipelining, respectively. For an integrated computer vision system, pipelined pseudoparallelism is valuable because temporal parallelism and spatial parallelism can be exploited. Many computer vision tasks, such as image understanding, pattern recognition, dynamic scene analysis, etc., can be cast as pipelined pseudoparallel algorithms.

Pipelined pseudoparallel algorithms can be mapped conveniently onto FCM II. FCM II can be partitioned into a set of various-size MIMD machines (or SISD, single instruction stream–single data stream, if the size is 1) by using the partitionable A/D bus. There are two procedures to map pipelined pseudoparallel algorithms: the decomposition of a task into a set of subtasks and the assignment of these subtasks onto FCM II. Using the partitionable bus and two memory sets diminishes the communication overhead. Any composition of subtasks in pipelined pseudoparallel algorithms may be mapped onto FCM II without the communication overhead. Of course, simple pipelining can also be mapped onto FCM II without the communication overhead. Therefore, FCM II itself may be used for an integrated computer vision system. The details of the mapping strategy are in [31,32,36].

A pseudo-binary tree is a binary tree structure that can be easily embedded into a hypercube topology such that a node in the hypercube may represent more than one node in a corresponding pseudo-binary tree [20,29]. The pseudo-binary tree is an efficient topology for distributing subimages and for collecting the local results in the hypercube multiprocessors. The reason for this is that all PEs in the hypercube are used for the pseudo-binary-tree implementation, whereas at most only half of all PEs are used for a binary tree implementation. The pseudo-binary tree can be embedded not only into the hypercube topology but also into FCM. See [31,32,36] for more details.

In mapping the pseudo-binary tree onto FCM, no communication overhead (no message passing) occurs [31,32,36]. In contrast, the communication overhead for implementing the pseudo-binary tree can significantly limit the speed-up, as on the hypercube multiprocessor. In addition, no memory conflict occurs because only one PE in each partition performs the merging procedure. Instead, only switching and control times exist. Moreover, general tree topologies may also be embedded into FCM. The embedding procedure for general tree topologies into FCM is similar to that for the pseudo-binary tree. Thus, tree-structured algorithms may be implemented on FCM without the communication overhead and any memory contention.

## 3.4 Comparisons with Other Architectures

We discuss the comparisons between FCM and other architectures. The first subsection presents FCM versus iPSC/1; and the second describes FCM versus a single-bus multiprocessor with an external shared memory.

### FCM versus iPSC/1

iPSC/1 provides only message passing, whereas FCM supports message passing via the communication bus, and shared memory via the variable-space memory. The time for the data I/O and data sharing on iPSC/1 includes controller-to-PE communication and PE-to-PE communication, which significantly degrade the performance [20,31,32,38]. As $N$ increases, the communication overhead increases, and the efficiency sharply decreases.

In contrast, for the data I/O and data sharing on FCM, only marginal switching and control times are needed if the data locality is guaranteed. Therefore, the overhead for parallel processing is small. In contrast, iPSC/1 requires the communication overhead, even if the data locality is guaranteed.

### FCM versus a Single-Bus Multiprocessor with an External Common Memory

The most notable difference between FCM and a single-bus multiprocessor is the topology. FCM uses the dynamically partitionable (reconfigurable) bus, whereas the single-bus multiprocessor uses a common bus. Moreover, the variable-space memory in FCM, which is advantageous for data merging and the data I/O, is quite different from a shared memory in the single-bus multiprocessor.

The performance indices of bus-based multiprocessors are well described [25]. Since a bus has a bandwidth limit, the bus suffers from a bottleneck. However, FCM prevents the bottleneck when the switch sets are open. Then, the memory bandwidth can be increased. Of course, if a PE attempts to access an item in a nonadjacent memory module, the switch sets between the PE and the memory module are closed. Then, this group becomes a tightly coupled partition, and a memory access passes through the arbiter, as in the single-bus system. Alternatively, the communication bus can also be used between two PEs without holding the other PEs in that partition. When the data locality is guaranteed, the switch sets can be open and the memory bandwidth can be increased. As described previously, FCM supports both message passing via the communication bus and shared memory via the variable-space memory, whereas the single-bus multiprocessor provides only shared memory.

## 3.5 The Performance Evaluation of FCM

The simulations of common computer vision algorithms are undertaken on the proposed architectures and compared with the implementation of these on the hypercube machine. The advantages of the proposed models over the hypercube model for such algorithms are illustrated. Region labeling, one of the basic operations in computer vision, is chosen for the performance evaluation. A new parallel algorithm for region labeling has been proposed for hypercube multiprocessors and is described elsewhere [38]. Median filtering is used for preprocessing in many computer vision tasks. Even though median filtering is not an intermediate-level vision, it is chosen for a performance comparison.

Parallel algorithms for region labeling and median filtering are implemented on iPSC/1 and simulated on FCM by using iPSC/1. A timing analysis by actual implementation is used. In other words, all possible time components based on the computational models described in [31,32,36] are measured. See [31,32,36] for more details.

If a task is computation-bounded and its data locality is guaranteed, a linear speed-up may be expected. Even with the conservative assumptions, the switching and control times on FCM are much smaller than the computation time. Hence, bottlenecks due to CU, the communication bus, and the control bus, mainly for control but not for data sharing are minimal. Thus, FCM may have a good scalability. FCM can also be used for more general tasks. Intermediate-level vision tasks, array processing, pipelined algorithms, pipelined pseudoparallel algorithms, and tree-structured algorithms are a few examples. FCM is well-suited for tasks where the data locality is guaranteed.

# 4 VisTA/3: A Flexibly Coupled Hypercube Multiprocessor for High-Level Vision

Even though FCM can be exploited for various types of algorithms, it may have disadvantages in some applications. For example, if there is no data locality or no regular communication patterns between PEs, switch sets should be closed and FCM may not achieve a good performance. In contrast, the hypercube multiprocessor, which is a general-purpose architecture, can be used for a wider range of applications. Moreover, a hypercube is a powerful topology into which various topologies can be embedded [29]. However, it also has disadvantages: the communication overhead and the inefficient data I/O [31,32,38]. To minimize these disadvantages of FCM and the hypercube multiprocessor, the flexibly (tightly/loosely) coupled hypercube multiprocessor (FCHM), a coarse-grained MIMD architecture, is proposed for high-level vision.

For high-level vision tasks, such as image understanding and scene analysis, a variety of algorithms are used, such as parallel search algorithms, pattern matching, graph isomorphism/subisomorphism, decision-making algorithms, and network consistency maintenance. These algorithms require semantic processing involving knowledge-based inference. This type of processing is suitable for symbolic computation.

## 4.1 The Architecture of FCHM

Figure 5 shows FCHM. The architectural aspects of FCHM are similar to those of FCM. The main difference between FCHM and FCM is the interconnection network: one is a dynamically partitionable hypercube topology (FCHM), and the other is a dynamically partitionable bus topology (FCM). FCHM is a coarse-grained MIMD machine designed for symbolic processing.

In Fig. 5a, the oval represents one PE and one memory module which realize the FCHM model I (FCHM I). The rectangle in Fig. 5b represents IOP. Each PE shown in Fig. 5c may have two memory modules, which provide a buffering capability and realize the FCHM

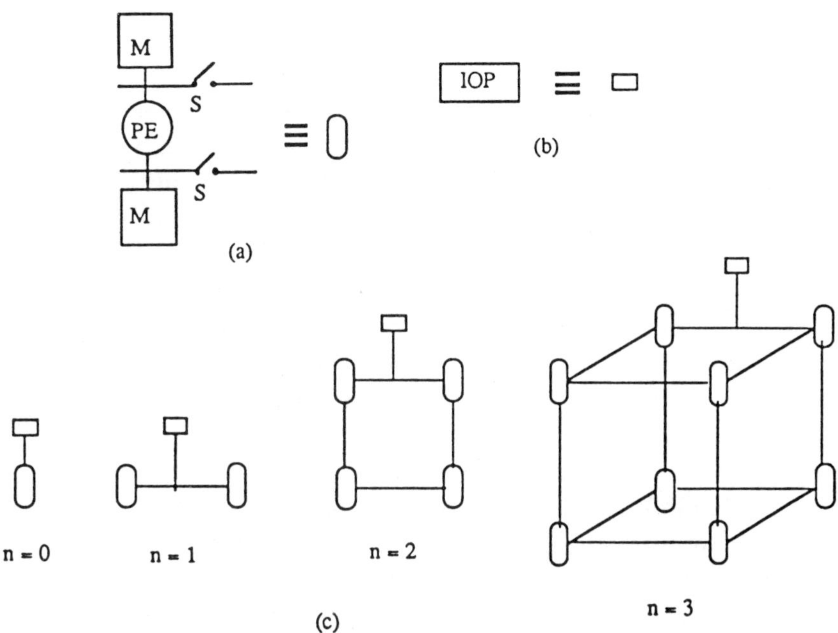


Figure 5: The flexibly coupled hypercube multiprocessor (FCHM).

model II (FCHM II). The control unit (CU) is omitted for simplicity. Figure 5d shows various dimensions of FCHM.

As in FCM, FCHM also has the variable space memory scheme, in which a set of neighboring memory modules can be merged by a dynamically partitionable bus. In addition, each PE has dedicated communication links connected to neighboring PEs as in existing hypercube machines. Hence, FCHM can support both message passing and shared memory.

Each PE contains its own local memory for storing program and intermediate results. The variable-space memory is used only for data. IOP is directly connected to the variable-space memory in order to input and output data efficiently without any communication.

In contrast, existing hypercube multiprocessors do not have separate memories for the data and the program. Thus, PE-to-PE and controller-to-PE communication are required for the data I/O and data sharing, which significantly degrade the performance [31,32,38]. IOP can input and output data by treating the collection of memory modules as a single module. This scheme can significantly reduce the data I/O overhead. In contrast to hypercube multiprocessors, the data I/O on FCHM needs only marginal switching and control times.

As in FCM, FCHM can be dynamically reconfigured into various types of partitions, such as fully loosely coupled, fully tightly coupled, partially loosely coupled, and partially tightly coupled partitions. For data sharing, communication links can be used for loosely coupled partitions, and the variable-space memory can be used for tightly coupled partitions. Even in tightly coupled partitions, communication links can be used for message passing. Thus, as in FCM, FCHM supports both message passing and shared memory.

To combine data in neighboring memory modules, only the switching time to close the switch set is needed instead of message passing. This scheme can significantly reduce the communication overhead. Since the architectural features of FCHM are quite similar to those of FCM, the details of FCHM are omitted. Pipelining, pipelined pseudoparallelism, tree-structured algorithms, grid and multigrid algorithms, multiprocessing, etc., may be efficiently mapped onto FCHM as well as onto the hypercube topology.

## 4.2 The Performance Evaluation of FCHM

Search algorithms are often used for high-level computer vision tasks including AI applications. There are many search algorithms. Among them, exhaustive search is one of the simplest algorithms. A parallel algorithm for exhaustive search is implemented on iPSC/1 and simulated on FCHM by using iPSC/1. The controller on iPSC/1 divides the whole search space into a set of subspaces and distributes each subspace into each PE. The controller broadcasts the target to be searched to every PE. As soon as each PE receives the target, it executes exhaustive search. After a PE finds the target, the PE sends the found signal to the controller. The data I/O time is much larger than the computation time on iPSC/1. Thus, the data I/O time is dominant on the hypercube, while the data I/O time is negligible on FCHM II. As the size of the search space increases, the computation time increases on both architectures. However, the data I/O time linearly increases only on iPSC/1 but this time is negligible on FCHM. The performance of FCHM shows a significant improvement [36].

Exhaustive search is an I/O-bounded task on iPSC/1. On the other hand, most of the data I/O time diminishes on FCHM. Hence, exhaustive search, an I/O-bounded task on the hypercube, turns into a computation-bounded task on FCHM. If the data I/O time is neglected, an almost linear speed-up may be achieved on iPSC/1. However, the actual speed-up is insignificant. This case clearly shows why the I/O time should be considered in a realistic performance evaluation. More details are in [36].

# 5 VisTA: Integrating the Three Architectures into a Composite Model

This section addresses the integration of three parallel architectures for a composite computer vision system, called VisTA. There are several ways to integrate different architectural layers. For example, pyramidal architectures use a large number of communication links between layers [39,41], and the UMass IUA uses shared memories and communication links [44]. However, the former requires large communication links and has a communication overhead, while the latter may cause memory contentions.

In contrast with these schemes, the connection scheme of VisTA between the three different architectures is a pipelined scheme. Figure 6 shows the overall connection scheme of three parallel architectures. This connection is the pipelined scheme with a distributed control rather than a hierarchical or pyramidal scheme. The pipelined scheme can meet the temporal parallelism in most vision tasks.

Since each architecture is modularized and independent, it can be built separately. Then IOPs can connect these architectures. IOP1

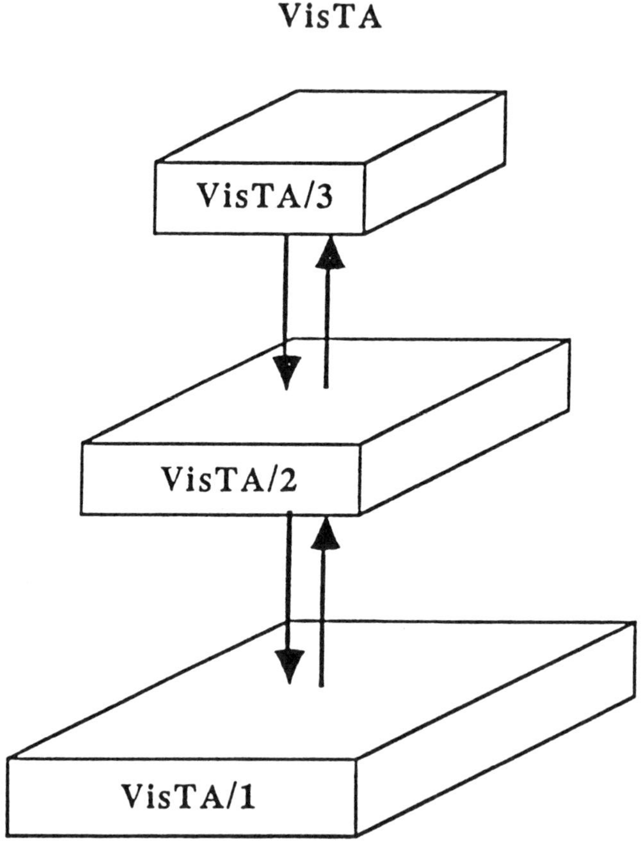


Figure 6: The overall scheme for an integrated computer vision system.

and IOP2 are used to transfer data between two architectures. IOP1 has the capability of a column-parallel (or row-parallel) I/O for SliM and the addressing scheme for the variable-space memory in FCM. IOP2 has the addressing scheme for FCM and FCHM. The data transfer is bidirectional. Even if a task is required to process alternately between stages, it can be easily implemented. Each of the proposed architectures is designed to have a buffering capability. Thus, the I/O time between stages may be negligible, if the computation time is larger than the I/O time.

Since there is no shared memory between layers, memory contention never occurs. Instead, IOPs can transfer data between stages without the communication overhead because each architecture has a buffering capability. The scheme can significantly reduce the number of communication links between two layers. This scheme contrasts with that in pyramidal architectures, where a large number of communication links should be used between layers.

As discussed earlier, two types of parallelism exist in computer vision tasks: temporal parallelism and spatial parallelism. Most computer vision tasks include both types of parallelism, as in pipelined pseudo parallelism. To meet real-time applications, both types of parallelism should be fully used. Pipelining that exploits temporal parallelism can be realized through the integrated three-stage pipeline architecture, that is, VisTA. Moreover, pipelining and pipelined pseudoparallelism can also be realized within FCM and FCHM. Array processing or multiprocessing can achieve the spatial parallelism. Array processing can be realized by SliM and multiprocessing can be realized by FCM or FCHM. Therefore, VisTA may efficiently exploit both types of parallelism, and may be well-suited for a general-purpose computer vision system.

# 6 Concluding Remarks

To alleviate the disadvantages of existing parallel architectures, to meet the three-level hierarchy in computer vision, and to improve performance, three new parallel architectures for the three different levels of computer vision have been developed: (1) VisTA/1–SliM for low-level vision; (2) VisTA/2–FCM for intermediate-level vision; and (3) VisTA/3–FCHM for high level vision. These architectures are pipelined into VisTA for a general-purpose computer vision system. The proposed architectures are evaluated through simulations and analytical models. Each of the proposed architectures shows performance improvements in its class.

SliM for low-level vision diminishes the disadvantages of existing mesh-connected architectures, such as the inter-PE communication overhead, complicated interconnections, and the data I/O overhead. SliM is a fine-grained, massively parallel SIMD architecture. SliM has several unique features, namely the sliding memory plane that alleviates the inter-PE communication overhead, and the bit-serial communication bit-parallel computation scheme that gives high speed, saves the area of the VLSI, and reduces the number of pins. Moreover, the virtual communication links for diagonal neighboring PEs can be realized by using two sliding memory plane shifts or the connection modes. Therefore, SliM reduces the disadvantages of existing mesh-connected architectures. The performance of SliM shows improvements [34–36].

FCM for intermediate-level vision alleviates the disadvantages of existing multiprocessors, such as the communication overhead in loosely coupled multiprocessors (multicomputers), memory contentions in tightly coupled multiprocessors, and the data I/O overhead due to inefficient data I/O schemes. The unique feature–the variable-space memory scheme–in which a set of neighboring memory modules can be merged into one shared memory, has been developed to realize FCM. This memory can be either a shared memory or a local memory, and is advantageous for the data I/O. FCM provides both types of mechanisms for data sharing, that is, message passing and shared memory. Parallel algorithms for computer vision are simulated on the proposed FCM architectures by using iPSC/1. The performance evaluation of FCM shows improvements over that of iPSC/1 [31,32,36]. FCM is well-suited for tasks where the data locality is guaranteed.

To minimize the disadvantages of existing hypercube architectures, such as the communication and data I/O overheads, and to broaden the relatively narrow range of applicability of FCM, FCHM has been proposed. FCHM was developed for high-level vision. The difference between FCHM and FCM is the interconnection network: the former is based on a dynamically partitionable hypercube topology; the latter is based on a dynamically partitionable bus topology. FCHM provides various types of partitions and supports both types of mechanisms for data sharing: message passing and shared memory. The parallel exhaustive search algorithm is simulated on FCHM by using iPSC/1. The performance of FCHM shows a significant improvement over that of iPSC/1. As mentioned earlier, the data I/O time, which is usually neglected, could be critical for real-time applications. Therefore, the data I/O time should be considered for a realistic performance evaluation.

In the end, these proposed architectures are pipelined into VisTA for a general-purpose computer vision system including an image-understanding system. Within each of the proposed architectures, spatial parallelism can be exploited. In addition, either each architecture or the whole pipelined system can realize temporal parallelism. This pipelined scheme with a buffering capability can reduce the number of communication links in multilayer architectures and eliminate the possibility of memory contentions in shared memories between layers.

This research mainly concerns architectural issues and does not discuss implementation issues in detail. More detailed implementation issues are possible areas for future research. Even though these architectures have been developed for computer vision tasks, they can also be used for more general-purpose tasks. The applicability of each of the proposed architectures is also a possible area for future research.

## Bibliography

[1] D. P. Agrawal and R. Jain, *A pipelined pseudoparallel system architecture for real-time dynamic scene analysis,* IEEE Trans. Comput., vol. C-31, Oct. 1982, pp. 952–962.

[2] G. H. Barnes, R. M. Brown, M. Kato, D. J. Kuck, D. L. Slot-

nick, and R. A. Stokes, *The ILLIAC IV computer,* IEEE Trans. Comput., vol. C-17, Aug. 1968, pp. 746–757.

[3] K. E. Batcher, *Design of a massively parallel processor,* IEEE Trans. Comput., vol. C-29, Sep. 1980, pp. 836–840.

[4] F. A. Briggs, K. S. Fu, K. Hwang, and B. W. Wah, *PUMPS architecture for pattern analysis and image database management,* IEEE Trans. Comput., vol. C-31, Oct. 1982, pp. 969–983.

[5] A. N. Choudhary and J. H. Patel, *A parallel processing architecture for an integrated vision system,* Proc. Int. Conf. Parallel Processing, Aug. 1988, pp. 383–387.

[6] P. E. Danielsson, *The time-shared bus–A key to efficient image processing,* Proc. Int. Conf. Pattern Recognition, 1980, pp. 296–299.

[7] R. Davis and D. Thomas, *Systolic array chip matches the pace of high-speed processing,* Electronic Design, vol. 32, no. 22, Oct. 1984, pp. 207–218.

[8] J. D. Dessimoz, J. Birk, R. Kelley, and J. Hall, *A vision system with splitting bus,* Proc. 1981 IEEECS Workshop Comput. Architect. for PAIDM, Nov. 1981, pp. 62–66.

[9] M. J. B. Duff, *Review of the CLIP image processing system,* Proc. Nat. Comput. Conf., 1978, pp. 1055–1060.

[10] M. J. B. Duff, ed., Intermediate-Level Image Processing, Academic Press, 1986.

[11] T. Ericsson and P-E. Danielsson, *LIPP - A SIMD multiprocessor architecture for image processing,* Proc. 10th Ann. Int. Symp. Comput. Architect., 1983, pp 395–400.

[12] Z. Fang, X. Li, and L. M. Ni, *On the communication complexity of generalized 2-D convolution on array processors,* IEEE Trans. Comput., vol. 38, no. 2, Feb. 1989, pp. 184–194.

[13] T. J. Fountain, *A survey of bit-serial array processor circuits,* in M. J. B. Duff, ed., Computing Structures for Image Processing, Academic Press, 1985, pp. 1–13.

[14] T. J. Fountain, K. N. Matthews, and M. J. B. Duff, *The CLIP7A image processor,* IEEE Trans. PAMI, vol. 10, May 1988, pp. 310–319.

[15] F. A. Gerritsen, *A comparison of the CLIP4, DAP and MPP processor-array implementations,* in M. J. B. Duff, ed., Computing Structures for Image Processing, Academic Press, 1983, pp. 15–30.

[16] W. D. Hillis, The Connection Machine, MIT Press, 1985.

[17] L. Kohn and S. W. Fu, *A 1 000 000 transistor microprocessor,* Proc. 1989 Int. Solid-State Circuits Conf. Digest of Technical Papers, Feb. 1989, pp. 54–55.

[18] T. Kushner, A. Y. Wu, and A. Rosenfeld, *Image processing in ZMOB,* Proc. IEEECS Workshop Comput. Architect. for PAIDM, 1981, pp. 88–95.

[19] T. Kushner, A. Y. Wu, and A. Rosenfeld, *Image processing on MPP,* Pattern Recognition, vol. 15, 1982, pp. 121–130.

[20] S. Y. Lee and J. K. Aggarwal, *Exploitation of image parallelism via the hypercube,* Second Conf. Hypercube Multiprocessors, Sep. 1986.

[21] S. Y. Lee and J. K. Aggarwal, *Parallel 2-D convolution on a mesh connected array processor* IEEE Trans. PAMI, vol. PAMI-9, July 1987, pp. 590–594.

[22] S. P. Levitan, C. C. Weems, A. R. Hanson, and E. M. Riseman, *The UMass image understanding architecture,* in L. Uhr, ed., Parallel Computer Vision, Academic Press, 1987, pp. 215–248.

[23] H. Li and M. Maresca, *Polymorphic-Torus: A new architecture for vision computation,* Proc. IEEECS Comput. Architect. for PAMI, Oct. 1987, pp. 176–183.

[24] M. Maresca, M. A. Lavin, and H. Li, *Parallel architectures for vision,* in Proc. IEEE, vol. 76, Aug. 1988, pp. 970–981.

[25] M. A. Marsan, G. Balbo, and G. Conte, *Performance Models of Multiprocessor Systems,* MIT Press, Cambridge, 1986.

[26] R. Miller, V. K. Prasanna Kumar, D. Reisis, and Q. F. Stout, *Meshes with reconfigurable buses,* Proc. MIT Conf. Advanced Research in VLSI, 1988, pp. 163–178.

[27] S. F. Reddaway, *DAP - A distributed processor array,* Proc. First Ann. Symp. Comput. Architect., 1973, pp. 61–65.

[28] A. P. Reeves, *A systematically designed binary array processor,* IEEE Trans. Comput., vol. C-29, Apr. 1980, pp. 278–287.

[29] Y. Saad and M. H. Schultz, *Topological properties of hypercubes,* Res. Rep. YALEU/DCS/RR-389, June 1985.

[30] C. L. Seitz, *The cosmic cube,* Comm. ACM, vol. 28, Jan. 1985, pp. 22–33.

[31] M. H. Sunwoo and J. K. Aggarwal, *Flexibly coupled multiprocessors for image processing,* in Proc. Int. Conf. Parallel Processing, vol. I, Aug. 1988, pp. 452–461.

[32] M. H. Sunwoo and J. K. Aggarwal, *Flexibly coupled multiprocessors for image processing,* Journal of Parallel and Distributed Computing, vol. 10, no. 2, Oct. 1990, pp. 115–129.

[33] M. H. Sunwoo and J. K. Aggarwal, *A sliding memory plane array processor,* Proc. Second Symp. Frontiers '88 Massively Parallel Computation, Oct. 1988, pp. 537–540.

[34] M. H. Sunwoo and J. K. Aggarwal, *A sliding memory plane array processor for low level vision,* Proc. 10th Int. Conf. Pattern Recognition, June 1990, pp. 312–317.

[35] M. H. Sunwoo and J. K. Aggarwal, *A vision tri-architecture (VisTA) for an integrated computer vision system,* Proc.

DARPA Image Understanding Benchmark Workshop, Oct. 1988.

[36] M. H. Sunwoo and J. K. Aggarwal, *VisTA: An integrated vision tri-architecture system,* Tech. Rep., TR-89-6-57, Computer and Vision Research Center, Univ. Texas, Austin, September 1989.

[37] M. H. Sunwoo and J. K. Aggarwal, *VisTA for a general purpose computer vision system,* Proc. Int. Conf. Pattern Recognition, June 1990, pp. 635–641.

[38] M. H. Sunwoo, B. S. Baroody, and J. K. Aggarwal, *A parallel algorithm for region labeling,* Proc. 1987 IEEECS Workshop Comput. Architect. for PAMI, Oct. 1987, pp. 27–34.

[39] S. Tanimoto, *A pyramidal approach to parallel processing,* Proc. 10th Ann. Int. Symp. Comput. Architect., 1983, pp. 372–378, pp. 3–17.

[40] S. L. Tanimoto, *Architectural issues for intermediate-level vision,* in M. J. B. Duff, ed., Intermediate-Level Image Processing, Academic Press, 1986.

[41] L. Uhr, *Layered recognition cone networks that process, classify and describe,* IEEE Trans. Comput. vol. 21, 1972, pp. 758–768.

[42] S. H. Unger, *A computer oriented toward spatial problems,* Proc. IRE, vol. 46, Oct. 1958, pp. 1744–1750.

[43] R. S. Wallace and M. D. Howard, *HBA vision architecture : Built and benchmarked,* Proc. IEEECS Workshop Comput. Architect. for PAMI, 1987, pp. 209–216.

[44] C. Weems, *Some sample algorithms for the image understanding architecture,* Proc. DARPA Image Understanding Workshop, 1988, pp. 127–138.

[45] C. Weems, E. Riseman, A. Hanson, and A. Rosenfeld, *An integrated image understanding benchmark: Recognition of a 2 1/2D mobile,* Proc. DARPA Image Understanding Workshop, 1988, pp. 111–126.

[46] S. Yalamanchili, K. V. Palem, L. S. Davis, A. J. Welch, and J. K. Aggarwal, *Image processing architectures: A taxonomy and survey,* Progress in Pattern Recognition, vol. II, pp. 1–37, 1985.

# Part II

# Parallel Algorithms

# Optimal Image Computations on Reduced Processing Parallel Architectures

HUSSEIN M. ALNUWEIRI
*Computer Engineering Department*
*King Fahd University of Petroleum and Minerals*
*Dhahran, Saudi Arabia*

and

V. K. PRASANNA KUMAR
*Department of Electrical Engineering - Systems*
*University of Southern California*
*Los Angeles, California*

## 1 Introduction

Processor-time trade-offs are of fundamental importance in understanding the complexity and performance of parallel computations. Driven by technological limitations, hardware cost, and flexibility, several schemes have been proposed for implementing large-size computations on parallel architectures of fixed-size, or on architectures having a reduced number of processors. The major goal of such schemes is to keep the number of processors (or the processing chip-area, if implemented in VLSI) independent of the problem size and subject only to hardware cost, and other practical considerations. Such considerations are particularly important for problems on digitized images. With increasing image resolution, a processor array for a $1024 \times 1024$ image with a fixed number of pixels, say eight, per processor requires more than $10^5$ processors. Design and implementation cost of such large arrays may be prohibitive, not to

Parallel Architectures and
Algorithms for
Image Understanding




ISBN 0-12-564040-4

mention limitations due to I/O bandwidth, programming, and testing methodologies. Furthermore, if this array is required to handle larger size images, say images of size $2048 \times 2048$, then processor-time trade-offs must be addressed again.

This chapter presents several parallel architectures with a large memory and a reduced number of processors for parallel-image computations. The memory size is proportional to the image size. However, the number of processors can be varied over a wide range while maintaining processor-time optimal performance. Several parallel architectures will be considered, including the reduced mesh of trees (RMOT), mesh-connected modules (MCM), linear arrays, two dimensional meshes, hypercubes, and shuffle-exchange networks. It should be emphasized here that direct mapping of parallel techniques from a specific organization onto a smaller version of the same organization generally does not lead to linear processor-time trade-off. New techniques based on combining efficient parallel and sequential algorithms must be developed. These techniques will be illustrated by several examples. The following section identifies the computation and communication requirements of several image problems. Section 3 defines a basic set of image problems. Section 4 derives processor-time optimal algorithms for several image problems on the above mentioned architectures.

# 2 Computation and Communication Requirements for Image Problems

Given a problem on an image of size $N(= n \times n)$ pixels, which can be solved in an optimal sequential time of $T(N)$ units, the problem will require $\Omega(T(N)/p)$ time on a parallel organization with $p \leq N$ processors. A parallel algorithm for a given problem is said to be *processor-time optimal* if the product of the number of processors and the parallel execution time is equal to the sequential complexity of the problem. In parallel and distributed processing, a substantial amount of time is usually spent in routing messages among the processors. Therefore, efficient techniques should be developed for partitioning and moving data among the processors. Careful analysis of the problems is needed to derive such techniques. The following is a list of some basic features of computations in medium and higher-level vision and image analysis:

1. Images naturally divide into subregions representing objects, shades, lines, polygons, regular patterns, etc. Such regions can be represented by a smaller amount of data using border representation, run-length codes, etc. An image represented in such compressed forms can be handled by a smaller number of processors.

2. A wide class of image problems can be solved using a divide-and-conquer procedure. To solve a problem on an image $I$ one can first subdivide the image into smaller parts (subimages), solve the problem independently within each subimage, then merge the results from the subimages to obtain a final solution. An outline of this procedure is presented in Section 3.1. In many applications, only data pertaining to the boundary pixels of each subimage is needed for the merge procedure. The boundary data is much smaller than the original image data, and thus, fewer processors are needed by the merge procedure. Adaptations of this procedure will be considered in Section 4 on several parallel architectures.

3. Based on their communication requirements, image problems can be classified into three categories [1]: local, regular global, and irregular global. Definitions and examples of each category are presented in Fig. 1. It is clear that irregular-global computations impose the most stringent demands on the communication capabilities of the parallel architecture. The orthogonal-access architectures presented in Section 4 are very well suited to such problems, as are hypercubes and shuffle-exchange networks.

Several other features can be used to characterize image computations. However, the above classification is most useful for our discussion. In general, these features imply that efficient parallel architectures for image computations must be communication-efficient.

- **Local computations:** The computation performed on a certain pixel $p$ is a function of the pixels in a relatively small neighborhood of $p$. Examples include gradient operators for edge detection, morphological operators, convolution, and correlation operators.
- **Regular global computations:** The computation performed on a certain pixel $p$ is a function of other pixels at a relatively large distance from $p$. However, these pixels lie in predetermined (data-independent) locations within the image or the underlying data structure. Examples include image transforms such as the Fourier transform, Walsh-Hadamard transform, etc.
- **Irregular global computations:** The computation performed on a certain pixel $p$ is a function of other pixels whose exact location is not predetermined but is data-dependent. Computing geometric properties of images (such as convexity and nearest neighbors) is a good example of such computations.

Figure 1: Classification of image problems.

However, the number of processors can be reduced. In fact, the number of processors should be chosen so as to balance the time taken to perform data movement (communication) and the time taken to perform computations on the local data in each processor.

# 3 A Repertoire of Image Problems

The image labeling problem will be used to illustrate the algorithmic techniques employed by the parallel organizations considered in this chapter. Histogramming and Hough transform computations will be used to illustrate the communication efficiency of the RMOT and MCM organizations. These and related image problems are introduced in this section, and well-known approaches to solve them are also briefly discussed.

## 3.1 Labeling connected components

A black and white (binary) image may consist of several connected regions of black pixels on a white background. A maximally connected region is called a connected-component or figure. Assigning a unique label to each such component is a fundamental problem in image analysis and vision. Several parallel solutions to this problem have been proposed [6]. A well-known solution strategy on the MCC is the divide-and-conquer approach of Nassimi and Sahni [20]. This approach has been implemented on several other parallel organizations. Major steps of this approach are reviewed as a prelude to the labeling algorithms presented in the next section.

To label an $n \times n$ image, the image is first partitioned into $k^2$ subimages of size $m \times m$ each, where $m = n/k$. Each subimage is labeled independently, then the labels are merged to produce a labeling of the complete image. The procedure can be applied recursively to the subimages. It is important to observe that only the boundary pixels of each subimage need to be processed by the merge procedure. Consider merging two adjacent subimages $I_1$ and $I_2$ each of size $m \times m$ pixels, and assume that each subimage has been labeled independently. The merge procedure consists of correcting the labels of figures that are connected across the boundary between $I_1$ and $I_2$, since such figures have different labels in each subimage. The adopted approach is based on the construction of a bipartite graph $G = (V_1, V_2, E)$ representing the connectivity among figures in the two subimages. $V_1$ and $V_2$ are two sets of vertices with each vertex in $V_1$ (respectively, $V_2$) representing the label of a figure with at least one pixel on the boundary of $I_1$ (respectively, $I_2$), and $E$ is a set of edges such that $(u, v) \epsilon E$ if there are two figures labeled $u \epsilon V_1$ and $v \epsilon V_2$ that are connected across the boundary between $I_1$ and $I_2$ (see Fig. 2). This graph will be referred to as the boundary-connectivity graph. Merging the labels in the two subimages can be performed by first labeling the connected components of the graph $G$, then assigning the computed labels to the figures represented by the vertices.

## 3.2 The Hough Transform

The Hough transform is most commonly used for straight line detection in binary images [13]. The transform can be computed in two stages. The first stage accumulates evidence for the existence of certain lines. The second stage selects the lines to be reported based on some decision criteria (voting process).

A straight line in the plane can be uniquely identified by two parameters; its minimum distance from the origin ($\rho$) and the clockwise angle of the perpendicular to the line from the horizontal ($\theta$). These two parameters are related by the line equation $\rho = x \cos\theta + y \sin\theta$, where $(x, y)$ is a point on the line. Straight line detection in an image is done first by transforming each image point $(x, y)$ into a line (in fact, a sinusoidal curve) in the parameter-space defined by $\rho$ and $\theta$. Note that image points lying on the same line defined by the parameters $(\rho_i, \theta_i)$ are transformed into curves intersecting at point $(\rho_i, \theta_i)$ in the parameter-space. If the number of curves intersecting at a certain point in the parameter-space is above a certain threshold, then the image line parameterized by this point is reported. This idea can be used to implement the Hough transform using the two-stage method mentioned above. For computational purposes, the parameter space is quantized into rectangular cells defined by $k$ $\theta-$values

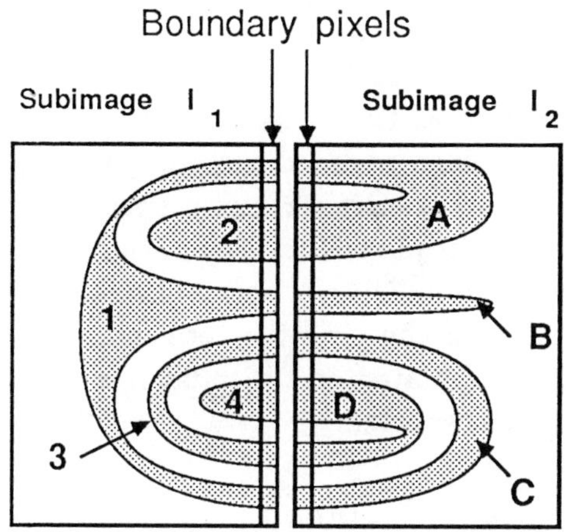


Merging two labeled subimages

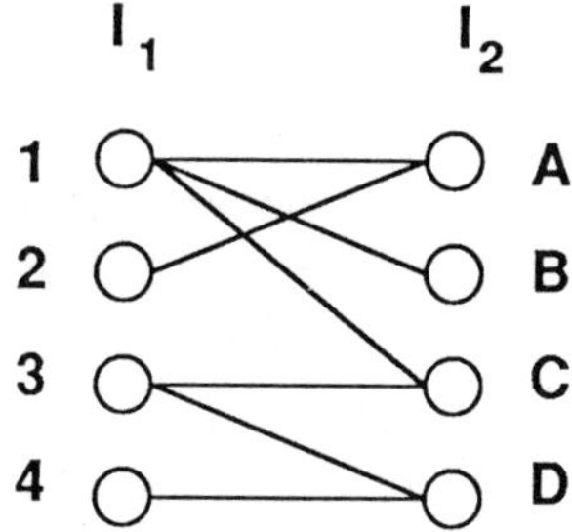


Boundary Connectivity Graph

**Figure 2: Image labeling by divide-and-conquer.**

and $m$ $\rho-$values. The first stage is performed by associating with each cell in the parameter space, an accumulator which counts the number of lines passing through the cell. The computation is usually performed in $k$ steps. In step $i$, $1 \leq i \leq k$, the $\rho-$values of all image points $(x, y)$ are computed for the same $\theta_i-$value. The counts in the accumulator cells are then updated accordingly. This updating step can be implemented by a histogramming operation using $\rho-$values as the keys. Each step requires $O(n^2)$ operations on an $n \times n$ image, and thus all $k$ steps require $O(kn^2)$ operations in the worst case. The second stage consists of checking the total number of intersections reported by each accumulator, and then using a decision criterion to choose the lines to be reported.

### 3.3 Related Image Problems

Parallel algorithms for a number of representative image problems will be considered in the next section. The problems include histogramming, computing nearest neighbors, and computing convex hulls. Briefly, histogramming is a *key counting* operation on gray-level images and it produces a count of the number of pixels in each gray-level. Nearest neighbor problems in a black and white image are concerned with computing a closest black pixel for each image pixel, or computing a nearest figure (connected component) for each figure in the image. Convexity problems are concerned with computing *convex hulls* of point sets. The convex hull of a set of planar points is the minimum area convex polygon containing them. In digitized images, convexity is defined on pixels that can be viewed as planar points having integer coordinates.

## 4 Reduced Parallel Architectures for Image Computations

In this section, several communication efficient architectures for image computations are presented. These architectures include the RMOT organization, the MCM organization, the hypercube, and shuffle-exchange networks. In each of these organizations, the number of processors can be scaled over a wide range while maintaining processor-time optimality. The basic approach for solving image problems on such architectures is to decompose computations into parallel communication phases and sequential computation phases. Data reduction and efficient routing techniques are used to speed up communication operations, while powerful sequential techniques are utilized by each processor in computations performed on its local data. Extensions of these techniques to architectures with limited communication capabilities such as linear arrays are also discussed.

## 4.1 Image Processing on the RMOT Organization

The reduced mesh of trees (RMOT) architecture [2, 4] consists of $n$ processing elements (PEs)[1] each having row and column access to an $n \times n$ array of memory modules such that $PE_i$ can access the modules in the $i$th row and the $i$th column of the array. To avoid memory access conflicts all PEs are allowed to perform either row access or column access at the same time but not both. The organization of the RMOT is shown in Fig. 3 for $n = 4$. The PEs have basic arithmetic-logic capabilities and all their internal registers and data paths are $O(\log n)$-bit wide. Also, each memory module consists of a fixed number of $O(\log n)$-bit registers each constituting one memory location within the module.

The RMOT organization belongs to a class of orthogonal-access architectures, which has been studied by several authors [2, 4, 24, 27]. The row-column access capabilities of the organization provide a new and efficient medium for exploring parallel algorithms. Parallel computations can be implemented on the organization by decomposing them into a sequence of orthogonal phases in each of which computations are performed either on rows or on columns of the memory. Such access capabilities allow the RMOT to perform global image operations and dense data movement very efficiently. For example, the RMOT can sort $n^2$ integers stored in its memory in $O(n)$ time which is optimal [4]. Note that this is the same time as that taken

[1]The terms processor and PE will be used alternatively throughout the chapter.

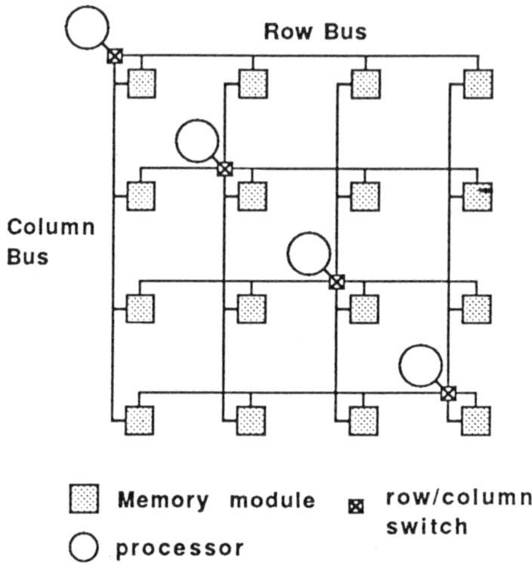


Figure 3: RMOT with four PEs.

by a mesh or a pyramid computer with $O(n^2)$ PEs to sort $n^2$ numbers. Moreover, if the number of integer keys to be sorted is $m$, where $n^{3/2} \leq m \leq n^2$, an RMOT with $n$ PEs can sort these keys in $O(m/n)$ time. These results are of considerable importance to image and graph algorithms since the keys involved in sorting are usually integers, such as pixel labels, pixel coordinates, and vertex numbers. In the following, optimal parallel techniques for several image problems are presented for the RMOT.

## Image Labeling

Labeling an $n \times n$ image can be performed in $O(n)$ time on an RMOT with $n$ PEs. The RMOT solution is based on the divide-and-conquer approach combined with efficient data reduction and movement techniques to yield optimal performance. The basic procedure is as follows: Partition the $n \times n$ image into $n$ subimages each of size $\sqrt{n} \times \sqrt{n}$, and store each subimage in one memory column, as shown in Fig. 4. Each PE can label the subimage in its memory column in $O(n)$ time

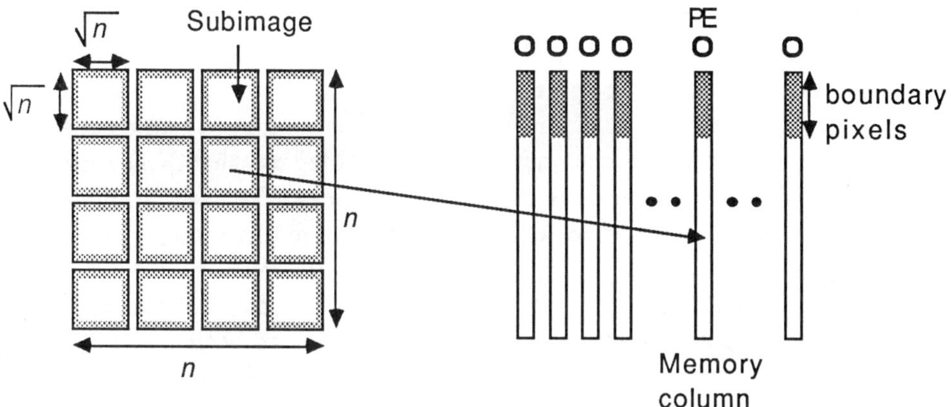


Figure 4: Image mapping for component labeling on the RMOT.

using a sequential algorithm. A final labeling of the $n \times n$ image can be obtained by merging the labels of the pixels on the boundaries of the $n$ subimages. Since each subimage has $(4n^{1/2} - 4)$ boundary pixels, the total number of pixels to be considered by the merge procedure is $\Theta(n^{3/2})$. The boundary labels can be merged using a parallel graph connectivity technique. The boundary-connectivity graph introduced in Section 3.1 has $O(n^{3/2})$ edges. Constructing this graph and labeling its connected components can be done in $O(n)$ time on an RMOT with $n$ PEs [4]. The above procedure finds the correct labels for the pixels on the boundary of each subimage. Each PE can then propagate these labels to the internal pixels of the subimage stored in its memory column. This can be done in $O(n)$ time, and thus, the total time taken by the algorithm is $O(n)$. Therefore, an RMOT with $n$ PEs only can solve the image labeling problem in the same time as that taken by a two-dimensional mesh computer with $n^2$ PEs [20].

### Histogramming and Image Enhancement

Computing the histogram of an $n \times n$ gray-level image can be performed in $\Theta(n)$ time on an RMOT with $n$ PEs. The histogram is computed by sorting the pixels by their gray-level values, then computing the sum of pixels in each gray-level by scanning the memory rows and columns. Since these values are integers, the $\Theta(n)$ time parallel radix-sort technique mentioned earlier can be used.

To enhance the contrast or the dynamic range of an image, some pixels on the inner or outer boundaries of gray-level regions may have to be reassigned new gray-level values. The process of reassigning gray-level values to pixels to produce an image with a specific histogram is called *histogram modification* or *histogram equalization*. Using a fixed number of radix-sort operations and row-column scans, an RMOT with $n$ PEs can perform histogram modification operations in $O(n)$ time [1].

### Feature Detection Using the Hough Transform

The Hough transform can be implemented using a number of histogramming steps. As mentioned in Section 3.2, updating the accumulators for each $\theta-$value can be viewed as computing the histogram of the pixels using their $\rho-$value as a key. Thus, the Hough transform for an $n \times n$ image can be computed in $O(kn)$ time on an RMOT with $n$ PEs, where $k$ is the number of discrete values of $\theta$. Note that this time is optimal since an equivalent sequential computation would take $O(kn^2)$ time.

The RMOT communication capabilities can be further exploited to implement dynamically quantized pyramids (DQP) for the Hough transform [9]. In this case, the parameter space is subdivided into cells of various sizes. Such multiresolution environments are useful for reducing the computational requirements of detecting objects other than straight lines. For example, representation of circles requires three parameters (center location $(x, y)$ and radius $r$ [8]). Thus, the parameter-space is three-dimensional and fixed-interval quantization may produce a very large number of cells even for moderate-size images. Given an $r-$dimensional DQP with $N = n^2$

cells, one step of computation involving all the cells can be implemented in $O(n)$ time on an RMOT with $n$ PEs, which is optimal. This result follows from the fact that any communication pattern on $n^2$ nodes (cells in this case) can be realized in $\Theta(n)$ time on an RMOT with $n$ PEs [2].

## 4.2 Image Algorithms on the MCM Organization

A useful enhancement of the RMOT can be achieved by incorporating it as a module (node) in a mesh structure. This is the basis of the mesh-connected modules (MCM) organization. One distinct feature of the MCM is that PEs can communicate through a shared memory as well as direct interprocessor links.

The MCM organization consists of $p$ PEs and $\Theta(n^2)$ memory locations [5]. The MCM is organized as a $k \times k$ mesh-connected array of basic modules (BMs), where $1 \leq k \leq n$. Each BM is an RMOT organization with $q$ PEs $(PE_0, \cdots, PE_{q-1})$, $1 \leq q \leq n/k$; and a $q \times q$ array of memory modules each having $\Theta((n/kq)^2)$ locations. In addition, each $PE_i$ of a BM is connected to $PE_i$ in each adjacent BM. It is assumed that $O(\log n)$ bits can be moved across each bus or data link in a constant amount of time. An MCM can be specified by the three parameters $n, k$, and $q$ defined above, where $1 \leq k \leq n$ and $1 \leq q \leq n/k$. We use the notation MCM$(n, k, q)$ to denote an MCM having $\Theta(n^2)$ words of memory and being organized as a $k \times k$ array of BMs, each having $q$ PEs. The basic organization of an MCM$(n, 4, 4)$ is shown in Fig. 5.

### Implementing Parallel Algorithms

The two-level structure of the MCM implies a two-level structure on the algorithms developed for the MCM: module-algorithms and communication-algorithms. Several problems can be solved by recursively partitioning the MCM into submeshes of BMs, solving the subproblem in each submesh, then merging the results. Using the special access capabilities of the MCM, efficient techniques for moving, partitioning, and reducing data have been developed [5]. These techniques lead to processor-time optimal parallel solutions for a wide class of

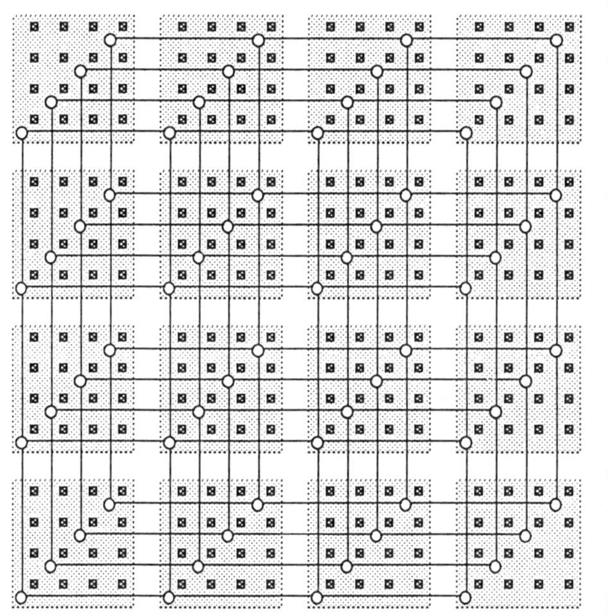




**Figure 5: The mesh-connected modules (MCM) organization.**

problems on digitized images. For example, given an $n \times n$ black and white image mapped onto the memory array of an MCM$(n, k, q)$ such that each pixel is stored in one memory location, the following image problems can be solved in $O(k+n^2/p)$ time using $p$ PEs, where $1 \leq p \leq n^{3/2}$, and $k \leq n^{2/3}$:

1. labeling all image connected components.
2. computing the convex hull of each component.
3. computing a smallest enclosing box for each component.
4. computing nearest neighbors of pixels and components.
5. histogramming when the number of gray-levels is $O(n^2/k^2)$.

The general approach to solving the above problems is based on a two-phase technique [5]: The first phase solves the problem independently within each basic module using an RMOT algorithm; the second phase merges the results recursively after performing data reduction.

### Comparison with Pyramids

The efficient communication capabilities of the MCM make its performance comparable to that of other parallel organizations with a larger number of processors. Compared to the pyramid computer [19], the processor-time product of the MCM for the previously listed problems is clearly superior. For example, the problems of computing the connected components of an image and computing all closest figures take $O(n^{1/2})$ time on a pyramid computer with $O(n^2)$ PEs. The MCM can also solve these problems in $O(n^{1/2})$ time, using $n^{3/2}$ PEs only. Processor-time tradeoffs on the MCM can be also compared with similar tradeoffs on reduced mesh-connected computers. Processor-time optimality has been achieved previously on a $\sqrt{p} \times \sqrt{p}$ reduced mesh in which each PE is supplied with a local memory of size $O(n^2/p)$ words [18]. It has been shown that such a mesh provides $O(\sqrt{p} + n^2/p)$ time solutions for the problems listed above, which is processor-time optimal when $1 \leq p \leq n^{4/3}$. The MCM provides optimal solutions for the same set of problems over a wider range, namely $1 \leq p \leq n^{3/2}$. The minimum time taken by such problems on the MCM is $O(n^{1/2})$, while for the reduced mesh this time is $O(n^{2/3})$. Moreover, the reduced mesh can be viewed as a special instance of the MCM when each basic module consists of a single PE. Thus, the techniques developed for the MCM can be implemented directly on the reduced mesh.

## 4.3 Hypercube and Shuffle-Exchange Algorithms

Hypercube-based computers are communication-efficient parallel organizations, which can provide polylogarithmic time solutions to a wide class of problems. A hypercube with $N = 2^k$ nodes (processors) is called a $k$-dimensional cube or simply a $k$-cube. Two processors are connected by a link if the binary representations of their indices differ in exactly one bit. Thus, in a $k$-cube each processor is connected to $k$ other processors. Image labeling will be used to illustrate the efficiency with which a hypercube computer can be used to solve image problems (see [11] for alternate techniques). However, issues related to data movement and embedding meshes on hypercubes must be discussed first.

Several algorithms for intermediate- and high-level image problems involve the use of pointer-based structures and graph theoretic techniques. The communication requirements for such techniques are usually complex and data-dependent. Two important operations for performing this type of communication are the random access read (RAR) and the random access write (RAW) operations introduced in [21]. In such operations, each processor $P_i$ has a record $r_i$ having a key $h_i$, a destination field $d_i$ containing the index of another processor, and a data field containing one or more data elements. In a RAR operation, each processor $P_i$ reads the data field of record $r_j$, where $d_i = j$. In a RAW operation, each processor $P_i$ copies the data field of its record into the data field of record $r_j$, where $d_i = j$. Conflicts may arise in RAW operations whenever two or more processors send data to the same processor. Such conflicts can be resolved in a number of ways, including storing (in the destination processor) the record with the minimum key, or storing the sum of the data in the received records. In [21], it was shown that both of these operations can be implemented by a constant number of sorting steps.

RAR and RAW operations can be performed in $O(\log^2 N)$ time on a hypercube of size $N$, with each each processor holding one record. Faster algorithms can be used to implement these operations if the number of records to be routed is less than the number of processors. Nassimi and Sahni [22] presented $O(\log N)$ time algorithms for performing RAR and RAW on $R$ records using a hypercube of size $N = R^{1+\epsilon}$ processors, where $0 < \epsilon \leq 1$.

Several image computations may require the processors of the hypercube to be arranged as a two-dimensional mesh. This can be done by assigning indices to the mesh nodes according to *reflected gray-code* (RGC) numbering [10]. A reflected gray-code sequence of length $n$ is a sequence $A(n) = a_1, a_2, \cdots, a_n$ of $n$ elements each represented by $\log n$ bits, such that any two consecutive elements of the sequence differ in exactly one bit. Note that in the RGC sequence $A(n)$, $a_n$ and $a_1$ are also defined to be consecutive. An $n \times n$ mesh can be mapped on a hypercube of size $N = n^2$ by assigning node $(i, j)$ of the mesh, $1 \leq i, j \leq n$, to processor $a_i a_j$ of the hypercube, where $a_i, a_j \epsilon A(n)$, and $a_i a_j$ is a $(2\log n)$-bit number obtained by concatenating the binary codes of $a_i$ and $a_j$. An example of mapping a $4 \times 4$ mesh onto a hypercube with 16 nodes is shown in Fig. 6. Note that in order to use this mapping the hypercube is assumed to have *independent communication* capability, that is, each node can use one of its links along a certain dimension independent of the dimensions used by other nodes. Under this mapping scheme, the hypercube can simulate mesh algorithms directly with no loss in times.

The shuffle-exchange network [26] can perform several computations in the same time as a hypercube with the same number of processors. However, such computations have the restriction that simultaneous communication steps on the hypercube can use links along the same dimension only. In this case, an algorithm that takes $T(m)$ time on a hypercube with $M = 2^m$ processors can be performed in $O(T(m))$ time on a shuffle-exchange network with the same number of processors. The shuffle-exchange network has the advantage

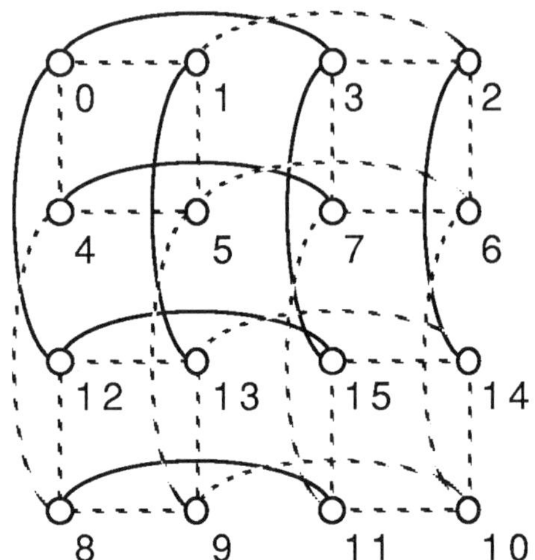


Figure 6: Mapping a $4 \times 4$ mesh onto a hypercube.

that each of its nodes has degree three only, regardless of the network size. The algorithms presented later for the hypercube can be implemented in the same asymptotic time on a shuffle-exchange network of the same size.

## Image Labeling on the Hypercube

Labeling an $n \times n$ image on a hypercube computer with $N = n^2$ processors can be performed in $O(\log^2 N)$ time by using the divide-and-conquer technique outlined in Section 3.1. It is assumed that the image is mapped onto the hypercube such that each $k \times k$ subimage is stored (one pixel per processor) in a subcube of size $k^2$. The algorithm is based on recursively partitioning an $n \times n$ image into $n$ subimages each of size $\sqrt{n} \times \sqrt{n}$, labeling the subimages, and then merging their labels [11]. Merging the labels is done by constructing a boundary connectivity graph representing connectivity among all subimages, and computing the connected components of the graph.

Such a graph has $\Theta(n^{3/2}) = \Theta(N^{3/4})$ edges and its connected components can be computed in $O(\log n)$ iterations using the connectivity algorithm proposed in [25]. The data movement required by each iteration of this algorithm can be performed using the $O(\log N)$-time RAR and RAW operations mentioned previously. Let $T(r)$ denote the time taken to label the connected components of an $r \times r$ image using the labels computed for its $\sqrt{r} \times \sqrt{r}$ subimages. The time complexity of the labeling algorithm can then be expressed by the recurrence $T(r) = T(\sqrt{r}) + \log^2 r$, for $r = 2^{2p}$ and $\log n \geq p \geq 1$, which has the solution $T(n^2) = O(\log^2 n)$.

## Image Labeling on Fixed-Size Hypercubes

The previous algorithm can be modified to solve the image labeling problem on a fixed-size cube. The main modification involves the initial steps of the computation. In the following, a processor-time optimal hypercube algorithm is presented to solve the image labeling problem in $O(N/M)$ time, where $N = n \times n$ is the image size, $M$ is the number of processors, and $1 \leq M \leq N/\log^2 N$. It is assumed that each processor has a local memory of size $\Theta(N/M)$ words, and that the image is partitioned such that each processor has a subimage of size $\sqrt{N/M} \times \sqrt{N/M}$.

The algorithm strategy is dependent on the number of processors used. If $1 \leq M \leq N^{2/3}$, a hypercube algorithm can be obtained by embedding a $\sqrt{M} \times \sqrt{M}$ mesh on the hypercube, then simulating the reduced-mesh algorithm (discussed in Section 4.2) to compute the connected components of the image. Thus, for the previous range of $M$, the hypercube algorithm takes $O(N/M)$ time, which is optimal. If $M \geq N^{2/3}$, the algorithm proceeds in two phases. The first phase partitions the hypercube into subcubes of size $(N/M)^2$ processors each, such that each subcube has a subimage of size $(\frac{N}{M})^{3/2} \times (\frac{N}{M})^{3/2}$. By simulating a reduced mesh algorithm, each subcube can label the connected components of its subimage in $O(N/M)$ time. The second phase merges the labels on the boundaries of the subimages recursively. The technique involves merging the boundary labels in each group of $k$ adjacent subcubes using their boundary connectivity graphs. Note that each subcube has $(N/M)^2$ processors and

$\Theta((N/M)^{3/2})$ boundary pixels; that is, its boundary connectivity graph has $\Theta((N/M)^{3/2})$ edges. Thus, the number of edges in $k$ subcubes is $\Theta(k(N/M)^{3/2})$ while the number of available processors is $k(M/N)^2$. By choosing a sufficiently small $k$, the $O(\log N)$ time RAR and RAW operations mentioned earlier can be used to perform the necessary routing of data elements (graph edges). The time complexity of the second phase can be described by the recurrence equation given previously for a hypercube of size $N$. Thus, the time complexity of the second phase is $O(\log^2 N)$ and the total time complexity of the algorithm is $O(N/M + \log^2 N)$, which is optimal for $1 \leq M \leq N/\log^2 N$.

## 4.4 Image Algorithms on Linear Arrays

Linear arrays of processors have been used or proposed to provide parallel solutions to a wide variety of problems. Examples of available linear-array computers include the CMU Warp [7], the SLAP array [14], and the PPPE [15]. Linear arrays have several attractive features that make them suitable for VLSI implementation. These features include simplicity of interconnection, modularity, amenability to simpler fault tolerance techniques, and low I/O bandwidth requirements as compared with other array processors with more complex interconnection networks.

The basic linear array model consists of $p$ processors, $1 \leq p \leq n$, indexed 0 through $p-1$, with each processor $P_i$ connected by bidirectional links to its immediate left and right neighbors if they exist (see Fig. 7). The bandwidth of each link is $\Theta(\log n)$ bits. Each processor also has a local memory of $O(n^2/p)$ words, each word consisting of $\Theta(\log n)$ bits. Also, each processor can access one word from its memory or communicate one word of data to one of its neighbors in $O(1)$ time. Finally, a processor can perform a basic logic or arithmetic operation on a fixed number of words in $O(1)$ time.

When considering solutions in which global transfer of data is required, several factors can complicate their implementation on linear arrays. The main sources of inefficiency are the small communication bandwidth and the large communication diameter. To overcome such shortcomings, efficient techniques for data reduction and movement must be developed. Several such techniques have been proposed in [3, 12]. These techniques reduce the communication time by minimizing the amount of data transfer over communication links as well as minimizing the communication distance throughout a computation. The main goal is to make the total computation time be dominated by the time of the local computations performed by each processor rather than by the time taken for communication. The following mapping scheme can be used to attain such results.

## Image Mapping

The $n \times n$ image is partitioned into subimages of size $\sqrt{n} \times \sqrt{n}$, and each subimage is stored in one processor. The mapping of subimages onto the processors is done according to the shuffled row-major indexing scheme.

**Shuffled row major distribution:** In this distribution, the image is partitioned into a $\sqrt{p} \times \sqrt{p}$ array of squares, each of size $n/\sqrt{p} \times n/\sqrt{p}$. The square in the $i$th row and $j$th column is denoted by $S(i,j)$. Let $q = \log\sqrt{p} - 1$, and let $(i_q i_{q-1} \ldots i_0)$ and $(j_q j_{q-1} \ldots j_0)$ be the binary representations of the numbers $i$ and $j$, respectively. In the shuffled row-major assignment, $S(i,j)$ is assigned to processor $P_k$, where the binary representation of $k$ is $(i_q j_q i_{q-1} j_{q-1} \ldots i_0 j_0)$. An example of this assignment is shown in Fig. 7.

When using divide-and-conquer techniques, this mapping has the advantage that subimages of size $k\sqrt{n} \times k\sqrt{n}$, $1 \leq k \leq \sqrt{n}$, are stored in $k^2$ adjacent processors. Thus, it reduces the communication distance overhead since processing each subimage requires data to move among a smaller subset of processors (that is to say, $k^2$ processors for a $k\sqrt{n} \times k\sqrt{n}$ subimage).

## Image Algorithms

Using efficient mapping and data movement techniques, a linear array with $n$ PEs can provide $O(n)$ time solutions to several problems

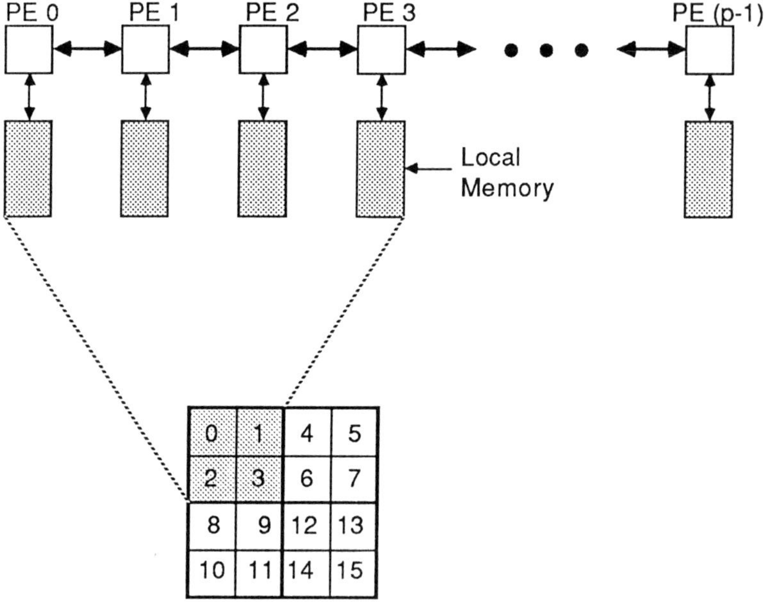


**Figure 7: Linear array model and image mapping.**

on an $n \times n$ image, which is the same as the time taken by a two-dimensional mesh with $n^2$ processors. The image labeling computation provides a good demonstration of the linear array techniques and will be considered here in some detail. The algorithm is based on a divide-and-conquer technique [3].

Initially, each processor labels the $\sqrt{n} \times \sqrt{n}$ subimage in its local memory. This can be done in $O(n)$ time using a sequential labeling algorithm. The subimages are then merged recursively to label subimages of larger size. The merge procedure consists of $\log \sqrt{n}$ stages. In stage $i$, $1 \leq i \leq \log \sqrt{n}$, the boundary pixels in each group of four adjacent subimages, each of size $(k/2)\sqrt{n} \times (k/2)\sqrt{n}$, are merged to label the pixels of the $k\sqrt{n} \times k\sqrt{n}$ subimage containing them, where $k = 2^i$. Note that each group of four subimages is contained in a group of $k^2$ adjacent processors. Merging the boundaries of each such group is performed sequentially using a single processor. This processor can be chosen to be the lowest indexed processor in the processor-group containing the four subimages. Since the number of boundary pixels in each group of four subimages is $8k\sqrt{n} - 16$, merging the boundary labels can be done sequentially in $\Theta(k\sqrt{n})$ time by the chosen processor of each group. Also, the communication distance over which the pixels are moved is at most $k^2$. Thus, in stage $i$, moving the data into the chosen processor can be done in $O(k^2 + k\sqrt{n})$, where $k = 2^i$, and the total time taken by the merge procedure is

$$\sum_{i=1}^{\log \sqrt{n}} (2^{2i} + 2^i\sqrt{n}) = O(n).$$

Since only boundary pixels of subimages are considered in each stage of the merge procedure, some internal pixels may hold old incorrect labels at the end of the procedure. These labels can be updated in $O(n)$ time by using a top-down recursive procedure to propagate correct boundary labels to internal pixels.

A number of other global image problems can be solved in $O(n)$ time on a linear array with $n$ PEs. Such problems include computing nearest neighbors of pixels and figures, computing area, perimeter, and moment of each figure. These problems take $O(n)$ time on an $n \times n$ mesh. Computing the convex hull of each figure needs somewhat more complicated data movement than the earlier problems. However, a linear array can solve this problem in $O(n \log n)$ time using $(n/\log n)$ PEs [3], which is processor-time optimal. In addition, the above techniques can be implemented on a fixed-size linear array with $p$ processors, where $1 \leq p \leq n$. In this case, the time taken to label an $n \times n$ image is $O(n^2/p)$ which is processor-time optimal.

### Acknowledgments

This research was supported in part by NSF under grant IRI-8710836 and in part by AFOSR under grant AFOSR-89-0032.

## Bibliography

[1] H. M. Alnuweiri, Communication-Efficient Parallel Architectures and Algorithms for Image Computations, Ph.D. Dissertation, Department of Computer Engineering, U.S.C., Los Angeles, CA, 1989.

[2] H. M. Alnuweiri and V. K. Prasanna Kumar, *A reduced mesh of trees organization for efficient solutions to graph problems*, Proc. of the 22nd Annual Conference on Information Science and Systems (CISS), 1988, pp.

[3] H. M. Alnuweiri and V. K. Prasanna Kumar, *Optimal geometric algorithms for fixed-size linear arrays and scan line arrays*, Proc. IEEE Conference on Computer Vision and Pattern Recognition, 1988, pp. 931-936

[4] H. M. Alnuweiri and V. K. Prasanna Kumar, *Optimal image computations on reduced VLSI architectures*, IEEE Transactions on Circuits and Systems, 1989, pp. 1365-1375.

[5] H. M. Alnuweiri and V. K. Prasanna Kumar, *Processor-time optimal parallel algorithms for digitized images on mesh-connected processor arrays*, to appear in Algorithmica.

[6] H. M. Alnuweiri and V. K. Prasanna Kumar, *Parallel architectures and algorithms for image component labeling*, Technical Report, IRIS 253, University of Southern California, 1989.

[7] M. Annaratone, E. Arnould, T. Gross, H. T. Kung, M. Lam, O. Menzilcioglu, K. Sarocky, and J. A. Webb, *The Warp computer architecture, performance, and implementation*, IEEE Transactions on Computers, C-36, pp. 1523-1538.

[8] D. H. Ballard, *Generalizing the Hough transform to detect arbitrary shapes*, Pattern Recognition, vol. 13, 1981, pp. 111-112.

[9] R. P. Blanford, *Dynamically optimized pyramids for Hough vote collection*, IEEE Workshop on Computer Architecture for Pattern Analysis and Machine Intelligence, 1987.

[10] T. E. Chan and Y. Saad, *Multigrid Algorithms on Hypercube Computers*, IEEE Transactions on Computers, c-35, 1986.

[11] R. Cypher, and J. L. C. Sanz, L. Snyder, *Hypercube and shuffle-exchange algorithms for image component labeling*, IEEE Workshop on Computer Architecture for Pattern Analysis and Machine Intelligence, 1987, pp. 5-10.

[12] K. Doshi and P. Varman, *Optimal graph algorithms on a fixed-size linear array*, IEEE Transactions on Computers, c-36, 1987. pp. 460-470.

[13] R. O. Duda and P. E. Hart, *Using Hough transform to detect lines and curves in pictures*, Communications of the ACM, vol. 15, 1972, pp. 11-15.

[14] A. I. Fisher, *Scan line array processors for image computations*, International Conference on Computer Architecture, 1986, pp. 338-345.

[15] E. B. Hinkle, J. L. C. Sanz, A. K. Jain, and D. Petkovic, *$P^3E$ new life for projection-based image processing*, Journal of Parallel and Distributed Computing, vol. 4, 1987, pp. 45-87.

[16] J. Ja'Ja' and R. M. Owens, *An architecture for a VLSI FFT processor*, INTEGRATION the VLSI Journal, vol. 1, 1983, pp.

[17] J. L. Little, G. Blelloch, and T. Cass, *Algorithmic techniques for computer vision on a fine-grained parallel machine*, IEEE Transactions on Pattern Analysis and Machine Intelligence, PAMI-11, 1989, pp. 244-257.

[18] R. Miller and Q. F. Stout, *Varying diameter and problem size on mesh-connected computers*, Proc. International Conference on Parallel Processing, 1985, pp. 697-699.

[19] R. Miller and Q. F. Stout, *Data Movement Techniques for the Pyramid Computer*, SIAM Journal on Computing, vol. 2, 1987, pp. 38-60.

[20] D. Nassimi and S. Sahni, *Finding connected components and connected ones on a mesh-connected parallel computer*, SIAM Journal on Computing, vol. 9, no. 4, 1980, pp. 744-757.

[21] D. Nassimi and S. Sahni, *Data broadcasting in SIMD computers*, IEEE Transactions on Computers, vol. c-30, no. 2, 1981, pp. 101-107.

[22] D. Nassimi and S. Sahni, *Parallel permutations and sorting algorithms and a new generalized connection network*, Journal of the ACM, vol. 29, no. 3, 1982, pp. 642-667.

[23] Y. Saad and M. Schultz, *Topological properties of hypercubes*, IEEE Transactions on Computers. vol. c-37, no. 7, 1988, pp. 867-872.

[24] I. D. Scherson and Y. Ma, *Analysis and applications of an orthogonal access multiprocessor*, Journal of Parallel and Distributed Computing, vol. 7, 1989, pp. 232-255.

[25] Y. Shiloach and U. Vishkin, *An $O(\log n)$ parallel connectivity algorithm*, Journal of Algorithms, vol. 3, 1982.

[26] H. Stone, *Parallel processing with the perfect shuffle*, IEEE Transactions on Computers, vol. c-20, 1971, pp.

[27] P. S. Tseng, K. Hwang, and V. K. Prasanna Kumar, *A VLSI based multiprocessor architecture for implementing parallel algorithms*, Proc. International Conference on Parallel Processing, 1985.

# Efficient Parallel Algorithms for Intermediate-Level Vision Analysis on the Reconfigurable Mesh

RUSS MILLER
*State University of New York at Buffalo*
*Buffalo, New York*

and

V. K. PRASANNA KUMAR and
DIONISIOS I. REISIS
*University of Southern California*
*Los Angeles, California*

and

QUENTIN F. STOUT
*University of Michigan*
*Ann Arbor, Michigan*

## 1 Introduction

In this chapter, we consider a model of computation that captures fundamental properties of *CHiP* [12, 33], mesh computers augmented with broadcast buses [1, 4, 27, 34], the *bus automaton* [5], the *polymorphic-torus network* [15], and the *coterie network* in the *content addressable array parallel processor (CAAPP)* of the image un-

Parallel Architectures and
Algorithms for
Image Understanding




ISBN 0-12-564040-4

derstanding architecture [31, 32]. We use the term *mesh with reconfigurable bus* or *reconfigurable mesh* to describe this model. We introduce a number of fundamental data movement operations, which we then incorporate into algorithms to solve problems involving images. These algorithms are asymptotically superior to previous algorithms for the aforementioned reconfigurable architectures. They also show that the reconfigurable mesh can provide more efficient solutions to problems than can other mesh-based architectures. In fact, we are able to give solutions to certain problems that are more efficient than those possible for the PRAM.

In Section 2, we define the reconfigurable mesh. Section 3 illustrates the power of the reconfiguration scheme in basic operations on data, as well as in sparse data movement, by giving efficient implementations for fundamental data movement operations such as random access read-write, data reduction, and parallel prefix. These global operations form the foundation of algorithms appearing later in the chapter, and rely on the ability to reconfigure the bus in a variety of ways. Section 4 presents algorithms that exploit the fundamental data movement operations introduced in Section 3 to develop efficient solutions to several image problems. Section 5 serves as the conclusion.

## 2 Mesh with Reconfigurable Bus

The mesh with reconfigurable bus (reconfigurable mesh) of size $N$ consists of an $N^{1/2} \times N^{1/2}$ array of processors connected to a grid-shaped reconfigurable broadcast bus, where each processor has four locally controllable bus switches, as shown in Fig. 1. The switches allow the broadcast bus to be divided into subbuses, providing smaller reconfigurable meshes. For a given set of switch settings, a *subbus* is a maximal connected subset of the processors. Other than the buses and switches, the reconfigurable mesh is similar to the standard mesh in that it has $\Theta(N)$ area, under the assumption that processors, switches, and a link between adjacent switches occupy unit area. Notice that by setting the switches properly, subrow (column) buses can be created within each row (column), subreconfigurable

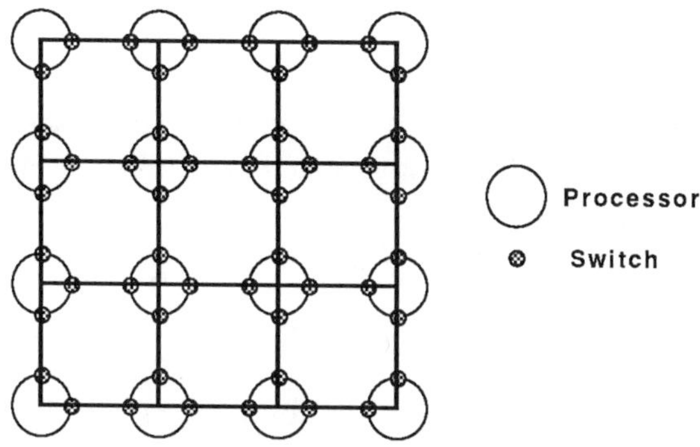


Figure 1: Reconfigurable mesh

meshes can be created, a global broadcast bus can be created, a bus can be created within sets of contiguously labeled processors, and so forth.

We consider two models of bus arbitration in this chapter. The *exclusive write model*, which mimics the exclusive write capability of the *exclusive write PRAM (EW PRAM)*, allows only one processor to broadcast to a subbus shared by multiple processors at any given time. We assume that the value broadcast consists of $O(\log N)$ bits. The *common write model*, which mimics the common write version of the *concurrent write PRAM (CW PRAM)*, allows multiple processors simultaneously to broadcast to the same subbus so long as they all broadcast the same value and it is only a single bit. The focus of this chapter is on the exclusive write reconfigurable mesh. In fact, all algorithms presented in this chapter are for the exclusive write model except for the component labeling algorithm associated with Theorem 4.1, which uses the common write model.

Two computational models will be discussed in this chapter with respect to the delay that a broadcast requires. The *unit-delay model* will assume that all broadcasts take $\Theta(1)$ time, as is the assumption in [4, 27, 29, 34, 35] for models that assume various broadcasting strategies. We will also consider the *log delay model,* in which it is assumed that each broadcast takes $\Theta(\log s)$ time to reach all the processors connected to its subbus, where $s$ is the maximum number of switches in a minimum switch path between two processors connected on the bus.

# 3 Data Movement Using Reconfigurable Buses

Data movement operations form the foundation of numerous parallel algorithms for machines constructed as an interconnection of processors. In fact, algorithms that are designed in terms of fundamental abstract data movement operations [23] provide the possibility of portability to architecturally related machines. Therefore, the algorithms given in this chapter will be described in terms of such operations.

In this section, a variety of these fundamental operations are given for the reconfigurable mesh. We first introduce a technique called *bus splitting*, which shows how the processors can exploit the ability to control locally the effective size of subbuses. This technique is introduced by way of an example. Suppose we want to compute the logical OR of $N^{1/2}$ bits of data stored one bit per processor in the $i$th row of the reconfigurable mesh, storing the result in processor $P_{i,0}$, for all $0 \leq i \leq N^{1/2} - 1$. This can be accomplished as follows. Set the switches so that each row is connected by a disjoint subbus. Next, each processor $P_{i,j}$ that has a one as its data value *splits* its bus by setting its eastern switch to disconnect its row bus. Then, each processor $P_{i,j}$ that has a one as its data value broadcasts the one on its subbus. Processor $P_{i,0}$, for all $0 \leq i \leq N^{1/2} - 1$, will receive on its row subbus the westernmost one in its row, if such a value exists. Note that if it is desired to find the logical OR of the data stored in all processors, then first the OR of each row can be determined followed by the OR of these values in the first column. Alternatively, the logical OR of the data in all processors can be determined by setting the switches so that all processors are connected by a single linear bus (following the snakelike indexing), and then using a single bus splitting step, where each processor that contains a one splits the bus by disconnecting the switch between itself and its successor. A broadcast then informs processor $P_{0,0}$ as to the logical OR of the values.

**Proposition 3.1** *Given a reconfigurable mesh of size $N$, in which each processor stores a bit of data, the logical OR of the data in each row (column), or in the entire reconfigurable mesh, can be determined in $\Theta(1)$ time using the unit-delay model, and in $\Theta(\log N)$ time using the log-delay model.* □

The reconfigurable mesh can be superior to other parallel models for some computations. Consider, for example, computing the exclusive OR (EXOR) of $N^{1/2}$ values stored in a row of the mesh. It should be noted that in [11] it has been shown that the exclusive OR cannot be computed in $\Theta(1)$ time on a PRAM using a polynomial number of processors. The ability to reconfigure the bus of the reconfigurable mesh, however, allows us to compute the EXOR function in $\Theta(1)$ time using the unit-delay model. Assume that the PEs in row 0 have a bit. First, the EXOR of the bits in the even numbered PEs is computed. If PE$(0, 2j)$ has a one, PEs in the $2j$th column and in the $(2j+1)$th column set the switches such that the incoming signal from PE$(2i, 2j-1)$ is routed to PE$(2i+2, 2j+1)$. If PE$(0, 2j)$ has a zero then the incoming signal from PE$(2i, 2j-1)$ is routed to PE$(2i, 2j+1)$. Using this setting, the EXOR of the bits in the even numbered PEs in row 0 can be computed in $\Theta(1)$ time in the unit-delay model. Repeating this idea on the data in odd-numbered PEs and combining the results, we have the following.

**Proposition 3.2** *Given a reconfigurable mesh of size $N$, the exclusive OR (EXOR) of $N^{1/2}$ bits of data, initially stored one bit per processor in a row (column), can be computed in $\Theta(1)$ time using the unit-delay model, and in $\Theta(\log N)$ time using the log-delay model.* □

The previous result can be extended in a natural fashion to the following.

**Corollary 3.1** *Suppose on a reconfigurable mesh of size $N$, each processor in row (column) $j$ stores a bit of data $d_j$, $0 \leq j \leq N^{1/2}-1$. The prefix computation of $\mathcal{F}_j$, where $\mathcal{F}_j = \sum_{i=0}^{j} d_i$ is to be stored in row $j$, $0 \leq j \leq N^{1/2}-1$, can be performed in $\Theta(1)$ time in the unit-delay model, and in $\Theta(\log N)$ time in the log-delay model.* □

Many algorithms are designed to reduce data at intermediate stages of the algorithm. It is, therefore, often useful to be able to perform efficiently fundamental operations on reduced sets of data. The maximum of $N^{1/2}$ values $x_0, \ldots, x_{N^{1/2}-1}$ initially stored in a row of a reconfigurable mesh of size $N$ can be determined as follows. First, column broadcasts can be used so that every processor $P_{i,j}$ contains a copy of $x_j$. Next, within every row $i$, processor $P_{i,i}$ uses a row broadcast to inform all processors $P_{i,j}$ of the value of $x_i$, $0 \leq i,j \leq N^{1/2}-1$. At this point, every processor $P_{i,j}$ contains a copy of $x_i$ and $x_j$. Next, every processor computes the Boolean result of $x_j < x_i$. In every column $j$, the logical OR of these results (using the algorithm associated with Proposition 3.1 to store the result in $P_{0,j}$) can be used to decide whether or not $x_j$ is a maximum. Notice that a result of zero in $P_{0,j}$ indicates that $x_j$ is a maximum, while a one indicates that it is not. Since there may be more than one processor in row 0 storing the maximum value, bus splitting in row 0 is used to inform $P_{0,0}$ as to the maximum value, which can then be broadcast to all processors. Notice that the minimum can be computed similarly.

**Proposition 3.3** *Given a reconfigurable mesh of size $N$, in which no more than one processor in each column stores a data value, the maximum (minimum) of these $O(N^{1/2})$ data items can be determined in $\Theta(1)$ time using the unit-delay model, and in $\Theta(\log N)$ time using the log-delay model.* □

By a somewhat more complicated sequence, Valiant's PRAM algorithm for finding the maximum [39] can be simulated on a reconfigurable mesh to find the maximum of $N$ values, assuming they are stored one value per processor. Assume that the mesh is divided into $N^{1/2}$ disjoint blocks of size $N^{1/4} \times N^{1/4}$. Suppose the maximum of the data in each block has been determined. Then, we need to determine the maximum of $N^{1/2}$ values using $N$ processors in the array. After moving the data to appropriate locations, this can be done in $\Theta(1)$ time using Proposition 3.3 in the unit-delay model. Recursively applying this idea leads to an algorithm with running time that obeys the recurrence $T(N) = T(N^{1/2}) + \Theta(1)$ in the unit-delay model and $T(N) = T(N^{1/2}) + \Theta(\log N^{1/2})$ in the log-delay model.

**Proposition 3.4** *Given a set of data items $S$ of size $N$ stored one per processor on a reconfigurable mesh of size $N$, the maximum (minimum) value of $S$ can be determined in $\Theta(\log\log N)$ time using the unit-delay model, and in $\Theta(\log N)$ time using the log-delay model.* □

Combining the above approach with Proposition 3.2 leads to

**Corollary 3.2** *Given a set $S$ of $N$ bits stored one per processor on a reconfigurable mesh of size $N$, the EXOR of all items in $S$ can be computed in $\Theta(\log\log N)$ time using the unit-delay model, and in $\Theta(\log N)$ time using the log-delay model.* □

*Parallel prefix* is an important operation that can be used to sum values, broadcast data, solve problems in image processing, solve graph problems, and so forth [13]. In the following, we assume a row major order indexing of the processors. Assume processor $P_i$, $0 \leq i \leq N-1$, initially contains data element $a_i$. The parallel prefix problem requires every processor $P_i$, $0 \leq i \leq N-1$, to determine the $i$th initial prefix $a_0 \otimes a_1 \otimes \cdots \otimes a_i$, where $\otimes$ is a binary associative operator. Parallel prefix can be computed in every row (or column) of the reconfigurable mesh simultaneously in $\log_2 N^{1/2}$ iterations by setting switches appropriately, broadcasting, and updating values at each iteration. Using the computed values in each row, parallel prefix over the entire mesh can be computed [17], giving the following results.

**Lemma 3.1** *Given a set $S = \{a_i\}$ of $N$ values, distributed one per processor on a reconfigurable mesh of size $N$ so that processor $P_i$ contains $a_i$, $0 \leq i \leq N-1$, and a unit-time binary associative operation $\otimes$, in $\Theta(\log N)$ time using the unit-delay model, and in $\Theta(\log^2 N)$ time using the log-delay model, the parallel prefix problem can be solved so that each processor $P_i$ knows $a_0 \otimes a_1 \otimes \ldots \otimes a_i$.* □

It is often desirable to model PRAM algorithms on other machines. The CRCW PRAM consists of a set of processors and a shared memory in which concurrent reads from the same memory location are allowed, as are concurrent writes to the same location. In the case of concurrent writes, a predefined scheme is used to decide which value succeeds. In order efficiently to simulate the CRCW PRAM, one must be able efficiently to simulate the concurrent read and concurrent write properties. Define *random access read (RAR)* to be a data movement operation that models a concurrent read, in which each processor knows the index of another processor from which it wants to read data [25]. Similarly, a *random access write (RAW)* will model a concurrent write in that each processor knows the index of a processor that it wishes to write to [25]. In case of multiple writes to the same processor, a tie-breaking scheme is used, such as minimum or maximum data value, or arbitrarily letting one value succeed. Such data movement operations on SIMD computers using $N$ processors can be performed in the same time as it takes to sort $N$ numbers. However, on the reconfigurable mesh, we give algorithms whose running times depend on the number of data items to be moved.

The algorithms we give in this section are actually concerned with more general versions of these operations. The operations that we consider have PEs attempting to read or write information based on keys, where the key may or may not be the index of a processor. In order to maintain consistency during concurrent read and concurrent write operations, it will be assumed that there is at most one *master record*, stored in some processor, associated with each unique key. In a concurrent read, each PE generates a fixed number of request records, where each *request record* specifies a key that the PE wishes to receive information about. In a concurrent write, each PE generates a fixed number of update records, where each *update record* specifies the key and data field corresponding to the key that the PE wishes to update. It should be noted that for many applications, a PE will maintain master records and also generate request or update records. The data movement is accomplished by first moving the data to a compact region of the reconfigurable mesh, making disjoint copies of the data throughout the mesh, and using mesh connected computer data movement techniques within local copies of the data to distribute the data to its destination [17].

**Lemma 3.2** *Given a reconfigurable mesh of size $N$, in $O(k^{1/2})$ time using the unit-delay model, and in $O(k^{1/2} \log N)$ time using the log-delay model, $k$ data items may be moved in a RAR or RAW, where $k \leq N$.* □

Another useful operation for implementing image algorithms is data reduction. Assume that each processor has at most one record having a key field and a data field. Data reduction will perform an associative binary operation on the data of records having the same key. At the end of the data reduction operation, each processor with key $x$ will have the result of the operation performed over all data items with key $x$. The basic idea of the algorithm is to merge data in blocks. Initially, data reduction is performed in $O(k^{1/2})$ time using a sort-based mesh computer algorithm within blocks of size $k$. Once this is complete, blocks are merged iteratively, while continuing to reduce data, until the data is reduced over the entire mesh [17].

**Proposition 3.5** *Given an associative binary operator $\otimes$, data reduction can be performed on $k$ distinct keys in $\Theta(k^{1/2} + \log N)$ time on a reconfigurable mesh of size $N$ under the unit-delay model, and in $\Theta(k^{1/2} \log N + \log^2 N)$ time under the log-delay model. At the end of the operation each processor knows the result of applying $\otimes$ over all data items with its key.* □

# 4 Intermediate-Level Vision Tasks on the Reconfigurable Mesh

In this section, we illustrate the power of the reconfigurable mesh by giving efficient parallel algorithms to solve image problems. Many of the solutions rely on the fundamental data movement operations given in the previous section. We also show that the reconfigurable mesh can exploit its numerous communication patterns to simulate efficiently the pyramid computers.

## 4.1 Simulating Pyramid Computations

In this section, we show that the reconfigurable mesh can efficiently simulate the pyramid, for which numerous efficient vision algorithms already exist. A pyramid computer (pyramid) of size $N$ is a machine that can be viewed as a full, rooted, quaternary tree of height $\log_4 N$, with additional horizontal links so that each horizontal level is a mesh. It is often convenient to view the pyramid as a tapering array of meshes. A pyramid of size $N$ has at its base a mesh of size $N$, and a total of $\frac{4}{3}N - \frac{1}{3}$ processors. The levels are numbered so that the base is level 0 and the apex is level $\log_4 N$. A processor at level $i$ is connected via bidirectional unit-time communication links to its nine neighbors (assuming they exist): four siblings at level $i$, four children at level $i-1$, and a parent at level $i+1$. An embedding of the pyramid of base size $N$ onto a reconfigurable mesh of size $N$ can be generated by using the standard H-tree embedding of the layers above the pyramid's base onto its base, and using the natural map of the pyramid's base onto the reconfigurable mesh. Using this, one can partition the pyramid communication links into four sets, namely the mesh edges of the base, the mesh edges of all levels above the base, the parent-child edges connecting each even layer with the layer above, and the parent-child edges connecting each even layer with the layer below. For each of these sets there is a natural planar layout resulting in each node having degree four or less. Each set can in turn be naturally mapped into four collections of subbuses, giving a total of 16 collections of subbuses to simulate all the pyramid connections.

**Lemma 4.1** *Given a pyramid algorithm $\mathcal{A}$ taking $T(N)$ time on a pyramid of base size $N$, on a reconfigurable mesh of size $N$, $\mathcal{A}$ can be simulated in $O(T(N))$ time on the unit-delay model, and in $O(T(N)\log N)$ time on the log-delay model.* □

## 4.2 Image Algorithms

Many problems involving digitized images can be solved efficiently on the reconfigurable mesh. The input for these problems is an $N^{1/2} \times N^{1/2}$ digitized image distributed one pixel per processor on a reconfigurable mesh of size $N$ so that processor $P_{i,j}$ stores pixel

$(i, j)$. The pixels are either black or white, where the interpretation is a black image on a white background. The problems that we examine focus on figures (connected components) and determining properties of the figures. The reconfigurable bus plays an important role in image algorithms, since it can be used to create a subbus within every figure so that information can be extracted about all figures concurrently. Indeed, a multilevel system for image understanding is being built, with a configurable bus system for low-level image processing [24, 32]. The first result of this section provides an algorithm to label efficiently the figures of an image. In the following, the common write model is assumed.

**Theorem 4.1** *Given an $N^{1/2} \times N^{1/2}$ digitized image mapped one pixel per processor onto the processors of a reconfigurable mesh of size $N$, in $\Theta(\log N)$ time in the unit-delay model, and in $\Theta(\log^2 N)$ time under the log-delay model, the figures (connected components) can be labeled.*

*Proof:* In parallel, every processor examines the pixel in each of its four neighbors and sets its four switches so that a connection is maintained only between neighboring black pixels. This $\Theta(1)$ time operation creates a subbus over every figure. Using subbuses in parallel a unique label can now be assigned to every figure by a standard bit polling algorithm, as follows. Initially, all processors with a black pixel are active. At the $i$th iteration, all active processors with a one in the $i$th bit of their unique processor index, send a one to the bus. (Note that this requires the concurrent write capability of the bus.) If no processor sends a one to the bus, then the algorithm proceeds to the next iteration, while if at least one processor sends a one to the bus, then only those processors that sent a one remain active. During the $i$th iteration, every processor with a black pixel records the $i$th bit of its final component label, which is a one if a one is read from the bus, and is a zero otherwise. The label of a figure will be the maximum index of any PE containing a pixel of the figure. □

For all results concerning distance or convexity, each pixel is treated as being an integer lattice point, rather than a small square. The next result is concerned with determining a nearest figure to every figure. The distance between figures $F$ and $G$ is $\min\{d(f,g) \mid f \in F, g \in G\}$, where $d$ is the Euclidean distance. On the reconfigurable mesh, a nearest figure to each figure can be determined in two stages. In the first stage, a nearest figure to each boundary pixel of all figures is determined. Then, using a bottom-up merge, a nearest figure to each figures is identified [17].

**Theorem 4.2** *Given an $N^{1/2} \times N^{1/2}$ digitized image mapped one pixel per processor onto the processors of a reconfigurable mesh of size $N$, in $O(\log^2 N)$ time in the unit-delay model, and in $O(\log^3 N)$ time under the log-delay model, a nearest figure to each figure can be determined.* □

As we have shown, the reconfigurable mesh is particularly useful when the amount of essential data remaining can be rapidly reduced. For images, one common form of data reduction is to represent a figure by its extreme points, that is, by the corners of the smallest convex polygon containing the figure. It is particularly useful to enumerate the extreme points. A standard enumeration scheme is to start with the easternmost extreme point (if there are two easternmost points, start at the northernmost of them), and number the extreme points in counterclockwise order. Enumerated extreme points store not only their number, but the numbers and locations of the preceding and following extreme points.

**Theorem 4.3** *Given an $N^{1/2} \times N^{1/2}$ digitized image mapped one pixel per processor onto the processors of a reconfigurable mesh of size $N$, in $O(\log^2 N)$ time in the unit-delay model, and in $O(\log^3 N)$ time under the log-delay model, the extreme points of the convex hull can be enumerated for every figure.*

*Proof:* We use a bottom-up divide-and-conquer approach. Assume that the image has been partitioned down the center, and that in each half the extreme points of each figure restricted to that half have been enumerated. We show how to use this information to find the extreme points of the entire figure. Note that this is needed only for figures crossing the center; the others are finished.

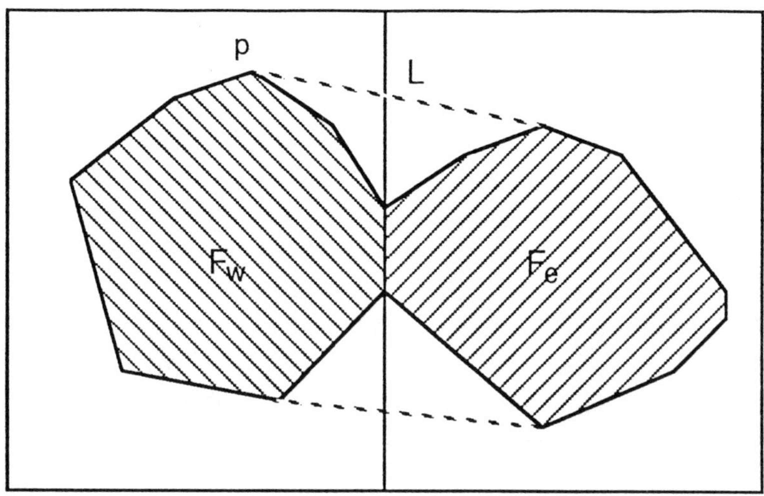


Figure 2: Tangent lines for combining convex hulls

For each figure $F$ crossing the center, let $F_w$ denote the portion of $F$ on the western half, and let $F_e$ denote the portion of $F$ on the eastern half. We will locate the top and bottom tangent lines, shown in Fig. 2, and their four points of intersection with $F$. Extreme points of $F_w$ and $F_e$ are extreme points of $F$ if and only if they do not lie within the quadrilateral formed by these four points of intersection. The process of locating these two tangent lines is similar, so we will explain only finding the northernmost one, denoted $L$. Let $p$ denote the westernmost point of intersection of $F$ and $L$, respectively. We will show how to locate $p$, with a similar procedure used to locate the easternmost point of intersection of $F$ and $L$.

Let $e$ be an edge of the convex hull of $F_w$, and $l_e$ a line collinear with $e$. If all points of $F_e$ lie on the same side of $l_e$ as $F_w$ does, then $p$ precedes the second endpoint of $e$ in the counterclockwise ordering, while if some points of $F_e$ lie on the opposite side of $l_e$ as $F_w$ does, then $p$ follows the first endpoint of $e$. This fact can be used to generate a binary search procedure to find $p$. Each iteration of the binary search consists of broadcasting an oriented edge of the convex hull of $F_w$, and then determining if any points of $F_e$ lie on the opposite side. (An oriented edge gives the equation of the line and a normal vector toward the half-plane containing $F_w$). Notice that each iteration of the binary search reduces the candidate edges remaining by half. The broadcasting from $F_w$ is done by the first extreme point of the edge. For the response from $F_e$, we have to ensure that only one processor responds (assuming the EW model). Suppose a processor $P_r$ contains the extreme point of $F_e$ such that a line parallel to $l_e$ passing through the extreme point in $P_r$ will have all the rest of $F_e$ on the side determined by the given normal to $e$. Then $P_r$ is responsible for responding, since all of $F_e$ lies on the proper side of $e$ if and only if the extreme point stored in $P_r$ does. (It is possible that there is an edge of $F_e$ parallel to $l_e$, and having $F_e$ on the proper side, in which case the processor storing the first endpoint of the edge, in the enumeration, is responsible for responding.)

The binary search to locate $p$, and each of the other three points of intersection of the tangent lines with $F$, takes $O(\log N)$ iterations, each of which takes $\Theta(1)$ time in the unit-delay model. Once the four extreme points are known, in $\Theta(1)$ time the extreme points in the quadrilateral formed by these points can be eliminated, and the extreme points can be renumbered. Therefore, in the unit-delay model the time obeys the recurrence $T(N) = T(N/2) + O(\log N)$, which is $\Theta(\log^2 N)$. □

We now turn our attention to problems related to a single set of black pixels, not necessarily connected. We first show how two disjoint convex hulls can be merged on a reconfigurable mesh, and then recursively use this in a result that gives efficient algorithms to enumerate the extreme points, determine the diameter, determine a smallest enclosing box, and determine the smallest enclosing circle of an arbitrary set of pixels.

**Lemma 4.2** *Suppose $S_1$ and $S_2$ are sets of extreme points representing two disjoint convex hulls, $|S_1| = |S_2| = k$. Given $S_1$ and $S_2$ each stored one point per processor in a row of a $k \times k$ reconfigurable mesh, the extreme points of $S_1 \cup S_2$ can be determined in $\Theta(1)$ time in the unit-delay model, and in $O(\log k)$ time under the log-delay model.*

*Proof:* Let the extreme points be stored in processors $P_1 \ldots P_k$ such that the $i$th processor stores the the $i$th extreme point of $S_1$ and the $i$th extreme point of $S_2$. The algorithm relies on being able to find the two tangent lines from a point $A$ outside of $S_1$ to the convex hull defined by $S_1$ in $\Theta(1)$ time using the unit-delay model, and in $O(\log k)$ time using the log-delay model. Suppose that every processor $P_1 \ldots P_k$ knows the point $A$. Then, each such processor $P_i$ computes the angle formed by the $x$ axis and the line through the $i$th point of $S_1$ and $A$. Let $w$ be the index of the processor having the westernmost southernmost extreme point. The angles in processors $P_1 \ldots P_w$ form a bitonic sequence. Also, a bitonic sequence is formed by the angles in processors $P_w \ldots P_k$. Thus, a processor $P_m$ having the maximum (minimum) angle can easily identify itself by examining the contents of processors $P_{m\pm1}$. Notice that the minimum and the maximum angles correspond to the tangent lines from $A$ to the convex hull defined by $S_1$.

Using the above idea, the two convex hulls defined by $S_1$ and $S_2$ can be merged as follows. Initially, the points in $S_1$ are stored one per processor in $P_{0,j}$, $0 \leq j \leq k-1$, as are the points of $S_2$.

1. Copy $S_1$ and $S_2$ to each row of the mesh. This is done for each set by a column broadcast.

2. Broadcast the $i$th point of $S_2$ to all processors in the $i$th row of the mesh.

3. Processor $P_{i,j}$ computes the angle formed between the $i$th point of $S_2$ and the $j$th point of $S_1$, with respect to the $x$ axis. The maximum and the minimum angles in each row are then detected by comparing angles in neighboring processors. Let $a_{min_i}$ and $a_{max_i}$ denote the the minimum and the maximum angles computed in the $i$th row. Using a broadcast in each row, these values can be stored in $P_{i,0}$, $0 \leq i \leq k-1$.

4. The common tangents to the two sets of extreme points are $\max(a_{min_i})$ and $\min(a_{max_i})$, which are computed using Proposition 3.3.

Since each step of the algorithm requires a fixed number of computations and bus operations, the running time is as claimed. □

The following theorem shows how to enumerate the extreme points of a single arbitrary set $S$ of pixels, and then uses the extreme points to determine additional properties of $S$. The diameter of $S$ is $\max\{d(p,q)|p,q \in S\}$, where $d$ is the Euclidean distance. A smallest enclosing box of $S$ is a (not necessarily unique) rectangle of minimal area that contains $S$, and the smallest enclosing circle of $S$ is the circle of minimal area that contains $S$.

**Theorem 4.4** *Given an $N^{1/2} \times N^{1/2}$ digitized image mapped one pixel per processor onto the processors of a reconfigurable mesh of size $N$, in $\Theta(1)$ time in the unit-delay model, and in $\Theta(\log N)$ time under the log-delay model, several geometric properties of a (not necessarily connected) set $S$ of pixels can be determined. These properties include marking and enumerating the extreme points of the convex hull, determining the diameter, and determining a smallest enclosing box.*

*Proof:* These algorithms are based on being able quickly to reduce the $N$ pieces of data to $O(N^{1/2})$ pertinent pieces of data from which the solution can be obtained. First we mark and enumerate the extreme points, and then we use these points to solve the remaining problems.

The algorithm for finding and enumerating the extreme points of a given set $S$ of pixels (distributed over an $N^{1/2} \times N^{1/2}$ mesh) is as follows.

1. Let $w_i$ and $e_i$ denote the westernmost and easternmost points, respectively, of $S$ in the $i$th row, $0 \leq i \leq N^{1/2} - 1$. Each of these can be identified by a bus splitting operation.

2. Divide the mesh into disjoint row blocks, each of size $N^{1/4} \times N^{1/2}$. Each such row block has a subset of points identified in step 1, which consists of no more than $2N^{1/4}$ points. Let $L_i$ and $R_i$ denote the sets of westernmost and easternmost points, respectively, located in the $i$th row block. Compute the convex hull of $L_i$ and $R_i$ using the $N^{3/4}$ processors of the $i$th row block as follows.

(a) Divide each row block into disjoint subblocks of size $N^{1/4} \times N^{1/4}$. Using a row broadcast, each subblock of the $i$th row block can store a copy of both $L_i$ and $R_i$.

(b) Use the $j$th subblock to decide whether or not $w_j$ is an extreme point of $L_i$ as follows. Consider $w_j$ as the origin and determine for both the upper and lower half-planes the points of $L_i$ located at the minimum and maximum angles relative to $w_j$. Then $w_j$ is an extreme point of $L_i$ if and only if it is not contained in the convex hull of these four points. These minimums and maximums can be determined by using Proposition 3.3. The extreme points of $L_i$ can be enumerated using Corollary 3.1. The extreme points of $R_i$ are computed similarly.

3. Using row and column broadcasts, the resulting sets $L_i^*$ and $R_i^*$ of extreme points in the $i$th row block are moved to each subblock of the $i$th row block and to the $i$th subblock of each row block. Using Lemma 4.2, in block $(i, j)$ the common tangent lines between $L_i$, $L_j$, $R_i$, and $R_j$ can be computed.

4. The previous step results in $O(N^{1/4})$ pairs of tangent lines in each row block. Compute the slope of these lines with the $x$ axis and compute the minimum and the maximum such angle, using Proposition 3.3. From this, the extreme points of $L_i^*$ and $R_i^*$, which are the extreme points of $S$, can be determined. These points can be enumerated using Corollary 3.1.

The algorithm uses a constant number of broadcast and bus splitting operations and thus the time is as claimed.

The diameter of the set of black pixels is easily determined once the extreme points have been marked. To do this, for each extreme point the maximum distance to any other extreme point is computed, and the maximum of these distances is the diameter. Note that the number of extreme points of a set of pixels in a grid of size $N^{1/2} \times N^{1/2}$ is $O(N^{1/3})$ [40]. To compute the farthest pixel to each extreme point, the mesh is partitioned into $N^{1/3}$ disjoint blocks of size $N^{1/6} \times N^{1/2}$ each. Using broadcast operations, the $i$th extreme point can be moved to the $i$th block and distributed to all processors in the block. Using broadcast operations, the extreme points of $S$ are moved to each row of the mesh, residing in the first $N^{1/3}$ columns. Within the $i$th block, divide the portion in the first $N^{1/3}$ columns into $N^{1/6}$ subsquares of size $N^{1/6} \times N^{1/6}$. Within each subsquare there are $N^{1/6}$ extreme points. Use Proposition 3.3 to find the maximum distance from any of these to the $i$th extreme point. Now within the $i$th block there are $N^{1/6}$ distances, one per subsquare. Move these to the leftmost subsquare, and again determine the maximum. This is the maximum distance from the $i$th extreme point to any other extreme point. The maximum of the resulting $O(N^{1/3})$ distances is the diameter and it can be computed using Proposition 3.3. Each stage takes constant time in the unit-delay model, or $O(\log N)$ time in the log-delay model, giving the time as claimed.

To compute a smallest enclosing box, use the fact that a smallest enclosing box has one of the edges of the convex hull collinear with one of its sides [10]. The other sides of the box can be determined by computing the extreme points tangent to each side of the box. Use row and column broadcasts so that every processor $P_{i,j}$ contains hull edge $e_{i,j}$. Then, each column $i$ will be used to compute a smallest box that contains an edge collinear with $e_i$ by determining points tangent to the other three sides of the box. This can be done by bus splitting operations since the distances of the extreme points from the line collinear with the hull edge form a bitonic sequence along the column responsible for the edge. Finally, the minimum of these $O(N^{1/3})$ values is computed. □

# 5 Conclusion

This chapter has introduced the reconfigurable mesh as a model of computation that captures salient features common to a number of reconfigurable architectures. We have presented efficient fundamental data movement operations, as well as efficient solutions to fundamental image problems. Many problems in low-level image analysis can also be solved using these techniques. Additional results in using the reconfiguration scheme and details of the algorithms presented in this chapter can be found in [17].

This work was motivated by a number of parallel systems being built which provide reconfigurable connections between processors. New advances in holography and other optical techniques offer certain advantages compared with traditional electronic systems, which can be exploited to provide reconfigurable interconnections [3, 7].

## Acknowledgments

The work of Russ Miller was supported in part by the National Science Foundation under grants DCR-8608640 and IRI-8800514.

The work of V. K. Prasanna Kumar was supported in part by the National Science Foundation under grant IRI-8710863.

The work of Dionisios I. Reisis was supported in part by DARPA under contract F 33615-84-K-1404 monitored by the Air Force Wright Aeronautical Laboratory.

The work of Quentin F. Stout was supported in part by the National Science Foundation under grant DCR-8507851, and by an Incentives for Excellence award from Digital Equipment Corporation.

# Bibliography

[1] A. Aggarwal, *Optimal bounds for finding maximum on array of processors with k global buses*, IEEE Transactions on Computers, vol. C-35, no. 1, 1986, pp. 62-64.

[2] H. M. Alnuweiri and V. K. Prasanna Kumar, *Efficient image computations on VLSI arrays with reduced hardware*, Proc. of IEEE Workshop on Computer Architectures for Pattern Analysis and Machine Intelligence, October, 1987.

[3] T. E. Bell, *Optical Computing: A field in flux*, IEEE Spectrum, 1986.

[4] S. H. Bokhari, *Finding maximum on an array processor with a global bus*, IEEE Transactions on Computers, vol. C-33, no. 2,

1984, pp. 133-139.

[5] D. M. Champion and J. Rothstein, *Immediate parallel solution of the longest common subsequence problem*, Proc. of International Conference on Parallel Processing, 1987, pp. 70-77.

[6] C. R. Dyer, *A VLSI pyramid machine for hierarchical parallel image processing*, Proc. of IEEE Conference on Pattern Recognition and Image Processing, 1981, pp. 381-386.

[7] Mary M. Eshaghian and V. K. Prasanna Kumar, *VLSI electro-optical computers for signal and image processing*, Proc. of Third International Conference on Supercomputing, 1988.

[8] V. K. Prasanna Kumar and D. Reisis, *VLSI arrays with reconfigurable buses*, Tech. Report, CRI-87-48, Computer Research Institute, University of Southern California, September 1987.

[9] D. Reisis and V. K. Prasanna Kumar, *VLSI arrays with reconfigurable buses*, Proc. of International Conference on Supercomputing, 1987.

[10] H. Freeman and R. Shapira, *Determining the minimal-area enclosing rectangle for an arbitrary closed curve*, Communications of ACM, vol. 18, 1975, pp. 409-413.

[11] M. Furst, J. Saxe and M. Sipser, *Parity, circuits and polynomial time hierarchy*, Proc. of IEEE symposium on Foundations on Computer Science, 1981, pp. 260-270.

[12] K. S. Hedlund and L. Snyder, *Wafer scale integration of configurable, highly parallel processors*, Proc. of International Conference on Parallel Processing, 1982, pp. 262-264.

[13] R. E. Ladner and M. J. Fischer, *Parallel prefix computation*, Journal of ACM, vol. 27, 1980, pp. 831-838.

[14] F. T. Leighton, *Parallel computations using Mesh of Trees*, Technical eport, MIT, 1982.

[15] H. Li and M. Maresca, *Polymorphic-Torus network*, Proc. of International Conference on Parallel Processing, 1987, pp. 411-414.

[16] R. Miller, V. K. Prasanna Kumar, D. Reisis, and Q. F. Stout, *Meshes with reconfigurable buses*, Proc. of the MIT Conference on Advanced Research in VLSI, 1988, pp. 163-178.

[17] R. Miller, V.K. Prasanna Kumar, D. Reisis, and Q. F. Stout, *Parallel computations on reconfigurable meshes*, to appear in IEEE Trans. on Computers.

[18] R. Miller and Q. F. Stout, *Convexity algorithms for pyramid computers*, Proc. of International Conference on Parallel Processing, 1984, pp. 177-184.

[19] R. Miller and Q. F. Stout, *Computational geometry on a mesh-connected computer*, Proc. of International Conference on Parallel Processing, 1984, pp. 66-74.

[20] R. Miller and Q. F. Stout, *Geometric algorithms for digitized pictures on a mesh-connected computer*, IEEE Transactions on Pattern Analysis and Machine Intelligence, PAMI-7, 1985, pp. 216-228.

[21] R. Miller and Q. F. Stout, *Data movement techniques for the pyramid computer*, SIAM Journal on Computing, vol. 16, no. 1, 1987, pp. 38-60.

[22] R. Miller and Q. F. Stout, *Some graph and image processing algorithms for the hypercube*, SIAM Conference on Hypercube Multiprocessor, 1987, pp. 418-425.

[23] R. Miller and Q. F. Stout, Parallel Algorithms for Regular Architectures, MIT Press, 1990.

[24] J. G. Nash and D. B. Shu, *The image understanding architecture*, Proc. of 21st Annual Asilomar Conference on Signals, Systems and Computers, 1987.

[25] D. Nassimi and S. Sahni, *Data broadcasting in SIMD computers*, IEEE Transactions on Computers, vol. C-30, no. 2, 1981, pp. 101-107.

[26] M. H. Overmars and J. Van Leeuwen, *Dynamically maintaining configurations in the plane*, Proc. of 12th Annual Symposium on Theory of Computing, 1980.

[27] V. K. Prasanna Kumar and C. S. Raghavendra, *Array processor with multiple broadcasting*, Proc. of Annual Symposium on Computer Architecture, 1985.

[28] V. K. Prasanna Kumar and M. Eshaghian, *Parallel Geometric algorithms for digitized pictures on mesh of trees organization*, International Conference on Parallel Processing, 1986, pp. 270-273.

[29] V. K. Prasanna Kumar and D. Reisis, *Parallel image processing on enhanced arrays*, International Conference on Parallel Processing, 1987, pp. 909-912.

[30] A. Rosenfeld, *Parallel image processing using cellular arrays*, IEEE Computer, 1983, pp. 14-20.

[31] D. B. Shu, J. G. Nash, and C. Weems, *The image understanding architecture and applications*, in J. Sanz, ed., Advances in Machine Vision, Applications and Architectures, Springer Verlag, 1988.

[32] D. B. Shu, J. G. Nash, and C. Weems, *A multiple level heterogeneous architecture for image understanding*, Proc. International Conference on Pattern Recognition, 1990.

[33] L. Snyder, *Introduction to the configurable highly parallel computer*, Computer, 15(1), 1982, pp. 47-56.

[34] Q. F. Stout, *Mesh connected computers with broadcasting*, IEEE Transactions on Computers, vol. C-32, 1983, pp. 826-830.

[35] Q. F. Stout, *Meshes with multiple buses*, Proc. of 27th IEEE Symposium on Foundations of Computer Science, 1986, pp. 264-273.

[36] Q. F. Stout, *Pyramid computer algorithms optimal for the worst-case*, in L. Uhr, ed., Parallel Computer Vision, Academic Press, 1987.

[37] S. L. Tanimoto, *A pyramidal approach to parallel processing*, Proc. of International Symposium on Computer Architecture, 1983, pp. 372-378.

[38] L. Uhr, Algorithm-Structured Computer Arrays and Networks, Academic Press, 1984.

[39] L. G. Valiant, *Parallelism in comparison problems*, SIAM Journal on Computing vol. 3, 1975.

[40] K. Voss and R. Klette, *On the maximum number edges of convex digital polygons included into a square*, Friedrich-Schiller Universitat Jena, Forchugsergebnisse, Nr. N/82/6.

# Experiments in Component Labeling in a Parallel Computer

**DENNIS PARKINSON**
*Center of Parallel Computing*
*Queen Mary and Westfield College, University of London*
*London, England*
and
*Active Memory Technology*
*Reading, England*

## 1 Introduction

The task of labeling components in images is an important initial step in many image–understanding strategies. Algorithms for component labeling have many features in common with problems in network analysis, such as connectivity, reachability and shortest paths. The growth of parallel computing has led to a number of publications proposing algorithms for component labeling. A common feature of most algorithms is to assume that the number of processors exactly matches the number of pixels. In real life this may not be true. The common case will be one in which the number of processors is less than the number of pixels. In this paper we evaluate some alternative strategies for component labeling of 512 × 512 bit images using a 32 × 32 processor array. The motivation for this work was not to develop a new algorithm but to evaluate the relative performance of well–known algorithms when applied to a real, practical architecture. Not all processors arrays are identical, and the optimum algorithm may depend strongly on details of the operations directly supported

Parallel Architectures and
Algorithms for
Image Understanding




ISBN 0-12-564040-4

by a given particular hardware and software environment. The next section therefore discusses the specific details of the AMT DAP 510 hardware used in this study.

# 2 The AMT DAP Hardware and Software Environments

## 2.1 Hardware

All the experiments described here were carried out on an AMT DAP 510 [1] with 8 MB of memory and equipped with a video display terminal supporting 1024 × 1024 pixels at eight bits per pixel. The DAP 510 is a 1024 processor SIMD system with each processor having 64K bits of private memory. The interprocessor communication network has two components : (1) A nearest neighbor two-dimensional mesh (NEWS), and, (2) a set of row and column highways, which give properties similar to the 'edge registers' of [2]. For this application, an important property of the highways is their ability to broadcast a given scalar simultaneously to all processors in the array.

An important tool in the development of any image–processing algorithm is the ability to view the effects of each algorithmic step. The DAP 510 has a video display screen, which can reflect the instantaneous state of a megabyte of the data space, treating it as a 1024 × 1024 by eight-bit color image. The user's space is treated as a "Frame Store" for the video so that any algorithmic effect that changes the contents of that data memory is immediately reflected on the display screen. In the project described here, we caused the screen to display the instantaneous state of the labels at every stage of the computation. We were able therefore to monitor the time history of the labeling algorithms and immediately understand which parts of our test images were contributing most to the running time.

## 2.2 Software

All our experiments were programmed using an array extension to FORTRAN 77 called FORTRAN PLUS. The latest release of FORTRAN PLUS allows the user to specify data parallel operations of arrays of arbitrary size; the compiler undertakes the task of splitting the operations into subsets, matching the real size of the machine. As a simple example consider the following task. Suppose at some stage in a computation we have a 256 × 512 array of eight-bit values which we want to call IMAGE_1, and we want to create another 256 × 512 array called IMAGE_2 with pixel values three greater than those of IMAGE_1. The data may be declared as follows:

```
INTEGER*1 IMAGE_1(*256,*512),IMAGE_2(*256,*512)
```

and the operation is then simply

```
IMAGE_2=IMAGE_1 + 3
```

A very important data type in the language is a logical variable. Arrays of logical variables can represent black and white images, but are also frequently used as "masks" to provide conditional processing.

If we have declared a variable SUBSET as follows,

```
LOGICAL SUBSET(*256,*512)
```

We can subtract 5 from those pixel values in IMAGE_1 that exceed 100, by the code

```
SUBSET=IMAGE_1.GT.100

IMAGE_1(SUBSET)=IMAGE_1 - 5
```

The index on the left-hand side of the above assignment can be considered a mask, which modifies the assignment so that it is active only where the corresponding element in the mask is true. Alternatively, we are allowed to write

```
IMAGE_1(IMAGE_1.GT.100)= IMAGE_1 - 5
```

where a logical expression is used to control which elements of IM-

AGE_1 are altered. Our image-processing application requires operations in which we compare values corresponding to two different locations in the image (usually nearest neighbors). The FORTRAN PLUS language uses "Shift Functions" or operators for this purpose. The statement

```
IMAGE_2 = IMAGE_1 + SHNP(IMAGE_1,1)
```

performs the operation

```
IMAGE_2(I,J) = IMAGE_1(I,J) + IMAGE_1(I+1,J) for all I,J
```

with IMAGE_1(257,J) being taken as zero. The SHNP function is read as "shift north plane" and returns an array conformal with its first argument, which is treated as if it had been shifted north a given distance (specified by the second argument). The plane specified that, at the edges, zeros are to be placed in the appropriate positions. Cyclic shifts are also provided as well as shifts in each of the four directions (north,east,south and west). These shift operators are fundamental tools for programming our image–labeling algorithms. There are many more features to the language, but the only other features, that we need to describe our algorithms is the ability to do a global test on a logical array. The expression ANY(SUBSET) has scalar value "true" if any element of the logical variable SUBSET is true. In the later sections we will show further examples of the language, but first we shall discuss the set of test images used in our experiments.

## 3 The Test Image Set

To prove the validity of the algorithms and provide a set of benchmarks for relative performance, we have used a set of 12 artificially generated images. The image set has been chosen in a somewhat arbitrary manner but chosen to contain "difficult" objects. All the images are 512 ×512.

Image 1– "Simple square": a two-color image formed by placing a square with side 430 in the center of the field.

Image 2– "Swiss flag": image with the cross arms 420 pixels long and 100 pixels wide.

Image 3– "Four Square": four small squares each 100 $\times$ 100 pixels located with NW corners at (200,200), (200,400), (400,200) and (400,400).

Image 4– "Vertical Blind": 32 vertical stripes each 16 pixels wide. Sketches of Images 1–4 are shown in figure 1 and 2.

Image 5– "Diagonals": a series of stripes of varying width sloped at 450 from the southwest corner to the northeast corner.

Image 6– "Chevron": An image similar to image 5 in the top 256 rows but with the stripes sloping the opposite way in the lower rows. The stripes in the lower half have different colors than those in the top half.

Image 7– "Wedding cake": an image containing eight nested squares.

Images 8 and 9 are modifications of image 7 with bridges joining some of the squares. Sketches of Images 5–9 are shown in figure 3 and 4

Image 10– "The spiral": A square spiral of width 10 pixels winding its way into the center.

Image 11– "Characters": An array of characters obtained by magnifying a proportionally spaced character set so that each character is approximately 100$\times$100 pixels. The characters are arranged in four rows with @ S X o # in the first row; 8 A M T a in the second; N Z ! e % F in the third; and W A $ ? Q in the last row. These characters were chosen because of their special shapes.

Image 12– "The mobile" A multicolored image of a mobile, specified by DARPA for an image-understanding benchmark. The image

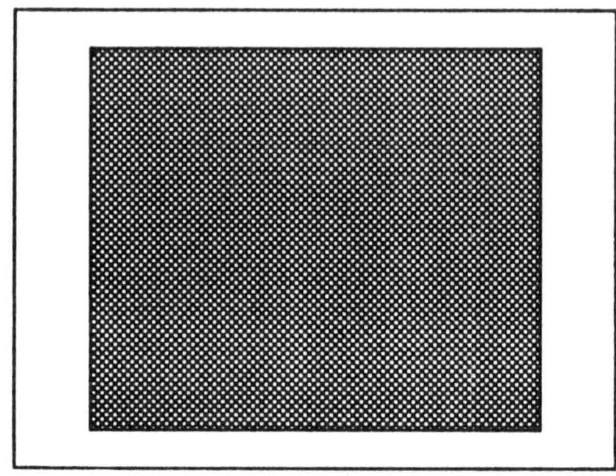

IMAGE 1

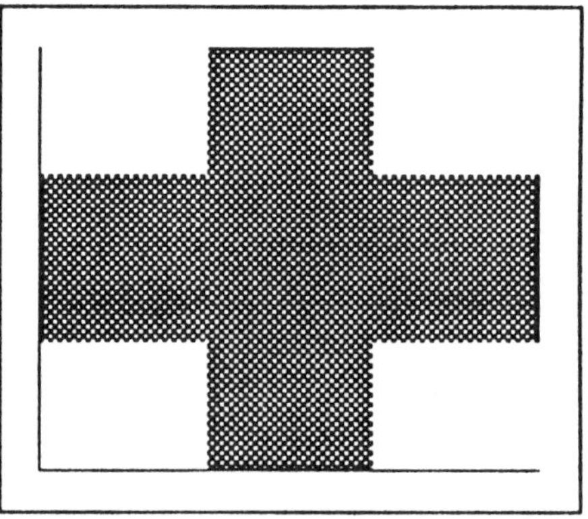

IMAGE 2

**Figure 1: Images 1 and 2.**

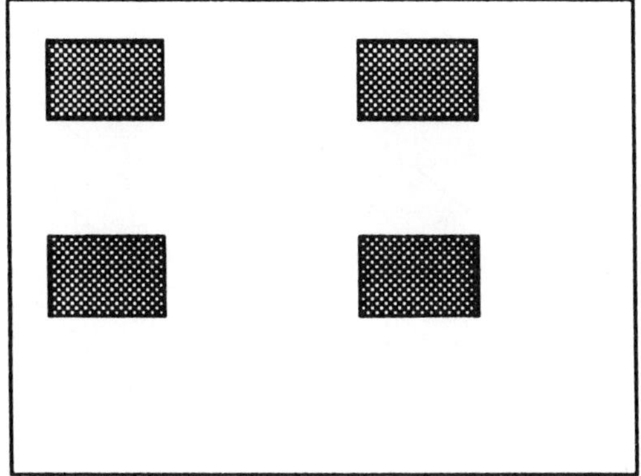

IMAGE 3

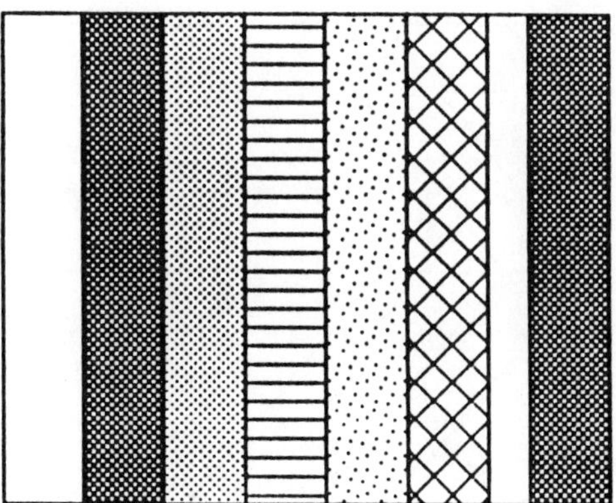

IMAGE 4

**Figure 2: Images 3 and 4.**

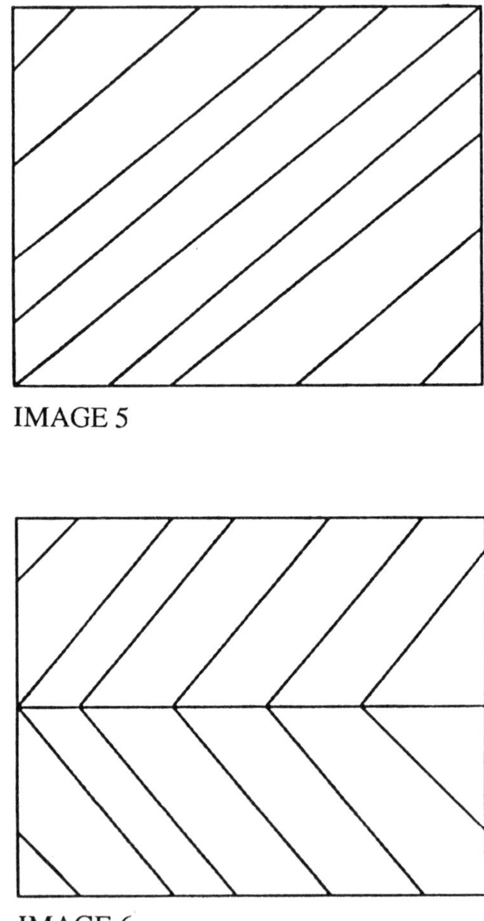


**Figure 3: Images 5 and 6.**

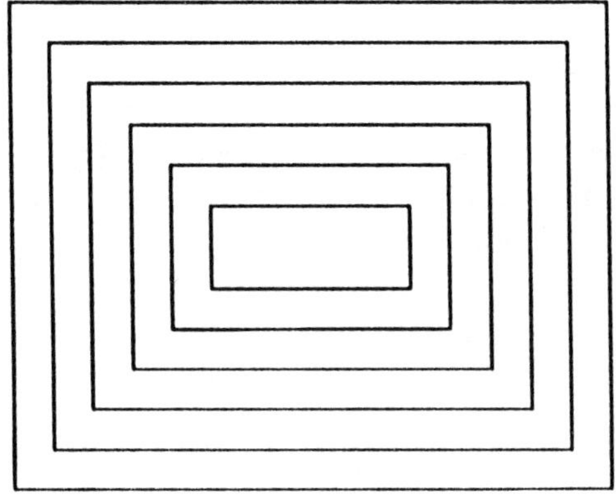


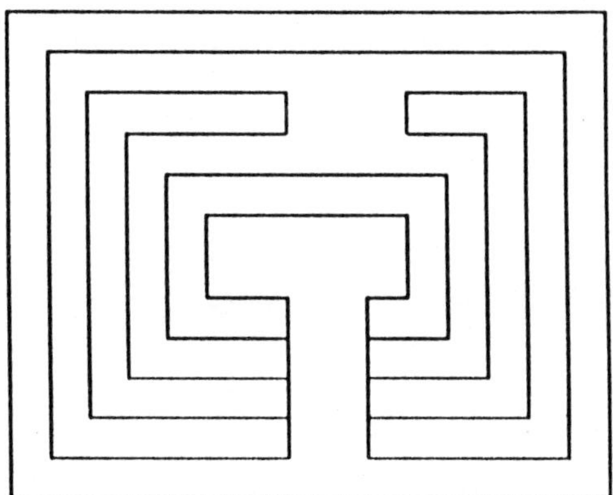


**Figure 4: Images 7, 8, and 9.**

has a number of overlapping rectangles of variable aspect ratios and orientations.

# 4 Algorithm 1

We suppose we have an n × n image of colored pixels. We define a component to be a connected set of pixels with identical color values. For this study we defined "connected" to be the four neighbor NEWS window. The extension to eight neighbors is simple. We define algorithm 1 to be the following well–known algorithm. For each point in the image allocate a unique tentative label. (We shall use a simple set of integers from 1 to $n^2$ assigned in the usual FORTRAN ordering of the elements of an array, although any other ordering would be valid.)

**Step 1** At each pixel location compare two adjacent pixels. If the two pixels' values are the same, set the local label to the smaller of itself and the value of its neighbor. Repeat for all four directions.

**Step 2** If any label has changed value in step 1, then repeat step 1; otherwise halt.

In the DAP programming language, the algorithm is trivial to program.

```
   INTEGER*3          LABELS(*512,*512),OLD_LABELS(*512,*512)
   INTEGER*1          PIXELS(*512,*512)
10 OLD_LABELS=LABELS
   LABELS(PIXELS.EQ.SHNP(PIXELS,1).AND.LABELS.LT.SHNP(LABELS))=SHNP(LABELS)
   LABELS(PIXELS.EQ.SHEP(PIXELS,1).AND.LABELS.LT.SHEP(LABELS))=SHEP(LABELS)
   LABELS(PIXELS.EQ.SHSP(PIXELS,1).AND.LABELS.LT.SHSP(LABELS))=SHSP(LABELS)
   LABELS(PIXELS.EQ.SHWP(PIXELS,1).AND.LABELS.LT.SHWP(LABELS))=SHWP(LABELS)
   IF(ANY(LABELS.NE.OLD_LABELS)) GOTO 10
```

The labels are stored at three bytes (24 bits) precision to allow sufficient precision to cover the $2^{18}$ different initial labels. The results

| Image | 1 | 2 | 3 | 4 | 5 | 6 | 7 | 8 | 9 | 10 | 11 | 12 |
|---|---|---|---|---|---|---|---|---|---|---|---|---|
| | 52 | 43 | 34 | 28 | 28 | 17 | 53 | 74 | 69 | 725 | 39 | 57 |

Table 1: Times in seconds for Algorithm 1 applied to test images

obtained for this algorithm are shown in Table 1 and can only be described as disappointing!

The reasons for the poor performance became obvious when we watched the video display. The only useful work is done on a wavefront, which propagates from a corner of each component. In the simple case of a single–color image, the number of times that Step 1 is obeyed is 1024. In more complex images, the number of times Step 1 will be obeyed is governed by the size of the largest component in the image and the "diameter" of that component. By diameter, we mean the shortest path totally within the component joining the two most extreme pixels. A spiral is a very pathological type of component that leads to diameters of nearly $n^2/2$ in a $n \times n$ image. Not only was the performance very bad for the pathological spiral image but the performance is bad for the Mobile image where the objects are relatively small. A component of that image is, however, the background, which has a very complex structure. An algorithm that identified the background as a special value would have improved the performance in that case, but we want to search a general algorithm. We also feel that a good algorithm should not have a performance that varies so strongly with the details of an individual image. The factor of 43 between the fastest and slowest image is, we believe, unsatisfactory. Algorithm 1 has a worst–case operation count $O(n^4)$ for a $n \times n$ image. If we have $m \times m$ physical processors, these operations are done $m \times m$ at a time, but we will still have to perform up to $\frac{n^4}{m^2}$ steps in the worst case. The running time of the algorithm is very strongly dependent on the image, but we can expect best performance on images consisting purely of many very small components. A fundamental fault of Algorithm 1 is that it can only propagate information one pixel location at a time. To improve the performance we need to propagate information over longer distances; we therefore examine the following algorithm.

# 5 Algorithm 2

For Algorithm 2 we adopt a strategy in which we propagate information as far as possible in a given direction before switching directions. We also reduce the number of times we perform pixel comparisons. First consider propagation of a label in the northerly direction. We use an auxiliary logical array :

```
LOGICAL EQUAL_PIXELS(*512,*512)
```

The pair of statements

```
EQUAL_PIXELS = IMAGE.EQ.SHNP(IMAGE,1)
LABELS(EQUAL_PIXELS.AND.SHNP(LABELS,1).LT.LABELS)=SHNP(LABELS,1)
```

performs the same work as the first substep in Algorithm 1. We now perform a recursive doubling algorithm, propagating the information as far as possible :

```
    I=1
101 EQUAL_PIXELS=EQUAL_PIXELS.AND.SHNP(EQUAL_PIXELS,I)
    LABELS(EQUAL_PIXELS.AND.SHNP(LABELS,I).LT.LABEL)=SHNP(LABELS,I)
    I=I*2
    IF(ANY(EQUAL_PIXELS)) GOTO 101
```

By such a code the value at the lowest end of a continuous set of equal pixel values can be propagated to the top value in only $\log_2 p$ steps, where $p$ is the vertical line length of equal pixels. The algorithm should be faster than the simple nearest neighbor algorithm for two reasons :

(1) References to eight-bit IMAGE data have been replaced by references to the single-bit data EQUAL_PIXELS.

(2) The $\log_2 p$ is very much less than $p$ when we have images with large areas of equal pixel values.

The coding for the total algorithm becomes

```
10   OLDLABELS=LABELS
     EQUAL_PIXELS= IMAGE.EQ.SHNP(IMAGE,1)
     LABELS(EQUAL_PIXELS.AND.SHNP(LABELS,1).LT.LABELS)=SHNP(LABELS,1)
     I=1
101  EQUAL_PIXELS=EQUAL_PIXELS.AND.SHNP(EQUAL_PIXELS,I)
     LABELS(EQUAL_PIXELS.AND.SHNP(LABELS,I).LT.LABEL)=SHNP(LABELS,I)
     I=I*2
     IF(ANY(EQUAL_PIXELS)) GOTO 101
     EQUAL_PIXELS= IMAGE.EQ.SHEP(IMAGE,1)
     LABELS(EQUAL_PIXELS.AND.SHEP(LABELS,1).LT.LABELS)=SHEP(LABELS,1)
     I=1
102  EQUAL_PIXELS=EQUAL_PIXELS.AND.SHEP(EQUAL_PIXELS,I)
     LABELS(EQUAL_PIXELS.AND.SHEP(LABELS,I).LT.LABEL)=SHEP(LABELS,I)
     I=I*2
     IF(ANY(EQUAL_PIXELS)) GOTO 102
     EQUAL_PIXELS= IMAGE.EQ.SHSP(IMAGE,1)
     LABELS(EQUAL_PIXELS.AND.SHSP(LABELS,1).LT.LABELS)=SHSP(LABELS,1)
     I=1
103  EQUAL_PIXELS=EQUAL_PIXELS.AND.SHSP(EQUAL_PIXELS,I)
     LABELS(EQUAL_PIXELS.AND.SHSP(LABELS,I).LT.LABEL)=SHSP(LABELS,I)
     I=I*2
     IF(ANY(EQUAL_PIXELS)) GOTO 103
     EQUAL_PIXELS= IMAGE.EQ.SHWP(IMAGE,1)
     LABELS(EQUAL_PIXELS.AND.SHWP(LABELS,1).LT.LABELS)=SHWP(LABELS,1)
     I=1
104  EQUAL_PIXELS=EQUAL_PIXELS.AND.SHWP(EQUAL_PIXELS,I)
     LABELS(EQUAL_PIXELS.AND.SHWP(LABELS,I).LT.LABEL)=SHWP(LABELS,I)
     I=I*2
     IF(ANY(EQUAL_PIXELS)) GOTO 104
     IF(ANY(LABELS.NE.OLDLABELS)) GOTO 10
```

This algorithm was tested using the test image set with dramatic improvements. Table 2 presents the results.

The improvement over algorithm 1 is dramatic but the performance for the spiral is still poor. Watching the algorithm perform confirms the expectation that the cost of Algorithm 2 is governed not

| Image | 1 | 2 | 3 | 4 | 5 | 6 |
|---|---|---|---|---|---|---|
| | 1.5 | 1.8 | 1.2 | .8 | 8.1 | 4.9 |
| Image | 7 | 8 | 9 | 10 | 11 | 12 |
| | 1.5 | 3.0 | 2.4 | 17.3 | 3.3 | 4.5 |

Table 2: Times in seconds for Algorithm 2 applied to test images.

by the diameter but by the number of turns. The number of turns is roughly the number of times a shortest path following the diameter changes direction and is reflected directly in the number of times we go around the outer loop in algorithm 2. The number of corners is particularly bad for the spiral.

# 6 Finite Parallelism Modifications

The two basic algorithms have carried an implied assumption that we have 512 × 512 processors, and we have expected the compiler to translate from the implied 512 × 512 degrees of parallelism into the actual 32 × 32 on our real target architecture. Although the compiler performs this task very efficiently, we cannot expect it to change the underlying algorithm. The next step is therefore to consider the 512 × 512 images as a 16 × 16 array of subimages each 32 × 32. Suppose we have two adjacent subimages that touch along one edge. Suppose that we have used a labeling algorithm independently to label each of the subimages. If we consider the set of edge values along the touching edge in each of the two images, comparing two adjacent image values can tell us if we want to propagate a label from one subimage into the other. However, we know that if a label value at the edge of a subimage should be changed, then all equal label values no matter where they are, must be changed in the same fashion. The edge registers discussed in Section 2 are ideal for these operations. These operations may be programmed on the DAP by the following code :

```
      INTEGER*3 LABEL(*32,*32,16,16),BROADCAST_LABEL,OLD_LABEL
      INTEGER*1 IMAGE(*32,*32,16,16)
      LOGICAL MATCH_PIXELS(*32),CHANGE_LABELS(*32)
      INTEGER INDEX
      DO 1 I=2,16
      DO 11 J=1,16
      MATCH_PIXELS=IMAGE(32,,I-1,J).EQ.IMAGE(1,,I,J)
      IF(.NOT.ANY(MATCH_PIXELS)) GOTO 11
10    CHANGE_LABELS=MATCH_PIXELS.AND.(LABEL(32,,I-1,J).LT.LABEL(1,,I,J))
      IF(.NOT.ANY(CHANGE_LABELS)) GOTO 11
      INDEX=ELN(CHANGE_LABELS)
      BROADCAST_LABEL=LABEL(32,INDEX,I-1,J)
      OLD_LABEL=LABEL(1,INDEX,I,J)
      LABELS(LABELS.EQ.OLD_LABEL,I,J)=BROADCAST_LABEL
      GOTO 10
11    CONTINUE
1     CONTINUE
```

The above code causes all labels to be broadcast down the image in subimage blocks. Similar code performs broadcasts in the other three directions. There are two points about notation, which may be unclear to the reader :

(1) When an index is omitted, all values of that index are implied. Hence, IMAGE(1,,I,J) specifies all elements in the first row of the I,Jth subimage.

(2) The function ELN returns the element number of the first true value in its logical array argument.

This subimage-matching strategy has been tested using Algorithms 1 and 2 to label the subimages. We call these modified algorithms 1M and 2M. Table 3 shows the results obtained.

The results show considerable improvements over the base algorithms, and we are pleased to note that the variation of times is considerably less than those of the raw, maximally parallel algorithms. The performance on the spiral is particularly good. The efficiency of the compiler in handling the 512 $\times$ 512 degrees of parallelism is

| Image | 1 | 2 | 3 | 4 | 5 | 6 |
|---|---|---|---|---|---|---|
| 1M | 3.4 | 3.4 | 3.4 | 3.2 | 5.4 | 4.4 |
| 2M | .94 | .95 | .94 | .80 | 2.54 | 1.84 |
| Image | 7 | 8 | 9 | 10 | 11 | 12 |
| 1M | 3.4 | 3.7 | 3.6 | 3.9 | 4.4 | 4.1 |
| 2M | .89 | 1.04 | 1.04 | 1.46 | 1.35 | 1.42 |

Table 3: Times in seconds for Algorithms 1M and 2M applied to test images.

| Algorithm | 1 | 2 | 1M | 2M |
|---|---|---|---|---|
| Lines of FORTRAN | 10 | 50 | 50 | 100 |

Table 4: Complexity of programming the algorithms.

evident when we note that Algorithm 1M is not always as good as Algorithm 2. Image 5 is the worst-case performance due to a clash between our choice of ordering the operations in the N–E–S–W order and the optimal for that image, which would prefer a N–W–S–E ordering.

# 7 Discussion

In any comparison of algorithms, one should take into account the programming difficulty. It is therefore of interest to count the number of executable lines of code written to implement the four algorithms. Approximate numbers are presented in Table 4.

The numbers are approximate because, as usual, there is a trade-off that one can make between lines of code and clarity. We could have written shorter codes, but they would have been less easy to understand. We believe that the figures in Table 4 fairly represent the relative difficulty of programming the algorithms. It is interesting to see that the performance of the algorithms follows the same trend! Further improvements are certainly possible, for instance, the need to carry 24 bits for the label information is not justified in the fastest algorithms. A reprogramming that carried fewer bits in the labels would certainly give greater speed, as would writing in lower level languages than FORTRAN.

The work presented here is an extension of some unpublished work with black and white images done during the summer of 1986 by the author and Rhys Francis of La Traube University, Melbourne. Many of the test images were conceived by Dr. Francis. The coding, which represents the generation of test images, represented a greater expenditure of effort than the actual labeling algorithms presented here.

# Bibliography

[1] D. Parkinson, D. J. Hunt, and K. S. MacQueen, *The AMT DAP 500,* Proc. of 33rd IEEE Computer Conference, San Francisco, 1988, pp. 196–199.

[2] V. K. Prasanna Kumar and C. S. Raghavendra, *Array Processor with Multiple Broadcasting,* Journal of Parallel and Distributed Computing, vol. 4, 1987, pp. 173–190.

# Image Transformations on Hypercube and Mesh Multicomputers

**SANJAY RANKA**
*Department of Computer and Information Science*
*Syracuse University*
*Syracuse, New York*

and

**SARTAJ SAHNI**
*Department of Computer Science and Engineering*
*University of Florida*
*Gainesville, Florida*

## 1 Introduction

Since transformations on two-dimensional images are very computationally intensive, several authors have developed parallel algorithms for these. For example, Rosenfeld [10] developed pyramid algorithms for shrinking and expanding. Using his algorithms, a $2^k$ step resampled shrinking and expanding of an $N \times N$ image can be performed in $O(k)$ time on a pyramid with an $N \times N$ base and height $k$ [1]. For unresampled shrinking and expanding, [10] develops an $O(k^2)$ algorithm for a one-dimensional binary image. The generalization of this algorithm to two-dimensional images results in a pyramid algorithm of complexity $O(2^k)$. The unresampled algorithm of [10] does

[1] *Throughout this chapter, we assume N is a power of two.*

Parallel Architectures and
Algorithms for
Image Understanding





ISBN 0-12-564040-4

not generalize to the case of gray-scale images. In this chapter, we develop hypercube algorithms for unresampled shrinking-expanding. Our algorithms may be applied to binary as well as gray-scale images. Our algorithm for a $2^k$ – *step* shrinking or expanding on an $N \times N$ image takes $O(k)$ time on an $N^2$ processor MIMD hypercube, $O(\log N)$ time on an $N^2$ processor SIMD hypercube, and $O(2^k)$ time on an $N \times N$ SIMD and MIMD mesh.

Lee et al. [3] developed parallel algorithms for image translation, rotation, and scaling. Their algorithms are for a mesh-connected multicomputer. Their algorithms are able to perform the above operations on an $N \times N$ binary image in $O(N)$ time, when an $N \times N$ processor mesh is available. We show how these operations can be performed for a gray-scale image in $O(\log N)$ time using an $N^2$ processor hypercube. Additionally, we develop mesh algorithms for translation, rotation, and scaling that complete in $O(N)$ time and use only $O(1)$ memory per processor. Although these operations can be performed in these time and space bounds using random access writes [4], our algorithms are elegant and have smaller constant factors associated with the complexity.

In section 2 we describe our hypercube and mesh models. Section 3 and 4 discuss image mapping and some basic data movement operations. In section 5, our algorithms for shrinking and expanding are developed. Algorithms for translation, rotation, and scaling are presented in sections 6, 7, and 8, respectively.

# 2 Multicomputer Model

The important features of an SIMD multicomputer and the programming notation we use are as follows :

1. There are $P$ processing elements connected together via an interconnection network. Different interconnection networks lead to different SIMD architectures. Each processing element (PE) has a unique index in the range $[0, P-1]$. We shall use brackets [ ] to index an array and parentheses ( ) to index PEs. Thus, A[$i$] refers to the $i$th element of array A and A($i$) refers

to the A register of PE $i$. Also, A[$j$]($i$) refers to the $j$th element of array A in PE $i$. The local memory in each PE holds data only (that is, no executable instructions). Hence, PEs need to be able to perform only the basic arithmetic operations (that is, no instruction fetch or decode is needed).

2. There is a separate program memory and control unit. The control unit performs instruction sequencing, fetching, and decoding. In addition, instructions and masks are broadcast by the control unit to the PEs for execution. An *instruction mask* is a Boolean function used to select certain PEs to execute an instruction. For example, in the instruction

$$A(i) := A(i) + 1, \quad (i_0 = 1),$$

   $(i_0 = 1)$ is a mask that selects only those PEs whose index has bit 0 equal to 1. That is, odd indexed PEs increment their A registers by 1. Sometimes we shall omit the PE indexing of registers, so, the above statement is equivalent to the statement

$$A := A + 1, \quad (i_0 = 1).$$

3. We shall consider the following interconnection networks:

   (a) *Hypercube*: A $p$-dimensional hypercube network connects $P = 2^p$ PEs (Figure 1a). Let $i_{p-1}i_{p-2}\cdots i_0$ be the binary representation of the PE index $i$. Let $\overline{i_k}$ denote the complement of bit $i_k$. A hypercube network directly connects pairs of processors whose indices differ in exactly one bit. That is, processor $i_{p-1}i_{p-2}\cdots i_0$ is connected to processors $i_{p-1}\cdots\overline{i_k}\cdots i_0$, $0 \le k \le p-1$. We use the notation $i^{(b)}$ to represent the number that differs from $i$ in exactly bit $b$.

   (b) *Mesh* : A $P = N \times N$ mesh connects $N^2$ PEs that are logically arranged as a two-dimensional array (Figure 1b). Each PE has a unique index from $(0\cdots N-1, 0\cdots N-1)$.

PE$(i,j)$ is connected to PE$((i-1)$ *mod* $N$, $j)$, PE$((i+1)$ *mod* $N$, $j)$, PE$(i$, $(j-1)$ *mod* $N)$, and PE$(i$, $(j+1)$ *mod* $N)$. Sometimes we will use a one dimensional indexing of the mesh. This is obtained using the standard row major mapping in which $(i,j)$ is mapped $iN+j$.

4. Interprocessor assignments are denoted using the symbol $\leftarrow$;

   intraprocessor assignments are denoted using the symbol $:=$. Thus, the assignment statement

   $$B(i^{(2)}) \leftarrow B(i), \quad (i_2 = 0)$$

   on a hypercube is executed only by those processors whose bit 2 is equal to 0. These processors transmit their B-register data to the corresponding processors whose bit 2 is equal to 1.

5. In a *unit route*, data may be transmitted from one processor to another if it is directly connected. We assume that the links in the interconnection network are unidirectional. Hence, at any given time, data can be transferred either from PE $i$ $(i_b = 0)$ to PE $i^{(b)}$ or from PE $i$ $(i_b = 1)$ to PE $i^{(b)}$. For example, on a hypercube, the instruction

   $$B(i^{(2)}) \leftarrow B(i), \quad (i_2 = 0)$$

   takes one unit route, whereas the instruction

   $$B(i^{(2)}) \leftarrow B(i)$$

   takes two unit routes.

6. Since the asymptotic complexity of all our algorithms is determined by the number of unit routes, our complexity analysis will count only these.

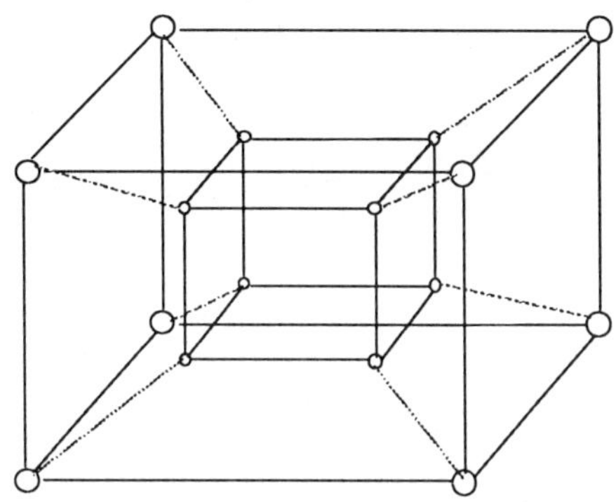

(a) 16 processor hypercube.

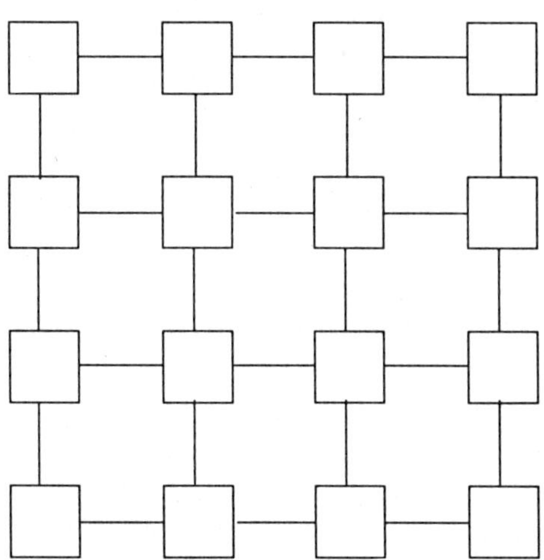

(b) A 16 node mesh
end-around connections are not shown.

Figure 1: Interconnection networks.

The features, notation, and assumptions for MIMD multicomputers differ from those of SIMD multicomputers in the following way: there is no separate control unit and program memory. The local memory of each PE holds both the data and the program that the PE is to execute. At any given instance, different PEs may execute different instructions. In particular, in an MIMD hypercube, PE $i$ may transfer data to PE $i^{(b)}$, while PE $j$ simultaneously transfers data to PE $j^{(a)}$, $a \neq b$.

# 3 Image Mapping

In the case of a mesh, the pixel in position $[i, j]$ of the image is mapped to processor $(i, j)$ of the mesh. For a hypercube, a two-dimensional grid view is needed. Figure 2a gives a two-dimensional grid interpretation of a dimension four hypercube.

This is the binary reflected gray code mapping of [1]. An $i$ bit binary gray code $S^i$ is defined recursively as follows :

$$S_1 = 0,\ 1; S_k \ = \ 0[S_{k-1}], 1[S_{k-1}]^R,$$

where $[S_{k-1}]^R$ is the reverse of the $k$-1 bit code $S_{k-1}$ and $b[S]$ is obtained from $S$ by prefixing $b$ to each entry of $S$. So, $S_2 =$ 00, 01, 11, 10 and $S_3 =$ 000, 001, 011, 010, 110, 111, 101, 100.

If $N \ = \ 2^n$, then $S_{2n}$ is used. The elements of $S_{2n}$ are assigned to the elements of the $N \times N$ grid in a snakelike row major order [12]. In this mapping, grid elements that are neighbors are assigned to neighboring hypercube nodes.

Figure 2b shows an alternate embedding of a $4 \times 4$ image grid into a dimension 4 hypercube. The index of the PE at position $(i,\ j)$ of the grid is obtained using the standard row major mapping of a two-dimensional array onto a one-dimensional array [2]. That is, for an $N \times N$ grid, the PE at position $(i,\ j)$ has index $iN + j$. Using the mapping, a two-dimensional image grid $I[0 \cdots N-1,\ 0 \cdots N-1]$ is easily mapped onto an $N^2$ hypercube (provided $N$ is a power of 2) with one element of $I$ per PE. Notice that in this mapping, image elements that are neighbors in $I$ (that is, to the north, south, east, or west of one another) may not be neighbors (i.e., may not be directly

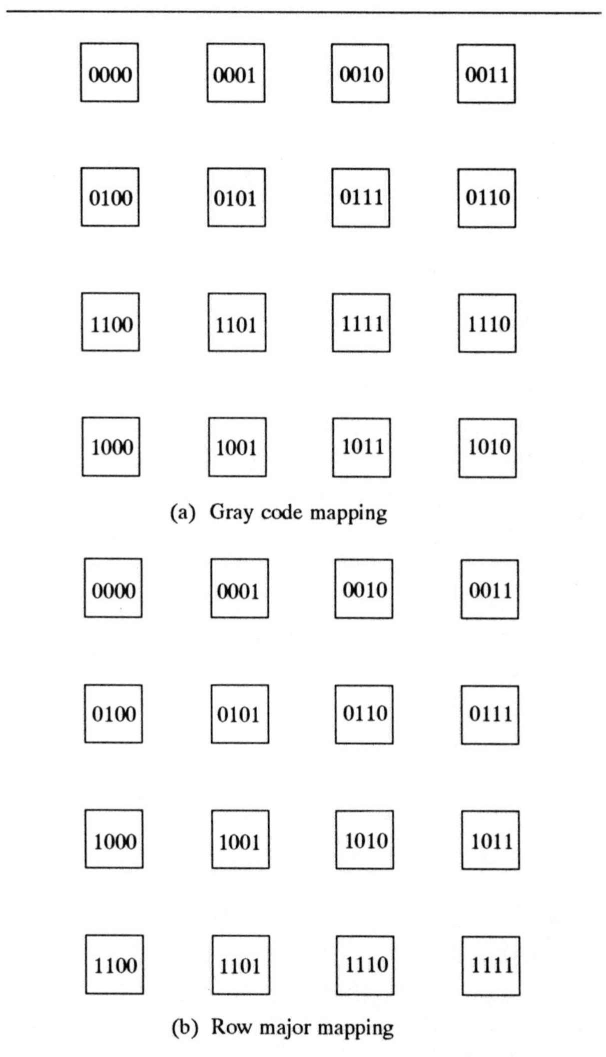


Figure 2: A 16 PE hypercube viewed as a 4 X 4 grid

connected) in the hypercube. This does not lead to any difficulties in the algorithms we develop.

We will assume that images are mapped using the gray code mapping for all MIMD hypercube algorithms and the row major mapping for all SIMD hypercube algorithms.

# 4 Basic Data Manipulation Operations

## 4.1 SIMD Shift

$SHIFT(A, i, W)$ shifts the $A$ register data circularly counterclockwise by $i$ in windows of size W. That is, $A(qW + j)$ is replaced by $A(qW + (j - i) \bmod W)$, $0 \leq q < (P/W)$. $SHIFT(A, i, W)$ on an SIMD hypercube computer can be performed in $2 \log W$ unit routes [6]. A minor modification of the algorithm given in [6] performs $i = 2^m$ shifts in $2 \log (W/i)$ unit routes [7]. The wraparound feature of this shift operation is easily replaced by an end-off *zero* fill feature. In this case, $A(qW + j)$ is replaced by $A(qW + j - i)$, as long as $0 \leq j - i < W$ and by 0 otherwise. This change does not increase the number of unit routes. The end-off shift will be denoted $ESHIFT(A, i, W)$. Both $SHIFT$ and $ESHIFT$ can be done, in a straightforward way, in $|i|$ unit routes on an SIMD mesh.

## 4.2 MIMD Shift

When $i$ is a power of two, $SHIFT(A, i, W)$ on an MIMD computer can be performed in $O(1)$ unit routes. An MIMD shift of 1 takes one unit route, of 2 takes two unit routes, of $N/2$ takes four, and the remaining power of two shifts take three routes each. For any arbitrary $i$ the shift can be completed in $3(\log W)/2 + 1$ unit routes on an MIMD computer hypercube [8]. On an MIMD mesh, the operation is easily performed with $|i|$ unit routes. As in the case of the SIMD shift, the MIMD shift is also easily modified to an end-off *zero* fill shift without increasing the number of unit routes.

## 4.3 Row and Column Reordering

These are special cases of the random access write (RAW) operation defined in [4]. We assume an $N \times N$ array logical view of an $N^2$ PE hypercube. In a row reordering, the destination processor, $dest(p)$, for data in any PE is another PE in the same row. The $dest(p)$ values in each row of the $N \times N$ processor array are either nondecreasing left to right for all rows or nonincreasing left to right for all rows. Because of this monotonicity of the *dest* values, the required reordering can be done in $O(d \log N)$ where $d$ is the maximum number of processors in any row that have the same *dest*. In case only one of the many data destined to the same processor is to survive, the time can be reduced to $O(\log N)$. This reduction requires that the surviving data be selected by some associative operation like min or *max*. The algorithm for this is obtained from the RAW algorithm of [4] by omitting the sort step.

Column reordering is the column analog of row reordering. It is performed in an analogous manner. Both operations take $O(N)$ time on a mesh.

# 5 Shrinking and Expanding

Let $I[0 \cdots N-1,\ 0 \cdots N-1]$ be an $N \times N$ image. The *neighborhood* of the image point $[i, j]$ is defined to be the set

$$nbd(i,\ j) \ = \ \{[u,\ v]\,|\,0 \le \ u < N,\, 0 \le \ v < N,\ max\{|u-i|, |v-i|\} \le \ 1\}.$$

The *q-step shrinking* of I is defined in [10] and [11] to be the $N \times N$ image $S^q$ such that

$$S^q[i,\ j] \ = \ \min_{[u,v] \in\ nbd(i,\ j)} \{I[u,\ v]\},\ q \ = \ 1,\ 0 \le \ i < N,\ 0 \le \ j < N$$
$$S^q[i,\ j] \ = \ \min_{[u,v] \in\ nbd(i,\ j)} \{S^{q-1}[u,\ v]\},\ q > 1,\ 0 \le \ i < N,\ 0 \le \ j < N.$$

Similarly, the *q-step expansion* of I is defined to be an $N \times N$ image $E^q$ such that

$$E^q[i,\ j] \ = \max_{[u,v]\in\ nbd(i,\ j)} \{I[u,\ v]\},\ q \ = \ 1$$
$$E^q[i,\ j] \ = \max_{[u,v]\in\ nbd(i,\ j)} \{E^{q-1}[u,\ v]\},\ q > 1$$

for all $0 \leq \ i, j < N$.

When the images are binary, the min and max operators in the above definitions may be replaced by *and* and *or* respectively. Let $B_{2q+1}[i,j]$ denote the block of pixels:

$$\{[u,\ v] \mid 0 \ \leq \ u < N,\ 0 \leq \ v < N,\ max\{|u-i|, |v-i|\} \ \leq \ q\}.$$

Then $nbd(i,\ j) \ = \ B_3[i,\ j]$. In [11], it is shown that

$$S^q[i,\ j] \ = \min_{[u,v]\in\ B_{2q+1}(i,\ j)} \{I[u,\ v]\} \qquad (1)$$
$$E^q[i,\ j] \ = \max_{[u,v]\in\ B_{2q+1}(i,\ j)} \{I[u,\ v]\}$$

for all $0 \leq \ i, j < N$.

Our remaining discussion of shrinking and expanding will explicitly consider shrinking only. Our algorithms for shrinking can be easily transformed to expanding algorithms of the same complexity. This transformation simply requires the replacement of every min by a max and a change in the *ESHIFT* fill in from -$\infty$ to $\infty$. In the case of binary images the min and max operators may be replaced by *and* and *or*, respectively, and the *ESHIFT* fill-in of -$\infty$ and $\infty$ by 1 and 0, respectively.

Let $R^q[i,j]$, for all $0 \leq \ i, j < N$, be defined as follows :

$$R^q[i,\ j] \ = \min_{[i,v]\in\ B_{2q+1}(i,\ j)} \{I[i,\ v]\}. \qquad (2)$$

From Eqn. 1, it follows that for all $0 \leq \ i, j < N$

$$S^q[i,\ j] \ = \min_{[u,j]\in\ B_{2q+1}(i,\ j)} \{R^q[u,\ j]\}. \qquad (3)$$

When an $N \times N$ image is mapped onto an $N \times N$ MIMD or SIMD hypercube or mesh using the mappings of Section 2, the rows and columns of the mappings are symmetric. Consequently, the algorithms to compute $R^q$ and $S^q$ from Eqs. 2 and 3 are very similar. Hence, in the sequel we consider the computation of $R^q$ only. In keeping with the development of [11], we assume $q = 2^k$.

## 5.1 MIMD Hypercube Shrinking

On an MIMD hypercube $R^q$ for $q = 2^k$ may be computed using the algorithm of Program 1. The computation of $R$ is done in two stages. These are obtained by decomposing Eqn. 2 into

$$\begin{aligned} left^q[i, j] &= \min_{[i,v] \in B_{2q+1}(i, j), v \le i} I[i, v] \\ right^q[i, j] &= \min_{[i,v]_{v \ge i} \in B_{2q+1}(i, j)} I[i, v] \\ R^q[i, j] &= \min\{left^q[i, j]\ right^q[i, j]\} \end{aligned}$$

for all $0 \le i, j < N$.

One may verify that following the first **for** loop iteration with $i = a$, $left(p)$ is the minimum of the pixel values in the left $2^a$ processors and that in its own $I$ register, $0 \le a < k$. To complete the computation of $left(p)$ we need also to consider the pixel value $2^k$ units to the left and on the same image row. This is done by a rightward shift of $2^k$. The shift is done by rows (that is, blocks of size $N$) with a fill-in of $\infty$. A similar argument establishes the correctness of the second-stage computation of *right*.

Since a power-of-two MIMD shift takes $O(1)$ time, it follows that the complexity of procedure *MIMDShrink* is $O(k)$. Once $R^q$, $q = 2^k$, has been computed, $S^q$ may be computed using a similar algorithm.

## 5.2 SIMD Hypercube Shrinking

Since a shift of $2^i$ in a window of size $N$ takes $O(\log(N/2^i))$ time on an SIMD hypercube, a simple adaptation of *MIMDShrink* to SIMD hypercubes will result in an algorithm whose complexity is $O(k \log N)$. We can do better than this using a different strategy.

```
procedure MIMDShrink;
{Compute R^q for q = 2^k on an MIMD hypercube}

begin
        {Compute min. of the left 2^k pixels on the same row}
        {MIMDEShift does an ∞ fill instead of a 0 fill}
        left(p) := I(p);
        for i := 0 to k - 1 do
        begin
                C(p) := left(p);
                MIMDEShift(C, 2^i, N);
                left(p) := min {left(p), C(p)};
        end
        C(p) := I(p);
        MIMDEShift(C, 2^k, N);
        left(p) := min {left(p), C(p)};

        {Compute min. of the right 2^k pixels on the same row}
        right(p) := I(p);
        for i := 0 to k - 1 do
        begin
                C(p) := right(p);
                MIMDEShift(C, -2^i, N);
                right(p) := min {right(p), C(p)};
        end
        C(p) := I(p);
        MIMDEShift(C, -2^k, N);
        right(p) := min {right(p), C(p)};
        R(p) := min {left(p), right(p)};
end;
```

Program 1 - MIMD computation of $R^q$.

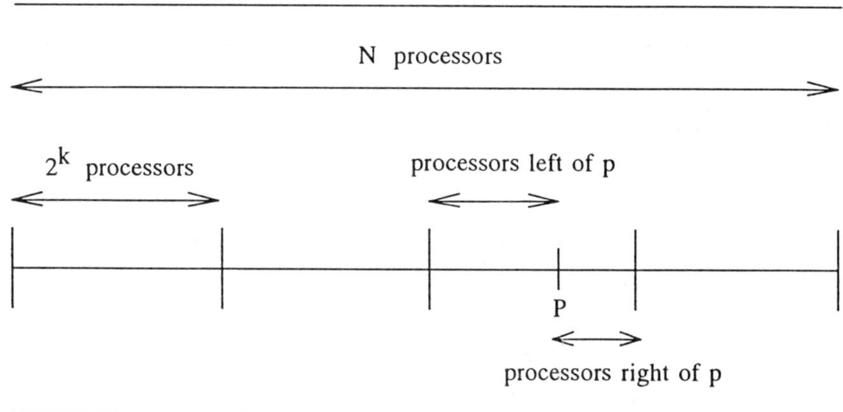


Figure 3: $2^k$ blocks of processors.

The $N \times N$ image is mapped onto the $N \times N$ hypercube using the row major mapping. $R^q$ for $q = 2^k$ may be computed by considering the $N$ processors that represent a row of the image as comprised of several blocks of size $2^k$ each (see Fig. 3).

Each processor $p$ computes

*left(p)* = minimum of pixel values to the left of $p$ but within the same $2^k$ block

*right(p)* = minimum of pixel values to the right of $p$ but within the same $2^k$ block.

Now, $R^q(p)$ is the minimum of

1. I($p$)
2. *left(p)*
3. *right(p)*
4. *left*($p + q$) provided $p + q$ is in the same row
5. *right*($p - q$) provided $p - q$ is in the same row.

Note that this is true even if $q$ is not a power of two and we use $k = \lfloor \log_2 \rfloor$ in the definition of *left* and *right*. *left(p)* and *right(p)* for $2^k$ blocks may be computed by first computing these for $2^0$ blocks,

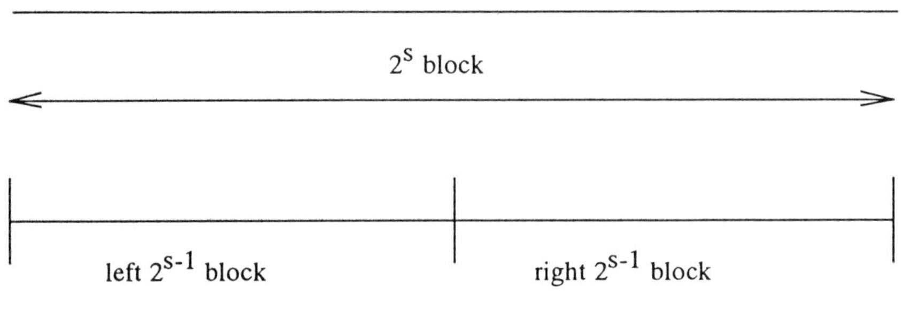


Figure 4: $2^s$ blocks of processors

then for $2^1$ blocks, then $2^2$ blocks, and so on. Let *whole(p)* be the minimum of all pixels in the block that currently contains PE $p$. For $2^0$ blocks, we have

$$left(p) = right(p) = \infty; whole(p) = I(p).$$

Each $2^s$ block for $s > 0$ consists of two $2^{s-1}$ blocks as shown in Fig. 4. One is the left $2^{s-1}$ block and the other the right $2^{s-1}$ block. The PEs in the left $2^{s-1}$ block have bit $s-1 = 0$; while those in the right one have bit $s-1 = 1$. Let us use a superscript to denote block size. So, $left_s(p)$ denotes *left(p)* when the block size is $2^s$. We see that when $p$ is in the left $2^{s-1}$ block,

$$\begin{aligned}
left^s(p) &= left^{s-1}(p) \\
right^s(p) &= \min\{right^{s-1}(p), whole^{s-1}(p + 2^{s-1})\} \\
whole^s(p) &= \min\{whole^{s-1}(p), whole^{s-1}(p + 2^{s-1})\},
\end{aligned}$$

and when $p$ is in the right $2^{s-1}$ block,

$$\begin{aligned}
left^s(p) &= \min\{left^{s-1}(p), whole^{s-1}(p - 2^{s-1})\} \\
right^s(p) &= right^{s-1}(p) \\
whole^s(p) &= \min\{whole^{s-1}(p), whole^{s-1}(p - 2^{s-1})\}.
\end{aligned}$$

Program 2 implements the strategy just developed. Its complexity is $O(\log N)$. The algorithm can also be used when $q$ is not a power of two by simply defining $k = \lfloor \log q \rfloor$. The complexity remains $O(\log N)$.

### 5.3 Shrinking on SIMD and MIMD Meshes

The operations required to shrink on a mesh are readily performed in $O(2^k)$ time.

## 6 Translation

This operation requires moving the pixel at position $[i, j]$ to the position $[i + a,\ j + b], 0 \leq i < N,\ 0 \leq j < N$, where $a$ and $b$ are given and assumed to be in the range $0 \leq a,\ b \leq N$. Translation may call for image wraparound in case $i + a \geq N$ or $j + b \geq N$. Alternatively, pixels that get moved to a position $[c,\ d]$ with either $c \geq N$ or $d \geq N$ are discarded and pixel positions $[i,\ j]$ with $i < a$ or $j < b$ get filled with zeros. Regardless of which alternative is used, image translation can be done by first shifting by $a$ along rows (circular shift for wraparound or zero-fill right shift for no wraparound) and then shifting by $b$ along rows. Unless $a$ and $b$ are powers of two, the time complexity is $O(\log N)$ on both an SIMD and an MIMD hypercube. When $a$ and $b$ are powers of two, the translation takes $O(1)$ time on an MIMD hypercube. The shifting needed for the translation takes $O(|a| + |b|)$ time.

## 7 Image Rotation

The $N \times N$ image I is to be rotated $\theta$ degrees about the point $[a,\ b]$ where $a$ and $b$ are integers in the range $[0,\ N - 1]$. Following the rotation, *pixel*$[i,\ j]$ of I will be at position $[i', j']$ where $i'$ and $j'$ are given by [9]:

$$i' = \lceil (i - a)\cos\theta - (j - b)\sin\theta + a \rceil$$

---

```
procedure SIMDShrink;
{Compute R^q for q = 2^k on an SIMD hypercube}

begin
    {Initialize for 2^0 blocks}
    whole(p) := I(p);
    left(p) := ∞;
    right(p) := ∞;

    {Compute for 2^(i+1) blocks}
    for i := 0 to k - 1 do
    begin
        C(p) := whole(p);
        C(p) ← C(p^(i));
        left(p) := min {left(p), C(p)}; (p^(i) = 1)
        right(p) := min {right(p), C(p)}; (p^(i) = 0)
        whole(p) := min {whole(p), C(p)};
    end

    R(p) := min {I(p), left(p), right(p)};
    SIMDEShift(left, -q, N);
    SIMDEShift(right, q, N);
    R(p) := min {R(p), left(p), right(p)};
end; { of SIMDShrink }
```

---

Program 2 - SIMD computation of $R^q$

$$j' = \lceil (i - a)\sin\theta + (j - b)\cos\theta + b \rceil.$$

The equations for $i'$ and $j'$, may be simplified to

$$\begin{aligned} i' &= \lceil i\cos\theta - j\sin\theta + A \rceil \\ j' &= \lceil i\sin\theta + j\cos\theta + B \rceil, \end{aligned} \quad (4)$$

where $A = a(1 - \cos\theta) + b\sin\theta$
and $B = b(1 - \cos\theta) - a\sin\theta$.

We first consider rotations of $\theta = 180^0, 90^0, -90^0$, and $|\theta| \leq 45^0$. Then we show that a rotation of an arbitrary $\theta$, $0 \leq \theta \leq 360^0$ can be performed using the algorithms for these special cases.

### 7.1 $\theta = 180^0$

In this case,

$$\begin{aligned} i' &= -i + a \\ j' &= -j + b. \end{aligned}$$

The rotation can be performed as follows:

**Step 1:** [Column reordering] Each processor, $p$, sets $dest(p) = -i + a$ where $i$ is the row number of the processor. Next, a column reordering as described in Section 4.3 is done.

**Step 2:** [Row reordering] Each processor, $p$, sets $dest(p) = -j + b$ where $j$ is the column number of the processor. Next, a row reordering as described in Section 4.3 is done.

Note that the *dest* values in each column in *Step 1* and those in each row in *Step*2 are in decreasing order. *Step 1* sends all pixels to their correct destination row while *Step 2* sends them to the correct column. The column and row reordering of *Steps* 1 and 2 can be replaced by column and row reversal followed by a shift. Since a reversal can be done in $O(\log N)$ time [5], the complexity of a $180^0$ rotation on a hypercube is $O(\log N)$, regardless of how the RAW's of *steps* 1 and 2 are accomplished. On a mesh, its complexity is $O(N)$.

### 7.2 $\theta = \pm 90^0$

The case $\theta = 90^0$ and $\theta = -90^0$ are quite similar. We consider only the case $\theta = 90^0$. Now,

$$\begin{aligned} i' &= -j + a + b \\ j' &= i - a + b. \end{aligned}$$

The steps in the rotation are:

**Step 1:** [Transpose] Transpose the image so that $I^{new}[i, j] = I^{old}[j, i]$

**Step 2:** [Column reorder] Each processor sets $dest(p) = a + b - i$, where $i$ is the row number of the processor. Next, a column reordering (cf. Section 4.3) is done.

**Step 3:** [Shift] A rightward shift of $-a + b$ is performed on each row of the image.

Note that in a $90^0$ rotation the pixel originally at $[i, j]$ is to be routed to $[-j + a + b, i - a + b]$. Step 1 routes the pixel to position $[j, i]$; Step 2 routes it to $[a + b - j, i]$; and Step 3 to $[a + b - j, i - a + b]$. The transpose of *Step*1 can be performed on a hypercube in $O(\log N)$ time using the algorithm of [5]. The overall complexity is $O(\log N)$ on a hypercube.. Once again, the column reordering of *Step*2 can be done by a column reversal followed by a shift. This does not change the asymptotic complexity. On a mesh, the three steps can be completed in $O(N)$ time.

### 7.3 $|\theta| \leq 45^0$

We explicitly consider the case $0 \leq \theta \leq 45^0$ only. The case $-45^0 \leq \theta < 0$ is similar. The steps for the case $0 \leq \theta \leq 45^0$ are

**Step 1:** [Column reorder] Set $dest(p) = \lceil i \cos\theta - j \sin\theta + A \rceil$, where $i$ is the row number and $j$ the column number of processor $p$. Since $j$ is the same in a column, $dest(p)$ is nondecreasing in each column. Hence, a column reordering can be done as described in Section 4.3. All data with the same destination are routed to that destination.

**Step 2:** [Row reorder] Set $dest(p) = \lceil i\tan\theta + j\sec\theta - A\tan\theta + B\rceil$, where $i$ and $j$ are, respectively, the row and column numbers of processor $p$. A row reordering may be performed as described in Section 4.3.

**Step 3:** [Shift] Pixels that need to be shifted left by one along rows are shifted.

Step 1 sends each pixel to its correct destination row. Since $0 \le \theta \le 45^0$, $1/\sqrt{2} \le \cos\theta \le 1$. Hence, each processor can have at most two pixels directed to it. The column reordering of Step 1 is done such that both these reach their destination. Following this, the pixels in the processor at position $[i, j]$ originated in processors in column $j$ and row

$$\frac{i + j\sin\theta - A - \delta}{\cos\theta},$$

where $0 \le \delta < 1$ accounts for the ceiling function in Eqn. 4. From Eqn. 4, it follows that these pixels are to be routed to the processors in row $i$ and column $j = \lceil y\rceil$, where $y$ is given by

$$\begin{aligned} y &= \left(\frac{i + j\sin\theta - A - \delta}{\cos\theta}\right)\sin\theta + j\cos\theta + B \\ &= i\tan\theta + j\left(\frac{\sin^2\theta + \cos^2\theta}{\cos\theta}\right) - A\tan\theta - \delta\tan\theta + B \\ &= i\tan\theta + j\sec\theta - A\tan\theta + B - \delta\tan\theta. \end{aligned}$$

In Step 2, the pixels are first routed to the column $\lceil i\tan\theta + j\sec\theta - A\tan\theta + B\rceil$. Then, in Step 3, we account for the $\delta\tan\theta$ term in the formula for $y$. For $0 \le \theta \le 45^0$, $\tan\theta$ is in the range $[0, 1]$. Since $0 \le \delta < 1$, $0 \le \delta\tan\theta < 1$, the pixels need to be shifted left on the rows by at most 1. Note that since $1 \le \sec\theta \le \sqrt{2}$ for $0 \le \theta \le 45^0$, $dest(p)$ is different for different processors on the same row. One readily sees that on a hypercube, $O(\log N)$ time suffices for the rotation, and $O(N)$ time is sufficient on a mesh.

### 7.4 $0 \leq \theta \leq 360^0$

Every $\theta$ in the range $[0, 360]$ can be cast into one of these forms:

(1) $-45 \leq \theta' \leq 45$

(2) $\pm 90 + \theta', \quad -45 \leq \theta' \leq 45$

(3) $\pm 180 + \theta', \quad -45 \leq \theta' \leq 45$

Case 1 was handled in the last subsection. Cases 2 and 3 can be done in two steps. First a $\pm 90^0$ or a $180^0$ rotation is done (note that a $180^0$ and a $-180^0$ rotation are identical). Next a $\theta'$ rotation is performed. This two-step process may introduce some errors because of end-off conditions from the first step. These can be eliminated by implementing all rotations as wraparound rotations and then having a final cleanup step to eliminate the undesired wraparound pixels.

## 8 Scaling

Scaling an image by $s$, $s \geq 0$, around position $[a, b]$ requires moving the pixel at position $[i, j]$ to the position $[i', j']$ such that [3]:

$$i' = \lceil si + a(1 - s) \rceil$$

$$j' = \lceil si + b(1 - s) \rceil$$

$$0 \leq i, j < N.$$

In case $i' \geq N$ or $j' \geq N$, the pixel is discarded. If two or more pixels get mapped to the same location, then we have two cases:

1. Only one of these is to survive. The surviving pixel is obtained by some associative operation such as max, min, average etc.

2. All pixels are to survive.

When $s > 1$, then in addition to routing each pixel to its destination pixel, it is necessary to reconnect the image boundary and fill in the inside of the objects in the image [3]. The pixel routing can be done in $O((\log N)/s)$ time on a hypercube and in $O(N/s)$ time on a mesh when $s < 1$ and all pixels to the same destination are to survive. In all other cases, pixel routing takes $O(\log N)$ time on a hypercube and $O(N)$ time on a mesh. The routing strategy is to perform a row reordering followed by a column reordering. Reconnecting the boundary and filling require $O(\log N)$ time on a hypercube and $O(N)$ time on a mesh.

# 9 Conclusions

We have developed efficient hypercube and mesh algorithms for image shrinking, expanding, translation, rotation, and scaling. All our algorithms require $O(1)$ memory per PE. The complexity of each operation on an $N^2$ PE hypercube is $O(d \log N)$ and on an $N \times N$ mesh is $O(dN)$, where $d$ is the maximum number of data that is destined to any processor.

### Acknowledgments

The research reported in this chapter was supported in part by the National Science Foundation under grants DCR84-20935 and MIP 86-17374.

# Bibliography

[1] T. E. Chan and Y. Saad, Multigrid algorithms on hypercube multiprocessor, IEEE Transactions on Computers, vol. C-35, Nov. 86, pp. 969–977.

[2] E. Horowitz and S. Sahni, Fundamentals of Data Structures in Pascal, Computer Science Press, 1985.

[3] S. Y. Lee, S. Yalamanchali, and J. K. Agarwal, Parallel Image Normalization on a Mesh Connected Array Processor, Pattern

Recognition, vol. 20, no. 1, Jan 87, pp. 115–120.

[4] D. Nassimi and S. Sahni, Data Broadcasting in SIMD computers, IEEE Transactions on Computers, vol. C-30, no. 2, Feb. 1981, pp. 101–107.

[5] D. Nassimi and S. Sahni, Optimal BPC permutations on a cube connected computer, IEEE Transactions on Computers, vol. C-31, no. 4, Apr. 1982, pp. 338–341.

[6] V. K. Prasanna Kumar and V. Krishnan, Efficient Image Template Matching on SIMD Hypercube Machines, International Conference on Parallel Processing, 1987, pp. 765-771.

[7] S. Ranka and S. Sahni, Image Template Matching on an SIMD hypercube multicomputer, 1988 International Conference on Parallel Processing, Vol III, Algorithms & Applications, Pennsylvania State University Press, pp 84–91.

[8] S. Ranka and S. Sahni, Image Template Matching on MIMD hypercube multicomputers, 1988 International Conference on Parallel Processing, Vol III, Algorithms & Applications, Pennsylvania State University Press, pp 92–99.

[9] A. P. Reeves and C. H. Francfort, Data Mapping and Rotation Functions for the Massively Parallel Processor, IEEE Computer Society Workshop on Computer Architecture for Pattern Analysis and Image Database Management, 1985, pp. 412–417.

[10] A. Rosenfeld, A note on shrinking and expanding operations on pyramids, Pattern Recognition Letters 6 , Sept 1987, pp. 241–244.

[11] A. Rosenfeld and A. C. Kak, Digital Picture Processing, Academic Press, 1982.

[12] C. D. Thompson and H. T. Kung, Sorting on a mesh-connected parallel computer, Communications of the ACM, 1977, pp 263–271.

# Part III

# Implementations and Applications

# Architecture and Performance Evaluation of NETRA

ALOK N. CHOUDHARY
*Department of Electrical and Computer Engineering*
*Syracuse University*
*Syracuse, New York*

and

JANAK H. PATEL and NARENDRA AHUJA
*Coordinated Science Laboratory*
*University of Illinois*
*Urbana, Illinois*

## 1 Introduction

Computer vision has been regarded as one of the most complex and computationally intensive problems. Computer vision algorithms perform a variety of mathematical, signal processing, graph theoretic, and data manipulation computations. Thus, parallel processing has been the most widely accepted approach to solve computer vision problems.

Several multiprocessor architectures have been proposed for computer vision. Some of the common architectures include mesh connected, [7, 8, 1] pyramids, [4, 17, 20] array processors, systolic arrays (CMU Warp), [14, 9, 13] and hypercubes [10]. Most of these architectures are SIMD computers (with the exception of Warp and some hypercube machines) and hence are mainly suitable for low–level vision algorithms. However, low–level vision algorithms constitute only the first few steps in a vision system [21, 5]. Therefore, SIMD computers, such as those listed here, are not suitable for efficient implementation of complex vision systems. Several hierarchical and partitionable ar-

Parallel Architectures and
Algorithms for
Image Understanding


ISBN 0-12-564040-4

chitectures have been proposed that contain both SIMD and MIMD types of computing modules. Examples include PM4[3], PASM[19], REPLICA[15], INSPECTOR[16], and IUA[22]. Design of these architectures has addressed the issues of flexibility, partitionability, and reconfigurability, which are needed in an architecture for vision systems.

In this chapter we consider one such multiprocessor architecture called NETRA, which is highly reconfigurable and does not involve the use of complex interconnection schemes [5, 18]. The topology of NETRA is recursively defined and hence is easily scalable from small to large systems. It has a tree-type hierarchical architecture each of whose leaf nodes consists of a cluster of small but powerful processors connected via a programmable crossbar with selective broadcast capability. NETRA also provides shared memory as well as distributed memory computation paradigms.

The focus of this chapter is on the performance evaluation of clusters of NETRA. We show how a cluster can be reconfigured to perform computations in SIMD, MIMD, and systolic modes. The reconfiguration is obtained by programming the crossbar of cluster appropriately. We present performance evaluation of several common vision algorithms such as two-dimensional FFT, two-dimensional convolution, and median filtering. We present analytical performance results for some algorithms and compare them with implementation on a cluster simulation. It is shown that analytical performance results are very close to the implementation results.

This chapter is organized as follows. Section 2 contains a description of the NETRA. Section 3 shows how to map an algorithm onto a processor cluster in NETRA and describes different computation modes. In Section 4 we present performance analysis of various algorithms on a cluster. Implementation results are presented in Section 5. Furthermore, a comparison of analytical and implementation performance results is presented. Finally, in Section 6, a summary and concluding remarks are given.

# 2 Architecture of NETRA

Figure 1 shows the architecture of NETRA which consists of the following components :

1. a large number (1000–10000) of processing elements (PEs), organized into clusters of 16–64 PEs each.

2. a tree of distributing and scheduling-processors (DSPs) that make up the task distribution and control structure of the multiprocessor.

3. a parallel pipelined shared Global Memory and a global interconnection that links the PEs and DSPs to the global memory.

## 2.1 Processor Clusters

The clusters consist of 16–64 PEs, each with its own program and data memory. They form a layer below the DSP tree, with a leaf DSP associated with each cluster. PEs within a cluster also share a common data memory. The PEs, the DSP associated with the cluster, and the shared memory are connected together with a crossbar switch. The crossbar switch permits point-to-point communication as well as selective broadcast by the DSP or any of the PEs. Figure 2 shows the cluster organization using a 4×4 crossbar. The crossbar design consists of pass transistors connecting the input and output data lines. The switches are controlled by control bits indicating the connection pattern. If a processor of DSP needs to broadcast, then all the control bits in its row are made one. To connect processor $P_i$ to processor $P_j$, control bit $(i, j)$ is set to one and the rest of the control bits in row $i$ and column $j$ are set to zero.

Clusters can operate in an SIMD mode, a systolic mode, or an MIMD mode. Each PE is a general–purpose processor with a capability for high–speed floating–point operations. In an SIMD mode, PEs in a cluster execute identical instruction streams from private memories in a lockstep fashion. In the systolic mode, PEs repetitively execute an instruction or set of instructions on data streams from one or more PEs. In both cases, communication between PEs

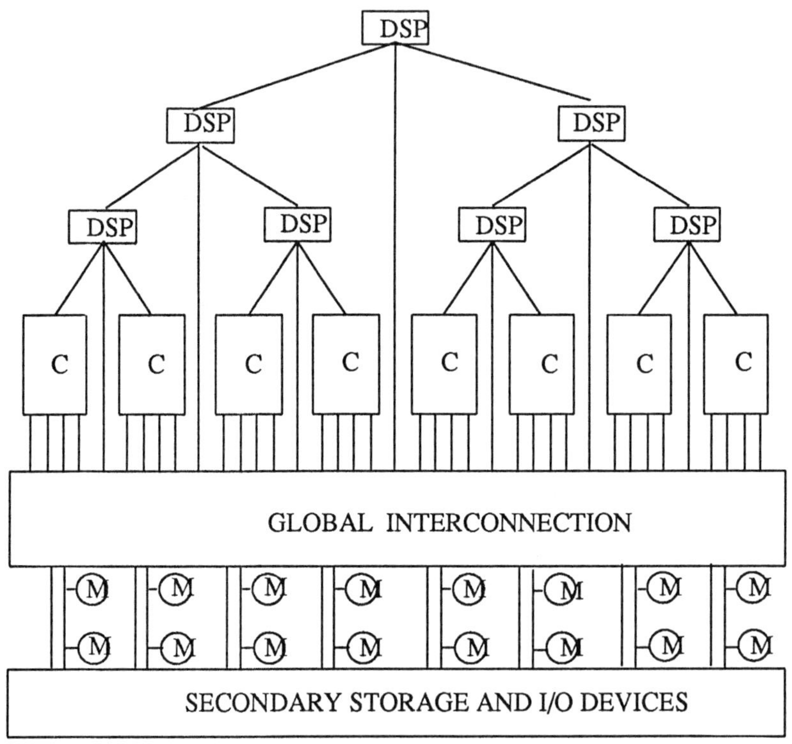


DSP : Distributing and Scheduling Processor
C : Processor Cluster M : Memory Module

**Figure 1: Organization of NETRA.**

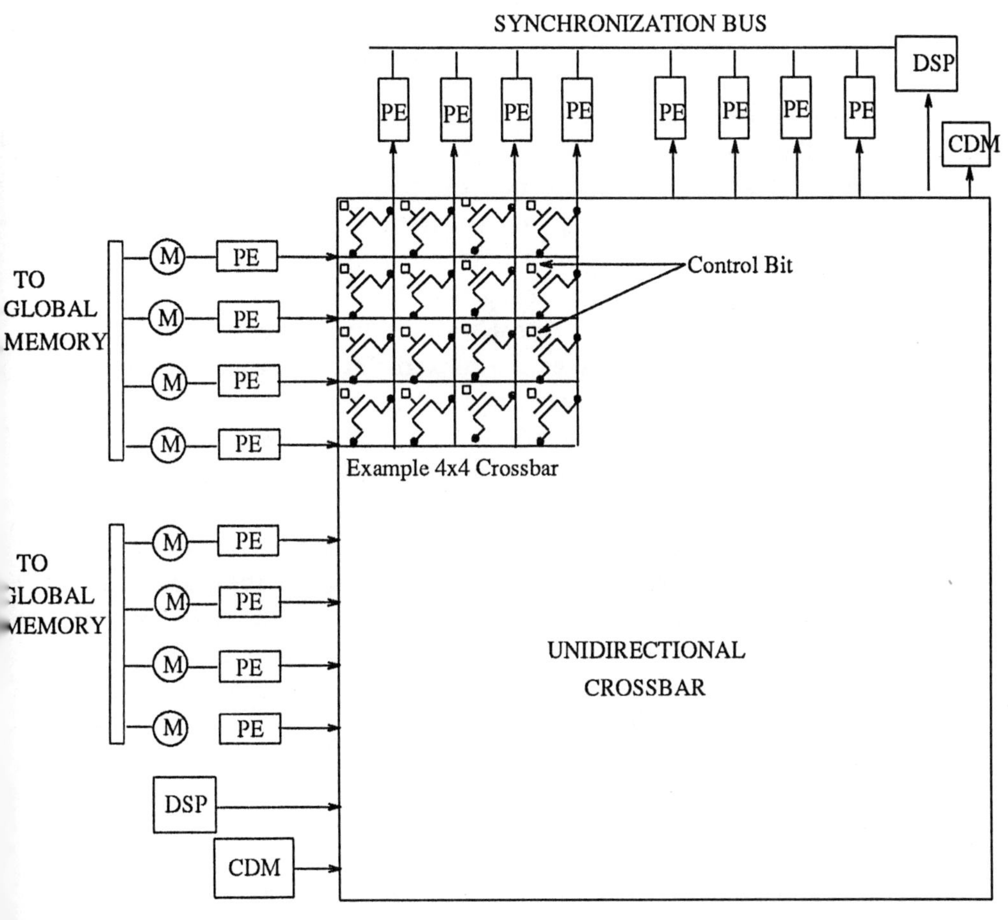


**Figure 2: Organization of a processor cluster. PE: processor, M: local memory, CDM: Common data memory.**

is synchronous. In the MIMD mode, PEs asynchronously execute instruction streams resident in their private memories. The streams may not be identical. To synchronize the processors in a cluster, a synchronization bus is provided, which is used by processors to indicate to the DSP that one or more processors have finished computation or that a processor wants to change the communication pattern. The DSP can either poll the processors or the processors can interrupt the DSP using the synchronization bus.

There is no arbitration in the crossbar switch. That is, the interconnection between processors has to be programmed before processors can communicate with each other. Programming a crossbar requires writing a communication pattern into the control memory of the crossbar. A processor can alter the communication pattern by updating the control memory as long as it does not conflict with the existing communication pattern. The DSP associated with the cluster can write into the control memory to alter the communication pattern. The most common communication patterns such as linear arrays, trees, meshes, pyramids, shuffle-exchanges, cubes, broadcast, can be stored in the memory of the crossbar. These patterns need not be supplied externally. Therefore, switching to a different pattern in the crossbar can be fast because switching only requires writing the patterns into the control bits of the crossbar switches from its control memory.

## 2.2 The DSP Hierarchy

The DSP tree is an n-tree with nodes corresponding to DSPs and edges to bidirectional communication links. Each DSP node is composed of a processor, a buffer memory, and a corresponding controller.

The tree structure has two primary functions. First, it represents the control hierarchy for the multiprocessor. A DSP serves as a controller for the subtree structure under it. Each task starts at a node on an appropriate level in the tree, and is recursively distributed at each level of the subtree under the node. At the bottom of the tree, the subtasks are executed on a processor cluster in the desired mode (SIMD or MIMD) and under the supervision of the leaf DSP.

The second function is that of distributing the programs to leaf DSPs and the PEs. Vision algorithms are characterized by a large number of identical parallel processes that exploit the spatial parallelism and operate on different data sets. It would be highly wasteful if each PE issued a separate request for its copy of the program block to the global memory because it would result in large unnecessary traffic through the interconnection network. Under the DSP-hierarchy approach, one copy of the program is fetched by the controlling DSP (the DSP at the root of the task subtree) and then broadcast down the subtree to the selected PEs. Also, DSP hierarchy provides communication paths between clusters to transfer control information or data from one cluster to others. Finally, the DSP tree is responsible for global memory management.

## 2.3 Global Memory

The multiport global memory is a parallel-pipelined structure as introduced in [2]. Given a memory (chip) access time of $T$ processor-cycles, each line has $T$ memory modules. It accepts a request in each cycle and responds after a delay of $T$ cycles. Since an $L$-port memory has $L$ lines, the memory can support a bandwidth of $L$ words per cycle.

Data and programs are organized in memory in *blocks*.Blocks correspond to 'units' of data and programs. The size of a block is variable and is determined by the underlying tasks and their data structures and data requirements. A large number of blocks may together constitute an entire program or an entire image. Memory requests are made for blocks. The PEs and DSPs are connected to the global memory with a multistage interconnection network.

The global memory is capable of queuing requests made for blocks that have not yet been written into. Each line (or port) has a memory-line controller (MLC), which maintains a list of read requests to the line and services them when the block arrives. It maintains a table of *tokens* corresponding to blocks on the line, together with their length, virtual address, and full–empty status. The MLC is also responsible for virtual memory management functions.

Two main functions of the global memory are input–output of

data and program to and from the DSPs and processor clusters, and to provide intercluster communication between various tasks as well as within a task if a task is mapped onto more than one cluster.

### 2.4 Global Interconnection

The PEs and the DSPs are connected to the global memory using a multistage circuit-switching interconnection network. Data are transferred through the network in pages. A page is transferred from the global memory to the processors, which is given in the header as a destination port address; and the header also contains the starting address of the page in the global memory. When the data are written into the global memory, only starting address needs to be stated. In each case, end-of-page may be indicated using an extra flag bit appended to each word. For further details of the NETRA the reader is referred to [5, 18, 6].

## 3 Computation Modes and Mapping in a Cluster

In this section we describe two computational modes for a processor cluster, namely, SIMD mode and systolic mode. An important characteristic in reconfiguring in different modes is that it can be achieved by simply programming the crossbar connections. The design of the crossbar permits fast enough communication links so that systolic computations can be performed even though the processors and interconnection network are general–purpose [5].

The computation modes are described using a mapping of a matrix multiplication algorithm. The MIMD mode of computation is described in the next section along with performance analysis.

### 3.1 Computation Modes

The clusters in NETRA provide SIMD, MIMD, and systolic capabilities. Consider matrix multiplication operation. We will show how it can be performed in SIMD and systolic modes. Assume that the computation requires obtaining matrix $C = A \times B$. For simplicity, also assume that the cluster size is $P$ and the matrix dimensions are $P \times P$. Note that this assumption is made to simplify the example description. In general, any arbitrary–size computation can be performed independent of the data or cluster size.

## SIMD Mode

The algorithm can be mapped as follows. Each processor is assigned a column of the $B$ matrix, that is, processor $P_i$ is assigned column $B_i$. Then the DSP broadcasts each row to the cluster processor, which computes the inner products of the rows with their corresponding columns in lockstep fashion. Note that the elements of the A matrix can be continuously broadcast by DSP, row by row without any interruptions, and therefore, efficient pipelining of data input, multiply, and accumulate operations can be achieved. Figure 3a illustrates an SIMD configuration of a cluster. The following pseudo code describes the DSP and processor ($P_k$'s program, $0 \leq k \leq P-1$) programs.

**SIMD Computation**

| DSP | $P_k$ |
|---|---|
| 1. FOR i=0 to i=P-1 DO | 1. - |
| 2. connect(DSP,$P_i$) | 2. - |
| 3. out(column $B_i$) | 3. in(column $B_i$) |
| 4. END_FOR | 4. - |
| 5. connect(DSP, all) | 5. - |
| 6. FOR i=0 to i=P-1 DO | 6. $c_{ik} = 0$ |
| 7. FOR j=0 to j=P-1 DO | 7. FOR j=0 to j=P-1 DO |
| 8. out($a_{ij}$) | 8. in($a_{ij}$) |
| 9. END_FOR | 9. $c_{ik} = c_{ik} + a_{ij} * b_{jk}$ |
| 10. END_FOR | 10. END_FOR |

In the previous code, the computation proceeds as follows. In the first three lines, the DSP connects with each processor through the crossbar and writes the column on the output port. That column

**Systolic Computation**

| **DSP** | $P_i$ |
|---|---|
| 1. FOR i=0 to i=P-1 DO | 1. - |
| 2. connect(DSP,$P_i$) | 2. - |
| 3. out(column $B_i$) | 3. in(column $B_i$) |
| 4. out(row $A_i$) | 4. in(column $A_i$) |
| 5. END_FOR | 5. - |
| 6. connect($P_i$ to $P_{i+1}$ *mod* $P$) | 6. $c_{ii} = 0$ |
| 7. - | 7. FOR j=0 to j=P-1 DO |
| 8. - | 8. $c_{ii} = c_{ii} + a_{ij} * b_{ji}$ |
| 9. - | 9. out($a_{ij}$), in($a_{i-1j}$) |
| 10. - | 10. END_FOR |
| 11. - | 11. repeat 7–10 for each new row |

is input by the corresponding processor. In Statement 5, the DSP connects with all the processors in a broadcast mode. Then, from Statement 6 onward, the DSP broadcasts the data from matrix A in row major order, and each processor computes the inner product with each row. Finally, each processor has a column of the output matrix. It should be mentioned that the code describes the operation in principle and does not exactly depict the timing of operations.

## Systolic Mode

The same computation can be performed in a systolic mode. The DSP can reconfigure the cluster in a circular linear array after distributing columns of matrix B to processors as before. Then DSP assigns row $A_i$ of matrix $A$ to processor $P_i$. Each processor computes the inner product of its row with its column and at the same time writes the element of the row on the output port. This element of the row is input to the next processor. Therefore, each processor receives the rows of matrix A in a systolic fashion, and the computation is performed in the systolic fashion. Note that the computation and communication can be efficiently pipelined. In the code, it is

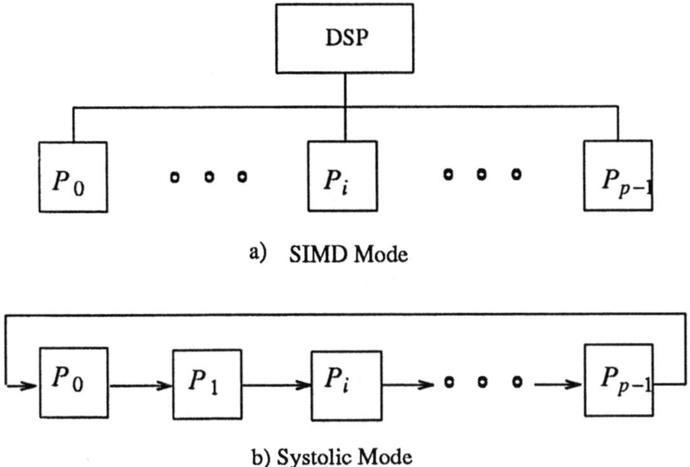


Figure 3: An example of SIMD and systolic modes of computation in a cluster. a) SIMD mode. b) MIMD mode.

depicted by Statements 7–10. Each element of the row is used by a processor and immediately written onto the output port, and at the same time, the processor receives an element of the row of the previous processor. Therefore, a processor computes new element of the $C$ matrix from the new rows it receives every $P$ cycles. Again, note that the code describes only the logic of the computation and does not include the timing information. Figure 3b illustrates a systolic configuration of a cluster.

## 3.2 Mapping Parallel Algorithms on a Cluster

There are two main considerations in the mapping of parallel algorithms onto a cluster. First is selection of a computation mode such as SIMD, MIMD, or systolic, and the second is the number of available processors on a cluster and selection of the best way to map the algorithm. The methodology we use for mapping parallel algorithms is multidimensional, divide and conquer, with medium–grain to large–grain parallelism. An individual task (in the following discussion 'task' and 'algorithm' are used interchangeably) can be efficiently mapped using spatial parallelism, because most of the vision algorithms are performed on two-dimensional data.

Assume that there are $P$ processors in a cluster. First, program and data are loaded onto the DSP of the cluster. Both in the case of SIMD or MIMD mode, the program is broadcast to the processors. The data division depends on the particular algorithm. If an algorithm is mapped in SIMD or systolic mode, then the compute and communication cycles will be intermixed. If an algorithm is mapped in MIMD mode, then each processor computes its partial results and then communicates with others to exchange or merge data.

The total processing time in mapping a task consists of the following components: time of program loading onto the cluster of processors ($t_{pl}$), data loading and partitioning time ($t_{dl}$), computation time of the divided subtasks on the processors ($t_{cp}$), which is the sum of the maximum processing time on a processor $P_i$ and intracluster communication time ($t_{comm}$), and the result report time ($t_{rr}$). $t_{dl}$ consists of three components: (1) data read time from the global memory ($t_r$) by the cluster DSP, (2) crossbar switch set-up time ($t_{sw}$), and (3) the data broadcast and distribution time to the cluster processors ($t_{br}$). The total processing time $\tau(P)$ of the parallel algorithm is given by

$$\tau(P) = t_{pl} + t_{dl} + t_{cp} + t_{rr}, \tag{1}$$

where

$$t_{dl} = t_r + t_{sw} + t_{br}. \tag{2}$$

If the computation and communication do not overlap, then

$$t_{cp} = \mathrm{MAX}_{1 \leq i \leq P} (t_{Pi}) + t_{comm}; \tag{3}$$

if computation and communication completely overlap, then

$$t_{cp} = \mathrm{MAX} ( \mathrm{MAX}_{1 \leq i \leq P} (t_{Pi}) , t_{comm} ). \tag{4}$$

In Eqs. 1–4, $t_r$ depends on the effective bandwidth of the global interconnection network.

# 4 Performance of Parallel Algorithms on a Cluster

In the following we illustrate how algorithms can be mapped in SIMD, systolic, and MIMD modes onto a cluster, and show how algorithms from different classes can be mapped onto the cluster. In the evaluation we discuss the computation and communication requirements for the algorithms. Table 1 shows the parameters used for performance evaluation. These parameters are used for all the analysis and implementation unless specified otherwise.

## 4.1 Two–dimensional convolution

A two–dimensional convolution of an $N \times N$ image $I(i,j)$, $0 \leq i, j \leq N$, with a kernel $W(i,j)$, $0 \leq i, j \leq w$, can be expressed as follows :
$G(i,j)$

$$= \sum_{m=j-\frac{w}{2}}^{m=j+\frac{w}{2}} \sum_{n=i-\frac{w}{2}}^{n=i+\frac{w}{2}} I(n,m) * W((i + \frac{w}{2} - n) \bmod w, (j + \frac{w}{2} - n) \bmod w).$$

In other words, each point in the output is replaced by a weighted sum of a window $wxw$ around it. This mapping will illustrate how to map algorithms in SIMD and systolic modes on a processor cluster when the number of processors is much smaller than the problem size. Figure 4 shows a cluster of 64 processors. The interconnection

| | |
|---|---|
| Total No. of Processors $N_p$ | 512 |
| Cluster Size $P_c$ | 8–128 |
| No. of Processors/Port $P_p$ | 4 |
| Image Size $N \times N$ | 512 × 512 |
| Memory Modules $M$ | 128 |
| Processor Speed | 5 MIPS, 5 MFLOPS |
| Network Speed (Block Transfer) | 20 Mbytes/Sec. |

Table 1: Paramters for performance evaluation.

between processors shows an abstract representation of all the connections required to perform the convolution operation. However, all the connections are not needed at the same time.

Each pixel is logically mapped onto a separate processor (as if there were as many processors available as there are pixels). Actually, the image is folded and multiple pixels are mapped onto one processor. The image is folded in two dimensions in a wraparound fashion, both left to right and top to bottom. For a cluster size $P$, (assume $P = pxp$), each processor has $M = N^2/P$ pixels in its local memory. In general, pixel $(i, j)$ ; $0 \leq i \leq N-1$, $0 \leq j \leq N-1$ is mapped to processor $((imodp), (jmodp))$. Therefore, this mapping preserves the adjacency of any two pixels even though the image is folded.

Figure 4 shows the flow of the distribution of data for window size $5 \times 5$. A small window is embedded in a larger one, and therefore, the same connections can be used for a larger window size with the addition of new connections for extra steps. The algorithm performs the convolution by each processor distributing its pixel values to the neighborhood in a pipelined manner.

In the following algorithm, north, south, east and west neighbors are defined in wraparound fashion. At any step, all the processors have the same neighbor connection. Figure 4 shows how processor (3,3)'s values will be distributed. All the processors follow the same pattern.

The algorithm works as follows. The DSP broadcasts the convolution weights to all the processors. Each processor multiplies its $M$ pixels with the central weight value. The intermediate values are stored in the running variable for each of the $M$ pixels. The image is then shifted in a spiral manner (as shown in Fig. 4). If the image is shifted north, then the processors now multiply the pixel values with the south weight. This process is repeated $w^2 - 1$ times , that is, once for each weight.

We make the following observations. First, the mapping is independent of problem or cluster size. That is, this mapping will work for all problem sizes. Second, the number of times the interconnection needs to be changed depends only on the convolution kernel size.

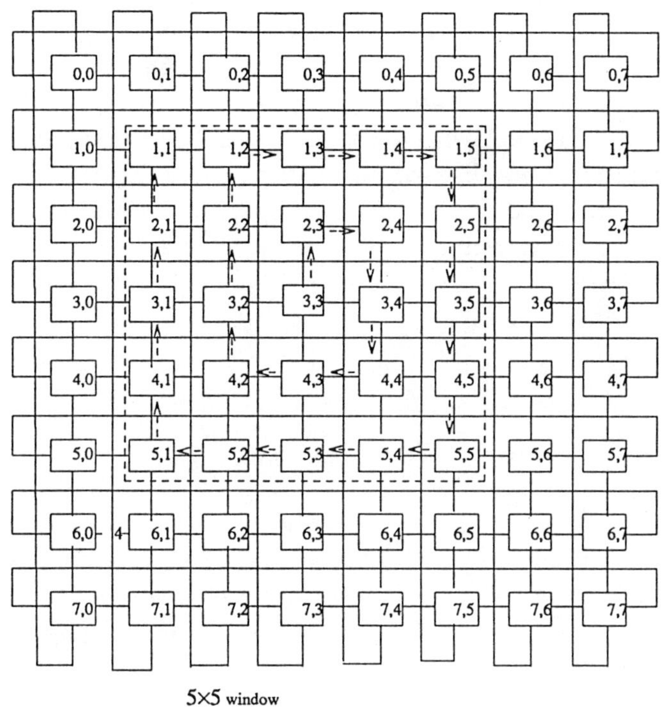


**Figure 4: Mapping on the cluster for convolution.**

Furthermore, at any time only one input and one output connection are required. By storing the connection patterns in the crossbar memory the switching time is negligible. Third, it is possible to overlap the computation and communication by writing the pixel to the output port as soon as it is multiplied by the appropriate weight in the current processor. The above algorithm illustrates that SIMD algorithms can be mapped efficiently onto the processor clusters using the flexibility and programmability of the interconnection.

The computation time decreases as the number of processors increases. The communication time per pixel depends only on the kernel size. The following formulas present the computation and communication times in terms of multiplication and addition operations. The factor $t_{fl}$ denotes the floating-point speed of a processors in terms of its normal instruction execution speed.

$$\begin{aligned} t_{cp} &= 2 \times t_{fl} \times \lceil \frac{N^2}{P} \rceil \times w^2 \\ t_{comm} &= \lceil \frac{N^2}{P} \rceil \times w^2, t_{sw} = w^2 - 1 \\ t_{tot} &= \max(t_{cp}, t_{comm} + t_{sw}) \end{aligned}$$

Figure 5 shows the performance of the two-dimensional convolution on a processor cluster. The processing time has been computed assuming a 2 MFLOP processor. The figure shows two speed-up graphs, one with communication overlap and the other without additive communication. The computation time decreases linearly as the number of processors increases. The total communication time per processor also decreases linearly, but the communication time per pixel computation remains constant. The important observation one can make is that it is essential that the communication and computation overlap to obtain linear speed-ups. However, if the interconnection speed is not matched with the computation speed, then overlap will not be possible. Having a fast crossbar without arbitration delays provides the necessary communication speed to obtain linear speed-ups. Note that since computation and communication can overlap, this mapping also illustrates how systolic algorithms can be mapped.

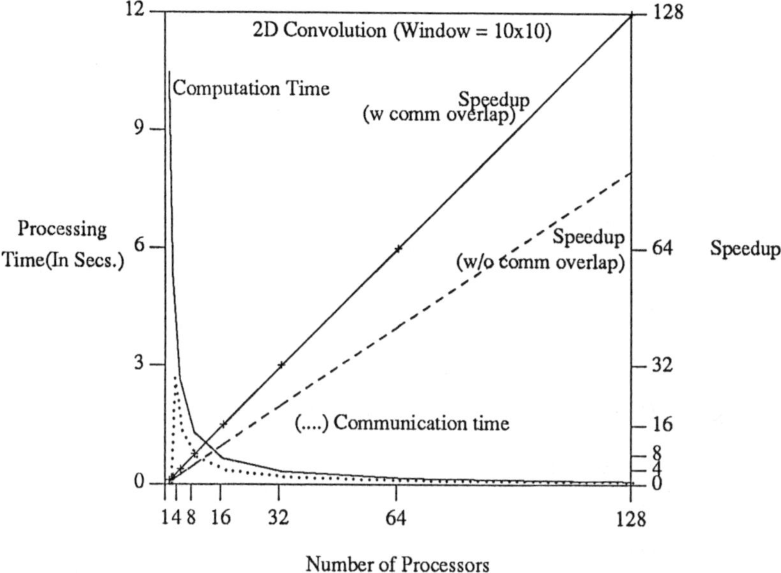


Figure 5: Performance of two-dimensional convolution on a processor cluster.

## 4.2 Separable Convolution

Separable convolution is a two-dimensional convolution broken into two one-dimensional convolutions. For applications such as computation of zero crossings, separable convolution performs well [12]. The main advantage of separable convolution is that the computation requirements per pixel are reduced from $2w^2$ to $4w$. We show how it can be mapped on a cluster. This example also illustrates how an algorithm can be mapped in MIMD mode on a cluster.

The data is decomposed among the processors as follows. Each processor is assigned $N/P$ rows of the data. Processor $P_i$ gets rows $(i-1) \times N/P$ to $i \times N/P - 1$. Each processor computes convolution along the rows using a window of size $w$. Once processor $i$ finishes convolution along the rows, it needs rows $(i-1) \times N/P - w/2$ to $(i-1) \times N/P - 1$ from processor $P_{i-1}$, and similarly, it needs the bottom $w/2$ rows from $i \times N/P$ to $i \times N/P + w/2 - 1$ from processor $i+1$. Therefore, a processor needs to communicate with only two

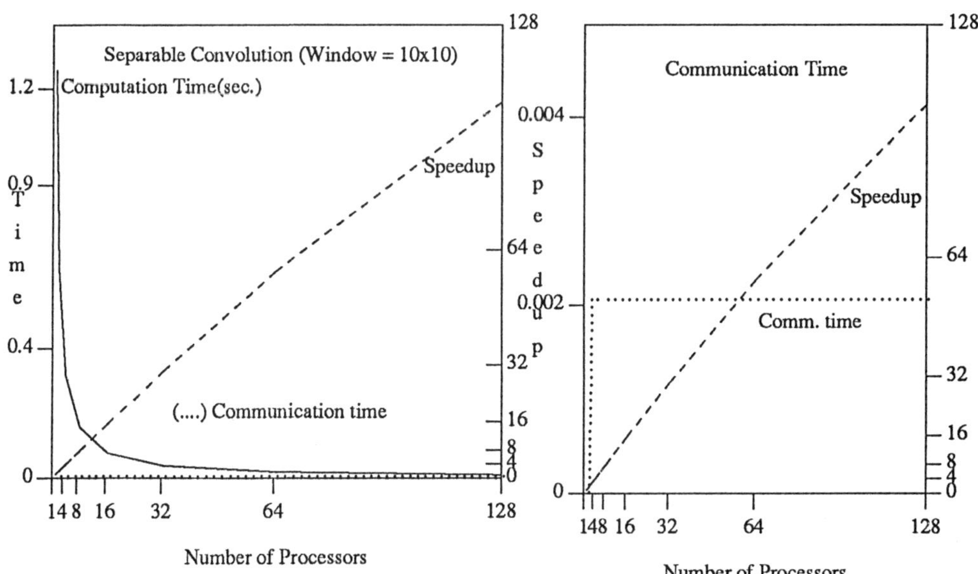


**Figure 6: Performance of separable convolution on a processor cluster.**

processors to obtain the desired intermediate data. The boundary processors $P_0$ and $P_{P-1}$ need only to communicate with one other processor. Note that if the granule size with each processor is less than $w/2$ (that is, $N/P < w/2$), then the processors need to exchange data with the number of processors given below by $t_{sw}$. Now, each processor computes convolution along the columns in its granule. The following are computational and communication requirements of the algorithm:

$$t_{cp} = \frac{t_{fl} \times N^2 \times 4 \times (w/2 + 1)}{P}$$
$$t_{comm} = 2 \times N \times w$$
$$t_{sw} = \lceil \frac{w \times P}{N} \rceil.$$

The amount of computation per pixel in separable convolution is a function of $w$ for a $w \times w$ kernel, unlike in two-dimensional convolution, where it is a function of $w^2$. The amount of communication in separable convolution is fixed as shown in Fig. 6. Therefore, the speed-up is not as much as in the case of 2D convolution. There are two reasons for smaller speedup. First, the communication is not decomposable as a function of the number of processors, because each processor needs to exchange $w/2$ rows of intermediate results with two adjacent processors. Second, since the computation per pixel itself is small, the communication overhead as a fraction of computation time is large.

### 4.3 Two-dimensional FFT (2D-FFT)

A nice property of 2D-FFT is that it can be performed in two decomposable steps : a one-dimensional N-point FFT along the rows followed by a one-dimensional N-point FFT of the intermediate results along the columns, or vice versa. We use this property to map 2D-FFT on the cluster processors. The algorithm consists of three phases : computing 1D-FFT along rows, transposing the intermediate results, and computing 1D-FFT along the columns. In the first phase each processor is assigned $N/P$ rows. Let's denote the sequence of rows with processor $P_i$ as Granule($i$). Also, let's divide each granule into $P$ equal blocks of size $N^2/P^2$ as shown in Fig. 7.

A block $B(i,j)$ denotes a block of size $N^2/P^2$ with processor $P_i$, $0 \leq j \leq P-1$. Each processor, computes the 1D-FFT along the rows of its granule. Then in the second phase, the processors communicate with each other in the following manner to transpose the intermediate results. A processor $P_i$ sends block $B(i,j)$ to processor $P_j$ for all $0 \leq j \leq P-1$, $j \leq i$. Each processor needs to communicate and exchange a block with every other processor in the cluster. However, by performing the communication systematically, the transpose can be achieved without any conflict as described in the algorithm. Finally, each processor computes 1D-FFT along the columns.

The 1D-FFT for size $N$ can be done in $O(N \log N)$ time [11]. The constant of multiplication is six, that is, to perform $N$-point 1D-FFT it takes approximately $6N \log N$ floating point operations. Therefore, the computation time for the above algorithm is (for both row and column),

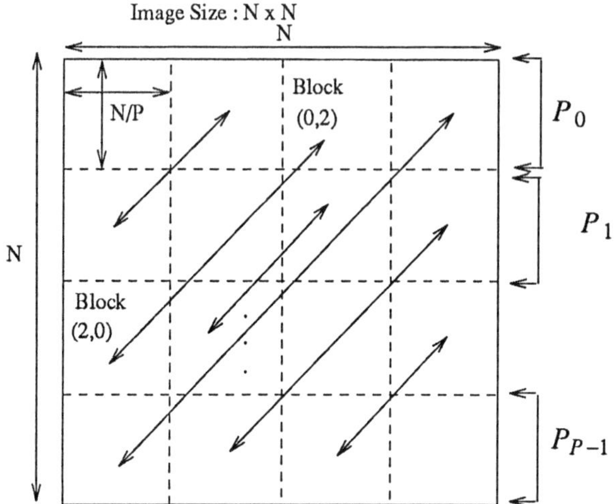


The figure shows data exchange needed to transpose intermediate data.

Figure 7: An example of mapping 2D-FFT onto four processors.

$$t_{cp} = \frac{12 \times t_{fl} \times N \times N \times \log_2 N}{P}.$$

The communication time to transpose the intermediate results is

$$t_{comm} = 2 \times (P - 1) \times N^2/P^2,$$

and the number of switch settings is

$$t_{sw} = P - 1.$$

One important observation is that in this above mapping both the computation and communication times reduce as the number of processors increases. In other words, both computation and communication are decomposable for parallel processing. Therefore, if the communication is achieved without conflicts (as in our case), we can obtain linear speed-ups.

Figures 8 and 9 show the performance 2D-FFT on a processor cluster. From Fig. 8 we can observe that almost linear speed-up can

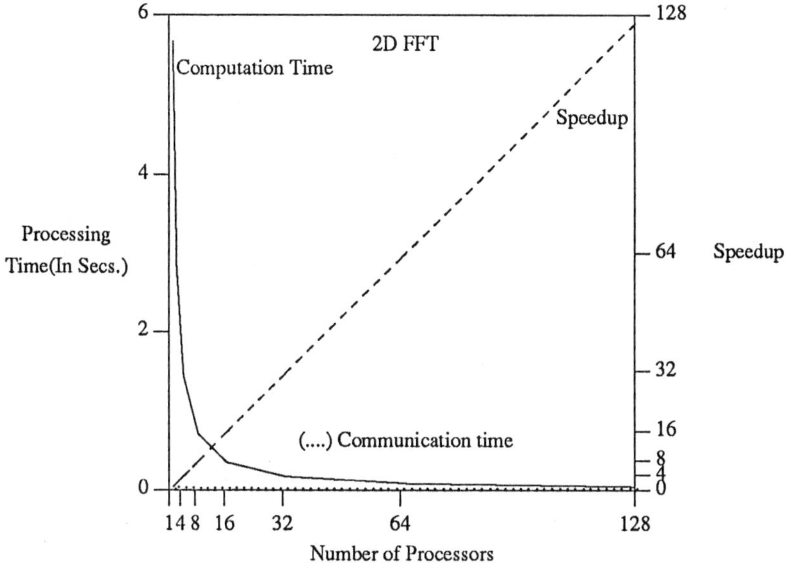


Figure 8: Performance of 2D-FFT on a processor cluster.

be obtained. The variation of the communication time as a function of the processor is shown in Fig. 9. Note that the communication time curve follows the computation time curve in its shape and the communication is completely decomposable.

# 5 Parallel Implementation Results

This section contains implementation of some algorithms on a simulated processor cluster. A cluster was simulated on an Intel iPSC/2 hypercube multiprocessor. The performance results capture all the overheads associated with parallel programming, and therefore, the results are very accurate. Also, we show through the example of a 2D-FFT algorithm that the analysis presented in the previous section is very close to the implementation results. We present performance results for four algorithms in this section. Two algorithms are 2D-FFT and separable convolution. The other algorithm (median filtering) is part of the image understanding benchmark algorithms developed

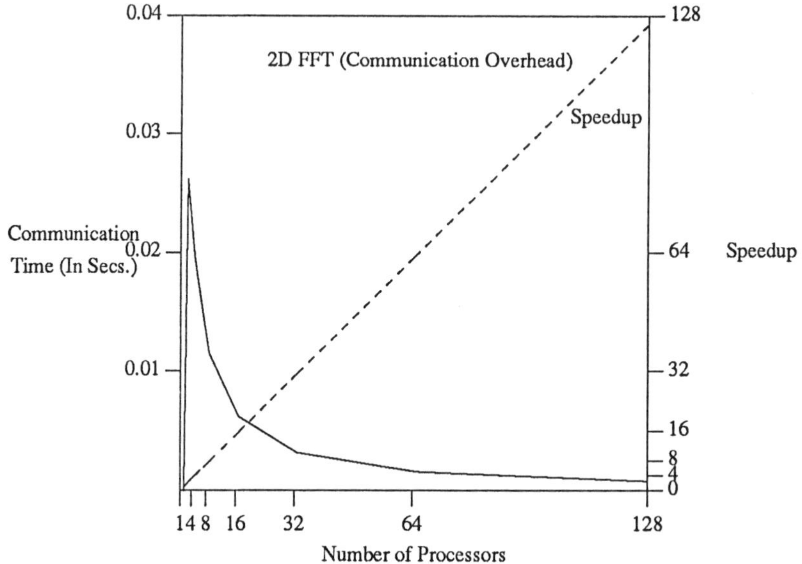


Figure 9: Communication time for 2D-FFT on a processor cluster.

by Weems et al.[21].

## 5.1 2D-FFT

A mapping of 2D-FFT has been described in the previous section. Figure 10 shows the performance of 2D-FFT on a 16-processor cluster. Other parameters are the same as given in Table 1. Solid lines in the graph show the computation times for analysis (symbol +) and implementation. We observe that the analytical results are very accurate. However, the implementation times are a little more than that given by analysis because implementation captures the overhead of index management, etc., which is not included in the analysis.

The graph also shows the corresponding speed-ups for both cases. Note that speed-ups obtained through analysis and implementation are almost the same and are practically indistinguishable. Figure 11 shows graphs for the communication time. Again, implementation and analytical results are very close to each other.

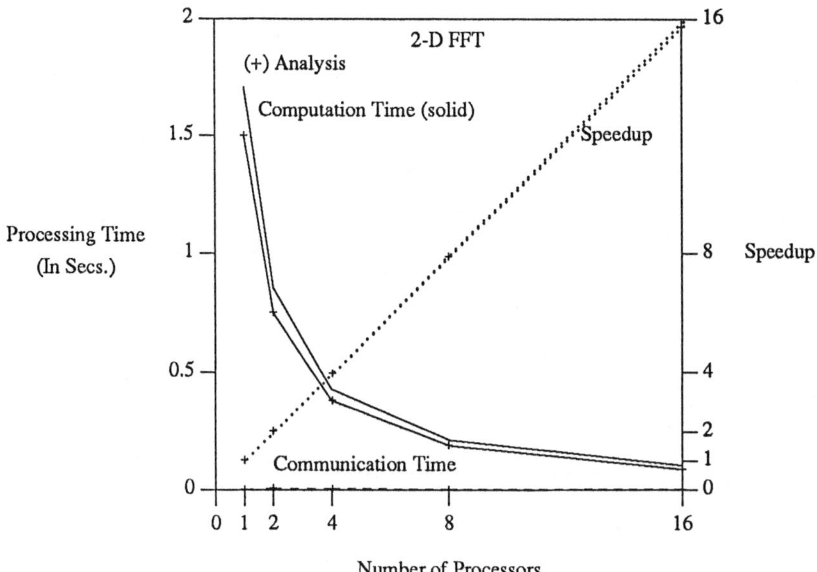


**Figure 10: Performance of 2D-FFT on a cluster (analysis and implementation).**

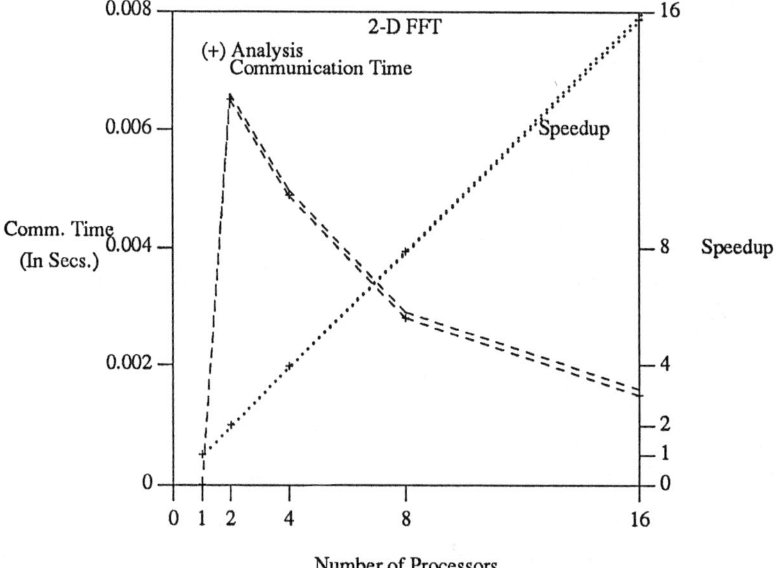


**Figure 11: Communication time for 2D-FFT.**

| Separable Convolution | | | | | | |
|---|---|---|---|---|---|---|
| | Window 10x10 | | | | | |
| No. Proc. | Fl. Point K. Ops | Other K. Ops | Comp. Time (ms.) | Comm. Setup | Comm. K Bytes | Comm. Time(ms.) |
| 1 | 3932 | 3932 | 2607 | 0 | 0 | 0 |
| 2 | 1966 | 1966 | 1310 | 2 | 20 | 4.09 |
| 4 | 983 | 983 | 658 | 3 | 20 | 4.09 |
| 8 | 492 | 492 | 332 | 3 | 20 | 4.09 |
| 16 | 246 | 246 | 169 | 3 | 20 | 4.09 |

Table 2 : Separable convolution implementation results.

## 5.2 Separable Convolution

Table 2 shows the performance for separable convolution implementation on a 256 $\times$ 256 image with window 10 $\times$ 10. The table shows the major computation operations in the algorithm, which include floating-point operations as well as integer operations. The fifth column shows the number of times connection in the crossbar needs to be changed during the algorithm execution, and the sixth column contains the rounded value of the amount of data communicated in kilobytes. The table shows that the communication time is very small compared to the computation time, and therefore, good speed-ups are obtained.

## 5.3 Median Filtering

The image understanding benchmark provided the serial version of the programs and the data [22]. We present results for one of the algorithms, namely median-filtering. Table 3 shows the performance results for the median filtering algorithm. The algorithm was evaluated on the same data set. Size of the median filter was 5 $\times$ 5. Data are partitioned along the rows. Each processor is allocated an equal number of rows and two boundary rows in each direction. There is no need for communication during the algorithm execution. Median filtering does not involve any floating-point multiplication or addition operations (only comparison operations are needed). Table 3 shows that we can obtain good speed-ups on a cluster for median filtering.

| Median Filtering (Test) | | | | | | |
|---|---|---|---|---|---|---|
| No. Proc. | Proc. Time(sec.) | Data load Time(Sec.) | Result Output Time(sec.) | Data Input Time(sec.) | Total Time(sec.) | Speed up |
| 1 | 60.36 | 0 | 0 | 0.008 | 60.37 | 1 |
| 2 | 30.17 | 0.056 | 0.056 | 0.008 | 30.30 | 1.99 |
| 4 | 15.19 | 0.056 | 0.056 | 0.008 | 15.31 | 3.94 |
| 8 | 7.72 | 0.056 | 0.056 | 0.008 | 7.85 | 7.70 |
| 16 | 3.99 | 0.056 | 0.056 | 0.008 | 4.11 | 14.68 |
| 32 | 1.90 | 0.056 | 0.056 | 0.008 | 2.02 | 29.93 |

Table 3 : Median filtering.

## 6 Concluding Remarks

In this paper we have studied the performance of a multiprocessor architecture called NETRA, which is highly reconfigurable and does not involve the use of complex interconnection schemes. Its processing power is concentrated in clusters of powerful processors connected through flexible and programmable crossbars with selective broadcast capability. We showed how a cluster can be reconfigured in various modes of computation. Also, we presented the performance of several algorithms on a cluster. It was observed that almost linear speed-ups can be obtained by choosing an appropriate mode of computation. Furthermore, we presented a comparison of analytical and implementation results and showed that analytical results are very accurate. Furthermore, we presented a comparison of analytical and implementation results.

**Acknowledgments**

This research was supported in part by the National Aeronautics and Space Administration under contract NASA NAG-1-613.

# Bibliography

[1] K. Batcher, *Design of a massively parallel processor,* IEEE Transactions on Computers, vol. 29, 1980, pp. 836–840.

[2] F. A. Briggs and E. S. Davidson, *Organization of semiconductor memories for parallel-pipelined processors,* IEEE Transactions on Computers, Feb. 1977, pp. 162–169.

[3] F. A. Briggs, K. S. Fu, J. H. Patel, and K. H. Huang, *PM4–A reconfigurable multiprocessor system for pattern recognition and image processing,* 1979 National Computer Conference, pp. 255–266.

[4] V. Cantoni, S. Levialdi, M. Ferretti, and F. Maloberti, *A pyramid project using integrated technology,* Integrated Technology for Parallel Image Processing, Academic Press, London, 1985, pp. 121–132.

[5] A. N. Choudhary, *Parallel architectures and parallel algorithms for integrated vision systems,* Ph.D. Thesis, University of Illinois, University of Illinois, Urbana-Champaign, August, 1989.

[6] A. Choudhary, J. Patel, and N. Ahuja, *NETRA–A parallel architecture for integrated vision systems I: architecture and organization,* IEEE Transactions on Parallel and Distributed Processing (submitted).

[7] M. J. B. Duff, *CLIP 4: a large scale integrated circuit array parallel processor,* IEEE Intl. Joint Conf. on Pattern Recognition, November 1976, pp. 728–733.

[8] M. J. B. Duff, *Review of the CLIP image processing system,* National Computer Conference, 1978, Anaheim, Calif., pp. 1055–1060.

[9] T. Gross, H. T. Kung, M. Lam, and J. Webb, *WARP as a machine for low-level vision,* IEEE International Conference on Robotics and Automation, St. Louis, Mar. 1985, pp. 790–800.

[10] D. Hillis, The Connection Machine, MIT Press, Cambridge, 1985.

[11] E. Horowitz and S. Sahni, Fundamentals of computer algorithms, Computer Science Press, 1984.

[12] A. Huertas and G. Medioni, *Detection of intensity changes with subpixel accuracy using Laplacian–Gaussian masks,* IEEE Transactions on Pattern Analysis and Machine Intelligence, Sep., 1986, pp. 651–664.

[13] H. T. Kung, *Systolic algorithms for the CMU Warp processor,* Tech. Rep. CMU-CS-84-158, Dept. of Comp. Sci., CMU, Pittsburgh, Sep. 1984.

[14] H. T. Kung and J. A. Webb, *Global operations on the CMU WARP machine,* Proceedings of 1985 AIAA Computers in Aerospace V Conference, pp. 209–218.

[15] Y. W. Ma and R. Krishnamurti, *The architecture of REPLICA–a special-purpose computer system for active multi-sensory perception of 3-dimensional objects,* Proceedings International Conference on Parallel Processing, 1984, pp. 30–37.

[16] W. A. Perkins, *INSPECTOR–A computer vision system that learns to inspect parts,* IEEE Transactions on Pattern Analysis and Machine Intelligence, Nov. 1983, pp. 584–593.

[17] D. H. Schaefner, D. H. Wilcox, and G. C. Harris, *A pyramid of MPP processing elements–experience and plans,* Hawaii Intl. Conf. on System Sciences, 1985, pp. 178–184.

[18] M. Sharma, J. H. Patel, and N. Ahuja *NETRA: An architecture for a large scale multiprocessor vision system,* Workshop on Computer Architecture for Pattern Analysis and Image Database Management, IEEE Computer Society, Miami Beach, Fla., Nov., 1985, pp. 92–98.

[19] H. J. Siegel, L. J. Siegel, F. C. Kemmerer, P. T. Muller, H. E. Smalley, and S. D. Smith, *PASM–a partitionable SIMD/MIMD system for image processing and pattern recognition,* IEEE Transactions on Computers, C-30, Dec. 1981, pp. 934–947.

[20] S. L. Tanimoto, *A hierarchical cellular logic for pyramid computers,* J. of Parallel and Distributed Processing, vol. 1, 1984, pp. 105–132.

[21] C. Weems, A. Hanson, E. Riseman, and A. Rosenfeld, *An integrated image understanding benchmark: recognition of a 2 1/2 D mobile,* IEEE Conference on Computer Vision and Pattern Recognition, Ann Arbor, Mich., June 1988.

[22] C. C. Weems, S. P. Levitan, A. R. Hanson, E. M. Riseman, J. G. Nash, and D. B. Shu, *The image understanding architecture,* COINS Tech. Rep. 87-76, University of Massachusetts, Amherst.

# Geometric Arithmetic Parallel Processor: Architecture and Implementation

**EUGENE L. CLOUD**
*Martin Marietta Electronic Systems*
*Orlando, Florida*

## 1 Introduction

This monograph presents description and the rationale for the geometric arithmetic parallel processor ($GAPP^{TM}$)[1]. The introduction includes the description of the conditions that promoted the GAPP development. In section 2, the objectives of this development and their impact on the architecture are presented. Section 3 provides a definition of terms specific to GAPP. Section 4 describes the processing element itself. Section 5 addresses the development of the integrated circuit or chip design composed of a number of these GAPP cells. Section 6 discusses the considerations involved in the design of an architecture to accommodate arrays of these chips. The seventh section addresses system parameters. Section 8 describes the placement of the arrays of chips to satisfy a systems concept. Two separate systems implementations are discussed, which satisfy the same basic architectural requirements but which have decidedly different systems partitions and therefore different performance capability. The final section, Section 9, provides a summary.

In the mid-1970s, the military defined a need for nighttime air-to-ground attack mission capability. Thermal images, created from radiated heat in the infrared (IR) spectrum, provide the ability to

[1]GAPP is a trademark of Martin Marietta Corporation.

Parallel Architectures and Algorithms for Image Understanding





ISBN 0-12-564040-4

carry out this mission. Scanning IR sensors were developed that could look in front of low-flying, high-speed aircraft, thus the term forward looking IR or FLIR. These scanning sensors produce pictures similar to normal black-and-white television images.

As an adjunct to the inherent ability to "see" in the dark provided by the FLIR, digital technology and pattern recognition techniques had advanced sufficiently to envision a system that could automatically detect desired targets while ignoring undesired clutter in thermal images. When developed, such a system would greatly aid the air crew. This detection system constitutes one form of image-understanding as applied to a military situation.

The operational environment of a military aircraft imposes severe constraints on the performance of an image-understanding system. Images arrive at the rate of thirty or more images per second. Each image may contain more than a quarter of a million digital picture elements or pixels, and each pixel may be composed of eight or more bits. All images must be processed as they arrive. Systems installed on military aircraft must be small, light-weight, and reliable, and must consume little power. Image understanding systems must be easily programmable. They must also be affordable. It is within this context that the geometric arithmetic parallel processor was invented and developed to satisfy these constraints.

In 1981, Dr. Wlodzimierz Holsztynski joined Martin Marietta in Orlando. Dr. Holsztynski's previous cellular automata work, as a mathematician, had provided him with an understanding of the computational requirements for logical processing in image understanding. The problem definition, as it existed upon his arrival, stimulated the invention of the GAPP concept. Subsequently, a patent [13] was issued covering this invention.

## 2 Objectives

The objective desired from the GAPP architecture was programmable real-time processing speed in a form reducible to tactical size packages. A secondary objective was to develop an architecture relevant to a number of applications, that is, to achieve universality, at least in the mathematical sense. Holsztynski has shown that GAPP processing elements are universal.[3] This includes translation-invariant transformations (finite window transformations) which constitute most image-processing computations and noninvariant transformations.

Real-time processing speed is the overwhelming driving force. If the processor can't keep up with the arrival rate of the data, then it is not operating in real-time. If the processor is not operating at real-time rates, then it doesn't matter if it can be packaged in a small size. The nature of the image-understanding problem suggests that an array of processing elements connected together in such a way as to provide efficient access to neighboring data, in the geometrical sense, is an appropriate solution. Further, operating these processors in lockstep as a single-instruction, multiple-data (SIMD) machine obtains very high computational speeds and minimizes control problems.

The objective of image processing for image understanding is to transform and concentrate the relatively low informational content of individual pixel values into high-value informational content packets. The absence of an individual pixel usually does not destroy all information. The real-time systems task is to process this high speed stream of pixels and concentrate the information. This means that processors that deal with higher informational content are included in the system, but are not in the image data stream. Instead, these processors are part of the image-processing control and understanding portion of the system.

# 3 Definitions

The term GAPP is used in a variety of contexts. The three major uses are defined here, and a definition of real-time is given also.

*GAPP cell or GAPP processing element:* This refers to the processing element described in the Holsztynski patent[13] and its variations. The cell design is detailed in section 4.

*GAPP chip:* An array of GAPP cells implemented in a silicon integrated circuit.

*GAPP array:* An array of GAPP chips arranged and connected together in such a way as to form a contiguous processor. A single GAPP chip is the smallest array possible. Usually all of the array elements receive exactly the same instruction at the same time.

*Real-Time:* The processing of every input data value within the time frame required to acquire that data.

# 4 Cell Design

The GAPP cell described in the patent follows the three basic principles set forth in [3]. These are (1) the cell must achieve universality; (2) the number of cells on a chip should be maximized; and (3) the functions performed by the computational components of the element should be kept simple.

Universality of the cell means that the element can perform all transformations. The computational component of the GAPP cell, a one-bit full adder–subtracter, meets this requirement. It is not the minimum component, but it is nearly so. The compromise made was between simplicity and utility. The minimum element, a nand gate, is almost unusable in a practical sense because the number of machine cycles required to accomplish higher-level functions becomes excessive. The half adder, as a minimum element, might satisfy. However, the increase in utility gained by using the full-adder/subtracter outweighs the lost efficiency.

The full adder–subtracter can be implemented in silicon on a small area of a chip. Therefore, it becomes practical and realistic to put a large number of these cells on a chip. The second principle is satisfied by retaining the simplicity of the computational element.

The third principle is also satisfied by limiting the computational element to be a one-bit full adder–subrtracter. As noted previously, this element is universal and simple. This element is a three-input, three-output device. This means that most of the computational elements' components are busy on every clock cycle. The three input elements are always involved, and usually, two of the three outputs are required. The objective is to keep all elements of the cell busy at all times. If all elements are fully involved, then maximum efficiency has been obtained.

The cell design is shown schematically in [7]. It consists of three parts: the four one-bit latches or registers with their associated input multiplexers, the one-bit full adder–subtracter (hereafter referred to as the adder), and the 128-bit random access (RAM) data memory.

The four registers are designated NS (north-south), EW (east-west), C (carry/borrow or conditional) and CM (communications). Three of the registers, NS, EW, and C always provide the input data to the one-bit full adder. The fourth provides a communications path, which does not interfere with the computation activity of the cell. The selection of the source of data, which loads the registers, is controlled by each register's input multiplexer. Similarly, there is a multiplexer that selects the data direction and source with respect to the RAM. The sources associated with each register and RAM are: C{C, RAM, NS, EW, CY, BW, 0, 1}, NS{NS, RAM, N, S, EW, C, O}, EW{EW, RAM, E,W, NS, C, O}, CM{CM, RAM, CMS, 0}, and RAM{read, CM, C, SM}.

The C register multiplexer has eight possible inputs. The NS and EW registers have seven inputs. The CM has four inputs. The RAM has one output, a read control line, and three inputs. Each of these five multiplexers is independent and all can be thought of as bit fields in the cell instruction or control word. There are $8 \times 7 \times 7 \times 4 \times 4 = 6,272$ independent combinations of useful instructions that can be generated for this set of multiplexers. The settings of the multiplexer control lines constitute the machine instruction set of the cell and, since it is SIMD, also of the GAPP array. The control of the processing element is achieved by 13 control lines. The number of possible combinations from thirteen control lines is 8,192. The efficiency of the control word is 6272/8192 or about 76.5%. The only additional signals required, beyond the clock, are the seven address lines necessary to select the RAM cell for read–write operations. The cells are totally controlled by twenty bits of control and address information.

All arithmetic is performed in a bit-serial manner. All logical operations are performed on one-bit logical variables. The power of GAPP is not achieved due to the power of the individual processing element, but because of the exact opposite–the simplicity of the processing element. The simplicity permits the assembly of very large arrays that are controllable. The aggregation of the simple cells into large arrays enable processing throughput equaling giga-operations per second. Examples of some complex algorithms that take advantage of this architecture are contained in [1, 6, 5].

The cell's data memory is equivalent to eight 16-bit registers, which is similar to 8/16 bit microprocessors. Although there are problems that require more data memory than is provided within the cell, high-speed access to this memory is easily achieved as part of the overall system architecture. Since one of the major design drivers is to obtain a large number of cells per chip, the cell's memory size is a reasonable compromise.

The output of every NS register is always connected as an input to an OR gate. In the chip and system design this output can be used to implement system-wide global output. Similarly, the ability to set the C register to either a one or a zero, along with the ability to write the C registers content to memory, provides an efficient way to broadcast global values to all cells.

## 5 Chip Design

The cell design discussed in section 4 was implemented in silicon by Martin Marietta's licensee, NCR Corp. of Ft. Collins, Colorado. The second version of the chip (GAPP-II) contained 72 cells per chip organized, as a $6 \times 12$ array. This chip geometry provides eight more cells per chip than an $8 \times 8$ organization, while minimizing the package pin count. The NCR two-micron CMOS process chip that is available commercially is designated as NCR45CG72. It was announced in a series of articles in [4, 9, 12, 14, 10]. This chip achieves an equivalent eight-bit add rate of 28.8 million adds per second at a 10 MHz clock frequency. This is predicated on 25 clocks per add, which yields 400,000 adds per second per cell.

Every field in an instruction operates on all cells in the array.

When a reference is made to any of the instruction field mnemonics, (EW, NS, C, CMS, and RAM[adr]), it is the same as addressing a geometric plane containing as many points as there are cells in the array. This has the effect of usefully creating extremely large words. The number of bits involved is given by

$$\text{bits/clock} = \text{number of fields active} \times \text{array size in cells.}$$

Processing rates are defined in terms of the number of bits in a single plane accessed on a single clock. For a single chip, the rate of nine bytes (72/8) per clock, or 90 megabytes per second at 10 MHz is realized.

# 6 Arrays–General Design

Larger GAPP arrays are constructed by connecting chips together. The chips are packaged with pin outs arranged to facilitate point-to-point wiring for the east–west, north–south and communications lines. It is possible to make these signal connections on a single layer of a multi–layer printed circuit board. The control and address lines must also be distributed to every chip in the array along with clock power and ground.

A single chip could have 48 bits of I/O on a given clock: six bits of input at CMS, six bits of output at CMN and either input or output at the edge pairs of north–south and east–west. This is equivalent to 60 MB of I/O at a 10 MHz clock frequency. It is more normal, however, to treat only the CMS and CMN as true I/O ports. These provide 1.5 bytes of I/O per clock or 15 MB per second. As chips are added in the EW dimension, the input–output bandwidth to the array increases directly as the number of chips increases, and increases proportionately to the processing speed. SIMD processors sometimes are data–starved because of limited I/O bandwidth.

Arrays of GAPP chips are connected together to form GAPP modules, which are of convenient size, while maximizing the number of cells in the array. There are special applications that need different-sized arrays. Two different array printed circuit board modules will be described subsequently in this chapter. These boards are connected together to form larger arrays. GAPP arrays are synchronous systems. Since every cell in every chip is clocked at the same time on the array clock cycle, critical requirements for power supply decoupling and response times, as well as control and data line termination, are imposed.

In some algorithms, it is desirable to have the array topology appear as a toroid. In this case, the array's NS northern edge connects in a wraparound fashion to the arrays' NS southern edge, and its eastern edge connects to its western edge. In other instances it is desirable to have the array appear as a long spiral, connecting the northern edge to the southern edge shifted by one place. The simple toroid has most often been the treatment of choice.

# 7 System Parameters

Image-understanding architectures must accommodate the breadth of algorithmic techniques while handling large volumes of data. They also must be fully programmable. Digital images by their very nature are large arrays of data. Data volumes between 262,144 pixels for a 512 × 512 image to more than a million for 1024 × 1024 images are common. Rates greater than 30 images per second are normal.

For real-time GAPP systems, two major parameters determine the GAPP array size: input data rate, and algorithm size. Using the standard television frame rate provides $33\frac{1}{3}$ ms per frame processing time. Suppose the algorithm requires exactly $33\frac{1}{3}$ ms to execute. Then the array size must equal the total number of pixels in the frame to maintain real-time operation. If a million pixels are produced in one thirtieth of a second, all processing on those million pixels must be accomplished in one frame time. When the algorithm execution time equals the frame time, the limit for maintaining real-time operation in a single array has been reached.

The Sobel [7, 8] 3 × 3 neighborhood image-processing operator requires 540 instruction cycles. At 10 MHz this is about 617 Sobels per frame.

The preceding discussion illustrates that a large number of powerful image-processing operators, such as Sobel, can be executed in a 30 Hz frame time. If the algorithms that accomplish the initial operations of image understanding are relatively short, then large images can be divided into smaller windows and still maintain real-time processing.

Systems for real-time image processing must accommodate the sensor data acquisition parameters. The system design must accommodate and manage dynamic algorithm selection and execution as a function of the acquisition parameters on a frame-by-frame basis.

There are two basic types of results from image-understanding systems: images and informational records. In most systems both types are desired at some stage. The images are used for display or algorithm development and informational records for reporting the location of the object of interest. Dealing with these results impose additional system I/O requirements and increase the bandwidth and data-handling functions.

## 8 System Design

An image-understanding system contains many functional blocks. In the case being described here, the target recognizer for military applications, the GAPP array is one functional block that is part of the overall system. In these systems GAPP has been assigned the computational intensive low-level image-processing load. The SIMD array with its natural geometric relationship is very well-suited to these processes. The array, however, is not the total system.

This section describes two generic system implementations, which both perform the automatic target recognition function. At the top level they can both be represented by the same block diagram as shown in Fig. 1.

At the top level, this image-understanding architecture contains three major components. These are the image processor (IP), the data extractor (DE) and the analysis hardware (AH). The image processor is the GAPP array and its SIMD controller. The data extractor is composed of high speed, custom design hardware–software for information extraction. The analysis hardware section is composed primarily of general-purpose serial processors. As data are

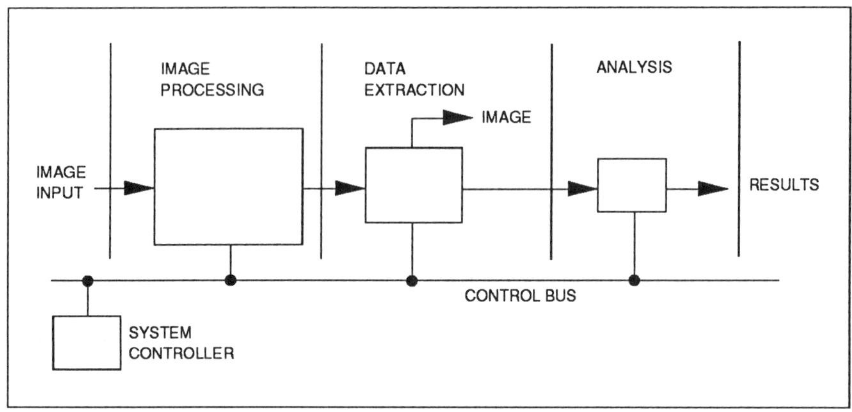


Figure 1: Image-understanding processor components.

processed from left to right through the functions, the information content of those data that are kept is increased by the value of the processes that have been performed.

The IP executes a set of algorithms, which enhances the input image by noise removal, performs edge detection, executes size and shape filtering and nominates objects as having characteristics of those of interest. The IP outputs a plane that contains a flag at the objects' position. These nominated objects are target-like and worthy of further processing.

The DE is responsible for identifying the object by detecting the flag wherever it is in the plane and extracting the associated object from the image. If the system includes output display requirements and symbology annotation, then the DE performs that function also. If the system is only an image processor, then post-DE components are not required.

The AH section makes the final decision regarding the nominated objects. Appropriate algorithms, either model-based or statistical classifiers, are used to make the final decision about an object. Either the object is a target and reported as such, or it is clutter and discarded.

The control function is kept out of the image data path and therefore does not have to compete for bus bandwidth. The control function provides for program storage, execution data storage (such as lookup table initialization), and signaling and handshake control among the elements of the system. The control function is the synchronizer of the system. The front-end processing begins when there are sufficient data to fill the GAPP array. The DE function starts when a frame or subframe has been processed. The analysis function begins when objects are presented for a decision. Each of these functions (image processing, data extraction, analysis, and control) are executed by one or more computers (treating the GAPP array as a single computer). The machine is a true multiprocessor computer, containing both serial and SIMD processes. Most GAPP-based systems are in fact MIMD (multiple instruction multiple data) processors, containing a nonhomogeneous processor suite.

The image-processor section is shown in more detail in Fig. 2. This unit contains three interfaces, the GAPP array, and the SIMD controller for the array. The three interfaces are the image interface to the sensor, the output buffer interface to the data extractor, and the control interface. The sensor interface provides image data to the input buffer. The input buffer is an array of standard memory parts. It is addressable by both the sensor interface and the GAPP array. The memory design must accommodate any difference that might exist between clock speeds of the GAPP array clock and the sensor data clock. The sensor interface writes data into the input buffer using narrow to moderate word length (16 or 48 bits per word). The GAPP array reads data from the input buffer in very long words, which are the width of the array in the EW dimension. Changing the effective word length dramatically changes the time required to empty an input buffer and load the GAPP array. The GAPP array is composed of one or more modules containing GAPP chips. The array forms the image-processing engine.

The output buffer is a dual memory system, which is written to by the GAPP under control of the array output buffer address generator. Data are written using the same very long word format as the read operation. Dual buffers are used so that the array may write to the output buffer throughout the frame time while the other section of the output buffer is being scanned by the data extractor. In some implementations, direct reintroduction of data from the output

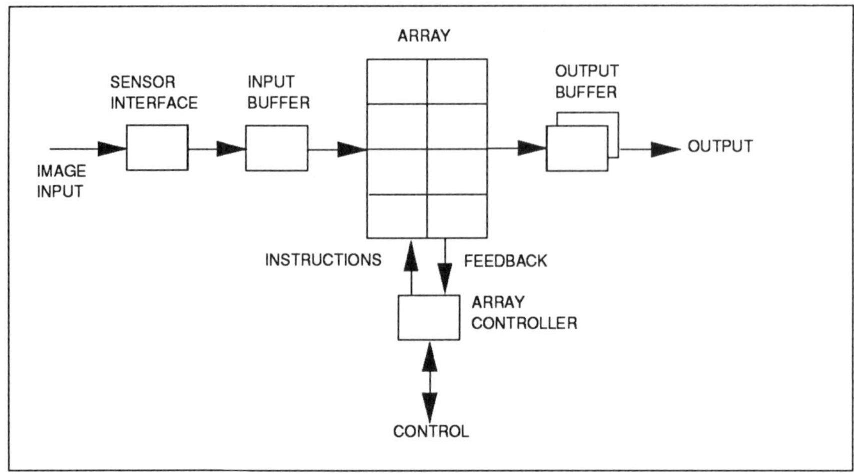


Figure 2: The image-processor block diagram.

buffer to the input of the array is provided. This means that the output buffer can be used as virtual memory storage for intermediate variables from the array data memory. Also, the output buffer can be used to store fixed data masks and fixed array constants, with easy and rapid reloads into the array.

The array controller is the final component of the image processor. It sequences through the memory containing the fully expanded machine instructions for the GAPP cells. In most implementations, one instruction is output to the array for execution for each access to instruction memory. This provides a cost-effective, very high-speed approach since each instruction is output at the array clock speed. It is cost-effective because commercial memory parts tend to decrease in cost-per-bit at a fairly rapid rate. The array controller also provides the ability to interface the global OR output of the array to the system controller, and also provides for the broadcast of global constants via the C register set–reset instructions (1 or 0). The array controller interfaces with the control bus to accept the download of the algorithms in machine executable form, establish constants and accept revised values as the processing progresses. The array controller provides health and status information on the array to the

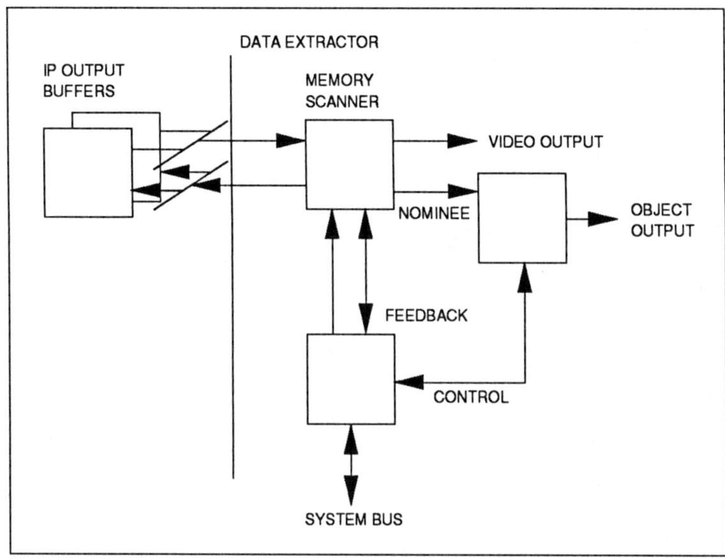


Figure 3: Data extractor function.

system controller.

The Data Extractor section is shown in Fig. 3. It consists of three sections which interface with the IP output buffers, object output to the analysis section, the video output to the video annotation section, and the system bus interface.

The memory-scanner section generates addresses to the output buffer memory section, which is not currently being written to by the array. The scanner accesses data words and detects the presence of flags. The lines from the scanner to the output buffers represent the addresses and the lines from the output buffer to the scanner represent the actual data. Nominees or candidate objects are further processed to ensure that only isolated objects are passed along to the analysis section. The control section provides interface to the system bus. It accepts commands to specify the operation of the scanner and candidate or nominee processor. The control section also provides feedback, and health and status information to the system controller.

The analysis section contains two independent optional parts: the post-processor and the video annotation. The post-processor section is usually composed of one or more serial computers. These have been implemented as MIL-STD-1750A computers, 680xx computers, SUN[2] or VAX[3] computers depending upon the system application. The function of these processors is to perform the final decision process.

The system controller function shown in Fig. 1 has been implemented by a number of general-purpose computers. These include IBM PC[4], SUN, VAX, and 680xx single-board computers. Some are resident directly on the system bus; others have been implemented via a remote process through bus interface hardware.

Two approaches have been created to implement the generic architecture shown. Both are modular and can contain all of the elements described here, or they may be tailored to perform a specific image understanding function.

## 8.1 First-Generation Implementation

The system implementation structure is greatly influenced by the choice of the control bus. In 1983, when the decision was made to begin development of the first-generation system, two major bus structures were in use: MULTIBUS[5] and VME.[6] The MULTIBUS was chosen for this implementation primarily because of the design team's familiarity with MULTIBUS in previous work. MULTIBUS provides 16-bit data path and 24-bit addressing (16 MB of address space), and eight interrupts.

The image-processor portion of the system is partitioned as shown in Fig. 4. It consists of a sensor interface (SI), three input buffers (IB), four GAPP array boards, three output buffers (OB), and the GAPP controller (GC). All access to memories in the image-processing section from the MULTIBUS uses memory mapping to allocate address space. The memories on all boards are accessible from MULTI-

[2]SUN is the trademark of SUN microsystems.

[3]VAX is the trademark of Digital Equipment Corporation.

[4]IBM is the trademark of International Business Machines, Inc.

[5]Trademark of Intel Corp.

[6]Trademark of Motorola Corp.

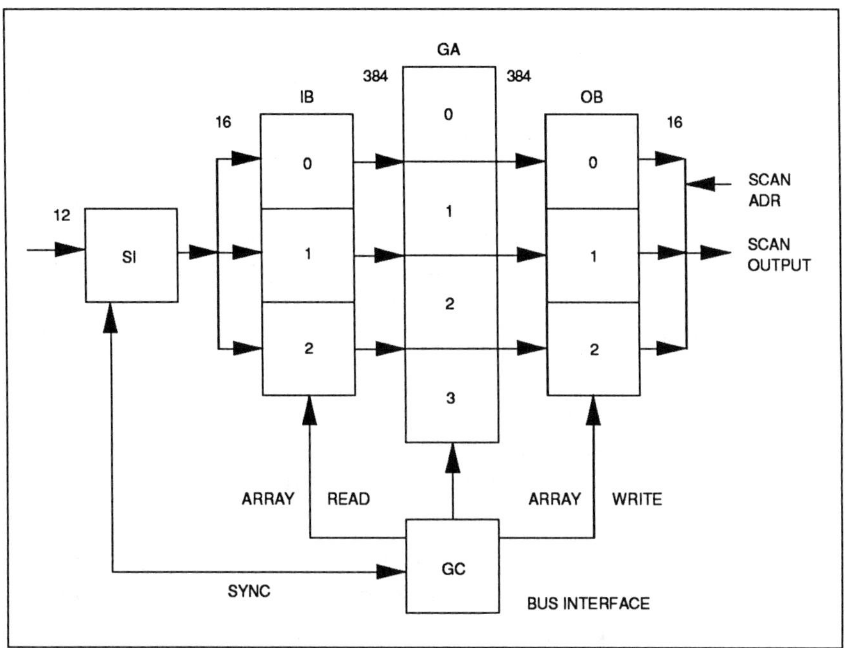


Figure 4: First-generation image processor.

BUS except for the data memories contained in the GAPP chips.

The GAPP controller provides the common control functions that cause the array to execute programs. The GC contains 256K 32-bit control words to store the fully expanded operational GAPP machine code. Of the 32 bits, 20 are used to control the array processor (command fields and address for the cells) See page 283). Two bits are used for input and output control. The remaining 10 bits are used to control the sequencer and to provide the ability to broadcast constants to the array. Multiple controllers can be used in parallel for larger programs. The GAPP controller also generates MULTIBUS interrupts to the system controller upon completion of the algorithm.

A sensor interface provides line receivers and data conditions as required. The SI also includes histogram circuitry and statistic capability. The interface provides data to the input buffer (IB) boards in a bit-parallel word serial data stream along with clocks and synchronization signals. A 12-bit-wide data path is necessary for the pixel information of interest. As shown in Fig. 4, the input data width to the SI is 12 bits per clock; from the SI to the IB, it is 16 bits per clock; from the IB into the GAPP array, it is 384 bits per clock.

The GAPP array boards use 144 chips on a single board. This produces an array of 10,368 cells per board. The array is organized as a 96 × 108 matrix. The array is constructed on a MUPAC[7] 347 board whose size is approximately 15 ×17 inches. Each module also contains receivers to provide the necessary drive for the control, address, and clock lines for each of the GAPP chips. Similarly, buffers are provided, which give access to the global OR result either at the board level or on an individual chip basis. Input of external data is provided by the CM lines along the 96-pin southern edge of the array. Output is supplied along the 96-pin northern edge of the array. In those systems that contain more than one of these modules, the east, west, north, and south connections are provided to their respective complimentary signals. The southern edge of the array is at the left nearest the IB.

The dual output buffers perform an analogous function to the input buffers. These memories are 16K bits per column. One buffer is connected to the array section, while the other is connected to the scanning direct memory access (DMA) processor contained in the data extractor section. The array section writes data to these memories in plane format.

Image processors of this architecture have been made, which contain a single GAPP array supported by the appropriate number of IB and OB boards. The largest system built, as of December 1988, contains eight of these boards or 82,944 processing cells. The system shown in Fig. 4 contains 41,472 cells organized as a 384 × 108 array.

The data extractor scans the output buffer memory. For applications where the output is to be an image the DMA scanner extracts all data values in plane format. It performs the process to reconstruct pixels for output to display subsystems or for storage. The scanning DMA is implemented using a 29116 microcontroller. All elements of this process are programmable. Different DMA controller algorithms

[7]Trademark of MUPAC Corp.

are available in real-time so that the size of the extraction area and other activities may be selected on a frame-by-frame basis.

The post-processing is performed by an enhanced MIL-STD-1750A instruction set computer and a 68000 microcomputer. The 1750A performs feature measurement and statistical classification when required. The 68000 performs temporal matching functions. For model-based systems the 1750A was dropped in favor of SUN computers.

System control is implemented by a 68000/010 microprocessor resident on the system bus. It contains nonvolatile storage either disk or PROM depending upon the application. The system controller communicates with a host computer or the remainder of the system. The controller downloads all volatile memory at start-up. In a multiple-user laboratory environment, the controller reloads memories upon command of the host.

Systems of this architecture have been built in military packages whose dimensions are about $6 \times 10 \times 10$ inches and whose weight is 40 pounds. It has a main array of $360 \times 108$ (38,880) cells. At a 10 MHz clock rate, the main array computes $15.5 \times 10^9$ eight-bit adds per second. This is about 25.9 million adds per cubic inch. In actual practice the machine is clocked at 6 MHz. Variations on the architecture have found application in laboratory rack mounted systems. The architecture has been interfaced to both IBM AT computers and SUN 3/x computers. This architecture has the advantage of producing a large number of cells on a single board. However, an operational array needs at least three boards–IB, GA, and OB–in addition to the array controller to function. The input–output time is fast, but it is not fixed.

## 8.2 Second-Generation Implementation

The second-generation implementation project was begun in early 1987, although systems design had been done in 1986. At that time the available bus structures were MULTIBUS, VME, and MULTIBUS II. After analysis and review the MULTIBUS II bus was chosen for the second generation. MULTIBUS II is a 32-bit-wide bus which supports 40 MB/s data transfers. It also supports message passing protocol, which permits the implementation of packet data transfers, which bounds the upper limit on the delay in responding to interrupts. The message-passing capability also permits distributed control of the system to be implemented so that new capabilities can be added without disturbing the existing functions. A board's functionality is isolated from the bus and the control structure. Each board that resides on the MULTIBUS II contains its own local 68010 processor, which implements a generic device interface as well as personalization of each board's specific functions. The generic device interface is common to all boards and includes the ability to send and receive messages on the multibus. All memory is local to each board [2].

The system-level block diagram is identical to the first generation but differs dramatically in detail. For an automatic target recognizer, the image-processor (IP) section is composed of three board types. The data-extraction section is composed of two board types, with a third to provide for video display functions. The analysis section has one custom board design and then employs multiple 68020/30 or RISC post-processors to achieve the final results. System control is hosted on a 68020/30 single board MULTIBUS II processor.

The second-generation IP section is shown in Fig. 5. Compared with Fig. 4, it can be seen that the board count has remained the same at 12 boards but the number of board types has been reduced from five to three. Ten boards implement the input buffer, GAPP array, and output buffer functions. Each of these boards contains 88 GAPP chips. The number of GAPP cells has therefore gone from 41,472 in first generation to 63,360 in second generation. This is more than a 50% increase in GAPP cells in the same board count and is clearly a better solution.

The sensor interface function is performed by the serial IO controller, SIOC. This board contains circuits to descramble pixels, provide a window that can limit the pixels allowed into the system, and provide an image-compression function. Also, the board contains statistics gathering and histogram functions similar to the first-generation SI board. The SIOC also contains a lookup table, (LUT), and a vertical-to-horizontal converter. The data are placed into FIFOs for output to the input buffer. This allows for 'cycle stealing'–

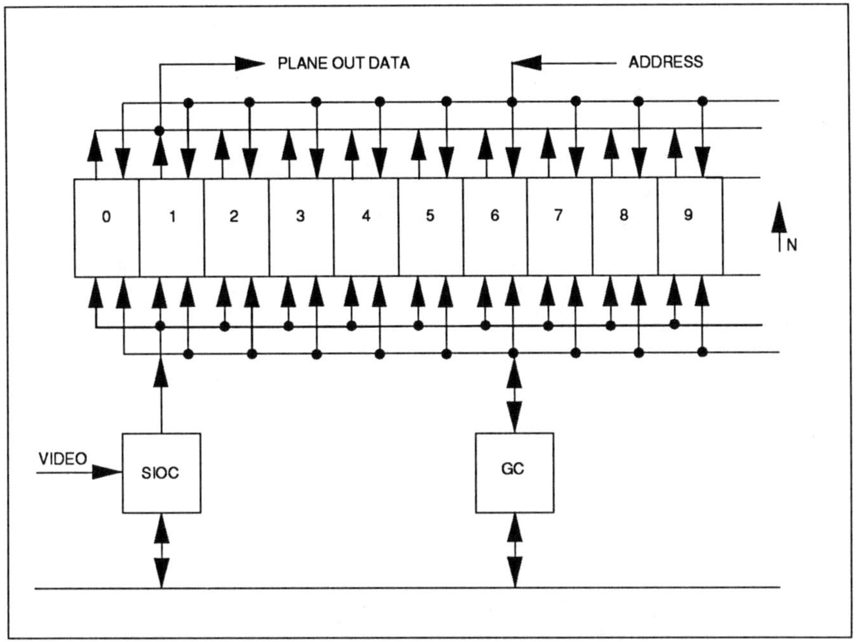


Figure 5: Second generation image processing section.

like operations when the GAPP modules are loading data from the IB. The address generation for writing to the IB is performed on the SIOC. The 48-bit-wide corner turn data bus is connected to each GAPP module.

The GAPP module shown in Fig. 6 contains both the input buffer and output buffer as well as the GAPP array itself. The module is 48 bits wide in the EW dimension, as are the IB and the dual OB sections. The IB section is either 16 or 64K bits deep depending on the choice of memory chips.

The GAPP array section contains 88 chips organized as an $8 \times 11$ array which yields a $48 \times 132$ cell map (6,336). Two of these modules obtain about 20% more cells than the functionally equivalent first-generation IB, GA, and OB module group. The global OR of all 88 chips is provided as an output from the board.

The dual output buffer section contains two 64K-deep, 48-bit-

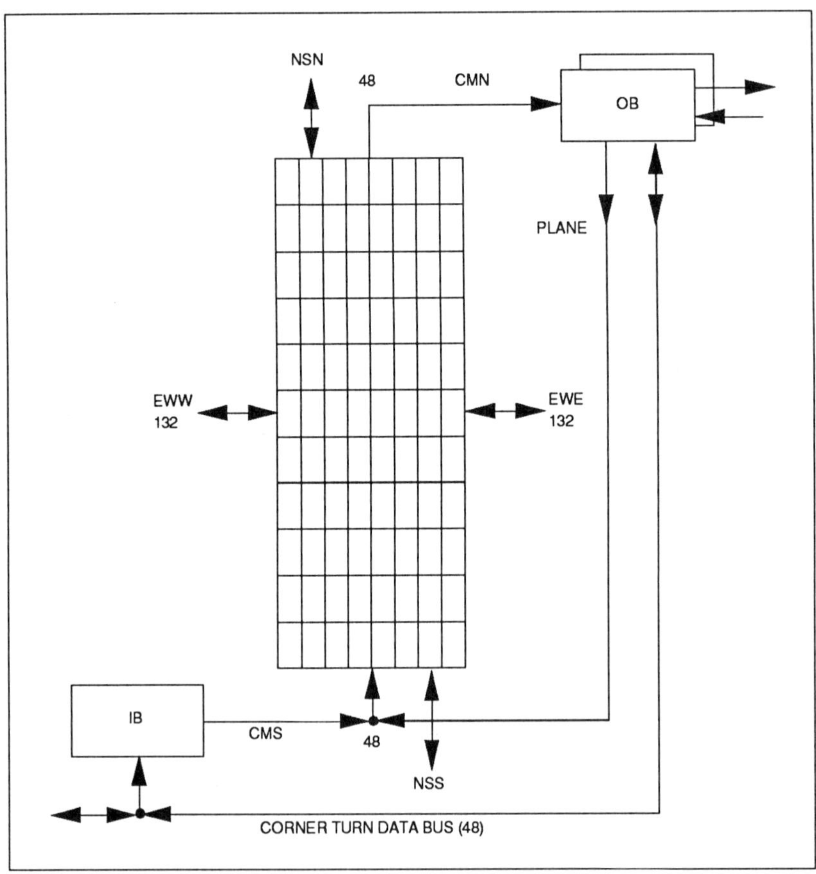


**Figure 6: Second-generation GAPP module.**

wide memories. As in the first generation, one section "faces" the array while the other is connected to the data extractor section of the system. The 48-bit-wide corner turn bus (the same as the SIOC input bus) is also available to the GAPP controller. This means that data can be input and output from the array via the GAPP controller. A minimum system can be constructed, which contains only two boards: the GAPP controller and the GAPP array module. An additional path is provided from the output buffer section to the input CMS lines of the array. This allows the output buffer to be used temporarily to store intermediate results from the array and then later read these data back into the array for further processing. The output buffer can be used to implement a virtual storage scheme for array data.

Because every GAPP module contains its own input and output buffer sections, the time required to input an array full of data is independent of the array organization. Every module can be loaded in 132 clocks times the number of data bit planes. GAPP modules are not resident on MULTIBUS II; this means that they do not occupy MULTIBUS II address space. Diagnostic access is provided via the GAPP controller.

The second-generation GAPP controller performs the same main functions as the first-generation controller plus the following: IB and OB address generation, subframe order control, array input–output interface control, and diagnostics and MULTIBUS II interface. The controller's main function is to store and broadcast to the array the machine instructions to be executed. For this purpose, the controller contains 1 MB of main instruction memory organized as 32-bit × 256K words. The sequencer supports looping repeat of instruction sequences. The controller contains start vector programmability to allow different algorithm functions to be executed out of sequence, which permits complex algorithm execution order changes to be made as a function of the acquisition parameters. The controller's functions and interface to MULTIBUS II are managed by a local 68010 microprocessor. The diagnostic ports interface to the GAPP modules' corner turn data bus. This permits access to the input and output buffer memories on all GAPP modules in the system.

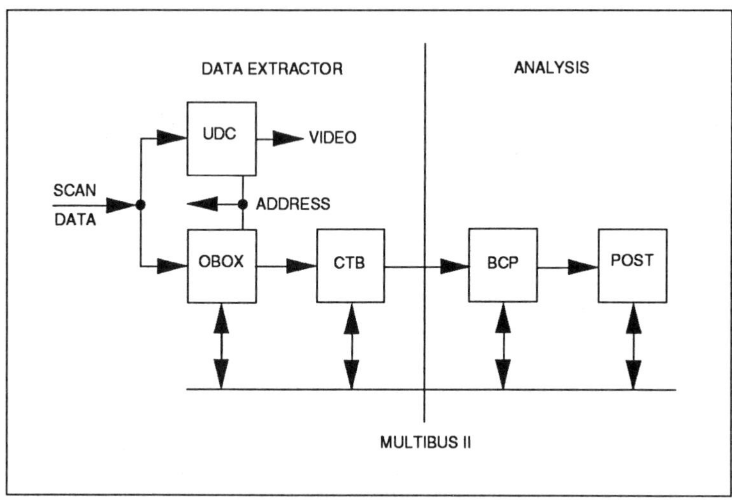


Figure 7: Second-generation post array processing.

The data extraction and analysis sections of the target recognizer are depicted in Fig. 7. All modules in this section are optional in the system configuration. All but the video display controller VDC, are needed for statistical target recognition work. The video extraction and output function is performed by the VDC. The data extraction function for candidate objects is performed by the output buffer data extractor (OBDX). These two boards share the scan bus common to all GAPP modules. These boards arbitrate for control of the scan bus.

The OBDX may be configured for a number of applications. Simple reports of object presence and extent are accomplished by the minimum configuration. Extraction and formatting of data for post-processing require the full capability configuration. In this application, conversion from planes to pixels and object overlap removal are required. The OBDX interfaces to the MULTIBUS II using the generic device interface implemented by the 68010 and the message passing coprocessor.

The candidate target buffer (CTB), provides buffer storage for nonoverlapped single candidate objects. The CTB can support up to eight independent postprocessing channels. The number of channels is dependent upon the object density per unit time extracted from the front-end process and by the postprocessing analysis execution time. The CTB includes an interface to MULTIBUS II.

The postprocessing analysis stream consists of one custom design, built-in function co-processor (BCP), and one general-purpose militarized 68020/30 single-board computer, which performs the postprocessor controller (PPC), function. The BCP consists of interfaces to the CTB, the 68020, a sequencer and microcode store, an arithmetic and logic unit (ALU), and two multiply accumulators. The data extracted from the image processor include the original image values for the local neighborhood around the object's centroid. Additionally, each pixel has information relating to its relative properties attached to the intensity. Pixels may now be up to 48 bits long, but note that the quantity of pixels is reduced a thousand fold. The BCP computes features used in the classifier calculations performed by the postprocessor 68020. The BCP does not have an interface to the MULTIBUS II. It is rather a true coprocessor to the 68020, similar in functionality to a floating-point processor, although it operates on larger operands. The execution time of the BCP is a function of the size of the object presented to it.

The PPC is a general-purpose-single-board, militarized computer in most cases. Since this machine is performing the execution of the classifier, any capable serial computer can be used. For laboratory or workstation applications, a special interface called the generic interface (GI), is available. This permits parallel input and output data flow to the image processor as well as the download of all code for all elements from the host processor. When coupled with companion compatibility cards personalized to each host, the machine may be connected to IBM AT, SUN or VAX/APTEC[8] combination.

The video display controller VDC, is a major system interface card. It can accept external analog (RS170 or RS343) or digital video and output annotated analog or digital video. In this mode,

[8]APTEC I/O computer is the trademark of APTEK Inc.

the results of automatic recognition are multiplexed with the video under control of an on-board graphics coprocessor. The VDC can extract and convert planes of data from the output buffer into pixels for display or for return to the front end of the system. Data can be extracted and sent back to a host if the GI is present, or back to the SIOC if some global operation is required.

The second-generation system architecture components and their functions have been described. Together they constitute a functionality that can implement a wide range of image-understanding systems. One benchmark for some elements of the system is the Abingdon Cross [11]. The GAPP processor ranks high in the list.

# 9 Summary

The rationale behind the image-understanding system approach, based on GAPP chips, has been presented along with the motivations that led to its development. Examples of these systems are shown in Fig. 8. These systems have sometimes been described as SIMD GAPP processors. The system architecture does indeed contain, as its major compute component, a SIMD GAPP array. However, the SIMD section is oriented primarily toward the image-processing function. Image understanding is a higher-level function. To that end, the image-understanding system described here contains other computing capabilities. Specifically, any image-understanding system must of necessity extract facts from the image. This is the proper role of the image processor. The interpretation of the meaning of those facts is the image-understanding function. In the systems described, this function is carried out by one or more processors whose individual cpu's are many times more powerful than the simple GAPP cell. It is appropriate that this is so because the data on which the more powerful processor operates contain more significant information than the simple pixel processed by the cell. The GAPP array has always been a peripheral to a higher-order processor. It is a highly efficient image-array processing engine. More than 12,000 GAPP chips have been produced and used in systems as of 1989.

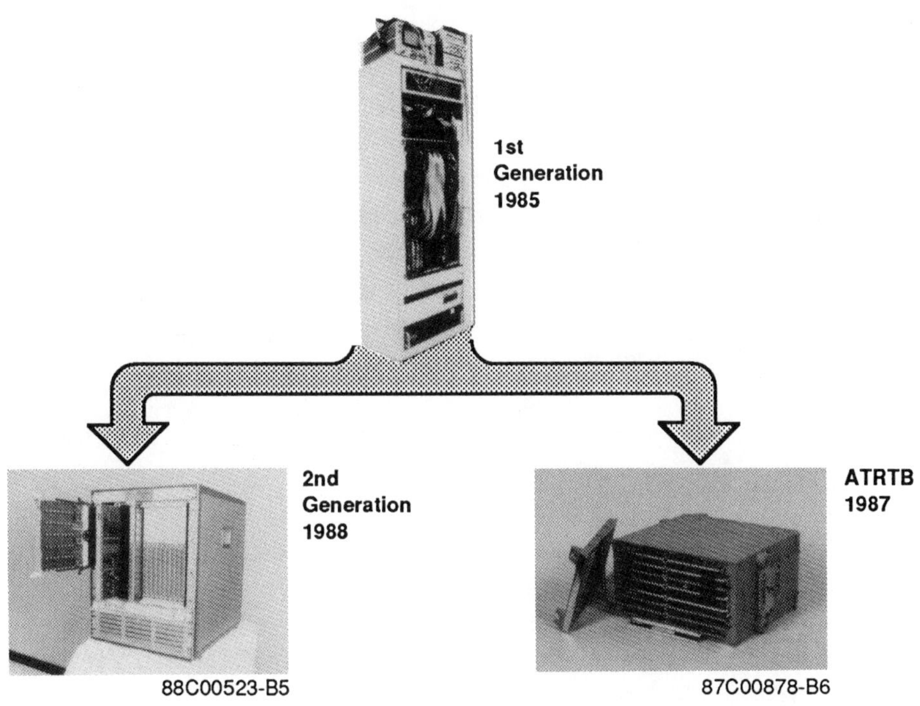


Figure 8: The image-understanding processor family.

**Acknowledgments**

Corporations form teams to develop concepts, and so it was with the exploitation of the GAPP. This author was selected as the first principal investigator for the project that developed the first working model. This team also developed the first-generation system architecture. The principal designer was W. K. Johnson. This author subsequently led the team that developed the first tactically packaged implementation which can be fitted into high-performance aircraft. The principal designer of that effort was M. S. Tomassi.

R. N. Jackson led the team that developed the second-generation system architecture and the team assigned to the algorithm development effort. The principal designer was A. Abercrombie. The first second-generation system was designed and built, first under the leadership of S. P. Buchanan and later under R. N. Jackson. The principal designers were M. Danagher, R. Wood, J. Deam, and L. Coulter.

# Bibliography

[1] Joe R. Brown, Melissa M. Garber and Steven F. Venable, *Artificial neural network on a SIMD architecture*, Proceedings of the 2nd Symposium on the Frontiers of Massively Parallel Computation, October 10–12, 1988, held at George Mason University, pp. 43–47.

[2] Eugene L. Cloud, *The geometric arithmetic parallel processor*, Proceedings of The 2nd Symposium on the Frontiers of Massively Parallel Computation, October 10–12, 1988, held at George Mason University, pp. 373–381.

[3] Eugene Cloud and Wlodzimierz Holsztynski, *Higher efficiency for parallel processors*, Professional Program Record 14, Computer Vision, IEEE SOUTHCON/84, Jan 17–19, 1984, pp. 1–15.

[4] Ronald Davis and Dave Thomas, *Systolic array chip matches the pace of high-speed processing*, Electronic Design, October

31, 1984, 207–218.

[5] Arthur V. Forman Jr., Arthur Chang, Patrick Walker and John Selvage, *An implementation of the two-dimensional discrete Fourier transform on the Geometric Arithmetic Parallel Processor*, SPIE Proceedings 8–11 August 1989, San Diego, California, Applications of Digital Image Processing XII, vol. 1153, pp. 400–411.

[6] Arthur V. Forman Jr. and Daniel J. Sullivan, *Pararallel algorithms for automatic target indentification using $CO_2$ laser radar imagery*, SPIE Proceedings 8–11 August 1989, San Diego, California, Real Time Signal processing XII, vol. 1154, pp. 167–176.

[7] *Geometric arithmetic parallel processor*, (NCR45CG72), data sheet, NCR Microelectronics Division, 2001 Danfield Ct., Ft. Collins, Colorado, 80525.

[8] Rafael C. Gonzales and Paul Wintz, Digital Image Processing, 2nd edition, Addison-Wesley, p. 337.

[9] Wyndham Hannaway, Gary Shea and William R. Bishop, *Handling real-time images comes naturally to systolic array chip*, Electronic Design, November 15, 1984, 289–300.

[10] Alexis Koster, Norman Sondak and Paul Sullivan, *Systolic arrays fill the bill as data-base management heads for gigabyte range*, Electronic Design, January 10, 1985, pp. 349–356.

[11] Kendall Preston, Jr., *The Abington Cross benchmark Survey*, COMPUTER, July 1989, IEEE Computer Society, pp. 9–18.

[12] Winthrop W. Smith, Jr. and Paul Sullivan, *Systolic array chip recognizes visual patterns quicker than a wink*, Electronic Design, November 29, 1984, pp. 257–266.

[13] US Patent Number 4,739,474.

[14] Lyle Wallis, *Associative memory calls on the talents of systolic array chip*, Electronic Design, December 13, 1984, pp. 217–226.

# The SLAP Image Computer

**ALLAN L. FISHER**
*Carnegie Mellon University*
*Pittsburgh, Pennsylvania*

and

**PETER T. HIGHNAM**
*Schlumberger Laboratory for Computer Science*
*Austin, Texas*

## 1 Introduction

A *scan line array processor* (SLAP) is an SIMD linear array that supports high-performance real-time image-processing. The Carnegie Mellon University SLAP Project [9, 11, 13] has designed a prototype SLAP system that includes Processing Elements (PEs) implemented in custom VLSI, and an optimizing high-level language compiler. We describe the hardware and software components of the CMU SLAP system. We also include a description of the directional-based compilation technique [10] for optimizing grid computations, SLAP algorithms, and performance estimates for compiled SLAP programs.

## 2 Scan Line Array Processor

Image computations take a variety of forms. The *iconic* form generates a new image from an input image on a pixel-for-pixel basis, using neighborhood values in the computation. The usual linear and nonlinear filters fall within this class. A variety of operations perform a data-reduction task, creating a summary or measurement of




ISBN 0-12-564040-4

one or more image attributes. Histograms, Hough transforms, and blob parameter measurements are all examples of this. The dominant characteristic of the iconic operations is the tremendous computational bandwidth required. A SLAP includes a large number of processors for this purpose. The data reduction operations are distinguished by their need to summarize results from entire images; a SLAP has a fast "global" computational unit to assist in the collation and correlation of results computed within the system. The reduction operators generate low-volume results that do not impose too much strain on a typical workstation bus. Figure 1 shows the varying data bandwidths within a SLAP system. The computational and I/O burden is entirely off-loaded from the host.

## 2.1 Pipelined Computation, Input, and Output

Typically an image moving between major components within an image-processing system does so as a stream of pixels. A SLAP operates on each row or "scan line" as it arrives; a distinct PE receives each image column. The usual mode of operation for a SLAP is therefore to "sweep" down an image as shown in Fig. 2. Each SLAP PE communicates directly with just its two nearest neighbors. Input and output of image rows is achieved by a video rate shift register built into the array. This is a similar mechanism to that used in the MPP [7], AMT DAP [1], CLIP 7A [16] and AIS [5]. The advantage is that a scan line can be shifted in at the same time as earlier scan lines are being processed and a result scan line is being shifted out (Fig. 2.1). Pipelining input, output, and computation in this way minimizes the impact of I/O on performance, which is substantial in a real-time image-processing system.

## 2.2 SIMD Vector

The SIMD paradigm minimizes overhead costs for instruction decoders, instruction memory, and control flow logic. SIMD control also simplifies inter-PE communication because instruction execution is lockstep. A SLAP's only high-bandwidth communication routes are the nearest neighbor connections. Compared with a grid machine,

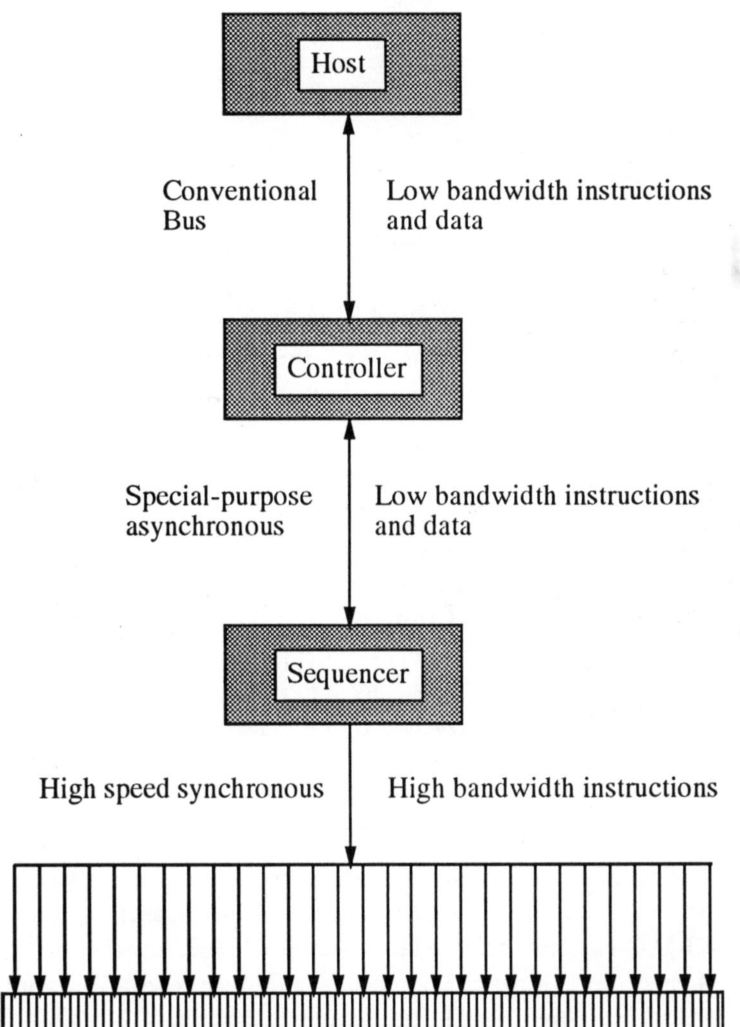


Figure 1: SLAP structure.

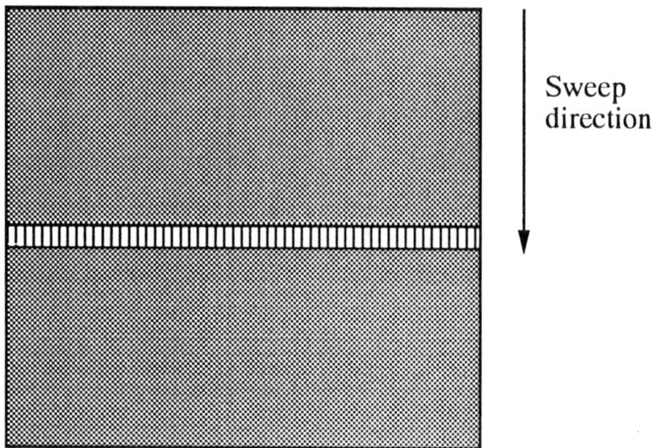


Figure 2: A SLAP sweeps an image.

a SLAP has only a moderate number of processors. This fact can be used to advantage to invest hardware resources in more powerful processing elements (PEs). Images rarely have binary pixels. Thus, the majority of arithmetic operations performed during the processing of an image are on multibit operands, generating multibit results. Therefore, the PE word size can and should be quite large. We see large integers as a good compromise between bit-serial and floating point processing for an image processor.

The Achilles' heel of any SIMD machine is local inflexibility. In order to provide for data-dependent computation, nearly every such architecture provides for conditional execution, whether centralized as in ILLIAC-IV [3] or handled locally to each PE. Another important type of flexibility is provided by local address generation ability in each PE. This capability is found in ILLIAC and in other large-word SIMD machines. It is not found in the majority of bit-serial machines, because address generation, storage and communication would dwarf the rest of the processor. The CM2 [6] and BLITZEN [2] are the only exceptions to this rule of which we are aware. The CM2 approach employs logic already provided to utilize floating-

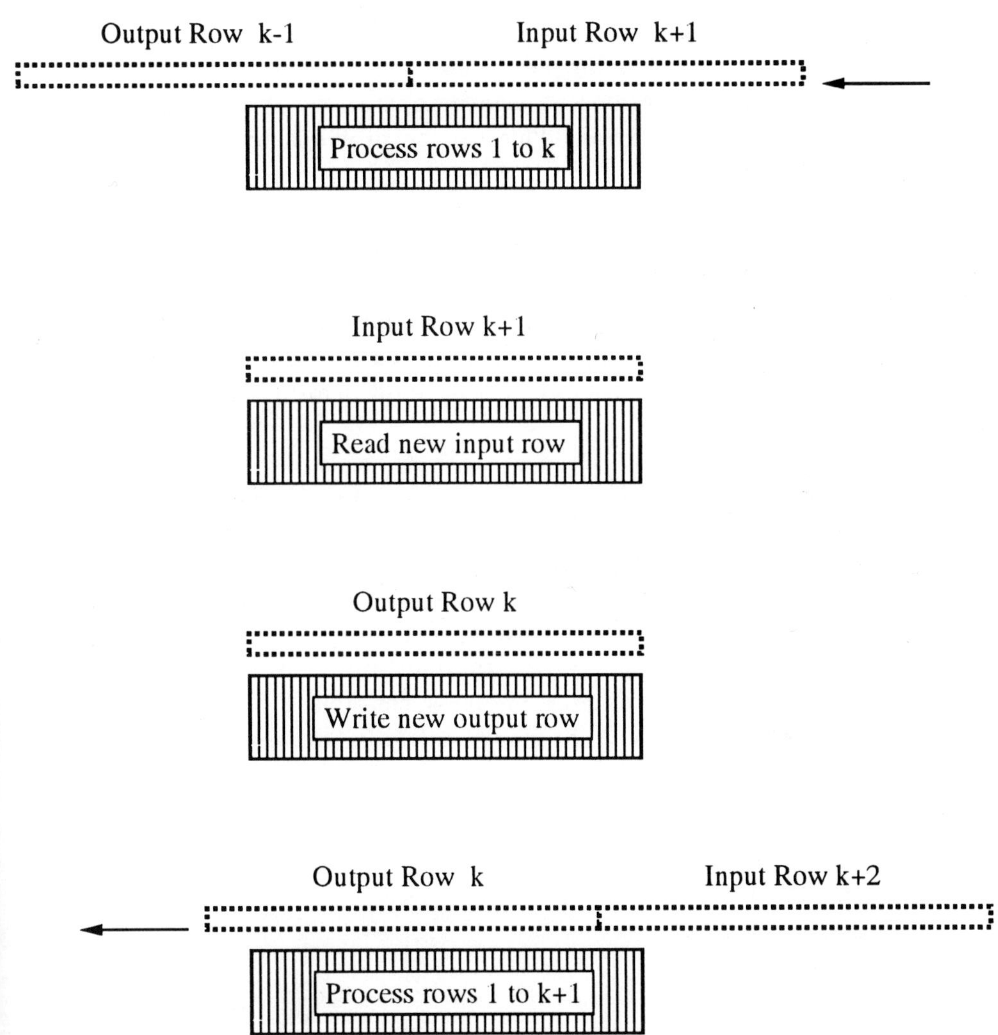


Figure 3: A SLAP pipelines input, output, and computation.

point accelerators. A third type of flexibility is the provision for single cycle shift and rotation operations with locally determined distances, crucial to flexible and efficient bit-field manipulations. All three mechanisms are provided in a SLAP PE.

Instruction sequencing needs feedback from the PE vector for data reduction operations, associative operations or calculations with data-dependent runtimes. This can be provided by simply adding "virtual" PEs to the vector extremes and by a simple, single-bit line that computes the wired-OR of contributing PEs.

The linear organization offers great leverage in terms of scaling with technology or image size. Any number of processors can be packed onto a chip without changing its pinout. The same comment applies to circuit boards, when the on-board PEs are organized as a vector only the extremes of which have off-board connectivity.

# 3 Overview of the SLAP Prototype

The structure of the CMU SLAP closely follows that shown in Fig. 1. A system contains a controller, a sequencer, a vector of processing elements, and some commercial A/D boards for video I/O. In this section we describe the system components. The following section discusses the PE in detail. Figure 4 contains a block diagram of the prototype design. The design is optimized for 512 × 512 images. The overall system size for the prototype would be three Sun boards, including two vector boards (each containing 256 PEs) and one controller-sequencer board that also contains four transposing image buffers.

## 3.1 Controller

The controller is a conventional microprocessor (MC68030) programmed in C. The controller selects and orders the execution of modules on the sequencer-vector. The controller has its own code and data memory. There are also image buffers that can be used as alternative source and destination for video rate imagery. These buffers can be accessed directly or transposed.

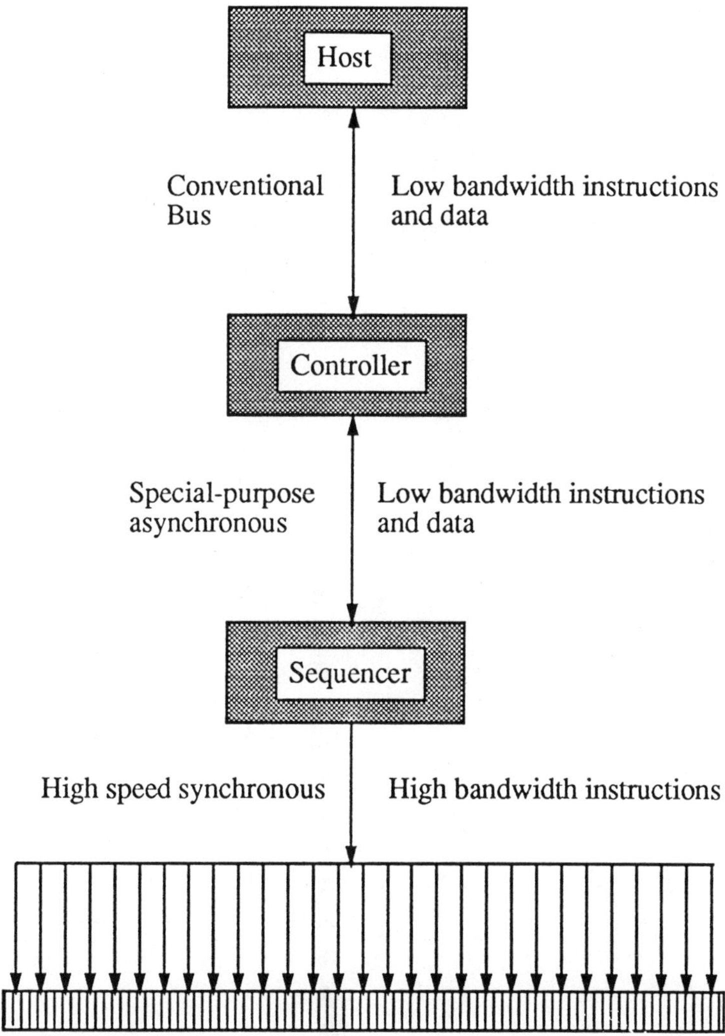


Figure 4: SLAP controller and sequencer.

## 3.2 Sequencer

The sequencer and the PE vector operate in lockstep. The sequencer is constructed from bit-slice components that provide a word size of 16 bits. There is a scratchpad memory of 64k words. The instruction memory includes the control bits for both the sequencer and the vector and is a little more than 100 bits wide, of which the PE component is 26 bits. In one cycle (100 ns) the sequencer's ALU can perform additive and logical instructions; a small number of cycles are required for multiplicative operations.

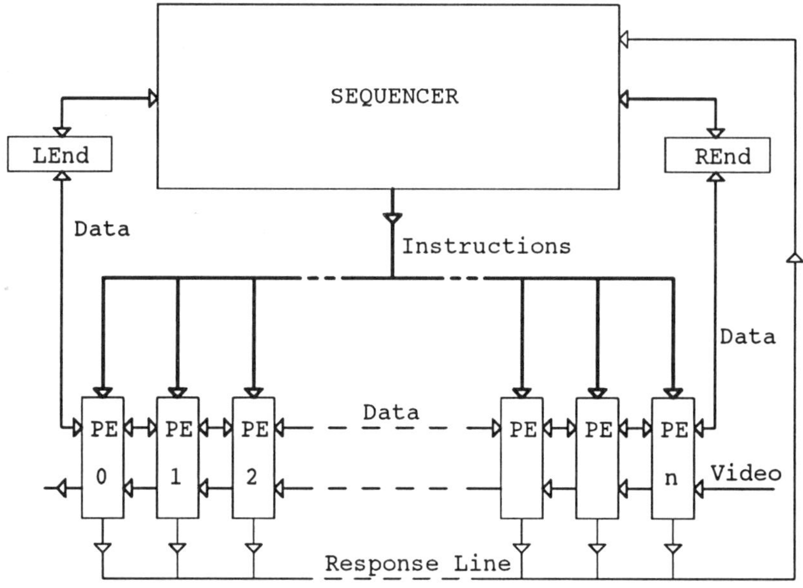


Figure 5: Block diagram of a SLAP sequencer and PE vector.

There are several communication routes between the sequencer and the vector:

- Literals (compile-time and run-time constants) are inserted into instruction fields and broadcast from the sequencer to all

PEs.

- The sequencer includes registers that function as virtual PEs, neighbors to the real PEs on the vector's extremes. These registers facilitate bidirectional communication. The sequencer includes a mechanism that permits the vector extremes to be tied directly together, forming a PE ring.

- The sequencer can use a single-bit line that holds the wired-OR of a single-bit register in all of the PEs to make branching decisions.

### 3.3 Vector

The vector is constructed from custom CMOS chips each of which holds four PEs (Fig. 6). The PE design is discussed in detail later in this chapter. Interesting properties of the PE units include the following:

- There is a decoder on-chip shared by the coresident PEs. The decoder supports the three-stage pipeline in the PE data path. The decoder is also able to sequence the multicycle multiplicative operations independently of the instruction stream.

- Each PE chip has associated SRAM chips. There is no external control logic: memory addresses are supplied via the neighbor communication lines, data is transferred using video shift register pins, and bank selection is provided by the sequencer.

## 4 The SLAP Processing Element

The premises for the PE design [14] were that the word size should provide adequate precision for most computer vision applications, that each PE would have independent addressing ability, that the familiar "IF-THEN-ELSE" style of conditional programming would be available, that multiplication would be supported, and that the exploitation of parallelism within a nontrivial PE would be possible.

Two implementation constraints were those common to any high-performance VLSI design: PE area and pin count. Inter-PE communication is supported solely by immediate-neighbor links. This connectivity is inexpensive, and yet augmented by the essentially free communication of data between pixel positions within each image column, the system has an interesting connectivity.

Speedups from parallelism inside a processor are gained from multiple functional units and pipelining. While a completely horizontal instruction format is impractical for any but the simplest PE design, saving a single cycle via concurrency can yield a large increase in throughput for the short loops often found in image-processing code. The compromise adopted is an instruction format combining vertical and horizontal components: a straightforward two-address instruction field and fields for critical functionality (such as the inter-PE communication). The "vertical" field is decoded on-chip, guiding data path activity over three successive clock cycles. The horizontal fields each dictate an action concurrent with one of the three phases.

As will be seen later, the mix appears to be a good one in terms of utilization of PE resources. The pipeline has no interlocks. The inter-PE communication, the conditional control management, and the two functional units, shifter and **ALU**, can all operate concurrently. The first two have their own control fields. Generally, the **ALU** or the shifter would be in operation. However, during multi-cycle multiplication and division sequences, the **ALU** is isolated and controlled without additional instruction bits by the on-chip decoder. When such a sequence is in progress the remainder of the data path is available.

The data path control part of each instruction is split by the decoder into three pipelined phases corresponding to "READ; COMPUTE; WRITE." Thus, in any cycle, three instructions are controlling sections of the data path. This scheme is supported in the design by two buses: the **A** bus is loaded during the READ phase; the **B** bus is loaded with the result from the COMPUTE phase, and written from in the WRITE phase. The PE memory is a dual-ported register file, reading from **B** and writing to **A**. The data path is illustrated in Fig. 7 .

## 4.1 Local Control

When a uniprocessor executes a conditional branch, it jumps past code that it will not execute. In the SIMD model, every processor receives every instruction. The PE design contains the idea of "protected state" and a mechanism to mimic closely the serial IF-THEN-ELSE model. A local context control value is kept in a sleep counter (**SC**). When the value in the **SC** exceeds zero the PE will not permit its protected state (register file, address registers, external memory, **RLR**, **VSR**) to be written. The value in **SC** represents the depth of nesting of conditional statements since the PE initially rendered itself inactive. A distinct field in the instruction controls the operation of this mechanism.

## 4.2 Instruction Decoder

All PEs on a chip share a single decoder. The decoder plays three roles :

1. It expands broadcast instruction bits into control signals for the PEs.

2. It provides a three-stage pipeline of the control bits. The simple instruction formats and the definition of instruction phases require little sophistication. The decoder retains the original instruction bits in a three-step shift register. Combinational logic specific to each instruction phase decodes the appropriate instruction field in each shift-register position.

3. It autonomously sequences multiplicative operations in the PEs. The multiplicative instructions involve only the ALU and associated registers. The decoder will initiate such operations on command. The decoder will then provide the appropriate PE control signals in every subsequent cycle until an instruction is received that terminates the operation. Thus, the decoder has two mutually exclusive flags that, when set, cause control signals to be provided regardless of the current instruction buffer contents. Non-ALU PE components can be controlled as before.

## 4.3 Implementation and Performance

The initial chip implementation used $2\mu$ CMOS [14]. Each chip contains 56,669 transistors, implementing four 16-bit processing elements and a pipelining decoder. The instruction rate is 10 MHz. The chip receives two clocks. One clock drives the instruction execution while the other, faster clock is used for the independent video stream. The die is 7.9mm × 9.2mm in a 108-pin PGA package. The power dissipation is 0.5 Watt.

A 512 PE system running at 10 MHz would deliver up to 5.12 billion 16-bit integer operations (additive or logical) per second, while simultaneously performing real-time image I/O. For a system dealing with 512 × 512 images at 30 frames per second this rate translates to about 640 operations per pixel.

A selection of image-processing codes has been implemented on a single processor of a Cray YMP, rated at 280 MFlop/s. Figure 8 illustrates the SLAP speedups over the Cray. The figure indicates the speedup that one would expect if one Cray 64-bit floating-point operation were considered equivalent to one SLAP 16-bit integer operation. The timings assume that the image is 512 × 512 and that the SLAP has 512 PEs. The Cray codes were implemented in Cray FORTRAN; the SLAP timings were derived from SLAP assembler. All codes were vectorized on the Cray. The speedup figures were computed using the numbers from the assembler SLAP implementations in an attempt to factor out the quality of the Cray FORTRAN compiler.

The binary filter operation assembles a nine-bit address from neighboring pixels. The address is then used as the address in a table of binary values. The SLAP implementation pipelines the assembly of an address as it scans down the image; the Cray implementation computes the address at each position independently. The SLAP implementation stores the table in a compact form (redundantly) within every PE that requires a local address, a local shift, and a mask to extract the requisite value. The histogram on the SLAP involves a postimage pass accumulation phase that reduces the speedup. The convolution involves multiplication. On a SLAP, when the operands are unknown at compilation time each multiply operation requires around ten cycles. The median like the binary filter can be pipelined as the SLAP sweeps down the image. Thus, the cost of sorting is amortized on the SLAP.

## 4.4 PE Design Issues

The processing-element design was developed over many iterations using a suite of image-processing operation kernels as the yardstick. The use of kernels is an acceptable paradigm in image processing because the variety of computation can be captured in just a few forms. We worked to ensure that the design was well-suited for each kernel and that fast code was not difficult to generate by a compiler. The kernels were augmented with code fragments that move data laterally within the vector because lateral communication bandwidth is at a premium. Below we enumerate PE features and the computations that influenced their inclusion.

1. *Pipelining* is a standard technique in conventional processor design for decreasing the average operation time. Pipelining can have disadvantages: (a) constraints are imposed on operand accessing, and (b) the pipeline must be emptied and refilled around branches. The constraints and the pipeline empty-refill can be enforced by hardware pipeline interlocks or implicitly in the code generated by a compiler. The SLAP PE has a short "open" pipeline. The small length reduces the penalty for empty-refill and reduces the distance (in cycles) between when an operand can be read and written. The availability of operands on **B** as an operand for a succeeding operation provides a simple expression chaining ability.

2. *Symmetric functionality* allows a simple code generator to generate code that catches transient values, preventing unnecessary load and store operations. In the PE design this generally required little more than providing some input selection logic before each functional unit.

3. *Local address generation* was identified for inclusion in the PE design from the outset. Address generation was included from

the outset because it gave our powerful processing elements the ability to perform fast internal sorts and independent table accesses. Local addressing was refined into static address registers for source and destination as distinct address registers were found to be effective in the shipment of indexed data blocks among PEs.

4. *Rotation and shifting by locally determined amounts* permits the PE locally to select fields within a word. This is found when making a reference into a compressed lookup table, for example. The alternative code would use conditional control to permit each PE to identify and obey the relevant instruction sequence.

5. *Autonomously sequencing multiplicative operations in the decoder* in combination with the logical isolation of the ALU is a simple mechanism for releasing the instruction stream. Multiply, divide, and modulos are all multicycle operations in the PE because we did not feel that the logic necessary for single-cycle execution was justified. In fact, the actual number of cycles that are executed can be made dependent upon the results of compiler subrange analysis. The decoder requires only a small amount of state to record which (if any) of the operations are being executed. When such state is set, the decoder sets the ALU control lines in each cycle. The released instruction bandwidth is available for any non-ALU operation. In particular, the sequencer is able to load tabular data into the PEs.

6. *The main PE instruction format has distinct communication and conditional control fields.* These are natural consequences of the design goal to minimize the effects of the linear connectivity and SIMD conditionality overhead. The conditional control field in the last instruction of a statement sequence within a conditional structure is easily utilized. Lateral communication can operate concurrently with intra-PE operations.

7. *The PE instruction format has a second format* that enables large global values (such as table entries) to be efficiently broad-

cast (for example, binary filters or connected components tables of label equivalence).

8. *Multiprecision integer operation support is built into the PEs* because some operations require more than 16 bits of dynamic integer range (for instance, convolutions with large mask values).

# 5 Directionals

Image-processing codes that achieve high utilization on an SIMD machine require largely similar computations to be carried out at every position within the domain of interest. This style of computation can be characterized as position-independent. The sequential expression of this style typically uses loop indices to specify the center of a computation whose operands are drawn from positions specified using relative offsets. The *directional* marker for expression graphs within a compiler [10] changes the optimization focus from array-loop expression analysis into algebraic transformations. In the standard form the offset values imply memory addressing. In an SIMD form the directional notation can be mapped directly to communication between processing sites. Directionals have been shown to be a good source of information for conventional algebraic expression optimization methods. We have found them to be particularly effective in combination with common subexpression elimination (CSE).

A directional is functionally a unary operator indicating a communication operation along a mesh axis. Thus for a two-dimensional grid there are four directionals: left, right, up, and down. We provide a set of rules for manipulating directionals that augments the usual set of algebraic operations found in compilers. We have shown that even a simple greedy heuristic application of the rules can be very effective in reducing the communication and computation time of an SIMD program. Our experiments include an isolated rule-based optimizer and a high level language optimizing compiler for the SLAP system [15]. An example transformation is shown below. A $2 \times 2$ summation (applied simultaneously to all points on a two-dimensional grid),

```
result :=  pixel +  left pixel +  up pixel +
      up left pixel
```

becomes

```
temp   := pixel +  up pixel
result := temp +  left temp
```

The optimizer, in conjunction with a CSE phase (again, a standard compiler component) has been shown to minimize the operation count in a symmetric linear filter and reduce by one third the multiplicative work in a common edge operator.

The directional markers can be usefully augmented with an additional operator **nomove** that is inserted initially above all global variables and constants. As **nomoves** are propagated within the expression forest along with the communication directionals, subtrees are automatically identified for execution on the scalar component of the SIMD system or compile-time evaluation.

# 6 SLAP Programming

A SLAP is programmed at two levels. A *harness*, written in C, executes on the controller. The harness selects and initiates modules that execute on the sequencer controlling sequencer and vector computations. Modules are generally written in the SLANG high- level language. SLANG is a programming language for the implementation of medium- and low-level image operations. The language directly supports appropriate programming models for image computations. A SLANG programmer enjoys implicit video synchronization and convenient image plane data reference support. A SLANG program provides a compiler with precise information on data reference patterns that can be readily exploited. SLANG has the structure of a conventional imperative language.

In the SLANG programming model, a programmer can write code that treats the system as a linear array, ignoring the video data transport mechanism. Within a special construct, **pass**, code is written that will be executed at every pixel position (the **grid** and **apply** models) or on every row of the incoming image (the **scanline** model). Values that are computed at other pixel positions can be referenced using relative offsets within a program. Bidirectional data motion between the vector and the sequencer is specified by addressing the left and right image borders.

A SLANG program resembles a conventional statically scoped language. The only numeric type is integer. Variables have two orthogonal attributes: dimensionality and locality. A variable can be scalar or array and **global** or **local**. The meaning of **local** is somewhat context dependent but all **global** variables exist only in the sequencer. Variables declared to be **local** outside a **pass** statement are replicated in all PEs. The locality of a variable declared within a **pass** statement depends upon the **pass** type: **grid** and **apply** variables are logically replicated at every position in a virtual image; **scanline** variables are replicated one to a column with a lifetime of one scanline.

There is a typical selection of control constructs (**if**, **while**, **for**, **repeat**, and **loop**). The controlling parameters for all the iterative constructs must be **global**. The condition controlling the **if** can be **local** or **global**. The significant digression is in inter-PE communication; values on other PEs are accessed by using directionals as explicit communication operators that provide implicit communication synchronization. Routines are provided to invoke harness-level actions from a module. As an example, a binary filter coded in SLANG is shown here:

```
slang binfilt()
begin
  var addr , look_up_table[ 32 ] : local ;
  addr := 0 ;
  pass( scanline , in ( im0 ) , out ( im1 ) )
  begin
        var entry , position : local ;
         addr := ( addr shiftl 3 ) or
               ( left im0 shiftl 2 ) or
               ( right im0 shiftl 1 ) or
               im0 ;
     entry    := look_up_table[ addr and 0o37 ] ;
     position := ( addr and 0o740 ) shiftl -5 ;
     im1      := ( entry shiftl -position ) and 1
  end
end.
```

## 6.1 A SLANG Compiler

SLANG constructs are generally transformed into SLAP object code in a straightforward manner. The SLANG compiler's most complex task is to map **pass** statements to the linear array. The bulk of the compilation time is spent exploiting common characteristics of image-processing programs. The different phases are as follows:

1. *Loop unrolling.* Those loops that have known bounds during compilation are in general unrolled. This uncovers a significant number of constant folding opportunities per unrolled body instance. This is combined with a constant propagation scheme.

2. *Conditional statement elimination.* Constant folding can determine the logical value of a condition during compilation. This results in the compiler eliding (or just simplifying) the iterative or conditional statement to which it belongs. In an SIMD machine, the simplification of conditional statements is an excellent optimization.

3. *Directional optimization and common subexpression elimination.* The expression subgraphs of the program are manipulated using directional information. The goal is to reduce the number of communication steps and to detect common subexpressions. The common subexpressions are broken out and placed as assignments to temporary variables within the program's statement graph. The use of directionals permits the compiler to identify a new class of common subexpressions specific to SIMD. Of course, CSE does not require directionals to be used.

4. *Pass conversion.* The computation expressed within a **pass** must be remapped before code can be generated for the SLAP. Additionally, when external images are involved in a **pass** there are video synchronization issues. The computation is recast from the two-dimensional abstraction to the one-dimensional machine. The conversion requires the introduction of buffers to hold vertically offset values.

# 7 Performance

The prototype SLANG to SLAP compiler generates SLAP control words. The compiler has been instrumented to permit the effectiveness of a number of different compiler optimizations to be determined. Our analysis includes estimates of the effectiveness of the two optimization components that have not been fully implemented: peephole and schedule. The bottom line is that without peephole and schedule the average SLANG module sees a performance improvement of about a factor of three when all the optimizations are applied. The numbers reported are for the operation code execution time only, ignoring image I/O time unless the image resides in off-chip memory.

The module set is a suite of 16 image-processing modules coded in SLANG, including histogram, median filter, binary filter, and Hough transform. Ten of the 16 modules were generated from programs written in the Apply language [17] using a program developed by

Shigeru Sasaki. Eleven of the modules use a **grid pass**, four modules use a **scanline pass**, and one module uses an **apply pass**. The average length of a module is 63 lines. All modules employ horizontal directionals; ten modules use vertical directionals. Simple counts of directional operators in the code mask the compile-time extent of directionals because many are embedded in loops whose extent is discovered during compilation. Eleven of the modules perform multiplicative operations in the PEs. All of the module timings are for 512 × 512 images held in off-chip memory.

Compiler switches are used to vary the optimization selection:

- *Constants.* The compiler folds constant expressions and elides or simplifies statements whenever possible. This can be disabled. When a compile-time constant value is assigned to a variable or to an array element using a compile-time constant index, that value is conservatively associated with the entity and used in its place. This is referred to as constant propagation and can be disabled.

- *Loops.* Loops are unrolled before and after any **pass** structures are translated into their **for** equivalents. Loop unrolling and constant folding are iterated exhaustively. Each unroll can instantiate more constants (from expressions that previously involved the loop index variable). The unrolling operations can both be stopped. The maximum number of times that a loop is unrolled is also controllable.

- *Directionals.* Directionals are by default elevated as much as possible to increase directional interaction opportunities. The incurred cost is the implementation of temporary buffers to handle vertical directionals. All directional optimization can be disabled. Another compiler option forces all vertical directionals down to the leaves of the expression graph. This reduces the directional optimizations that can be applied but removes the need for temporary buffers.

- *Common subexpression elimination.* Each time a common subexpression is identified and exploited, temporary storage is required. In general, the savings in terms of redundant operations should be worthwhile. There is a trade-off in the SLAP PEs because off-chip storage access is expensive. CSE can be turned off.

- *Multiplicative operations.* The PE ALU is able to perform a multiplicative operation in fewer than the number of cycles needed for full word operations when the maximum size of the operands is known at compile-time. This can be turned off.

- *Registers.* There are operations that require significant amounts of memory. The effect of large on-chip register files can be simulated.

The results are initially summarized as geometric means that are then expressed as ratios using the results of not applying any optimizations as the base case. We discuss the effectiveness of the compiler using examples from the generated assembler.

## 7.1 Basic Results

Table 1 contains the results summarized as geometric means and expressed normalized against the no-optimization case. The combined effects of all optimizations yields almost a factor of three performance increase. As a means of reducing the effects on measurements due to coding in SLANG we evaluate the various compiler optimizations using marginal change on performance. The most significant optimization contributions (measured) each yield marginal improvements of almost a factor of two when all other optimizations are applied. The rightmost column in the table records the impact of including an optimization using as the percentage performance increase over when it is not being used (100.0 * (time - best) / time). The lower portion of the table reports the results of not performing certain pairs of optimizations. These are included to demonstrate optimization interactions, which are discussed below.

As expected, the relationship between directional optimization and common subexpression elimination (CSE) is close. In the absence of normalized, directional optimization execution time increases

| Optimization | Mean | Contribution |
|---|---|---|
| *No optimizations* | 1.000 | |
| *All optimizations* | 0.348 | 100.0% |
| *No loop unrolling* | 0.682 | 49.0% |
| *No common subexpression elimination* | 0.488 | 28.7% |
| *No constant propagation* | 0.457 | 23.9% |
| *No directional analysis* | 0.426 | 18.3% |
| *Vertical directionals moved to leaves* | 0.385 | 9.6% |
| *No multiplicative optimization* | 0.383 | 9.1% |
| *No loop unrolling and no constant propagation* | 0.688 | 49.4% |
| *No CSE and no directional optimization* | 0.641 | 45.7% |
| *No CSE and vertical directionals moved to leaves* | 0.575 | 39.5% |

Table 1: Geometric means of normalized execution times.

from 0.348 to 0.426, or by 22.4%. In the absence of CSE, run time increases from 0.348 to 0.488, or by 40%. However, when both CSE and directional optimization are removed the time increases to 0.641, or by 86.2%. The directional optimization elevates directionals within the expression trees, necessitating additional buffer storage. The manipulation of the buffers is largely similar and hence amenable to CSE, which reduces the cost imposed by directional optimization. CSE itself has no costs in terms of buffered storage (although temporaries are generally required) but is able to exploit common subtrees below different directionals.

With a little care we can examine the relationship between CSE and directional optimization applied horizontally and vertically. One of the compiler switches permits us to force all vertical directionals to the leaves of the expression tree. This removes the need for temporary buffers at the expense of (a) optimization opportunities, and

(b) a net increase in the number of directionals. We will treat the results of pushing all verticals down to the leaves as not applying any vertical directional optimizations. Table 2 demonstrates the relative effectiveness of different options in the CSE/directional optimization spectrum.

The column labeled Improvement is the percentage gain from not applying any directional optimization to applying both. Without CSE the vertical to horizontal numbers (56.9% to 43.1%) would seem to indicate that the former is advantageous. However, the horizontal-only figure includes the cost for the verticals moved to leaves, which is accentuated by the absence of CSE to reduce the buffer access costs. When CSE is present we see a more correct picture that reflects the buffer cost for vertical optimization.

| Optimization | No CSE | | CSE | |
|---|---|---|---|---|
| | Mean | Improvement | Mean | Improvement |
| Neither | 0.641 | 0.0% | 0.426 | 0.0% |
| No Vertical | 0.575 | 43.1% | 0.385 | 52.6% |
| No Horizontal | 0.554 | 56.9% | 0.389 | 47.4% |
| Both | 0.488 | 100.0% | 0.348 | 100.0% |

Table 2: Interactions of directional optimization and CSE.

Constant propagation and folding are used to evaluate loop control expressions. Unrolled loops instantiate constants in place of loop variables and thereby provide more opportunities for constant manipulation. Our results indicate that the effects are by no means orthogonal. Independently unrolling and propagation provide 49.0% and 23.9% performance increases, respectively. However, their combined effect is only slightly better (49.4%) than that of unrolling alone. This indicates the advantages of loop unrolling. It also indicates the preponderance of simple loops in the module suite.

Optimizing multiplicative operators using information on the range of the operands yields a respectable improvement of 9.1%. This derives almost entirely from local multiplication optimization (from inspection of the modules). There are also multiplications hidden from the programmer that might be performed by the PEs (such as accessing local arrays using local expressions).

In order to provide an idea of the absolute performance of the code on SLAP, we have also coded two modules in the SLAP assembly language and compared the timing results to those obtained from compiled code. The results are shown in the Assembler column in Table 3. The Original values are for the compiler generated code; Scheduled code is derived from the output of the SLANG compiler after sequencer and PE instructions have been coscheduled. We found no improvement after peephole optimization on the compiled code. The scheduling improvement derives almost entirely from overlapping PE and sequencer operations. Employing the instruction stream during off-chip access and multiplicative operations was not found to be amenable to simple local analysis because the operations that could use the free positions are generally not local in the code. The Convolution and Hough lines in the table reflect the fact that the inner loops are simple and that the only substantial advantage to be gained is from sequencer/PE code overlap. The Hough code contains a number of very simple inner loops. Each loop is iterated 56 times. The code for the loop body is approximately one-third global and two-thirds local. The global component in the scanline loops involves identifying, retrieving, and using the next move entry for line motion. The post-pass loops' global component identifies array elements to update. Thus, the advantage we show for assembler and scheduling of the Hough can be largely realized by loop unrolling and constant folding in the global code segment.

| Module Name | Original | Scheduled | Assembler |
|---|---|---|---|
| Convolution | 1.00 | 0.67 | 0.67 |
| Median | 1.00 | 0.85 | 0.61 |
| Hough | 1.00 | 0.70 | 0.62 |

Table 3: Impact of scheduling and hand-coding.

We have found that the compiler's fairly simple code generator invariably exploits the PE's conditional control hardware using the dedicated instruction field. The code generator also does a good job of chaining long expressions within the PEs.

## 8 Hough transform

The Hough transform [4] is a global image operation that is a popular benchmark for vision systems. The form of the transform used here assists in the identification of straight lines within an image. The sequential implementation takes $O(n^2\theta)$ time to map image points to an accumulator matrix in which each cell represents one straight line. After all image points have contributed a vote for each line that they might be on, the accumulator matrix is scanned and the most popular lines are reported. The SLAP implementation performs $O(\theta)$ operations per scanline, which can be achieved within one scanline time. The SLAP algorithm [12] uses a Bresenham-style [8] digital, straight line generation technique to direct the motion of the accumulator bins along the lines that they represent. The SLAP examines a single image twice: the second pass is over the transposed image to capture all line orientations. The computation requires less than three frame times.

## 9 Summary

The SLAP project has produced a system design that is capable of useful real-time vision computations. The PEs and the system structure have been designed and the PEs implemented as custom VLSI. An optimizing compiler for a high-level language has been built for the system that exploits a novel optimization technique. Algorithms, that are extremely effective, have been implemented on the SLAP, including a Hough transform.

The SLAP processing element demonstrates a number of features that are unusual for an SIMD computer. The word size (16 bits) allows the PE to demonstrate features that significantly ameliorate the local inflexibility of SIMD: local addressing, local shift control, conditional control hardware. The PE design process was also able to make use of conventional processor design guidelines: open pipeline, symmetric functional units. There are features of the PE that have not yet been fully explored, but which we have every reason to believe will be fruitful. In particular, scheduling of intra-PE and PE-sequencer activities.

The directional approach to SIMD optimization has been shown to be effective. There are other computational contexts that are similar in form to image-processing, such as finite difference calculations. We are exploring the utility of directional-based manipulation in this and other areas.

### Acknowledgments

In addition to the authors, the SLAP project has involved Todd Rockoff, Juan Leon, Shigeru Sasaki, and John Zsarnay. We are grateful to Jon Webb for access to Apply routines.

## Bibliography

[1] Active Memory Technology, 16802 Aston Street, Irvine, CA 92714. *Distributed Array Processor*, 1986.

[2] R. Heaton, D. Blevins, and E. Davis, *A bit-serial VLSI array processing chip for image processing*, Journal of Solid-State Circuits, 25(2), 1990, pp. 364-368.

[3] R. M. Hord, The Illiac IV, the First Supercomputer,. Computer Science Press, 1982.

[4] P. V. C. Hough, *Methods and means to recognize complex patterns* U.S. Patent 3,069,654, 1962.

[5] L. A. Schmitt and S. S. Wilson, *The AIS-5000 parallel processor*, IEEE Transactions on Pattern Analysis and Machine Intelligence, 10(3), 1988, pp. 320-330.

[6] G. L. Steele, Jr, *Connection machine model CM-2 technical summary*, Thinking Machines Incorporated, April 1987. Report Number HA87-4.

[7] K. E. Batcher, *Design of a massively parallel processor*, IEEE Transactions on Computers, C-29(9)1980, pp. 836-840

[8] J. E. Bresenham, *Algorithm for computer control of a digital plotter*, IBM Systems Journal, 4(1), 1965, pp. 25-30.

[9] A. L. Fisher and P. T. Highnam, *Real-time image processing on scan line array processors*, In IEEE Computer Society Workshop on Computer Architectures for Pattern Analysis and Image Database Management, 1985, pp. 484-489.

[10] A. L. Fisher and P. T. Highnam, *Communication and code optimization in SIMD programs*, International Conference on Parallel Processing, 1988, pp. 84-88.

[11] A. L. Fisher and P. T. Highnam, *Programming considerations in the design and use of a SIMD image computer*, Frontiers '88 : The Second Symposium on the Frontiers of Massively Parallel Computation, 1988, pp. 683-690.

[12] A. L. Fisher and P. T. Highnam, *Computing the Hough transform on a scan line array processor*, IEEE Transactions on Pattern Analysis and Machine Intelligence, 1989. Presented in the IEEE Computer Society Workshop on Computer Architecture for Pattern Analysis and Machine Intelligence, October 1987.

[13] A. L. Fisher, P. T. Highnam, and T. E. Rockoff, *Scan line array processors : work in progress*, DARPA Image Understanding Workshop, 1988, pp. 625-633.

[14] A. L. Fisher, P. T. Highnam, and T. E. Rockoff, *A four-processor building block for SIMD processor arrays*, Journal of Solid-State Circuits, 25(2), 1990, pp. 369-375.

[15] A. L. Fisher, J. Leon, and P. T. Highnam, *Design and performance of an optimizing SIMD compiler*, Frontiers of Massively Parallel Computation, 1990.

[16] T. J. Fountain, K. N. Matthews, and M. J. B. Duff, *The CLIP7A image processor*, IEEE Transactions on Pattern Analysis and Machine Intelligence, 10(3), 1988, pp. 310-319.

[17] R. S. Wallace, J. A. Webb, and I. C. Wu, *Machine-independent image processing: performance of Apply on diverse architectures*, 3rd International Conference on SuperComputing, 1988.

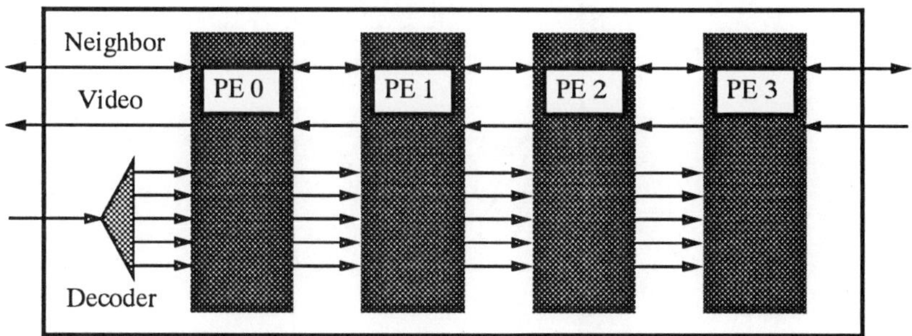


Figure 6: Processor chip organization.

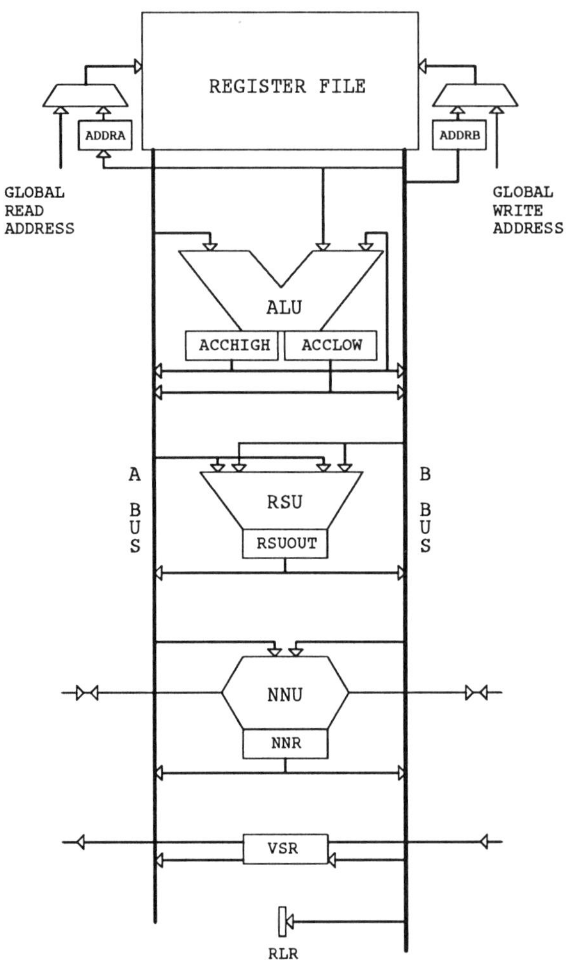


Figure 7: SLAP processing element data path.

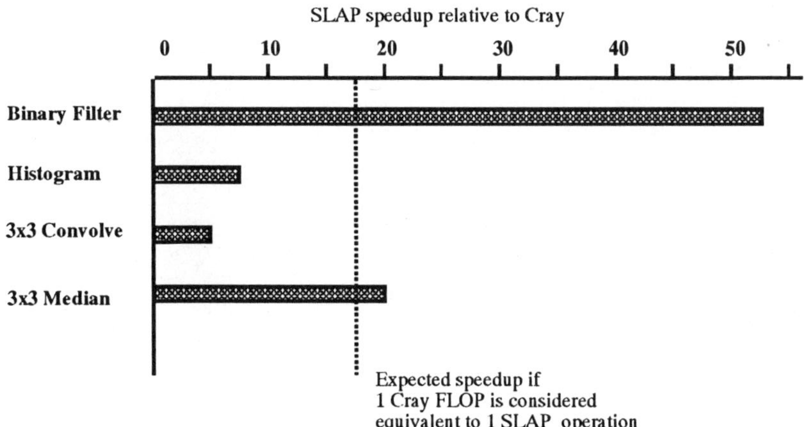


Figure 8: SLAP speedups relative to cray.

# Real-Time Image Understanding with the Associative String Processor

**ANARGYROS KRIKELIS**
*Aspex Microsystems Ltd.*
*Uxbridge, England*

## 1 Introduction

Image-understanding applications are characterized by the need to provide a rapid response to information derived from a high-speed continuous data stream. For example, real-time image understanding using noninterlaced (60 Hz) raster-scanned image frames requires the completion of all processing tasks (including data input and output) within a frame time of 16.7 msec, suggesting processing rates of 10–1000 GOPS (giga operations per second; (for example, $10^9$ eight-bit additions per second)) and input data rates approaching 1 GB/s. It is the requirement for such high performance, unattainable by sequential architectures, that can be achieved only with massively parallel processing.

Image-understanding systems, especially systems used in real-time applications, need to support continuous data input and attempt the rapid detection, analysis, and decision making (based on understanding or recognition) of pictorial information and determination of some appropriate response, as indicated in Fig. 1.

Sensors may include some form of visual, thermal, electromagnetic, or nuclear radiation energy and applications include remote sensing, surveillance and tracking in aerospace, avionics, and autonomous navigation, and increasingly in biomedical sciences. In

Parallel Architectures and Algorithms for Image Understanding


ISBN 0-12-564040-4

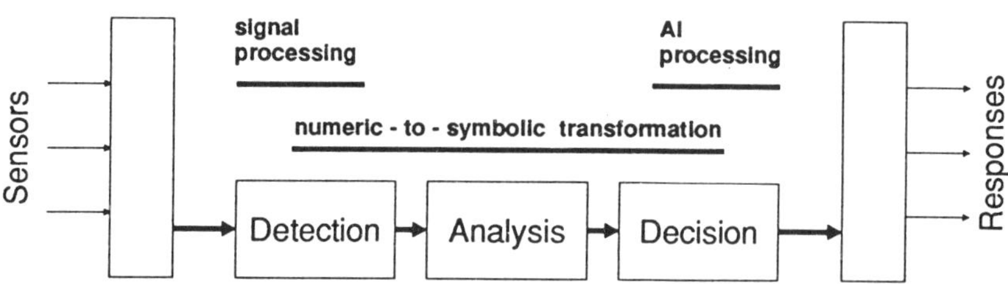


Figure 1: Real-time image-understanding system.

particular, real-time image-understanding systems appear very attractive to any form of robotic applications.

Typical detection tasks range from image reconstruction or restoration (to compensate for sensor nonuniformities, aging, and eventual failure), through filtering (to improve signal-to-noise ratios and enhance particular image features) to correlation (to discriminate relevant image information from background clutter).

Typical analysis tasks range from grouping data associated with meaningful objects, through specific transforms for feature extraction and edge or contour following (to establish feature connectivity), to object quantification (for length or area measurement or center-of-mass coordination), and listing of relevant object properties.

Typical decision tasks range from pattern matching (correlation of invariant object descriptors with model descriptions) and navigation of semantic networks, through hypothesis analysis, to interpretation of object-related information to facilitate decision making and response determination.

However, such end-to-end processing (that is to say, problem solving) systems encompass a sequence of tasks, from signal processing through some form of numeric-to-symbolic data conversion (usually achieving considerable data reduction), to AI (artificial intelligence) processing. Indeed, image understanding tasks are not solely confined to the low-level arithmetic operations on two-dimensional arrays typical of early (that is, first-generation) parallel computing, but the wide variety of tasks also includes higher-level operations on more complex data structures (for example, sets, tables, trees, or graphs). Moreover, the nature of image-understanding environments ensures dynamically changing functionality requirements as sensor technology and application understanding improve.

## 2 Architectures for Image-Understanding

An ideal real-time image-understanding system would instantaneously process each data sample on input, as indicated in Fig. 1, and consequently, the traditional approach to the implementation of such systems is a pipeline of different processors, with each stage being dedicated to a specific task, which is executed on the fly as data flush through its processor. Indeed, there are a number of image-understanding systems based on this approach [2, 13]. Clearly, in order to process a continuous stream of data samples, the task processing rate of the first stage of the pipeline must match the maximum input data rate. However, the performance of each subsequent processor in the pipeline can be optimized to reduce the overall latency delay of the output response.

Such spatial partitioning of task parallelism implies that the scaling of overall parallel processing power, to match the everchanging (input-to-output) complexities and performance requirements of different parallel computing applications, entails adjusting the length of the pipeline with the insertion or removal of high-performance hardware stages. Indeed, although the rate of data transfer between stages reduces rapidly as computation proceeds along the pipeline, particular tasks may, nevertheless, be based on quite complex algorithms, requiring the high-speed execution of very many low-level operations (for example, image-filtering operations in the very early stages of image understanding).

This ad hoc optimization of different processors and the emphasis on high-speed data flow between processors restrict opportunities for microelectronics and packaging technologies to reduce the number of expensive and error-prone interconnections and thereby to overcome the engineering problems discussed previously. Indeed, development, manufacture, and maintenance costs for a range of such unique (that is, low-volume) modules will inevitably remain high (compared with high-volume standard parts) and system durability will be difficult to maintain. Moreover, the expense of redundant processors in irregular parallel computing pipelines is likely to render attempts at fault-tolerance cost-ineffective. Consequently, such machines are unlikely to comply with the engineering constraints of real-time image-understanding systems discussed in the previous section.

The traditional approach to overcoming these problems would be with a regular parallel computing pipeline of identical stages (for example, the linear systolic array [8]). Real-time, on the fly processing can still be achieved, but the output response now suffers a latency delay, which depends on the length of the pipeline (that is, the number of stages).

By balancing processing rate with input data rate, the uniform pipeline processor gains undoubted speed advantages for the early stages of image understanding. However, lack of architectural and programming flexibility would severely reduce the efficiency of the numeric-to-symbolic data conversion process and AI processing, which dominate the latter processing stages of image understanding, for which the common processing stages are not so well suited.

Finally, it is interesting to note that such homogeneous pipeline architectures derive little benefit from the experimental observations, that for most real-time image-understanding systems the numeric-to-symbolic data conversion process may reduce the output data volume by several orders of magnitude (with respect to a given input data volume), and that application requirements for processing and input data rates are normally significantly different.

Architectural alternatives to dedicated pipelines, which attempt to take advantage of the above criticisms and observations, are massively parallel processors based on homogeneous MIMD (multiple-instructions, multiple-data) or SIMD (single-instruction, multiple-data) array processing, pyramidal structures, and multiprocessing. Such architectures comprise an ensemble of processing units (in the case of massively parallel up to hundreds of thousands) which intercommunicate via global memory or sending messages through an interconnection network. In this case, the necessary process is achieved by first distributing data elements over the identical processors of the architecture and then executing successive tasks on the stored data. In addition, such temporal partitioning of task parallelism must be supported by data buffering to ensure that task processing rates are independent of input and output data rates.

To be cost-effective for integrated real-time image-understanding applications, such parallel computer architectures would need to satisfy the following computational requirements.

1. application flexibility
2. architectural scalability
3. computational efficiency, by avoiding
   - sequential processing overheads, associated with the input and output of data values
   - inefficient processor allocation, resulting in redundant sequential processing and low concurrency within the processor ensemble and interprocessor communication network, due to a mismatch between the applied parallelism of the computer and the natural (data-level) parallelism of the data structure being processed
   - sequential processing overheads, associated with the initialization and scheduling of the concurrent execution of mutually exclusive processes/operations, resulting in inefficient exploitation of natural (control-level) parallelism in the algorithmic requirement
   - sequential processing due to requirements for the storage and processing of scalar (as opposed to vector) data (for example, during the calculation of intermediate results)
   - parallel processing overheads, due to the initialization and synchronization of interprocessor communication (which would not be suffered by a sequential processor); for example, navigating irregular tree-structured data on an orthogonal array processor could entail much routing through

redundant processors with significant control and communication overheads

4. pipelining data input

5. inter-processor communication network configurability

6. overlapping sequential and parallel processing

7. programmability.

Consequently, for integrated real-time image understanding, the new generation (that is, second generation) of massively parallel processors must satisfy significantly different application and design requirements than their first-generation predecessors.

# 3 The ASP Architecture

Based on the encouraging results emerging from research into parallel computing technology at Brunel University and being developed by Aspex Microsystems Ltd., ASP (associative string processor) modules comprise highly versatile parallel processing building blocks for the simple construction of fault-tolerant massively parallel processors [9, 10, 11]. Indeed, according to application requirements, an appropriate combination of ASP modules would be plugged into the control bus of Data Communications Network of an appropriate modular ASP system, as indicated in Fig. 2.

An ASP module comprises an MIMSIMD (multiple-instruction control of multiple-SIMD (single-instruction stream, multiple-data stream)) parallel-processing structure of intercommunicating ASP substrings, each supported with an ASP data buffer (ADB) and an ASP control unit (ACU), as shown in Fig. 3 and Fig. 4. The ASP module also incorporates a single control unit (CU) and multiple data interfaces (DIs), to connect to the system rack.

Based on a fully programmable, reconfigurable, and fault-tolerant homogeneous parallel-processing architecture, ASP modules offer considerable application flexibility, maintaining computational efficiency over a particularly wide range of applications, due to

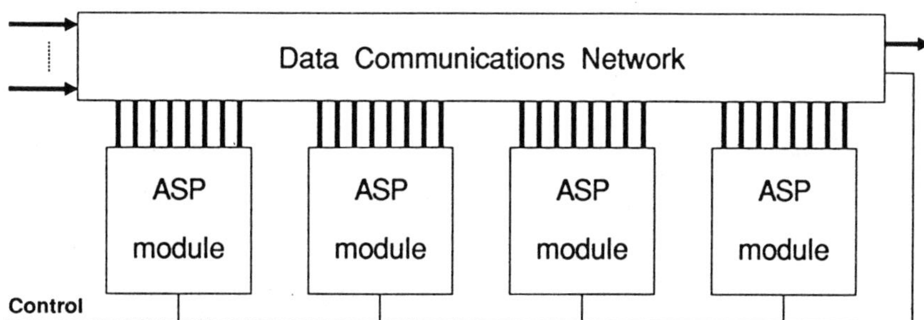


Figure 2: Modular ASP system.

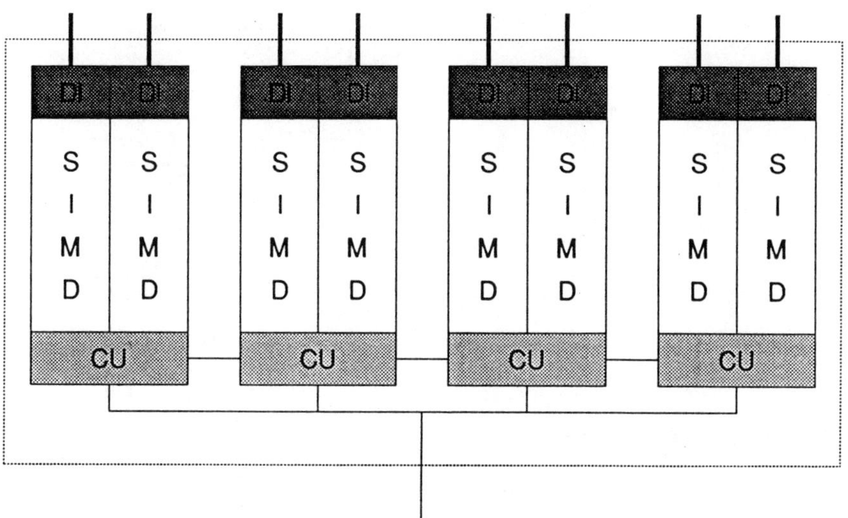


Figure 3: ASP module.

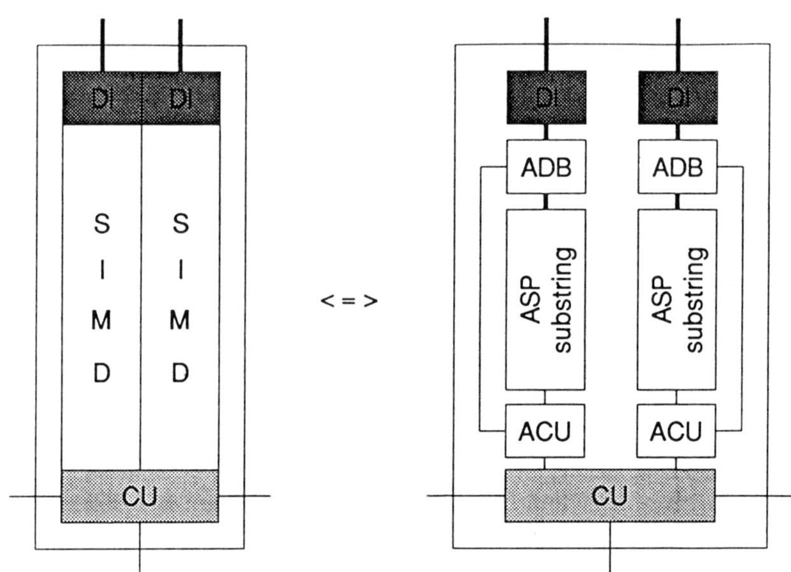


Figure 4: ASP module implementation.

1. simple configuration of ASP modules to simplify the development of systems, which are well matched to functional application requirements;

2. pipelining and overlapping input–output data transfers (via the data communications network) with parallel processing (within ASP substrings), by separating input–output from processing with the ASP data buffers (ADBs);

3. overlapping of sequential processing in the ASP Control Units (ACUs) with parallel processing (in ASP substrings); and

4. mapping different application data structures to a common string representation within ASP substrings (supporting content-addressing, parallel-processing, and a reconfigurable interprocessor communication network).

The numeric-to-symbolic data conversion process is achieved by first distributing data elements over the identical processors of the ASP substrings and then executing successive tasks on the stored data. Such temporal partitioning of task parallelism ensures that task processing rates are independent of input data rate, due to data buffering with ADBs, and scaling of overall parallel processing power simply entails adjusting the number and length of ASP substrings. Indeed, the uniformity of ASP substrings provides a much cheaper medium for scaling than the expensive processors of a dedicated pipeline.

## 3.1 ASP Substrings

An ASP substring is a programmable, homogeneous, and fault-tolerant fine-grain, SIMD massively parallel processor incorporating a string of identical APEs (associative processing elements), a reconfigurable interprocessor communication network, and a vector data buffer for fully overlapped data input–output [9, 10], as indicated in Fig. 5.

As shown in Fig. 6, each APE incorporates a 64-bit data register and a six-bit activity register, a 70-bit parallel comparator, a single-bit full-adder, four status flags (C to represent arithmetic carry, M

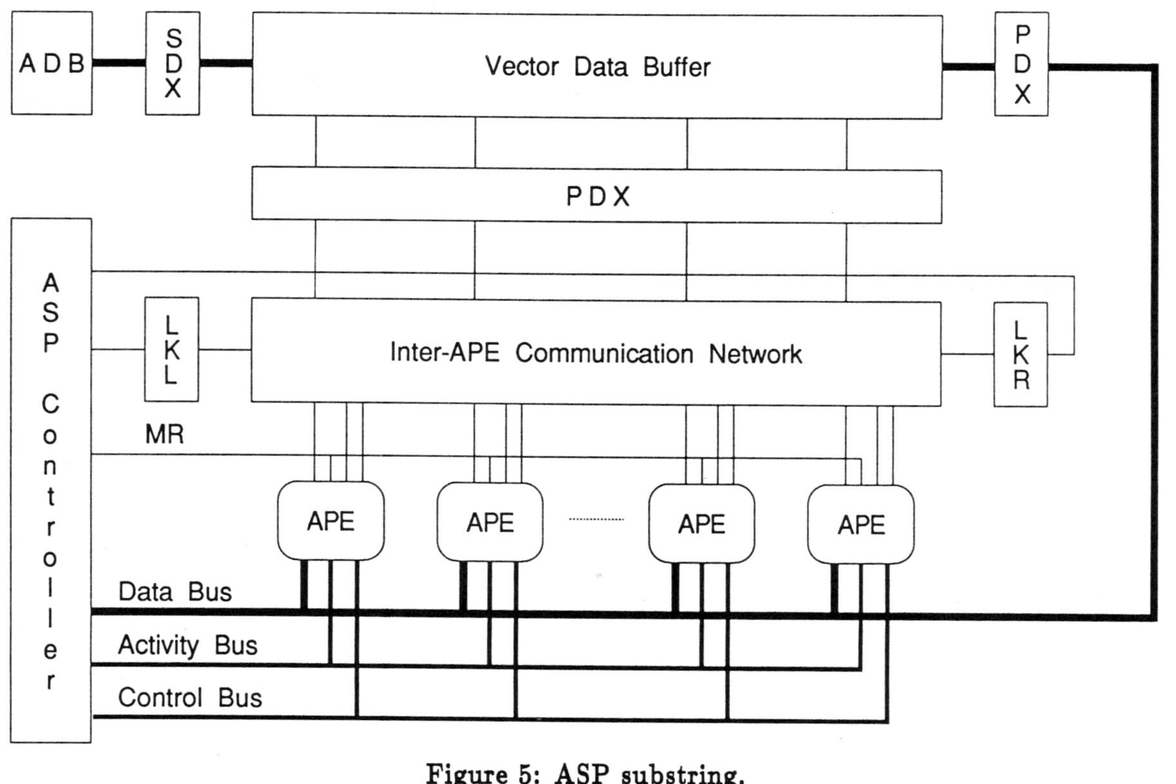


**Figure 5: ASP substring.**

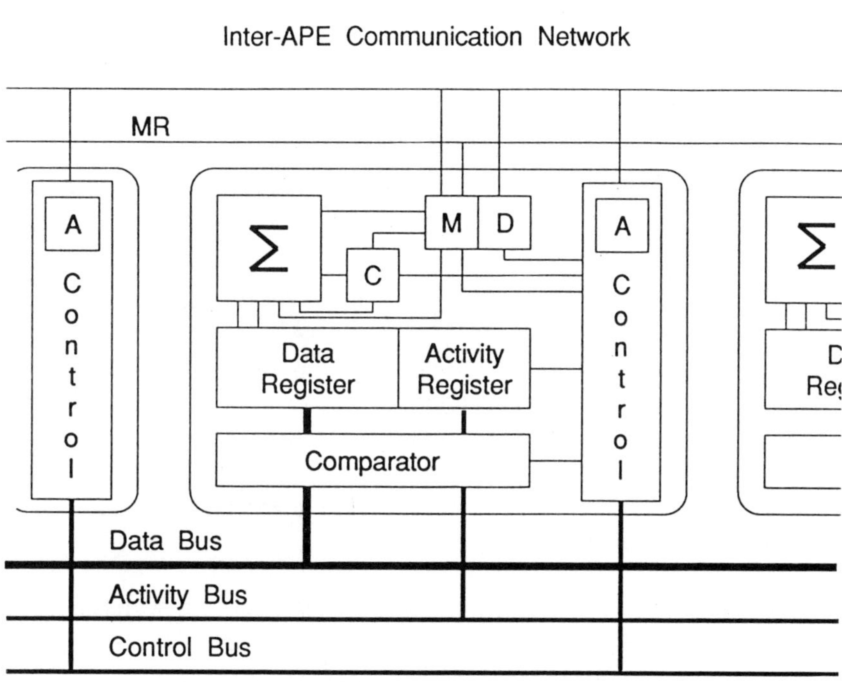


Figure 6: Associative Processing Element (APE).

and D to tag matching and destination APEs and A to activate selected APEs), and control logic for local processing and communication with other APEs.

In operation, the signal to data processing sequence indicated in Fig. 1, is achieved by first distributing data elements over the APE data registers and then executing successive tasks on the stored data. Indeed, each ASP substring supports a form of set processing, in which a subset of active APEs (that is, those which match scalar data and activity values broadcast from the ACU) support scalar–vector (that is, between the ACU and data registers) and vector–vector (that is, within data registers) operations. Matching APEs are either directly activated or source inter-APE communications to indirectly activate other APEs. A match reply line in the control interface provides feedback on whether none or some APEs match.

## 3.2 Inter-APE Communications Network

The inter-APE communications network implements a simply-scalable, fault-tolerant, and dynamically reconfigurable tightly coupled APE interconnection strategy, which supports cost-effective emulation of common network topologies: arrays (such as, vector, matrix and binary n-cube), tree networks, graph networks (for example, semantic networks), address permutation networks(such as exchange, shuffle and butterfly networks) and shifting networks.

Most significantly, the APE interconnection strategy supports simple unlimited modular network extension, via the LKL and LKR (link left and right) ports, as indicated in Fig. 5, to enable tailoring of parallel processing power to match user requirements.

In fact, the APE interconnection strategy supports two modes of inter-APE communication:

(1) *circuit-switching*: asynchronous, bidirectional single-bit communication to connect APE sources and corresponding APE destinations of high-speed activation signals, implementing a fully connected, dynamically configured (programmer-transparently) permutation and broadcast network for APE selection and inter-APE routing functions;

(2) *packet-switching*: synchronous bidirectional multibit communication, via a high-speed bit-serial shift register for data or message transfer between APE groups.

Thus, the interconnection strategy adopted for ASP substrings supports a high degree of parallelism for local communication and progressively lower degrees of parallelism for longer distance communication.

At an abstract level, and assuming a programmable connection between the ends of a chain of ASP substrings (that is, LKL and LKR ports shown in Fig. 5), the inter-APE communications network can be considered a hierarchical chordal-ring structure, with the chords bypassing APE blocks (and groups of APE blocks), as indicated in Fig. 7, to

(1) *accelerate inter-APE communication signals*: APE blocks not including destination APEs are automatically bypassed for both circuit-switched and (if required) packet-switched modes of inter-APE communication and, if appropriate for the former mode, activated in a singlestep;

(2) *provide APE block defect/fault-tolerance*: APE blocks failing a test routine, either in manufacture or service, are switched out of the string, such that defective or faulty blocks are simply bypassed.

### 3.3 Data Input–Output

The data communications network supports pipelining of continuous input data streams, by routing input data through the (optional) hierarchy of double-buffered global and local ADBs. The network and global ADBs also enable data transfer between parts of selected global and local ADBs, respectively.

At the lowest level of the data buffering hierarchy, the vector data buffer (shown in Fig. 5) supports a dual-port exchange of vector-data (that is, output dumped and input loaded in a single step) with alternating primary data exchange (PDX) and secondary data exchange (SDX), as illustrated in Fig. 8.

The bit-serial PDX, between the vector data buffer and APEs, performs a very high bandwidth (that is, APE-parallel) data exchange via the inter-APE communications network. With a lower bandwidth (APE-sequential), the bit-parallel SDX provides a data exchange between the vector data buffer and a local or global ADB or the data communications network, which is overlapped with parallel processing and therefore does not present a sequential processing overhead.

Thus, ADBs fulfil a dual purpose; to create a processing window (that is, decoupling task processing rates from input data rates at the expense of a latency delay in the output response), and to enable data transfer to be fully overlapped with parallel processing in

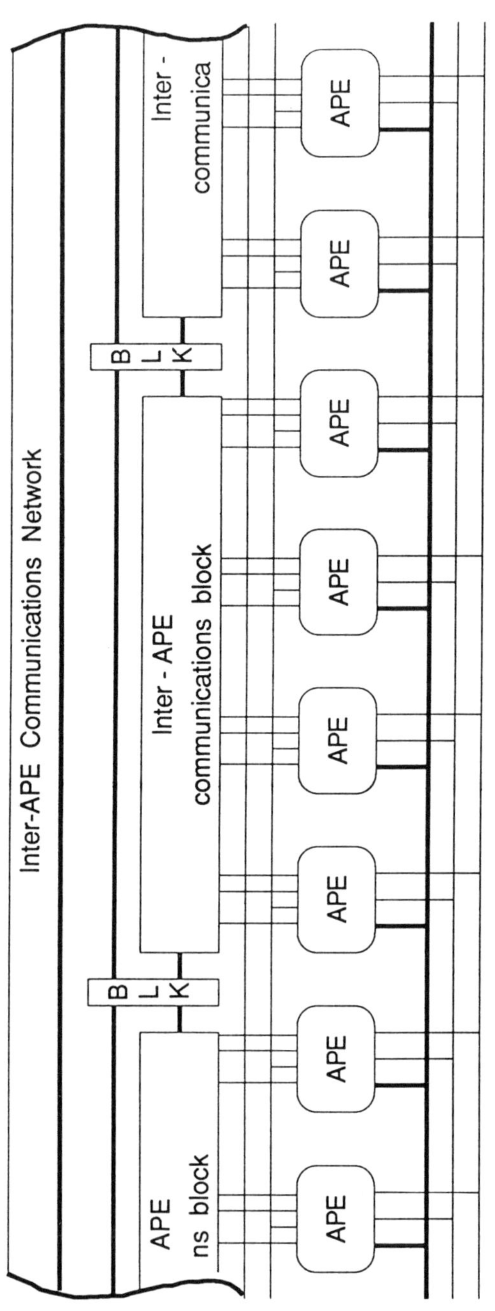


**Figure 7: ASP block bypassing.**

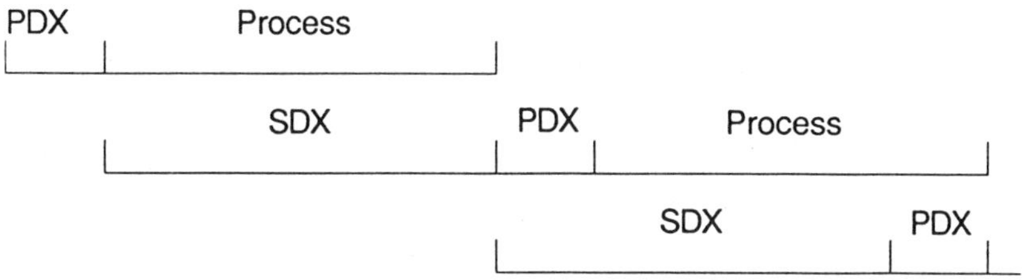


Figure 8: ASP data I/O.

the ASP substrings (thereby eliminating sequential processing overheads, which could otherwise be responsible for significant loss of computational efficiency).

## 3.4 ASP Architecture Summary

ASP architecture offers considerable application flexibility, maintaining high efficiency (in computation and communication) over a particularly wide range of signal and data processing, due to

1. simple configuration of ASP modules to simplify the development of MIMD–SIMD massively parallel processing systems, which are well matched to functional application requirements;

2. pipelining and overlapping input–output data transfers (via the data communications network) with parallel processing (within ASP substrings), by separating input–output from processing with local and global ADBs and vector data buffers;

3. overlapping of sequential (scalar) processing (in local or global ACUs) with parallel processing (in ASP substrings);

4. mapping different application data structures to a common string representation within ASP substrings (supporting content addressing, parallel processing and a reconfigurable interprocessor communication network);

5. elimination of processor (location) addressing, for the purposes of

   - achieving unlimited architectural scalability
   - implementing cost-effective fault-tolerance with simple (hierarchical) bypassing of faulty processor substrings, which until failure occurs are available for parallel processing
   - further minimization of sequential processing overheads;

6. minimization of interprocessor data movement, with highspeed activity transfer between processor subsets and insitu processing.

The progress of ASP hardware and software research heralds the development of highly versatile and fault-tolerant building blocks for the construction of massively parallel processors, with significant benefits, compared with contemporary parallel processing implementations. Indeed, the forecasts of Table 1 summarize the potential of the thin-profile SEM-E-compatible [14] massively parallel processing module.

Based on extrapolation of experimental results, the first four forecasts are fairly conservative. Since a performance of 1 TOPS (1000 GOPS) could be achieved with only 10 ASP modules within an eighth of a cubic foot, allowance for a similarly miniaturized global controller and data communications network (see Fig. 2) would suggest that a target of 1 TOPS/$ft^3$ is achievable.

| | |
|---|---|
| Configuration | 1, 2 or 4 MIMSIMD blocks |
| Performance | 100 GOPS (12-bit adds at 40 MHz) |
| Maximum I/O bandwidth | 640 Mbytes/sec (at 20 MHz) |
| Number of processors | 65,536 |
| Package | 6.4" x 5.88" x 0.3" |
| Power dissipation | < 100 Watts (i.e. > 1 GOPS/W) |

Table 1: ASP module design targets.

# 4 Image-Understanding with the ASP

In contrast to many of the systems designed to date, the ASP-based image-understanding approach described in this article is designed to work with object data-bases containing a number of models and to process each scene in parallel for instances of each model object. The ASP approach is applicable to both two- and three-dimensional object domains.

The general framework for the approach is massive parallel hypothesis generation and test. Whereas image-understanding algorithms traditionally use some form of constraint-based tree search, in ASP searching is effectively replaced by hypothesis generation and parameter space clustering. In this scheme, image features in the scene serve as events, while features of each model serve as expectations waiting to be satisfied. Hypotheses arise whenever an event satisfies an expectation.

On the ASP, objects known to the system are represented simply as a collection of features, generally straight line segments and their intersections at corners. Each feature is assigned to its own APE. A single object is therefore distributed over a number of APEs, enabling each feature to participate actively in the solution.

Features useful for hypothesis generation are those that constrain the position and orientation of a matching model object. A single point, line, or patch of color is by itself not sufficient. In a two-dimensional world, however, the intersection of two lines that matches an expected model corner can be used to generate a hypothesis that an instance of the model object exists, albeit translated and rotated such that the corresponding features come into alignment.

In a typical implementation of an image-understanding scenario using the ASP, an unknown scene is first digitized and loaded into the ASP as an array of pixels, one per APE, with image lines concatenated. Edge points are marked and straight line segments are fitted to edge points using a least-squares estimate. Intersecting lines are grouped into corner features and matched in parallel with corresponding corner features in the model data-base.

Whenever a match between an image and a model feature occurs, a hypothetical instance of the corresponding model object is created and projected into the image plane. A hypothesis-clustering scheme, related to the Hough transform, is next applied to order hypotheses according to the support offered by mutually supportive hypotheses. Although this still leaves many interpretations for each image feature, the ASP can rapidly accept or reject thousands of hypotheses in parallel using templatelike verification steps based on its associative processing nature.

Verification results from having each instance check the image for evidence supporting each of its features in parallel. Hypotheses having strong support for their expected features are accepted over those with little support. Expected features of an object that are occluded or obscured in the scene do not rule out the hypothesis, they only weaken the confidence the system has in the object's existence. Competitive matching between instances for each image feature finally resolves any conflicts that arise in the overall scene interpretation.

The remainder of this contribution reports on the ASP performance in a number of independent image-understanding benchmarks and compares it with a number of existing and proposed image-understanding architectures.

# 5 ASP Performance in Independent Image-Understanding Benchmarks

The field of image understanding provides a strong incentive for massively parallel processors, due to the large data volume, high data rate and algorithmic complexity of its computational tasks. Indeed, researchers involved in the areas of algorithm and system development for real-time image understanding need high performance that is easy to use (including programming) and is cost-effective. Not surprisingly, therefore, the image-understanding workers were among the first to attempt the establishment of realistic benchmarks for massively parallel processors. Early independent image-understanding benchmarking attempts, besides the performance figures stated by most of the commercial purveyors attempting to promote their machines, included the Abingdon Cross problem [15] and the Tanque Verde benchmark suite.

More recent and more coherent attempts to construct independent image-understanding benchmarks emerged from the DARPA image-understanding community and the LAA project at CERN (European Organization for Nuclear Research).

One of the goals of the DARPA strategic computing program is to develop algorithms and computer architectures for artificial vision tasks. These goals are tied to another of the DARPA's projects, (the autonomous land vehicle), which aims to develop robotic devices that would sense and interpret their environment, accept high-level commands, and plan their way around obstacles to carry out their missions.

The purpose of the DARPA-sponsored benchmarks is to attain greater understanding of the types of architectures needed at various levels of the image-understanding problem by requesting a comparative study of parallel computer architectures. The motivation for the study was based on the fact that although many architectures have been designed or built that can be used for image-understanding tasks, very little was known about their relative capabilities.

One of the activities of the LAA project at CERN is the investigation of the suitability of using fine-grained parallel computers in the data-acquisition system of experiments at high-energy particle physics accelerators. Implementing feature-extraction algorithms for pictures like the one shown in Fig. 9 on such computer architectures, may allow the development of triggers or the compaction of fine-grain data, leading to the reduction of event rates and/or data volumes [17].

## 5.1 DARPA Image-Understanding Benchmark I

A set of benchmark problems based on image-understanding computational tasks was defined [19] and distributed to various parallel architecture groups. Each of the benchmarks was defined as a self-contained task; no attempt was made to structure the benchmarks into a coherent sequence of operations representative of image understanding processing scenario.

The benchmark algorithms deal with the following tasks:

1. edge detection (including convolution, zero crossing detection and border following);
2. connected component labeling;
3. Hough transform computation;
4. computation of the convex hull, the Voronoi diagram, and the minimum spanning tree of a set of points in the plane;
5. visibility for a set of opaque triangles in three-dimensional space;
6. finding subgraphs of a given graph that are isomorphic (that is, similar) to another given graph;
7. finding the minimum cost path between two vertices of an edge-weighted group;

Tasks 1–3 handle pixel arrays. Tasks 4 and 5 deal with manipulation of the geometric data of a scene. Tasks 6 and 7 deal with relational structures and operations, which are very useful in

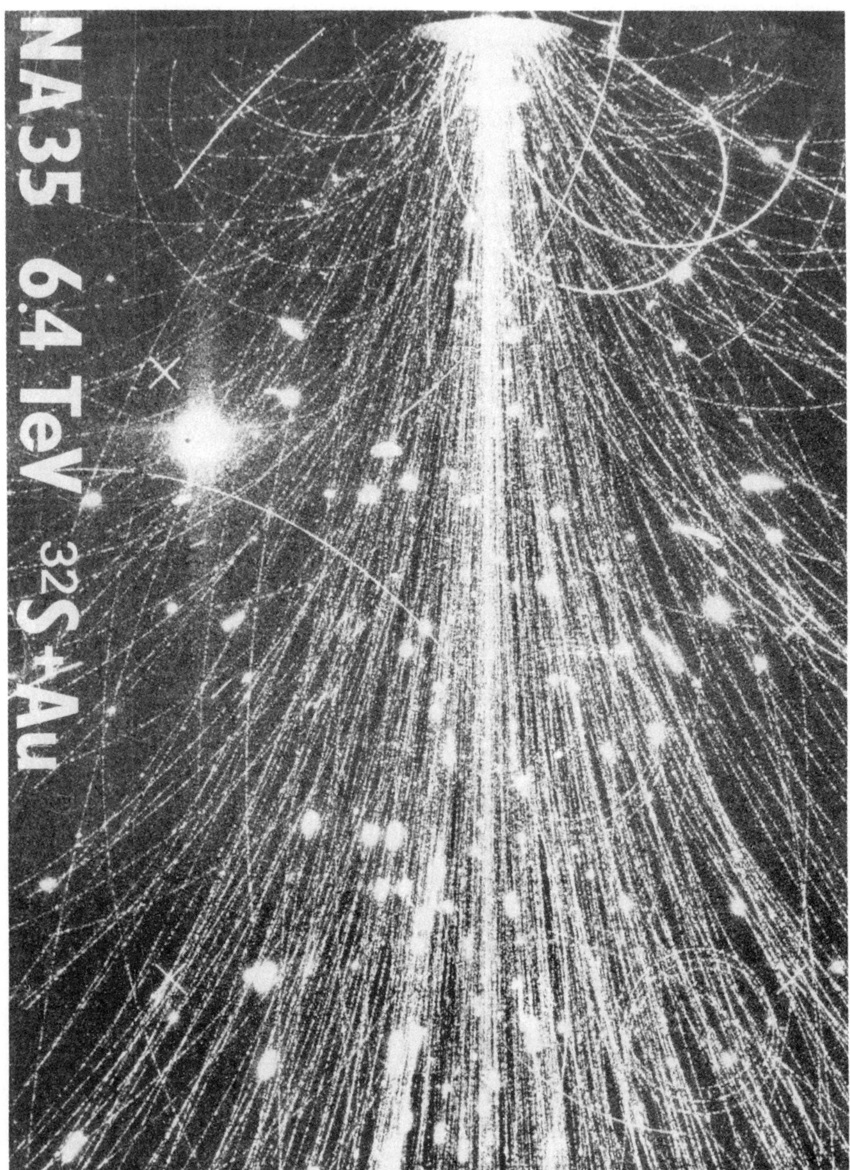


Figure 9: Streamer chamber picture for feature (i.e., tracks) extraction.

relating sensed data with data-base data (for example, maps) for image-understanding applications.

All the tasks span a range of problems representative of those that might be encountered at successive levels of the image-understanding process.

A number of parallel computer architectures have used the benchmark suite to evaluate their performance for image understanding tasks. These include

1. medium-grain systolic arrays ( CMU's WW-Warp, PC-Warp and, iWarp [1];

2. fine-grain SIMD arrays (columbia NON-VON [5], Thinking Machines Connection Machine (CM-1) [4], and Aspex ASP;

3. fine-grain MIMD/SIMD array processors (University of Massachusetts and Hughes Research Laboratories IUA [Image Understanding Architecture] [20].

To ease comparative evaluation, Table 2 indicates the performance of the benchmarked parallel architectures normalized against the performance of the ASP architecture. The entries in Table 2 indicate how slow the other machines are in comparison with the ASP. The reported performance figures for component labeling and graph matching could not be normalized because they were based in different assumptions. Nonentries mean that no performance figure was reported for the corresponding task.

The results of the benchmark [7, 19] clearly indicate that the overall performance of the ASP is close to the top performance of the IUA machine, and both architectures, based on associative processing, have generally much better performance figures than the alternative parallel architectures.

## 5.2 DARPA Image-Understanding Benchmark II

The purpose of the second DARPA-sponsored benchmark was to study performance of (mainly) parallel computer architectures on

| | WW Warp | PC Warp | iWarp | Non-Von | CM-1 | IUA | ASP |
|---|---|---|---|---|---|---|---|
| Laplacian | 458.7 | 437.5 | 9.7 | 2.5 | 3.75 | 0.2 | 1 |
| Zero-crossing | 43589.7 | 12820.5 | 2000.0 | | | | 1 |
| Border following | | 20000.0 | 12545.4 | | | 3.6 | 1 |
| Hough transform | 14.3 | 2.4 | 0.4 | 2.9 | 5.0 | 0.2 | 1 |
| Convex hull | 3.7 | 3.7 | 1.8 | | 83.3 | 6.2 | 1 |
| Voronoi diagram | | 26.4 | 12.7 | | | 4.5 | 1 |
| Minimum spanning tree | 1.9 | 1.9 | 0.5 | 0.4 | 26.8 | 1.5 | 1 |
| Visibility | 3.1 | 3.1 | 0.3 | 0.8 | 7.7 | 0.5 | 1 |
| Minimum cost-path | 93.3 | 4.6 | 1.7 | 2.7 | 3.3 | 66.7 | 1 |

**Table 2: DARPA image-understanding benchmark I. Comparative performance results.**

a set of integrated operations selected to be representative of typical image-understanding tasks. Although the method specified in the benchmark definition may not be the best approach for image-understanding in general, or for any given parallel machine, it was thought that the activity would help to achieve a better understanding of the requirements for a general image-understanding architectured and of the performance bottlenecks in different types of machines, and to provide insight about the impact parallelism can have on problems of communications and control across representations and algorithms.

The DARPA image understanding benchmark II was designed to address the need for an image-understanding benchmark that transcends several different data structures and algorithms typical of the iconic-to-symbolic transformation of real-world vision applications. The specification of the benchmark [21] was distributed to more than 25 academic and industrial groups in (sequential) C language coding.

The benchmark task suite involved recognizing an approximately specified $2\frac{1}{2}$ D *mobile* sculpture composed of rectangles within each image pair, given images from intensity and range sensors. The test images were designed so that neither by itself was sufficient to form a complete match.

The object to be recognized was a collection of rectangles of various sizes, brightness, two-dimensional orientations, and depths. It can be thought of as a semirigid mobile consisting of suspended rectangles floating in space with fixed spatial relationships. To simplify the tasks, each rectangle was oriented normal to the $z$-axis (the viewing axis), and the image was constructed under orthographic projection. The model that was provided of the object was approximate in the sense that the sizes, orientations, and depths of the rectangles as well as their spatial relationships were constrained to within given tolerances.

The rectangles that made up the object were interspersed with additional extraneous rectangles in the scene from which the two images were taken. These additional rectangles may have occluded portions of the mobile object, and some of the adjacent rectangles in the scene may have had very similar brightness.

For clarity of relative comparison, Table 3 indicates the performance of the benchmarked architectures normalized against the performance of the ASP architecture [16, 6, 22]. The entries in Table 3 indicate how slow the other machines are in comparison with the ASP.

Despite the fact that the ASP architecture has been designed for highly compact implementation and especially for cost-effectiveness, rather than optimized for high performance, it was pleasing to note that ASP has fared better than the any other of the benchmarked architectures, with the IUA architecture performing second best. On reflection this is not so surprising, since the application flexibility of the ASP architecture is well-suited to the wide task variation defined for the benchmark. Indeed, the result reinforces the claim that application flexibility (to avoid processing bottlenecks) rather than raw speed is a fundamental architectural requirement for real-world image-understanding applications.

Unfortunately, the DARPA benchmarks neglected size, weight, power, and cost factors. Indeed, had implementation size and cost of the computer architectures been taken into account, the results would have demonstrated a considerably greater advantage for the ASP.

It is also interesting to note that, as in the previous DARPA image-understanding benchmark, associative-processing–oriented parallel computer architectures, such as the IUA machine and ASP architecture, generally achieve much better performance figures than alternative parallel architectures.

## 5.3 LAA Benchmark

The goal of the LAA benchmark was to get a clear understanding of the problems involved in implementing trigger algorithms on parallel structures, and to assess the difficulties and limitations of embedding such structures in data acquisition systems. To this end, a set of representative benchmarks was defined and was used to evaluate several commercially available parallel processor systems, both in hardware implementations and simulation.

The benchmark algorithms deal with the following seven tasks:

| | Sun 4/280 | Alliant FX/80 (8 proc.) | Sequent Symmetry 81 (8 proc.) | Warp | CM-2 (64K proc.) | IUA | ASP |
|---|---|---|---|---|---|---|---|
| Overhead | 4780.5 | 10643.9 | 7231.7 | 4243.9 | 304.9 | 17.0 | 1 |
| Component labelling | 200.0 | 312.9 | 694.3 | 177.2 | 4.4 | $2.6 \times 10^3$ | 1 |
| Find rectangles | 232.9 | 723.6 | 315.1 | 1794.5 | 68.5 | 4.3 | 1 |
| Median | 17853.7 | 7142.7 | 18597.6 | 10634.1 | 18.3 | 0.7 | 1 |
| Sobel | 16808.8 | 5573.5 | 22735.3 | 705.9 | 11.8 | 4.0 | 1 |
| Graph matching | 2333.3 | 1731.2 | 2611.1 | 166.7 | | 5.3 | 1 |
| Match verification | 360.9 | 147.8 | 3986.7 | 602.6 | | 0.3 | 1 |
| Result presentation | 3795.4 | 4229.5 | 24454.5 | 5136.4 | | 2.1 | 1 |
| **Total** | **1185.8** | **951.5** | **2054.5** | **780.9** | | **1.3** | **1** |

**Table 3: DARPA image-understanding benchmark II. Comparative performance results.**

1. peakfinder
2. generic pattern recognition
3. fixed neighborhood calorimeter cluster analysis
4. variable neighborhood calorimeter cluster analysis
5. missing energy calculation
6. Hough-transform–based trackfinding
7. gray-level histogramming–based trackfinding.

The tasks are defined in terms of FORTRAN code and input and result data are supplied with the benchmark definition, to facilitate testing of the implementation.

The architectures that were evaluated included the sequential VAX 8300 system, a pipeline system (that is, the MaxVideo system [2] by Datacube), and three parallel architectures (the NCR GAPP [3], the AMT DAP 510/610 [18], and Aspex ASP).

To ease comparative evaluation, Table 4 indicates the performance of the benchmarked parallel architectures normalized against the performance of the ASP architecture. The entries in Table 4 indicate how slow the other machines are in comparison with the ASP. Nonentries mean that no performance figure was reported for the corresponding task.

The results of the benchmark [12] indicate that the ASP architecture has the better overall performance. Indeed, the ASP architecture, compared with RISC processors available in 2–4 years, has a performance ratio ranging from 2 to $2 \times 10^4$ in favor, whereas the second in performance architecture, the MaxVideo, can only perform 1–170 times better than existing RISC processors.

## 6 Summary

The use of the ASP architecture has been proposed for the implementation of image–understanding systems. The simple configuration of

| | VAX 8300 | MaxVideo | GAPP | DAP | ASP |
|---|---|---|---|---|---|
| Peakfinder | 2.1 x $10^6$ | 1239.3 | 2.1 | 555.6 | 1 |
| Pattern recognition | 266.8 | 12.1 | 7.6 | | 1 |
| Fixed neighbourhood Calorimeter cluster analysis | 555.5 | 15.2 | 1.8 | | 1 |
| Variable neighbourhood Calorimeter cluster analysis | 4200.0 | | 5.2 | | 1 |
| Missing energy calculation | 153.8 | | 61.5 | | 1 |
| Hough transform | 523.1 | 0.9 | 18.3 | | 1 |
| Grey-level histogram | 184.5 | 0.9 | 238.1 | | 1 |

Table 4: LAA–CERN benchmark. Comparative performance results.

ASP modules simplifies the development of MIMD/SIMD massively parallel processing systems, which are well matched to the functional requirements of image understanding and capable of delivering TOPS performance necessary for real-time system implementation.

Indeed, ASP modules offer the architectural flexibility (that is, configurability, programmability, and infinite scalability) required to maintain high computational efficiency across the wide task variation of numeric and symbolic processing of typical image-understanding applications. The suitability of the ASP architecture for image understanding has The suitibility of the ASP architecture for image-understanding has been confirmed with its consistent top performance in a number of independent benchmarks. If implementation size and cost of the computer systems are taken into account, the results will demonstrate a considerably greater advantage for the ASP.

**Acknowledgments**

The author expresses his gratitude to past and present members of Aspex Microsystems Ltd., Computer Architecture and Parallel Computing Technology groups at Brunel University, and the NA35 and LAA collaborations at CERN.

This work was supported in part by the US SDIO Innovative Science and Technology Office, monitored by the Office of Naval Research (contract number N00014-87-J-1247).

## Bibliography

[1] M. Annaratone, E. Arnould, T. Gross, H. T. Kung, M. Lam, O. Menzilcioglu, and J. A. Webb, *The warp computer: architecture, implementation and performance,* IEEE Transactions on Computers, vol. C-36, no. 12, Dec. 1987, pp. 1523–1538.

[2] DATACUBE: *Maxvideo User Manual*

[3] R. Davis and D. Thomas, *Systolic array chip matches the pace of high-speed processing,* Electronic Design, Oct. 31, 1984, pp. 207–218.

[4] D. Hillis, The Connection Machine, MIT Press, Cambridge, Massachusetts, 1986.

[5] H. A. H. Ibrahim, J. R. Kender, and D. E. Shaw, *Low-level image analysis tasks on fine-grained tree-structured SIMD machines,* Journal of Parallel and Distributed Computing, Vol. 4, No. 3, Academic Press, 1987, pp. 546–574.

[6] A. Krikelis, I. Kossioris, and R. M. Lea, *Performance of the ASP on the DARPA architecture benchmark II,* Proceedings of DARPA Image Understanding Benchmark Workshop, Avon Conn., Oct. 1988, pp. 21–29.

[7] A. Krikelis, and R. M. Lea, *Performance of the ASP on the DARPA architecture benchmark,* Proceedings of Frontiers 88,

2nd Symposium on the Frontiers of Massively Parallel Computation, Fairfax Virginia, October 1988, pp. 483–486.

[8] H. T. Kung, *Why systolic architectures?*, IEEE Computer, Volume 15, No. 1, January 1982, pp. 37–46.

[9] R. M. Lea, *The ASP: a cost-effective parallel microcomputer,* IEEE Micro, October 1988, pp. 10–29.

[10] R. M. Lea, *ASP modules: cost-effective building blocks for real-time DSP systems,* Journal of VLSI Signal Processing, Vol. 1, August 1989, pp. 61–76.

[11] R. M. Lea, *A WSI image processor*, in Wafer Scale Integration (E. Swartzlander ed.), Kluwer Academic Publishers, 1988, Chapter 5.

[12] S. Lone, R. K. Bock, Y. Ermolin, W. Krischer, C. Ljuslin, and K. Zografos, *Fine-grain parallel computer architectures in future triggers,* CERN report CERN-LAA RT/89-05, September 1989. Also submitted for publication to Nuclear Instrumentation and Methods in Physics Research.

[13] R. M. Lougheed and D. L. McCubbrey, *Multiprocessor architectures for machine vision and image analysis,* Proceedings of International Conference on Parallel Processing, 1985, pp. 493–497,

[14] R. Morgan and M. Soraya, *Future military avionics applications of wafer-scale technology,* In Proceedings of IEEE International Conference on Wafer Scale Integration ( E. Swartzlander, and J. Brewer eds.), IEEE Computer Society Press, San Francisco, 1989, pp. 1–12.

[15] K. Preston, Jr., *Benchmark results-the Abingdon Cross,* in Evaluation of Multicomputers for Image Processing ( L. Uhr, K. Preston , Jr., S. Levialdi, and M. J. B. Duff eds.) Academic Press, 1986, pp. 23–54.

[16] *Proceedings of DARPA IU Benchmark Workshop,* Avon, Conn., Oct. 1988.

[17] F. Pulhofer, D. Rohrich, and R. Keidel, *Track recognition in digitized streamer chamber pictures,* Nuclear Instruments and methods in Physics Research A263, 1988, pp. 360–367.

[18] S. F. Reddaway, *DAP-A distributed array processor,* Proceedings First Annual Symposium on Computer Architecture, Florida, 1973, pp. 61–65.

[19] A. Rosenfeld, *A report on the DARPA image understanding architectures workshop,* Proceedings of DARPA Image Understanding Workshop, Los Angeles, Calif., February 1987, pp. 298–301.

[20] C. C. Weems, S. P. Levitan, A. Hanson, E. Riseman, D. B. Shu, and G. J. Nash *The image understanding architecture,* in International Journal of Computer Vision, Vol. 2, Kluwer Academic Publishers, Boston, 1989, pp. 251–282.

[21] C. C. Weems, E. Riseman, A. Hanson, and A. Rosenfeld, *An integrated image understanding benchmark: recognition of a 2 $\frac{1}{2}$-D mobile,* Proceedings of DARPA Image Understanding Workshop, Cambridge, Mass., April 1988, pp. 111–126.

[22] C. C. Weems, E. Riseman, A. Hanson, and A. Rosenfeld, *A report on the results of the DARPA integrated image understanding benchmark exercise,* Proceedings of DARPA Image Understanding Workshop, Palo Alto, Calif., May 1989, pp. 165–192.

# A Multiple-Level Heterogeneous Architecture for Image Understanding

**DAVID B. SHU and J. GREG NASH**
*Hughes Research Laboratories*
*Malibu, California*

## 1 Introduction

Computer vision processing requires the intelligent interpretation of large two-dimensional arrays of sensor data. Except for very restricted applications, it remains one of the most computationally intractable domains of artificial intelligence (AI) research. Rapid progress toward a general computer vision capability can be achieved only with a digital parallel-processing system specifically designed from the ground up to support autonomous, model-knowledge–based interpretation of sensor data.

Tens of computer vision system research programs are now under way, all associated with available machines or various prototypes. They cover a wide range of Flynn's [1] taxonomies (SIMD, MSIMD, MIMD, MISD), network topologies (bus, hypercube, ring, mesh, pyramid, one- and two-dimensional systolic), data path widths (bit-serial, bit-parallel), and data path types (fixed point, floating point). However, our image-understanding architecture (IUA) [10, 9] – being developed jointly by Hughes Research Laboratories and the University of Massachusetts at Amherst – is the first digital parallel-processing system custom designed for computer vision processing that relies heavily on AI techniques to classify objects.

Unlike most parallel-processing computer vision systems, ours

This chapter is based on a "Multiple-Level Heterogenous Architecture for Image Understanding," from *Proceedings of the 10th International Conference on Pattern Recognition*; Atlantic City, New Jersey, June 16-21, 1990; pp. 629-634. ©1990 IEEE.

Parallel Architectures and
Algorithms for
Image Understanding





ISBN 0-12-564040-4

can handle the entire range of vision algorithms, rather than just a single class of numeric or symbolic computation. That capability is the architectural equivalent of mating a numeric processor with a symbolic processor at a fine grain. Although a variety of computer vision architectures now exist, nearly all have been designed–or work best–for one domain only. For example, most are SIMD machines, which severely limits their applicability beyond low-level processing. Moreover, virtually all other systems have limited associative capabilities. We know of just one with a similar architecture: the Warwick pyramid machine being developed in England [2].

The capabilities of the IUA have already been demonstrated in our own mapping tests and various DARPA benchmark exercises, the most comprehensive of which was conducted in 1989 [11]; selected 1989 DARPA results are listed in in Table 1. That exercise, which tested the ability of various machines to perform a comprehensive spectrum of low-, intermediate-, and high-level vision algorithms, clearly revealed the superior performance potential of our IUA compared with other systems. Even when low-level processing alone is considered, the IUA performs well, as indicated by the 1989 Abingdon Cross [3] benchmark measurements listed in Table 2. That analysis compared E40 low-level computer vision architectures, including a previous-generation IUA, on the basis of speed normalized to the array size.

Previous publications [3,7–10], present efficient IUA-based solutions to a variety of problems, such as finding the minimum spanning tree and minimum-cost path, connectivity, graph matching, line finding, large-window convolutions, Hough transformations, region feature extraction, and neural computations. They demonstrate that, in addition to its unique capabilities, the IUA is a powerful system for conventional computing tasks.

Associativity gives the IUA a powerful ability to obtain high-bandwidth feedback between high-level control and low-level processing. Feedback signals are usually the result of reduction operations; associativity produces O(1) reductions, compared with the $O(\log n)$ typical of conventional parallel processors. The effective query bandwidth between the low and high levels of the IUA can be as high as

| Processing Level | Processing Time (s) for Various Machines | | | | |
|---|---|---|---|---|---|
| | Sequent | Alliant | Warp[a] | CM-2[b] | IUA |
| Low | 66 | 31 | 28 | 0.6 | 0.03 |
| Intermediate | 3 | 2 | <1 | —[c] | 0.01 |
| High | 181 | 23 | 27 | —[c] | 0.03 |
| Total | 250 | 56 | 56 | —[c] | 0.07 |

[a]Developed by Carnegie-Mellon University (CMU).

[b]Developed by Thinking Machine.

[c]The CM-2 was not tested at this processing level.

**Table 1: Selected 1989 DARPA IU benchmark comparisons.**

| Processor | Relative Speed |
|---|---|
| IUA (64x64 PEs) | 1.6 |
| Warp[a] | 0.006 |
| DAP[b] (64x64 PEs) | 1.0 |
| GAPP[c] | 0.1 |

[a]Developed by Carnegie-Mellon University (CMU).

[b]Developed by American Memory Technology.

[c]Developed by National Cash Register.

**Table 2: Selected 1989 Abingdon Cross benchmark comparisons.**

100 GB comparisons per second. Special hard-wired adder trees are embedded in the bottom level of the bit-serial array to accumulate results rapidly and hence accelerate feedback. Consequently, data can be processed in parallel and in place.

## 2 IUA Architecture

**System Acronyms**

*ACU*: array control unit

*ARL*: ACU resident language

*CAAPP*: content-addressable array parallel processor

*CISM*: CAAPP-ICAP shared memory

*ICAP*: intermediate communications associative processor

*IMU*: image mapping unit

*ISSM*: ICAP-SPA shared memory

*IUA*: image understanding architecture

*MPL*: main processor language

*SCSM*: SPA-CAAPP shared memory

*SPA*: symbolic processing array

*TCB*: transfer control block

The three-level structure of the full-scale IUA, shown in Fig. 1, supports the hierarchy of abstractions necessary for the various representations and operations needed for efficient computer vision processing. Each level is constructed to perform the suite of tasks most appropriate for a specific level of abstraction.

The CAAPP, which is an SIMD 1K×1K mesh-connected array of bit-serial processing elements (PEs), is optimized to perform SIMD

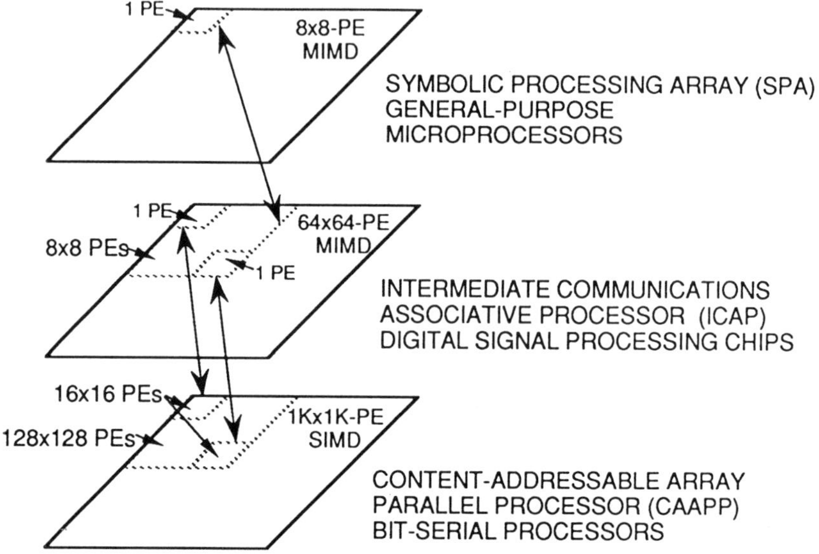


**Figure 1: Full-scale image-understanding architecture.**

neighborhood operations and rapidly to obtain summary information on groups of pixels. A special network at this level allows simultaneous processing of different regions. The CAAPP is also capable of primitive symbolic processing that requires manipulation of only short strings of data–for example, Boolean operations.

The ICAP, which is a multistage network-connected array of $64 \times 64$ numerically powerful digital signal processing (DSP) chips (where each chip comprises just one PE), is designed to support the CAAPP-level operations with fast numeric computations (primarily floating-point) and to execute symbolic schema. All higher-level grouping and matching operations, based on stored models or other relevant knowledge, are carried out here. The CAAPP and the ICAP communicate via a shared memory. Each CAAPP PE has access to a large backing-store memory that is dual-ported with the ICAP. The backing store is also referred to as the CAAPP-ICAP shared memory (CISM). Each ICAP PE is spatially associated with the $16 \times 16$ CAAPP PEs directly beneath it and, if necessary, will perform floating-point operations for data related to that set of PEs. The ICAP level is directed by control strategies generated at the SPA level.

The SPA comprises an $8 \times 8$ array of powerful general-purpose microprocessors for performing the high-level symbolic operations that generate the overall IUA processing plan. For example, numerous domain experts can run at this level as part of the image decomposition process, each assigning tasks to be carried out at the ICAP and CAAPP levels. The SPA and the ICAP communicate via the ICAP–SPA shared memory (ISSM); and the SPA and the CAAPP through the SPA–CAAPP shared memory (SCSM). The SPA views the lower levels as an intelligent global shared memory; thus, its processes are decoupled from and unlimited by the localism of information in the image. In addition, at any given time, one or more SPA PEs will be performing tasks associated with system-level functions such as I/O.

## 3 Programmer's Model

The IUA application programmer will view the system as a shared-memory symbolic processor, part of the shared memory being dual-ported with an iconic processor, as shown in Fig. 2. The iconic processor supports parallel instructions in an SIMD mode and distributed processing in an MIMD mode. This model is similar to any superscalar microprocessor having integer and floating-point units that run concurrently. Data stored in the dual-port memory array of Fig. 2 can be processed by either the symbolic or the iconic unit, but in most cases one will be more efficient and will thus incur less overhead.

Ultimately, we will program the IUA in standard high-level languages (e.g., LISP, C, FORTRAN, Ada), which we will call the main processor languages (MPLs). Extensions of those languages will provide several levels of parallelism, each requiring a unique level of overhead. The MPL-plus-extension packages will be designed to mask the details of the IUA iconic architecture and make the MPL programs

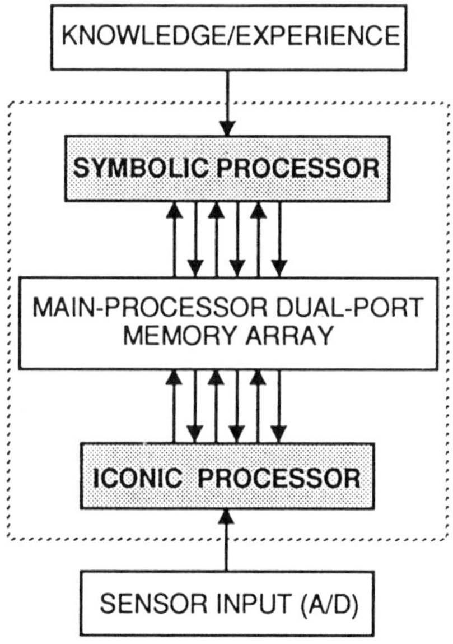


Figure 2: Abstraction of programmer's model.

more portable. The SPA platform compiler will map different levels of parallelism, specified by the MPLs and their extensions, to the three IUA levels. Normally, coarse- and very-coarse-grained parallelism will be assigned to the SPA level and fine-grained operations to the ICAP and CAAPP levels, whereas the location of medium-grained computations will depend on the specific compiler. We have already described a LISP-based MPL that features (a) parallelism and (b) grouping operations [9]. However, further development of MPLs depends strongly on the introduction of standard language extensions. For example, to date, only FORTRAN 77 provides a standardized set of data-parallel extensions (FORTRAN 8X).

The interface between the SPA and the iconic-processor array control unit (ACU) will be more sophisticated than the set of simple parallel instructions used to support MPLs. It will contain libraries of ACU macros and subroutines in scalar, SIMD, and distributed

MIMD modes. Rather than being processed by the MPL compiler, they will be treated as memory-mapped devices and linked as such. Thus, there will be two ways to program the iconic processor: control it directly with the MPL via the compiler, or use an ACU resident language (ARL), such as FORTRAN 8X or C*, to write the device-driver–like macros and subroutines, which would then be called by an MPL and linked as a library. Initially, we will program the IUA by the latter method. In the future, however, we will develop MPL extensions to support the full-scale IUA architecture.

Although the MPL and the ARL could be the same language, our programmer's model makes part of the ARL memory space inaccessible to the MPL, to simplify the porting of iconic processor programs to various commercial symbolic platforms.

As shown in Fig. 3, the dual-port memory array in Fig. 2 is partitioned into two I/O buffers: "regular" on the left of the iconic processor and "irregular" on the right. The regular part–the SCSM–contains highly structured data, such as tables, images, and matrices, and can be processed in the SIMD mode with great efficiency. The irregular part–the ISSM–contains less structured data, such as lists, sparse matrices, and frame instances, suitable for distributed medium-grained processing.

To develop ACU macros and subroutines, the iconic processor can be treated as a separate computer. As shown in Fig. 3, it can be viewed as having a CPU (the iconic processor itself) and three memory segments: the working memory (that is, the CISM) and both the regular and irregular I/O buffers. The working memory stores the program variables and is available to either the fine-grained CAAPP processor or the medium-grained ICAP processor, as appropriate. The regular I/O buffer can be accessed only by the CAAPP, whereas the irregular buffer can be accessed only by the ICAP. The CISM is accessible to the ACU resident language but not the main processor language.

A major function of the iconic processor, after some initial fine-grained SIMD operations, is to tranform highly structured data (such as two-dimensional images) from the regular buffer into less structured data (such as symbolic frame instances or linked lists) for stor-

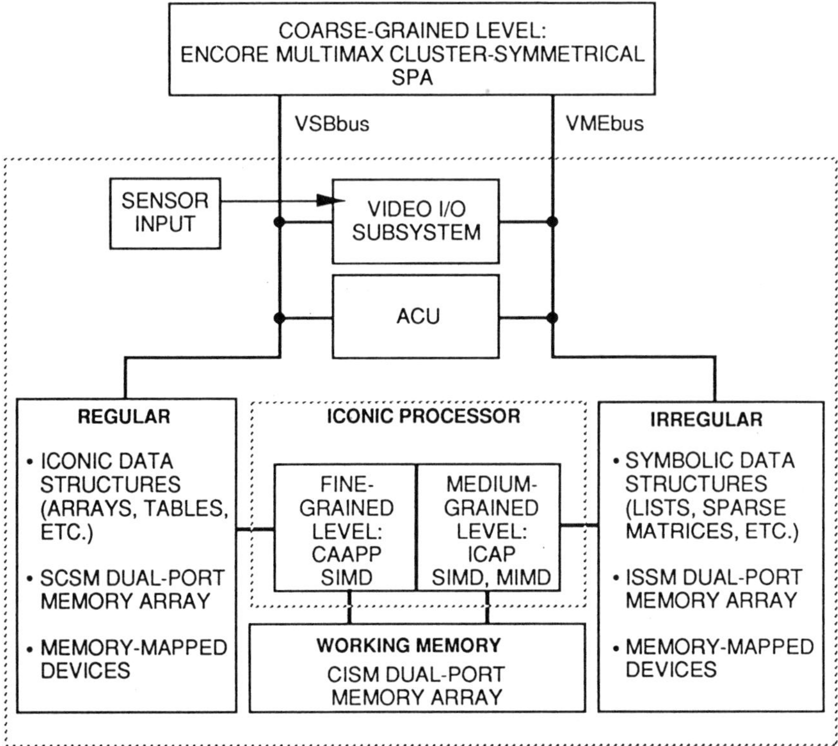


**Figure 3: Realization of programmer's model based on Encore Multimax SPA.**

age in the irregular buffer. When the ICAP is running in an SIMD mode, it is a coprocessor from the CAAPP point of view. However, since the coprocessor instruction could be an ICAP subroutine, it is much more flexible than a purely SIMD machine because it can carry out sophisticated operations. For example, adjacent ICAP PEs can operate asynchronously with respect to each other by executing their own code independently. In addition, the ICAP can suspend a process that is waiting for synchronization and execute tasks in an MIMD distributed multiprocessing mode, as described in subsection 5.3. Therefore, the ACU macros and subroutines are classified into two categories: SIMD for the CAAPP–ICAP array and MIMD for the ICAP alone.

# 4 Hardware

The lowest level of the IUA uses full custom VLSI chips. The other two levels are served by commercial processors.

## 4.1 1/64th-Scale IUA Prototypes

The 1/64th-scale prototype will be used as the fundamental building block of the full-scale system.

### First Generation

DARPA funded a 1/64th-scale IUA first-generation prototype consisting of 16 "supernode" processor boards, each having four 64-PE CAAPP chips, four Texas Instruments (TI) TMS320C25 (hereafter called TI C25) fixed-point DSP chips for the ICAP level, 2.5 MB of dual-port video random-access memory (VRAM), and 256 KB of static random-access memory (SRAM). In addition, we use a SUN 3 as a node for the SPA level. The total prototype system (detailed in [10]) therefore contains 4K bit-serial PEs at the CAAPP level and 64 TI C25 DSP chips.

A "concentrator board" is used to obtain summary information from the SOME–NONE lines and adder tree outputs, as well as status information from the TI C25 processors. Moreover, an "interconnect" board allows the processors to communicate among themselves in a bit-serial mode.

A CAAPP chip [4] has been fully tested alone and in a 1 × 2 array to ensure functionality both within and between chips. In addition, a full subunit–consisting of a CAAPP chip, a TI C25, VRAM, and SRAM–was tested by loading the CAAPP from the distributed SCSM frame buffer, processing the data, transferring the processed data from the CAAPP to an off-chip backing store (the CISM), and having the TI C25 run a program to obtain data from the random-access port of the CISM and transfer it to the ISSM connected to a VMEbus. The entire 1/64th-scale prototype is now being fabricated and assembled.

### Second Generation

We are now buildin a modified version of the 1/64th-scale IUA prototype capable of 2 GFLOPS/4 GOPS and having a 384-MB memory. It contains 256-element CAAPP chips and TI TMS320C30 (hereafter called TI C30) floating-point DSP chips; the board form factors, etc., are unchanged. The basic board design for this version is shown in Fig. 4.

The 256-element CAAPP chip is constructed by arraying four 64-element CAAPP chips and scaling the geometry to 1–5m feature sizes. Compared with the DARPA-funded prototype, the new version will have four times greater integration, 300 times better floating-point performance, and far more software support at the DSP level. Our "extended" prototype will allow us to build a 16K-element IUA for a cost far below that of similar systems now on the market.

The major hardware features of the second-generation Hughes integrated IUA prototype–which has the MIMD, MSIMD, and SIMD capabilities needed for computer vision processing–together make the architecture unique:

1. hierarchical organization;

2. three heterogeneous levels of processing;

3. 256-element bit-serial CAAPP:

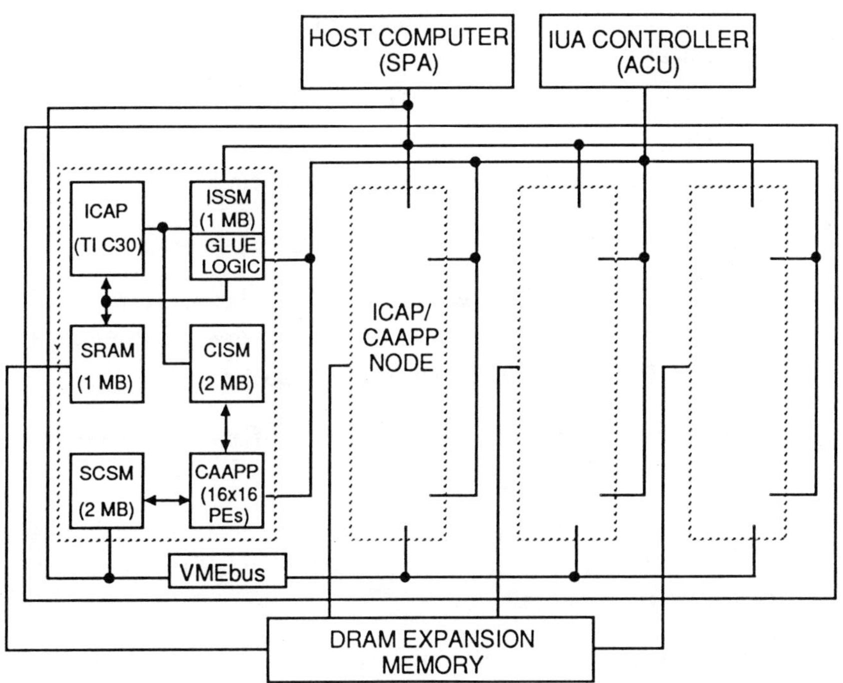


**Figure 4: IUA board containing 1K CAAPP PEs (16 boards per 1/64th-scale prototype).**

- coterie network (an implementation-efficient programmable network for local–global communication)
- large, double-buffered, off-chip, dual-port VRAM memory (128 K bits/PE)
- large, local on-chip memory (320 bits/PE)
- efficient corner turning to convert from bit-parallel to bit-serial
- local response lines (SOME–NONE) for each PE, with on-chip wired-OR between all PEs
- on-chip adder tree for response counting;

4. sophisticated VMEbus-based video I/O subsystem:
   - variety of microprocessor-controlled data-transfer modes to CAAPP array, such as region of interest, thinned arrays
   - MAXbus interface to Datacube boards;
5. distributed frame buffer providing an 8-GB/s effective data-transfer rate;
6. mid–level DSP-array (TI C30) modular message-passing network, providing a peak bandwidth of 4 GB/s for transfers between DSP elements;
7. highly integrated CAAPP bit-serial array and DSP array;
8. concentrator board to summarize responses rapidly from all processors;
9. three blocks of dual-port VRAMs, each connecting adjacent levels of the IUA, to facilitate information transfer between levels. The three blocks are together controlled by an efficient custom 10,000-gate glue logic circuit to arbitrate and control access to them;
10. efficient implementation–1024 CAAPP PEs and four TI C30 DSP chips per triple-height VMEbus board;
11. VMEbus interface.

## 4.2 Other Components of the Full-Scale IUA

### SPA Level

The SPA level is designed to perform AI-based computations that are tightly coupled to the strong numerical capabilities of the IUA's lower two levels. However, its complexity and the lack of appropriate software make construction of a custom subsystem expensive. Alternatively, we could use one of the newly available shared-memory multiprocessors, such as the Encore Multimax. That approach would allow us to exploit the abundant software (both application and system) already on the market, as well as enabling us to simulate various architectural configurations of SPA components. Here we briefly describe how the second approach could be implemented, using the Encore Multimax.

The Encore multiprocessor incorporates a high-speed shared bus with hierarchical caches. In the future, the Multimax will be based on the Motorola 88000-series reduced-instruction-set computer (RISC) processor (four 88K chips per board), which provides about 40 VAX MIPS. Various combinations of memory (64 MB/board), processors, and I/O cards (VMEbus interface, Ethernet) are possible. Three parallel languages (LISP, Ada, FORTRAN) and a multithreaded operating system (Mach) are already available for the Multimax.

The Encore VMEbus Subsystem Interface (VSI) allows the Multimax nanobus to communicate with both the VMEbus and the VSB-bus. The nanobus sees them as memory-mapped devices. The Nanobus access window is a decoded address range within the Nanobus memory address space; it can be used by Multimax processors to access the VME/VSBbus resident memory. The current Encore Gigamax supports multiple VSIs.

In the projected full-scale IUA model presented in Fig. 3, the VMEbus is connected to the irregular (ISSM) portion of the main-processor dual-port memory; and the VSBbus, multiplexed with the video I/O subsystem, is connected to the regular (SCSM) portion. Thus, the SCSM can obtain array data from either the VSBbus or the video input. Further, the VSBbus allows the Multimax processors to obtain data stored in the SCSM while simultaneously accessing the

VMEbus.

The VSI gives all processors and programs in Multimax shared access to the IUA main-processor dual-port memory shown in Fig. 2. Further, on the Multimax, the symmetry of operations between processors allows any process in any Multimax processor to transparently use the iconic portion of the IUA in time-shared operation. Therefore, parallel SIMD-mode instructions and MIMD-mode distributed processing are both available to any process.

## Array Control Unit

The ACU is the hardware controller for the iconic array processors. Each IUA "crate" (1/64th-scale prototype) contains one ACU to control the 16-VMEbus board subsystem, which comprises the 128 × 128 CAAPP processors and the 64 TI C30 ICAP processors. The ACU directs a continuous stream of instructions toward the CAAPP–ICAP array, while efficiently supporting the virtual machine targeted by the high-level language compiler. It is organized hierarchically in order to maximize CAAPP efficiency. The ACU relies heavily on fast associative feedback of information from the CAAPP level. To keep the CAAPP PEs busy, therefore, it must be able to act on that information rapidly.

The CAAPP incorporates three levels of control. At the highest level, the SPA directs processing with response time in hundreds of microseconds. At the intermediate level, the macrocontroller portion of the ACU reacts in tens of microseconds. At the lowest level, the microcontroller responds in $0.125\mu s$ via dedicated hardware.

The central component of the ACU is the controller, a powerful RISC general-purpose data processor that has local memory and VME–VSBbus ports for interfacing with an Encore Multimax. SPA commands to an IUA crate are essentially remote procedure calls to an ACU controller, which while executing a call, may in turn direct the SIMD CAAPP–ICAP or the MIMD ICAP to perform specified tasks.

The remaining hardware components of the ACU allow the controller to command and synchronize with the CAAPP and the ICAP. The ACU must supply all CAAPP instructions at a rate of 8 MHz.

Although the controller is a powerful RISC computer, it cannot produce CAAPP instructions at the required rate. It may require 10–20 RISC instructions to produce each CAAPP instruction, necessitating an 80–160 MIPS controller. However, the CAAPP instruction generator markedly reduces the throughput requirements for the ACU controller. It performs the field substitution and simple address arithmetic necessary to generate multiple CAAPP instructions from a single controller command. It also reads blocks of data from the controller's memory and outputs them as CAAPP instructions, freeing the controller to handle subroutine calls. Moreover, the CAAPP instruction generator contains a first-in, first-out (FIFO) instruction-output-rate buffer to avoid CAAPP processing stalls caused by a transient inability of the controller and the instruction generator to produce the required number of CAAPP instructions.

The ICAP controller generates ACU controller interrupts in response to ICAP conditions, such as the assertion of ICAP DONE bits, and also causes interrupts at the ICAP. In addition, it allows the ACU controller to load code into the ICAP's local SRAM and perform a number of other useful operations. In normal IUA operation, the ICAP controller merely senses and signals events passing between the ACU controller and the ICAP. Information is transferred between the ACU controller and the ICAP via the ISSM.

## Video I/O Unit

A salient feature of the video I/O subsystem is its ability to select a subset of the available image data, stored in a cache connected to a video input or VMEbus, and transfer the selected data to the SCSM associated with a particular node in the processor array. A sophisticated strategy for mapping all or part of an image onto a processor array allows the extraction of low-resolution information from high-resolution frame buffers, as well as reducing the communication bandwidth required between the image store and the array. Once the data are stored in the SCSM array, the available bandwidth between the SCSM and the processor array is 512 GB/s for the full-scale IUA system, which will comprise 4K nodes. Each node will contain one ICAP chip, one CAAPP chip, and one SCSM block.

The video I/O subsystem contains two parts: commercial boards from the Datacube MaxVideo family, and our custom image mapping unit (IMU). Notable features of the MaxVideo family are the high-speed video data buses and the clock bus that run across the top of the cards. A Datacube Digimax card is suitable for real-time image acquisition and display. The MAXbus is used by the IMU for real-time video data transfers between MaxVideo cards and the SCSM array.

The IMU has a cache memory and, on command, transfers selected image data to or from its cache to one or more SCSM nodes. The SCSMs are dual-port, 1 Mbit VRAMs with 25 ns serial access time; they supply data to or receive data from the CAAPP chips at 32 MHz on a 64 bit CAAPP bus (that is, 256 MB/s per CAAPP chip). This load-or-store operation occurs simultaneously for all 4K CAAPP chips in the IUA (with a resulting 1 TB/s bandwidth). The current prototype is designed for 16 MHz operation.

The source, destination, and nature of a transfer are defined by data supplied, by either the SPA or the ACU, in a very compact single block called the transfer control block (TCB). Image data are similarly transferred from the SCSMs to a cache RAM. Images may be mapped as follows:

1. *Region of interest* (ROI): A rectangular area containing a scene of interest;

2. *Partition*: a rectangular, contiguous, nonoverlapping subdivision of a ROI. A partition is mapped onto an arbitrary rectangular set of CAAPP chips;

3. *Patch*: a rectangular, contiguous, nonoverlapping subdivision of a partition. A patch is mapped onto a single $16 \times 16$ PE CAAPP chip;

4. *Dilute segment*: a rectangular subdivision of a patch. A dilute segment contains only selected noncontiguous pixels and is mapped to one byte of data for each of the 256 PEs on a CAAPP chip;

5. *Dense segment*: a 256-pixel square.

## 4.3 Projected Full-Scale IUA

A full-scale IUA, based on today's technology, could be constructed by combining one Encore Gigamax with eight Multimax clusters, as Fig. 5 shows. The Multimax configuration comprises five 88K cards (400 MIPS), one UIC cache interface, two VSIs, and two MEM memories (128 MB). That configuration would be coupled with eight 1/64th-scale subsystems, or crates, each having its own ACU. Each VSI would be connected to an IUA cabinet comprising four crates.

Multiple 1/64th-scale units could operate synchronously, with one ACU as the master and the rest as slaves. Any process running in the Gigamax would have access to the 1K×1K CAAPP array (256 GOPS) and the 4K ICAP distributed array (128 GFLOPS). Multiple crates could also operate asynchronously, each controlled by its own ACU. The programmer's model is not changed for the full-scale IUA.

# 5 Software

No single language best serves every purpose or application. The programmer's model of the IUA shows both data- and control-parallel processing, suggesting that the IUA can support all high-level languages equally well. However, no existing language can handle the parallelism required at every level of the IUA. It is very difficult to define a language that embodies both data- and control-parallel processing, or intermediate forms such as multiassociative processing, as well as synchronous MIMD. It is equally hard for a compiler to choose, for a given context, the most appropriate level of parallelism for mapping onto the available set of parallel hardware.

Since we wish to focus on optimizing the IUA architecture rather than developing custom software, we will, for efficiency, obtain the latest commercially available high-level language–compiler technology for each level of the IUA as an interim means for making the IUA hardware available for demonstration and evaluation as soon as possible. Later, however, we will develop new compiler technology and new language constructs specifically for the IUA.

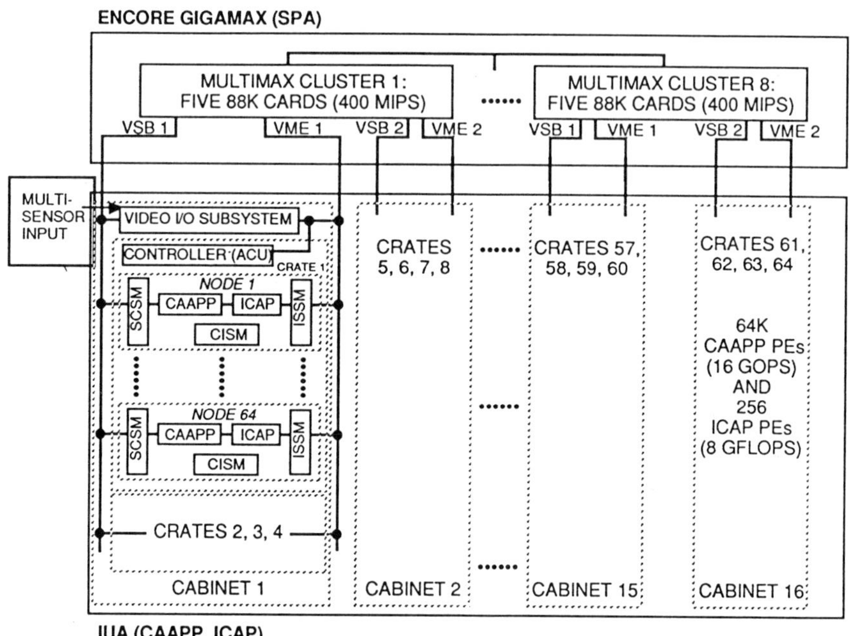


**Figure 5: Projected full-scale IUA configuration based on Encore Multimax clusters and 1/64th-Scale IUA crates.**

# 6 SPA Level

At the SPA level, if we use the Encore Multimax, then we can accommodate most major high-level languages. Since the Multimax sees the IUA as a VME/VSBbus memory-mapped device, any program, regardless of language, can call the device driver. Thus, all ACU macros and subroutines will be available to the user throughout linking with no extra effort except the need to remember their properties and functions; otherwise, he or she must custom-develop them by programming in the ARL. Writing efficient codes, however, may require some knowledge of the IUA iconic processor architecture.

## 6.1 ACU Level

The ARL programmer will see a single CPU comprising three parts: a scalar processor (the ACU controller), a fine-grained SIMD array (the CAAPP), and a medium-grained SIMD–MIMD array (the ICAP). A given ARL routine may use any combination of the three–for example, the CAAPP together with the SIMD part of the ICAP, or exclusively the distributed MIMD part of the ICAP. Since the ACU controller and the ICAP incorporate standard commercial components, extensive software support is available. We are therefore concentrating on the SIMD CAAPP software. The language selected for the CAAPP will be the main ARL. The ICAP may have subroutines written in different languages, but they can be treated only as coprocessor instructions by the ARL compiler or as libraries by the linker.

## 6.2 ICAP Level

ICAP software will be written in C as a collection of tasks interacting through device monitors. One possibility would be to use the Spectron Microsystems SPOX software package, which contains a TI C30 real-time kernel as well as facilities to write tasks and monitors in C. The SPOX package would give us a single-processor multitasking facility. Multiprocessing would be implemented using message passing through device monitors created with SPOX. The monitors can be configured to manage TI C30 network links or the ISSM.

The ICAP synchronizes with the ACU by using TI C30 interrupts and ICAP DONE bits. From the point of view of an ARL programmer, ICAP hardware would be managed by SPOX, which acts as a server subsystem. ICAP services to the CAAPP and the ACU can be grouped in two categories–synchronous (such as running in an SIMD mode as a CAAPP coprocessor) and asynchronous (such as message passing)–depending on the method used by the ICAP to schedule the service request. Services are requested by sending a message to the ICAP, with an ACU or SPA write to ISSM, followed by an ACU interrupt of the ICAP.

Synchronous services (SIMD mode) are carried out by the ICAP immediately and completely, taking priority over asynchronous services. While executing any single synchronous request, the ICAP will not work on any previously received asynchronous task, nor will it accept a new synchronous or asynchronous service request. Synchronous service requests are thus completed in the order generated by the ACU. Asynchronous service requests (distributed MIMD mode) are queued on the ICAP as independent tasks, executing only when synchronous requests are not being serviced. Asynchronous service requests may be completed in any order. Completion is signaled by an ICAP message to the ACU or the SPA.

The ICAP, with extensive libraries of DSP functions, provides general-purpose computational services to the CAAPP and the ACU. For example, it can perform calculations that do not use CAAPP data-parallel operations, or carry out floating-point multiplications that actually execute faster on the ICAP than on the CAAPP. The ICAP also provides message-passing communication services. Messages can be transferred between arbitrary ICAP source and destination processors within the IUA over ICAP serial links. Communications can be requested only as asynchronous services.

There are four ICAP TI C30 processors on a single IUA supernode board, as Fig. 4 shows. Each can access a shared memory. The IUA may be configured in a variety of sizes ranging up to 1024 supernodes. For message routing, the closely coupled super-node appears as a versatile eight-link device able to source, sink, or forward messages through the common expansion memory. With no additional hardware, the eight-link supernodes can be interconnected in a variety of networks at roughly comparable average internode distances to the 1K-node hypercube network. The connected network is the hardware backbone of the ICAP communication services subsystem. A powerful interconnection scheme is thus provided solely by the TI C30 ICAP chips, a four-node common memory on a supernode board, and wires; no routing hardware is necessary.

The SPOX-supported device monitor allows ICAP nodes to route tasks asynchronously by accessing a table of routing decisions. More global issues–for example, how the routing tables are constructed and how the unique names used in routing are assigned–are decided at the system level. Either the SPA or the ICAP can perform those tasks.

Fig. 6 shows the overall structure of the ICAP service software. The SPOX kernel controls all task scheduling. The application initialization and services subsystem carries out the generalized functions needed by the three subsystems, which run at differing levels of priority. Synchronous tasks are scheduled by ACU-to-ICAP interrupts and preempt all other tasks. Once the ACU has scheduled any synchronous task, it cannot schedule another synchronous task until the one already being executed has been completed. Thus, synchronous tasks must run quickly. The message-routing subsystem has second priority, since delays there usually obstruct multiple ICAP processors.

Asynchronous tasks have the lowest priority. They are scheduled and signal their completion by receiving and sending messages from or to the ACU or the SPA. Such tasks are normally specific permanent routines enabled by specific messages. In addition, an asynchronous "metatask" may accept messages of the form "run the code fragment located at memory address XXX." Such a metatask would not be scheduled by the ACU. Instead, it would automatically be initiated by the application initialization and services subsystem.

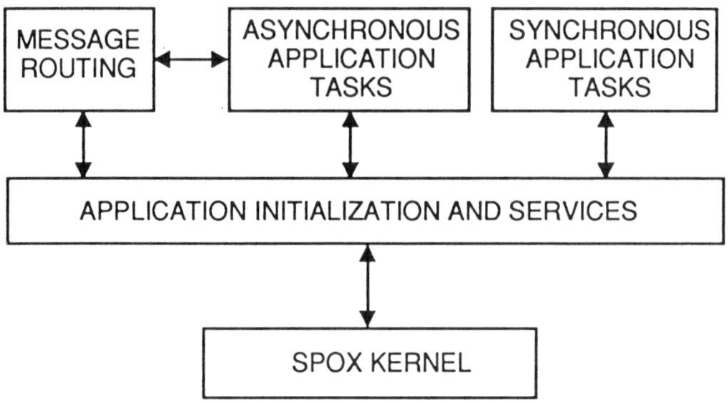


Figure 6: ICAP top-level software.

# 7 CAAPP Level

The University of Massachusetts at Amherst has fully instrumented VAX- and SUN-based IUA simulators, an assembler, a linker, compilers, and debugger packages. All debugger packages are written in C for ease of rehosting to other platforms. University staff have also developed three programming languages for the CAAPP: a C-syntax assembler that allows us to write CAAPP instructions in a C framework, a FORTH interpreter, and an Apply compiler. The C framework makes all control structures and other facilities of the C language available to the user. The FORTH interpreter is interactive and extensible. The first two languages both require the programmer to understand the CAAPP architecture. The Apply compiler gives us access to a package of more than 100 low-level operators running on the Warp at CMU. In addition, an extensive arithmetic subroutine library, including byte, integer, and many standard functions, provides the basis for a compiler run-time library.

To complement our current software package, we will develop a

FORTRAN or C compiler with parallel extensions that can invoke both the CAAPP and the ICAP. The ICAP layer will be accessed through C routines. That strategy requires the definition of an intermediate code, which will be a virtual machine specifically targeted for FORTRAN 8X and C*.

# 8 Conclusions

The architecture described in this paper supplies the basis for high-performance computer vision processing. Further, our programmer's model frees application programmers from the complicated task of controlling three-level heterogenous processor arrays; they are able to work in the familiar setting of a single processor and associated memory block.

Our projected full-scale IUA will be capable of 128 GFLOPS/256 GOPS using today's technology. However, even our second-generation 1/64th-scale prototype (2 GFLOPS/4 GOPS with 384 MB of memory) will be useful for computer vision research and development. It will provide 16K PEs and have sufficient memory to handle efficiently image sizes much larger than the number of PEs. We have also designed a sophisticated video I/O subsystem. It will support intelligent transfer of data to a distributed frame buffer that will be able to sustain rates to and from the bit-serial SIMD array of 512 GB/s for a full-scale IUA.

A commercial multiprocessor, such as the Encore Multimax, would give the user access to parallel languages (LISP, Ada, FORTRAN) as well as modern operating systems (Mach) and debuggers (Parasight). We plan to develop a FORTRAN 8X or C compiler to program both the bit-serial level (fixed-point) and the intermediate DSP level (floating-point) in an SIMD mode. Further, we will port code such as the Spectron Microsystems SPOX C-based software package to support the MIMD mode of multitasking and multiprocessing at the DSP level. Ultimately, we will develop custom software for the full-scale IUA.

**Acknowledgments**

The work described here was funded by the Defense Advanced Research Projects Agency, Information Science and Technology Office, under contract DACA76-86-C-0015.

# Bibliography

[1] M. J. Flynn, *Very high-speed computing systems*, Proc. IEEE, vol. 54, Dec. 1966, pp. 1901–1909.

[2] G. R. Nudd, T.J. Atherton, S.C. Clippingdale, R.M. Howarth, N.D. Francis, D.J. Kerbyson, R.A. Packwood, G.J. Vaudin and D.W. Walton, *WPM: A multiple-SIMD architecture for image processing,* Proc. Third International IEE Conference on Image Processing and Its Applications (London, July 1989), pp. 161–165.

[3] K. Preston, Jr., *The Abingdon Cross benchmark survey,* Computer, vol. 22, no. 7, July 1989, pp. 9–18.

[4] D. B. Shu, L. W. Chow, J. G. Nash, and C. C. Weems, *A content addressable array parallel processor,* Proc. Workshop on VLSI Signal Processing III, (R. W. Brodersen and H. S. Moscovitz eds.), IEEE Computer Society Press, New York, 1988, pp. 120–128.

[5] D. B. Shu and J. G. Nash, *The Gated Interconnection Network for dynamic programming,* in Concurrent Computations, (S. K. Tewksbury, B. W. Dickinson, and S. C. Schwartz eds.), Plenum, New York, 1988, pp. 645–658.

[6] D. B. Shu and J. G. Nash, *Minimum spanning tree algorithm on an image understanding architecture,* in Proc. SPIE, Vol. 939, Hybrid Image and Signal Processing, (D. P. Casasent and A. G. Tescher, eds.), SPIE, Bellingham, Wash., 1988, pp. 212–228.

[7] D.B. Shu, J. G. Nash, and M. M. Eshaghian, *Connectivity, convexity, and proximity on an enhanced mesh-connected computer,*

presented at the 4th Annual Parallel Processing Symposium, Fullerton, Calif., April 1990.

[8] D. B. Shu, J. G. Nash, M. M. Eshaghian, and K. Kim, *Straight-line detection on a gated-connection VLSI network,* presented at the 10th IEEE International Conference on Pattern Recognition, Atlantic City, N.J., June 1990.

[9] D. B. Shu, J. G. Nash, and C. C. Weems, *image understanding architecture and applications*, in Advances in Machine Vision, (J. L. C. Sanz ed.), Springer-Verlag, New York, 1988, pp. 297–355.

[10] C. C. Weems, S. P. Levitan, A. R. Hanson, E. M. Riseman, D. B. Shu, and J. G. Nash, *The image understanding architecture* Int. J. Computer Vision, vol. 2, no. 3, Jan. 1989, pp. 251–282.

[11] C. C. Weems, E. M. Riseman, A. R. Hanson, and A. Rosenfeld, *A report on the results of the DARPA integrated image understanding benchmark exercise,* Proc. DARPA Image Understanding Workshop (Palo Alto, Calif., May 1989), Morgan Kaufmann Publishers, San Mateo, Calif., 1989, pp. 165–192.

# Preliminary Results from the DARPA Integrated Image-Understanding Benchmark Exercise

**CHARLES C. WEEMS, EDWARD RISEMAN, and ALLEN HANSON**
*Computer and Information Science Department*
*University of Massachusetts at Amherst*
*Amherst, Massachusetts*

and

**AZRIEL ROSENFELD**
*Center for Automation Research*
*University of Maryland*
*College Park, Maryland*

## 1 Introduction

The computational challenge presented by knowledge-based image understanding has yet to be satisfied by any parallel architecture. The challenge is not merely to provide fast processing, but also to supply the necessary varieties of operations. In addition to I/O and pixel processing, a vision system must be able to organize extracted image features via perceptual grouping mechanisms, locate relevant models in a potentially vast store of knowledge and compare them to partial models derived from the input data, generate hypotheses concerning the environment of the sensor, resolve conflicting hypotheses




ISBN 0-12-564040-4

to arrive at a consistent interpretation of the environment, manage and update stored knowledge, and so on.

Traditional supercomputing benchmarks may be useful in estimating the performance of an architecture on some types of image-processing tasks, but those benchmarks have little relevance to the majority of the processing that takes place in a vision system. Nor has there been much effort to define a vision benchmark for supercomputers, since those machines in their traditional form have usually been viewed as inappropriate vehicles for knowledge-based vision research. However, now that parallel processors are becoming readily available, and because they are viewed as being better suited to vision processing, researchers in both machine vision and parallel architecture are taking an interest in performance issues with respect to vision.

The next section summarizes the first DARPA vision benchmark. Other benchmarks that have been proposed for vision are described in [3, 7, 12]. Section 3 presents an overview of the benchmark task. The complete specification for the task can be found in [10]. Section 4 discusses the results from running the benchmark on the SUN-3, SUN-4, Alliant FX-80, Sequent Symmetry 81, and CMU WARP. Benchmark results for simulations of the UMass/Hughes Image Understanding Architecture, and Aspex Associative String Processor, plus partial results for the Connection Machine and Intel iPSC-2, are also discussed in that section. The numerical timings and validation output are presented in the appended tables. The numerical results are preliminary in that no reduction of the data or compensation for technology differences has been performed.

## 2 Review of the Previous DARPA Benchmark Effort

In 1986, a benchmark was developed at the request of the Defense Advanced Research Projects Agency (DARPA). It was a collection of vision-related tasks (Table 1). A workshop was held in Washington, DC, in November 1986 to present the results of testing the benchmark on several machines, with those results summarized in

[8]. The consensus of the workshop participants was that the results cannot be compared directly for several reasons. First, no method was specified for solving any of the problems. Thus, in many cases, the timings were more indicative of the knowledge or cleverness of the programmer than of a machine's true capabilities. Second, no input data was provided and the specifications allowed a wide range of possible inputs. Thus, some participants chose to test a worst-case input, while others chose "average" input values that varied considerably in difficulty.

The workshop participants pointed out other shortcomings of the benchmark. Chief among these was that because it consisted of isolated tasks, the benchmark did not measure performance related to the interactions between the components of a vision system. For example, there might be a particularly fast solution to a problem on a given architecture if the input data are arranged in a special manner. However, this apparent advantage might be inconsequential if a vision system does not normally use the data in such an arrangement, and the cost of rearranging the data is high. Another shortcoming was that the problems had not been solved before they were distributed. Thus, there was no canonical solution on which the participants could rely for a definition of correctness, and there was even one problem for which it turned out there was no practical solution.

The issue of having a ground truth, or known correct solution, was considered very important, since it is difficult to compare the performance of two architectures when they produce different results. For example, is an architecture that performs a task in half the time of another really twice as powerful if the first machine's programmer used integer arithmetic while the second machine was programmed to use floating point, and they thus obtained significantly different results? Since problems in vision are often ill-defined, it is possible to argue for the correctness of many different solutions. In a benchmark, however, the goal is not to solve a vision problem but to test the performance of different machines doing comparable work.

The conclusions from the first DARPA benchmark exercise were that the results should not be directly compared, and that a new benchmark should be developed that addresses the shortcomings of the preceding benchmarks. Specifically, the new benchmark should test system performance on a task that approximates an integrated solution to a machine vision problem. A complete solution with test data sets should be constructed and distributed with the benchmark specification. And every effort should be made to specify the the benchmark in such a way as to minimize the opportunities for taking shortcuts in solving the problem. The task of constructing the new benchmark, to be called the Integrated Image Understanding Benchmark, was assigned to the vision research groups at the University of Massachusetts at Amherst and the University of Maryland.

Following the 1986 meeting, a preliminary benchmark specification was drawn up and circulated among the DARPA image understanding community for comment. The benchmark specification was then revised, and a solution was programmed on a standard sequential machine. In creating the solution, several problems were discovered and the benchmark specification was modified to correct those problems. The programming of the solution was done by the group at the University of Massachusetts and the code was then sent to the group at the University of Maryland to verify its validity, portability, and quality. The group at Maryland also reviewed the solution to verify that it was general in nature and neutral with respect to any underlying architectural assumptions. The Massachusetts group developed a set of five test cases, and a sample parallel solution for a commercial multiprocessor.

In March 1988, the benchmark was released and made available from Maryland via network access, or by sending a blank tape to the group in Massachusetts. The benchmark release consisted of the sequential and parallel solutions, the five test cases, and software for generating additional test data. The benchmark specification was presented at the DARPA Image-Understanding Workshop, the International Supercomputing Conference, and the Computer Vision and Pattern Recognition conference [10]. More than 25 academic and industrial groups, listed in Table 2, obtained copies of the benchmark release. Nine of those groups developed either complete or partial versions of the solution for an architecture. A workshop was held in October 1988 in Avon Old Farms, Connecticut, to present those results to members of the DARPA research community. As with the previous workshops, the participants spent a session developing a critique of the benchmark and making recommendations for the design of the next version.

Next, we review the benchmark task and summarize the results that were based on hardware execution or on instruction-level simulation of the benchmark. Groups from the University of Texas at Austin and the University of Illinois also presented estimated results for proposed architectures [9, 2], respectively, which are not included here. Also not included are results from Active Memory Technology for its DAP array processor that are for a set of independent image-processing tasks only somewhat related to the benchmark problem. Finally, we present recommendations for improving the benchmark.

# 3 Benchmark Task Overview

The overall task that is to be performed by this benchmark is the recognition of an approximately specified two-and-a-half-dimensional "mobile" sculpture in a cluttered environment, given images from intensity and range sensors. The intention of the benchmark designers is that neither of the input images, by itself, is sufficient to complete the task.

The sculpture is a collection of two-dimensional rectangles of various sizes, brightnesses, two-dimensional orientations, and depths. Each rectangle is oriented normal to the $z$ axis (the viewing axis), with constant depth across its surface, and the images are constructed under orthographic projection. Thus an individual rectangle has no intrinsic depth component, but depth is a factor in the spatial relationships between rectangles, hence the notion that the sculpture is two-and-a-half-dimensional.

The clutter in the scene consists of additional rectangles, with sizes, brightnesses, two-dimensional orientations, and depths that are similar to those of the sculpture. Rectangles may partially or completely occlude other rectangles. It is also possible for a rectangle to disappear when another rectangle of the same brightness or slightly greater depth is located directly behind it.

A set of models is provided that represents a collection of similar sculptures, and the recognition task involves identifying the model that best matches the object present in the scene. The models are only approximate representations of sculptures in that they allow for slight variations in component rectangle's sizes, orientations, depths, and the spatial relationships between them. A model is constructed as a tree structure where the links in the tree represent the invisible links in the sculpture. Each node of the tree contains depth, size, orientation, and intensity information for a single rectangle. The child links of a node in the tree describe the spatial relationships between that node and certain other nodes below it. The intensity and depth sensors are precisely registered with each other and both have a resolution of $512 \times 512$ pixels. There is no averaging or aliasing in either of the sensors. A pixel in the intensity image is an 8-bit integer grey value. In the depth image a pixel is a 32-bit floating-point range value. The intensity image is noise-free, whereas the depth image has added Gaussian noise.

A set of test images is created by first selecting one of the models in a set. The model is then rotated and translated as a whole, and its individual elements are then perturbed slightly. Next, a collection of spurious rectangles is created with properties that are similar to those in the chosen model. All of the rectangles (both model and spurious) are then ordered by depth and drawn in the two image arrays. Last, an array of Gaussian-distribution noise is added to the depth image array.

Figure 1 shows an intensity image of a sculpture alone, and Fig. 2 shows the sculpture with added clutter.

Processing in the benchmark begins with some low-level operations on the intensity and depth images, followed by some grouping operations on the intensity data that result in the extraction of candidate rectangles. The candidate rectangles are used to form partial matches with the stored models. For each model, it is possible that multiple hypothetical poses will be established. The benchmark then proceeds through the model poses, using the stored information to probe the depth and intensity images in a top-down manner. Each

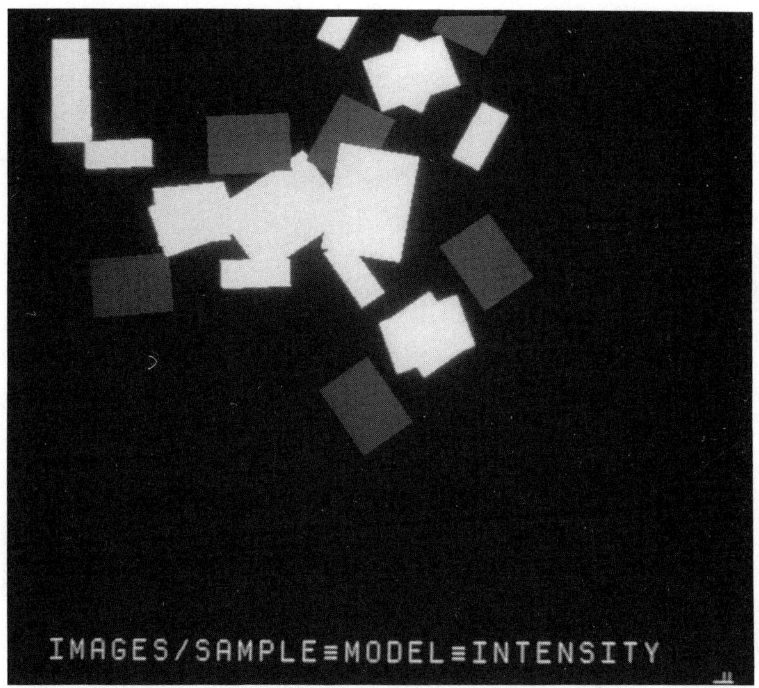


Figure 1: Intensity image of model alone.

and position information. It is possible for the match strength to be as low as zero when there is no supporting evidence for the match and a lack of strong evidence that the rectangle is absent, as in the case of a rectangle that is entirely occluded by another. After a probe has been performed for every unmatched rectangle in the list of model poses, an average match strength is computed for each pose that has not been eliminated. The model pose with the highest average match strength is selected as the best match, and an image is generated that

Figure 2: Image of model with clutter.

probe can be thought of as testing an hypothesis for the existence of a rectangle in a given location in the images. Rejection of a hypothesis, which only occurs when there is strong evidence that a rectangle is actually absent, results in elimination of the corresponding model pose.

Confirmation of the hypothesis results in the computation of a match strength for the rectangle at the hypothetical location, and an update of its representation in the model with new size, orientation, highlights the model in the intensity image.

Table 3 lists all of the steps that make up the complete benchmark task. The benchmark specification requires that this set of steps be applied in implementing a solution. Furthermore, for each step, a recommended method is described that should be followed whenever possible. However, in recognition of the fact that some methods simply may not work, or will be extremely inefficient for a given architecture, implementors are permitted to substitute other methods for individual steps. When it is necessary for an implementation to differ from the specification, the implementor is expected to supply a justification for the change. If possible, it is also urged that a version of the implementation be written and tested with the recommended method so that the difference in performance can be determined.

# 4 Results

Only a few of the participants had time to complete the entire benchmark exercise and test it on all five of the data sets. It was common to underestimate the effort required to implement the benchmark, and several who had said they would provide timings were unable to complete even a portion of the task prior to the workshop. Despite requests to groups that did not attend the workshop that they submit belated results to be included in this report, no new benchmark reports have been received. Thus, the results presented here are those that were provided by the workshop participants. In a few cases, the results have been updated, corrected, or amended since they were originally presented.

Care must be taken in comparing these results. For example, no direct comparison should be made between results obtained from actual execution and those that were derived from simulation [1]. No matter how carefully a simulation is carried out, it is never as accurate as direct execution. Likewise, no comparison should be made between results from a partial implementation and a complete one. The complete implementation must account for overhead involved in the interactions between subtasks, and even for the fact that the program is significantly larger than for a partial implementation. Consider that a set of subtasks might appear to be much faster than their counterparts in a complete implementation simply because less paging is required to keep the code in memory. It is also unwise to compare the raw timings directly, even for similar architectures, without considering the differences in technology between systems. For example, a system that executes a portion of the benchmark in half the time of another is not necessarily architecturally superior if it also has a clock rate that is twice as high or if it has twice as many processors.

In addition to the technical problems involved in making direct comparisons, there are other considerations that must be kept in mind. For example, every participant expressed the view that given more time to tune their implementation, the results for their architecture would improve considerably. What is impressive in many cases is not the raw speed increase obtained, but the increase with respect to the amount of effort required to obtain it. While this has more to do with the tools available for developing software for an architecture than with the architecture itself, it is still important in evaluating the overall usefulness of the system. Another major consideration is the ratio of cost to performance, since many applications can afford to sacrifice a small amount of performance in order to reduce the cost of the implementation. In other applications, the size or weight or power consumption of a system may be of greater importance than all-out speed. One of the purposes of this exercise has been merely to assemble as much of this data as possible so that the performance results can be evaluated with respect to the requirements of each potential application of an architecture.

Thus, in what follows, there is no single best architecture and there are no winners or losers. Each has its own unique merits and drawbacks, of which none are absolute. To play down the direct comparison of raw timings, the results for each architecture will be presented separately. The order of presentation is random, except that the sequential solution is presented first to provide a performance baseline, and then complete parallel implementations are presented, followed by partial implementations. Results that were based on theoretical estimations are not included in this report. The timings in all of the tables are in seconds, for the sake of consistency. Where a timing is zero, it indicates that the processing time was less than the resolution of the timing mechanism employed. Blanks in the tables indicate values that were omitted from the reports that were supplied by the implementors.

## 4.1 Sequential Solution

The sequential solution to the benchmark was developed in C on a SUN-3/160 workstation. The solution contains roughly 4600 lines of code, including comments. The implementation was designed for maximum portability and has been successfully recompiled on several different systems. The only portion that is system-dependent is the actual result presentation step, which uses the graphics primitives provided for drawing on the workstation's screen. The implementation differs from the recommended method on the connected component labeling step by using a standard sequential method for computing this well-defined function. The sequential method is designed to minimize array accesses and their corresponding index calculations, which is not a problem for array processors, but incurs a significant time penalty on a sequential machine.

Timings have been produced for the sequential code running on all five data sets, and on three different machine configurations. The configurations are a SUN-3/160 (a 16 MHz 68020 processor) with 8 MB of RAM, a SUN-3/260 (a 25 MHz 68020) with 16 MB of RAM, and a SUN-4/260 (a 16 MHz SPARC processor) with 16 MB of RAM. The extra RAM on the latter two machines did not affect performance, since the benchmark was able to run in 8 MB without paging. The 3/260 was equipped with a Weitek floating-point coprocessor, while the 3/160 used only the standard 68881 coprocessor. These results have been corrected since the workshop, where some questions arose as to their validity due to a difference in the number of connected components extracted. It was determined that the original results were obtained with a faulty copy of the data set, and the problems vanished when the proper data were used. Table 4 shows the results for the SUN-3/160, Table 5 shows the SUN-3/260 results, and Table 6 gives the execution times for the SUN-4/260. The timings were obtained with the standard system clock utility, which has a resolution of 20 msec on the SUN-3 systems and 10 msec on the SUN-4.

## 4.2 Alliant FX-80 Solution

The Alliant FX-80 consists of up to eight computational elements and up to 12 I/O processors that share a physical memory through a sophisticated combination of caches, buses, and an interconnection network. The computational elements communicate with the shared memory via the interconnection network, which links them to a pair of special-purpose caches that in turn access the memory over a bus that is shared with the I/O processor caches. The FX-80 differs from the older FX-8 primarily in that the computational elements are significantly faster.

Alliant was able to implement the benchmark on the FX-80 in roughly one programmer-week. The programmer who built the implementation had no experience in vision and, in many cases, did not even bother to learn how the benchmark code works. The implementation was done by rewriting the system dependent section to use the available graphics hardware, compiling the code with Alliant's vectorizing and globally optimizing C compiler, using a profiling tool to determine the portions of the code that used the greatest percentage of CPU time, inserting compiler directives in the form of comments to break implicit dependencies in four sections of the benchmark, and recompiling the new version of the code. Alliant provided results for five configurations of the FX-80, with one, two, four, six, and eight computational elements.

To save space, only two of the configurations are represented here. Table 7 shows the execution times for a single FX-80 computational element, and Table 8 shows the results for an FX-80 with eight elements. Another point that was noted by Alliant is that the C compiler is a new product and does not yet provide as great a degree of optimization as their FORTRAN compiler (a difference of up to 50% in some cases). They expect to see significantly better performance with later releases of the product.

## 4.3 Image-Understanding Architecture

The image-understanding architecture (IUA) is being built by the University of Massachusetts and Hughes Research Laboratories specifically to address the problem of supporting real-time, knowledge-based vision. The architecture consists of three different parallel processors that are arranged in a hierarchy that is tightly coupled by layers of dual-ported memory between the processors. The low-level processor in the hierarchy is a bit-serial, processor-per-pixel, SIMD, associative array. The intermediate-level processor is an MIMD array of 4096 16-bit digital signal processors that can communicate via an interconnection network. Each intermediate-level processor shares a dual-ported memory segment with 64 low-level processors. The high level is a multiprocessor that is designed to support AI processing and a blackboard model of communication through a global shared memory, which is dual-ported with a segment of the intermediate-level processor's memory. A detailed description of the architecture can be found in [11].

Because the architecture is still under construction, an instruction-level simulator was used to develop the benchmark implementation. The simulator is programmed in a combination of FORTH and an assembly language which has a syntax that is similar to Ada or Pascal. The benchmark was developed over a period of about six months, but much of that time was spent in building basic library routines and additional tools that were generally required for any large programming task.

A 1/64th scale version of the simulator (with 4096 low-level, 64 intermediate-level, and one high-level processor) runs on a SUN workstation, and was used to develop the initial benchmark implementation. The implementation was then transported to a full-scale IUA simulator running on a Sequent Symmetry multiprocessor. At the time of the Avon workshop, several errors remained in the full-scale implementation, but these have since been corrected.

Table 9 presents the results from the IUA simulations with a resolution of one instruction time (0.1 $\mu$sec). There are several points to note about these results. Because the processing of different steps can be overlapped in the different processing levels, the sum of the individual step timings does not always equal the total time for a segment of the benchmark. Some of the individual timings represent average execution times, since the intermediate level processing takes place asynchronously and individual processes can vary in their execution time. For example, the time for all of the match-strength probes is difficult to estimate since probes are created asynchronously and their processing is overlapped. However, the time for a step such as match extension takes into account the span of time required to complete all of the subsidiary match-strength probes. Finally, it should be mentioned that the intermediate-level processor was greatly underutilized by the benchmark (only 0.2% of its processors were activated), and the high-level processor was not used at all. The low-level processor was also idle roughly 50% of the time while awaiting requests for top-down probes from the intermediate level.

## 4.4 Aspex ASP

The associative string processor (ASP) is being built by the University of Brunel and Aspex Ltd. in England [6]. It is designed as a general-purpose processing array for implementation in wafer-scale technology. The processor consists of 262,144 processors arranged as 512 strings of 512 processors each. Each processor contains a 96-bit data register and a 5-bit activity register. A string consists of 512 processors linked by a communication network that is also tied to a data exchanger and a vector data buffer. The vector data buffers of the strings are linked through another data exchanger and data buffer to another communication network. One of the advantages of this arrangement is a high degree of fault tolerance. The system can be built with 1024 VLSI devices, or 128 ULSI devices, or 32 WSI devices. Estimated power consumption is 650 watts. The processor clock and instruction rate is 20 MHz. Architectural changes that would improve the benchmark performance include increasing the number of processors (improves performance on K-curvature, median filter, and Sobel), increasing the speed of the processors and communication links (linear speedup on all tasks), and adding a separate controller to each ASP substring (gives approximately an 18%

increase overall).

Because the system is still under construction, a software simulator was used to implement and execute the benchmark. The benchmark was programmed in an extended version of Modula-2 over a period three months by two programmers, following a three-month period of initial study of the requirements and development of a solution strategy. A Jarvis's March algorithm was substituted for the recommended Graham Scan method on the convex hull. Table 10 lists the benchmark results for the ASP. Timings were not provided for several of the steps in the model-matching portion of the benchmark, because a different method was used that solved the task with a data-parallel approach. Startup and model input times were not listed separately. The miscellaneous time under overhead accounts for the input and output of several intermediate images. The miscellaneous time under the section that extracts rectangles from the intensity image accounts for the output and subsequent input of data records for corners and rectangles. Some data rearrangement took place as part of these I/O operations.

## 4.5 Sequent Symmetry 81

The Sequent Computer Systems Symmetry 81 multiprocessor consists of multiple Intel 80386 microprocessors, running at 16.5 MHz, connected via a shared bus to a large shared memory. The particular configuration used to obtain these results included 12 processors (one of which is reserved by the system), each with an 80387 math coprocessor, and 96 MB of shared memory. The test system also contained the older A-model caches, which induce a considerably greater level of traffic on the shared bus than the newer B-model caches. An improvement of 30% to 50% in the overall performance is claimed with the new caching system. Sequent was to have provided timings for a system with the improved cache, but they have not yet done so. The timings presented in Table 11 were obtained by the benchmark developers at UMass as part of their effort to ensure the portability of the benchmark to different systems.

About a month was spent developing the parallel implementation for the Sequent. The programmer who did the work was familiar with the benchmark, but had no previous experience with the Sequent system. Part of the development period was spent back-porting modifications to the sequential version of the benchmark in order to enhance its portability. The low-level tasks were directly converted to a parallel implementation by dividing the data sets among the processors in a manner that completely avoided write-contention. About half of the development time was spent adding the appropriate data-locking mechanisms to the model-matching portion of the benchmark, and resolving problems with timing and race conditions.

It was possible to obtain timings only for the major steps in the benchmark, because the Sequent operating system does not provide facilities for accurately timing individual child processes. The benchmark was run on configurations of from one to eleven processors, with the optimum time being obtained with eight or nine processors. Additional processors resulted in an overall reduction in performance, which was due to a combination of factors. As the data sets were divided among more processors, the ratio of processing time to task creation overhead decreased so that the latter came to dominate the time on some tasks. We also believe that some of the tasks reached the saturation point of the shared bus at about eight or nine processors since one run that was observed on a B-model cache system showed performance to improve with more processors. The table shows the performance obtained for a single processor running the sequential version of the benchmark, to provide a comparison baseline, and the performance on the optimum number of processors for each data set.

## 4.6 Warp

The CMU WARP is a systolic array consisting of ten high-speed floating-point processing elements in a linear configuration [5]. Processing in the WARP is directed by a host processor, such as the SUN-3/60 workstation that was used in executing the benchmark. The benchmark implementation was programmed by one person in two weeks, using a combination of the original C implementation and subroutines written in Apply and W2. The objective of the implementation was to obtain the best overall time, rather than the best time for each task. While it would seem that the latter guarantees the former, consider that the WARP and its host can work in parallel on different portions of a problem. Thus, even though the WARP could perform a step in one second that requires four seconds on the host, it is better to let the host do the processing if it would otherwise sit idle while the WARP is computing. Thus the WARP implementation of the benchmark exploits both the tightly coupled parallelism of the WARP array, and the loosely coupled task-level parallelism present in the benchmark.

Table 12 lists the results for the WARP. Timings were not provided for a few of the steps, but the totals include all of the processing time. The Miscellaneous category under Overhead is the time required for downloading code to the WARP array at various stages of the processing. A figure for the total system time was provided, rather than a breakdown of system time by task. The overall Total includes the system time, which is listed on the line below the Total. Note that sums of the times for the individual steps will not equal the Total time because of the task-level parallelism that was used.

## 4.7 Connection Machine

The Thinking Machines Connection Machine model CM-2 is a data-parallel array of bit-serial processors that are linked by an $N$-dimensional hypercube router network [4]. In addition, for every 32 of the bit-serial processors, a 32-bit floating-point coprocessor is provided. Connection Machines are available in configurations of 8192, 16384, 32768, and 65536 processing elements. Results were provided for direct execution on the three smaller configurations, and extrapolated to the largest configuration. The development team at Thinking Machines spent about three programmer-months converting the low-level portion of the benchmark into 2600 lines of *LISP, which is a data-parallel extension to Common LISP. There was not enough time to implement the intermediate and top-down processing portions of the benchmark before the workshop, and other projects have taken priority over completing the benchmark since then. However, there was also some concern as to whether the Connection Machine would be the best vehicle for implementing the other portions, since they are more concerned with task parallelism than data parallelism. It was suggested that if the model data base included several thousand models to be matched, then an appropriate method might be found to take advantage of the Connection Machine's capabilities.

Table 13 summarizes the results for the Connection Machine on the low-level portion of the benchmark, with times rounded to two significant digits (as provided by Thinking Machines). A 32K-processor CM-2 with a Data Vault disk system and a SUN-4 host processor was used to obtain the results. Results were supplied for only one data set, and did not indicate which one was used. It is interesting to note that several of the tasks saw little speedup with the larger configurations of the Connection Machine. Those tasks involved a collection of contour values that had been mapped into 16K virtual processors, which are enough to operate on all of the contour points in parallel, and so there was no advantage in using more physical processors than virtual processors. It was suggested that the Connection Machine might thus be used to process the contours for several images at once in order to make use of the larger number of processors. On the other hand, for those tasks that are pixel oriented, 256K virtual processors were used and therefore a proportional speedup can be observed as the number of processors increases.

## 4.8 Intel iPSC-2

The Intel Scientific Computers iPSC-2 is a distributed memory multiprocessor that consists of up to 128 Intel 80386 microprocessors that are linked by a virtual cut-through routing network, which simulates point-to-point communications. Each of the microprocessors can have up to 8 MB of local memory, and an 80387 arithmetic coprocessor. The benchmark implementation for the iPSC-2 was developed by the University of Illinois at Urbana-Champaign using C with a library that supports multiprocessing. The group had only enough time to implement the median filter and Sobel steps of the low-level depth image-processing. However, they did run those portions on five different machine configurations, with one, two, four, eight, and 16 processors, and on four of the five data sets. Table 14 presents their results, which are divided into user time and system time (including data and program load time, and output time).

## Acknowledgments

This work was supported in part by the Defense Advanced Research Projects Agency under contract number DACA76-86-C-0015, monitored by the U.S. Army Engineer Topographic Laboratories.

We would like to thank Claire Bono, Chris Brown, C.H. Chien, Larry Davis, Todd Kushner, Ram Nevatia, Keith Price, George Reynolds, Lew Tucker, and Jon Webb for their many helpful comments and suggestions in response to the draft benchmark specification.

For their efforts in designing, programming, and debugging the sequential and Sequent Symmetry solutions to the benchmark, we would like to thank Poornima Balasubramaniam, Sunit Bhalla, Chris Connoly, John Dolan, Martin Herbordt, Michael Scudder, Lance Williams, and especially Jim Burrill.

For providing benchmark results on other architectures we also thank Alok Choudhary, R. M. Lea, A Krikelis, I. Kossioris, Lew Brown, Dan Mezynski, Jon Webb, Lew Tucker, Steven Levitan, Mary Jane Irwin, Sunit Bhalla, Martin Herbordt, Michael Scudder, Michael Rudenko, and Jim Burrill.

And, for their many suggestions for improvements to the benchmark we again thank all of the above, plus Jake Aggrawal, Thomas Binford, Martin Fischler, Prasanna Kumar, Daryl Lawton, Randall Nelson, Karen Olin, Dennis Parkinson, Tomaso Poggio, Tony Reeves, Arnold Rosenberg, and Myung Sunwoo.

# Bibliography

[1] Robert J. Carpenter, *Performance measurement instrumentation for multiprocessor computers*, Report NBSIR 87-3627, U.S.

Department of Commerce, National Bureau of Standards, Institute for Computer Sciences and Technology, Gaithersburg, MD, 1987, p. 26.

[2] A. N. Choudhary, *Parallel architectures and parallel algorithms for integrated vision systems*, Ph.D. Thesis, University of Illinois, Urbana-Champaign, August 1989.

[3] M. J. B. Duff, *How not to benchmark image processors*, in L. Uhr, K. Preston, S. Levialdi, and M. J. B. Duff, eds., Evaluation of Multicomputers for Image Processing, Academic Press, 1986.

[4] Daniel W. Hillis, The Connection Machine, MIT Press, 1986.

[5] H. T. Kung and Onat Menzilcioglu, *WARP: A programmable systolic array processor*, Proc. SPIE Symp., Vol. 495, Real-Time Signal Processing VII, 1984.

[6] R. M. Lea, *ASP: A cost-effective parallel microcomputer*, IEEE Micro, 1988, pp. 10-29.

[7] Kendall Preston, Jr., *Benchmark results: The Abingdon Cross*, L. Uhr, K. Preston, S. Levialdi, and M. J. B. Duff, eds., Evaluation of Multicomputers for Image Processing, Academic Press, 1986.

[8] A. R. Rosenfeld, *A report on the DARPA image-understanding architectures workshop*, Proceedings of the 1987 DARPA Image-Understanding Workshop, 1987, pp. 298-302.

[9] M. H. Sunwoo and J. K. Aggarwal, *VisTA: An image understanding architecture*, in V. K. Prassana Kumar, ed., Parallel Architectures and Algorithms for Image-Understanding, Academic Press, 1990.

[10] Charles C. Weems, Allen Hanson, Edward Riseman, and Azriel Rosenfeld, *An integrated image-understanding benchmark: recognition of a 2 1/2 D "mobile"*, Proceedings of the 1988 DARPA Image-Understanding Workshop, 1988, pp. 111-126.

[11] Charles C. Weems, ven P. Levitan, Allen R. Hanson, Edward M. Riseman, David B. Shu, and J. Gregory Nash, *The image-understanding architecture*, International Journal of Computer Vision, vol. 2, 1989, pp. 251-282.

[12] Charles C. Weems, Allen Hanson, Edward Riseman, and Azriel Rosenfeld, *A report on the DARPA integrated image-understanding benchmark exercise*, Proceedings of the, DARPA Image-Understanding Workshop, 1989, pp. 165-192.

| 11x11 Gaussian Convolution of a 512x512 8-bit Image |
|---|
| Detection of Zero Crossings in a Difference of Gaussians Image |
| Construct and Output Border Pixel List |
| Label Connected Components in a Binary Image |
| Hough Transform of a Binary Image |
| Convex Hull of 1000 Points in 2-D Real Space |
| Voronoi Diagram of 1000 Points in 2-D Real Space |
| Minimal Spanning Tree Across 1000 Points in 2-D Real Space |
| Visibility of Vertices for 1000 Triangles in 3-D Real Space |
| Minimum Cost Path Through a Weighted Graph of 1000 Nodes of Order 100 |
| Find all Isomorphisms of a 100 Node Graph in a 1000 Node Graph |

Table 1: Tasks from the First DARPA Image Understanding Benchmark

| International Parallel Machines | Hughes AI Center |
|---|---|
| Mercury Computer Systems | University of Wisconsin |
| Stellar Computer | George Washington University |
| Myrias Computer | University of Massachusetts* |
| Active Memory Technology | SAIC |
| Thinking Machines* | Eastman Kodak |
| Aspex Ltd.* | University College London |
| Texas Instruments | Encore Computer |
| IBM | MIT |
| Carnegie-Mellon University* | University of Rochester |
| Intel Scientific Computers* | University of Illinois* |
| Cray Research | University of Texas at Austin* |
| Sequent Computer Systems* | Alliant Computer* |

* Indicates Results Presented at the Avon Workshop

Table 2: Distribution List for the Second DARPA Benchmark

| **Low-Level, Bottom-Up Processing** | |
|---|---|
| **Intensity Image** | **Depth Image** |
| Label Connected Components | 3x3 Median Filter |
| Compute K-Curvature | 3x3 Sobel and Gradient Magnitude |
| Extract Corners | Threshold |
| **Intermediate Level Processing** | |
| Select Components with 3 or More Corners | |
| Convex Hull of Corners for Each Component | |
| Compute Angles Between Successive Corners on Convex Hulls | |
| Select Corners with K-Curvature and Computed Angles Indicating a Right Angle | |
| Label Components with 3 Contiguous Right Angles as Candidate Rectangles | |
| Compute Size, Orientation, Position, and Intensity for Each Candidate Rectangle | |
| **Model-Based, Top-Down Processing** | |
| Determine all Single Node Isomorphisms of Candidate Rectangles in Stored Models | |
| Create a List of all Potential Model Poses | |
| Perform a Match Strength Probe for all Single Node Isomorphisms (see below) | |
| Link Together all Single Node Isomorphisms | |
| Create a List of all Probes Required to Extend Each Partial Match | |
| Order the Probe List According to the Match Strength of the Partial Match Being Extended | |
| Perform a Probe of the Depth Data for Each Probe on the List (see below) | |
| Perform a Match Strength Probe for Each Confirming Depth Probe (see below) | |

Table 3: Steps that Compose the Integrated Image Understanding Benchmark

| |
|---|
| Update Rectangle Parameters in the Stored Model for Each Confirming Probe |
| Propagate the Veto from a Rejecting Depth Probe Throughout the Corresponding Partial Match |
| When No Probes Remain, Compute Average Match Strength for Each Remaining Model Pose |
| Select Model with Highest Average Match Strength as the Best Match |
| Create the Output Intensity Image, Showing the Matching Model |
| **Depth Probe** |
| Select an X-Y Oriented Window in the Depth Data that will Contain the Rectangle |
| Perform a Hough Transform Within the Window |
| Search the Hough Array for Strong Edges with the Approximate Expected Orientations |
| If Fewer than 3 Edges are Found, Return the Original Model Data with a No-Match Flag |
| If 3 Edges are Found, Infer the Fourth from the Model Data |
| Compute New Size, Position, and Orientation Values for the Rectangle |
| **Match-Strength Probe** |
| Select an Oriented Window in the Depth Data that is Slightly Larger than the Rectangle |
| Classify Depth Pixels as Too Close, Too Far, or In Range |
| If the Number of Too Far Pixels Exceeds a Threshold, Return a Veto |
| Otherwise, Select a Corresponding Window in the Intensity Image |
| Select Intensity Pixels with the Correct Value |
| Compute a Match Strength Based on the Number of Correct vs. Incorrect Pixels in the Images |

Table 3: (continued)

| Data Set | Sample | | Test1 | | Test2 | | Test3 | | Test4 | |
|---|---|---|---|---|---|---|---|---|---|---|
| | User | System | User | System | User | System | User | System | User | System |
| Total | 794.94 | 2.94 | 335.96 | 2.10 | 326.84 | 2.40 | 549.3 | 2.52 | 550.26 | 2.90 |
| Overhead | 4.02 | 1.06 | 4.06 | 0.88 | 4.50 | 1.14 | 4.60 | 1.04 | 4.58 | 0.94 |
| Miscellaneous | 2.24 | 0.04 | 2.18 | 0.04 | 2.16 | 0.06 | 2.12 | 0.02 | 2.10 | 0.02 |
| Startup | 0.02 | 0.00 | 0.04 | 0.00 | 0.02 | 0.04 | 0.00 | 0.02 | 0.02 | 0.00 |
| Image input | 0.60 | 0.68 | 0.58 | 0.54 | 1.32 | 0.78 | 1.50 | 0.74 | 1.42 | 0.66 |
| Image output | 0.24 | 0.30 | 0.30 | 0.28 | 0.06 | 0.24 | 0.06 | 0.24 | 0.08 | 0.26 |
| Model input | 0.92 | 0.04 | 0.96 | 0.02 | 0.94 | 0.02 | 0.92 | 0.02 | 0.96 | 0.00 |
| Label connected components | 27.40 | 0.38 | 27.46 | 0.36 | 28.12 | 0.28 | 27.86 | 0.36 | 27.88 | 0.36 |
| Rectangles from intensity | 6.42 | 0.08 | 4.00 | 0.14 | 4.34 | 0.04 | 5.36 | 0.08 | 5.10 | 0.24 |
| Miscellaneous | 2.06 | 0.06 | 1.84 | 0.02 | 1.94 | 0.02 | 1.94 | 0.02 | 1.92 | 0.06 |
| Trace region boundary | 0.52 | 0.02 | 0.28 | 0.02 | 0.38 | 0.00 | 0.42 | 0.00 | 0.38 | 0.06 |
| K-curvature | 1.62 | 0.00 | 0.80 | 0.00 | 0.82 | 0.00 | 1.22 | 0.00 | 1.10 | 0.00 |
| K-curvature smoothing | 1.26 | 0.00 | 0.62 | 0.00 | 0.70 | 0.00 | 0.96 | 0.00 | 1.02 | 0.02 |
| First derivative | 0.46 | 0.00 | 0.22 | 0.02 | 0.24 | 0.00 | 0.28 | 0.02 | 0.22 | 0.02 |
| Zero-crossing detection | 0.26 | 0.00 | 0.06 | 0.00 | 0.04 | 0.00 | 0.18 | 0.00 | 0.24 | 0.02 |
| Final corner detection | 0.20 | 0.00 | 0.16 | 0.02 | 0.18 | 0.02 | 0.28 | 0.02 | 0.16 | 0.04 |
| Count corners | 0.00 | 0.00 | 0.00 | 0.02 | 0.02 | 0.00 | 0.00 | 0.02 | 0.00 | 0.00 |
| Convex hull | 0.02 | 0.00 | 0.00 | 0.02 | 0.00 | 0.00 | 0.02 | 0.00 | 0.04 | 0.00 |
| Test for right angles | 0.00 | 0.00 | 0.02 | 0.02 | 0.00 | 0.00 | 0.04 | 0.00 | 0.00 | 0.00 |
| Final rectangle hypothesis | 0.02 | 0.00 | 0.00 | 0.00 | 0.02 | 0.00 | 0.02 | 0.00 | 0.02 | 0.02 |
| Median filter | 246.06 | 0.60 | 118.62 | 0.26 | 92.58 | 0.28 | 90.70 | 0.22 | 90.66 | 0.24 |

Table 4: Sun-3/160 Results

| | | | | | | | | | | |
|---|---|---|---|---|---|---|---|---|---|---|
| Sobel | 135.3 | - 0.18 | 133.14 | 0.16 | 135.92 | 0.18 | 135.12 | 0.16 | 135.14 | 0.28 |
| Initial graph match | 24.4 | 0.06 | 24.94 | 0.06 | 26.02 | 0.02 | 68.30 | 0.14 | 67.48 | 0.14 |
| Match data rectangles | 0.14 | 0.00 | 0.10 | 0.02 | 0.08 | 0.02 | 0.26 | 0.04 | 0.24 | 0.00 |
| Match links | 0.22 | 0.00 | 0.06 | 0.00 | 0.08 | 0.00 | 0.74 | 0.00 | 0.58 | 0.02 |
| Create probe list | 0.00 | 0.00 | 0.00 | 0.00 | 0.00 | 0.00 | 0.02 | 0.00 | 0.02 | 0.00 |
| Partial match | 24.04 | 0.06 | 24.78 | 0.04 | 25.86 | 0.00 | 67.28 | 0.10 | 66.64 | 0.12 |
| Match strength probes | 24.02 | 0.06 | 24.74 | 0.02 | 25.82 | 0.00 | 66.64 | 0.10 | 65.82 | 0.12 |
| Window selection | 0.02 | 0.00 | 0.02 | 0.00 | 0.00 | 0.00 | 0.12 | 0.02 | 0.10 | 0.02 |
| Classification and count | 24.0 | 0.06 | 24.72 | 0.02 | 25.82 | 0.00 | 66.50 | 0.06 | 65.70 | 0.08 |
| Match extension | 326.54 | 0.50 | 11.46 | 0.12 | 18.72 | 0.20 | 202.58 | 0.32 | 204.68 | 0.44 |
| Match strength probes | 72.88 | 0.10 | 3.28 | 0.00 | 5.80 | 0.06 | 47.82 | 0.06 | 42.00 | 0.06 |
| Window selection | 0.08 | 0.00 | 0.00 | 0.00 | 0.00 | 0.00 | 0.08 | 0.02 | 0.10 | 0.00 |
| Classification and count | 72.80 | 0.10 | 3.28 | 0.00 | 5.80 | 0.06 | 47.72 | 0.02 | 41.88 | 0.06 |
| Hough probes | 253.32 | 0.38 | 8.16 | 0.12 | 12.84 | 0.12 | 153.76 | 0.22 | 161.98 | 0.36 |
| Window selection | 0.00 | 0.00 | 0.00 | 0.00 | 0.00 | 0.00 | 0.08 | 0.02 | 0.02 | 0.02 |
| Hough transform | 252.20 | 0.36 | 8.10 | 0.12 | 12.78 | 0.12 | 151.86 | 0.16 | 160.34 | 0.28 |
| Edge peak detection | 1.08 | 0.02 | 0.06 | 0.00 | 0.06 | 0.00 | 1.76 | 0.00 | 1.54 | 0.02 |
| Rectangle parameter update | 0.04 | 0.00 | 0.00 | 0.00 | 0.00 | 0.00 | 0.04 | 0.02 | 0.04 | 0.00 |
| Result presentation | 24.80 | 0.00 | 12.28 | 0.04 | 16.64 | 0.02 | 14.78 | 0.00 | 14.74 | 0.02 |
| Best match selection | 0.00 | 0.00 | 0.00 | 0.00 | 0.00 | 0.00 | 0.02 | 0.00 | 0.00 | 0.00 |
| Image generation | 24.80 | 0.00 | 12.28 | 0.04 | 16.64 | 0.02 | 14.76 | 0.00 | 14.74 | 0.02 |

Table 4: (continued)

| Statistics | | | | | |
|---|---|---|---|---|---|
| Connected components | 134 | 35 | 34 | 114 | 100 |
| Right angles extracted | 126 | 99 | 92 | 210 | 197 |
| Rectangles detected | 25 | 21 | 16 | 42 | 39 |
| Depth pixels > threshold | 21256 | 14542 | 12898 | 18584 | 18825 |
| Elements on initial probe list | 381 | 19 | 27 | 400 | 249 |
| Hough probes | 55 | 3 | 5 | 97 | 93 |
| Initial match strength probes | 28 | 20 | 15 | 142 | 142 |
| Extension mat. str. probes | 60 | 3 | 5 | 110 | 97 |
| Models remaining | 2 | 1 | 1 | 2 | 1 |
| Model selected | 10 | 1 | 5 | 7 | 8 |
| Average match strength | 0.64 | 0.96 | 0.94 | 0.84 | 0.88 |
| Translated to | 151,240 | 256,256 | 257,255 | 257,255 | 257.255 |
| Rotated by (degrees) | 85 | 359 | 114 | 22 | 22 |

Table 4: (continued)

| Data Set | Sample | | Test1 | | Test2 | | Test3 | | Test4 | |
|---|---|---|---|---|---|---|---|---|---|---|
| | User | System | User | System | User | System | User | System | User | System |
| Total | 293.42 | 5.96 | 130.48 | 2.06 | 116.96 | 2.56 | 191.38 | 3.38 | 192.38 | 3.20 |
| Overhead | 2.26 | 0.66 | 2.46 | 0.58 | 2.76 | 0.68 | 2.50 | 0.94 | 2.72 | 0.72 |
| Miscellaneous | 1.28 | 0.00 | 1.24 | 0.00 | 1.24 | 0.02 | 1.22 | 0.02 | 1.22 | 0.00 |
| Startup | 0.02 | 0.00 | 0.00 | 0.00 | 0.00 | 0.02 | 0.00 | 0.04 | 0.02 | 0.00 |
| Image input | 0.30 | 0.50 | 0.50 | 0.50 | 1.00 | 0.48 | 0.76 | 0.72 | 0.92 | 0.54 |
| Image output | 0.18 | 0.14 | 0.26 | 0.08 | 0.06 | 0.16 | 0.06 | 0.14 | 0.08 | 0.18 |
| Model input | 0.48 | 0.02 | 0.46 | 0.00 | 0.46 | 0.00 | 0.46 | 0.02 | 0.48 | 0.00 |
| Label connected components | 14.14 | 0.38 | 14.20 | 0.26 | 14.10 | 0.36 | 14.46 | 0.12 | 14.40 | 0.26 |
| Rectangles from intensity | 3.60 | 0.14 | 2.36 | 0.02 | 2.44 | 0.04 | 3.12 | 0.04 | 2.90 | 0.08 |
| Miscellaneous | 1.28 | 0.02 | 1.12 | 0.00 | 1.22 | 0.02 | 1.26 | 0.00 | 1.08 | 0.00 |
| Trace region boundary | 0.28 | 0.02 | 0.20 | 0.00 | 0.18 | 0.00 | 0.14 | 0.02 | 0.26 | 0.04 |
| K-curvature | 0.82 | 0.02 | 0.44 | 0.02 | 0.42 | 0.00 | 0.68 | 0.00 | 0.48 | 0.02 |
| K-curvature smoothing | 0.78 | 0.02 | 0.26 | 0.00 | 0.42 | 0.02 | 0.50 | 0.00 | 0.56 | 0.00 |
| First derivative | 0.20 | 0.02 | 0.16 | 0.00 | 0.10 | 0.00 | 0.18 | 0.00 | 0.26 | 0.00 |
| Zero-crossing detection | 0.02 | 0.02 | 0.04 | 0.00 | 0.06 | 0.00 | 0.18 | 0.00 | 0.14 | 0.00 |
| Final corner detection | 0.20 | 0.00 | 0.12 | 0.00 | 0.04 | 0.00 | 0.18 | 0.00 | 0.04 | 0.00 |
| Count corners | 0.00 | 0.00 | 0.00 | 0.00 | 0.00 | 0.00 | 0.00 | 0.00 | 0.00 | 0.00 |
| Convex hull | 0.02 | 0.00 | 0.00 | 0.00 | 0.00 | 0.00 | 0.00 | 0.20 | 0.04 | 0.00 |
| Test for right angles | 0.00 | 0.00 | 0.02 | 0.00 | 0.00 | 0.00 | 0.00 | 0.00 | 0.04 | 0.00 |
| Final rectangle hypothesis | 0.00 | 0.00 | 0.00 | 0.00 | 0.00 | 0.00 | 0.00 | 0.00 | 0.00 | 0.02 |
| Median filter | 112.50 | 1.20 | 59.86 | 0.42 | 42.64 | 0.46 | 42.64 | 0.34 | 42.72 | 0.54 |

Table 5: Sun-3/260 Results

| | | | | | | | | | | |
|---|---|---|---|---|---|---|---|---|---|---|
| Sobel | 38.96 | 2.04 | 38.12 | 0.38 | 37.90 | 0.44 | 38.02 | 0.74 | 38.14 | 0.42 |
| Initial graph match | 6.10 | 0.06 | 6.06 | 0.02 | 6.38 | 0.20 | 17.02 | 0.30 | 16.80 | 0.14 |
| Match data rectangles | 0.08 | 0.00 | 0.06 | 0.00 | 0.04 | 0.00 | 0.14 | 0.02 | 0.12 | 0.00 |
| Match links | 0.10 | 0.00 | 0.04 | 0.00 | 0.04 | 0.00 | 0.30 | 0.00 | 0.26 | 0.00 |
| Create probe list | 0.00 | 0.00 | 0.00 | 0.00 | 0.00 | 0.00 | 0.00 | 0.00 | 0.00 | 0.00 |
| Partial match | 5.92 | 0.06 | 5.96 | 0.02 | 6.30 | 0.20 | 16.58 | 0.28 | 16.42 | 0.14 |
| Match strength probes | 5.90 | 0.06 | 5.94 | 0.02 | 6.30 | 0.20 | 16.34 | 0.22 | 16.04 | 0.14 |
| Window selection | 0.00 | 0.00 | 0.00 | 0.00 | 0.00 | 0.00 | 0.10 | 0.02 | 0.02 | 0.00 |
| Classification and count | 5.90 | 0.06 | 5.94 | 0.02 | 6.30 | 0.18 | 16.24 | 0.18 | 16.02 | 0.10 |
| Match extension | 109.18 | 1.28 | 3.78 | 0.14 | 6.02 | 0.22 | 69.32 | 0.76 | 70.42 | 0.74 |
| Match strength probes | 17.54 | 0.02 | 0.78 | 0.00 | 1.40 | 0.00 | 11.60 | 0.06 | 10.20 | 0.10 |
| Window selection | 0.04 | 0.00 | 0.00 | 0.00 | 0.00 | 0.00 | 0.04 | 0.00 | 0.04 | 0.00 |
| Classification and count | 17.50 | 0.02 | 0.78 | 0.00 | 1.40 | 0.00 | 11.56 | 0.06 | 10.16 | 0.08 |
| Hough probes | 91.44 | 1.26 | 3.00 | 0.12 | 4.62 | 0.20 | 57.30 | 0.66 | 59.80 | 0.64 |
| Window selection | 0.04 | 0.00 | 0.00 | 0.00 | 0.00 | 0.00 | 0.04 | 0.02 | 0.02 | 0.00 |
| Hough transform | 90.64 | 1.24 | 2.98 | 0.12 | 4.60 | 0.20 | 56.40 | 0.64 | 59.00 | 0.62 |
| Edge peak detection | 0.76 | 0.02 | 0.02 | 0.00 | 0.02 | 0.00 | 0.82 | 0.00 | 0.78 | 0.02 |
| Rectangle parameter update | 0.00 | 0.00 | 0.00 | 0.00 | 0.00 | 0.00 | 0.04 | 0.00 | 0.00 | 0.00 |
| Result presentation | 6.68 | 0.00 | 3.64 | 0.00 | 4.72 | 0.00 | 4.30 | 0.20 | 4.28 | 0.02 |
| Best match selection | 0.00 | 0.00 | 0.00 | 0.00 | 0.00 | 0.00 | 0.00 | 0.00 | 0.00 | 0.00 |
| Image generation | 6.68 | 0.00 | 3.64 | 0.00 | 4.72 | 0.00 | 4.30 | 0.02 | 4.28 | 0.02 |

Table 5: (continued)

| Statistics | | | | | |
|---|---|---|---|---|---|
| Connected components | 134 | 35 | 34 | 114 | 100 |
| Right angles extracted | 126 | 99 | 92 | 210 | 197 |
| Rectangles detected | 25 | 21 | 16 | 42 | 39 |
| Depth pixels > threshold | 21256 | 14542 | 12898 | 18584 | 18825 |
| Elements on initial probe list | 381 | 19 | 27 | 400 | 249 |
| Hough probes | 55 | 3 | 5 | 97 | 93 |
| Initial match strength probes | 28 | 20 | 15 | 142 | 142 |
| Extension mat. str. probes | 60 | 3 | 5 | 110 | 97 |
| Models remaining | 2 | 1 | 1 | 2 | 1 |
| Model selected | 10 | 1 | 5 | 7 | 8 |
| Average match strength | 0.64 | 0.96 | 0.94 | 0.84 | 0.88 |
| Translated to | 151,240 | 256,256 | 257,255 | 257,255 | 257,255 |
| Rotated by (degrees) | 85 | 359 | 114 | 22 | 22 |

Table 5: (continued)

| Data Set | Sample | | Test1 | | Test2 | | Test3 | | Test4 | |
|---|---|---|---|---|---|---|---|---|---|---|
| | User | System | User | System | User | System | User | System | User | System |
| Total | 117.21 | 3.80 | 40.19 | 2.45 | 38.88 | 2.06 | 78.41 | 2.64 | 80.15 | 2.69 |
| Overhead | 2.49 | 1.85 | 2.34 | 1.58 | 2.43 | 1.36 | 2.62 | 1.46 | 2.66 | 1.45 |
| Miscellaneous | 1.23 | 1.20 | 1.17 | 0.81 | 1.24 | 0.70 | 1.45 | 0.77 | 1.43 | 0.74 |
| Startup | 0.02 | 0.03 | 0.00 | 0.05 | 0.03 | 0.02 | 0.01 | 0.05 | 0.01 | 0.06 |
| Image input | 0.33 | 0.48 | 0.27 | 0.58 | 0.33 | 0.47 | 0.35 | 0.46 | 0.38 | 0.47 |
| Image output | 0.10 | 0.11 | 0.12 | 0.10 | 0.05 | 1.11 | 0.05 | 0.10 | 0.09 | 0.09 |
| Model input | 0.52 | 0.02 | 0.50 | 0.02 | 0.50 | 0.04 | 0.50 | 0.04 | 0.49 | 0.04 |
| Label connected components | 4.39 | 0.35 | 4.29 | 0.27 | 4.31 | 0.23 | 4.36 | 0.26 | 4.33 | 0.28 |
| Rectangles from intensity | 1.01 | 0.09 | 0.68 | 0.00 | 0.67 | 0.04 | 0.86 | 0.10 | 0.87 | 0.04 |
| Miscellaneous | 0.31 | 0.05 | 0.32 | 0.00 | 0.27 | 0.02 | 0.33 | 0.05 | 0.32 | 0.02 |
| Trace region boundary | 0.06 | 0.01 | 0.04 | 0.00 | 0.04 | 0.01 | 0.04 | 0.00 | 0.03 | 0.00 |
| K-curvature | 0.21 | 0.00 | 0.05 | 0.00 | 0.11 | 0.00 | 0.08 | 0.00 | 0.08 | 0.00 |
| K-curvature smoothing | 0.22 | 0.00 | 0.16 | 0.00 | 0.15 | 0.00 | 0.21 | 0.01 | 0.22 | 0.00 |
| First derivative | 0.12 | 0.00 | 0.09 | 0.00 | 0.06 | 0.00 | 0.14 | 0.00 | 0.08 | 0.00 |
| Zero-crossing detection | 0.04 | 0.01 | 0.01 | 0.00 | 0.00 | 0.01 | 0.02 | 0.00 | 0.04 | 0.00 |
| Final corner detection | 0.04 | 0.01 | 0.01 | 0.00 | 0.03 | 0.00 | 0.02 | 0.02 | 0.06 | 0.00 |
| Count corners | 0.00 | 0.00 | 0.00 | 0.00 | 0.00 | 0.00 | 0.00 | 0.00 | 0.00 | 0.02 |
| Convex hull | 0.00 | 0.00 | 0.00 | 0.00 | 0.00 | 0.00 | 0.01 | 0.01 | 0.00 | 0.00 |
| Test for right angles | 0.00 | 0.00 | 0.00 | 0.00 | 0.00 | 0.00 | 0.01 | 0.00 | 0.01 | 0.00 |
| Final rectangle hypothesis | 0.01 | 0.01 | 0.00 | 0.00 | 0.00 | 0.00 | 0.00 | 0.00 | 0.03 | 0.00 |
| Median filter | 30.33 | 0.20 | 14.47 | 0.17 | 11.14 | 0.16 | 11.16 | 0.14 | 11.15 | 0.19 |
| Sobel | 11.21 | 0.95 | 11.26 | 0.17 | 11.17 | 0.10 | 11.11 | 0.30 | 11.15 | 0.30 |

Table 6: Sun-4/260 Results

| | | | | | | | | | | |
|---|---|---|---|---|---|---|---|---|---|---|
| Initial graph match | 3.41 | 0.01 | 3.36 | 0.10 | 3.53 | 0.01 | 10.01 | 0.09 | 9.83 | 0.11 |
| Match data rectangles | 0.03 | 0.00 | 0.00 | 0.03 | 0.02 | 0.00 | 0.05 | 0.01 | 0.04 | 0.02 |
| Match links | 0.07 | 0.00 | 0.01 | 0.01 | 0.02 | 0.00 | 0.22 | 0.01 | 0.18 | 0.00 |
| Create probe list | 0.03 | 0.00 | 0.02 | 0.00 | 0.01 | 0.00 | 0.12 | 0.00 | 0.12 | 0.01 |
| Partial match | 3.28 | 0.01 | 3.33 | 0.06 | 3.48 | 0.01 | 9.62 | 0.07 | 9.49 | 0.08 |
| Match strength probes | 3.27 | 0.10 | 3.33 | 0.60 | 3.47 | 0.01 | 9.44 | 0.07 | 9.30 | 0.08 |
| Window selection | 0.00 | 0.00 | 0.01 | 0.00 | 0.00 | 0.00 | 0.01 | 0.00 | 0.04 | 0.01 |
| Classification and count | 3.15 | 0.00 | 3.23 | 0.06 | 3.38 | 0.01 | 8.85 | 0.05 | 8.65 | 0.02 |
| Match extension | 60.98 | 0.26 | 2.06 | 0.12 | 3.35 | 0.08 | 36.18 | 0.23 | 38.10 | 0.26 |
| Match strength probes | 9.89 | 0.02 | 0.45 | 0.00 | 0.79 | 0.00 | 6.63 | 0.02 | 6.06 | 0.02 |
| Window selection | 0.00 | 0.00 | 0.00 | 0.00 | 0.00 | 0.00 | 0.03 | 0.01 | 0.01 | 0.00 |
| Classification and count | 9.60 | 0.00 | 0.44 | 0.00 | 0.78 | 0.00 | 6.12 | 0.00 | 5.56 | 0.02 |
| Hough probes | 50.99 | 0.21 | 1.61 | 0.12 | 2.56 | 0.08 | 29.32 | 0.20 | 31.77 | 0.22 |
| Window selection | 0.03 | 0.00 | 0.00 | 0.00 | 0.01 | 0.00 | 0.09 | 0.01 | 0.07 | 0.00 |
| Hough transform | 50.65 | 0.12 | 1.60 | 0.11 | 2.54 | 0.07 | 28.86 | 0.08 | 31.32 | 0.12 |
| Edge peak detection | 0.15 | 0.00 | 0.01 | 0.00 | 0.01 | 0.00 | 0.24 | 0.02 | 0.21 | 0.00 |
| Rectangle parameter update | 0.03 | 0.01 | 0.00 | 0.00 | 0.00 | 0.00 | 0.03 | 0.01 | 0.06 | 0.00 |
| Result presentation | 3.37 | 0.01 | 1.67 | 0.00 | 2.24 | 0.00 | 2.07 | 0.00 | 2.02 | 0.00 |
| Best match selection | 0.06 | 0.00 | 0.02 | 0.00 | 0.02 | 0.00 | 0.10 | 0.00 | 0.04 | 0.00 |
| Image generation | 3.31 | 0.01 | 1.65 | 0.00 | 2.22 | 0.00 | 1.97 | 0.00 | 1.98 | 0.00 |

Table 6: (continued)

| Statistics | | | | | |
|---|---|---|---|---|---|
| Connected components | 134 | 35 | 34 | 114 | 100 |
| Right angles extracted | 126 | 99 | 92 | 210 | 197 |
| Rectangles detected | 25 | 21 | 16 | 42 | 39 |
| Depth pixels > threshold | 21254 | 14531 | 12892 | 18579 | 18822 |
| Elements on initial probe list | 381 | 19 | 27 | 389 | 248 |
| Hough probes | 55 | 3 | 5 | 93 | 92 |
| Initial match strength probes | 28 | 20 | 15 | 142 | 142 |
| Extension mat. str. probes | 60 | 3 | 5 | 105 | 97 |
| Models remaining | 2 | 1 | 1 | 2 | 1 |
| Model selected | 10 | 1 | 5 | 7 | 8 |
| Average match strength | 0.64 | 0.96 | 0.94 | 0.84 | 0.88 |
| Translated to | 151,240 | 256,256 | 257,255 | 257,255 | 257,255 |
| Rotated by (degrees) | 85 | 359 | 114 | 22 | 22 |

Table 6: (continued)

| Data Set | Sample | | Test1 | | Test2 | | Test3 | | Test4 | |
|---|---|---|---|---|---|---|---|---|---|---|
| | User | System | User | System | User | System | User | System | User | System |
| Total | 204.858 | 2.531 | 102.700 | 1.861 | 93.311 | 1.828 | 136.759 | 3.049 | 139.130 | 3.032 |
| Overhead | 7.968 | 0.776 | 7.925 | 0.777 | 7.897 | 0.775 | 7.900 | 0.764 | 7.895 | 0.763 |
| Miscellaneous | 0.627 | 0.030 | 0.585 | 0.033 | 0.559 | 0.033 | 0.554 | 0.030 | 0.554 | 0.031 |
| Startup | 0.030 | 0.031 | 0.029 | 0.033 | 0.029 | 0.031 | 0.029 | 0.032 | 0.029 | 0.029 |
| Image input | 5.692 | 0.515 | 5.691 | 0.051 | 5.691 | 0.505 | 5.697 | 0.509 | 5.690 | 0.504 |
| Image output | 1.039 | 0.175 | 1.039 | 0.179 | 1.038 | 0.183 | 1.039 | 0.171 | 1.040 | 0.177 |
| Model input | 0.580 | 0.021 | 0.058 | 0.017 | 0.580 | 0.018 | 0.580 | 0.017 | 0.580 | 0.019 |
| Label connected components | 16.917 | 0.268 | 16.830 | 0.258 | 16.800 | 0.253 | 16.948 | 0.247 | 16.930 | 0.259 |
| Rectangles from intensity | 2.760 | 0.590 | 1.791 | 0.267 | 1.874 | 0.252 | 2.312 | 0.681 | 2.286 | 0.643 |
| Miscellaneous | 1.005 | 0.231 | 0.928 | 0.097 | 0.931 | 0.094 | 0.986 | 0.255 | 0.983 | 0.239 |
| Trace region boundary | 0.312 | 0.078 | 0.172 | 0.021 | 0.183 | 0.019 | 0.255 | 0.062 | 0.221 | 0.054 |
| K-curvature | 0.592 | 0.037 | 0.287 | 0.017 | 0.308 | 0.017 | 0.438 | 0.045 | 0.432 | 0.045 |
| K-curvature smoothing | 0.362 | 0.037 | 0.176 | 0.018 | 0.188 | 0.017 | 0.269 | 0.045 | 0.264 | 0.044 |
| First derivative | 0.158 | 0.037 | 0.077 | 0.017 | 0.082 | 0.016 | 0.119 | 0.045 | 0.117 | 0.043 |
| Zero-crossing detection | 0.170 | 0.037 | 0.076 | 0.017 | 0.099 | 0.017 | 0.135 | 0.045 | 0.133 | 0.043 |
| Final corner detection | 0.135 | 0.042 | 0.060 | 0.022 | 0.069 | 0.022 | 0.103 | 0.051 | 0.101 | 0.049 |
| Count corners | 0.006 | 0.037 | 0.003 | 0.017 | 0.002 | 0.017 | 0.007 | 0.044 | 0.006 | 0.042 |
| Convex hull | 0.013 | 0.026 | 0.006 | 0.017 | 0.006 | 0.017 | 0.015 | 0.042 | 0.015 | 0.040 |
| Test for right angles | 0.006 | 0.013 | 0.005 | 0.011 | 0.004 | 0.009 | 0.009 | 0.022 | 0.008 | 0.021 |
| Final rectangle hypothesis | 0.003 | 0.013 | 0.003 | 0.011 | 0.002 | 0.009 | 0.006 | 0.022 | 0.005 | 0.021 |
| Median filter | 77.294 | 0.170 | 43.652 | 0.160 | 31.886 | 0.163 | 31.919 | 0.154 | 31.880 | 0.166 |

Table 7: Alliant FX-80 Single Processor Results

| | | | | | | | | | | |
|---|---|---|---|---|---|---|---|---|---|---|
| Sobel | 26.147 | 0.001 | 26.079 | -0.001 | 26.063 | 0.001 | 26.128 | 0.001 | 26.129 | 0.001 |
| Initial graph match | 2.458 | 0.088 | 2.397 | 0.063 | 2.569 | 0.055 | 7.117 | 0.368 | 7.011 | 0.373 |
| Match data rectangles | 0.067 | 0.023 | 0.051 | 0.012 | 0.046 | 0.014 | 0.129 | 0.047 | 0.111 | 0.041 |
| Match links | 0.067 | 0.002 | 0.024 | 0.004 | 0.022 | 0.004 | 0.262 | 0.013 | 0.214 | 0.023 |
| Create probe list | 0.002 | 0.001 | 0.002 | 0.001 | 0.002 | 0.001 | 0.005 | 0.001 | 0.006 | 0.003 |
| Partial match | 2.321 | 0.062 | 2.320 | 0.046 | 2.499 | 0.036 | 6.722 | 0.307 | 6.680 | 0.307 |
| Match strength probes | 2.305 | 0.045 | 2.303 | 0.032 | 2.486 | 0.024 | 6.502 | 0.228 | 6.429 | 0.229 |
| Window selection | 0.009 | 0.032 | 0.003 | 0.011 | 0.002 | 0.008 | 0.020 | 0.076 | 0.020 | 0.077 |
| Classification and count | 2.299 | 0.015 | 2.298 | 0.011 | 2.482 | 0.008 | 6.471 | 0.076 | 6.397 | 0.076 |
| Match extension | 68.025 | 0.385 | 2.149 | 0.083 | 3.817 | 0.091 | 42.243 | 0.600 | 44.806 | 0.584 |
| Match strength probes | 7.139 | 0.096 | 0.311 | 0.005 | 0.568 | 0.008 | 4.600 | 0.168 | 4.216 | 0.155 |
| Window selection | 0.009 | 0.032 | 0.000 | 0.002 | 0.001 | 0.003 | 0.15 | 0.056 | 0.014 | 0.052 |
| Classification and count | 7.125 | 0.032 | 0.310 | 0.002 | 0.566 | 0.003 | 4.576 | 0.056 | 4.193 | 0.052 |
| Hough probes | 60.754 | 0.202 | 1.833 | 0.068 | 3.241 | 0.071 | 37.330 | 0.301 | 40.320 | 0.312 |
| Window selection | 0.008 | 0.030 | 0.001 | 0.002 | 0.001 | 0.003 | 0.014 | 0.051 | 0.014 | 0.051 |
| Hough transform | 60.259 | 0.082 | 1.806 | 0.061 | 3.210 | 0.061 | 36.650 | 0.097 | 39.604 | 0.110 |
| Edge peak detection | 0.474 | 0.031 | 0.026 | 0.002 | 0.030 | 0.003 | 0.642 | 0.050 | 0.681 | 0.050 |
| Rectangle parameter update | 0.008 | 0.030 | 0.000 | 0.002 | 0.001 | 0.003 | 0.015 | 0.051 | 0.014 | 0.051 |
| Result presentation | 3.269 | 0.002 | 1.860 | 0.002 | 2.388 | 0.002 | 2.177 | 0.002 | 2.174 | 0.002 |
| Best match selection | 0.003 | 0.001 | 0.001 | 0.001 | 0.001 | 0.001 | 0.004 | 0.001 | 0.002 | 0.001 |
| Image generation | 3.266 | 0.001 | 1.859 | 0.001 | 2.387 | 0.001 | 2.174 | 0.001 | 2.172 | 0.001 |

Table 7: (continued)

| Statistics | | | | | |
|---|---|---|---|---|---|
| Connected components | 134 | 35 | 34 | 114 | 100 |
| Right angles extracted | 126 | 99 | 92 | 210 | 197 |
| Rectangles detected | 25 | 21 | 16 | 42 | 39 |
| Depth pixels > threshold | 21266 | 14542 | 12888 | 18572 | 18813 |
| Elements on initial probe list | 374 | 19 | 27 | 389 | 248 |
| Hough probes | 55 | 3 | 5 | 93 | 92 |
| Initial match strength probes | 28 | 20 | 15 | 142 | 142 |
| Extension mat. str. probes | 60 | 3 | 5 | 105 | 97 |
| Models remaining | 2 | 1 | 1 | 2 | 1 |
| Model selected | 10 | 1 | 5 | 7 | 8 |
| Average match strength | 0.65 | 0.96 | 0.94 | 0.84 | 0.88 |
| Translated to | 151,240 | 256,256 | 257,255 | 257,255 | 257,255 |
| Rotated by | 85 | 359 | 114 | 22 | 22 |

Table 7: (continued)

| Data Set | Sample | | Test1 | | Test2 | | Test3 | | Test4 | |
|---|---|---|---|---|---|---|---|---|---|---|
| | User | System | User | System | User | System | User | System | User | System |
| Total | 57.177 | 2.935 | 31.056 | 2.082 | 30.872 | 2.043 | 50.357 | 3.577 | 50.153 | 3.467 |
| Overhead | 7.940 | 0.847 | 7.903 | 0.825 | 7.897 | 0.813 | 7.891 | 0.820 | 7.899 | 0.822 |
| Miscellaneous | 0.601 | 0.042 | 0.558 | 0.039 | 0.558 | 0.039 | 0.553 | 0.041 | 0.560 | 0.058 |
| Startup | 0.030 | 0.056 | 0.029 | 0.047 | 0.029 | 0.042 | 0.029 | 0.043 | 0.029 | 0.033 |
| Image input | 5.690 | 0.549 | 5.695 | 0.541 | 5.691 | 0.532 | 5.690 | 0.542 | 5.690 | 0.536 |
| Image output | 1.039 | 0.173 | 1.040 | 0.172 | 1.038 | 0.177 | 1.039 | 0.173 | 1.039 | 0.173 |
| Model input | 0.580 | 0.023 | 0.580 | 0.021 | 0.580 | 0.017 | 0.580 | 0.017 | 0.580 | 0.017 |
| Label connected components | 6.930 | 0.295 | 6.864 | 0.272 | 6.849 | 0.270 | 6.979 | 0.273 | 6.992 | 0.272 |
| Rectangles from intensity | 2.776 | 0.686 | 1.799 | 0.314 | 1.882 | 0.295 | 2.329 | 0.785 | 2.309 | 0.751 |
| Miscellaneous | 1.010 | 0.277 | 0.931 | 0.120 | 0.934 | 0.113 | 0.994 | 0.303 | 0.990 | 0.290 |
| Trace region boundary | 0.312 | 0.084 | 0.172 | 0.023 | 0.183 | 0.022 | 0.227 | 0.071 | 0.224 | 0.063 |
| K-curvature | 0.594 | 0.042 | 0.287 | 0.020 | 0.308 | 0.019 | 0.438 | 0.051 | 0.433 | 0.049 |
| K-curvature smoothing | 0.364 | 0.042 | 0.176 | 0.019 | 0.189 | 0.019 | 0.270 | 0.052 | 0.267 | 0.050 |
| First derivative | 0.159 | 0.042 | 0.077 | 0.019 | 0.083 | 0.019 | 0.120 | 0.051 | 0.120 | 0.050 |
| Zero-crossing detection | 0.171 | 0.049 | 0.077 | 0.020 | 0.100 | 0.019 | 0.136 | 0.051 | 0.135 | 0.050 |
| Final corner detection | 0.136 | 0.048 | 0.060 | 0.028 | 0.070 | 0.025 | 0.103 | 0.057 | 0.130 | 0.055 |
| Count corners | 0.007 | 0.041 | 0.003 | 0.019 | 0.003 | 0.019 | 0.008 | 0.050 | 0.007 | 0.052 |
| Convex hull | 0.014 | 0.030 | 0.007 | 0.019 | 0.007 | 0.019 | 0.016 | 0.047 | 0.016 | 0.045 |
| Test for right angles | 0.006 | 0.016 | 0.005 | 0.013 | 0.004 | 0.010 | 0.010 | 0.025 | 0.009 | 0.023 |
| Final rectangle hypothesis | 0.004 | 0.015 | 0.003 | 0.013 | 0.002 | 0.010 | 0.007 | 0.026 | 0.005 | 0.023 |
| Median filter | 9.890 | 0.223 | 5.637 | 0.220 | 4.111 | 0.212 | 4.110 | 0.214 | 4.109 | 0.209 |

Table 8: Alliant FX-80 Results with Eight Processors

| | | | | | | | | | | |
|---|---|---|---|---|---|---|---|---|---|---|
| Sobel | 3.798 | 0.001 | 3.789 | 0.001 | 3.787 | 0.001 | 3.795 | 0.001 | 3.795 | 0.001 |
| Initial graph match | 2.455 | 0.123 | 2.399 | 0.094 | 2.569 | 0.086 | 7.130 | 0.485 | 7.014 | 0.459 |
| Match data rectangles | 0.068 | 0.048 | 0.052 | 0.028 | 0.046 | 0.033 | 0.131 | 0.102 | 0.112 | 0.083 |
| Match links | 0.068 | 0.004 | 0.024 | 0.009 | 0.022 | 0.009 | 0.263 | 0.030 | 0.213 | 0.020 |
| Create probe list | 0.002 | 0.001 | 0.002 | 0.001 | 0.002 | 0.001 | 0.005 | 0.001 | 0.006 | 0.004 |
| Partial match | 2.317 | 0.070 | 2.322 | 0.055 | 2.499 | 0.043 | 6.732 | 0.351 | 6.682 | 0.351 |
| Match strength probes | 2.301 | 0.050 | 2.304 | 0.037 | 2.485 | 0.027 | 6.509 | 0.259 | 6.429 | 0.263 |
| Window selection | 0.004 | 0.017 | 0.004 | 0.012 | 0.002 | 0.009 | 0.023 | 0.087 | 0.025 | 0.087 |
| Classification and count | 2.294 | 0.017 | 2.298 | 0.012 | 2.482 | 0.009 | 6.473 | 0.085 | 6.390 | 0.087 |
| Match extension | 20.105 | 0.455 | 0.786 | 0.107 | 1.376 | 0.122 | 15.926 | 0.739 | 15.845 | 0.702 |
| Match strength probes | 7.121 | 0.111 | 0.311 | 0.006 | 0.567 | 0.009 | 4.609 | 0.195 | 4.219 | 0.185 |
| Window selection | 0.010 | 0.037 | 0.001 | 0.002 | 0.001 | 0.003 | 0.019 | 0.065 | 0.016 | 0.065 |
| Classification and count | 7.105 | 0.037 | 0.310 | 0.002 | 0.565 | 0.003 | 4.580 | 0.066 | 4.193 | 0.060 |
| Hough probes | 12.847 | 0.243 | 0.468 | 0.086 | 0.799 | 0.099 | 10.996 | 0.378 | 11.350 | 0.366 |
| Window selection | 0.008 | 0.033 | 0.001 | 0.002 | 0.001 | 0.003 | 0.014 | 0.057 | 0.014 | 0.057 |
| Hough transform | 12.353 | 0.110 | 0.441 | 0.078 | 0.767 | 0.086 | 10.315 | 0.151 | 10.629 | 0.140 |
| Edge peak detection | 0.472 | 0.034 | 0.026 | 0.002 | 0.030 | 0.003 | 0.645 | 0.057 | 0.682 | 0.057 |
| Rectangle parameter update | 0.009 | 0.033 | 0.000 | 0.002 | 0.001 | 0.003 | 0.013 | 0.056 | 0.014 | 0.057 |
| Result presentation | 3.265 | 0.002 | 1.859 | 0.002 | 2.382 | 0.002 | 2.178 | 0.002 | 2.173 | 0.002 |
| Best match selection | 0.003 | 0.001 | 0.001 | 0.001 | 0.001 | 0.001 | 0.004 | 0.001 | 0.002 | 0.00 |
| Image generation | 3.262 | 0.001 | 1.858 | 0.001 | 2.381 | 0.001 | 2.174 | 0.001 | 2.171 | 0.001 |

Table 8: (continued)

| Statistics | | | | | |
|---|---|---|---|---|---|
| Connected components | 134 | 35 | 34 | 114 | 100 |
| Right angles extracted | 126 | 99 | 92 | 210 | 197 |
| Rectangles detected | 25 | 21 | 16 | 42 | 39 |
| Depth pixels > threshold | 21266 | 14542 | 12888 | 18572 | 18813 |
| Elements on initial probe list | 374 | 19 | 27 | 389 | 248 |
| Hough probes | 55 | 3 | 5 | 93 | 92 |
| Initial match strength probes | 28 | 20 | 15 | 142 | 142 |
| Extension mat. str. probes | 60 | 3 | 5 | 105 | 97 |
| Models remaining | 2 | 1 | 1 | 2 | 1 |
| Model selected | 10 | 1 | 5 | 7 | 8 |
| Average match strength | 0.65 | 0.96 | 0.94 | 0.84 | 0.88 |
| Translated to | 151,240 | 256,256 | 257,255 | 257,255 | 257,255 |
| Rotated by | 85 | 359 | 114 | 22 | 22 |

Table 8: (continued)

| Data Set | Sample | Test1 | Test2 | Test3 | Test4 |
|---|---|---|---|---|---|
| Total | 0.0844445 | 0.0455559 | 0.0455088 | 0.4180890 | 0.3978859 |
| Overhead | 0.0139435 | 0.0139435 | 0.0139435 | 0.0139435 | 0.0139435 |
| Miscellaneous | 0.0092279 | 0.0092279 | 0.0092279 | 0.0092279 | 0.0092279 |
| Startup | 0.0038682 | 0.0038682 | 0.0038682 | 0.0038682 | 0.0038682 |
| Image input | 0.0000020 | 0.0000020 | 0.0000020 | 0.0000020 | 0.0000020 |
| Image output | 0.0000020 | 0.0000020 | 0.0000020 | 0.0000020 | 0.0000020 |
| Model input | 0.0008302 | 0.0008302 | 0.0008302 | 0.0008302 | 0.0008302 |
| Label connected components | 0.0000596 | 0.0000596 | 0.0000596 | 0.0000596 | 0.0000596 |
| Rectangles from intensity | 0.0161694 | 0.0125489 | 0.0134704 | 0.0131378 | 0.0129635 |
| Miscellaneous | 0.0003227 | 0.0002421 | 0.0002010 | 0.0006216 | 0.0002421 |
| Trace region boundary | 0.0033792 | 0.0015472 | 0.0018672 | 0.0010912 | 0.0012832 |
| K-curvature | 0.0038256 | 0.0019936 | 0.0023136 | 0.0015376 | 0.0017296 |
| K-curvature smoothing | 0.0005525 | 0.0005525 | 0.0005525 | 0.0005525 | 0.0005525 |
| First derivative | 0.0003777 | 0.0003777 | 0.0003777 | 0.0003777 | 0.0003777 |
| Zero-crossing detection | 0.0000108 | 0.0000108 | 0.0000108 | 0.0000108 | 0.0000108 |
| Final corner detection | 0.0000118 | 0.0000118 | 0.0000118 | 0.0000118 | 0.0000118 |
| Count corners | 0.0000020 | 0.0000020 | 0.0000020 | 0.0000020 | 0.0000020 |
| Convex hull | 0.0036694 | 0.0019109 | 0.0015290 | 0.0025947 | 0.0026463 |
| Test for right angles | 0.0006122 | 0.0006009 | 0.0005906 | 0.0006421 | 0.0006421 |
| Final rectangle hypothesis | 0.0067877 | 0.0067877 | 0.0078821 | 0.0067877 | 0.0064229 |
| Median filter | 0.0005625 | 0.0005625 | 0.0005625 | 0.0005625 | 0.0005625 |

Table 9: Image Understanding Architecture Simulation Results

| | | | | | |
|---|---|---|---|---|---|
| Sobel | 0.0026919 | 0.0026919 | 0.0026919 | 0.0026919 | 0.0026919 |
| Initial graph match | 0.0121876 | 0.0076429 | 0.0066834 | 0.1124236 | 0.0822296 |
| Match data rectangles | 0.0029096 | 0.0015672 | 0.0013264 | 0.0134885 | 0.0106136 |
| Match links | 0.0088872 | 0.0056950 | 0.0049762 | 0.0985542 | 0.0712324 |
| Create probe list | 0.0000968 | 0.0001299 | 0.0001130 | 0.0009252 | 0.0008618 |
| Partial match | 0.0033786 | 0.0077033 | 0.0068704 | 0.1828976 | 0.1534418 |
| Match strength probes | 0.0009275 | 0.0011460 | 0.0012285 | 0.0025175 | 0.0212640 |
| Window selection | 0.0002100 | 0.0003000 | 0.0002700 | 0.0005700 | 0.0004800 |
| Classification and count | 0.0001043 | 0.0001490 | 0.0001341 | 0.0002831 | 0.0002384 |
| Match extension | 0.0300650 | 0.0017674 | 0.0024856 | 0.0899214 | 0.1277396 |
| Match strength probes | 0.0026500 | 0.0001146 | 0.0004095 | 0.0543250 | 0.0071766 |
| Window selection | 0.0006000 | 0.0000300 | 0.0000900 | 0.0012300 | 0.0016200 |
| Classification and count | 0.0002980 | 0.0000149 | 0.0000447 | 0.0006109 | 0.0008046 |
| Hough probes | 0.0068430 | 0.0003251 | 0.0005092 | 0.0084591 | 0.0109868 |
| Window selection | 0.0000675 | 0.0000045 | 0.0000090 | 0.0001755 | 0.0002385 |
| Hough transform | 0.0053010 | 0.0002223 | 0.0003036 | 0.0044499 | 0.0053477 |
| Edge peak detection | 0.0011745 | 0.0000783 | 0.0001566 | 0.0030537 | 0.0041499 |
| Rectangle parameter update | 0.0003000 | 0.0000200 | 0.0000400 | 0.0007800 | 0.0010600 |
| Result presentation | 0.0022826 | 0.0009452 | 0.0011944 | 0.0029768 | 0.0029766 |
| Best match selection | 0.0000404 | 0.0000403 | 0.0000405 | 0.0000406 | 0.0000397 |
| Image generation | 0.0022352 | 0.0009185 | 0.0011396 | 0.0029464 | 0.0029464 |

Table 9: (continued)

| Statistics | | | | | |
|---|---|---|---|---|---|
| Connected components | 134 | 35 | 34 | 114 | 100 |
| Right angles extracted | | | | | |
| Rectangles detected | 31 | 23 | 19 | 60 | 55 |
| Depth pixels > threshold | | | | | |
| Elements on initial probe list | | | | | |
| Hough probes | 44 | 5 | 8 | 84 | 100 |
| Initial match strength probes | 24 | 20 | 15 | 81 | 80 |
| Extension mat. str. probes | 20 | 1 | 3 | 41 | 54 |
| Models remaining | 3 | 1 | 1 | 2 | 1 |
| Model selected | 10 | 1 | 5 | 7 | 8 |
| Average match strength | 0.45 | 0.86 | 0.84 | 0.81 | 0.84 |
| Translated to | 151,240 | 256,256 | 257,255 | 257,255 | 257,255 |
| Rotated by | 85 | 359 | 113 | 23 | 23 |

Table 9: (continued)

| Data Set | Sample | Test1 | Test2 | Test3 | Test4 |
|---|---|---|---|---|---|
| Total | 0.1307200 | 0.0359600 | 0.0398100 | 0.1130700 | 0.1188200 |
| Overhead | 0.0008200 | 0.0008200 | 0.0008000 | 0.0008000 | 0.0008000 |
| Miscellaneous | 0.0002560 | 0.0002560 | 0.0002560 | 0.0002560 | 0.0002560 |
| Startup | | | | | |
| Image input | 0.0000512 | 0.0000512 | 0.0000512 | 0.0000512 | 0.0000512 |
| Image output | 0.0000512 | 0.0000512 | 0.0000512 | 0.0000512 | 0.0000512 |
| Model input | | | | | |
| Label connected components | 0.0392000 | 0.0228000 | 0.0228000 | 0.0348000 | 0.0313000 |
| Rectangles from intensity | 0.0033100 | 0.0029200 | 0.0028800 | 0.0031900 | 0.003350 |
| Miscellaneous | 0.0000761 | 0.0000860 | 0.0000842 | 0.0000795 | 0.0000734 |
| Trace region boundary | 0.0000047 | 0.0000047 | 0.0000047 | 0.0000047 | 0.0000047 |
| K-curvature | 0.0007800 | 0.0007800 | 0.0007800 | 0.0007800 | 0.0007800 |
| K-curvature smoothing | 0.0004500 | 0.0004500 | 0.0004500 | 0.0004500 | 0.0004500 |
| First derivative | 0.0000320 | 0.0000320 | 0.0000320 | 0.0000320 | 0.0000320 |
| Zero-crossing detection | 0.0000045 | 0.0000045 | 0.0000045 | 0.0000045 | 0.0000045 |
| Final corner detection | 0.0000018 | 0.0000018 | 0.0000018 | 0.0000018 | 0.0000018 |
| Count corners | 0.0000400 | 0.0000380 | 0.0000380 | 0.0000530 | 0.0000380 |
| Convex hull | 0.0003300 | 0.0002820 | 0.0002820 | 0.0003300 | 0.0003300 |
| Test for right angles | 0.0008800 | 0.0008400 | 0.0008400 | 0.0009500 | 0.0009200 |
| Final rectangle hypothesis | 0.0004500 | 0.0003800 | 0.0002900 | 0.0007600 | 0.0007000 |
| Median filter | 0.0007200 | 0.0007200 | 0.0005100 | 0.0006100 | 0.0005100 |

Table 10: Aspex ASP Simulation Results

| | | | | | |
|---|---|---|---|---|---|
| Sobel | 0.0006240 | 0.0006240 | 0.0006240 | 0.0006800 | 0.0006240 |
| Initial graph match | 0.0000090 | 0.0000090 | 0.0000090 | 0.0000090 | 0.0000080 |
| Match data rectangles | | | | | |
| Match links | | | | | |
| Create probe list | | | | | |
| Partial match | | | | | |
| Match strength probes | | | | | |
| Window selection | 0.0001200 | 0.0001320 | 0.0001080 | 0.0005500 | 0.0006400 |
| Classification and count | 0.0009500 | 0.0008850 | 0.0008650 | 0.0015400 | 0.0016000 |
| Match extension | 0.0835200 | 0.0001470 | 0.0001400 | 0.0002650 | 0.0002590 |
| Match strength probes | | | | | |
| Window selection | 0.0003000 | 0.0000240 | 0.0000360 | 0.0009200 | 0.0009800 |
| Classification and count | 0.0030000 | 0.0004050 | 0.0003520 | 0.0047200 | 0.0054500 |
| Hough probes | | | | | |
| Window selection | 0.0002880 | 0.0000240 | 0.0000360 | 0.0005800 | 0.0007300 |
| Hough transform | 0.0790000 | 0.0054000 | 0.0104000 | 0.0610000 | 0.0690000 |
| Edge peak detection | 0.0007700 | 0.0000640 | 0.0000990 | 0.0015400 | 0.0017600 |
| Rectangle parameter update | 0.0002160 | 0.0000090 | 0.0000100 | 0.0002340 | 0.0002360 |
| Result presentation | 0.0008500 | 0.0004400 | 0.0004700 | 0.0004700 | 0.0010300 |
| Best match selection | 0.0000250 | 0.0000150 | 0.0000150 | 0.0000280 | 0.0000150 |
| Image generation | 0.0007200 | 0.0003200 | 0.0003500 | 0.0008400 | 0.0009100 |

Table 10: (continued)

| Data Set | Sample | | Test1 | | Test2 | | Test3 | | Test4 | |
|---|---|---|---|---|---|---|---|---|---|---|
| | Single | Eight | Single | Eight | Single | Nine | Single | Eight | Single | Nine |
| Total | 889.66 | 251.33 | 300.34 | 73.88 | 282.71 | 77.87 | 562.15 | 174.96 | 578.14 | 139.72 |
| Overhead | 5.84 | 6.00 | 5.57 | 5.93 | 5.62 | 5.87 | 5.75 | 5.86 | 5.65 | 5.90 |
| System time | 3.60 | 9.40 | 2.00 | 5.40 | 2.10 | 6.40 | 2.80 | 7.60 | 2.90 | 8.80 |
| Label conn. components | 19.27 | 12.68 | 19.34 | 15.83 | 19.29 | 16.01 | 19.60 | 16.84 | 19.58 | 16.89 |
| Rectangles from intensity | 4.18 | 1.45 | 2.62 | 0.92 | 2.74 | 1.92 | 3.42 | 1.42 | 3.38 | 1.89 |
| Median filter | 239.24 | 31.00 | 114.12 | 15.25 | 85.81 | 11.08 | 85.83 | 11.45 | 85.79 | 11.11 |
| Sobel | 110.89 | 15.00 | 113.21 | 15.46 | 110.80 | 14.83 | 110.84 | 15.20 | 110.81 | 14.73 |
| Initial graph match | 18.52 | 3.08 | 18.53 | 3.76 | 19.90 | 4.35 | 52.53 | 7.21 | 51.63 | 7.17 |
| Match data rectangles | 0.17 | 0.04 | 0.11 | 0.03 | 0.09 | 0.03 | 0.26 | 0.13 | 0.22 | 0.06 |
| Match links | 0.19 | 0.24 | 0.06 | 0.20 | 0.06 | 0.65 | 0.74 | 0.29 | 0.59 | 0.78 |
| Create probe list | 0.01 | 0.00 | 0.01 | 0.01 | 0.01 | 0.01 | 0.01 | 0.01 | 0.01 | 0.01 |
| Partial match | 18.15 | 2.80 | 18.35 | 3.52 | 19.74 | 3.66 | 51.52 | 6.78 | 50.81 | 6.32 |
| Match extension | 470.90 | 161.34 | 16.16 | 5.97 | 24.08 | 9.38 | 271.07 | 103.99 | 288.21 | 69.10 |
| Result presentation | 20.82 | 20.78 | 10.80 | 10.76 | 14.47 | 14.43 | 13.11 | 12.99 | 13.09 | 12.93 |

Table 11: Sequent Symmetry 81 Results

| Statistics | | | | |
|---|---|---|---|---|
| Connected components | 34 | 33 | 113 | 99 |
| Right angles extracted | 99 | 92 | 210 | 197 |
| Rectangles detected | 21 | 16 | 42 | 39 |
| Depth pixels > threshold | 14533 | 12891 | 18582 | 18817 |
| Elements on initial probe list | | | | |
| Hough probes | 3 | 5 | 97 | 93 |
| Initial match strength probes | 20 | 15 | 142 | 142 |
| Extension mat. str. probes | 3 | 5 | 110 | 97 |
| Models remaining | 1 | 1 | 2 | 1 |
| Model selected | 1 | 5 | 7 | 8 |
| Average match strength | 0.96 | 0.93 | 0.84 | 0.87 |
| Translated to | 256,256 | 257,255 | 257,255 | 257,255 |
| Rotated by | 359 | 114 | 22 | 22 |

Table 10: (continued)

| Data Set | Sample | Test1 | Test2 | Test3 | Test4 |
|---|---|---|---|---|---|
| Total | 43.60 | 20.30 | 22.30 | 58.10 | 55.30 |
| System | 3.00 | 2.30 | 2.50 | 4.30 | 4.90 |
| Overhead | | | | | |
| Miscellaneous | 3.56 | 2.24 | 2.30 | 5.52 | 7.30 |
| Startup | 5.76 | 6.04 | 5.96 | 5.88 | 6.00 |
| Image input | 3.52 | 3.72 | 5.40 | 5.34 | 5.34 |
| Image output | | | | | |
| Model input | 1.30 | 1.18 | 1.02 | 1.08 | 1.06 |
| Label connected components | 3.98 | 4.04 | 4.60 | 4.54 | 4.56 |
| Rectangles from intensity | | | | | |
| Miscellaneous | | | | | |
| Trace region boundary | | | | | |
| K-curvature | 3.14 | 2.24 | 2.20 | 2.272 | 2.54 |
| K-curvature smoothing | 1.38 | 0.64 | 0.78 | 0.98 | 0.90 |
| First derivative | 0.42 | 0.24 | 0.28 | 0.34 | 0.40 |
| Zero-crossing detection | 0.32 | 0.06 | 0.12 | 0.14 | 0.22 |
| Final corner detection | 0.16 | 0.10 | 0.12 | 0.22 | 0.20 |
| Count corners | 0.02 | 0.02 | 0.04 | 0.06 | 0.06 |
| Convex hull | 0.02 | 0.00 | 0.02 | 0.08 | 0.06 |

Table 12: Results for the Warp

| | | | | | |
|---|---|---|---|---|---|
| Test for right angles | 0.00 | 0.00 | 0.02 | 0.02 | 0.02 |
| Final rectangle hypothesis | 0.04 | 0.00 | 0.02 | 0.02 | 0.04 |
| Median filter | 10.70 | 8.70 | 1.38 | 1.40 | 2.00 |
| Sobel | 0.48 | 0.48 | 0.72 | 0.94 | 0.92 |
| Initial graph match | 0.42 | 0.24 | 0.22 | 1.22 | 1.38 |
| Match data rectangles | 0.20 | 0.16 | 0.16 | 0.40 | 0.68 |
| Match links | 0.22 | 0.08 | 0.06 | 0.82 | 0.70 |
| Create probe list | | | | | |
| Partial match | | | | | |
| Match strength probes | | | | | |
| Window selection | | | | | |
| Classification and count | | | | | |
| Match extension | 24.80 | 3.64 | 4.58 | 38.60 | 41.20 |
| Match strength probes | 9.10 | 2.64 | 2.86 | 13.60 | 13.50 |
| Window selection | 0.02 | 0.02 | 0.02 | 0.24 | 0.18 |
| Classification and count | 9.00 | 2.56 | 2.82 | 13.20 | 13.10 |
| | | | | | |

Table 12: (continued)

| | | | | | |
|---|---|---|---|---|---|
| Hough probes | 15.30 | 0.96 | 1.68 | 23.30 | 25.80 |
| Window selection | 0.02 | 0.00 | 0.02 | 0.12 | 0.06 |
| Hough transform | 12.80 | 0.88 | 1.44 | 19.30 | 20.00 |
| Edge peak detection | 2.38 | 0.08 | 0.22 | 3.80 | 5.58 |
| Rectangle parameter update | 0.02 | 0.00 | 0.00 | 0.00 | 0.08 |
| Result presentation | 2.60 | 2.26 | 2.52 | 2.24 | 2.26 |
| Best match selection | 0.02 | 0.00 | 0.00 | 0.02 | 0.02 |
| Image generation | 2.54 | 2.20 | 2.46 | 2.16 | 2.18 |
| | | | | | |
| | | | | | |
| | | | | | |
| Statistics | | | | | |
| Total match strength probes | 91 | 23 | 20 | 247 | 239 |
| Hough probes | 58 | 3 | 5 | 97 | 95 |

Table 12: (continued)

| Configuration | 8K | 16K | 32K | 64K |
|---|---|---|---|---|
| | | | | |
| Total (low level tasks only) | 1.26 | 0.91 | 0.71 | 0.63 |
| Overhead | | | | |
| Miscellaneous | | | | |
| Startup | 0.10 | 0.10 | 0.10 | 0.10 |
| Image input | 0.155 | 0.155 | 0.155 | 0.155 |
| Image output | | | | |
| Model input | | | | |
| Label connected components | 0.34 | 0.21 | 0.14 | 0.10 |
| Rectangles from intensity | | | | |
| Miscellaneous | | | | |
| Trace region boundary | 0.44 | 0.30 | 0.23 | 0.17 |
| K-curvature | 0.019 | 0.019 | 0.018 | 0.018 |
| K-curvature smoothing | 0.0056 | 0.0055 | 0.0062 | 0.0055 |
| First derivative | 0.00038 | 0.00037 | 0.00037 | 0.00037 |
| Zero-crossing detection | 0.00021 | 0.00020 | 0.00019 | 0.00019 |
| Final corner detection | 0.0058 | 0.0053 | 0.0053 | 0.0053 |
| Count corners | 0.018 | 0.016 | 0.016 | 0.016 |
| Convex hull | 0.041 | 0.038 | 0.039 | 0.038 |
| Test for right angles | | | | |
| Final rectangle hypothesis | | | | |
| Median filter | 0.082 | 0.041 | 0.025 | 0.015 |
| Sobel | 0.052 | 0.026 | 0.014 | 0.008 |

Table 13: Results for the Connection Machine on the Low-Level Portion

| Configuration | 1 | | 2 | | 4 | | 8 | | 16 | |
|---|---|---|---|---|---|---|---|---|---|---|
| | User | System | User | System | User | System | User | System | User | System |
| Median Filter | | | | | | | | | | |
| Sample | 176.47 | 0.00 | 87.93 | 11.52 | 43.46 | 11.23 | 22.27 | 3.1 | 11.14 | 3.82 |
| Test | 75.45 | 0.00 | 37.72 | 10.88 | 18.99 | 10.84 | 9.66 | 3.15 | 4.84 | 3.87 |
| Test2 | 60.84 | 0.00 | 30.36 | 11.48 | 15.25 | 11.45 | 7.63 | 3.73 | 3.81 | 4.19 |
| Test3 | 60.83 | 0.00 | 30.36 | 11.12 | 15.25 | 11.23 | 7.63 | 3.49 | 3.82 | 4.03 |
| Sobel | | | | | | | | | | |
| Sample | 78.63 | 0.00 | 39.32 | 3.53 | 19.68 | 3.00 | 9.84 | 2.37 | 4.92 | 2.91 |
| Test | 80.82 | 0.00 | 40.42 | 3.47 | 20.25 | 2.89 | 10.15 | 2.43 | 5.10 | 2.82 |
| Test2 | 80.82 | 0.00 | 40.42 | 1.46 | 20.25 | 1.99 | 10.15 | 1.87 | 5.10 | 2.50 |
| Test3 | 78.63 | 0.00 | 39.31 | 2.62 | 19.68 | 2.51 | 9.84 | 2.17 | 4.92 | 2.69 |

Table 14: iPSC-2 Results for Median Filter and Sobel Steps

# Part IV

# Software Environments

# Software Computer Vision Environments for Parallel Computers

**ANTHONY P. REEVES**
*School of Electrical Engineering*
*Cornell University*
*Ithaca, New York*

## 1 Introduction

The high computation requirements and the real-time constraints associated with computer vision applications have resulted in considerable interest in the utilization of parallel computing resources. Most computer vision applications may be considered to involve two main computation phases: an image preprocessing phase and an object identification phase. Although both phases typically involve large amounts of computation they embody different computation paradigms. Highly parallel, special-purpose hardware has been developed for a number of computer vision applications, especially for low-level image processing. Of current interest is how heterogeneous multicomputer systems can be effectively used for computer vision applications.

The central issues for efficient use of parallel resources are the decomposition of the tasks into appropriate subtasks and distribution of these tasks to the appropriate computation resource. There are two fundamental approaches to the task decomposition issue for parallel processing: functional decomposition and data partitioning.

Many current software systems for computer vision are already organized in a functional manner and it is reasonably simple to ex-

Parallel Architectures and
Algorithms for
Image Understanding





ISBN 0-12-564040-4

tend such systems to the functional decomposition approach. We discuss this approach in the context of the VISIX software system for computer vision. VISIX is a portable computer vision software environment that has been used for a number of years on serial computers for research applications.

The data-partitioning approach typically involves significant additional programming organization. A high-level environment for multicomputer systems called Paragon will be discussed, which has facilities for both the function decomposition and data-partitioning paradigms.

Current parallel programming environments are at an early stage of development. Interprocessor data management is specified by explicit mechanisms to transfer messages or to share data. The challenge for utilizing highly parallel multicomputer systems is to implement architecture-specific functions, such as data distribution and dynamic load balancing, without requiring the programmer to know the detailed organization of the available parallel resources.

The remainder of this paper is organized in four main sections. Section 2 considers the VISIX computer vision system, and in section 3 an example of an application implemented with VISIX in a functional decomposition parallel environment is presented. Section 4 outlines the concepts of Paragon, a parallel programming environment that supports data partitioning, and, in section 5, Paragon program features are illustrated with program segments that implement several basic image-processing functions.

## 2 The VISIX System

VISIX is a UNIX-based software computer vision system. It is typical of many visions systems that have been developed for computer applications on conventional serial computers. The initial version of VISIX was designed to provide three services: a library of computer vision algorithms, programming tools for developing new vision algorithms, and convenient access to special image-oriented computer devices [5, 4, 1].

The algorithm library is realized by a set of compiled programs that share a common set of protocols for parameter specification and data format. In general, these programs are written in conventional C or FORTRAN with programming tools for parameter parsing and data access. VISIX takes advantage of UNIX features such that any program may be used as a *filter*; that is, as an element of a pipeline of concurrent processes. Furthermore, a number of algorithms are implemented by command scripts (shell files) that invoke a number of simpler VISIX programs; this gives the appearance to the user of a single program although the implementation involves a set of interacting concurrent processes.

A consistent command line syntax is used for all VISIX programs. If a VISIX program is to be used with a non-VISIX data file, then all needed file header information may be specified on the command line.

## 2.1 VISIX Functions

The VISIX system involves over 200 program modules some of which are simply shell files that invoke a number of other modules. The general philosophy is to encapsulate single functions in a simple module rather than develop complex modules that contain a number of orthogonal or partitionable functions. We can categorize the image-processing modules of VISIX by the functions they perform. This breakdown for the current version of VISIX follows; the numbers in parentheses (after the functions) indicate the number of modules of that type:

1. image pixel operations (16): These operate on the individual pixels of the image. Examples include image thresholding and histogram equalization;

2. image filter operations (18): each of these involves using a small window operator on each pixel's local neighborhood. Examples of these operations include convolution and edge detection.

3. image transform operations (24): these transforms compute each output element as a function of a large number of input elements. These operations include the FFT and the radon

transform which are statically organized, and the Hough transform and image warping, in which the computation is data-dependent;

4. feature extraction operations (32): these functions reduce image data to a different feature form (for example, computing moment feature vectors to represent image segments). Typically, the result from one of these functions is a feature vector rather than an image matrix;

5. feature processing operations (24): these operations perform some processing on feature vectors; both data input and output are usually in the form of feature vectors. Typical operations for this class include normalization for translation and rotation, etc., and object matching.

## 2.2 Data Structures

In most vision systems image data files are usually organized by an initial header data structure that contains size and other image parameters, followed by the image data, which are typically a large matrix of pixels. In VISIX the header information includes the image size, the pixel format, the number of channels in the image, and the sequence of commands that were used to generate the file. This information is used by VISIX programs to check the file format and to set up the appropriate memory allocation. An appropriate header is generated for each output file.

Experience with VISIX has led to the following set of file formats:

1. Image formats: The image is considered as a two-dimensional matrix; pixel formats include bit, signed byte, unsigned byte, integer, and real. An image may have multiple channels, for example, red, green, and blue; channels may be interleaved by pixel, by row, or by image;

2. Fixed length features: Feature vector files frequently contain description information of different image regions. For example, image regions may be represented by the set of fourth order

moments. Each feature vector consists of subheader that contains information such as the location and class of the image region, and a data section that contains the feature information;

3. Variable length features: The variable length format is similar to the fixed-length format except that the length of each vector data segment may be different; each vector is preceded with its vector length. This is useful for image features such as a boundary chain code where the number of data elements depends on the perimeter of the image region;

4. Image sets: The concept of an image set is to have a sequence of image (or sets of feature vectors) in a single file structure. This is especially useful for temporal sequences of data.

These data structures have been found conveniently to cover most computer vision applications. Two other formats that are currently being developed are for computer graphics and for relational graphs.

## 2.3 Parallel Execution

The filter capability of VISIX programs offers a simple, direct method of using parallel resources in a UNIX environment. Using the standard UNIX command line syntax, it is possible to set up a pipeline of concurrent processes that may automatically take advantage of any available parallel resources. A VISIX addition to the UNIX shell facility enables a pair of pipelines to be merged into a third pipeline.

A useful feature of VISIX is the ability to process a set of images of unknown length using the image set data format. It is simple to set up a pipeline of processing stages that processes images as they become available. In this way, the process setup time is avoided for each image after the first.

Early parallel experiments with VISIX centered on a network of distributed computers [4][1]. A problem with pipelines that span different computers is that the internal data representation of these machines may be different. One of the parameters in the VISIX data header specifies the machine on which the data created. In this way,

| Operation | Time (secs.) | | Input data |
|---|---|---|---|
| | set-up | each image | each image |
| Preprocessing | 1.5 | 1.5 | 10,000 |
| Threshold and Moment generation | 0.9 | 4.1 | 10,000 |
| Moment normalization | 0.6 | 0.1 | 300 |
| Vector reduction | 0.5 | 0.01 | 300 |
| Vector balancing | 0.4 | 0.1 | 300 |
| Object matching | 17.5 | 9.5 | 300 |
| Result analysis (type, location, orientation) | 2.5 | 2.5 | 80 |

Table 1: An object-recognition example.

automatic data format conversions between different machine types are possible. More recent work that has focused on a multicomputer environment is discussed in the next section.

# 3 A Functional Decomposition Example

A simple object-recognition application implemented with VISIX modules has been tested on a number of different parallel multicomputer environments to demonstrate the method of function distribution. The task of the application is to identify a set of airplane images [6]. Each input to the system consists of a $96 \times 96$ image of a single object (an airplane). In the experiment a sequence of several hundred images in a VISIX image-set file was processed by a seven-stage pipeline of VISIX modules. The functions of these stages and the times that they required are shown in Table 1.

The image preprocessing consisted of a local mean filter. From Table 1, we see that the time to set up this module is initially 1.5 seconds and that then the time to process each $96 \times 96$ image is 1.5 seconds. These times are for a single processor of an Encore Multimax computer. The second stage computes the moments of the image region greater than a preset threshold (the airplane object), then the third stage normalizes this moment set with respect to size,

| Condition | Time (secs.) | |
|---|---|---|
| | set-up | each image |
| Single processor | 25 | 18.0 |
| Four processors | 24 | 9.8 |
| Four proc. and partitioned matching | 13 | 5.6 |
| Four proc. plus hypercube | 40 | 4.3 |

Table 2: Multicomputer Object Recognition Performance

location, and in-plane rotation. The fourth stage simply selects a subset of the normalized moments to be used for object identification. The fifth stage performs *variance balancing* for each moment vector, which is a normalization procedure based on the statistics of the object model database. Object matching is performed by a nearest neighbor match of the object's feature vector to a data base of 3000 precomputed vectors. A large setup time is required for this stage to read in the object data base. Finally, the best match is used to determine the type and orientation of the object in the image.

The last column in Table 1 gives the number of bytes that enter the given module for each image. For the first stages a large amount of information is needed to represent the raw image data. The amount of processing for each element is relatively small and the data transfer rate is a significant consideration. However, once the object region has been reduced to feature vector form, it may be represented by much less information and the data transfer rate is of much less importance. This behavior is typical of many computer vision applications.

The results of running this demonstration experiment on a number of multicomputer configurations are given in Table 2.

The first test involved running all modules on a single Encore processor. The result is very close to adding the times given for the individual stages given in Table 1. For the second test a UNIX pipeline was set up on a four-processor Encore Multimax; task scheduling was performed by the standard Encore UNIX system. The speed-up for this case was approximately two rather than the optimal four. This was due to the time required for the slowest stage (object matching). Since this stage involves an exhaustive search, it was simple to partition it into a pipeline of four stages, each of which was assigned one quarter of the object data-base. The results for the partitioned matching in Table 2 show that the speed-up is now about 3.2. For a final demonstration, the matching stage was partitioned into 32 stages and assigned to an Intel hypercube with 32 nodes. The total time for each image is now only slightly larger that for the remaining slowest stage on the Encore (moment generation).

This experiment demonstrates that a limited amount of speed-up may be simply achieved by using functional decomposition and parallel resources. However, a requirement for speed-up is that the application must decompose into a large number of functional components that have similar time requirements; the system is constrained by the speed of the slowest stage. This pipeline organization may be highly appropriate when a heterogeneous set of parallel resources are available. For example, it might be possible to augment a shared memory multicomputer with a highly parallel processor array for image preprocessing and feature extraction, and a special function processor for shape matching.

# 4 The Paragon Programming Environment

Conventional vision systems, as outlined in the previous sections, are able directly to take advantage of a limited amount of parallel resources. However, additional capabilities are necessary to take advantage of emerging, more highly parallel, computing resources.

Paragon is an experimental programming environment which is intended for the convenient and efficient programming of such resources. It consists of a programming language, that permits algorithms that naturally exhibit data parallelism to be more conveniently expressed, together with a run-time environment, which permits the task-management strategies to be adapted to the available parallel computer resources.

Paragon is designed to be an efficient programming environment for a wide range of parallel computer systems, especially homogeneous and heterogeneous multicomputer systems. It incorporates features of the task manager in the run-time environment, but its language also attempts to provide semantic constructs that permit the programmer to specify task management information at a high level. The key new features of the Paragon paradigm are as follows:

1. clear language semantics that do not require the overspecification typical of conventional serial languages;

2. facilities for the programmer to specify task-management information at the problem level without explicit references to hardware features;

3. a sophisticated run-time environment that may embody concepts of task management, dynamic load balancing, fault tolerance, and possibly some automatic algorithm selection.

The goals of Paragon are considered in more detail in [3]. An initial implementation has been developed for Paragon that currently runs on serial processors, the Intel iPSC/2 hypercube and on transputer networks. The first Paragon language is based on the SIMD model of computation and is implemented, for convenience, by a C++ package. Two novel concepts of the current Paragon environment are the use of *array shapes*, which is a data abstraction used to construct distributed array data structures, and a *rectangular block* data partitioning strategy that permits efficient run-time array data redistribution. These are considered in more detail in the following two sections. Further details of the current Paragon implementation and these novel features are given in [2].

## 4.1 Task Management

The decomposition of a problem into a set of subtasks and the effective management of these subtasks are unique features of software environments for multicomputer systems. The classical serial environment consists of two major components: the user program and the operating system, as outlined below.

1. *The user program:* Typically, the user develops a program in a high-level language. This program specifies the implementation of an algorithm without regard to the hardware details

of the system; device management is performed by explicit or implicit calls to the operating system. Special hardware utilization is achieved by means of optional special constructs in the programming language, such as vector instructions to take advantage of a pipelined vector processor.

2. *The Operating System*: The main functions of the operating system are to manage the sharing of resources between different tasks and to provide device access, through system calls, to these tasks.

On multicomputer systems *task management* is necessary. This consists of four main functions: *task decomposition, subtask allocation, subtask scheduling,* and *subtask communication*. Task decomposition on a conventional multiuser distributed system is achieved by the multiplicity of processes generated by the different users; it is not necessary to decompose these processes into smaller units. There is little interdependency among these processes and the operating system can perform all the other task management functions; no special programming language constructs are necessary. On a parallel system that supports a single application, effective task decomposition of the application into a number of subtasks, which may be highly interdependent, is a much more difficult problem. It is not clear if this decomposition should be the responsibility of the operating system or the user.

New programming environments need to be developed, which can take full advantage of multicomputer resources for single-user scientific applications. Such systems should have provisions for graceful fault tolerance, dynamic load balancing, automatic algorithm selection, and automatic task decomposition and allocation.

## 4.2 Array Shapes

At the programming language level, the Paragon *shape* is similar in concept to an array type with the difference that the former does not have an associated base type. When a distributed array, called a *parray*, is declared, it must be identified with both a shape and a base type. Semantically, the shape has a more important significance in that it also specifies the distribution of the parray data across the parallel processing resources. All parrays that are declared for a given shape will have the same data distribution. If at run-time a shape is redistributed, then all its derived parrays must also be redistributed, although, in some cases, a lazy redistribution policy may be possible. Array shapes may be defined based on other array shapes, but such derived shapes are not required to have the same distribution strategy. Assignments between parrays based on different shapes are permitted if the shapes are compatible. To be compatible, two shapes must specify the same number of array dimensions and corresponding dimensions must be of the same size; however, the shapes may have different distributions.

Explicit distribution of shapes can be used to specify data transfers between resources. For example, if the shape of one parray is specified to be located on a file device and the shape of a second parray specifies a distribution on a set of processors, then an assignment between these two parrays will have the effect of moving the data between the file device and the processors. This mechanism can be used for both file I/O and for explicitly moving data between different processing resources.

## 4.3 Rectangular Block Partitioning

The distribution of parrays in Paragon on the hypercube and transputer testbeds currently involves a rectangular block strategy. This strategy affects only the first two dimensions of a parray, which are the distributed dimensions. Each processor is assigned a rectangular partition of the parray data. The rectangular shape simplifies the maintenance of spatial locality and, where appropriate, the use of vector processor libraries. This organization is suitable for dynamic redistribution of data structures in a distributed parallel environment.

Our initial experiments have demonstrated how data can be transparently redistributed to achieve processor fault tolerance. When a faulty processor is detected, the distributed data structures are reconfigured so that no data are allocated to a faulty processor. We have shown that in general the performance of the reconfigured system is proportional to the number of active fault-free processors.

A multiple block strategy is planned for the next Paragon implementation in which each processor may be responsible for a set of rectangular partitioned segments of a parray. With this strategy finer control of the data distribution is obtained at the cost of higher data fragmentation within processors. The balance between data fragmentation and load distribution quality will be studied in our research.

# 5 Programming in Paragon

The novel features of the current version of Paragon which permit the transparent utilization of parallel resources through data partitioning, are illustrated by several image-processing program examples.

## 5.1 Data Parallel Program Constructs

The SIMD foundations of the Paragon language include total array expressions, and primitive permutation, reduction, and broadcast functions. These facilities are suitable for efficiently implementing most low-level shift-invariant image-processing operations. The use of these features is illustrated with a convolution example.

The convolution of an array $x$ by a $K1 \times K2$ kernel $k$ is given by

$$y_{\alpha,\beta} = \sum_{m=0}^{K1} \sum_{n=0}^{K2} k_{m,n} x_{\alpha+m,\beta+n}.$$

In a typical application, $y$ and $x$ are the same size and have large dimensions, while $k$ has much smaller dimensions. A possible C program for implementing this convolution is shown in Fig. 1. To simplify this example, elements close to the edge of the image are not computed. This program involves four loops: the two outer loops consider each pixel in turn and the two inner loops process all elements of the convolution kernel. Most of the parallelism is available in the two outer loops.

```
#define ksize 5;
#define isize 512;

int kernel[ksize][ksize];
int image[isize][isize];
int result[isize][isize];
int i1, i2, k1, k2, tsize;

. . .
tisize = isize - ksize + 1;
for(i1 = 0; i1 < tisize; i1++)
  for(i2 = 0; i2 < tisize; i2++) {
    result[i1][i2] = 0;
    for(k1 = 0; k1 < ksize; k1++)
      for(k2 = 0; k2 < ksize; k2++)
        result[i1][i2] += image[i1 + k1][i2 + k2] * kernel[k1][k2];
  }
```

Figure 1: Convolution in C.

One problem with the conventional serial program style is the overspecification of program loops. The order in which the computations are to be performed is explicitly stated by the **for** loops. For the given algorithm, order is not important and a suitable program construct could simply indicate to do the operation for all elements of the image matrix and for all elements of the kernel. This overspecification is undesirable for both the programmer and the compiler; the program is harder to read and the parallel compiler must be more complex to extract the parallelism. Efficient implementation on parallel resources may require reordering the operations; when given an explicit order, the compiler must perform a dependency analysis to determine that a different ordering is equivalent. In some cases there is not enough information in the program to do a complete dependency analysis.

A Paragon program that can distribute the image arrays across parallel resources is shown in Fig. 2. The two outer program loops are

```
int kernel[ksize][ksize];
shape  imshape (isize, isize);
parray image(imshape, INT);
parray result(imshape, INT);
int k1, k2;

. . .
  result = 0;
  for(k1 = 0; k1 < ksize; k1++)
    for(k2 = 0; k2 < ksize; k2++)
      result += shift(image, k1, k2) * kernel[k1][k2];
```

Figure 2: Convolution in Paragon.

replaced by parallel expressions that process all pixels of the image at the same time. The **shift** function is a built-in Paragon permutation function which shifts all elements of its first parray argument by the amounts specified in the following arguments. It is possible also to replace the inner two loops by implicit parallelism in Paragon. If the kernel is declared to be a parray, then the following statement completely specifies the convolution:

```
    result = sum( skewrep( skewrep(image, 3, ksize,1), 4, ksize,2)
*
                    rep( rep( kernel, 1, imsize), 2, imsize), 3, 4);
```

The **rep** function replicates a parray along a new dimension; the second argument specifies the dimension and the third argument specifies its size. The **skewrep** function is similar to the **rep** function except that the replicated data is skewed along the dimension specified by the last argument. The image is skew replicated along dimensions 3 and 4 to produce a parray of size isize $\times$ isize $\times$ ksize $\times$ ksize and the kernel matrix is replicated along dimensions 1 and 2 to produce a parray of the same size. The **sum** function is a built-in Paragon function that sum-reduces a parray identified by its first argument along the dimensions specified by the following arguments. The convolution is performed by multiplying the two replicated parrays together (element by element) and then sum-reducing the parrays over the dimensions of the kernel (corresponding to the inner two program loops of the C program).

This second formulation illustrates an alternative programming style that specifies the maximum degree of parallelism by explicitly enlarging the data structures. We call this approach *extended* parallelism since it usually involves the implicit specification of data structures that are larger than any explicitly declared data structures. On a given parallel implementation, the cost of actually replicating the data may be very high; however, an intelligent compiler may be able to generate code that avoids any actual replication. Which of these two styles is the best is still an open question. In Paragon both styles are currently supported.

## 5.2 Data-dependent Program Constructs

The data parallel or SIMD programming paradigm is not suitable for the expression of all computer vision algorithms for multicomputers. Some experimental programming constructs are being explored with Paragon that permit the concise expression of a class of data-dependent algorithms. The objective is to provide high-level synchronization constructs that are as transparent to the programmer as possible.

The first construct is called **within** and is used when all elements of a parray are to be accessed. This construct is illustrated with a program to compute the Hough transform in Paragon in Fig. 3. The program is similar to a conventional serial program except that the two program loops that are normally required to scan all elements of the magnitude parray are replaced by the **within** construct. This construct executes its associated program block with all valid pairs of $i1$ and $i2$. A further constraint is that within the controlled program block, the named variable " magnitude" cannot be changed; that

```
int kernel[ksize][ksize];
shape  imshape (isize, isize);
parray magnitude(imshape, INT);
parray direction(imshape, FLOAT);
parray accum(imshape, INT);
int i1, i2, rho, theta, threshold;
float ascale;

. . .
  accum = 0;
  within(magnitude, i1, i2){
    if (magnitude[i1][i2] > threshold){
      theta = direction[i1][i2];
      rho = i1 * cos(theta) + i2 * sin(theta);
      accum[rho, theta * ascale] += 1;
    }
  }
```

Figure 3: The Hough transform in Paragon.

is, it is set to be read only. The **within** construct permits the system to execute different iterations on different processors. Making the scanned variable read-only prevents nondeterministic program behavior.

This is only a partial solution, however; in general, it would be necessary to lock all parrays that are accessed. Similarly, all parrays that are updated need to perform a barrier synchronization at the end of the program block to ensure that no update messages are still pending.

A second construct, called **without**, is used in a manner analogous to **within** but, in this case, scans the indices of a parray that is to be updated. The **without** program construct is illustrated with a program to compute an image rotation in Fig. 4. As in the previous example, the new **without** construct is used to scan all elements of

```
shape  imshape (isize, isize);
parray image(imshape, INT);
parray result(imshape, INT);
int i1, i2, r1, r2;
float theta;

. . .
  result = 0;
  without(result, r1, r2){
    i1 = r1 * cos(theta) + r2 sin(theta);
    i2 = r2 * cos(theta) - r1 sin(theta);
    if( i1 >= 0 && i1 < isize && i2 >= 0 && i2 < isize)
      result[r1][r2] = image[i1][i2];
  }
```

Figure 4: Image rotation in paragon.

a parray in the controlled program block; the program is very similar to a conventional program that would involve two program loops to provide all valid pairs of values for $r1$ and $r1$. The difference in this case is that the program specifies a parray to be updated rather than a parray to be read. The **without** construct ensures that, in a parallel environment, a barrier synchronization on "result" occurs before the program block is exited.

The final two example programs implement the calculation of an image histogram. The histogram $h$ of an $n \times n$ image $x$ that has $g$ possible gray levels is specified by

$$h_k = \sum_{i=0}^{n-1} \sum_{j=0}^{n-1} x_{i,j} \equiv k.$$

A direct implementation of this equation in Paragon is shown in Fig. 5 and an extended parallel implementation can be expressed in Paragon by

```
hist = sum( rep(image, 3, g) ==
            rep( rep( indx(h,1), 1, isize), 2, isize),1,2);
```

The built-in Paragon function **indx** creates an index matrix for the specified parray and dimension. The parray returned by **indx** has the same shape as its argument.

```
shape  imshape (isize, isize);
parray  image (imshape, INT);
int shist[g];
int k;

. . .
  for(k=0; k < g; k++)
    shist[k] = sum (image == k, 1, 2);
```

Figure 5: Simple histogram generation in paragon.

However, both of these solutions require $O(n^2g)$ operations. If we use the fact that each pixel contributes to only one element of the histogram then an $O(n^2)$ solution is possible, which is shown in Fig. 6. This program involves both a **without** structure to synchronize the updates of "hist" and a **within** strucuture to scan through all elements of "image". In this case, we do not need to scan through the indices of "hist", therefore, none are specified in the **without** statement.

## 6 Conclusion

Two paradigms for software environments for programming parallel computers for computer vision applications have been considered: functional decomposition and data partitioning. The concept of the first approach is to take a modular vision system developed for a

```
shape  imshape (isize, isize);
shape  hshape (g);
parray  image (imshape, INT);
parray  hist (hshape, INT);
int i, j;

...
  hist = 0;
  without(hist)
    within(image, i, j)
      hist[image[i][j]] += 1;
```

Figure 6: Efficient histogram generation in paragon.

serial processor and use the capabilities of the standard operating system to utilize the parallel hardware resources. This functional decomposition approach may be appropriate when the amount of available parallelism is relatively low or when special software modules are available to interface to special-purpose hardware (for example, the use of the Intel hypercube in the VISIX example).

The concept of the data-partitioning approach is to formulate the basic program in a language suitable for parallel-processing environments. This requires the development and implementation of languages that permit the system to perform data partitioning. The advantage of this approach is that a much higher degree of parallelism may be utilized. Programming environments for convenient data partitioning are still at an early stage of development. Also, advanced run-time environments need to be developed, including dynamic restructuring but also maintaining data locality within processors. Examples of our current research environment, Paragon, have been presented.

# Bibliography

[1] J. D. Bruner and A. P. Reeves, *An image processing system with computer network distribution capabilities*, 1982 Pattern Recognition and Image Processing Conference, June 1982, 447–450.

[2] A. L. Cheung and A. P. Reeves, *The Paragon multicomputer environment: a first implementation*, Technical report EE-CEG-89-9, Cornell University, July 1989.

[3] A. P. Reeves, *Paragon: a parallel programming paradigm for multicomputer systems*, Technical report EE-CEG-89-3, Cornell University, January 1989.

[4] A. P. Reeves, *A structured image processing computer system*, 5th International Conference on Pattern Recognition, December 1–4, 1980.

[5] A. P. Reeves., *VISIX 2.0 users manual*, Technical report, July 1989.

[6] A. P. Reeves, R. J. Prokop, S. E. Andrews, and F. P. Kuhl, *Three dimensional shape analysis using moments and fourier descriptors*, IEEE Transactions on Pattern Analysis and Machine Intelligence, vol. 10(6), 1988, 937–943.

# Data Parallelism: Image Understanding and the Connection Machine System

**LEWIS TUCKER**
*Thinking Machines Corporation*
*Cambridge, Massachusetts*

## 1 Introduction

In recent years scientists have seen a profound increase in the need for high-speed computing. Investigators in computer vision, needing to process megabytes of data in near real-time, have long recognized the limitations of current computing platforms and have driven the search for alternative parallel computer architectures.

In this chapter we will examine one such approach: data parallelism, exemplified by the architecture and programming model of the Connection Machine system. Through discussion and examples of its application to problems in image understanding, we will stress the conceptual side of algorithm development under this programming style. It is hoped that the reader will gain an appreciation and understanding of the representational and computational issues that unlock the power of massively parallel architectures. "Thinking parallel" will hopefully be shown to be a natural way to approach computation problems and permit vision scientists readily to apply massively parallel systems to a broad range of interesting problems.

Data parallelism most of all is a conceptual approach that emphasizes the parallelism inherent in problems with large amounts of data. In general, data parallelism is realized in a single-instruction, multiple-data (SIMD) architecture. A single program directs the operation of thousands of processors each operating on different pieces

Parallel Architectures and
Algorithms for
Image Understanding




ISBN 0-12-564040-4

of data. Although at first this may not appear to be particularly useful, we hope to show how this simple notion is in fact easy to comprehend and apply to any number of different situations.

# 2 Architecture of the Connection Machine System

The Connection Machine system, developed in part under DARPA sponsorship, is a commercially available, massively parallel supercomputer capable of achieving extremely high execution rates. Employing up to 65,536 individual processing elements, the Connection Machine (CM-2) system has shown sustained performance above 2500 million instructions per second (MIPS) on a variety of applications. Floating-point performance, enhanced by hardware accelerators, permits execution in excess of 3,500 million 32-bit floating-point operations per second (MFLOPS). Total memory capacity of the Connection Machine system is 2 GB. Each processing element has access to 32,768 bytes of local memory and, through the communications network, access to any arbitrary location in the machine (see Fig. 1).

Processors are connected by a 12-dimensional hypercube. This supports interprocessor communication for both regular, mesh-type operations, as well as hardware-assisted routing between arbitrary processor locations.

Input–output (I/O) operations are supported by a high-speed bus. Total aggregrate I/O capacity is in excess of 400 MB per second. Peripheral devices include a 20 GB parallel mass storage unit (DataVault) and a high-resolution display device.

The interested reader is referred elsewhere for more detailed information [7, 9].

## 2.1 Front-End System

Program control over the Connection Machine processing array is provided by a traditional front-end computer such as a VAX or SUN. This has several advantages. All of the usual operating system func-

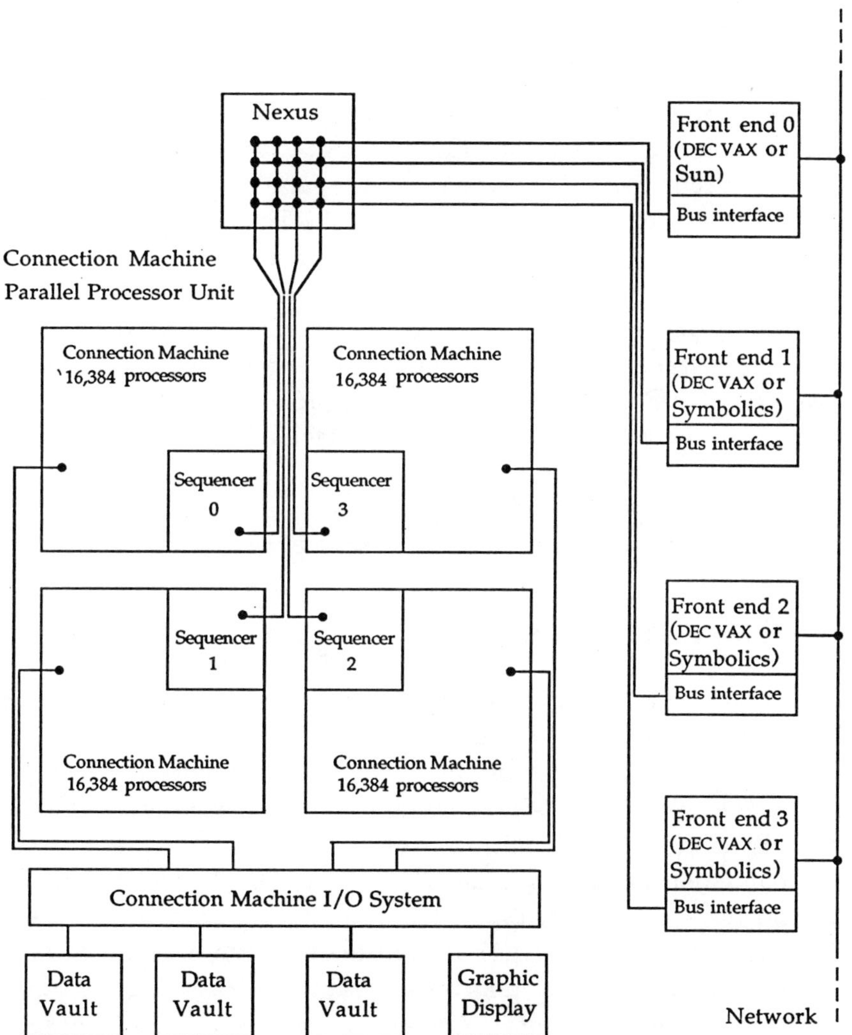


**Figure 1: Architecture of CM-2.**

tions, file systems, network interaction, and program development tools associated with a familiar front-end system are available to the user. During program execution, a single front-end process broadcasts instructions to the CM processors. This style of programming eliminates many of the difficulties and inefficiencies associated with synchronizing and controlling multiple processes.

In the course of its evolution, several parallel programming languages have been developed. PARIS, a low-level, assemblylike language, defines the machine model. Extensions to commonly used high-level languages such as FORTRAN, C, and common LISP have been developed. Each of these languages contains operators for evaluation on parallel variables held in Connection Machine memory. In evaluating the FORTRAN 8X expression: $A = B + C$, all processors compute in parallel the sum of local variables $B$ and $C$ and assign the result to variable $A$.

The development of new languages is an active area of research and we are sure to see new languages arise in the future.

# 3 Software Model

Throughout the rest of this chapter very little regard is given to the underlying topology (12-dimensional hypercube) of the Connection Machine. This is not meant to dismiss the importance of algorithms that specifically take advantage of particular network topologies. Hypercube-based multiwire communication strategies provide the foundation for an important class of parallel algorithms but are beyond the scope of this discussion. Instead, we hope to provide a kind of conceptual framework for considering general issues of relevance for effective use of massively parallel systems. The software model therefore only assumes the presence of a large number of parallel processing units connected by a communications network.

## 3.1 Physical and Virtual Processors

A particular architecture is often described by the number of physical processing elements. However, it is rare that a particular problem will fit the number of physical processors exactly.

A key element of data parallelism is therefore the notion of *virtual processors*. On the Connection Machine, physical processors simulate the operation of virtual processors many times greater than the actual available resource. Dynamic allocation of virtual processors is provided by low-level microcode, relieving the programmer from having to know the size of the actual machine. During the course of execution, any number of sets of virtual processors of different sizes and topologies may be allocated or deallocated according to the task requirements.

The relationship between the number of *virtual* and *physical* processing elements is termed the *virtual-processor ratio* (vp ratio). For example, at a vp ratio of eight, each physical processor simulates eight virtual processors. Hence, problems with much larger processor requirements than the physical size of the machine can be solved and are guaranteed to scale well with increasing processor resources.

In addition to describing the number of virtual processors, the user has control over their geometry. Grids of various sizes and shapes reflecting the structure of the problem define the neighboring relations between data elements. On the Connection Machine, the mapping between an $n$-dimensional grid and the underlying hypercube is accomplished by gray-coding the $x - y$ addresses into hypercube processor addresses.

In what follows, unless specifically noted, the terms processor and virtual processor will be used interchangeably.

## 3.2 Interprocessor Communication

Although various strategies for interprocessor communication is a much-debated topic in the computer architecture community, here we focus only on the communication primitives that form the basis for the data-parallel algorithms presented. In massively parallel systems, memory is distributed across processing elements (PEs), and communication is needed for nonlocal memory reference and data permutation.

Five basic modes of interprocessor communication will be described:

1. broadcast and reduce;
2. regular, grid-based;
3. general routing;
4. scans; and
5. spreads.

The simplest mode of communication is that performed by broadcasting a value from the front-end system to all PEs. A context flag within each PE controls which PEs receive the broadcast value. When large amounts of data must be loaded into the Connection Machine memory, the I/O mechanism is in general faster, but will not be discussed here. Other operations involving communication with the front-end system include reduction operations, such as min, max, and sum, which operate over all values in the active processor set.

Regular, grid-based communication is used with data arranged in an $n$-dimensional grid or torus. For example, each processor containing a pixel from a two-dimensional image may read the value of its neighbor to the north, east, west, or south. This mode is fast and collision-free.

Many problems, particularly those arising in middle- and high-level vision, cannot take advantage of predetermined, regular communication patterns. For example, to confirm a hypothesis it may be necessary to have processors sample the image space at arbitrary locations.

This mode of communication therefore requires general routing between processors. The Connection Machine employs special hardware router circuitry to route messages permitting all processors to read or write the contents of other processors at arbitrary locations. When messages are sent to the same destination, the user may optionally choose any one of a set of arithmetic or logical combining operations, such as add, multiply, or overwrite. A unique feature of the Connection Machine's router is its ability to perform this combining function as messages are being routed. The PARIS instructions SEND and GET perform general routing.

```
processor-number = [0   1   2   3   4   5   6]

A                = [3   2   6   4   3   2   1]

SB (segment bit) = [1   0   1   0   0   1   0]

Plus-scan(A)     = [0   3   5  11  15  18  20]

Max-scan(A)      = [0   3   3   6   6   6   6]

Segmented-copy
        (A, SB)  = [3   3   6   6   6   2   2]
```

Figure 2: Scan operators (plus, max, and segmented-copy) over the set A.

Scans [1] implement parallel prefix operations over a set of data elements and form an important new class of parallel computation and communication operations. As will be shown later, they are an integral part of many algorithms. A scan operator takes a binary associative operator $\oplus$, and an ordered set $(a_0, a_1, a_2, \ldots, a_n)$ and returns the set $(a_0, (a_0 \oplus a_1), \ldots, (a_0 \oplus a1 \oplus a2 \ldots \oplus a_n))$. Binary associative operators include plus, maximum, and minimum. Plus-scan with the operand $+1$ results in enumerating active processors. As will be shown later, enumeration is often used to compute new addresses for packing active elements into a smaller processor domain.

It is important to note that scans may also be performed over a sequence of processors partitioned into disjoint sets. This provides the algorithm designer with a mechanism for simulataneously processing data arranged into multiple, variable-length sets. Requiring specification of a segment bit to indicate the start of each partition, these operations are called *segmented scans* (see Fig. 2).

*Spread* is a communication primitive that takes one or more data elements and spreads them throughout a processor set. In the case of an $n$-dimensional grid, a spread may be used to copy an $n-1$ subspace along a single dimension. In the two-dimensional case this amounts to copying one column to all others. In three dimensions, a plane may be copied to all other planes. On the Connection Machine, scans and spreads are implemented using hypercube embedded binary trees and require a time proportional to that of a send.

# 4 Mapping Data to Processing Elements

When considering how to represent a problem on a parallel machine, consideration should be given to the assignment or mapping of data to processors to maximize processor utilization and minimize data movement.

Just as the issue of locality of memory reference plays an important role in the design of memory caching schemes for traditional computer systems, locality in large part determines the efficiency of data parallel algorithms. Access to nonlocal memory requires interprocessor communication, and excessive data movement significantly effects performance. Mapping of data onto the machine should therefore try to preserve locality.

"One element per processor" is a reoccurring theme in data parallel programming. Choosing what each element represents is not only important for clarity of expressions but is also central to effective processor utilization. Often the choice is clear. In image-processing tasks, assigning one pixel per processor is a natural approach and in general results in very high processor utilization. In other cases, the choice is not as clear. Consider the problem of model-based object recognition. Initially one might think of having one model per processor. Each model consists of a list of features. This, however, leads to under utilization if there is a large discrepancy between lengths of each model's feature list. Processors having simple models (short feature lists) would sit idle waiting for processors holding complex models to complete processing. A better choice would be to assign each model feature to a processor and use a set of processors to represent the entire model object (see Fig. 3). In this way we match the complexity of each model with an appropriate processor resource. Under this mapping, all model features may be processed in parallel and results may be accumulated using segmented scans.

Mapping problems onto parallel machines therefore requires that one give thought to the issue of choosing the right granularity and topology of the problem domain. In most cases, it is better to go back to the description of the problem itself rather than to rely on a previously implemented serial approach. Surprisingly, parallelism, which may be hidden in serial implementation, is often readily apparent in the original description.

# 5 Selected Data Parallel Algorithms

As can be seen from the previous discussion, there is a great deal of flexibility in deciding how to parallelize a particular problem. The algorithms that we describe here have been chosen because they reflect different approaches to solving problems using data parallel programming.

## 5.1 Line of Sight

In this first example we show how the parallel-prefix scan operator can transform what might appear to be an inherently serial algorithm to one that is fully parallel. The problem is for an observer on a hillside of varying elevation to determine the visibility of a light on top of a tower. Since any rise between the observer and the tower may block the view, a sequential traversal of the hillside at first seems necessary. The parallel-prefix max-scan operator accomplishes this in a single communication step.

Assume we have the situation pictured in Fig. 4. The light is on top of a tower at position $x_0$ and height $h_0$. The observer is at position $x_i$ with a corresponding elevation $h_i$. The angle of the line of sight between the observer and the light (relative to vertical) is $\theta = (\frac{\pi}{2}) + tan^{-1}(\frac{h_0-h_i}{x_i-x_0})$. Notice that if any location between the observer and the tower forms a greater incident angle with the light,

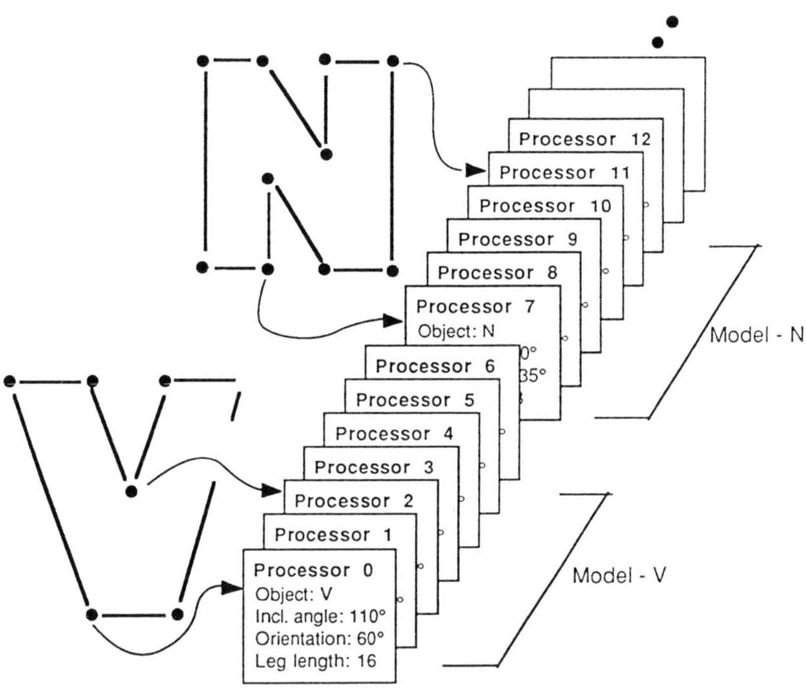


**Figure 3: Representation of object model using one feature per processor.**

then the observer will be in shadow. A scan permits us to combine communication with computation to compute this in parallel for all points on the terrain.

As shown, the $(x, h)$ pairs are arranged in sequentially ordered processors according to their distance from the tower. Each processor using its own distance $x_i$ and height $h_i$ computes $\theta$. A min-scan over $\theta$ returns in each processor, the minimum of $\theta$ at all preceding locations. Locations where $\theta$ is less than or equal to the result of the scan are on a line of sight with the tower. All others are hidden.

## 5.2 Line Drawing

Parallel line drawing shows how to bring to bear the greatest processing resource to the problem at hand. It illustrates the combined use of scans, and sends to distribute the computational requirement over a large set of processors.

The goal is to draw hundreds or thousands of lines in parallel. We are given a set of lines, one per processor, and wish to draw them into a two-dimensional image plane. Three virtual processor sets will be used: one for representing the lines to be drawn, another for the two-dimensional image, and a third as an intermediate domain of points on each line. (Lines may be displayed by sending the two-dimensional image plane to a display device.)

A serial algorithm for drawing a line starts at one of the line endpoints and sequentially sets pixels in an image array through which the line travels.

The naive approach to doing this in parallel would be to have each processor containing a line sequentially turn on (by a send operation) the requisite pixels in the image plane. This has several drawbacks: (1) the time it takes will be proportional to the longest line; and (2) unless we are drawing a number of lines greater than or equal to the number of processors, processors not holding lines will be idle. Since the time is determined completely by the longest line, this approach cannot benefit from increasing the number of available processors.

There are potentially two levels of data parallelism in this problem: the first is in the requirement to draw all lines; the second is in the points that make up each individual line. The problem with the

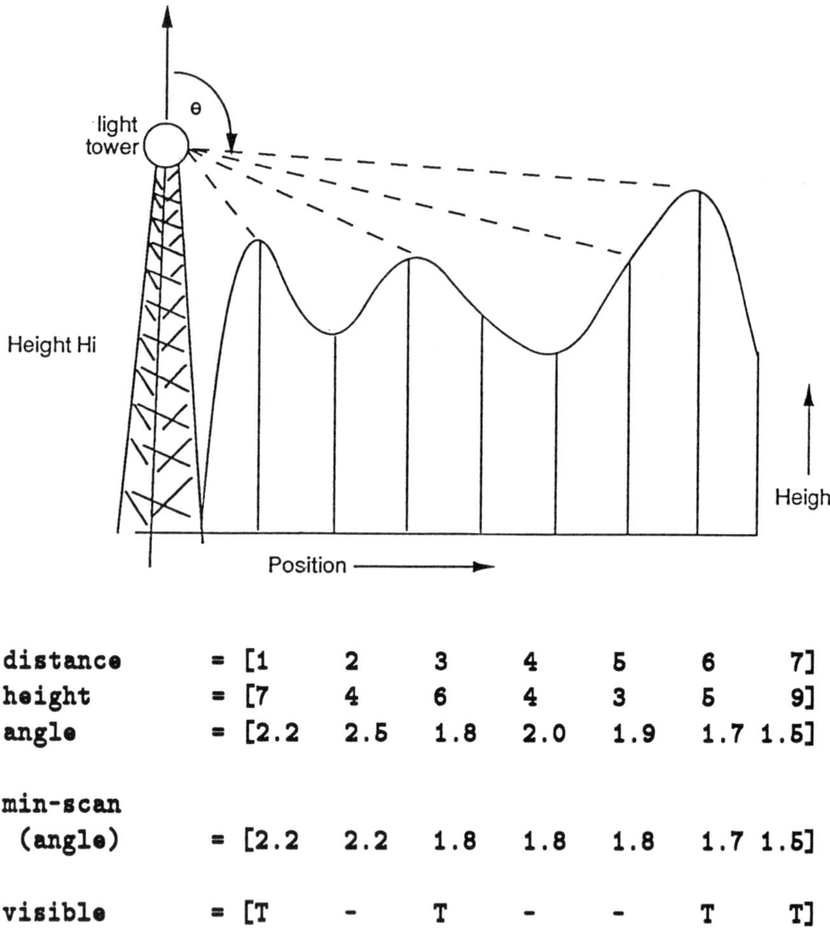


```
distance      = [1     2     3     4     5     6     7]
height        = [7     4     6     4     3     5     9]
angle         = [2.2   2.5   1.8   2.0   1.9   1.7 1.5]

min-scan
 (angle)      = [2.2   2.2   1.8   1.8   1.8   1.7 1.5]

visible       = [T     -     T     -     -     T     T]
```

Figure 4: Given a hillside and a light mounted on top of a distant tower, the problem is to find in parallel all locations that are on a line of sight with the the light. Using the min-scan operator, all visible locations are found in a single communication step.

naive approach is that only one level of parallelism is being exploited. In a sense, we've chosen the wrong granularity to exploit maximally the parallelism in line drawing.

What is required is a way to allocate processors for all points on all lines and have them compute and mark their locations in image space.

This fully parallel approach uses a programming idiom termed processor allocation, which works as follows (see Fig. 5). Each line processor determines the length in pixels of its line. This length determines how many processors need to be allocated to express the line in the point domain. By summing up the individual lengths, we can determine the total size required for this new vp-set domain. Partial sums, computed by a plus-scan gives the offset into the point domain for the beginning of each line to be drawn.

Using this offset, each line sends its parameters to the starting position of each point set, and a copy-scan spreads the parameters throughout.

Once the line information is expressed in the point domain, it remains to determine the image coordinated for each point on each line. An index for each pixel on each line is computed by a within segment enumeration. From the parameters of each line and pixel index, each point processor computes its image space location, which it marks by a send.

## 5.3 Contour Linking

Whereas in the line-drawing algorithm we started with a given number of lines and allocated a larger number of processors actually to draw the points on each line, here we are faced with an inverse situation. Points on the boundaries or contours of an object in an image typically occupy only a small fraction of the pixels in the image. Assuming that the representation of the image required a large number of virtual processors, it would be advantageous to use a much smaller processor domain (having a lower vp ratio) for subsequent processing of boundary points once identified.

This reduction in vp ratio can significantly improve the run-time of subsequent processing. What must be maintained, however, is

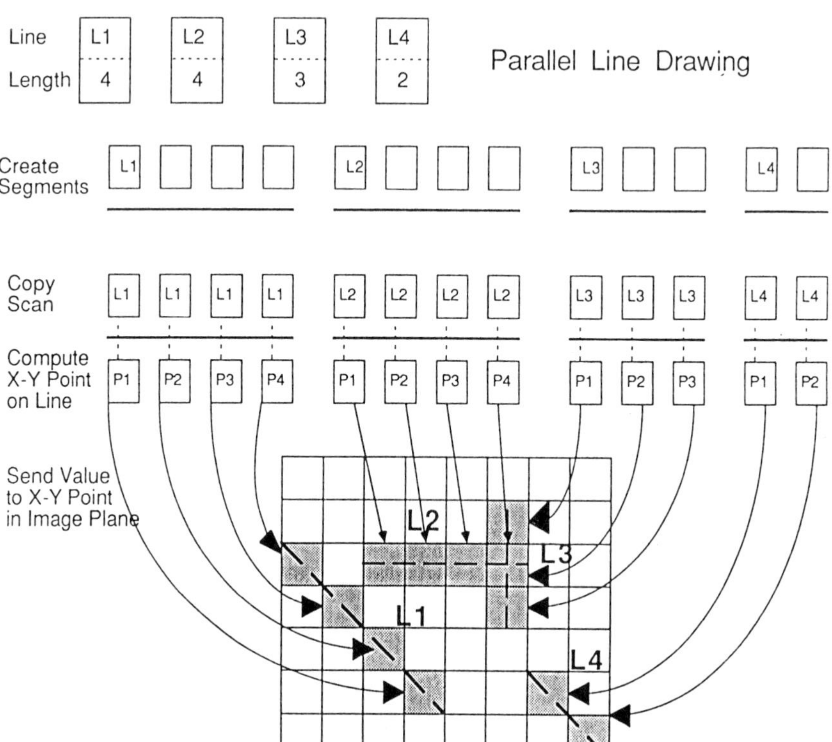


**Figure 5: Parallel line drawing. By allocating processors representing the points making up each line, we distribute the computational load over the largest number of processors.**

the topological relationship between contour points. The task is therefore to use the initial relationship between contour points in image space to form a linked list expressed in a contour-point-only virtual processor set.

We start with contour points marked in the image. Using grid-based operations each contour point finds the coordinates of the next point along the object's boundary. At this point, boundary points are linked together, but further operations in this domain would be performed at an unnecessarily high vp ratio. Many processors would not participate at all. To move the points to a reduced size, contour-point, vp set, we need to identify a unique destination for each point and recompute the address of each point's next neighbor. This relabeling is accomplished by an enumerate operation, which gives each processor a unique number ($1 \ldots n$ for $n$ selected processors). Then, in a single send, each point sends its coordinate information along with the address of its next neighbor to processors in the contour-set domain. Although the contour points are no longer physically adjacent, pointers maintain their ordering (see Fig. 6).

What we have done amounts to extracting from the image a linked-list type of structure and assigning each element of the list to an individual processor. By condensing the set of active elements down to only those required to represent the contour points, we have gained a substantial increase in effective processing capability.

## 5.4 Sequential Ordering by Pointer Jumping

In the previous example we were left with a linked-list representation of contour points. Neighboring points in image space are no longer in adjacent processors. Although reduction in the size of the required vp set was achieved, operations such as computing curvature or contour smoothing would now require general routing. To regain the locality required for grid or scan-base communication, one might want to reorder the data into sequentially ordered processors.

This reordering is accomplished by a parallel pointer-jumping (or distance doubling) algorithm.

Pointer jumping requires $\log N$ communication steps for a list of length $N$. Among other things, pointer jumping is used to propagate

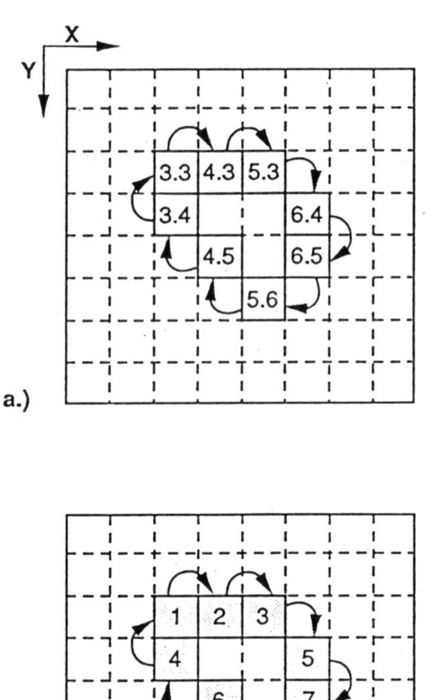


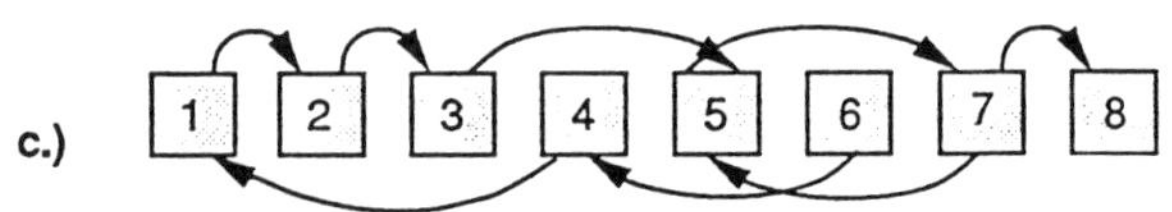


Figure 6: Contour points in image space are relabeled and packed into a compact, contour-point-only set of processors. Pointers between contour elements retain the adjacency relationship between points.

```
      -----------  {Pointer Jumping}  --------------

processor       = [0   1   2   3   4   5   6   7]
point           = [p0 p2  p3  p1  p7  p5  p6  p4]
next            = [3   2   7   1   -   6   4   5]
index           = [0   0   0   0   0   0   0   0]

        Send (index + 1) to index at next
        Get next from processor at next

index           = [0   1   1   1   1   1   1   1]
next            = [1   7   5   2   -   4   -   6]


        Send (index + 2) to index at next
        Get next from processor at next

index           = [0   2   3   1   3   5   3   3]
next            = [7   6   4   5   -   -   -   -]


        Send (index + 4) to index at next
        Get next from processor at next

index           = [0   2   3   1   7   5   6   4]
next            = [-   -   -   -   -   -   -   -]

Send point to processor at index

point           = [p0 p1  p2  p3  p4  p5  p6  p7]
```

Figure 7: Pointer jumping to enumerate in order a linked-list structure distributed across processors. In $\log N$ steps an ordered set of indices is produced which is used to rearrange points into sequential processors.

a label or value, find maximum or minimum, or enumerate in order the elements of the list. Here we need it to assign an index that can be used as a send address to rearrange the elements into sequential processors (see Fig. 7). At each step, processors send a newly computed index to their neighbors and modify their own pointers by reading their neighbors'. After $\log N$ steps, each index is used as a send address to rearrange the original points into sequential order.

## 5.5 Feature Matching

Matching is a fundamental operation in vision and in the context of a parallel machine takes on a number of different forms.

Consider the case of matching image features with those from a potentially large data base of models. Given $n$ image features, $m$ model features, and $p$ processors, we wish to find all $(n, m)$ pairs that meet certain matching criteria.

One approach would be to use the processors in an associative memory mode, iteratively broadcasting each of $n$ image features to the set of $m$ model features (previously stored on the machine). At each iteration $m$ pairs are formed.

An alternative approach is to create a two-dimensional virtual processor set of size $p = (n, m)$. Image features are sent to the first row of this processor set, model features to the first column, and a spread along each row and column brings together into each processor one $(n, m)$ pair.

When the product of $n$ and $m$ is large relative to the available processor resource but the number of pairs that will actually meet the matching criteria is small, the above approach results in a very sparse table of acceptable matches. In this case, an alternate approach employing a sort operation can prove useful. This approach assumes the presence of a single attribute expressible as an integer (such as the included angle of a corner feature), which may be used as the key. Sorting brings together features that share an identical key such that scans can be used to form the necessary relationships. This is illustrated in Fig. 8. To permit matching over a finite range of values, one need only expand the elements of the smaller set to cover the new possibilities. This approach requires only $O(n + m)$ processors at the expense of invoking a sort.

## 5.6 Evidence Accumulation

Recent work in model-based vision has focused on the development of methods to avoid the exponential search commonly associated with finding objects in unknown scenes. Approaches have included shape recognition using parameter space techniques [8, 6], transform space sampling [3], alignment [4] and geometric hashing [5, 2]. These highly parallel techniques attempt to combine weak evidence from local feature matches to build support for a specific model transformation.

In the context of a system for recognizing two-dimensional objects we will discuss projecting hypothesized poses into a parameter space such that evidence accumulates for likely hypotheses. Hypotheses simply identify the name and parameters of the model's position and orientation (pose) in the scene. Accumulated evidence is used to prune the number of hypotheses that must be verified, thereby reducing the overall computational cost. We start by matching image and model features. In the two-dimensional case we assume that the features are formed by the intersection of two line segments.

Geometric alignment of matching image and model feature produces a set of hypotheses that may number in the thousands for a typical scene. Notice, however, that if a model object in the scene has $n$ features, then within this set of hypotheses there must be $n$ identical (or nearly so) poses that arise from the "correct" association of corresponding image and model features.

The task is to find these sets of mutually supporting hypotheses in a multidimensional space. One approach would be to form a three-dimensional accumulator array covering all possible $(x, y)$ positions and orientations for each model object. Each hypothesis "votes" for an accumulator bin in this space. After the voting is complete, each hypothesis reads the total out of the corresponding accumulator location. Higher totals are indicative of greater evidence. On the Connection Machine, a dynamically created three-dimensional virtual processor accumulator array can be created and the communication primitive send with add used to accumulate the results.

The principal drawback of this is the rather large processor (or

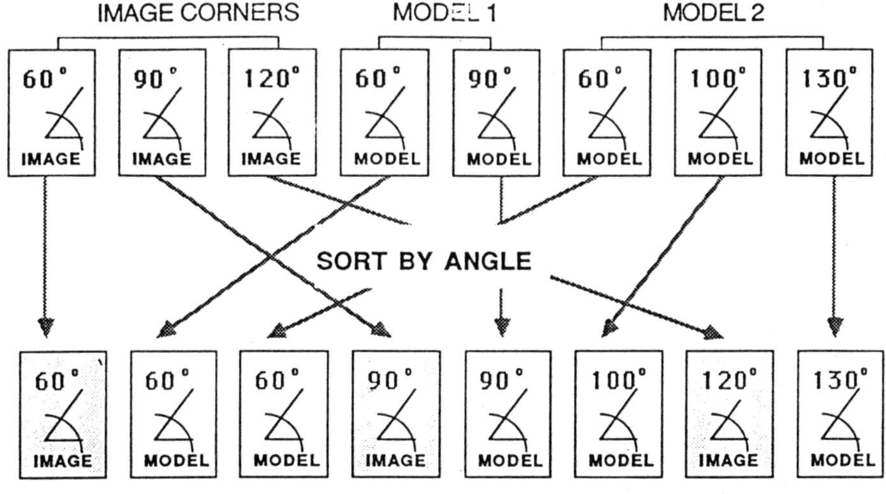


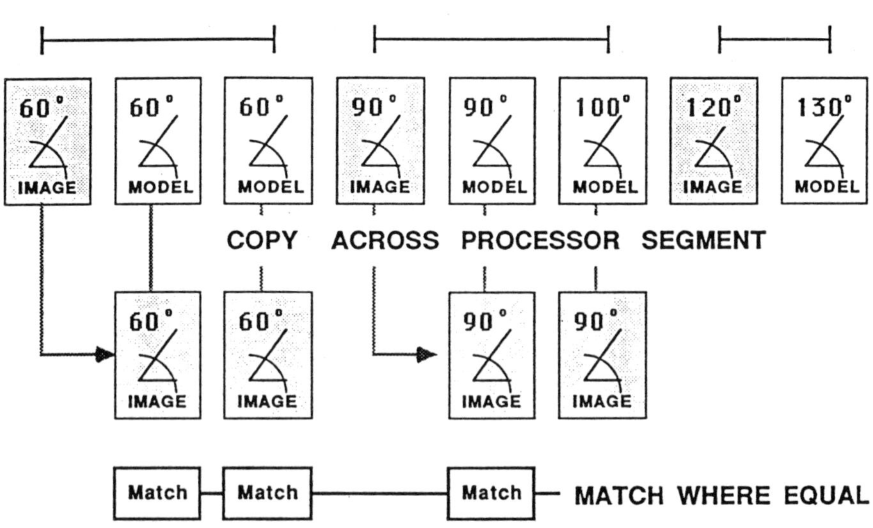


Figure 8: Feature matching using sort. Starting with a set of image and model corner features, the included angle of each feature is used as a key for matching. A sort followed by a scan matches model features with corresponding image features.

```
processor      = [0    1    2    3    4    5]
votes          = [1    1    1    1    1    1]

location-x     = [3    2    3    1    2    3]
location-y     = [5    5    5    4    5    5]
orientation    = [0    3    0    2    3    0]

                 Sort using location as a key
location-x     = [1    2    2    3    3    3]
location-y     = [4    5    5    5    5    5]
orientation    = [2    3    3    0    0    0]


                 Create segments where key changes
segment start  = [1    1    0    1    0    0]

                 Plus scan votes across segments
votes          = [1    1    2    1    2    3]

                 Spread totals from segment ends
votes          = [1    2    2    3    3    3]
```

Figure 9: Evidence accumulation using ordered scans. Using the location in parameter space as a key, create segments and count votes using plus scan.

memory) requirement for explicit representation of the accumulator array (which grows exponentially with the number of parameters.) To recognize objects in three-space, we would need a six-dimensional parameter space for each model in the data base. Discretizing each axis into 100 parts would require $10^{12}$ bins to represent each accumulator array.

An alternate approach avoids entirely explicit representation of the accumulator array. Instead of sending votes to an accumulator array, votes are sorted using their implied destination in parameter space as a key. This is illustrated in Fig. 9. Once sorted into a linear sequence of key values, the list is segmented wherever the value of the key changes and a segmented plus scan operator totals up the number of votes for each key. Any function that maps the parameters of each hypothesis to a location in the implied accumulator may be used to create the key. Control over the "coarseness" of the accumulator is thus easily accomplished. Generation of multiple keys for each hypothesis even permits overlapping or hierarchical schemes to be implemented.

# 6 Putting It All Together

If we examine how the modules of a two-dimensional object recognition system are integrated into an entire system [8], we see a general paradigm emerge. The overall system is illustrated in Fig. 10 and draws upon several of the algorithms of the previous sections. This system illustrates how the use of different virtual-processor-set domains results in easily understood representations for each stage in the processing.

We start by loading a set of models from a data base into a model-feature virtual processor set. Even though we spread features across processors, hundreds of models may be represented. An unknown image is acquired by a camera and loaded into a two-dimensional virtual processor set. Edge points, lines, and image corners are extracted. All features extracted from the image are next matched against those in the model data base. Wherever a match is found, a hypothesis specifying the model and its pose is created. An ev-

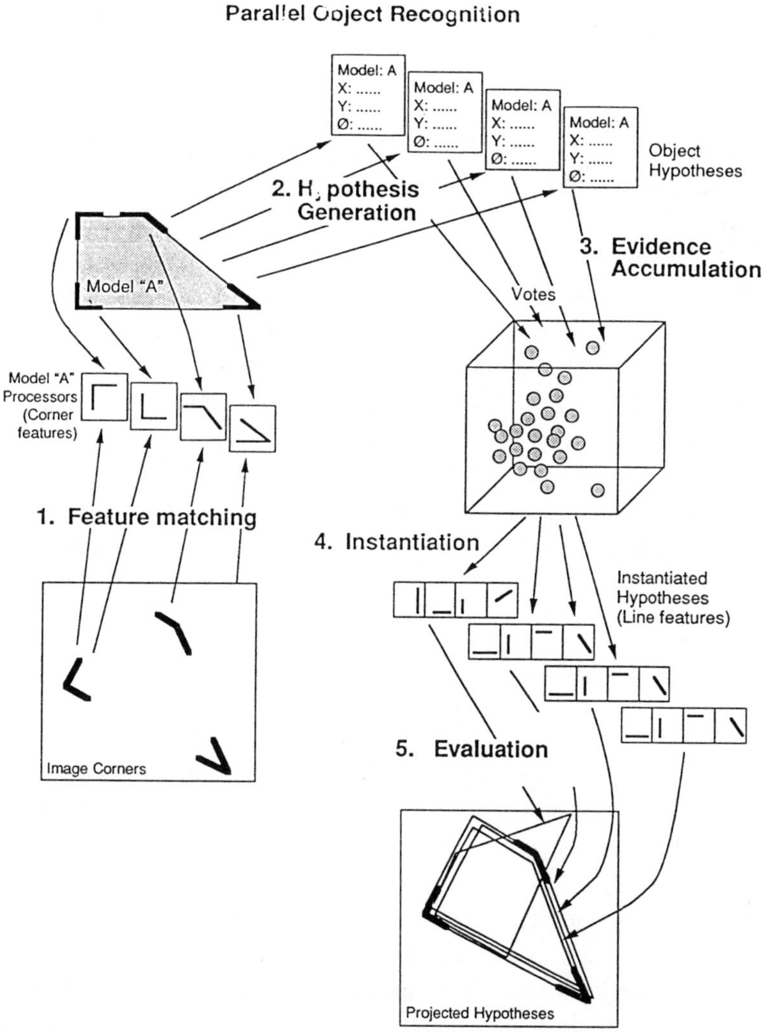

**Figure 10: Parallel model-based vision system for recognizing two-dimensional objects.**

idence accumulation stage filters out unlikely guesses. Hypotheses that have sufficient evidence are evaluated by instantiating the features of each model, projected into the image space. Each projected line feature, instead of being drawn, samples the image domain for confirming evidence that a line exists. A plus-scan over the instantiated features computes the overall confidence in each hypothesis. Competitive matching between hypotheses for features enforces a unique assignment of image features to models and results in a global interpretation of the scene.

The object recognizer illustrates well how an entire system may be implemented as a series of parallel stages. Once a model data base and image are loaded onto the Connection Machine, no further front-end data movement is required. The number of virtual processors varies from perhaps a few thousand (to represent the model features) to many tens of thousands during verification. The guiding principle was to distribute the work over as many processors as possible, changing representations into those best suited for each subtask. This resulted in an easy-to-code system that is both fast and robust.

# 7 Conclusion

In this chapter we have attempted to provide a framework and examples that illustrate how data parallelism may be applied to problems in image understanding. It is felt that our historical legacy of serial processing constrained our thinking and that parallel systems thereby open up new approaches toward computational problems. It is for this reason that we have concerned ourselves with general parallel constructs. In each case, parallelism was derived from the structure inherent in the problem. Emphasis is placed on bringing the greatest amount of processing power to the task at hand using only a few general notions such as dynamic virtual processors, parallel prefix scan operators, and simple communication primitives. It is hoped that the reader will have gained an appreciation for the power and ease of algorithm development on today's massively parallel systems.

## Bibliography

[1] G. Blelloch and J. Little, *Parallel solution to geometric problems on the scan model of computation,* AIM-952, MIT AI Laboratory, March 1987.

[2] O. Bourdon and G. Medioni, *Object recognition using geometric hashing on the Connection Machine,* submitted to 10th International Conference on Pattern Recognition, Atlantic City, 1990.

[3] T. Cass, *A robust parallel implementation of 2D model-based recognition,* Proceedings IEEE Conference on Computer Vision and Pattern Recognition, June 1988, pp. 879–884.

[4] D. P. Huttenlocher and S. Ullman, *Object recognition using alignment,* Proceedings 1st International Conference on Computer Vision, June 1987, pp. 102–111.

[5] Y. Lamdan and H. J. Wolfson, *Geometric hashing: A general and efficient model-based recognition scheme,* Proceedings of IEEE International Conference on Computer Vision, December 1988, pp. 218–249.

[6] D. Thompson, and J. L. Mundy, *Three-dimensional model matching from an unconstrained viewpoint,* Proceedings IEEE International Conference on Robotics and Automation, April 1987, pp. 208–220.

[7] Thinking Machines Corporation, Connection Machine Technical Summary, Cambridge, 1989.

[8] L. W. Tucker, C. R. Feynman, and D. M. Fritzsche, *Object recognition using the Connection Machine,* Proceedings IEEE Conference on Computer Vision and Pattern Recognition, June 1988, pp. 871–878.

[9] L. W. Tucker and G. Robertson, *Architecture and applications of the Connection Machine,* IEEE Computer, August 1988, pp. 26–38.

# Machine Independent Parallel Image Processing: Apply and Adapt

**JON A. WEBB**
*Department of Computer Science*
*Carnegie Mellon University*
*Pittsburgh, Pennsylvania*

## 1 Introduction

The Warp project at Carnegie Mellon [1] showed that it is possible to build, with ordinary engineering effort, quite powerful distributed memory parallel computers. iWarp [3] and other parallel computing projects are making these computers the most cost-effective source of new computing power. But efficient programming of these architectures remains difficult, particularly when machine-independence is concerned.

In the ideal case, parallel computers would run ordinary serial computer languages such as C or FORTRAN. But it is not yet possible efficiently to map serial languages onto parallel architectures, especially those with distributed memory. Another approach is to choose some common underlying programming method (such as message passing or LINDA [9] primitives) and map it onto all parallel architectures. This method has promise, but requires giving up efficiency when parallel computer features do not match the requirements of the underlying primitive: for example, exclusively using message passing in Warp would have required us to give up making use of Warp's systolic communications features, which allow us to overlap input and output with computation.

Parallel Architectures and
Algorithms for
Image Understanding




ISBN 0-12-564040-4

The programmer wants to make use of the features of a new parallel computer for efficiency without restricting the resulting program to be run just on the parallel architecture with those features. Specialized languages offer a way out of this paradox. These languages are specialized for a particular programming model and applications area. The compiler takes the program and maps it into a target source language (a language such as C with message passing, OCCAM, or W2) for a parallel computer.

The programming model supported by the specialized language is high-level enough so that the programmer is not directly aware of the parallel architecture features used to implement it. This keeps the programmer from doing things that restrict the program to a particular architecture. But the compiler implementor does make use of the specialized features, and this use is reflected in the greater efficiency of the resulting code.

Applications programming can be made easier because the specialized language can include features that make it easy to implement algorithms in the target applications area. The resulting programs can be easier to write than equivalent serial programs in C or FORTRAN. But the specialized language programs can be mapped efficiently onto a wide variety of architectures, and do not go out of date with the introduction of new architectures with new features.

Implementation of the compiler on a new architecture is not difficult, for several reasons. First, the compiler is really a translator, so the low-level details of language design are left to the designer of the native-language compiler. Second, the front end of the language is shared among all architectures, and only the back end has to be changed. Third, the language does not support a complete model of parallelism; only the particular programming model need be supported. This can enormously reduce the programming difficulty. For example, a language that supports message passing must allow any two processors to communicate; but in a specialized language based on data partitioning, only a method for partitioning data among processors and then recombining must be implemented. Fourth, the new architecture may share features with some previously mapped architecture, so that the new implementation can reuse the back-end module as well as the front end.

The Warp project developed three such languages, two of which (both specialized for image processing) are discussed here. (The third, AL, is specialized for scientific computing [14]). Apply allows the implementation of low-level local operations, such as point operations, edge detection, and smoothing. Apply has been mapped onto a wide variety of parallel computers with efficiency comparable to, and in some cases better than, hand-coded programs for the same machine. Adapt subsumes Apply, and allows the implementation of both local and global operations in the same programming model. Adapt allows the programmer to write such operations as histogram, Hough transform, and connected components, as well as the local operations supported by Apply.

I will discuss Apply and Adapt and describe how they have been used. Apply is more mature; it has been mapped onto more than a half dozen machines, and a library of about 100 Apply programs exists. Adapt is still under development; I present the concepts in Adapt, several Adapt algorithms, and results from an implementation of Adapt on a Warp machine.

# 2 Apply

Apply grew from the needs of computer vision researchers for low-level image-processing functions on a serial computer (originally, the VAX). It was only after it had been used for some time that it was mapped onto Warp. This background led to its generality and utility, and kept it from being restricted to a particular computer.

Apply will be described only briefly here; more detail is available elsewhere [10]. An Apply program is an Ada-like procedure that represents the inner loop of an image-to-image operation. An Apply implementation of the Sobel edge detector is shown in Fig. 1. The lines have been numbered for purposes of explanation.

Line 1 defines the input, output, and constant parameters to the function. The input parameter `inimg` is a window of the input image. Line 3 defines `horiz` and `vert` which are internal variables used to hold the results of the horizontal and vertical Sobel edge operator.

```
procedure sobel (inimg  : in array (-1..1, -1..1) of byte    -- 1
                          border 0,
                 mag    : out real)
is                                                             -- 2
   horiz, vert : integer;                                      -- 3
begin                                                          -- 4
   horiz := inimg(-1,-1) + 2 * inimg(-1,0) + inimg(-1,1) -    -- 5
            inimg(1,-1) - 2 * inimg(1,0) - inimg(1,1);
   vert := inimg(-1,-1) + 2 * inimg(0,-1) + inimg(1,-1) -     -- 6
           inimg(-1,1) - 2 * inimg(0,1) - inimg(1,1);
   mag := sqrt(horiz*horiz + vert*vert);                       -- 7
end sobel;                                                     -- 8
```

Figure 1: An apply implementation of Sobel edge detection.

Line 1 also defines the input image window. It is a $3 \times 3$ window centered about the current pixel processing position, which is filled with the value 0 when the window lies outside the image. This same line declares the constant and output parameters to be floating-point scalar variables.

The computation of the Sobel convolutions is implemented by the straightforward expressions on lines 5–7.

Images can be reduced or magnified in size by the use of special parameters added to the image declaration in the procedure header. If the `SAMPLE` parameter is used with an input image, the Apply operation is applied not at every pixel, but regularly across the image, skipping pixels as specified. For example `SAMPLE(2,3)` causes the Apply procedure to be applied every other pixel vertically and every third pixel horizontally. The resulting output image is thus reduced in size.

If the `ARRAY` parameter is used with an output image, then instead of a single pixel being produced by each application of the Apply procedure, a nonoverlapping array is produced. This makes the output image correspondingly larger.

The Apply programmer cannot control the order in which the Apply program is executed over the image. This makes it impossible for the Apply program to reuse intermediate results from processing adjacent pixels. But it is the key to the easy mapping of Apply programs onto parallel computers. Because the order is unrestricted, the entire image can be processed in parallel if there are as many processors as pixels, or it can be processed in sections, one section per processor, if there are fewer processors than pixels.

# 3 Implementations of Apply

The original implementation of Apply was done by Leonard Hamey of Carnegie Mellon. At this point, Apply was a C subroutine library that could be called to execute a per-pixel function across an image. The subroutine library used special buffering techniques to speed execution of the user routine.

Hamey implemented the first Apply compiler on Warp using a macro package. Later the first full Apply language was implemented by I-Chen Wu of Carnegie Mellon on Warp. Wu implemented a version of Apply that could process images with the image size specified at compile-time. At the same time, he implemented a code generator for FT (fault-tolerant) Warp that was used to generate test programs for this machine [4, 13].

In parallel with this, Richard Wallace and Ron Howard of Carnegie Mellon and Hughes Aircraft Corporation implemented an Apply compiler on the Hughes HBA. This compiler was used to generate demonstration programs and benchmark this machine [15].

These implementations of Apply were used to develop a performance comparison between Warp, the SUN, and the Hughes HBA [16].

Following this, Han Wang of the University of Leeds in England developed an Apply compiler for the Meiko Computing Surface. The first compiler was based on the SUN/C Apply code generator; later Wang developed an OCCAM code generator and performed experiments with different configurations of the Meiko [6, 12].

Wang also implemented a version of Apply on Warp that could generate Apply programs where the image size was specified at run-time. At compile-time, only the maximum image size was specified; at run-time, the actual partitioning of the image among processors was determined. This version of Apply is significantly slower than the fixed size image Apply (as discussed in section 7), but the increased flexibility more than makes up for this in most situations.

At the same time, Allan Fisher, Shigeru Sasaki, and Peter Highnam of Carnegie Mellon implemented Apply on the SLAP (scan line array processor) computer [7].

Recently, an implementation of Apply has been undertaken on the University of Massachusetts image-understanding architecture. An implementation of Apply on iWarp is under way at Intel Corporation.

When the first implementation of Apply on Warp was under way, it became clear that this language would allow us to implement and maintain a large library of image-processing software. Accordingly, Hudson Ribas of Carnegie Mellon implemented this library, called WEB. WEB consists of about 100 routines, and includes mode local low-level vision operations:

1. Basic image operations: image addition, subtraction, multiplication and division, including byte, real, and complex types. Also, image and, or, not, xor for byte images.

2. Gray-value transformations: thresholding, clipping, logarithm of image, requantize, shift, table-lookup.

3. Conversions: byte to real, real to byte, (real, imaginary) to (magnitude, phase).

4. Binary image processing: grow, shrink, extract border, Preston's operators, grassfire transform, connected components, halftoning.

5. Image-smoothing operations: median filter, edge preserving filter, adaptive smoothing, local maximum and minimum, iterative enhancement of noisy image, texture preserving averaging, etc.

6. Edge-detection operators: Canny, Sobel, Kirsch, Laplacian, Frei and Chen, Prewitt, Roberts, Robinson, iterative edge enhancement.

7. Convolution: one-dimensional, two-dimensional.

8. Multilevel image processing: image expansion and reduction, pyramid image generation.

9. Miscellaneous: color to black and white, magnitude, magnitude and direction, nonmaxima suppression.

Apply and WEB are still in daily use at Carnegie Mellon and at several other sites as some of the principal tools for programming vision operations on Warp.

# 4 Apply Performance

We will now compare performance of Apply implementation on the SUN, the Warp computer, and the Meiko Computing Surface. Table 1 gives the execution times of 10 programs on these machines, compared with commercial FORTRAN programs of identical function running on the SUN. (Some numbers are missing from the Warp W2 and Meiko columns because hand-coding Warp programs for local operations was abandoned once Apply became available, and the Meiko implementation did not support floating-point computation when these numbers were obtained.)

We see that the Apply-generated C code is usually faster than the FORTRAN code. This is surprising, because the Apply programs are shorter, as shown by the code length comparisons. The reason for the difference is that Apply employs a buffer transposition technique to replace array references that require multiplication for address calculations with array references that require only addition.

| Program<br>Apply lines/FORTRAN lines | SUN<br>Apply | SUN<br>FORTRAN | Warp<br>Apply | Warp<br>W2 | Meiko |
|---|---|---|---|---|---|
| Add constant to byte image.<br>2/3 | 1.7 | 3.1 | 0.073 | | 0.80 |
| Three by three four-connected binary image border detection.<br>13/15 | 1.9 | 3.5 | 0.21 | | 1.1 |
| Three by three eight-connected binary image border detection.<br>13/17 | 1.9 | 3.3 | 0.22 | | 1.4 |
| Clipping.<br>6/23 | 2.4 | 3.8 | 0.14 | | 0.95 |
| Divide real image by constant.<br>2/6 | 18 | 6.8 | 0.15 | | |
| Frei and Chen edge detection.<br>16/28 | 140 | 160 | 0.22 | 0.31 | |
| Edge-preserving filtering.<br>53/353 | 360 | 370 | 3.7 | | 14 |
| Prewitt operator (differential type).<br>10/18 | 28 | 36 | 0.20 | 0.21 | 2.2 |
| Prewitt operator (template type).<br>17/19 | 100 | 230 | 0.87 | 5.8 | 3.9 |

Table 1: Apply implementations and hand-written code. All images are $512 \times 512$, and all times are in seconds.

| Program<br>Apply lines/FORTRAN lines | SUN<br>Apply | SUN<br>FORTRAN | Warp<br>Apply | Warp<br>W2 | Meiko |
|---|---|---|---|---|---|
| Kirsch operator.<br>17/21 | 53 | 190 | 0.73 | 4.3 | |
| Roberts operator.<br>7/18 | 22 | 14 | 0.21 | 0.19 | |
| Robinson operator.<br>17/37 | 29 | 19 | 0.21 | 3.3 | 5.8 |
| Sobel operator.<br>7/18 | 23 | 33 | 0.27 | 0.21 | 1.5 |
| Iterative edge detection. | 18 | 19 | 0.78 | 0.51 | |
| Three by three local maximum.<br>11/53 | 19 | 33 | 0.75 | | 1.9 |
| Thresholding.<br>14/23 | 4.6 | 5.3 | 0.18 | | 0.85 |

Table 1: Continued.

Comparing the Warp Apply code with equivalent handwritten code, we see that the Warp Apply code is again faster. Here the difference comes from the use of a sophisticated I/O model in the Apply code. The programs generated by Apply overlap input, computation, and output. The same method could be used in the handwritten code, but it is difficult to implement such complex processing by hand. As a result, the Apply code is once again faster.

The Meiko times come from work by Han Wang of the University of Leeds. This implementation of Apply resulted from simple modifications to the Apply C code generator; essentially all that was changed was the underlying code for image access (later, Wang implemented an OCCAM code generator). The image access routines on the Meiko distribute rows of the image across the cells, whereas the access routines on the SUN use an image library to provide access to images stored in a number of different formats on disk or in frame buffers.

Several different implementations of Apply were tried to get the best performance. The Meiko allows the processors to be reconfigured statically. Configurations of processors in rings and two-dimensional arrays were tried. In the fastest implementation, the image started in the center of a two-dimensional array, and was passed out in four directions for processing by different quadrants of the processors. This resulted in the shortest communications paths, which was important for the fastest execution time, since I/O and computation use the same processor in the Meiko.

## 4.1 Lessons from Apply

Our experience with Apply in the Warp project led us to several conclusions about the utility of program generators for parallel architectures.

Program generators are useful for applications users of parallel computers. Apply has been used extensively in implementation of Warp programs at Carnegie Mellon and elsewhere; in algorithms where it could be used, it was used. Several Warp sites that developed image-processing programs on Warp used Apply. In fact, in response to this use we enhanced Apply–for example, the enhancement to allow Apply programs to specify the image size at run-time came about because of this use. It should be mentioned that this use was not required in any way; although applications users were expected to use Warp, they did not have to use Apply if they did not want to, since they could have implemented their programs in W2.

Program generators can also make programming parallel computers much easier and extend software lifetime. Before Apply, we found it difficult to build and maintain a library of even a dozen image-processing programs; using Apply, a graduate student was able to write the entire WEB library in one summer.

Program generators are useful for developers of parallel computers. With a few weeks' effort, Apply can be mapped onto a new parallel machine. (This mapping is even easier if the new machine is related to a previously mapped architecture, since the back-end module for the previous machine can be modified.) Once this is done, the entire WEB library of programs is available for testing simulators, comparing performance, testing correctness, and so on, for the new machine. Generating such a large library of code for a new computer is ordinarily quite difficult and can be a bottleneck in parallel computer development. Results from FT Warp, iWarp, the Meiko Computing Surface, and the Hughes HBA reflect this.

Program generators allow experimentation with parallel algorithms. By changing the back end of the Apply compiler, the implementor can compare different methods of implementing parallel programs and easily develop performance comparisons. (This was done in the Meiko Apply implementation.) In doing so, the implementor is not comparing the performance of a few different algorithms; he or she is actually comparing implementation techniques for a whole class of programs.

Program generators can address important efficiency issues in parallelism. For example, in distributing a row of data to the Warp cells, Apply-generated programs overlap I/O statements with program computations. In the best case, this can lead to a factor of three speed-up over nonoverlapped programs. This kind of issue is difficult to deal with in handwritten programs, since the generated code can be quite complicated.

Program generators can greatly increase the flexibility of programming the machine. Apply on Warp allows the user to distribute his or her code heterogeneously across the array, performing different functions in different groups of cells. This would be extremely difficult to do by hand, because of the need for proper balancing of input and output statements between groups of cells. But to the Apply programmer, manipulating such programs is simply a matter of adjusting compile-time parameters.

Program generators can make code more flexible and powerful. The original Apply compiler for Warp generated programs that could process only a certain size image, which was specified at compile-time. We modified Apply later so that it could also generate programs where the image size was specified at run-time; without modification, the WEB programs could be, and were, recompiled for the new model. When we wrote the original WEB code, we never anticipated that the image size would eventually be variable on Warp; and modifying handwritten code to use an image of varying size would have required prohibitive effort.

Program generators can give a remarkable degree of machine-independence to programs for parallel computers. Apply programs run efficiently on an architecturally wider variety of computers than programs written in any other language.

In spite of all these advantages, one serious deficiency remains: the range of algorithms that can be implemented in Apply is quite limited. It was to overcome partially this limitation that Adapt was developed.

## 5 Adapt

Adapt implements a programming model for global image processing called the *split-and-merge* method. In this method, which is commonly used in computing global operations on parallel computers, the input data structure is partitioned among processors, each processor computes an intermediate result separately, and then the intermediate results are combined to produce the final, global result. It can be shown that any image-processing operation that can be computed in raster or reverse-raster order can be computed with this model [17].

Adapt programs have two kinds of parameters: *global variables* and *images*. Global variables are broadcast to all processors (if input; here they correspond to Apply `const` parameters) or processed separately at different processors and then combined (if output). Images are split among processors as in Apply. In order to allow this, the Adapt programmer must divide an image-processing function into four parts:

First : an initialization function, which may be run at the beginning of any row of the image.

Next : a raster-order function, which is applied in raster order across the image (wrapped around the borders of the image). Each execution of the raster-order function is guaranteed to be preceded either by another execution of the raster-order function (for the previous pixel), or by the initialization function at the beginning of a row.

Combining : a merging function, which combines the outputs of any two image regions to produce an output for the concatenation of the two regions. In order to make programming easier, we stipulate that the combining function will be applied only to adjacent "swaths" (groups of consecutive rows) of the image.

Last : a termination function, which is applied once after the output of the entire image is computed.

It is not necessary to have all these parts in an Adapt program; only the **next** function is required if only images or images and global input variables are being processed, whereas the **next** and **combine** functions must be defined if images and global output variables are processed.

Because Adapt allows the programmer to reuse results from the previous pixel in the **next** function and restricts the **first** function to be run only at the beginning of a row, Adapt is fundamentally oriented toward partitioning the image by rows (although column-wise partitioning is still possible, as discussed in section 6). The reason is that the overhead of the combining function in image-processing programs usually restricts the usable parallelism to tens or hundreds of processors [17]. Thus, partitioning the image more finely than this is useless. Moreover, giving the programmer the convenience of processing row-wise is a great advantage in making programs easier to write and more efficient.

Adapt uses many concepts from Apply in order to make it easier to write Adapt programs. In particular, the programmer defines a rectangular window in each input image around the current pixel that can be accessed by the **next** function; the elements in this window are indexed just as they are in Apply, relative to the current pixel position. Adapt also uses Apply's Adalike syntax and allows the programmer to describe subsampling and image expansion operations. Thus, Adapt includes all of the Apply concepts while adding the ability to reuse intermediate results generated at a previous pixel and the ability to merge results from regions processed separately.

I will avoid giving syntactic details of Adapt and Adapt programs here to avoid complicating the paper. Instead, Adapt programs will be described informally. For example, an Adapt program for histogram is as follows:

**First** Initialize the histogram and the pixel count to zero.

**Next** Increment the histogram element corresponding to the current pixel and the pixel count.

**Combine** Add the two histograms.

**Last** Divide all elements in the histogram by the pixel count.

Depending on the target parallel processor, an Adapt program can be implemented in a wide variety of ways; all of these ways give a correct implementation, suited to the characteristics of the target machine. This will be considered in the next section.

## 6 Implementation of Adapt Programs

On a serial machine, an Adapt program can be implemented as shown in Fig. 6. In this implementation, the **first** function is executed once, at the beginning of the image, and then the **next** function is executed all across the image; finally, the **last** function is executed. The **combine** function is not executed at all.

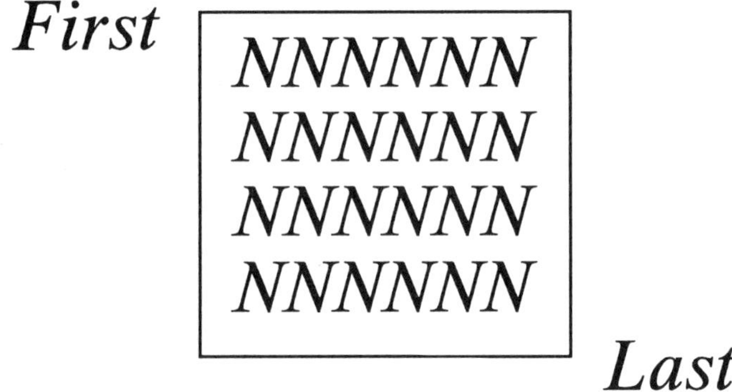


Figure 2: Serial implementation of Adapt.

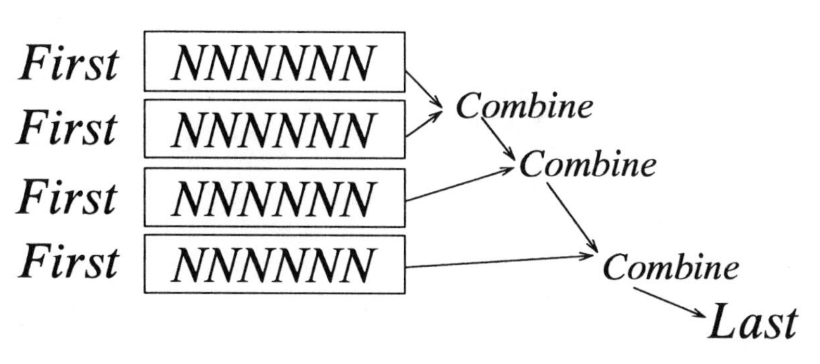


Figure 3: Row-partitioned implementation of Adapt.

On a parallel machine, the input image can be divided either by rows or by columns. If it is divided by rows, one possibility is shown in Fig. 6. Here each processor takes a horizontal swath of the image, and executes the **first** function at the beginning of the swath. The **next** function is executed by each processor across its swath. Then **combine** functions are used (here serially) to combine the results computed independently by the processors. Finally, the **last** function is executed.

If the image is partitioned by columns, a possible implementation is shown in Fig. 6. For each row, a processor executes the **first** function, then runs **next** functions across its portion of the image. Then it transfers its intermediate variables to another processor. This second processor runs **next** functions on its portion of the image, then transfers its intermediate results to a third processor. The last processor in this chain executes **next** functions on its portion of the image and then executes a **combine** function to combine the results just computed with the results for the previous portion of the image. After the entire image is processed, the **last** function is executed.

The column-partitioned implementation is less efficient than the row-partitioned implementation; intermediate results must be passed

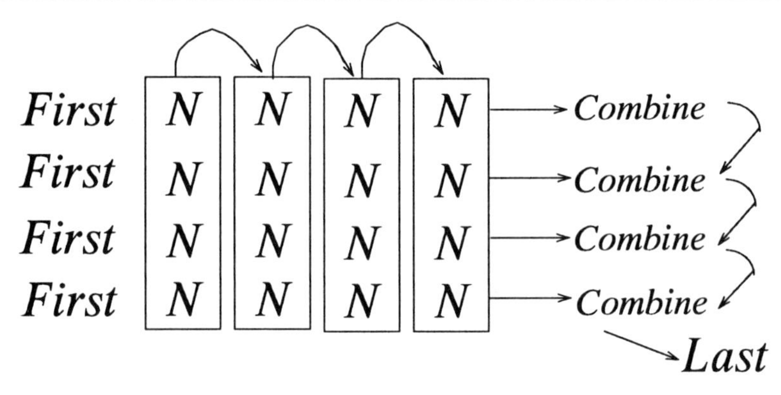


Figure 4: Column-partitioned implementation of Adapt.

between processors, and each processor must wait for the previous processor to complete before it can begin. (Of course, the processors may still be working all at the same time, in a pipeline.) The tight coupling between processors and the need for a lot of I/O may seriously reduce performance on many parallel computers. However, this implementation has some advantages: the amount of input image stored at each processor is smaller, allowing it to be used when the processors have small memories; the **combine** function is run in parallel with the **next**, while the row-partitioned implementation executes all the **combine** functions after all the **next** functions.

Of course, it is possible to combine the row- and column-partitioned methods to create greater parallelism.

It is the column-partitioned implementation that is used in the implementation of Adapt on the Carnegie Mellon Warp machine [1]. This was done primarily because the implementation of Adapt on Warp is based on the previous implementation of Apply, which used a column-partitioned method. The **first** function is executed on the first cell, **next** functions are run on this cell and the others, and the **combine** function is then run on the output cluster processor, which also runs the **last** function. This implementation also allows the **combine** and **last** functions to make use of large data structures that cannot be stored in the Warp cell's 32 KW memory.

We will now consider various Adapt programs and compare their performance to handwritten Warp programs.

# 7 Example Adapt Programs

We now present Adapt programs for several global operations. Performance figures are included here mainly to demonstrate the reality of actual running Adapt code, not to illustrate its efficiency. There are two sources of inefficiency in the current implementation:

1. Using the column-partitioned method has allowed early testing of Adapt programs, but the implementation suffers from serious performance limitations, particularly when the intermediate variables passed between processors exceed the size of the buffers between Warp cells (512 words). When this happens, each cell blocks until the next cell completes its processing, leading to complete loss of parallelism in the Warp array.

2. Adapt generates code for variable image sizes; the programmer specifies the largest image that will be supplied to the Adapt program at compile-time, and the actual image size is specified at run-time. This has several advantages for programmer convenience, but it leads to a significant increase in execution time, especially for programs that do little computation, for two reasons: many of the inner loops in the W2 code Adapt generates must have variable bounds, which the W2 compiler cannot pipeline efficiently, and a simpler I/O model is used that does not overlap input and output with computation.

By way of comparison, I present a few execution times of variable-size image Apply programs compared with their fixed-size image Apply program counterparts in Table 2. All programs were compiled for and executed on 512 × 512 images. The slowdown is 2.4 for the fastest program (addc1b) and decreases to 1.1 for the slowest (egpr). This should be taken into account when comparing performance of Adapt programs with their fixed-size handwritten counterparts.

| Program | Description | Fixed | Variable |
|---|---|---|---|
| Addclb | Add constant to image | 0.155 s | 0.378 s |
| Egsbl | Sobel operator | 0.485 s | 0.930 s |
| Egpr | Edge-preserving smoothing | 4.76 s | 5.10 s |
| Flwl0 | 3 × 3 convolution | 0.317 s | 0.649 s |
| Xconv | 1 × 41 convolution | 1.32 s | 1.64 s |

Table 2: Comparison of times for fixed- and variable-size image Apply programs.

## 7.1 Minimum Bounding Rectangle

The minimum bounding rectangle algorithm finds minimum upper-left and maximum lower-right coordinates of pixels of each color in a byte image. Written in Adapt, the program is

**First** Initialize all the coordinates to null.

**Next** If the upper-left coordinate of the current pixel is null, initialize it to the current coordinate. Set the lower-right coordinate of the current pixel to the current coordinate. (Note that this step takes advantage of raster-order processing to avoid unnecessary testing.)

**Combine** Set the upper-left coordinate of each rectangle to the minimum of the upper-left coordinates, and set the lower-right coordinate to the maximum of the lower-right coordinates, while ignoring null coordinates.

The Adapt program for minimum bounding rectangle executes in 8.46s on a $512 \times 512$ image, compared with 1.25s for the handwritten W2 code. This large difference is due primarily to passing the coordinate arrays between cells; these arrays total 1024 words in length, so that passing them between cells eliminates parallelism as discussed earlier.

## 7.2 Run-Length Encoding

In run-length encoding an image is compressed by encoding runs of same-colored pixels with a pair of numbers: the pixel value, and the length of the run. To make parallel image reconstruction easier, we augment the output with an array that gives the position of the start of each row of pixels in the run-length encoded image (and we split runs across the image boundaries). The Adapt program is

**Next** If at the first column, start a new run, noting the position of the row in the row start position matrix. If the current pixel is the same color as the previous, extend the run, otherwise start a new one.

**Combine** Concatenate the two runlength encoded matrices, appropriately modifying the row start positions.

Execution time for run length encoding implemented in this way is 2.91s. There is no comparable W2 program. As with minimum bounding rectangle, this time is considerably increased by the column-partitioned implementation; in this case it is the transfer of the row position matrix from cell to cell that considerably slows down the program.

A run-length encoded image can be converted back to the original with the following simple program:

**Next** If at the first column, set the pixel count and current pixel by looking up the appropriate position in the run-length encoded matrix. Then, if the pixel count is zero, take the next pixel value and pixel count from the run-length encoded matrix. Otherwise decrement the pixel count.

Note the use of the intermediate result (the current pixel value and count) from the previous pixel in this program. Without this facility, run-length decoding would be very inefficient. As described, the program runs on Warp in 0.271s.

## 7.3 Connected Components

Connected components is one of the more complex global image processing operations, and one that has been the subject of many different parallel implementations. In the implementation in Adapt, a global equivalence table is maintained. The algorithm runs in three passes.

In the first pass, horizontal connected runs are given the same label:

**Next** If at the beginning of a row, compute a unique label. If the current pixel is on, and so was the previous pixel, give the current pixel the current label. Otherwise compute a new unique label and assign it to the current pixel. If the current pixel is off, assign it zero.

The second pass forms the equivalence table. It uses an intermediate data structure to avoid having to pass the entire equivalence table, which can be quite large, between cells, and to avoid having to merge equivalence tables: this intermediate data structure is a list of labels to unify.

**First** Set the list of labels to unify to null.

**Next** Examine the current pixel and three pixels above and to the upper-left or upper-right of the current pixel. If they have different labels, add labels to the list of labels to unify as appropriate.

**Combine** Update the equivalence table, unifying labels according to the list of labels to unify.

In the third pass the equivalence table is applied to the image:

**Next** Look up each pixel in the equivalence table and assign it the appropriate value.

This entire algorithm takes 2.86s on a 512 × 512 image. This is considerably faster than the previous hand-coded W2 implementation of connected components on Warp [5], which takes 4.51s on the same image.

## 7.4 Median Filtering

Median filtering benefits enormously from the use of previous results. If the median of the window is computed independently at each pixel, at least $3n^2/2 - 3/2$ comparisons must be done in an $n \times n$ window [2]. (An Apply algorithm [10] achieves this bound for a $3 \times 3$ median filter by presorting kernel columns.) But by reusing results from the previous pixel the number of comparisons can be reduced further, using an algorithm suggested by Peter Highnam of Carnegie Mellon. The algorithm maintains a list of the $(n^2 + 1)/2$ smallest pixels in the kernel window.

**Next** Delete those elements from the list that came from the leftmost column. Sort the elements in the new rightmost column. Merge the new rightmost column with the list of the smallest elements to create a new sorted list. The largest element of the list is the new median.

This algorithm can be improved by using the histogram of the kernel pixels [11]. As the window is shifted the histogram is adjusted, removing the elements from the leftmost column and adding in the elements from the rightmost column. The number of elements less than the current median is also adjusted. The previous median is then moved up or down if necessary to become the new median.

We compare the performance of these algorithms for $512 \times 512$ images in Table 3. Note that Highnam's algorithm in Adapt is comparable in execution time to the optimized W2 code, taking into account Adapt's use of variable image sizes. The histogram-based algorithm performs remarkably well considering the column-partitioned implementation, which requires passing the histogram between cells. A row-partitioned implementation of this algorithm should perform even better than the hand-coded W2 implementation of Highnam's algorithm.

## 7.5 Quadtree

A quadtree is a compact representation of a binary image based on repeated quartering of the image until a region of a uniform color

| Algorithm | Time |
|---|---|
| Highnam's algorithm hand-coded in W2 (3 × 3 window) | 0.78 s |
| Highnam's algorithm in Adapt (3 × 3 window) | 1.85 s |
| Histogram-based algorithm in Adapt (3 × 3 window) | 1.34 s |
| Histogram-based algorithm in Adapt (15 × 15 window) | 4.68 s |

Table 3: Median-filter algorithms.

is reached. Quadtrees allow fast access to image pixels and fast manipulation of images; for example, image intersection is very fast.

Quadtree generation can be slow and is a natural target for parallelization. We present here an algorithm based on Gargantini's algorithm [8] for converting a raster image into a linear quadtree (a quadtree without pointers).

In a linear quadtree only the black regions of the image are represented. Each pixel has a quaternary code representing its position in the quadtree. The length of the code is the logarithm to the base two of the image size; the digit X is used to indicate a region not further subdivided. For example, the code "0XXXXXXXX" indicates the upper-left quarter of a 512 × 512 image; "02XXXXXXX" is the lower-left quarter of the upper-left quarter, "020000121" indicates pixel (130, 5), and so on.

In Gargantini's algorithm the image is scanned and a code is generated for each black pixel. All of these codes are then sorted. The sorted codes are then scanned and successive codes that indicate a filled black region are then merged: for example, successive codes 02113020, 02113021, 02113022, and 02113023 are replaced by the code 0211302X. Merging continues until each black region in the quadtree is represented by a single code in the list.

One way of implementing this algorithm in Adapt is

**Next** If the current pixel is black, generate its code based on the current row and column and insert it into a sorted binary tree.

**Combine** Merge the two binary trees.

**Last** Traverse the binary tree and convert it into a sorted linear array. While doing this, merge nodes as possible.

This algorithm preserves the performance characteristics of Gargantini's algorithm. The use of a binary tree to store the black pixel codes allows the cost of generating a new pixel to be $\log n$, when $n$ is the number of black pixels in the image. The **last** function takes time proportional to the number of pixels in the image.

# 8 Summary and Future Work

One of the principal results of the Warp project is the utility of program generators for programming distributed memory parallel computers. They allow the programmer to make use of special features of parallel computers to get the best efficiency without restricting his or her program to run on any particular computer.

I have discussed two such program generators, Apply and Adapt. Apply has been mapped onto a wide variety of architectures; the large library of Apply programs available makes Apply an attractive vehicle for aiding in machine development and benchmarking as well as applications programming.

Adapt significantly extends Apply by making it possible to compute global as well as local image-processing operations. I have described the fundamental concepts in Adapt and given several Adapt programs for different global image-processing operations. A first implementation of Adapt exists on Warp, and some Adapt programs already perform as well as, and even better than, hand-coded programs for Warp.

Future research on Adapt includes implementing Adapt on other architectures, especially iWarp, and careful examination of Adapt programs for important image-processing operations like connected components and image warping.

## Acknowledgments

Work on Adapt is being supported by a grant from Kodak Corporation.

# Bibliography

[1] M. Annaratone, E. Arnould, T. Gross, H. T. Kung, M. Lam, O. Menzilcioglu, and J. A. Webb, The Warp computer: architecture, implementation and performance, IEEE Transactions on Computers, vol. C-36, no. 12, December 1987, 1523–1538.

[2] S. Baase, Computer Algorithms: Introduction to Design and Analysis, Second Edition, Addison-Wesley, Reading, Mass., 1988.

[3] S. Borkar, R. Cohn, G. Cox, S. Gleason, T. Gross, H. T. Kung, M. Lam, B. Moore, C. Peterson, J. Pieper, L. Rankin, P. S. Tseng, J. Sutton, J. Urbanski, and J. Webb, iWarp: an integrated solution to high-speed parallel computing, Proceedings of Supercomputing '88, IEEE Computer Society and ACM SIGARCH, Orlando, Florida, November 1988, pp. 330–339.

[4] R. Cohn, H. T. Kung, O. Menzilcioglu, and S. Song, A highly reconfigurable array of powerful processors, Proceedings of SPIE Symposium, Vol. 975, Advanced Algorithms and Architectures for Signal Processing III, Society for Photo-Optical Instrumentation, August 1988, pp. 336–343.

[5] J. Deutch, P. C. Maulik, R. Mosur, H. Printz, H. Ribas, J. Senko, P. S. Tseng, J. A. Webb, and I-C. Wu, Performance of Warp on the DARPA architecture benchmarks, International Conference on Parallel Processing for Computer Vision and Display, Leeds, England, January 1988, pp. 336–343.

[6] P. M. Dew and H. Wang, Data parallelism and the processor farm model for image processing and synthesis on a transputer array, Proceedings of SPIE Symposium 977, Real Time Signal Processing XI, Society of Photo-Optical Instrumentation Engineers, August 1988, pp. 212–220.

[7] A. Fisher and P. T. Highnam, Communication and code optimization in SIMD programs. International Conference on Par-

allel Processing, IEEE Computer Society, University Park, PA, August 1988, vol. II, pp. 84–88.

[8] I. Gargantini, An effective way to represent quadtrees, Communications of the ACM, vol. 25, no. 12, 1982, 905–910.

[9] D. Gelertner, Generative communication in LINDA, ACM Transations on Programming Languages and Systems, vol. 7, no. 1, January 1985, 80–112.

[10] L. G. H. Hamey, J. A. Webb, and I-C. Wu, An architecture independent programming language for low-level vision, Computer Vision, Graphics, and Image Processing, vol. 48, 1989, 246–264.

[11] T. S. Huang, G. J. Yang, and G. Y. Tang, A fast two-dimensional median filtering algorithm, International Conference on Pattern Recognition and Image Processing, 1978, pp. 128–130.

[12] L. J. Manning, P. M. Dew, and H. Wang, Design and analysis of image-processing algorithms for programmable VLSI array processors, in Parallel Architectures and Computer Vision, Ian Page ed., Clarendon Press, Oxford, 1988, pp. 217–242.

[13] O. Menzilcioglu, Using powerful processors in a configurable systolic array architecture, Ph.D. thesis, Carnegie Mellon University, October 1988.

[14] P. S. Tseng, A parallelizing compiler for distributed memory parallel computers, Ph.D. thesis, Carnegie Mellon University, May 1989.

[15] R. S. Wallace and M. D. Howard, HBA vision architecture: built and benchmarked, Computer Architecures for Pattern Analysis and Machine Intelligence, IEEE Computer Society, Seattle, Wash., December 1987, pp. 209–215.

[16] R. S. Wallace, J. A. Webb, and I-C. Wu, Architecture independent image processing: performance of Apply on diverse architectures, Computer Vision, Graphics, and Image Processing, vol. 48, 1989, pp. 265–276.

[17] J. A. Webb, The divide and conquer model for parallel computation, September 1989, submitted for publication.

# The Image-Understanding Architecture and Its Programming Environment

**CHARLES C. WEEMS and JAMES H. BURRILL**
*Department of Computer and Information Science*
*University of Massachusetts*
*Amherst, Massachusetts*

## 1 An Overview of the IUA

### 1.1 Knowledge-based Vision

Computer vision encompasses a very wide range of processing requirements. At one level there are the standard image processing operations for smoothing, edge detection, histogramming, etc. At another level are the knowledge-based operations required to create an interpretation of an image.

Because of the disparity in abstraction between the two levels, computer vision is often viewed as having one or more intermediate levels. The intermediate levels are concerned with building up high-level knowledge from the results of low-level processing through mechanisms such as perceptual organization and grouping. Obviously, all three levels must be able rapidly to communicate and interact with each other [9].

Machines exist that are capable of working well at any one of these levels. However, no existing machine addresses the requirements of all levels. The image-understanding architecture (IUA) has been designed to support three distinct levels of processing and provide the types of communication required between levels [23].

Parallel Architectures and
Algorithms for
Image Understanding




ISBN 0-12-564040-4

## 1.2 Three Levels of Parallel Processing

A full-scale IUA contains a 512 × 512 array of low-level processors called the content addressable array parallel processor (CAAPP) with one processing element (PE) per pixel. The intermediate level is a 64 × 64 array of processors called the intermediate communications associative processor (ICAP). The top level is a symbolic processor array (SPA). Communication between the levels is accomplished using dual-ported memory layers between the levels. An ICAP processor, its memory, an 8 × 8 array of CAAPP PEs, and their associated memory all physically reside on one daughter board. The IUA is composed of mother boards, each containing 64 daughter boards. A full scale IUA would have 64 mother boards. The SPA processors are connected to the mother boards by a high-speed bus. See Fig. 1 for an overview of the three levels.

### The Low-Level Processor

The low-level processor in the IUA is an SIMD array of processing elements (PEs)-one per image pixel [3]. With one processor per pixel, very high processing rates can be achieved for most low-level computer vision operations. Instructions are issued to the PEs by the array control unit (ACU). Global feedback is provided to the ACU so that questions such as "Do any PEs have this value?" and "How many PEs have this value?" can be asked.

Added to this is the ability for individual processors to be temporarily deactivated depending on their local data, allowing operations such as "Any PE with a value greater than 10, set it to 10." Controlling processor activity is the primary mechanism for implementing branching in an SIMD processor.

Each processor has a set of five one-bit registers, a 320-bit explicitly managed cache memory, and access to 32k bits of backing store memory. Each PE also has two four-bit registers. These registers can be used for four- or eight-bit data movement. However, their main purpose is in controlling the coterie network described later. Each PE can access the memory of its four-way connected (north, east, south, west) neighbor via a mesh network, allowing windowing oper-

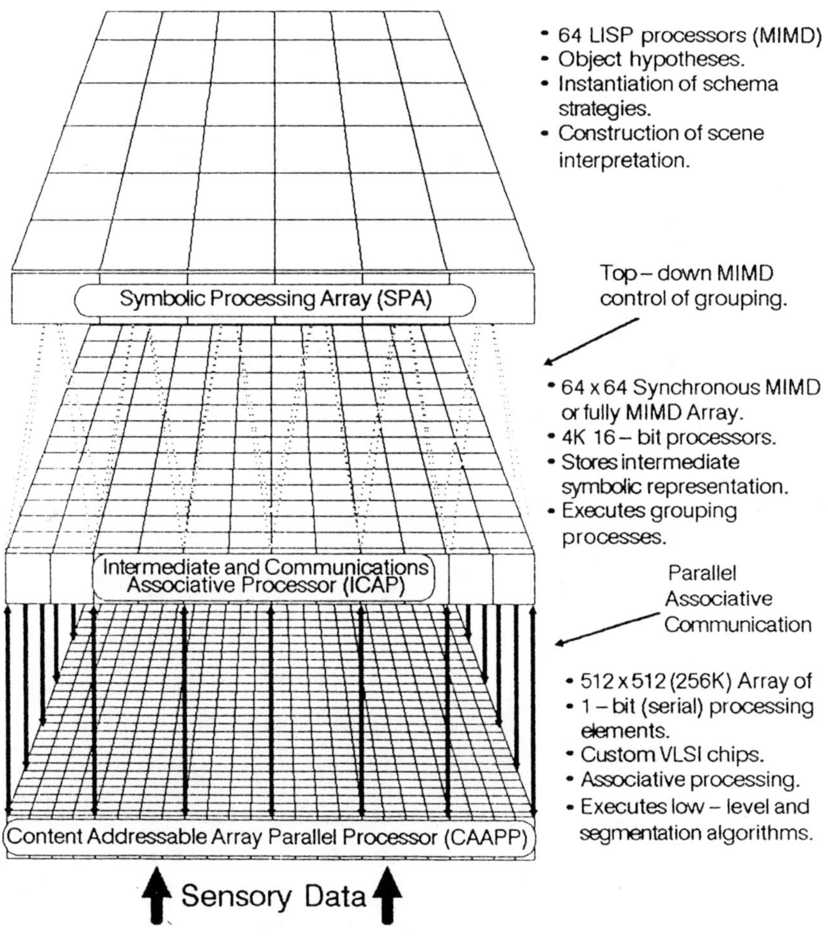
The Image Understanding Architecture
• 64 LISP processors (MIMD)
• Object hypotheses.
• Instantiation of schema strategies.
• Construction of scene interpretation.
Symbolic Processing Array (SPA)
Top – down MIMD control of grouping.
• 64 x 64 Synchronous MIMD or fully MIMD Array.
• 4K 16 – bit processors.
• Stores intermediate symbolic representation.
• Executes grouping processes.
Intermediate and Communications Associative Processor (ICAP)
Parallel Associative Communication
• 512 x 512 (256K) Array of
• 1 – bit (serial) processing elements.
• Custom VLSI chips.
• Associative processing.
• Executes low – level and segmentation algorithms.
Content Addressable Array Parallel Processor (CAAPP)
Sensory Data

**Figure 1: IUA Structure.**

ations such as smoothing. Each PE can add two bits and a carry to produce a result bit and a carry, allowing addition, subtraction, multiplication, and division of data of any length, bit-serially. Logical operations such as OR, AND, and exclusive OR are also available. See Fig. 2 for the complete instruction set.

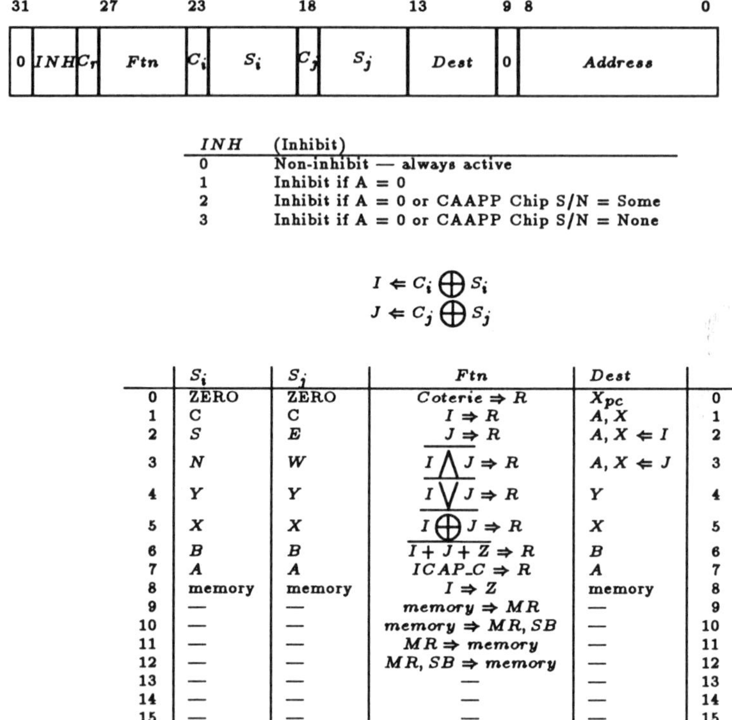


| *INH* | (Inhibit) |
|---|---|
| 0 | Non-inhibit — always active |
| 1 | Inhibit if A = 0 |
| 2 | Inhibit if A = 0 or CAAPP Chip S/N = Some |
| 3 | Inhibit if A = 0 or CAAPP Chip S/N = None |

$$I \Leftarrow C_i \oplus S_i$$
$$J \Leftarrow C_j \oplus S_j$$

| | $S_i$ | $S_j$ | *Ftn* | *Dest* | |
|---|---|---|---|---|---|
| 0 | ZERO | ZERO | *Coterie* $\Rightarrow R$ | $X_{pc}$ | 0 |
| 1 | C | C | $I \Rightarrow R$ | $A, X$ | 1 |
| 2 | *S* | *E* | $J \Rightarrow R$ | $A, X \Leftarrow I$ | 2 |
| 3 | *N* | *W* | $\overline{I \wedge J} \Rightarrow R$ | $A, X \Leftarrow J$ | 3 |
| 4 | *Y* | *Y* | $\overline{I \vee J} \Rightarrow R$ | *Y* | 4 |
| 5 | *X* | *X* | $\overline{I \oplus J} \Rightarrow R$ | *X* | 5 |
| 6 | *B* | *B* | $\overline{I + J + Z} \Rightarrow R$ | *B* | 6 |
| 7 | *A* | *A* | $ICAP\_C \Rightarrow R$ | *A* | 7 |
| 8 | memory | memory | $I \Rightarrow Z$ | memory | 8 |
| 9 | — | — | *memory* $\Rightarrow MR$ | — | 9 |
| 10 | — | — | *memory* $\Rightarrow MR, SB$ | — | 10 |
| 11 | — | — | $MR \Rightarrow$ *memory* | — | 11 |
| 12 | — | — | $MR, SB \Rightarrow$ *memory* | — | 12 |
| 13 | — | — | — | — | 13 |
| 14 | — | — | — | — | 14 |
| 15 | — | — | — | — | 15 |

$$Dest \Leftarrow C_r \oplus R$$

Figure 2: CAAPP PE instructions.

The five one-bit registers are

*A*: the activity register. The ACU can specify that only PEs whose A register is one participate in a particular operation.

*B*: a general purpose register.

$X$: the response register. The ACU can ask if any PE has its X register set to one or how many have the X register set to one, providing feedback to the ACU. The X register may also be used as a general-purpose register.

$Y$: a general purpose register.

$Z$: the carry register. This register is set to the carry from the addition operation and is an automatic operand to the addition operation.

Communication among CAAPP processors also involves a new and powerful variation on the nearest neighbor mesh called the coterie network [23]. This is similar to the reconfigurable buses proposed by Kumar and Raghavendra [11], Miller et al. [13] and the polymorphic torus proposed by Li and Maresca [12], but differs in that it allows general reconfiguration of the mesh, and multiple processors to write to the mesh at the same time. By adding the simple switch network shown in Fig. 3, it is possible, under program control, to create independent groups of processors that share a local associative some–none feedback circuit. The isolated groups of processors can then respond to globally broadcast instructions in a locally data-dependent fashion, called multiassociative processing, which permits parallelism to be employed with more flexibility. For example, suppose that an image is divided into a large number of regions, and that we wish to determine some attribute for each of the regions. In a typical SIMD architecture this would be done by sequentially selecting each region for analysis or in parallel by complex communication between neighbors where the attribute is computed via a propagating wave that checks region labels at each step. However, using the coterie network in the CAAPP, all regions can perform their own local evaluation in parallel without having to check region labels after one initial step of neighbor comparison.

The name coterie network is based upon the similarity of the isolated processor groups to a coterie: that is, a group of people who associate closely because of common purposes, interests, etc. Note that the coterie network is separate from the nearest neighbor mesh.

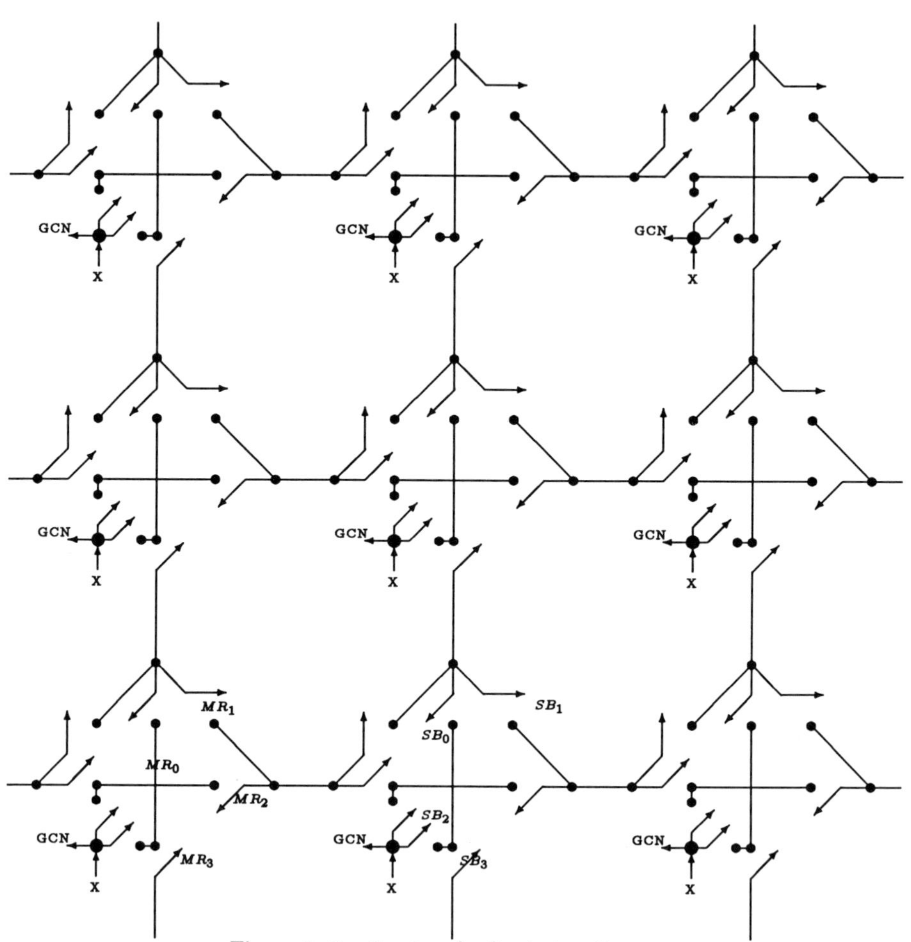


Figure 3: 3 × 3 network of coterie cells.

Creation of a set of coteries typically begins with opening all of the switches that link processors. Using the nearest neighbor mesh, the processors compare their own values with the values of their neighbors. They then close the switches that connect them to neighbors with similar properties, leaving open the switches that would connect them to dissimilar neighbors. Of course similarity can be defined by an operation such as a global broadcast of a threshold and a local comparison. In this way, processors with similar properties establish independent coteries. Among other things, each region of a segmentation could be a coterie of cells. Because the CAAPP processors can save and restore the switch settings that make up a set of coteries, it is possible to reconfigure the coterie network from one processor interconnection pattern to another by broadcasting a single instruction.

Within a coterie, there is a network of wire to which all of the processors are connected. Each active CAAPP processor may be instructed to output a bit onto its coterie's network and then read whatever bit value is currently on the network within its coterie. When more than one processor in a coterie tries to output a bit onto the network, the value that appears on the wire is the logical OR of the output bits of all of the processors in the coterie. The shared network is thus functionally equivalent to the global some–none feedback circuit except that its output is locally formed and only available within a coterie. In addition to its associative feedback function, the coterie network can be used to broadcast a value from a single processor to every member of the coterie. This is accomplished by first selecting a single processor within each coterie, using an associative search operation in parallel within all coteries. Subsequent instructions for placing a value onto the network will only be performed by these selected cells. However, all of the cells will perform the operations for reading the value that is on the network. The local feedback and broadcast processes can occur in every coterie in parallel.

To support communication between the CAAPP level and the intermediate level, the CAAPP–ICAP shared memory (CISM) is provided. This memory is accessible to the PEs with cache block transfers and to the ICAP level as extended addressing pages. It provides 32k bits of storage to each CAAPP PE on a daughter board and 256k bytes to each ICAP processor. Data may be passed from the PEs to the ICAP processors and back using this memory.

To provide access to visual data and the outside world, a separate memory is provided, called host-CAAPP shared memory (HCSM), which can store multiple frames of image data and pump it directly into each $8 \times 8$ block of CAAPP PEs. This allows an entire eight-bit image to be moved into PE memory in 7.2 microseconds.

## The ACU

One major design goal for the array control unit (ACU) was to maximize the rate at which instructions are issued to the CAAPP. This meant that the overhead for controlling loops, branches, and subroutine calls in the ACU had to be minimized. A second major design goal for the ACU was to minimize the cost of implementing a complete development environment for it. Preferably, the ACU would execute a commonly used instruction set so that software could be transported from an existing machine.

Clearly, the first goal required a custom processor, while the second goal dictated an off-the-shelf processor. The solution to this dilemma was to incorporate both into the ACU design. Thus, the ACU contains two separate processors that can issue instructions to the CAAPP (and control the ICAP as described below). The two processors are referred to as the macrocontroller and the microcontroller.

The macrocontroller is a standard RISC processor that brings with it the wide range of software tools that are available for that processor. It can issue instructions to the CAAPP in two ways. The simplest way is to take direct control of the instruction bus and write out data values that will be interpreted as instructions by the processor arrays. Even at its maximum rate, however, it can issue instructions only at about one half of the rate that the CAAPP can execute them. The second method for the macrocontroller to issue instructions is to issue subroutine calls to the microcontroller.

The microcontroller is a custom processor, driven by horizontal microcode. It is capable of issuing an instruction to the CAAPP every 100 nanoseconds, with minimal overhead for loop, branch, and subroutine control. The microcontroller will have a large library of CAAPP routines (ACU macros) in its program memory, any of which can be called by the macrocontroller. When the microcontroller completes execution of a CAAPP routine, it returns a status flag to the macrocontroller, which may then issue a new call.

The routine-calling mechanism permits the user to write applications in a high-level language for the macrocontroller, yet obtain good peak instruction rates for operations on the CAAPP.

### The ICAP Level

The ICAP level is designed to process the results from the low-level into an intermediate representation and store this information for access by the SPA level. The information at this level might be kept as a data base of extracted image events such as line segments or regions and associated information such as length, contrast, color, texture, etc. The ICAP is designed to access this information upon request from the top level. An example request might be "return all lines of length > 20 where one endpoint is near location (100,120)."

The ICAP level consists of an array of processors running in either synchronous-MIMD or pure-MIMD mode. Each ICAP processor is associated with an $8 \times 8$ tile of CAAPP PEs, and can access directly the CISM of its CAAPP subarray. The low-level processing places these results in the CISM where the ICAP may further process them.

The top level can make requests to the ICAP. The ICAP will either directly complete the request or *ask another ICAP for the information.* When a request must be satisfied from a separate ICAP, the ICAP processors communicate using a network described later.

To support the amount of data and processing required, each ICAP is a high-speed processor with significant amounts of data and program memory. Specifically, it is a Texas Instruments TMS320C25 DSP chip, which is a Harvard architecture processor designed for embedded digital signal processing applications [18]. Each ICAP processor has 128k bytes of data memory (IDM) and 128k bytes of program memory (IPM) and executes at an instruction rate of 5

MIPS.

A portion of each ICAP processor's data space is mapped through extended addressing into the CISM shared with the 64 associated CAAPP PEs. Using this memory, the ICAP and CAAPP can communicate massive amounts of information in parallel. The ICAP can also access the global feedback information from the associated $8 \times 8$ PE array.

Communication between ICAP processors is accomplished by the parallel communications switch (PARCOS) network [16]. This is a dynamically reconfigurable bit-serial network that uses the serial input and serial output ports on the TMS320C25 processor. The PARCOS network is built from custom VLSI chips that form a crossbar capable of storing patterns to specify the interprocessor connections. The patterns allow one-to-one or one-to-many configurations. The ability to select from 32 different patterns in one machine cycle permits optimal complex routing networks to be utilized for many algorithms.

The connection between an ICAP processor and the SPA processors is accomplished by using the ICAP–SPA shared memory (ISSM). The ICAP processor accesses this memory as an I/O device connected to one of its I/O ports. To the SPA processors, this is a shared random-access memory. A single ICAP processor may reference a segment (128k bytes) of the ISSM that is associated with it. An SPA processor may access any part of the ISSM.

The ICAP program memory is loaded with a large library of service routines upon system initialization. The way in which the ACU issues instructions to the ICAP is by storing a user program into ICAP program memory and then issuing an interrupt to the ICAP that causes it to jump to the user program. (The program is broadcast to all of the ICAP program memories in parallel.) An ICAP user program is typically just an execution script (written in C, FORTH, or assembly language) of calls to the ICAP library. Thus, the ACU and ICAP interact very little when a program is running in the ICAP; the exception is when the ICAP program reaches a global synchronization point–which must be mediated by the ACU. The ACU can also set the ICAP to operate in MIMD mode, by turning control over to a task queuing program in the ICAP processors. The queuing program reads execution scripts from the ISSM according to a predefined protocol. When the ICAP is executing in MIMD mode, it depends on the SPA to provide coordination of any required synchronization between ICAP processors.

The ACU thus supports the close interaction between the CAAPP and ICAP during the initial phases of interpreting an image. However, the ACU also permits the CAAPP and ICAP to work independently, with the ICAP taking directions from the SPA as the high-level interpretation processes come into play. This allows the CAAPP concurrently to perform additional low-level processing, such as integrating information from other sensors or starting to process the next image.

## The SPA Level

At the top level of the IUA is the symbolic processing array (SPA). This is a multiprocessor whose purpose is to support high-level symbolic processing. Each SPA processor is a complete computer and is connected to the rest of the IUA by its ability to access the ISSM in parallel. The spatial relation of an SPA processor to the machine as a whole is by software convention only.

The SPA processors will run a LISP-based blackboard system [7, 15, 5, 6], through which the various knowledge-based processes can communicate while cooperatively constructing an interpretation of an image and determining the relationships of the various image components to stored knowledge. From the point of view of the blackboard system, the CAAPP and ICAP will appear as knowledge sources at different levels of abstraction. Knowledge-based processes in the system can activate different processes in the CAAPP and ICAP either for the full array or for independent subarrays. Thus, the SPA processors operate in MIMD mode with communication through the blackboard. The detailed architecture of the SPA has not yet been fully defined. In the first prototype of the IUA, which is a 1/64th vertical slice of the full IUA, the SPA will be a single RISC processor. A separate research investigation within the UMass VISIONS project is currently exploring the implementation of cooperative algorithms and data structures using a commercially available shared-memory multiprocessor at the SPA level. This experience is providing additional direction to the future scaling up of the IUA at the SPA level.

Currently, the full SPA is envisioned as consisting of 64 or more processors, each capable of running LISP. Each processor will have some local memory and will have access to a global shared memory that will include the ISSM and the blackboard. The shared memory decouples the SPA processors from the locality of information in the image.

# 2 IUA Programming Environment

Writing programs for parallel processors and debugging those programs can be very difficult. For a machine the size of the IUA, the sheer amount of data that is processed at any one moment is staggering. We felt that the only way that we could successfully develop software to run on the IUA was by utilizing the even more powerful image-processing provided by the human visual system. We do not yet fully know how to prepare software using this power, but we do know how visually to display the state of the machine. Therefore, we decided to provide a simulator for the IUA that would let the programmer *see* the state of the machine.

As an example, consider a display of rectangles overlaid by points of high curvature. In this simple example, it would be easy to see immediately which points have been properly selected and which points have not. This focusing of attention quickly on the problem area and the visual clues provided greatly facilitate the process of correcting the software.

## 2.1 The IUA Simulator

The University of Massachusetts simulator for the image-understanding architecture provides a way of testing the design of, and developing the software for, the IUA [2]. The simulator runs on a SUN workstation under SunView and on a Sequent Symmetry parallel processor.

| Size | 1 | 2 | 4 | 8 |
|---|---|---|---|---|
| Mother boards | 1 | 4 | 16 | 64 |
| Daughter boards | 64 | 256 | 1024 | 4096 |
| PEs | 4096 | 16384 | 65536 | 262144 |
| ICAPs | $\leq 64$ | $\leq 256$ | $\leq 1024$ | $\leq 4096$ |

Table 1:

Several versions of the simulator exist on each machine and differ in the size of the IUA being simulated. The larger the IUA, the slower and larger is the simulation. The simulator supports IUA configurations with various numbers of mother boards as shown in Table 1.

Even with the smallest complement of mother boards, a complete IUA is usually not simulated due to limitations on the real memory available on the host computer and the desire to avoid page faults when running simulations. (Even the smallest configuration of the IUA contains 42 MB of RAM.) The amounts of CAAPP-ICAP shared memory (CISM), ICAP–SPA shared memory (ISSM), and ICAP data memory (IDM) are thus limited to that needed by the problem being run on the simulator. For the same reasons, the ICAP program memory (IPM) is considered to be read-only so that it need not be duplicated for all the processors.

The simulator on the SUN workstation is used to develop and debug programs because it provides an excellent visual presentation of the state of the IUA. The Sequent multiprocessor provides a much larger real memory, which can be accessed by multiple processors; thus, the Sequent version of the simulator is used to obtain timings on full-scale problems. The largest problem simulated to date is the DARPA integrated IU benchmark, which is a model-based object-recognition task [24, 25].

Using X-windows we could provide the same visual display from the Sequent simulator. However, the amount of data that would have to be sent over the network would slow down the simulation considerably. The remainder of this discussion will focus primarily on the SUN IUA simulator.

The simulator has been constructed in a modular fashion so that the various parts may be replaced easily for different needs such as allowing changes in the user interface, which varies from a keyboard interface on the Sequent to a full visual display on the SUN. The modularity also allows substitution of a 64-processor ICAP simulator module for a 16-processor ICAP simulator module when the primary simulation is at the ICAP level instead of at the CAAPP level.

### The User Console

The user console is a window under SunView, roughly 600 rows by 800 columns in size, leaving sufficient room to view other windows (such as a command window or editor) on the screen. This display is split into a left and right side. The left side is the *control panel* and the right side is the *display window*. See Fig. 4.

1. *Control panel*: The control panel contains displays of the one-bit CAAPP registers arranged as blocks of $64 \times 64$ pixels with one pixel per processor. For the smallest simulator this is the complete set of processors. For larger versions of the simulator, this is a subwindow into the $n \times n$ array of CAAPP processors. Associated with each register display is a *button*. Clicking this button with the mouse causes the display to be shown enlarged in the display window. Other buttons in the control panel cause other displays to appear in the display window or bring up *pop-up windows* for special operations such as loading and saving files. Having all of the registers shown at the same time allows the programmer to see the state of the CAAPP processors arranged in correspondence to images stored in the array.

2. *Display window*: The display window consists of a foreground and background display. The background display is always the programming terminal. The foreground display may or may not be present and shows the display selected by clicking a button in the control panel. The foreground display leaves the

bottom sixth of the programming terminal always visible. The programming terminal allows entry of commands and input to a running program. Output from a program can also be shown on the terminal.

Foreground displays include the following:

1. *PE Registers*: The selected PE register is displayed. The user can zoom in or out from a $2 \times 2$ processor display up to a display showing all the processors being simulated, even for a $512 \times 512$ simulation. Scroll bars on the sides indicate what portion of the complete array is being shown. Individual PE registers may be set or cleared by clicking with the mouse inside of the display window. The control panel shows the current row–column processor location selected by the mouse. See Fig. 5.

2. *PE memory*: A location in PE memory is shown. This display has the same functionality as the PE register display.

3. *Gray display*: The gray display shows a contiguous range of bits in PE memory as a gray-scale image. The user can zoom in or out from a $2 \times 2$ processor display up to a display showing all the processors being simulated. (Scroll bars on the sides indicate what portion of the complete array is being shown.) The user may select 1–32 bits in the range to be displayed. (The current SUN display in use can show 256 levels, but since using all 256 levels causes problems with the other SunView displays, only 128 levels, corresponding to the top seven bits of the range, are used.) The gray display may changed to an inverse gray or false color mode.

   The user may select a $3 \times 3$ pixel array with the mouse to be shown as numeric values in a pop-up window in either signed integer, unsigned integer, or IEEE floating-point format. The location in PE memory or CISM memory that is sampled may be different from the location shown in the gray display allowing an image to be used to guide exploration of other values that may not be visually informative when shown as an image.

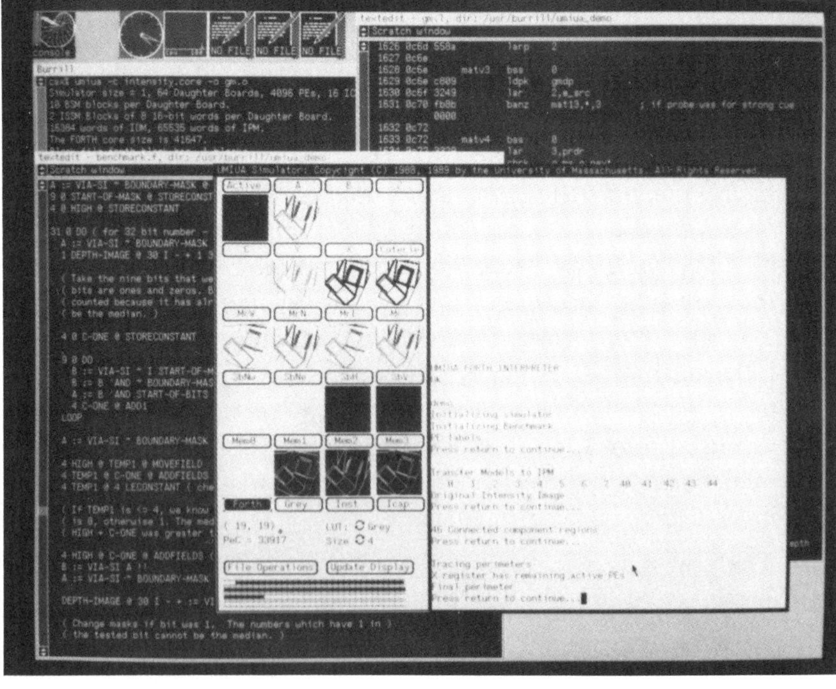


Figure 4: IUA simulator console.

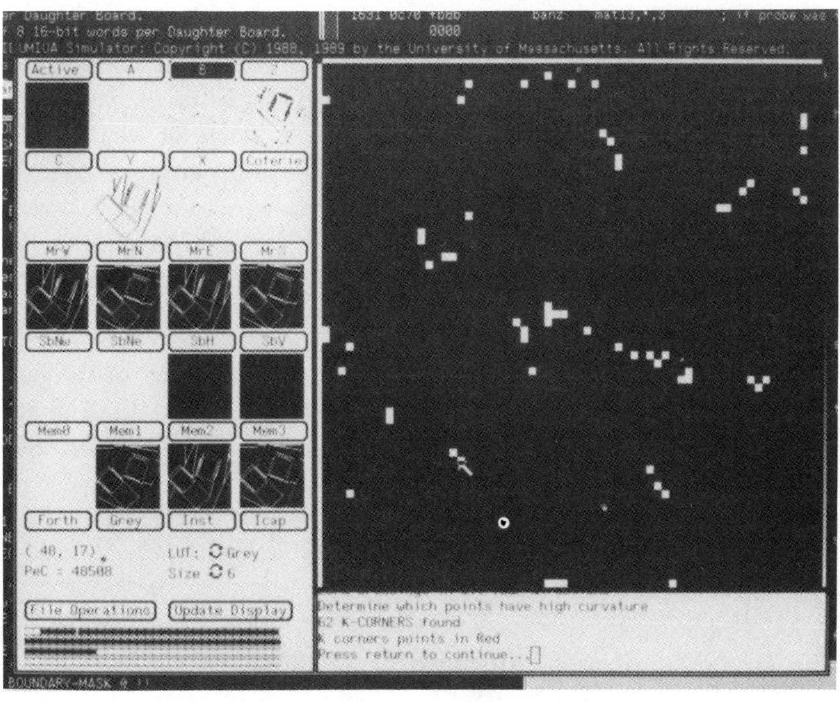


Figure 5: PE register display.

The gray display can be overlaid with red, green, and blue pixel maps. The overlay can be any of the PE registers or locations in PE memory. See Fig. 6.

4. *Coterie display*: The coterie display shows a graphic representation of the state of the switches and the the electrical charge in the network. Currently, the coterie display is limited to 32 × 32 PEs. A particular PE can be dragged to the center of the display with the mouse. Scroll bars on the side indicate what portion of the complete network is being displayed. Using function keys, individual switches can be opened or closed in the coterie network. See Fig. 7.

5. *ICAP display*: This display shows the complete set of registers for one ICAP processor. Also shown are all of the registers on the same daughter board (except for the CAAPP PE registers). When this display is selected, a pop-up window appears which may be used to select a particular daughter board, and a range of locations in IDM to be displayed. A range of locations in IPM, surrounding the current value of the program counter, is also shown. Up to four breakpoints may be set for the program running in the ICAP processors. Both the IDM range and the breakpoints may be selected using symbolic expressions. See Fig. 8.

6. *PE instruction display*: This is a scrollable display of the last 2048 instructions sent to the CAAPP by the ACU. The instructions are shown both in hex and in symbolic form. See Fig. 9.

All of the displays can be selected and manipulated by the user program running in the simulated ACU.

## The Daughter Board Simulator

The daughter board simulator simulates all of the PEs, CISM, ISSM, and glue logic. Although the IUA is made up of multiple daughter boards, the daughter board simulator does not simulate them one

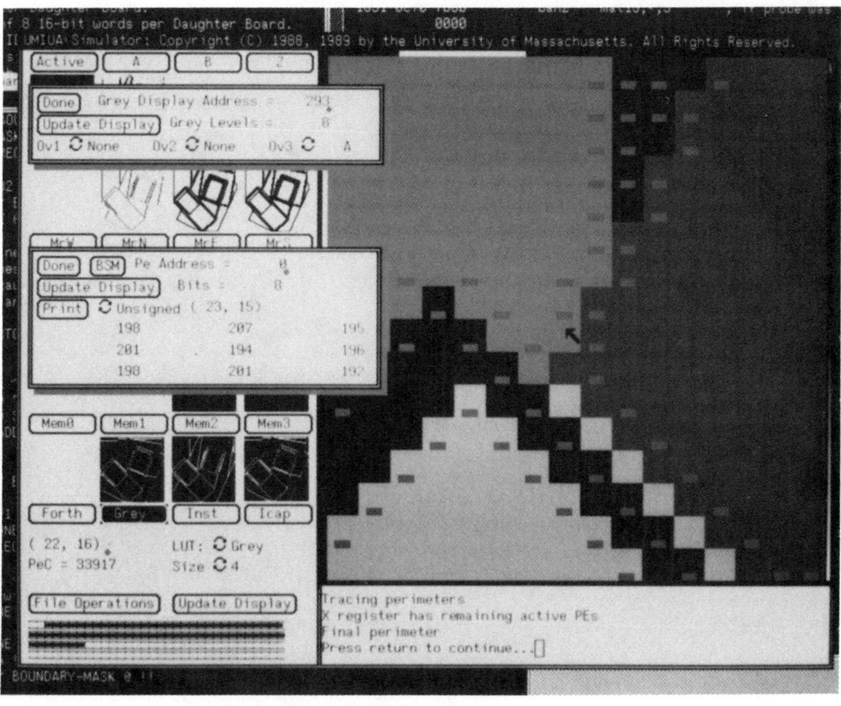


Figure 6: Gray display.

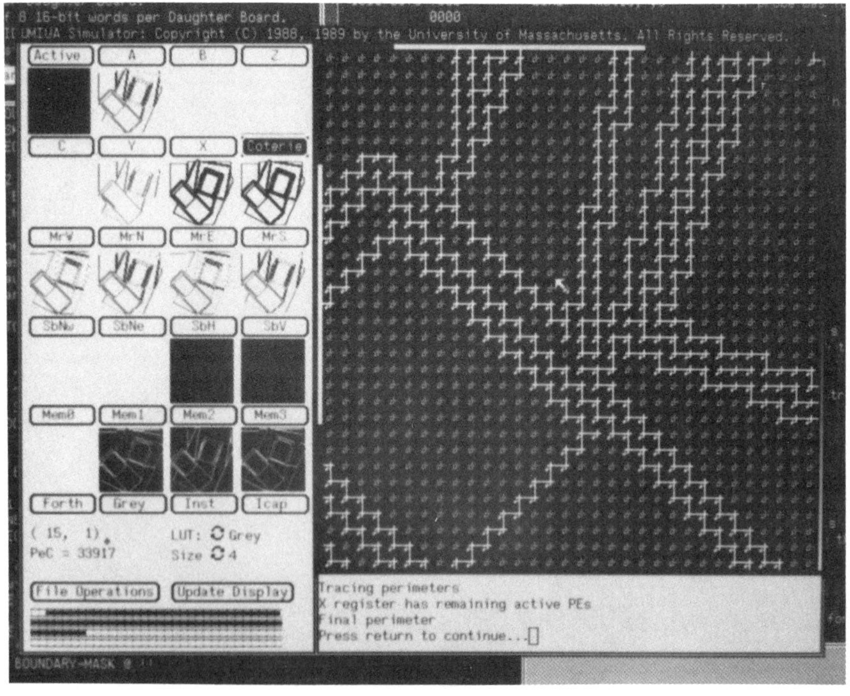


Figure 7: Coterie display.

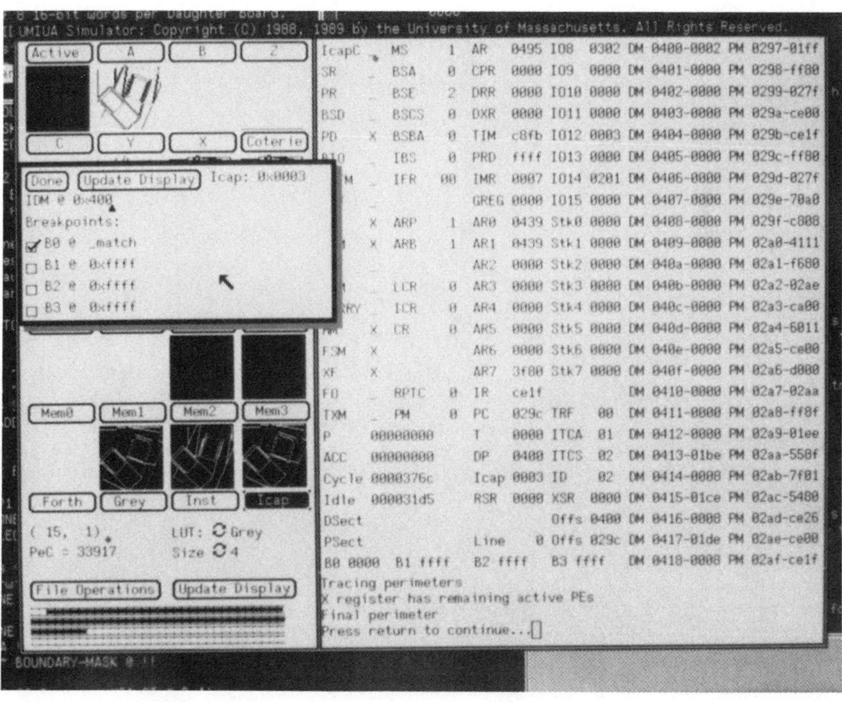


Figure 8: ICAP display.

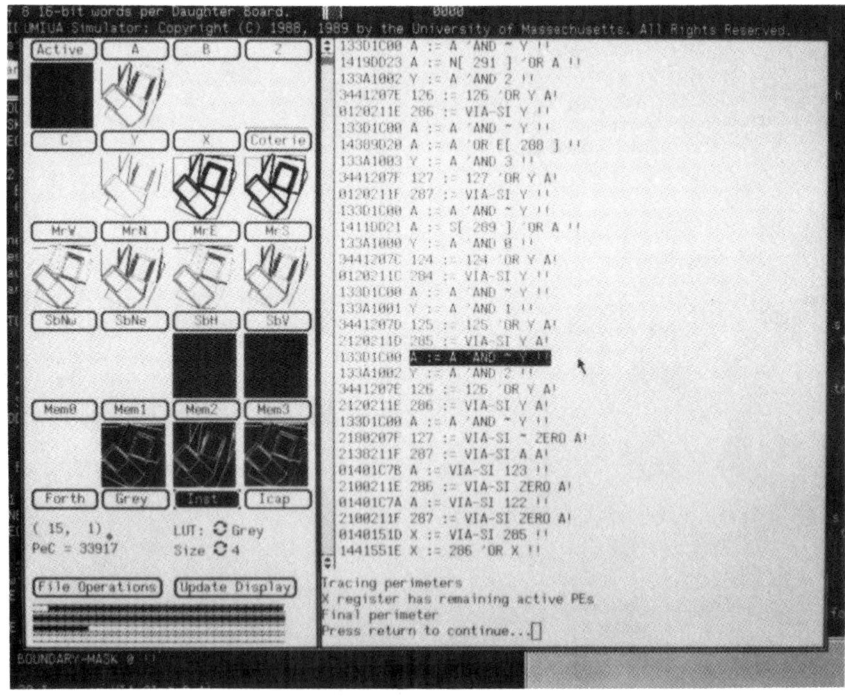


Figure 9: PE instruction display.

at a time. Instead, for efficiency, the PEs are simulated as a vector of processors. At those places where the geometry of the IUA is apparent, the simulation applies a board-by-board approach. For example, the instruction "zero the Z registers" is done for all PEs in a tight loop while the CISM operations are done board by board.

The daughter-board simulator receives instructions in the same form that the real daughter-boards receive instructions from the ACU. The instructions are sent on a simulated bus as 32 bit signals and are then decoded. This provides two benefits over a more tightly coupled scheme. First, the instruction stream on the bus is easily captured and can be used in exercising circuit boards under test. Second, using a bus allows quick construction of versions of the simulator that can utilize a parallel processor. In fact, we use the same daughter board code for both the SUN and Sequent simulators. A compile-time switch is used to select the data partitioning parallel code, which resides in only one subroutine. The parallel code is coupled with synchronizing check points that are no-ops in the nonparallel versions.

The computation of execution time is also simplified through the use of the simulated bus. Because the majority of instructions take a single clock cycle, an accumulator is used to count the instructions sent over the bus. An ACU overhead cost is also added as appropriate. (Microcontroller routines have lower per-instruction overhead.) For those operations such as `CISM Read`, where the result is not available immediately, the code that simulates the individual instruction adds the worst-case time to the accumulator. (In the multiprocessor version of the simulator, only one processor does the addition.) For the real machine, these variable length processes will be handled either by using feedback or by fixed-time idle loops in the ACU for the worst case. For the simulator, we took the second approach since we did not want to simulate the CISM finite state machine at the level needed to provide the correct timings using the feedback method.

The coterie network provided special problems in the simulation because it is really an analog circuit using electrical charge propagation. Because the cost of an analog simulation of the network is prohibitive, we simulated the charge propagation digitally, permitting us to simulate one cycle of 100 ns in approximately 18 milliseconds for a 512 × 512 PE simulator using nine processors on the Sequent multiprocessor. For the DARPA integrated IU benchmark, this would have required approximately 24 days of wall-clock time to run only one of the five test cases. An analysis of the problem showed that the configuration of the network was being changed infrequently with respect to the number of network operations performed. We thus modified the simulator to record a list of connected PEs whenever the network is reconfigured, and this information is used to accelerate the simulation of subsequent network operations using that configuration. The result is that the complete set of five IU benchmark test cases can be run in just two-and-one-half days on the Sequent. The user currently has the choice of running either the old or new simulation method with the new method as the default.

## The Programming Terminal

The programming terminal is an interactive interpreter that allows entry of commands and programs to manipulate directly the processing arrays. The IUA simulator has been designed so that this module of the simulator may be easily replaced by other modules. (Currently, the only module available is for interpreting the FORTH language [1]). A module for LISP could be provided as well. The interface consists of input and output streams from the simulator, a procedure call for issuing instructions to the CAAPP bus, and other procedure calls for changing the displays.

We felt that it was very important to provide an interactive environment so that the edit, compile, test loop would be very fast. The programmer can rapidly prototype code interactively and then reimplement the tested algorithm as an "ACU Macro" if desired.

FORTH is a threaded language. A few simple constructs are combined into ever more powerful constructs. Each construct is called a word. FORTH was selected because its interpreter is small and fast. We also had access to the source code for a FORTH implementation. New features such as floating-point operations were added, in addition to interfaces to the IUA simulator.

FORTH provides a quick way of changing a program and retrying it, or of just entering instructions. We provided a FORTH-based assembler for the CAAPP PE instructions so that the user is able to enter an instruction such as

```
A := B 'AND Y !!
```

and have it assembled and sent on the CAAPP bus. Each of the symbols (A, :=, B, etc.) are FORTH words that place information on the FORTH stack. This information is processed by the FORTH word to produce the CAAPP bus instruction. The special words provided to interface with the simulator allow FORTH to control all aspects of the simulation and act as the ACU.

A major extension to FORTH was the addition of IEEE floating-point format values along with words to operate on them. Words to convert from format to format are also provided.

The low-level processing portion of the DARPA Integrated IU benchmark was written mostly in FORTH with some of the simple ACU macros such as ADD-FIELDS written in C (C will be described in a later section). The major problem encountered with the use of FORTH was its flat name scoping, which prevented the FORTH code from being completely modular due to name conflicts (no vocabulary facility is available).

The following example is the definition of a FORTH word that adds two integer fields of the same length in PE memory.

```
( 1 ) : ADD-FIELDS ( length f1 f2 -- )
        ( Add field f2 to field f1 )
( 2 )   Z := ZERO !!
( 3 )   2 ROLL 1 - 0 DO
( 4 )    1 PICK I + >R X := R> A!
( 5 )    0 PICK I + DUP >R := X '+ R> A!
( 6 )   LOOP ;
```

Line 1 defines the word ADD-FIELDS. This word takes three arguments off the FORTH stack. The top stack value is the PE memory address of the second operand. The next stack value is the first operand–result field PE memory address. The third value is the length of the fields in bits. This argument protocol is documented with the comment in line 1. Line 2 clears the Z (carry) register in all PEs. Line 3 is a FORTH indexed loop. The 2 ROLL picks up the length value from the FORTH stack. If this value were 8, then line 3 would be equivalent to 7 0 DO, which would loop over the values 0, 1, 2, 3, 4, 5, 6, 7. The end of the loop is specified in line 6, which also ends the FORTH word. Line 4 generates the PE instruction "load the X register of the active PEs with the value from memory location `f2 + I`" where I is the loop index. The FORTH return stack is used as a temporary holding place for the value `f2 + I`. Line 5 generates the PE instruction `M[f1+I] := X + M[f1+I] A!` which causes the X register, the Z register, and memory location `f1 + I` to be added in all active PEs. The result is placed in memory location `f1 + I` and the carry goes to the Z register. For the FORTH statement `2 10 20 ADD-FIELDS`, the following PE instructions would be issued to add a pair of two-bit values at locations 10...11 and 20...21, with the result being stored back in locations 10...11:

```
Z := ZERO !!
X := M[20] A!
M[10] := X + M[] A!
X := M[21] A!
M[11] := X + M[] A!
```

### The ICAP Simulator

The ICAP simulator is structured to simulate one instruction from the first ICAP processor, one instruction from the next, and so forth. Because the ICAP processors run in MIMD mode, these instructions will probably be different. Since we did not want to pay the price of a gate level simulator, we chose to implement a functional simulator for the TMS320C25.

Because the simulation is on an instruction level, code written to use timing loops is not valid because the simulator will not maintain synchronization between the various ICAP processors. A disadvantage of this approach is that the timings are not exact. Our timing model uses the *average* time for an instruction with data in on-chip memory and instructions in off-chip memory. Our experience shows that approximately 90 percent of the data references are to the on-chip memory. With the TMS320C25 there is a large benefit to using a small amount of contiguous data memory, which is due not only to the on-chip data memory, but also to the addressing modes supported.

The full IUA will have 4096 ICAP processors. Each one will have 128k bytes of data memory and 128k bytes of program memory. This is a gigabyte of memory and is far more than the real memory available on any of the machines we have used to run the simulator. To prevent page faults, which would have drastically increased the elapsed time for any simulation, we reduced the number of ICAP processors and the amount of IDM and IPM available in the simulator. The IUA simulator can be easily reconfigured as to the number of ICAPs being simulated (independently of the size of the CAAPP array) and the size of IDM. The IPM is shared as read-only memory among all the ICAP processors. Even though the ICAP processors run independently, they all have the same programs loaded in IPM, which restricts the programmer to writing code that is not self-modifying.

Because there is a single system clock, the CAAPP and ICAP instruction streams are in approximate synchronization with roughly a two-to-one execute rate. Therefore, the IUA simulator executes two CAAPP instructions and then one instruction for each ICAP processor. Since an ICAP instruction may take more than one cycle, a particular ICAP processor is held up if its clock shows more time than the CAAPP has used.

The ICAP code is loaded into IPM by the ACU. The ACU can write the same program in every ICAP IPM directly using the CAAPP bus. The ACU can also write directly into any off-chip IDM location. Because the bus is a one-to-many bus, all ICAPs receive the same data and programs. However, it is also possible for the ACU to write a loader program into IPM that causes IPM to be loaded from ISSM by each individual ICAP processor. Since each ICAP processor sees a separate part of ISSM, each can be loaded with a different program. This mode of operating is not supported by the IUA simulator because there is only one IPM shared by every

ICAP processor.

Code for the ICAP processors can be written in either C or Assembler. The IUA simulator provides a loader for either special absolute code or for the TI COFF loader text format [19].

## The ACU and SPA

Whereas the full-scale IUA has one ACU and 64 SPA processors, the prototype hardware has one ACU and just one SPA. In the simulator, the ACU and SPA are the same computer and the simulator follows this simpler model regardless of how many PEs or ICAP processors are simulated. The ACU–SPA is the interactive module linked into the programmers terminal, which is currently the FORTH interpreter.

A separate module called the **acu_macros** is also part of the ACU. The ACU macros are procedures written in C for standard operations on the CAAPP such as ADD-FIELDS or FIND-GREATEST. On the real IUA, these macros will be stored in the microcode memory of the microcontroller that feeds the bus to the daughter boards. The ACU will request that a macro be executed with specified parameters, the microcontroller will execute the macro, substituting the parameters at the clock rate of the CAAPP while the ACU program sets up the next request. The approach taken in the simulator has been to identify which sequences of code should be in the microcode memory and what capabilities the microcontroller must have to efficiently execute those sequences. The ACU calls the macros via a special simulator interface procedure.

Also available to the user are User macros. These macros allow the user to provide procedures written and compiled in C, which can either be special code for an application or candidates for an ACU macro. Thus, the interactive programmer's terminal can still be used while taking advantage of the benefits of C. The cost to the user is that the simulator must be relinked whenever a change is made in the C code.

## 2.2 Programming Languages

The IUA can be programmed in various languages. Currently, separate compilers are used at each level of the IUA, and the only language that is available at every level is C. CAAPP FORTH has been discussed previously and its description will not be repeated here.

### CAAPP C

C is currently used to program the ACU and thus the CAAPP PEs. We use a special preprocessor to convert CAAPP PE instructions written in a high-level syntax into procedure calls that communicate with the PEs. The programmer must still be cognizant of the structure of the CAAPP PEs. As an example, a C program for doing an ADD-FIELDS in the PEs looks like this:

```
void add_fields(length,f1,f2)
int length; /* The length of the field */
int f1; /* Address of source and result field */
int f2; /* Address of other field */
{
int i;

  !! Z := ZERO !!
  for (i = 0; i < length; i++) {
   !! X := M[f2 + i] A!
   !! M[f1 + i] := X + M[] A!
   }
}
```

The !! signals the beginning of a parallel instruction to the preprocessor and the other !! or A! terminates the instruction. The statement

```
 !! X := M[f2 + i] A!
```

is converted to a call to a subroutine that sends a 32-bit instruction to the simulated CAAPP bus. The sense of this style of programming is that the programmer is writing assembly language programs in C.

Using C is not difficult because the programmer rarely has to work at such a low level. A large library of routines for doing the mundane arithmetic operations is available. These routines work with variable-size fields, and require the programmer to determine the size of a result from the sizes of the arguments. For example, multiplying a four-bit unsigned field with a seven bit unsigned field produces an 11-bit result. Other library routines for standard vision applications also exist.

In the future we will implement C* for the CAAPP [21]. This will ease the programmer's burden somewhat. But C* has two major failings when applied to the CAAPP. First, C* abstracts too much. An example is that it can not handle the variable-size fields that greatly increase the efficiency of the CAAPP. Second, C* is not designed to take advantage of the hardware for feedback and communication that makes the CAAPP particularly suited to computer vision. Constructs must be added for both. Our goal is that the resulting language will be a superset of C*.

Because we use variable-size fields in CAAPP processing, changing field sizes initially required all of the PE memory to be remapped by the programmer, which is a very error-prone process. We solved the problem by providing dynamic allocation of PE memory via allocation code in the ACU. When we have a true compiler for the CAAPP, a return to static mapping will be possible because the compiler will be able to optimize the mapping without error.

## Apply

Apply is a special-purpose, image-processing language developed at CMU for use on the Warp systolic array [8]. Apply is very good for expressing low-level image operations that are applied in a window on the image. Examples include Gaussian filtering, pixel averaging, median filters, etc. We have implemented Apply for the CAAPP [17]. It produces output that is acceptable to the C preprocessor described earlier. The Apply compiler produces code that uses the CAAPP PE memory as cache memory and the CISM as the real memory. This is an approach that we believe will generally be used in the implementation of higher level-languages.

There is a large body of Apply code available for the Warp, and having Apply for the CAAPP makes these routines available on the CAAPP. The following is an example of Apply code for performing a simple smoothing operation using a $3 \times 3$ window around each image pixel.

```
-- inimg - a 3 x 3 window centered around the
--         output pixel (outimg).
--         The border value is set to 128, which is a
--         midrange value.
--            -1,-1 | -1, 0 | -1, 1
--            ---------------------
--             0,-1 |  0, 0 |  0, 1
--            ---------------------
--             1,-1 |  1, 0 |  1, 1

procedure smooth(inimg: in array (-1..1, -1..1)
                          of byte border 128,
                 outimg: out byte)
is
  sum, i, j: integer; -- These local variables are local
                      -- to each pixel in the image.

begin
  sum := 0;           -- sum receives the total of the
                      -- input image window.

  for i in -1..1 loop
    for j in -1..1 loop
      sum := sum + inimg(i,j);
    end loop;
  end loop;

  outimg := (sum + 4) / 9; -- add 4 to round result.
                           -- The result is divided by
                           -- the number of pixels in
                           -- the input window.
```

```
end smooth;
```

The major limitation of Apply is that only spatially local operations fit the Apply paradigm. The DARPA integrated IU benchmark, for example, relied more on global communication among processors for which Apply was inappropriate.

## ICAP C

The C compiler for the ICAP implements the "standard" C of Kernighan and Ritchie [20]. No special provisions were made for the IUA. To make the ICAP programmer's job easier we have provided an ICAP monitor, which services requests for CISM, ISSM, and PARCOS operations. With the monitor, an ICAP processor can request ACU operations, respond to network operations, access CISM in a simplified manner, and send and receive information through ISSM.

In addition, a standard library is available to handle the normal C operations. This library was supplied with the C compiler for the TMS320C25 processor and was supplemented with routines specific to the IUA.

### Parallel Implementation of Common LISP

Because we currently have only a single processor at the SPA level, very little has been done about programming at this level beyond the use of existing languages and tools for the host processor. However, several groups at the University of Massachusetts have spent many years examining the nature of programming at this level. One major result has been the parallel implementation of Common LISP (PICL) [14]. This is a full common LISP implementation that currently runs on Sequent and Encore multiprocessors. Futures are the basis of this implementation. We plan initially to use PICL to program the SPA level.

A major project is the development of a language to support programming at all three levels of the IUA in an integrated manner. The language would be an extension of PICL.

PICL supports control parallelism of varying granularity, from nodes (supporting multiprocessors communicating over a network) to lightweight threads (function calls that can be executed in parallel). We would extend it to include data parallel constructs such as the alpha and beta operators from CM-LISP. The data parallel constructs would extend that range to a single control thread working on parallel data structures, and to multiple synchronized threads (such as applying alpha over an eval of a vector of functions). Such a language would be the first parallel language with sufficient generality to support all of the modes of parallelism embodied in the IUA.

Our initial development work will be to create a version of PICL that includes the data parallel constructs, and runs on the Sequent, Encore, and sequential hosts. This will provide a programmer's model under which software can be developed for the IUA, prior to the availability of the hardware.

The major technological issue is developing the algorithm for determining automatically which level of the IUA is most appropriate for a given operation. We believe, though, that we already have an approach to this problem that has potential to produce reasonable code, since the explicit nature of the parallelism in the language will simplify that task.

For example, as a first approximation, we know that the CAAPP will be the target of most data-parallel operations (except for certain floating-point operations and alpha-eval operations, which are best run on the ICAP); the ICAP will be the target of the fine-grained lightweight threads, although these may execute under an array of nodes (since PICL nodes support the style of message passing used in the ICAP), and the SPA will run the coarser-granularity modes. Eventually, there will be more sophisticated algorithms for distributing the processing that will provide better utilization.

## Generalized Blackboard

Many of the most advanced AI systems have required the communication of multiple complex processes. Blackboard systems that allow processes to post and read information independently have proven to be a popular and effective system design for such systems. At UMass research on distributed AI systems has led to the development of generalized blackboards where the organization of information can be structured for efficient storage and retrieval for a particular problem domain and set of processes.

The generalized blackboard system (GBB) [4] developed in Common LISP at UMass has turned out to be a very effective system development tool and has been widely distributed. In addition a parallel implementation of GBB has been developed to run in PICL on coarse-grained multiprocessors. Thus, an advantage of implementing PICL for the IUA is that it provides access to parallel GBB, and this will fill much of the AI processing needs for high-level vision.

## 2.3 Libraries

We currently have an extensive library of arithmetic subroutines for the CAAPP, including byte, integer, and floating-point arithmetic, and many of the standard transcendental functions [22]. Thus, we have the basis for a compiler run-time library. We also have implemented many vision subroutines, including various convolutions, filters, edge-preserving smoothing, convex hull, expand and contract morphological operators, connected component labeling, boundary tracing, windowed Hough transform, etc. In addition, we have implementations of the DARPA integrated IU benchmark, the Abingdon Cross benchmark, and an optical ray-tracing application (as an example of a nonvision application).

For the ICAP, in addition to the compiler run-time library, we have a library that supports communication via the serial ports, and synchronization with the ACU. We also have an implementation of the LINDA programming environment, originally developed at Yale (although it is very inefficient, as are most LINDA implementations). From the DARPA benchmark, we also have a model-matching algorithm that runs on the ICAP.

# 3 Summary

The image-understanding architecture consists of three distinct parallel processors, each supporting different modes and granularities of parallelism. Such a hardware environment, while necessary for the support of real-time computer vision, presents numerous challenges to the programmer.

First among these is the ability to visualize the state of the entire system, which we have addressed through the graphically oriented programmer's console in our simulator and the planned development environment. Second is the ability to interact with the system during development and debugging, which is supported by the mouse-based direct manipulation of the system through the software console, and by the interpretive language supported in the console's programming window.

A third challenge is programming the different levels of the IUA, which we have approached in two ways. Initially, the system will be programmed via a different dialect of a standard base language (C) at each level, and by special purpose languages (such as Apply). However, our eventual goal is to develop a general-purpose parallel programming language, based on parallel common LISP, that will support all of the modes of processing inherent in the IUA and automatically target object code for the appropriate portion of the architecture. The last challenge is to make effective use of the system without having to redevelop a vast amount of application software. We are addressing this through the existing libraries, and through the planned development of the KBVision system [10] and generalized blackboard for the IUA.

## Acknowledgments

This work was supported in part by the Defense Advanced Research Projects Agency under contracts DACA76-86-C-0015, and DACA76-89-C-0016, monitored by the U.S. Army Engineer Topographic Laboratory; by the Air Force Office of Scientific Research, under contract F49620-86-C-0041; and by a Coordinated Experimental Research grant from the National Science Foundation (DCR

8500332). Special thanks to Michael Scudder for supplying the Apply programming example.

# Bibliography

[1] L. Brodie, Starting FORTH, 2nd edition, Prentice-Hall Software Series, Prentice-Hall, Inc., Englewood Cliffs, N. J., 1987.

[2] J. Burrill, *UMASS IUA simulator*, COINS Dept., University of Massachusetts, 1989.

[3] J. Burrill, *IUA functional specification*, COINS Dept., University of Massachusetts, June 1988.

[4] D. Corkill and K. Gallagher, *A generic blackboard development system*, AAAI86, Aug. 1986, pp. 1008–1014.

[5] B. Draper, R. Collins, J. Brolio, J. Griffith, A. Hanson, and E. Riseman, *Tools and experiments in the knowledge-directed interpretation of road scenes*, Image-Understanding Workshop Proceedings, Morgan Kaufmann, Los Altos, Calif., 1987, pp. 178–193.

[6] B. Draper, R. Collins, J. Brolio, J. Griffith, A. Hanson, and E. Riseman, *The Schema System*, International journal of Computer Vision, vol. 2, no. 3, 1989, pp. 209–250.

[7] L. Erman et al., *The hearsay-II speech-understanding system: integrating knowledge to resolve uncertainty*, Computing Surveys, vol. 12, 1980, pp. 213–253.

[8] L. Hamey, J. Webb, and I-Chen Wu, *Low-level vision on Warp and the Apply programming model*, CMU-RI-TR-87-17, The Robotics Institute, Carnegie Mellon University, 1987.

[9] A. Hanson and E. Riseman, *The VISIONS image understanding system*, in Advances in Computer Vision, (C. Brown, ed.), Erlbaum Press, NJ., 1987. Also COINS TR 86-62, Univ. of Mass., Amherst, Mass., Dec. 1986, pp. 1–114.

[10] *The KBVision$^{TM}$ system, programmer's reference manual*, Amerinex Artificial Intelligence, Inc., Amherst, Mass., 1989.

[11] V. K. Prasanna Kumar and C. Raghavendra, *Array processor with multiple broadcasting*, Proc. 12th Annual Symp. on Computer Architecture, ACM Press, 1985, pp. 2–10.

[12] H. Li and Maresca, *Polymorphic torus network*, Proc. Intl. Conf. on Parallel Processing, Penn State Press, State College, Penn., 1987, pp. 411–414.

[13] R. Miller, V. K. Prasanna Kumar, D. Reisis and Q. Stout, USC Tech. Rept. IRIS No. 229, University of Southern California, Los Angeles, Calif., 1987.

[14] K. Murray and D. Corkill, Common LISP object representation strategies: The UMass concurrent and Common LISP implementation, COINS Tech. Report no. 88-35, COINS dept., Univ. of Mass.

[15] N. Nii, *The blackboard model of problem solving and the evolution of blackboard architectures*, AI Magazine, vol. 7, no. 2, 1986, pp. 38–53.

[16] D. Rana and C. Weems, *The ICAP parallel processor communications switch*, COINS Technical Report 89-02, COINS Dept., University of Massachusetts.

[17] M. Scudder, *Apply @ Umass user's manual*, August 1989.

[18] Texas Instruments, *TMS320C25 user's guide*, Texas Instruments, 1986.

[19] Texas Instruments, *TMS320C1x/TMS320C2x assembly language tools*, Texas Instruments, 1987.

[20] Texas Instruments, *TMS320C25 C compiler*, Texas Instruments, 1987.

[21] Thinking Machines Corporation, *Connection machine model CM-2 technical summary*, Technical Report HA87-4, April 1987, pp. 35–41.

[22] C. Weems, *Some sample algorithms for the image understanding architecture*, Proceedings of the 1988 DARPA Image Understanding Workshop, April 1988, Cambridge, Mass., pp. 126–138.

[23] C. Weems, D. Shu, et al., *The image understanding architecture*, International Journal of Computer Vision, vol. 2, no. 3, January 1989, pp. 251–282.

[24] C. Weems, E. Riseman, and A. Hanson, *An integrated image understanding benchmark: recognition of a 2 1/2 D "mobile,"* Proceedings of the 1988 DARPA Image Understanding Workshop, April 1988, Cambridge, Mass., pp. 111–126.

[25] C. Weems, E. Riseman, A. Hanson and A. Rosenfeld, *A report on the results of the DARPA integrated image understanding benchmark exercise*, Proceedings of the 1989 DARPA Image Understanding Workshop, May 1989, Palo Alto, Calif., 1989, pp. 165–192.

# Index